FIELDING'S
PARADORS, POUSADAS AND
CHARMING VILLAGES OF
SPAIN AND PORTUGAL

Other Fielding Titles

Fielding's Alaska Cruises and the Inside Passage
Fielding's America West
Fielding's Asia's Top Dive Sites
Fielding's Australia
Fielding's Bahamas
Fielding's Baja California
Fielding's Bermuda
Fielding's Best and Worst — The surprising results of the Plog Survey
Fielding's Birding Indonesia
Fielding's Borneo
Fielding's Budget Europe
Fielding's Caribbean
Fielding's Caribbean Cruises
Fielding's Caribbean on a Budget
Fielding's Diving Australia
Fielding's Diving Indonesia
Fielding's Eastern Caribbean
Fielding's England including Ireland, Scotland & Wales
Fielding's Europe
Fielding's Europe 50th Anniversary
Fielding's European Cruises
Fielding's Far East
Fielding's France
Fielding's France: Loire Valley, Burgundy & the Best of French Culture
Fielding's France: Normandy & Brittany
Fielding's France: Provence and the Mediterranean
Fielding's Freewheelin' USA
Fielding's Hawaii
Fielding's Hot Spots: Travel in Harm's Way
Fielding's Indiana Jones Adventure and Survival Guide™
Fielding's Italy
Fielding's Kenya
Fielding's Las Vegas Agenda
Fielding's London Agenda
Fielding's Los Angeles Agenda
Fielding's Mexico
Fielding's New Orleans Agenda
Fielding's New York Agenda
Fielding's New Zealand
Fielding's Paradors, Pousadas and Charming Villages of Spain and Portugal
Fielding's Paris Agenda
Fielding's Portugal
Fielding's Rome Agenda
Fielding's San Diego Agenda
Fielding's Southeast Asia
Fielding's Southern California Theme Parks
Fielding's Southern Vietnam on Two Wheels
Fielding's Spain
Fielding's Surfing Australia
Fielding's Surfing Indonesia
Fielding's Sydney Agenda
Fielding's Thailand, Cambodia, Laos and Myanmar
Fielding's Travel Tool™
Fielding's Vietnam, including Cambodia and Laos
Fielding's Walt Disney World and Orlando Area Theme Parks
Fielding's Western Caribbean
Fielding's The World's Most Dangerous Places™
Fielding's Worldwide Cruises

FIELDING'S
PARADORS, POUSADAS AND CHARMING VILLAGES OF SPAIN AND PORTUGAL

By

A. Hoyt Hobbs

Fielding Worldwide, Inc.

308 South Catalina Avenue

Redondo Beach, California 90277 U.S.A.

Fielding's Paradors, Pousadas and Charming Villages of Spain and Portugal

Published by Fielding Worldwide, Inc.

Text Copyright ©1997 A. Hoyt Hobbs

Icons & Illustrations Copyright ©1997 FWI

Photo Copyrights ©1997 to Individual Photographers

FIELDING WORLDWIDE INC.

PUBLISHER AND CEO	**Robert Young Pelton**
GENERAL MANAGER	**John Guillebeaux**
OPERATIONS DIRECTOR	**George Posanke**
ELECTRONIC PUBLISHING DIRECTOR	**Larry E. Hart**
PUBLIC RELATIONS DIRECTOR	**Beverly Riess**
ACCOUNT SERVICES MANAGER	**Christy Harp**
PROJECT MANAGER	**Chris Snyder**
MANAGING EDITOR	**Amanda K. Knoles**

PRODUCTION

Martin Mancha   **Ramses Reynoso**

Craig South

COVER DESIGNED BY	**Digital Artists, Inc.**
COVER PHOTOGRAPHERS — Front Cover	**Tony Stone Images**
Back Cover	**Robert Young Pelton/Westlight**
INSIDE PHOTOS	**Portuguese Tourist Office, Tourist Office of Spain, Marketing Ahead**

Inquiries should be addressed to: Fielding Worldwide, Inc., 308 South Catalina Ave., Redondo Beach, California 90277 U.S.A., ☎ *(310) 372-4474*, Facsimile *(310) 376-8064*, 8:30 a.m.–5:30 p.m. Pacific Standard Time.
Website: http://www.fieldingtravel.com
e-mail: fielding@fieldingtravel.com

ISBN 1-56952-119-0

Printed in the United States of America

Letter from the Publisher

In 1946, Temple Fielding began the first of what would prove a remarkable series of well-written, highly personalized guidebooks for independent travelers. Temple's opinionated, witty and oft-imitated books have now guided travelers for almost a half-century. More important to some was Fielding's humorous and direct method of steering travelers away from the dull and the insipid. Today, Fielding Travel Guides are still written by experienced travelers for experienced travelers. Our authors carry on Fielding's reputation for creating travel experiences that deliver insight with a sense of discovery and style.

Unforgettable. That's what you'll say after a vacation in Spain and Portugal the Fielding way. Hoyt Hobbs has been traveling through Europe for the past 25 years, searching for the dramatic, the little-known, the romantic attractions, and the pristine beaches that make Spain and Portugal some of the most entertaining countries in Europe. In *Fielding's Paradors and Pousadas*, Hoyt has created the perfect balance of entertainment and education, all with an eye to enhancing anyone's visit. You won't forget your trip to Spain and/or Portugal. Not with Fielding.

Today the concept of independent travel has never been bigger. Our policy of *brutal honesty* and a highly personal point of view has never changed; it just seems the travel world has caught up with us.

Enjoy your Iberian adventure with Hoyt Hobbs and Fielding.

RYP

Robert Young Pelton
Publisher and CEO
Fielding Worldwide, Inc.

Dedication

I gratefully dedicate this book to
Pilar Vico,
who makes all things possible.

ABOUT THE AUTHOR

Hoyt Hobbs

Hoyt Hobbs has traveled extensively throughout Europe and North Africa since 1973. He first visited Spain and Portugal in 1976 while living in the south of France, and was enchanted by the gentle beauty of the countryside and the warmth of the people. Quaint villages, graceful architecture, stunning beaches and savory cuisine drew him back again and again.

He wrote his first guidebook in 1979—to Egypt—when, after numerous trips, he had been unable to find a guidebook to his liking. Popular guides conveyed too little understanding of history and culture, while more scholarly books obscured interesting information within reams of detail. Reviewers applauded the balanced approach. *The Library Journal* said: "...with only this book [one can] enjoy a more comprehensive, efficient, and informative tour than is possible with any of the classical travel guides." According to *Traveler's Book Society* "...the level here is almost exactly right for the intelligent traveler....This is a book to travel with as well as to use in planning a tour..."

"This book is a model of specific, useful, honest travel advice and concise, vivid historical exposition," noted the *Chattanooga Times*, adding that "you ought to buy this book at once." In 1981 the Egypt guide was selected for publication as the first of the Fielding's country guides, followed by *Fielding's Spain* and *Fielding's Portugal*. Now he has applied his successful and informative approach to the special hotels of both countries.

Dr. Hobbs, an associate professor of philosophy at Long Island University, is widely read in history, architecture and cultural history. He is serious about food and wine and relishes making fresh discoveries, which he reports in this lively, comprehensive guide.

The author lives in New York City.

ACKNOWLEDGEMENTS

A project such as this could never have been completed without substantial assistance from a large number of people and organizations. It is a great pleasure to have an opportunity to publicly thank some of them.

I especially wish to thank Jorge Felner da Costa, director, ICEP/Portuguese National Tourist Office for his generous cooperation and interest in this project, and Sergio Lopes, director, *USA TAP/Air Portugal* for his kind attention and support.

I am exceedingly grateful to João Custódio of Enatur Pousadas de Portugal, Gloria Mello of TAP/Air Portugal, and Luis Reis of the Association of Hotels du Charmes for their gracious and enthusiastic assistance.

Abundant thanks to Manuel Ferreira Enes, José Almeida and Ruth Santiago for their many kindnesses on my behalf. I am grateful to our good friends Pamela Dailey and Arthur Krystal for timely and astute editorial assistance.

My debt to and affection for Pilar Vico of Travel Ahead is beyond measure. I am as constantly awed by the grace, efficiency and bubbling good humor with which she worked countless miracles as I am by her generous nature and warm friendship.

Lastly, I thank my friends and family for their patience and want them to know that, for better or worse, I am available again.

Fielding Rating Icons

The Fielding Rating Icons are highly personal and awarded to help the besieged traveler choose from among the dizzying array of activities, attractions, hotels, restaurants and sights. The awarding of an icon denotes unusual or exceptional qualities in the relevant category.

RATINGS: Fielding Award, Author Selection, Money Saver, Expensive, Quality, Warning, Danger, Inexpensive, Spacious, Cramped, Mild Disapproval, Timesaving

CULTURAL: Museum/Art, Interesting Architecture, History, Book Reference, Artistically Important, Musically Interesting, Cultural Archeology, Crafts, Theatre, Festivals

SIGHTS: Picturesque, Great Scenery, Market, Beaches/Resorts, Cultural, Fortress, Castles, Church

WHERE TO STAY: Simple, Luxurious, Cottage, Bed & Breakfast, Scenic, Business, Honeymoon, Chateau

TRAVEL TIPS: Arrival/Departure, By Air, By Water, By Train, By Car, Bus/Local Transit, Barge, River Boat, Calendar, Itinerary, Compass, Kids

ACTIVITIES

Downhill Skiing	X-country Skiing	Water Sports	Sailing	Scuba Diving	Snorkeling/ Diving	Deep-sea Fishing	Freshwater Fishing
Swimming	Hiking	Walking	Relaxing	Golf	Tennis	Horseback Riding	General Sports
Cycling	Workout	Spa	Camping	Off-Road	Boating	Rafting	Recreational Vehicle

SPECIAL INTEREST

Nightlife	Singles	Romantic	Nude Beaches	Lecture	Spectacular Cuisine	Wine Tasting	Shopping
Cafe Stops	Gardening	Pro Sports	Mystery	Gambling	Wildlife		

TABLE OF CONTENTS

PORTUGAL

LIST OF MAPS

SPAIN AND PORTUGAL

FIRST OF ALL

What's a parador—let alone a pousada?

Most often a parador is a fairy-tale place where real kings once slept, princes and princesses dreamed and courtiers roamed the halls. Sometimes, it's an ancient monastery—an aged edifice of architecture and art. Every once in a while, it's a modern building novel in concept or nestled in rustic mountains, artfully blended with nature.

In other words, a parador offers a very special place to lay one's head. Yet, special though paradors generally are, they welcome travelers accustomed to spending nights in Marriotts not Hiltons. Rates seldom exceed $100 for two. In sum, paradors provide memorable accommodations at moderate prices.

What entitles almost a hundred different hotels— ranging from 15th-century castles and 14th-century monasteries through spankingly new hotels of contemporary designs—to be called paradors? All are selected and managed by a quasi-government company— which has its good and bad sides, but mainly good. Here is how it all came about.

During the 1920s, as western Europe began its rush toward the twenty-first century, mass-production drove out handcrafts, ancient buildings gave way to modern structures, highways opened wilderness to the predations of modern life. Of course, there were advantages to all of this, but serenity, natural beauty and older graces were not among them. Increasingly Spain and Portugal attracted other Europeans (and, of course, Americans) who, at least on their vacations, craved older, quieter, natural ways. Spain and Portugal, although near industrialized France, Germany and England, lagged far behind the rest of the continent in modernization. Even as tourists flocked to both countries seeking the romance of pre-industrialized culture, they increasingly expected pampering before and after they hiked, fished, saw the sights or simply enjoyed Nature. Spain (and Portugal) relished the tourists' money but were unable to provide enough hot water, draft-free rooms, and private bathrooms.

Rather than meet this demand by erecting coldly modern hotels in its most popular tourist areas, Spain settled on a unique solution. Not yet having replaced the old with the new, she retained literally hundreds of medieval and Renaissance buildings from days of former glory. These were falling to ruin, in many cases, because their upkeep was prohibitive and they served no modern use.

By converting these ancient treasures into modern accommodations, while retaining original designs through intelligent renovation, Spain solved two problems at once. The result was aged castles and monasteries with modern plumbing, central heating, air conditioning, even saunas and conference rooms. Because renewal was much more costly than replacing an old building with a new one, only a national government could digest such a mammoth bill. At the time Spain was led by a fervent dictator, whose regime began appropriating old buildings and supplying cast to restore and refurbish them. So the parador program began.

The success of the parador idea led to its expansion according to two principles. If there were hotel-barren areas where tourists wanted to go or where the Spanish government wanted to entice them, old buildings were sought and renovated; if, however no appropriate structure existed, the government commissioned designs from outstanding Spanish architects. The second principle was the reverse of the priorities of the first. If an important old building would otherwise fall to ruin, the parador program would renovate even if there was no need for an additional hotel in that area, sometimes leading to one (or even two) paradors competing for the same tourists as nearby private hotels. Eventually 86 paradors dotted the country with more on the way.

Portugal's story follows a similar plot. It, too, was replete with stately castles, fortresses and monasteries that no longer served any purpose. It was the object of tourist travel, had a dictator (Salazar) at its helm, and had the example of neighbor Spain. In 1940 Portugal commissioned its first pousada, and the number has grown to 38 today.

So paradors and pousadas are housed in wonderful buildings, but what about their government management? Although, technically, both organizations are independent companies, private they are not. However, tourism is critical for Spain and Portugal so both countries try hard to please visitors. Perhaps not so surprisingly, then, the management works well. Staffs are eager, even if not at a level of those rare world-class hotels. Seldom will there be any complaint about service or cleanliness. The traditional downfall of paradors and pousadas had always been their food, but major efforts have raised culinary standards much above the traditional blandness.

Many paradors and pousadas are the finest hotels in their respective areas; some are utterly extraordinary; a few are ordinary as can be. We will call them as we see them which means we sometimes recommend you drive right past the local parador for a better choice.

But special accommodations by themselves are not sufficient reason to travel thousands of miles. Spain and Portugal must be worth the visit for their own sake.

Why Spain?

The reasons Spain hosts more visitors every year than any other country in Europe are clear. Spain warms travelers on sandy beaches, dazzles them with scenery, delights them with flavorful cuisine, and—most of all—surprises. Spain is not a European Mexico with mariachi music and Indian civilizations, but a different culture entirely. Spain is venerable, lively, cosmopolitan and graced with seminal architecture and art. These are her attractions, all packaged by a people whose friendliness and love of life endears her to all. Then, too, where else can European culture be sampled a stone's throw from your bedroom in a 15th-century palace?

There is cost to be considered as well. Western Europe has grown too expensive for the average American to consider for his vacation—with the sole exception of Iberia. Were it not for even less expensive Portugal, Spanish prices would be the lowest in Europe. Today a couple should budget almost $400 for each day in France, Germany, Italy or England, exclusive of transportation costs. Spain requires less than half as much.

Why Portugal?

Portugal has long been the continent's best-kept travel secret. Its people are warm, its sights memorable and, almost equally important, it remains affordable. True, the cost of flying there tops any American destination by several hundred dollars, but its hotels offer better value than ours and its good food is available for less, so careful choices of accommodations and dining can amortize the higher airfare away. And when you save a bundle on some lovely Portuguese ceramics, you can count that as a bonus. Portugal remains a viable option today, even when France, Italy and England do not.

Consider Portugal. While Europeans have flocked to its extraordinary beaches and graceful palaces for decades, those of us on the west side of the Atlantic still find Portugal a rare and wonderful surprise. Portugal offers some of the most beautiful beaches in the world and adds the cultural monuments that only a venerable European country can offer. Everyone retains the magical forests of Sintra and its three palaces in their hearts. Nor are you too late to make this discovery. Portugal has changed little over recent decades—except in some good ways, such as raising its hotels to world-class levels. The country remains unspoiled, its prices the lowest in Western Europe, its people unaffectedly friendly, and its sights pleasantly unfamiliar.

Why Not Both?

Spain, the third largest country in western Europe easily consumes all of a visitor's time. Portugal, though the size of one medium U.S. state packs enough within its borders to do the same. So in truth, there is no compelling reason to visit both during a single trip—unless you want only the best and want it immediately.

The fact is that Portugal and Spain are neighbors separated only by an imaginary border that requires nothing but a passport to cross. Distances, from the western half of Spain to Portugal, are manageable. For example, the trip from Madrid to Lisbon takes 7 hours by car, 9 hours by train or 20 minutes in the air. Portugal's magnificent Algarve beaches lie a two-hour drive away from Seville in Spain's south. From the parador in Spain's Mérida you can drive to the pousada in Portugal's Marvão for a visit and lunch before returning to Mérida for dinner.

Using This Guide

After introductory chapters on trip preparation, recommended itineraries follow showing how to tour the best as well as the offbeat along Spain's and Portugal's trail of paradors and pousadas. Then the book separates into a Spanish and Portuguese part. A background section on Spain explains the land, history and food. The sights and accommodations of Madrid follow, then the paradors of the center, the south, the north, and the east. Portugal begins, after an explanation of the land, history and food, with a chapter on Lisbon, followed by chapters on the pousadas of the center, the south, and the north. Each area chapter describes a territory whose most attractive sights can be visited during a three- or four-day stay in one centrally located city or town.

Changes

Although we've researched and inspected hundreds of hotels and restaurants over many visits, we're aware of the constantly changing landscape—improvements, declines or even closings that may have occurred too recently to be reflected in our reviews. If you locate some treasure we've missed, we'd love hearing about it; similarly, if you receive bad food or inadequate service in any of the establishments we recommend, we certainly want to know about that. While no hotel or restaurant can score perfectly every time, rude service is never acceptable. We welcome your comments and suggestions. Write us c/o Fielding Worldwide, 308 S. Catalina Avenue, Redondo Beach,

CA 90277, or FAX us at ☎ *(310) 376-8064*, 8:30 a.m.–5:30 p.m. Pacific Standard Time. Send e-mail to: fielding@fieldingtravel.com.

Our Rating System

Apart from giving you information about what is available to see and do in Spain and Portugal and some background about each country's history and culture, the most valuable assistance we can provide is to evaluate sights, monuments, and restaurants. For easy reference, we codify our opinions within a star system:

★★★★★	Outstanding anywhere in the world
★★★★	Exceptional, among the best in the country
★★★	Superior for a particular area of the country
★★	Good, a clear step above the average
★	Above average

PRACTICAL MATTERS

For Information

The tourist offices of Spain and Portugal are valuable resources for information.

Spain:

California   San Vicente Plaza Building, 8383 Wilshire Boulevard, Suite 960,
Beverly Hills, California 90211, ☎ (213) 658-7188; FAX (213) 658-1061

Canada   102 Bloor Street West, 14th Floor, Toronto, Ontario, Canada M5S 1M8,
☎ (416) 961-3131; FAX (416) 961-1992

England   56 St. James Street, London, SW1A 1LD,
☎ (4471) 499-0901; FAX (4471) 629-4257

Australia   203 Castlereigh Street, Ste. 21A, P.O. Box A-685, Sydney, NSW, Australia
2000, ☎ (02) 264-79-66

Portugal:

California   3440 Wilshire Boulevard, Suite 1616, Los Angeles, California 90010,
☎ (213) 380-6459

New York   590 Fifth Avenue, New York, New York 10036,
☎ (212) 345-4403; FAX (212) 764-6137

Canada   60 Bloor Street, West Suite 1005, Toronto, Ontario M4W 3BB,
☎ (416) 961-3131; FAX (416) 961-1992

England   22–25A Sackville Street, London WIX IDE,
☎ (0171) 494-1441

The U.S. booker for both paradors and pousadas is **Marketing Ahead, Inc.**
This company will reserve all paradors, pousadas and other first-class hotels,
providing you book at least three nights of your trip with them:

New York City

433 Fifth Avenue, New York, NY 10016, ☎ *(212) 686-9213; FAX (212) 686-0217.*

Travel to Spain and Portugal

By Plane

Direct flights to Spain depart from **New York City** (Iberia, TWA), **Newark** (Continental), **Dallas/Fort Worth** (American), **Atlanta** (Delta), **Miami** (Iberia, Aeromexico), **Washington, DC** (United), **Atlanta** (Delta), **Toronto** and **Montreal** (Air Canada and Iberia). Flight time is roughly seven hours from New York City to Madrid. Only Iberia and TWA fly every day to Madrid, the others four to five times a week. Iberia and Delta also fly daily from New York to Barcelona through Madrid. British Airways arranges connecting flights through **London** to various Spanish cities; Air France provides the same service through **Paris**; and KLM stops over at **Amsterdam**. All these can fly directly from their stopovers to Málaga, Barcelona or Madrid. In addition, charter flights abound.

Three airlines currently fly directly from the U.S. to Portugal: TAP (Air Portugal), TWA and Delta. All depart from **New York** (or Newark) daily, and land in Lisbon where connections to other cities can be made. TAP also provides frequent service from both **Montreal** and **Toronto** in Canada. Flight time from New York or Boston is a little more than 6 hours, two hours more from Canada, and six more from Los Angeles. However you fly, connecting flights from Lisbon can whisk you to Porto or to Faro in the Algarve.

Prices change with the seasons and are most expensive from June through mid-September and during Christmas and Easter; least expensive both from November to the middle of December and from the second of January through the first half of March; and between the two extremes at other times. Whatever the season, about $50 can be saved on a round-trip ticket by flying on weekdays.

Charter flights can be great bargains. Generally there is little or no flexibility in dates of travel, and advance payment is always required. Planes tend to be overcrowded, accommodations cramped. If you cancel your trip, you forfeit the entire price of the ticket, but the charter company may cancel its flight, up to ten days before scheduled departure, as long as it refunds your money. So if your charter leaves as scheduled, you can be sure it will be full—the company would have cancelled otherwise. Still, we have seen one-way flights from New York to Madrid for a very tempting $200. For more information ask your travel agent, check the travel section of the newspaper or try **Council Charter**, *205 East 42nd Street, New York, NY 10017 (☎ (800) 800-8222).*

Alternatively, ticket consolidators can provide tickets as cheaply as most charters with less risk. These firms sell at discounts the tickets that airlines were unable to at higher fares. Thus space will not be available for every flight, and never for popular times. But discounts range from 20 percent and more off standard fares. A sampling of consolidators is:

Access International	*101 West 31st Street, New York, NY 10016,* ☎ *(212) 465-0707; (800) 825-3633*
Travel Avenue	*10 South Riverside Plaza, Chicago, IL 60606,* ☎ *(800) 333-3335*
UniTravel	*1177 North Warson Rd., St. Louis, MO,* ☎ *(800) 325-2222*
Council Charter	*205 E. 42nd St., New York, NY 10017,* ☎ *(800)800-8222*
Sunline Express Holidays, Inc.	*607 Market St., San Francisco, CA 94105,* ☎ *(800) SUNLINE*
Travac	*989 Sixth Av., New York, NY 10018,* ☎ *(800) 872-8800*

By Car

Numerous border crossings link France with Spain. The most travelled are La Jonquera from Perpignan, on the extreme east coast, and Irún from Bayonne, on the extreme west coast. Both routes avoid mountain travel through the Pyrenees and remain open 24 hours a day, even through the winter. The most interesting Pyrenees route is through the tiny country of Andorra, enticing for its duty-free shopping. Portugal connects with Spain in 14 places, but the common crossings are from Élvas to Badajoz, in the center, from Valencia to Túy, in the north, and from the Algarve through Spain's Ayamonte in the far south.

By Train

Express trains leave Paris' Austerlitz station every evening, arriving at Madrid 13 hours later (or at Barcelona in 11-1/2 hours). The most modern train is the *Talgo* which currently departs from Paris at 8 p.m., and arrives at 8:30 a.m. in Chamartin station, Madrid. The Puerta del Sol is older, and leaves at 5:45 p.m. for a 9:55 a.m. arrival in Madrid. The Talgo also leaves for Barcelona from Paris at 9 p.m. for an 8:30 a.m. arrival. Sleeping accommodations must be reserved well in advance. Trains can also be picked up south of Paris, through Biarritz for Donostia (San Sebastian) and Madrid, and through Perpignan for Figueres and Barcelona on Spain's east coast. In most cases the train costs as much as flying and sometimes more.

Train service to Portugal all funnels through Madrid. The *Lusitania Express* leaves Madrid's Chamartin Station at 1:55 p.m. and 11 p.m. for arrival in Lisbon's Apolónia Station at 9:10 p.m. and at 8:45 a. m. The *Luiz de Camões*, in the daytime, is faster by a couple of hours. The reason the trip takes so long is that trains have to be changed at the Portuguese border because of wider-gauged Spanish rails.

In the other direction, the *Lusitania Express* leaves Lisbon at 9:45 p.m. for arrival in Chamartin Station at 8:55 a.m. A daylight train, the Luiz de Camões, is faster by more than an hour.

Costs

Although Spain and Portugal charge lower prices than other western European countries, they can no longer be considered inexpensive. Twenty years ago a moderate hotel charged $10 for a double, and the same amount bought a pleasant dinner for two with a house wine. Of course $10 bought more at home then too, but the loosening of government price controls on Spanish hotels and restaurants and the fall of the dollar have changed that situation even more drastically than inflation has.

Comfortable double rooms in moderately priced hotels in tourist areas and resorts cost about $100 ($130 in Madrid, Barcelona, and the Costa del Sol and Algarve in summer). The same room in a town less frequented by tourists will be 25 percent less. Count on $20 per person for an adequate dinner with wine. Gasoline is a significant expense as you will discover when you peel off almost $40 to fill up the tank. Museums in Spain average almost $4, twice that of Portugal. Thus, the current budget for a couple to travel modestly in Spain or Portugal in the high season of July and August averages a daily minimum of close to $200. This does not include transportation—either getting to or around the country. It is, however, about half the figure needed for France or Italy.

However, hotels drop their prices by at least 20 percent at times other than high summer and Christmas and Easter seasons. If a given city hosts a special festival, such as Seville with its April Fair or Pamplona with its San Fermin, top prices will also be charged at that time. At any other time of the year significant savings are possible. We list hotels by their high-season charges in this book; if traveling at other times, discount our listings by at least 20%.

When to Go: Climate and Seasons

In latitude Iberia sits opposite that part of the United States stretching from Boston to Baltimore, but because of proximity to the Mediterranean Sea its coastal climate is substantially warmer.

Spain's geography covers several different climates. The center, sealed from the sea by mountains north, south and west, experiences weather similar to most western European countries: hot summers, cold winters (but rarely with snow), low rainfall and low humidity. The north of Spain, especially the northwest—Galicia, Asturias and Cantabria—makes up for the aridity of the center. Santiago de Compostela averages five feet of rain annually, most of it falling in winter. On the other hand, the northwest is warmer in winter and cooler in summer than the central plateau. The most pleasant year-round temperatures in Spain are those of the eastern coast, from Catalonia to the Levant. Geographically a continuation of the French Riviera, it shares that climate, except for generally milder winters. Valencia averages 50 degrees in winter, Catalonia a few degrees less. August days reach 90, and swimming is comfortable in tepid 70-degree water through October. Almost all the rain falls in spring and autumn. The southern coastline of Spain enjoys the warmest winters in mainland Europe, with temperatures averaging 55 degrees in January. Almost no rain falls on the eastern half of this coast in summer, and not much during the rest of the year. Málaga boasts of almost 200 days of utterly cloudless skies. Coastal temperatures in August rise to mid or even high 90s.

Portugal's climate is more even, varying less than ten degrees between northern mountain cold and southern seaside warmth, with Lisbon experiencing almost exactly the temperatures as the Algarve. Winter corresponds to spring in our northeast; summer days seldom reach ninety or bring precipitation; spring and autumn are ideal sixty-degrees temperature-wise, but tend to be wet.

AVERAGE WEATHER IN SPAIN												
CITY		Jan.	Feb.	Mar.	Apr.	May	Jun.	Jul.	Aug.	Sep.	Oct.	Nov.	Dec.
ALMERIA (Southern Spain, 6 m/20 ft.)													
Avg High	°C	16	16	18	20	22	26	29	29	27	23	19	17
	°F	60	61	64	68	72	78	83	84	81	73	67	62
Avg Low	°C	8	9	11	13	15	18	21	22	20	16	12	9
	°F	46	47	51	55	59	65	70	71	68	60	54	49
Rainfall	mm	31	21	21	28	18	4	0	6	16	25	27	36
	in.	1.2	0.8	0.8	1.1	0.7	0.2	0	0.2	0.6	1.0	1.1	1.4

AVERAGE WEATHER IN SPAIN

CITY		Jan.	Feb.	Mar.	Apr.	May	Jun.	Jul.	Aug.	Sep.	Oct.	Nov.	Dec.
BARCELONA (Eastern Spain, 93 m/305 ft.)													
Avg High	°C	13	14	16	18	21	25	28	28	25	21	16	13
	°F	55	57	60	65	71	78	82	82	77	69	62	56
Avg Low	°C	6	7	9	11	14	18	21	21	19	15	11	8
	°F	43	45	48	52	57	65	69	69	66	58	51	46
Rainfall	mm	31	39	48	43	54	37	27	49	76	86	52	45
	in.	1.2	1.5	1.9	1.7	2.1	1.5	1.1	1.9	3.0	3.4	2.1	1.8
MADRID (Central Spain, 660 m/2165 ft.)													
Avg High	°C	9	11	15	18	21	27	31	30	25	19	13	9
	°F	47	52	59	65	70	80	87	85	77	65	55	48
Avg Low	°C	2	2	5	7	10	15	17	17	14	10	5	2
	°F	35	36	41	45	50	58	63	63	57	49	42	36
Rainfall	mm	39	34	43	48	47	27	11	15	32	53	47	48
	in.	1.5	1.3	1.7	1.9	1.9	1.0	0.4	0.6	1.3	2.1	1.9	1.9
SANTANDAR (Northern Spain, 66 m/217 ft.)													
Avg High	°C	12	12	14	15	17	20	22	22	21	18	15	13
	°F	53	54	58	60	62	68	71	72	70	65	59	55
Avg Low	°C	7	7	8	10	11	14	16	16	15	12	10	8
	°F	44	44	47	49	53	58	61	62	59	54	49	46
Rainfall	mm	119	88	78	83	89	63	54	84	114	133	125	159
	in.	4.7	3.5	3.1	3.3	3.5	2.5	2.1	3.3	4.5	5.2	4.9	6.3
SEVILLE (Central Spain, 9 m/30 ft.)													
Avg High	°C	15	17	20	24	27	32	36	36	32	26	20	16
	°F	59	63	69	74	80	90	98	97	90	78	68	60
Avg Low	°C	6	7	9	11	13	17	20	20	18	14	10	7
	°F	42	44	48	52	56	63	67	68	64	57	50	44
Rainfall	mm	66	61	90	57	41	8	1	5	19	70	67	79
	in.	2.6	2.4	3.5	2.2	1.6	0.3	0	0.2	0.8	2.8	2.6	3.1
CORUÑA (Northwestern Spain, 58 m/190 ft.)													
Avg High	°C	13	13	15	16	18	20	22	23	22	19	15	13
	°F	55	55	59	61	64	68	71	73	71	66	60	56
Avg Low	°C	7	7	8	9	11	13	15	15	14	12	9	8
	°F	45	44	47	48	51	55	58	59	57	53	49	46
Rainfall	mm	118	80	92	67	54	45	28	46	61	87	124	135
	in.	4.7	3.2	3.6	2.6	2.1	1.8	1.1	1.8	2.4	3.4	4.9	5.3

AVERAGE WEATHER IN PORTUGAL

CITY		Jan.	Feb.	Mar.	Apr.	May	Jun.	Jul.	Aug.	Sep.	Oct.	Nov.	Dec.
BRAGANZA (Northern Portugal, 720 m/2362 ft.)													
Avg High	°C	8	11	13	16	19	24	28	28	24	18	12	8
	°F	46	51	55	60	65	75	82	83	74	64	53	46
Avg Low	°C	0	1	3	5	7	11	13	13	10	7	3	1
	°F	32	33	38	40	45	51	55	55	50	44	38	33
Rainfall	mm	149	104	133	73	69	42	15	16	39	79	110	144
	in.	5.9	4.1	5.2	2.9	2.7	1.7	0.6	0.6	1.5	3.1	4.3	5.7
FARO (Southern Portugal, 36 m/118 ft.)													
Avg High	°C	15	16	18	20	22	25	28	28	26	22	19	16
	°F	60	61	64	67	71	77	83	83	78	72	66	61
Avg Low	°C	9	10	11	13	14	18	20	20	19	16	13	10
	°F	48	49	52	55	58	64	67	68	65	60	55	50
Rainfall	mm	70	52	72	31	21	5	1	1	17	51	65	67
	in.	2.8	2.1	2.8	1.2	0.8	0.2	0	0	0.7	2.0	2.6	2.6
LISBON (Central Portugal, 77 m/253 ft.)													
Avg High	°C	14	15	17	20	21	25	27	28	26	22	17	15
	°F	57	59	63	67	71	77	81	82	79	72	63	58
Avg Low	°C	8	8	10	12	13	15	17	17	17	14	11	9
	°F	46	47	50	53	55	60	63	63	62	58	52	47
Rainfall	mm	111	76	109	54	44	16	3	4	33	62	93	103
	in.	4.3	3.0	4.2	2.1	1.7	0.6	0.1	0.2	1.3	2.4	3.7	4.1
OPORTO (Northern Portugal, 95 m/312 ft.)													
Avg High	°C	13	14	16	18	20	23	25	25	24	21	17	14
	°F	56	58	61	65	67	73	76	77	75	69	62	57
Avg Low	°C	5	5	8	9	11	13	15	15	14	11	8	5
	°F	40	41	46	48	51	56	58	58	56	51	46	42
Rainfall	mm	159	112	147	86	87	41	20	26	51	105	148	168
	in.	6.3	4.4	5.8	3.4	3.4	1.6	0.8	1.0	2.0	4.1	5.8	6.6

Weather is pleasant the year round in Portugal. Spring and fall are ideal in the center of Spain, although summers can be uncomfortably hot and winters require bundling up. The northeast of Spain is best visited in summer, for winters bring frequent rain, though spring and fall are also pleasant. Catalonia and the Levant are balmy all year, their seas even swimmable in early fall, at least for those used to Maine bathing. Because of heat haze, Murcia is best in seasons other than summer. Barcelona, too, is not at its most enjoyable on steamy summer days. Andalusia remains pleasant year-long, though cool on winter evenings. However, nowhere in Spain is the weather ever inhospitable enough to prevent a trip.

Crowds are a consideration, too, in deciding when to visit. Spain doubles its population each summer, filling beaches, resort hotels and restaurants. In particular, August is the time when the Spanish themselves vacation, adding their numbers to beach crowds and leaving behind restaurants closed for vacation and raising prices to what the crowds will bear. Overall, spring would be the ideal season to cover Spain's terrain, and early summer months are preferable to crowded August.

For Portugal crowds are a concern only in the Algarve, but they are a major problem. Europeans adore Algarve beaches and book all the summer rooms by February. Reserve in January to avoid disappointment. Usually space in Lisbon is available the year round, however, special events may result in a scarcity of rooms.

Holidays and Special Events

The dates of holidays are important because businesses, certainly, and sights, possibly, will be closed. But holidays also offer the best opportunities to view and take part in the local color of the country.

Spain

National Holidays

All offices closed. When occurring near a weekend, the holiday becomes a four-day weekend.

Año Nuevo	*New Year.* Everyone is in the streets on New Year's Eve, and crowds gather in Madrid's Puerto del Sol munching grapes to the chiming of the clock at midnight.
Epifania del Señor	*Epiphany.* Presents are given to children, rather than on Christmas day.
San Jaime (mid-March)	*Saint James' day.*
Jueves Santo	*Maundy Thursday.*
Viernes Santo	*Good Friday.*
Dia de Pascua	*Easter Sunday.* Processions of floats in many towns bear holy statues.

May 1, Fiesta del Trabajo	*Labor Day.*
Asunción de la Virgen (mid-August)	*Assumption Day.*
October 12, Día Nacional de España	*Hispanic Day.*
November 1, Todos los Santos	*All Saints' Day.*
December 6, Constitución Española	*Constitution Day.*
Inmaculada Concepción (early December)	*Immaculate Conception.*
December 25, Natividad del Señor	*Christmas.*

Various regions and towns celebrate their own festivals at appointed times during the year. Check with the National Tourist Office of Spain for exact dates.

Carnival (mid-February)	Festive parades mark this festival before Lent.
March 24, Fallas	Processions of huge papier-mâché figures in Valencia.
Semana Santa (Easter week)	Processions of life-sized statues of the Holy Family, especially festive in Cádiz, Málaga, Seville, Toledo and Valladolid.
Viernes Santo	*Good Friday.* Processions of floats bearing holy statues in many towns (especially Seville, Málaga and Cádiz.
April Fair (the week after Easter)	Seville's picturesque festival where everyone dresses as if for *Carmen.*
Jerez Horse Fair (early May)	Horses, bullfighting and Flamenco.
San Isidro (late May)	Madrid's patron saint is celebrated for a week, and includes the best bullfights.
Corpus Christi (late June)	Processions, especially colorful in Toledo.
Running of the Bulls (early July)	Pamplona's famed macho festival.
Santiago Apóstol (end of July)	Feast of Santiago. Celebrated in odd numbered years only, i.e., not this year.
January 2, Granada	Commemoration of the end of the Reconquest.

Portugal

National Holidays—All offices close.

January 1	*Ano Novo*	New Year's Day
February (2nd week)	*Carnaval*	
Mid-April	*Sexta-feira Santa*	Good Friday
April	*Páscoa*	Easter
April 25	*Dia da Liberdade*	Liberation Day
May 1	*Dia do Trabalito*	Labor Day
June 10	*Dia da Portugal e da Camões*	Portugal and Camões Day
Mid-August	*Dia da Assuncão*	Assumption Day
October 5	*Dia da Republica*	Republic Day
November 1	*Todos os Santos*	All Saints' Day
December 1	*Restauração da Independencia*	Independence Day
Early December	*Imaculada da Concepção*	Immaculate Conception
December 25	*Dia de Natal*	Christmas

Various regions and towns celebrate their own festivals at appointed times during the year. See the discussion of the town in question for details, but they line up as follows:

1st half of January	Porto and Aveiro
2nd half of January	Aveiro; Évora
March Carnival	Throughout the country
April, Easter Week	Especially festive in Braga
1st half of May	Barçelos Fair
May 13	Pilgrimage to Fátima
May	Music festivals throughout the Algarve
Late June	Lisbon's St. Anthony fair; Porto's St John's Fair
June, last week	Évora's São João Festival
July-August	Estoril's music fair
August-!st weekend	Redondo Folk Festival
1st half of August	Folk Festival of Gualterianas in Guimarães

2nd half of August	Colorful "Lady of Agony" festival in Viana do Castelo; Agriculture and folk fair in Viseu
1st half of September	Dona da Nazaré festival in Nazaré
2nd half of September	Folk festivals throughout the Algarve
October 12–13	Fátima pilgrimage

Customs' Requirements

Both Spain and Portugal permit visitors to bring any items intended for personal use with them. This includes one carton of cigarettes and one liter of alcohol per adult. Expensive equipment—cameras, computers, etc.—should be registered with U.S. Customs before leaving the U.S. to ensure that they are not charged a duty on return. A proof of U.S. purchase will also suffice.

On the return home, U.S. Customs does not charge duty on a resident's first $400 of purchases for personal use or on gifts that accompany the traveler, providing his last allotment was claimed one month or more before. A family is permitted to pool its individual allotments as they wish. One carton of cigarettes is also duty-free for each adult, as are 100 cigars (not Cuban, of course), one liter of alcohol, and one bottle of perfume (if sold in the U.S, more otherwise). The next $1000 of personal merchandise or gifts is taxed at 10 percent. Above that amount, rates vary. Save receipts in case of questions. Antiques with proof from the seller that they are over 100 years old are duty-free, as are one-of-a-kind artworks.

Passports

The single requirement for the average tourist entering either Spain or Portugal is a valid passport. No shots are needed. No visa is necessary except for stays longer than 90 days (though this is seldom enforced) or to work in the country. Visa applications and information are available at the nearest Spanish emissary (**Spanish Embassy**: *2700 15th Street NW Washington, DC 20009,* ☎ *(202) 265-0190;* **Spanish Consulate**: *150 E. 58th Street, New York, NY 10155,* ☎ *(212) 555-4080)* or the Portuguese emissary (**Portuguese Embassy**: *2125 Kalorama Road NW, Washington, D.C. 20008,* ☎ *202-328-8610;* **Portuguese Consulate**: *630 Fifth Avenue, New York, NY 10111,* ☎ *(212) 246-4580).*

U. S. State Department passport agencies are located in Boston, Chicago, Honolulu, Houston, Los Angeles, Miami, New Orleans, New York, Philadelphia, San Francisco, Seattle, Stamford (CT) and Washington D.C. Federal or state courthouses also issue passports, as do many post offices.

Though not publicized or promised, renewals in person usually can be managed on an emergency basis in 24 hours at State Department offices. Frequent travelers may request double the normal 24 pages at no extra cost.

Hotels and Other Accommodations

The purpose of this book is to present paradors and pousadas for your selection, but there may be times when these hotels will not do. For example, there are no paradors in Madrid or Barcelona nor pousadas in Lisbon or Porto. Anyone staying in those cities needs another sort of accommodation. Then, sometimes the local parador or pousada isn't as good a choice as a private establishment nearby, either because it's less wonderful or because it threatens the budget. So, while we will describe all the paradors and pousadas and suggest itineraries based on them, we will add supplementary choices. (Incidentally, even if a special parador or pousada proves too expensive for spending the night, a lunch or dinner in its dining room allows a tour.)

Paradors and pousadas count as bargains because profit is not added to their tariffs. With the outstanding exceptions, noted above, of major cities that contain none, paradors and pousadas cover their respective countries well. It is a genuine treat to lodge your way around Spain and Portugal in these special hotels. We will discuss them all in the following pages, arranged by their location, and recommend and describe the surrounding sights, along with special restaurants.

Most people find that a night spent at an extraordinary hotel is at least the equal of a visit to a special museum or church. Paradors and pousadas monopolize any list of the great hotels of their respective countries. Here is a personal list of Spain's most extraordinary hotels (all expensive unless otherwise indicated) to whet your appetite. Note that more than half are paradors and that most of the establishments that crowd other paradors off the list do so with an elegance of service that also raises their prices far above parador levels.

Spain's Best

Parador Hostal de los Reyes Católicos	*Santiago de Compostela*
Parador Castillo de Sigüenza	*Sigüenza*
Alfonso XIII	*Seville (Very Exp.)*

Hotel De la Reconquesta	*Oviedo*
Ritz	*Madrid (Very Exp.)*
Santo Mauro	*Madrid (Very Exp.)*
Ritz	*Barcelona (Very Exp.)*
Parador San Marcos	*León*
Rector	*Salamanca*
Parador de Olite	*Olite (near Pamplona)*
Parador Duques de Cardona	*Cardona (near Barcelona)*
Parador Condes de Villalba	*Villalba (near Santiago de Compostela)*

For Portugal and her pousadas the story is similar. The best hotels in the country include at least five pousadas.

Portugal's Best

Palácio Seteis	*Sintra*
Pousada Santa Marinha	*Guimarães*
Hotel São Paulo	*Redondo near Évora*
Pousada Santa Maria	*Estremoz*
Infante de Sagres	*Porto*
Hotel da Lapa	*Lisbon*
Hotel Albatroz	*Cascais*
Vila Joya	*Albufeira (Algarve)*
Vilalara	*Armanção de Pêra (Algarve)*
Pousada de Palmela	*Palmela*
Pousada do Infante	*Sagres (Algarve)*
Pousada de São Lourenço	*Manteigas*

Money

Spanish money is called *pesetas*, abbreviated "ptas." Coins exist in denominations of 1, 2, 5, 10, 25, 50, 100, 200 and 500 pesetas, and bills bear denominations of 1000, 2000, 5000 and 10,000 pesetas. While the bills are unequivocal, coins arrive in a bewildering variety of sizes, shapes and colors.

What makes things difficult is that neither the size of a coin nor its color indicate its value. In particular, 100 and 500 pta. coins are easily confused. When it is not convenient to read the denomination, thickness is the best indicator of worth.

Portuguese money is called *escudos*. Each escudo is divided into 100 centavos, and prices are written in the form 1$00 with escudos to the left and centavos to the right (despite the fact that centavos hardly circulate). Coins exist in denominations of 1, 2.5, 5, 10, 20, 50, 100 and 200 escudos, while banknotes have the value of 500, 1000, 5000 and 10,000 escudos. Both 100 and 200 escudo coins have brass centers and can be detected by greater thickness than coins of lesser value.

At press time one U.S. dollar bought 175$escudos, which is to say that 100 escudos were worth 57 cents, but that is certain to fluctuate. One hundred and fifty-five pesetas were worth about $1. Incidentally, the "Travel" section of the Sunday *New York Times* quotes rates buying and selling foreign money in this country, not in Portugal or Spain, so its figures are low by twenty percent compared with what you will find when you arrive.

Banking hours in Portugal are similar to ours (from 8:30–3:00), but are more constricted in Spain—from 9 a.m. until 2 p.m. on weekdays only. However, the large **El Corte Inglés department store chain** in Spain changes money at bank rates and remains open when the banks are closed.

Popular credit cards are widely accepted in Spain, although Visa and MasterCard (called Eurocard in Spain) are recognized more generally than Amex or Diners' Club. Most restaurants, except very inexpensive ones, accept them, as do all first class and luxury hotels. Incidentally, payment by credit card ensures the best possible exchange rate.

Cash machines are growing common in Iberia. ATMs on the CIRRUS and PLUS systems will be found in large cities and they accept American bankcards, as well as Visa and MasterCard for cash advances. However, it is necessary to have a PIN number no longer than four digits. If yours is longer, the issuer of the card can change it for you before you depart. Amex cards can be used in such machines in Portugal but not Visa or MasterCards. However, Portugal's **Unicre-Unibanco** will dispense cash for those cards. The main office is at *Av. Antonio Augusto Aguiar 122.* in Lisbon.

Getting Around Spain and Portugal

By Car

When you drive in Iberia you discover how good U.S. roads really are. National highways there would be considered fair country roads here, yet they attempt to handle high traffic volume. And it is no fun at all driving behind a large truck with so much traffic in the other direction that passing proves impossible for miles. On the other hand, six-lane highways do exist and they are as speedy and well designed as our own. The problem is there are not enough such highways and, when not available in your direction, travel slows down.

The quality of a road and whether it is multi-laned is indicated by its letter designation. "A" followed by a number, as in A-1, means an *autopista* (*autoestrada* in Portugal), a well-paved four-lane or six-lane highway charging tolls *(peajes)* over most of its route. These roads will also have an "E" designation, since the major arteries in Europe are being systematically numbered throughout the European Economic Community. Toll roads charge truly exorbitant rates, but they do not pass through low-speed-limit villages, so save both time and gas.

"N" means a national road (*carratera Nacional*, or *Estrada Nacional*), and is followed by either a Roman or Arabic numeral. The number of digits in its designation tells how minor a road is. Thus, N203 will be a worse road than N10, acceptably paved but probably slower going. National roads are usually one lane in each direction and pass through towns and villages where speeds must be cut in half. The problem with only one lane going in your direction becomes painfully obvious when you're stuck behind a slow-moving vehicle. To help these roads become three-laned up steep hills, allowing an opportunity to pass. "D" and "C" prefixes designate even lesser roads, generally with more curves.

All are well marked with self-explanatory international highway symbols. However, except for super highways, these roads present astonishing hairpin curves, especially over the mountains, but sometimes on perfectly flat terrain. The curves are usually well marked, and preceded by signs indicating an appropriate speed, but stay alert.

Speed limits are 120 kilometers per hour (75 m.p.h.) on super highways, 100 (62 m.p.h.) on national highways, 90 (55 m.p.h.) on other roads, unless otherwise marked, and 60 (38 m.p.h.) to 40 in towns. Note that distances and speed limits will be measured in kilometers, approximately five-eighths of a mile. When passing, leave the left blinker on throughout your time in the passing lane, then signal right to return. Slow truckers will let you know when it is safe to pass them by signaling with their right blinker. Except for being occasionally more daring in passing, Spanish drivers are reasonably considerate and able.

Portuguese drivers are another story. The Portuguese are helpful and sweet in the normal conduct of their lives, but, as a psychologist friend reminds us, everyone needs an outlet for hostilities. The Portuguese find theirs in driving. Technically they are perfectly capable and they pilot fine machines, but they seem compelled to pass any vehicle that has the effrontery to be ahead of them and will do so under circumstances that will curl your hair. Need I add that they seem unaware of the speed limit? No wonder the Portuguese consistently earn the highest average accident rate in Europe. Drive defensively. Be aware that a car may pass you at any moment, even if the road behind seemed empty a second before. Most of all, be alert at the crest of any hill for some maniac, in the process of passing, driving straight toward you in your lane.

Gas is a major expense in Europe, costing three times what it does in the U.S. Posted gas prices are initially deceptive for Americans because they are quoted by the liter (slightly more than a quart), as opposed to per gallon. Stations are plentiful and remain open late throughout the country.

Car Rental

Although car rentals can be done on the spot, comparison shopping is easier from home and prices are lower. All major U.S. rental companies have Spanish subsidiaries. Your travel agent can make arrangements, or you can call directly for prices or reservations. Lesser known companies act as brokers to find the least expensive European rental for the type of car you specify. Generally, either Auto Europe or Europe by Car will have the lowest prices. Note that rentals will bill at 12–17 percent more than the price charged, because of Europe's VAT tax.

Despite the fact that the legal driving age in Spain is 18, most Spanish and some Portuguese rental agencies require a driver to be at least 21. Check in advance. Estimate about $380 per week for a compact car with automatic transmission, or about half that price for a smaller, manual-drive car without AC.

Avis	☎ *(800) 331-2112, or* ☎ *(800) 879-2847 in Canada.*
Auto Europe	☎ *(800) 223-5555, or* ☎ *(800) 458-9503 in Canada.*
Budget	☎ *(800) 527-0700.*
Dollar **(EuroDollar in Europe)**	☎ *(800) 800-6000.*
Europe by Car	☎ *(800) 223-1516 or* ☎ *(212) 581-3040.*
Foremost Euro-Car	☎ *(800) 272-3299, in California,* ☎ *(800) 272-3299.*
Hertz	☎ *(800) 654-3001 or* ☎ *(800) 263-0600 in Canada*
Kemwel	☎ *(800) 678-0678.*
National	☎ *(800) 227-3876.*

In addition, many rental companies and major airlines offer fly/drive packages that bundle airfare and car rental prices, frequently with very attractive savings.

An International Driving Permit is strongly recommended, for it is understood throughout Europe. Branches of the American Automobile Club can supply one. Bring along two passport-sized photos, a valid driver's license and a $5 fee. Incidentally, AAA has reciprocal arrangements with automobile clubs in Spain that provide similar services for AAA members from the U.S. **Real Automóvil Club de España** is located at *C. José Abascal, 10, Madrid 28003* (☎ *1-447-3200*). **Automovel Clube de Portugal**, located at *Rua Rosa Arango 24 in Lisbon* (☎ *01-736-121*), reciprocates in Portugal.

A good map is a necessity when driving. Old, haphazardly developed cities can be mazes of tiny, one-way streets. If aiming for the center, follow signs for "Centro."

By Plane

The cheapest way to fly from one city to another is to use free stopovers if they are included in your trans-Atlantic fare. Sufficient free stopovers may permit you to fly without additional charge. Check with your travel agent.

Until recently Spain had only one domestic airline—Avianco, affiliated with international Iberia Airlines, but competition today from Viva and Binter lowers prices that were already reasonable. Spain is a large country so flying is often the most convenient transportation. From Madrid, the longest flight to anywhere in Spain takes under one hour. Iberia always offers some inter-country special for foreign visitors. Currently on sale is a $300 pass (less out of season) for four cities of your choice, if purchased in conjunction with a ticket to Spain on Iberia Airlines. Barcelona is served by a shuttle plane (Puente Aereo) that leaves Madrid every half hour, and requires no reservation.

Portugal is so small that flying from one part of the country to another is rarely called for, nor does one see much of the country from 10,000 feet in the air. In a rush, both Porto in the north and Faro in the south's Algarve can be reached by Portugalia commuter flights from Lisbon that leave hourly, require no reservations and cost under $100.

By Train

Trains (and buses) beat planes when the distance is 200 miles or less because train stations are located downtown while airports are not.

Trains go almost everywhere in Spain, though not always directly. RENFE (Red Nacional de los Ferrocarriles Español) radiates from its hub in Madrid to the corners of the country. Travel is convenient along any continuous radius, but requires retracing tracks to reach cities on different lines. RENFE ticket offices are centrally located in large cities.

The best trains for speed and service are international trains (EC, IC, TER, Electrotren, Pendular and Talga). Intra-country *"expreso"* and *"rapido"* come next. Seville is served by the splendid new, high-speed AVE, complete with airplanelike earphones, that takes less than three hours. Smaller cities, however, are connected by Motorail, which corresponds to our commuter train systems. The price depends on the caliber of train and whether you choose to travel in first or second class. So many types of discounts are offered that anyone paying full fare has simply not asked—round-trips, senior citizens, families, youths and certain days of the week are all assigned one discount or another. Better than standing in line at the train station is to drop in to any travel agency in Spain that displays a yellow and blue RENFE sign. It costs no more.

Portuguese trains were British-built 75 years ago to the finest wide-gauge standards. In 1990, however, the Portuguese national rail system (CP) drastically cut service and maintenance. What remains is the romance of a train ride, though comfort and cleanliness are barely adequate. IR trains make fewer stops than regional trains and IC trains are faster still. Cerviço Alfas are the speediest of all, include dining facilities and are first-class only. They speed from Lisbon to Porto in under three hours for about $40 and to the Algarve in four and a half hours for about $50.

Restaurants

Restaurants in Spain and Portugal serve filling meals at about the price of restaurants at home. If the cost is slightly greater, the portions will be too. In Spain the problem is when these meals are served. The Spanish take siestas, which means they eat their big meal of the day at noon, just before a nap. Restaurants do not reopen for dinner until 8 p.m., at the earliest, or until 9 p.m. in metropolises such as Madrid or Barcelona. Hotel dining rooms are exceptions, since many of their guests can't wait so long to eat. Otherwise, when in Rome.... Portugal's dining hours are closer to what we are used to—7–10 p.m. for dinner.

The fundamental difference between northern European cuisines and those of the Spanish and Portuguese is the use of olive oil for sautéing, rather than butter products. Because the quality of available ingredients is outstanding throughout Spain and Portugal, even a modest restaurant can provide delicious tastes. Vegetables are grown for flavor, not for their capacity to survive early picking and travel, as in the U.S. Humble chicken retains the taste we have all but forgotten, and bread always tastes homemade.

Portuguese food tends to be simpler and blander than the Spanish version, more homey and filling than haute cuisine. Prices vary but prove to be about the same as a similar restaurant would charge at home. Best are the fresh fish, roast chicken and breads that bring out the peasant in all of us. Although charges, on average, are reasonable, if you want to trim costs, look for a restaurant specializing in *frango assado* or *churrascera*. Almost any such establishment will serve half of a delectable roast chicken, usually with *piri piri* (hot sauce) on the side and a heap of tasty french fries for about $10 with house wine. Another budget helper comes from stands or bars selling delicious steak sandwiches, *pregos*. Keep your eyes out for *pasteis de bacalhau*, delectable codfish cakes. There are also abundant pizza places. All restaurants offer an *ementa do dia* (menu of the day) that provides a full meal often at 75% of the cost of ordering separate dishes.

(One Portuguese practice to be aware of concerns the appetizers that generally come to your table as you peruse the menu. These are *not* free munchies. If you eat even one olive or piece of bread, you will be charged for that dish.)

Spanish food, on the other hand, can be as elevated as the French, although less for the sauces than for perfect cooking and seasoning. In no way should it be confused with Mexican cuisine which employs a different spice palette, degree of "heat" and ingredients. At its best Spanish food can be subtle and delectable, at its worst, it sinks to the heavy and greasy.

The Spanish love to dine out which generates an astonishing number of restaurants. In cities and towns, crowds wander the streets every evening, pause to study menus, and stop where their fancy dictates. Fortunately, few "tourist traps," where bad food is served at high prices, exist. Spain boasts some utterly splendid restaurants that rank with the best in the world. **Zalacaín** in Madrid and **Arzak** in Donostia (San Sebastian) both have Basque chefs, impeccable service and sublime food, at a price (about $65 dollars a person for Zalacaín, and $60 for Arzak).Even though restaurant prices are generally not exorbitant, eating out consumes the major part of most tourists' budgets. Costs can be reduced by ordering from the *Menú Turístico*, which all Spanish restaurants are obliged to offer (at least at lunch-time). This provides a three-course meal, usually including wine, and makes up for limited choices with savings of about half of à la carte orders. Many places offer *platos combinados* (combination plates), a filling meal and salad all on one plate, for five to 10 dollars, usually including wine on the side. Or try a sandwich *(bocadillo)* in any bar, or *tapas* (appetizers), enough for a meal in omnipresent tapas bars. Cafeterias and *auto-servicios* can be half the price of restaurants. And, should all else fail, major cities offer McDonald's and Kentucky Fried Chicken, just like at home—and at similar prices.

Shopping

Ceramics, leather, woven rugs, fashion, pearls, antiques and flea markets all call to the tourist's wallet in Spain. In Portugal ceramics, embroidered rugs, linens, antiques and, again, flea markets all pull out our purse strings.

Spain has been famous for **ceramics** since the time of the Moors, and its leather work so noted that "cordovan" became an English proper noun. Spain still produces colorful ceramics sold in a hundred shops at very attractive prices. The factories are located in Talavera de la Reina (near Toledo) and in the outskirts of Seville. Spain continues its tradition of fine **leather**, especially in Andalusia and in the famed Loewe's stores, with shoes best in Madrid, Barcelona and Seville.

Famed Majorca **pearls** can cost as much as 30 percent less in Spain. Spanish **antiques** have not yet escalated as precipitously as French, Italian or English articles; bargains, even in quality pieces, still exist. Costume **jewelry** is excellent and inexpensive. When one realizes that **gold** must be a minimum of 18 karat, one will see bargains. Colorful **rugs** can be spectacular. Toledo sells every kind of **weapon** imaginable, from copies of ancient swords, knives and guns to modern ones, from models to the real things.

The most entertaining shopping is to be found in local **flea markets**, in Madrid and elsewhere. Discussions of each city include the information.

Only the rare traveler can resist bringing **ceramics** home from Portugal. The pieces are delightful and range from elegant Vista Alegre productions through charming folk work to lovely modern copies of ancient designs. Vista Alegra ware approaches the finest French and English bone china, but prices are rigidly controlled by the factory so they are rarely less expensive than at Bloomingdale's. Purchases from the factory shop outside **Aveiro**, however, come from a grand selection offered nowhere else. On the other hand, traditional hand-crafted designs are sold all over Portugal. They include blue on white and polychrome copies of 16th- and 17th-century originals. Most are produced in **Condeixa** near Coimbra, where prices are lower than elsewhere. **Caldas da Raina**, also near Coimbra, is known for articles in the form of vegetables and fruit. **Barçelos**, in the north, produces charming folk-figurines, in addition to ubiquitous roosters. Painted and glazed tiles, called *azulejos*, can be purchased at many places, either individually or as composite scenes.

Arraiolos, near Évora, is the source of Portugal's famed **needlepoint carpets**; **Portalegre**, near Marvao in the Alentejo, produces fine hand-made **embroidered tapestries**. Several **Lisbon** shops carry lovely **lacework** from Madeira, although cheaper Chinese copies have demoted these from the buys they once were. Nonembroidered **linens**, however, remain outstanding buys in **Lisbon**, both for quality and price.

Lisbon is also known for **filigree** goldwork and silver. **Leather** of decent quality is available in the capital as well. **Antiques** are available in many areas, but the largest concentration is in Lisbon's **Bairro Alto**. Of course, **port** wines proliferate in Porto but are sold even in supermarkets throughout the country.

Time Zones and Official Hours

Clocks both in Spain and Portugal run six hours ahead of Eastern Standard Time in the U.S. Daylight saving time is observed in both countries from the last week in March to the end of September, so that during October the difference from E.S.T. declines to five hours.

The afternoon closings of shops, businesses, museums and monuments can be an avid tourist's bane, leaving him with nothing to do except eat or rest throughout the afternoon.

In Spain **banks** generally open from 8:30 a.m. until 2 p.m. on weekdays, but may close an hour earlier in summer. A few remain open until 5 p.m. on Thursday. **Shops** generally start business at nine or 10 Monday through Saturday, but close from one or two until three or four in the afternoon before opening again until eight in the evening. **Businesses** generally keep similar hours, except for being closed on Saturday. **Department stores** remain open throughout the day.

After closing for the afternoon hiatus, **museums** generally reopen until seven in the evening. However, in winter most museums and monuments close at six, rather than seven. Almost all museums close on Mondays and open only until one or two on Sundays. **Restaurants** open from one until four for lunch, then from nine or so until 11:30 or midnight for dinner. Of course, there are always exceptions.

It's a little more regular in Portugal. **Shops** open at 9 a.m. (or 10 a.m.), close for lunch at 1 p.m., then reopen at 3:00 until closing at 7 p.m. The few **department** stores and **shopping centers** remain open through the lunch period and, in the case of the shopping centers, may remain open until midnight. **Businesses** follow the regime of shops except for closing a half hour or an hour earlier. **Museums** generally open at 10 a.m., close for lunch from 12:30 p.m. until 2 p.m., then reopen until 5 p.m. Most are open every day except Monday.

Telephones, Electricity and Measurement

The telephone system is perfectly adequate, if somewhat slow. A local call costs 25 pesetas in Spain, 10 escudos in Portugal. To call Spain from the U.S. or Canada, dial 011 for international calls, 34 for Spain, and the Spanish telephone number, but drop the "9" in the Spanish area code. For example, the area code for Madrid is 91. To call Portugal from this side of the Atlantic, dial 011, 351 for Portugal, then the local Portuguese number. To call the U.S. or Canada from Spain, dial 07, for overseas, and 1 for the U.S. or Canada, plus the local area code and number. From Portugal the prefix is 097. To call the U.S. using an **AT&T** calling card, dial *900-99-11* for an American operator; using an **MCI** calling card, dial *900-99-14.*

To call a number in the same city in Spain just dial the local number, but to call a different city first dial 9, then the two or three digit area code, then the local number. In Portugal 0 accomplishes what 9 does in Spain.

Electricity in both Spain and Portugal runs at 220 or 240 volts, compared with 110 in the U.S. Unless an appliance has a 220 volt switch, it is likely to burn out in an Iberian socket when run at twice its power. Inexpensive converters are readily available in the U.S. Make sure you also buy an adapter for European sockets, which accept thin tubes, rather than our wider prongs.

Measures are metric, as in most of the world. Distance is measured in kilometers, volume in liters and weight in grams.

WHERE TO GO

Óbidos, with its steep, tiny streets and hilltop castle, charms tourists.

There is much to see and do with two entire countries under consideration—too much for any normal vacation trip. Let us tempt you with what is available. Afterwards we will recommend itineraries.

Topping any list of Spanish sights would be Andalusia's three great cities located close enough to each other to be covered in one trip. **Granada** must be seen for its Alhambra Palace, arguably the finest Muslim structure in the world and unlike any collection of buildings anywhere—perfect, exquisite and provoking. Together with its associated castle, fortified walls and the Generalife (summer palace nearby), it can be seen in half a day. Add the Capilla Real (Royal Chapel) with the tombs of Isabella and Ferdinand to the other sights in the city, and Granada can be explored in a day or two. An hour away lies **Córdoba** with its Mesquita, a perfectly preserved mosque. Inside, a forest of variegated columns incongruously houses a cathedral. The Mesquita, the lovely patios of the ancient Jewish Quarter, and the other sights of Córdoba consume one day. Two hours farther waits **Seville**, a beautiful city that contains the second best art museum in Spain, an immense cathedral and two resplendent examples of medieval Moorish-Christian architecture—the Alcázar and the Casa de Pilatos. At the minimum, Seville needs two days.

Next in priority is Madrid and the cities around it—Toledo, El Escorial, Segovia and Salamanca. **Toledo** is a virtual museum city overflowing with El Grecos. It possesses an awesome cathedral, an exquisite ancient synagogue, a fine art museum and more. Since Toledo lies within an hour of Madrid, visitors frequently make it a frenzied day-trip from the capital. An overnight stay would be better. **Madrid** is new in Spanish terms, but cosmopolitan and fun, combines pleasing sights with great museums. Two days hardly does justice to such a large and diverse city. A half-hour away, for a half-day excursion, stands **El Escorial**, a majestic complex of palace, church and monastery from the 16th century. An hour farther along is **Segovia**, with a genuine castle looking strikingly like the fantasy one at Disneyland, plus a grand cathedral and a dozen Romanesque churches all set on an imposing site—a visit requiring at least one hurried day. **Salamanca**, at least another full day, is surely the finest city in Spain that tourists ignore. It is a treasure-house of intricate Renaissance *plateresque* architecture, much of it preserved on the grounds of its university. Salamanca also boasts one of the great churches in Spain—the Romanesque **Catedral Vieja**.

Barcelona is a beautiful, cosmopolitan city offering much to do, pleasant walks while doing it and fine food to enjoy afterward. Beyond such simple pleasures, Barcelona bursts with so much architecture and art that it bids to be the one city in Spain to see if you can only see one. There is a fine cathedral standing in a preserved medieval quarter (the **Barri Gòtic**); the best Medieval and Renaissance museum in Spain (the **Museu de Arte de Catalunya**); some of the finest examples of modern art in the **Miró** and **Picasso museums**; and the astounding **Sagrada Familia** cathedral by Gaudí, to mention just the highlights. An absolute minimum stay in Barcelona demands three days.

Santiago de Compostela presents a great Romanesque cathedral set in the most beautiful of squares. Because one travels to Santiago to see only the cathedral and squares, it would be possible to spend a half day there, then continue on one's way. But no one wants to. Everyone sits, charmed and contemplative, regretting their time of departure. Just as grand, in a less insistent way, is the huge and flamboyantly Gothic cathedral of **Burgos**. Burgos is a lively, lovely town that should receive at least a full day of one's time. Outside the city stand a medieval convent and a Renaissance monastery, each a gem.

The state of Extremadura encompasses a variety of sights spread throughout pleasant scenery. **Mérida** preserves Roman buildings, **Cáceres** is a town of Renaissance houses, **Trujillo** invites with moody castle ruins and homes of the conquistadores, while **Guadalupe** monastery glitters mysteriously in the mountain's heights. **Extremadura** is small—a tour of the state requires only three days—and lies close to Madrid.

As to Portugal, **Lisbon** is the city most visited. While other European cities may be more grand, Lisbon has a character of its own, with enough sights to merit two full days. Elegant beaches surround Lisbon at **Estoril** and **Cascais** 14 miles west; lovely **Queluz Palace** waits six miles northwest; the magical forests of **Sintra**, described below, lie just 10 miles farther along; the imposing monastery of **Mafra** stands only 20 miles to the north; and stunning **Batalha** is close enough for a day trip. Enough wonders surround Lisbon to add at least two days more.

Portugal's most elegant spot is certainly the monastery at **Batalha**. For the 100 years it took to build this edifice, doting kings spared no expense to create a marvel. The ensemble of buildings composes an unusually harmonious whole, graceful in every detail. Batalha is an easy day trip from Lisbon that should not be missed. A visit can also include the nearby village of **Alcobaça**, which has a fine monastery of its own containing the romantic tombs of Inês de Castro and her lover, Pedro the Cruel. **Fátima** of the miracles is 10 miles east of Alcobaça.

Évora, due east of Lisbon, does not offer any one must-see sight, but contains a number of attractions in the lovely package of the town itself, and more wait nearby. Because Évora is located at Lisbon's latitude, a traveler could leave the capital early one morning, see Évora's sights before dark, stay the night in Estremoz at one of Portugal's most elegant pousadas, and spend the next day touring the fortified towns of **Estremoz**, **Évoramonte**, and lovely **Elvas**.

If you have an extra day, you could also include the embroidered carpets of **Arraiolos**, the antiques of **Borba** and the village of **Marvão** (discussed below).

Although **Marvão** is a fortified hilltop village of which Portugal has scores similar in age and condition, it differs by being the most charming. A stroll through the village provides enough mood for a half-day's sojourn. Marvão is a breeze of a day-trip from Évora, or can be reached directly from Lisbon in five hours by car.

Sintra, a mere 30 km from Lisbon, ranks near the top of any tourist's list both for its enchanted mountain site, and for its three castles—one from the 10th, another from the 16th, and one unbelievable fantasy from the 19th century. Spend the night and there's time to add the baroque royal palace of **Queluz**.

Tomar, 80 miles north of Lisbon, holds one special sight. Its monastery consists of a mysterious 12th-century church of the Knights Templar, graced by sublime cloisters. What makes a visit even more appealing is proximity to **Almourol**—Portugal's most romantic castle—sitting, as in a fairy tale, on the waters of the Tejo river. And less than half an hour away is the pilgrimage site of **Fátima**.

Coimbra is the major city on the road from Lisbon to Porto and offers plenty to do both in the city and around it. Coimbra contains the old buildings of Portugal's first university, a fine museum, and several interesting churches tumbling down a steep hill. **Condeixa-a-Nova**, 11 miles south, sells lovely ceramics and retains Roman ruins on its outskirts at **Conímbriga**. Twenty-five miles west is the resort of **Figueira da Foz**, with the Vista Alegre china factory and shop on its outskirts.

Travel to **Viseu**, 60 miles farther north. A stately cathedral stands on one side, a fine museum on another, and a perfect Portuguese baroque church graces the opposite end. If only the space between them were not a parking lot! A trip to Viseu can also be combined with **Guarda**, a village situated in the center of a score of medieval fortified hilltop villages, each more atmospheric than the next.

Porto is a city that still feels and looks like a 19th-century town. For all its attractive buildings and vivacity, it seems a kind of Portuguese Paris. Yes, there is port wine to be tasted, and plenty of it.

Close by is **Guimarães**, site of the country's oldest surviving castle where the first King of Portugal was born. Plus, there is a dramatic Renaissance palace and the most magnificent of all the pousadas, the grand **Santa Marinha**.

From Porto or Braga, **Bragança** is an exquisitely scenic 120-mile trip. Its old churches stand in lonely isolation behind mountains in an almost forgotten area of the country—a glimpse of an older way of life.

Beaches

Spain is almost surrounded by beach, close to 2400 miles of it, some on the Atlantic, but most on the Mediterranean. Europeans are well aware of both the quality and quantity of Spain's shore, arriving in sufficient droves every summer to double the population of the country.

The northern beaches—those on the Atlantic—are comprised of some looking like Scandinavian fjords, and others dotted with elegant resorts. A tour of these beaches can pleasantly fill a vacation. Start at Santiago and head east to the coastal **Rias**, headlands cut by river estuaries to form dramatic fjords. Or follow the coast east, pausing for days at Santillana del Mar,

Santander and Donostia (also called San Sebastian) to explore the **Costa Ver-de**. Or trace the route the other way around.

On the east coast, the rugged **Costa Brava** runs north from Barcelona for almost 100 miles, as cliffs and headlands are broken by tranquil coves. Though much development has taken place since the 1960s, pockets of scenic beach remain to remind us of rugged Maine, though thankfully warmer. South of Barcelona, along the 100 miles to Valencia, lies the **Costa del Azahar**, the Coast of Orange Blossoms. The land flattens, beaches widen and stretch, and the scent of orange blossoms indeed hangs in the spring air. Housing developments reach into that same air, but not to the degree that they do farther south on the Costas del Sol and Blanca. A few scattered towns manage to retain their charm; beaches are ample, with Peñiscola the best. Thus, sunning opportunities run for over 100 miles both north and south of Barcelona. Transportation is ample too—using either trains or buses it is perfectly feasible to visit both Barcelona and its adjacent beaches without a car.

The most popular beaches in Spain, in fact in all of Europe, form the southern coast of Spain. East to west spread the Costa Blanca, Costa del Sol and Costa de la Luz. The **Costa Blanca** is named for its fine white beaches that stretch for miles. Benidorm boasts of the best beaches in Spain, but the town itself is no longer attractive and space on the sand is hard to find at the height of the season. Nonetheless, there are pockets on this coast where crowds do not collect and bathing remains scenic and tranquil. The weather is wonderful—seldom are there clouds, let alone rain. The **Costa del Sol**, running from Gibraltar east to Almeria, is a different cup of tea. Beaches are gritty, pebbles in the shallows make wading difficult, and high-rise developments stretch as far as the eye can see. Why then do all the people come? To see all the other people, of course. These are Spain's most popular beaches by far and the most cosmopolitan and exciting, with crowded clubs, restaurants and bars. It is fun, and the sun shines almost every day, but such amusements are not cheap. West of Gibraltar begins the Atlantic Ocean and the **Costa de la Luz**. Beaches consist of sand rather than grit, the Atlantic sends true waves, fresh seafood is delicious and the crowds and prices dip below those on the Costa del Sol.

Portugal's southern extremity, the **Algarve**, consists of 200 km of the finest beaches in Europe, bar none. The water is an unpolluted blue-green; beaches are the finest white sand; and cliffs behind form exquisite rock formations and picture-postcard coves. Such perfection naturally attracts hordes of sun-seekers, yet the Algarve's prices are surprisingly low—generally lower than the less entrancing resorts along Spain's coast. Best of all, there remain areas at both ends of the Algarve that the crowds have not yet discovered. The Algarve is an easy day's travel from either Lisbon or Évora.

Fine beaches are also available near **Setúbal** within an hour's drive south of Lisbon. There are elegant resorts only a half-hour west of Lisbon at **Estoril**, with a casino, and at neighboring **Cascais**. About 20 miles west of Coimbra stretch long lovely beaches at **Figueira da Foz**. Halfway between Coimbra and Porto, less than 100 km west of Viseu, is the beach town of **Aveiro**, situated on a huge lagoon and divided by canals.

Castles

Do you want to see fortresses, the fabled castles of Spain? Here is a list of the best, all close to Madrid. The Alcázar in **Segovia** looks like a fairy-tale castle; and **Ávila**, not far from Segovia, is the most complete medieval fortified town in Europe (tied with Carcassone in France). Northeast of Ávila is the still-imposing castle of **Peñafiel**, with parts as old as the 10th century, the rest from the 15th. South of Madrid, on the way to Andalusia, is a massive 15th-century castle in **Belmonte**, complete with perimeter wall. Farther afield, the Alcázar of the Alhambra in **Granada**, along with its perimeter walls, calls insistently to the fortress lover, as do the walls of **Trujillo** in Extremadura. Would you like to spend the night in a castle? Near Madrid there is a large castle turned parador at **Siqüenza**, or, for more intimate fortress surroundings, the parador castle at **Alarcón**. Near Pamplona at **Olite**, an archtypical castle has been turned into another parador.

In Portugal at **Guimarães**, north of Porto, soar reconstructed 11th-century towers of the first castle of Portugal, where the parents of Afonso Henrique lived and in which he was born, to make it the cradle of the country. But the most magical castle of all is **Almourol**, perfectly situated on an island in the Tagus River, near Tomar. Built by the Knights Templar, this is the one castle lovers fantasize about.

Since medieval times Portugal had neighboring Spain to worry about, and so, during the 13th century, built a series of fortresses along the border. Twenty or so still ring the town of **Guarda**, 85 miles east of Coimbra. These were never palaces, but stout redoubts built to withstand sieges. Today their strong walls, generally with nothing inside them, allow the imagination to man the barricades. **Monsanto**, north of Évora, is probably the most dramatic.

More modern fortresses, that is to say from the 17th century, include the extensive "Vauban" style walls of Almeida, near **Guarda**, and Elvas, near **Évora**, that spread for miles. These are more than just massive walls to keep unwanted visitors out, but designs to entice an enemy into crossfires.

Palaces are in large supply in Portugal. Most impressive is the National Palace at **Sintra**, 200 years in the making, and unrestored. The restored Palace of the Dukes of Bragança, in **Guimarães** north of Porto, is a splendid 15th-century structure with elegant fittings. The palace at **Queluz**, near Lisbon, delicate and lovely, is a fitting contrast to the baroque munificence of the palace at **Mafra**. Try to include Pena Palace, also at **Sintra**, on your itinerary. Here the adjective "Victorian" takes on new meaning.

Passing the night in a castle or palace is even more enjoyable than just looking. The pousada of Rainha Santa Isabel in **Estremoz** is built inside the former grand palace. Pousada do Castilo in **Óbidos** provides a more rustic, medieval castle feel. Pousada Castelo de **Alvitó**, 85 miles from Lisbon near Beja in the Alentejo, is housed in a 15th-century Gothic fortress.

And while a monastery is not a palace, some are splendid enough to make the distinction academic. The grandest is Santa Marinha pousada in **Guimarães**. More intimate and older (14th-century) is the privately owned Hotel Convento de São Paulo, near **Évora**. The dining room of Pousada de **Palmela** is the former rectory of a 15th-century monastery, high on a hill.

Cathedrals

Anyone in pursuit of cathedral glories will find a profusion in Spain. In particular those in **Toledo**, **Burgos** and **Seville** represent the best and most impressive examples of the sumptuous Spanish Gothic. **León** presents the airier French model, and **Santiago de Compostela** , the acme of the Romanesque, while **Salamanca's** Catedral Vieja is a quietly moving church. The church at **El Escorial** and the cathedral at **Valladolid**, both by the architect Herrera, are imposing neo-classical structures.

Virtually every city and most towns will have a church of interest. And monasteries range from **Poblet**, near Barcelona (entirely restored, but moving nonetheless), to **Miraflores** and **Las Huelgas Convent**, older and more atmospheric (both in the suburbs of **Burgos**), to **El Escorial** (for its classical lines), and **Guadalupe** (full of religious mystery).

Portugal's cathedral pride is Santa Maria da Vitoria Monastery in **Batalha**, on which her great architects worked. Nearby **Alcobaça** is thrilling as well, as is the not too distant cathedral of **Coimbra**.

Charming Villages

Santiago de Compostela and **Segovia**, being large, stretch the village characterization, but both have that feel along with charm to spare. **Trujillo** is sleepy and picturesque. **Ronda**, in Andalusia, provides breathtaking vistas across the landscape. **Arcos de la Frontera**, also in Andalusia, offers views almost as stunning from either the parador or the tiny El Convento Hotel. **Peñiscola**, on the Costa del Azahar, offers vistas, miles of white beach and a lively town. **Donostia** on the Costa Verde is also much too large for the category, but its elegance immediately makes visitors forget that discrepancy.

Outside of a few cities and resort areas, Portugal consists of nothing but charming villages. Of course some of these villages are more charming than others, but those on the tourist circuit may be peopled by more gawkers than natives. For example, **Óbidos**, lost in time, charms everyone with its steep tiny streets and hilltop castle, and is a favorite of the tourists. You will not be alone there. **Marvão**, in the northern Alentejo, sites granite houses amid granite boulders for a unique picturesqueness, but you will not be alone there either. **Sintra** is deservedly famous as well, but provides enough surrounding forests to swallow up the touring throngs.

Our picks for the most picturesque place to visit would be **Buçaco** and **Sintra** forests on a quiet day; 17th-century **Amarante**, near Porto, peacefully overlooking the Tâmega on any day; and always **Bragança**, lost in time behind the Trás-o-Montes in the north.

The Best Paradors and Pousadas

The best paradors, in order, would be:

Rating	Parador	Town	Page
★★★★★	Hotel Reyes Católicos	Santiago de Compostela	*page 308*
★★★★★	Hostal San Marcos	León	*page 354*
★★★★	Duques de Cardona	Cardona	*page 420*
★★★★	Castelo de Santa Catalina	Jaén	*page 207*
★★★★	Marqués de Villena	Alarcón	*page 180*
★★★	La Concordia	Alcañiz	*page 430*
★★★★	Ferdinand II de León	Benavente	*page 343*
★★★	El Emperador	Hondarribia	*page 423*

The best pousadas are:

Rating	Pousada	Town	Page
★★★★★	Santa Marinha	Guimarães	*page 637*
★★★★	Rainha Santa Isabel	Estremoz	*page 548*
★★★★	Castelo de Alvito	Alvito	*page 544*
★★★★	Flor da Rosa	Flor da Rosa	*page 546*
★★★★	Palmela	Palmela	*page 517*
★★★★	Donha Maria I	Queluz	*page 512*
★★★★	Santa Cristina	Condeixa	*page 622*
★★★★	São Francisco	Beja	*page 561*

Itineraries

Since too much of even a good thing can tire, we recommend that days of sights be broken either by beach lolling or an extra day with nothing on the agenda in a town you enjoy. That same wisdom argues against overloading a trip with any single type of sight, whether castles, cathedrals or museums. Variety, as someone should have said, is the spice of vacations. Suggested itineraries follow, though we leave it up to you how to implement our advice to serve your own interests.

The following ten itineraries cover most of Spain in trips that vary in length from one week to 15 days. Any two itineraries may be combined to form trips of longer duration, and too-long itineraries may be shortened by omissions. As to the time estimates, we are aware that many travelers want to fill every minute with activity. Each itinerary assumes a first day consumed by travel, settling in a hotel and gaining bearings, and a last day taken up by departure arrangements, which in some cases might involve flying into Madrid for international connections. So, a week's itinerary comprises five sight-seeing days. Add to our itineraries whatever beach or rest days you wish.

IMPORTANT NOTE: Most museums in Spain are closed on Monday. If we list a museum for a day that falls on a Monday during your trip, interchange it with another day.

Madrid, seven days

This trip presents the flavor of Madrid and the Prado, one of the great museums of the world, as well as El Escorial, an imposing complex.

Day 1:   Travel to Madrid and settle into a hotel.

Day 2:   The Museo Nacional del Prado; Jardin del Retiro.

Day 3:   La Ciudad Antigua; Plaza Mayor; Convento Descalzes Reales; Convento de la Encarnación.

Day 4:   Excursion to El Escorial.

Day 5:   Museo Arqueológico Nacional; shopping; Museo Lázare Galdiano.

Day 6:   Palacio Real.

Day 7:   Departure.

Madrid and Toledo, seven days

This trip adds remarkable Toledo to the best of Madrid.

Day 1:   Travel to Madrid and settle into a hotel.

Day 2:   The Museo Nacional del Prado; Convento Descalzes Reales.

Day 3:   La Ciudad Antigua; Plaza Mayor; Palacio Real.

Day 4:   Museo Arqueológico Nacional; shopping; Museo Lázaro Galdiano.

Day 5:   Travel to Toledo; settle into a hotel; Cathedral; Santo Tomé.

Day 6:   Alcázar; El Tránsito Synagogue; Iglesia María Blanca; Santa Cruz Museum.

Day 7:   Return to Madrid and departure.

Note: If an extra day is available, the fairy tale castle of Segovia lies an hour north of Madrid, with El Escorial on the way.

Barcelona, seven days

This trip introduces the cosmopolitan city of Barcelona, its extraordinary collections of medieval and modern Spanish art, and the charm of Gaudí's architecture.

Day 1:   Travel to Barcelona and settle into a hotel.

Day 2:   Barri Gótic; Cathedral; Palau de la Generalitat.

Day 3:   Museo de Arte de Catalunya; Fondacion Joan Miró; Museu Arqueológico, if time.

Day 4:   Museu Maritím; Museu Picasso; and the Textile and Costume Museum.

Day 5:   Gaudí's works, including Sagrada Familia; shopping.

Day 6:   Ramblas and Palácio de la Virreina; Santa Maria del Mar.

Day 7:   Departure.

Note: This itinerary assumes flying directly to Barcelona. If landing in Madrid, you may need an extra day for travel to Barcelona, depending on connections. To include Madrid, add days two and three from the Madrid itinerary, but substitute the Museo Arqueológico Nacional for the Jardin del Retiro on the second day.

Madrid and Extremadura, eight days

This driving trip combines Madrid with a taste of the land which bred the Conquistadores. As a bonus it offers Roman ruins, a preserved Renaissance town and the holy monastery of Guadalupe.

Day 1:   Travel to Madrid and settle into a hotel.

Day 2:   The Museo Nacional del Prado; Museo Arqueológico Nacional.

Day 3:   La Ciudad Antigua; Plaza Mayor; Palacio Real.

Day 4:   Travel to Cáceres and settle into a hotel.

Day 5:   Ciudad Vieja and excursion to the Roman remains at Mérida.

Day 6:   Excursion to Trujillo.

Day 7:   Return to Madrid, visiting Guadalupe Monastery on the way.

Day 8:   Departure.

Seville, Granada, Córdoba, 10 days

This trip by car or train will give you the flavor of Andalusia, the Moors and Spanish architecture of the 14th and 15th centuries.

Day 1:   Travel to Madrid and settle into a hotel.

Day 2:   Travel to Seville and settle into a hotel. Cathedral; Torre Giralda.

Day 3:   Alcázar and gardens; Barrio de Santa Cruz; Museo Arqueológico.

Day 4:   Museo de Bellas Artes; Casa de Pilatos.

Day 5:   Travel to Córdoba and settle into a hotel. Mesquita.

Day 6:   Juderia; Alcázar and gardens; excursion to Medina el Azehara.

Day 7:   Travel to Granada and settle into a hotel. Cathedral and Capilla Real.

Day 8:   Alhambra; Palacio Carlos V; Generalife.

Day 9:   Albaicin; Cartuja, San Juan de Dios.

Day 10: Departure.

Note: Any number of beach days on the Costa del Sol or Costa de la Luz can easily be added to this itinerary. To include Madrid, add days two and three from the Madrid itinerary, but substitute the Museo Arqueológico Nacional for the Jardín del Retiro.

Old Castile, 10 days

This whirlwind trip, for which a car is necessary, includes the best castles, fine Renaissance architecture, two spectacular cathedrals and a Roman aqueduct.

Day 1: Travel to Madrid and settle into a hotel.

Day 2: Travel to Segovia and settle into a hotel, visiting El Escorial on the way.

Day 3: Roman aqueduct; Alcázar; Ciudad Vieja and Cathedral.

Day 4: Travel to Salamanca and settle into a hotel, visiting Ávila and Coca castle on the way.

Day 5: Plaza Mayor; Patio de las Escuelas; Catedral Vieja; travel to Valladolid and settle into a hotel.

Day 6: Collegio San Gregorio and the town. Travel to León and settle into a hotel.

Day 7: Cathedral; Saint Isadore; excursion to San Miguel de Escalada.

Day 8: Travel to Burgos and settle into a hotel, visiting Fromista on the way.

Day 9: Cathedral; the monastery of Miraflores; Las Huelgas convent; return to Madrid with optional stops at Santo Domingo de Silos and Pedraza de la Sierra.

Day 10: Departure.

Note: To include Madrid, add days two and three from the Madrid itinerary, but substitute the Museo Arqueológico Nacional for the Jardín del Retiro.

Santiago de Compostela, Galicia, and the Basque Counties, 12 days (or more)

In addition to the spectacular pilgrimage church of Santiago de Compostela, this driving trip offers rugged seacoast scenery and elegant beach resorts. Add days at Santillana del Mar, Santander, Laredo or Donostia (San Sebastian) for the beach.

Day 1: Travel to Madrid and settle into a hotel.

Day 2: Travel to Santiago de Compostela and settle into a hotel.

Day 3: Cathedral; Ciudad Antigua; Hostal do los Reyes Católicos.

Day 4: Excursion to Pazo de Oca, to ocean inlets at Mirador de la Curota an to Cabo Finisterre, the westernmost part of Europe.

Day 5: Travel via the coast to Oviedo and settle into a hotel, pausing at Mondoñedo.

Day 6: Ciudad Antigua; Cathedral; excursion to Santa Maria del Naranco.

Day 7: Travel along the coast to Santillana del Mar, Santander or Laredo.

Day 8: Explore the town.

Day 9: Travel along the coast to Donostia (San Sebastian), detouring for San Ignacio de Loyola Monastery.

Day 10: Ciudad Vieja; Mount Igueldo.

Day 11: Return to Madrid.

Day 12: Departure.

Note: From Santiago de Compostela an excursion can be made to Osera monastery and to Orense for its Cathedral and Old Town. The Altamira Caves lie outside of Santillana del Mar, but require advance permission to enter. Other painted prehistoric caves in the area that do not require permission are: Cueva Santimamine near Guernica on the way to Donostia; Cueva de Buxu in the Picos de Europa mountains between Oviedo and Santillana del Mar; Cueva el Castillo outside Puente Viesgo near Santillana del Mar; Cuevas Covalanas outside Ramales de la Victoria near Laredo; and Cueva Tito Bustillo outside Ribadesella on the way from Oviedo to Santillana del Mar. The road to Madrid goes through Burgos, with a magnificent Cathedral. To include Madrid, add days 2 and 3 from the Madrid itinerary, but substitute the Museo Arqueológico Nacional for the Jardin del Retiro.

Three Star Spain, 15 days

This trip covers the greatest sights in Spain, though it is light on local flavor and rest.

Day 1: Travel to Madrid and settle into a hotel.

Day 2: The Museo Nacional del Prado; the Museo Arqueológico Nacional.

Day 3: Plaza Mayor; Palacio Real; excursion to El Escorial.

Day 4: Travel to Toledo and settle into a hotel. Cathedral; Santo Tomé.

Day 5: El Transito Synagogue; Iglesia María Blanca; Iglesia San Roman; Santa Cruz Museum.

Day 6: Travel to Seville and settle into a hotel. Cathedral; Torre Giralda.

Day 7: Alcázar and gardens; Barrio de Santa Cruz; Casa de Pilatos.

Day 8:   Travel to Córdoba and settle into a hotel. Mesquita; Juderia; Alcázar and gardens.

Day 9:   Travel to Granada and settle into a hotel. Cathedral and Capilla Real.

Day 10:   Alhambra; Palacio Carlos V; Generalife.

Day 11:   Travel to Santiago de Compostela and settle into a hotel.

Day 12:   Cathedral; Hostal do los Reyes Católicos.

Day 13:   Travel to Barcelona and settle into a hotel. Barri Gótic; Cathedral.

Day 14:   Museo de Arte de Catalunya; Museus Miró and Picasso; Gaudí's works, including Sagrada Familia.

Day 15:   Departure.

Note: This itinerary assumes a departure from Barcelona. If leaving from Madrid one extra day may be needed for returning, depending on connections.

The five itineraries that follow offer different tastes of Portugal in trips of five to 11 days. They comprise sightseeing and travel through the countryside, but do not include stops at the beach. In particular, none incorporates a stay at any of the truly beautiful beaches of the Algarve, which are pleasant all year and provide fresh fish even when the air is too cool for swimming. Given that beaches line the west and south of the country and Portugal is narrow west to east, at almost any time during a trip one can break away to the ocean. The best beaches, those of the Algarve, are readily combined either with a visit to Lisbon or Évora. For example, in the "Lisbon, Évora, Marvão and Tomar" or "The Best of Portugal" itinerary, instead of traveling to Évora on day 4, you can head south to the Algarve instead. After sufficient sun and sand, one can continue to Évora to rejoin the itinerary.

Lisbon, 5 days

This tour covers the highlights of Lisbon and leaves time for shopping and strolling.

Day 1:   Travel to Lisbon and settle into a hotel.

Day 2:   Castello de São Jorge, the Alfama, the Cathedral and the Rossio.

Day 3:   São Roque, Igreja do Carmo, shopping in the Chiado, and a visit to the Calouste Gulbenkian museum. If time allows, add the Estufa Fria in the Parque Eduardo VI.

Day 4:   The Belém Tower, Hieronymite monastery, Carriage Museum, and Museum of Popular Art (all located in the suburb of Belém, 3 km from the center), stopping en route at the Museu Nacional de Arte Antiga.

Day 5:   Departure.

Lisbon and Its Environs, 7 days

This trip adds the elegance of Batalha and enchantment of Sintra to the best of Lisbon.

DAY 1:   Travel to Lisbon and settle into a hotel.

DAY 2:   Castello de São Jorge, the Alfama, the Cathedral and the Rossio.

DAY 3:   The Belém Tower, Hieronymite monastery, Carriage Museum, and Museum of Popular Art, stopping en route at the Museu Nacional de Arte Antiga.

DAY 4:   São Roque, Igreja do Carmo, shopping in the Chiado, and a visit to the Calouste Gulbenkian museum. If time allows, add the Estufa Fria in the Parque Eduardo VI.

DAY 5:   Travel to Batalha for the monastery, visiting Alcobaça on the way.

DAY 6:   Travel to Sintra for its palaces, visiting Queluz on the way.

DAY 7:   Departure.

Lisbon, Évora, Marvão and Tomar, 7 days

DAY 1:   Travel to Lisbon and settle into a hotel.

DAY 2:   Castello de São Jorge, the Alfama, the Cathedral and the Rossio.

DAY 3:   The Belém Tower, Hieronymite monastery, Carriage Museum, and Museum of Popular Art, stopping en route at the Museu Nacional de Arte Antiga.

DAY 4:   Travel to Évora and settle into a hotel; Roman temple; Cathedral and mansions.

DAY 5:   Travel to Tomar, visiting Elvas and Marvão on the way; settle into a hotel.

DAY 6:   Convent of Christ; return to Lisbon, visiting the castle of Almourol on the way.

DAY 7:   Departure.

Note: If additional time is available, instead of returning to Lisbon on day 6, continue to Batalha, visiting Alcobaça on the way. On the return to Lisbon visit Sintra and Queluz, if time allows.

Lisbon and North, 11 days

DAY 1:   Travel to Lisbon and settle into a hotel.

DAY 2:   Castello de São Jorge, the Alfama, the Cathedral and the Rossio.

DAY 3:   The Belém Tower, Hieronymite monastery, Carriage Museum, and Museum of Popular Art, stopping en route at the Museu Nacional de Arte Antiga.

DAY 4:   Travel to Batalha, visiting Sintra and Alcobaça on the way; settle into a hotel.

DAY 5:   Tour the monastery; travel to Tomar, visiting the castle of Almourol on the way; tour the monastery; settle into a hotel.

DAY 6:   Travel to Viseu, visiting Coimbra on the way; settle into a hotel.

DAY 7:   Cathedral; Museu Grão Vasco; tour of the village; travel to Guimarães; Paço dos Duques; Castelo; settle into hotel.

DAY 8:   Travel to Porto; settle into a hotel.

DAY 9:   Cathedral; São Francisco; Palácio Bolsa; tour of the port lodges.

Day 10:   Travel to Lisbon; settle into a hotel.

DAY 11:   Departure.

The Best of Portugal, 11 days

DAY 1:   Travel to Lisbon and settle into a hotel.

DAY 2:   Castello de São Jorge, the Alfama, the Cathedral and the Rossio.

DAY 3:   The Belém Tower, Hieronymite monastery, Carriage Museum, and Museum of Popular Art, stopping en route at the Museu Nacional de Arte Antiga.

DAY 4:   Travel to Évora and settle into a hotel; Roman temple; Cathedral and mansions.

DAY 5:   Travel to Tomar, visiting Elvas and Marvão on the way; settle into a hotel.

DAY 6:   Convent of Christ; travel to Batalha, visiting the castle of Almourol on the way; settle into a hotel.

DAY 7:   Tour of Batalha monastery; travel to Viseu; settle into a hotel; Cathedral; Museu Grão Vasco; tour of the village.

DAY 8:   Travel to Porto; settle into hotel.

DAY 9:   Cathedral; São Francisco; Palácio Bolsa; tour of the port lodges; travel to Sintra; settle into a hotel.

DAY 10:   Visit the three castles of Sintra; travel to Lisbon; settle into a hotel shopping in the Chiado, and the Calouste Gulbenkian museum, if time and energy allow.

DAY 11:   Departure.

SPAIN

BACKGROUND
FOR SPAIN

Olive groves are familiar sights near Toledo.

The Land and the People

The first and second surprises about Spain's geography are its size and lofty elevation. The country spreads over a quarter of a million square miles making it the third largest nation in Europe (after Russia and France). Only Switzerland comprises a higher average height—one Spanish peak tops 11,000 feet. Spain adds a third surprise with her people. This is not a country where the sun beams idly on guitar players while tourists loll on the sand. Although

47

abundant sand lines 2400 miles of coast, and guitars and sun are in evidence throughout, most of Spain is populated by city folk in business clothes and farmers in berets.

In shape Spain forms a 550-mile-wide by 400-mile-long shield, wider at the top and pointed at the bottom (the part that juts into the sea to reach for Gibraltar). Accidents of geography alone prevent it from belonging to Africa. A mere seven miles of sea separates Spain from Morocco, while its tie to Europe is a 300-mile tab of northern isthmus consisting of the towering Pyrenees. This mountain wall is the reason that, throughout its history, Spain dealt as much with the Moors across the sea to its south as with French to the north.

Climatically, Spain separates into three horizontal regions. The Pyrenees continue across to the northwest corner of Spain, there renamed the Cantabrian Mountains, completing a mountain barrier that seals the north of Spain from the rest. Rain clouds are held by these mountains to make the north green and wet. As opposed to this "wet Spain," the central part is arid. It is an immense, dusty plateau half a mile in altitude. This *Meseta* comprises **La Mancha,** where locals describe the climate as nine months of winter followed by three of hell. South of La Mancha stands a line of Sierra mountains to seal the cold from Andalusia, preserving a warm Mediterranean climate for the south.

Ancient provincial differences remain strong in Spain, although technically the country was unified 500 years ago and a recent political subdivision sliced the traditional provinces into smaller "departments." Still, old provinces mean more to the traveler, and to the Spanish, for they encompass cultural and artistic differences that the new alignment does not. Running across the north of Spain, west to east, are the original provinces of Galicia, Asturias, Cantabria, the Basque provinces, Navarre, Aragón and Catalonia.

Galicia, tucked into Spain's northwestern corner, is hilly, misty, green and cut by precipitous deep inlets from the sea like Norwegian fjords, called *rias.* Fishing is a major business. Inland, verdant topsoil barely covers a granite bed, making farming difficult. Farms therefore are small, raising corn, apples, lumber and some beef cattle. The name "Galicia" derives from the Celtic word that also gave us "Gaul" and "Wales," for originally this was the land of Celts and the countryside does bring Wales to mind. Here, in the eighth century, shepherds followed a bright light to a crypt of ancient bones, claimed to be those of Saint James. Christian Europe rejoiced. To house these relics, one of the greatest medieval monuments in the world was raised on the site—the Romanesque Cathedral of **Santiago de Compostela**.

East of Galicia, **Asturias**, **Cantabria** and the **Basque Provinces** present the same green and moist appearance and temperatures as Galicia, but their terrain is sedimentary rock instead of granite. Farms are consequently more fertile and larger, though growing crops similar to Galicia's. Asturian coal mines feed Spain's heavy industry, while the coast offers magnificent scenery and Donostia (San Sebastian), an elegant resort. All three provinces are home to Basques (*Vascos* in Spanish, *Euskaldi*, in their own tongue) in omnipresent berets, a people of enigmatic origin, language and robust national identity. Spain acknowledges their culinary expertise. Hard cider is the local drink (*sidra* in Spanish, *sagardua* in Basque). *Pelota*, *jai alai*, is the national sport, with a court in every village.

Navarre, next in line, is mountainous in the northeast, hilly in the northwest, and descends into cereal plains in the south. Rough stone houses sit on the mountains, and houses dug underground nestle into the plains. Vineyards cover the southeast near Ribera, next to the famous Riojas wine area. Navarre is dotted with medieval monasteries that once provided shelter for pilgrim hordes marching to holy Santiago de Compostela in Galicia. Pamplona, famous for its running of the bulls, is Navarre's capital.

The Pyrenees run through the north of **Aragón**, then descend to the basin of the Ebro River. Shut off from the tempering influence of the sea, Southern Aragón grows olives and grapes and boils in summer while freezing in winter. This was the homeland of Ferdinand the Catholic who married Queen Isabella of Castile. Aragón also lay on the pilgrims' path to Santiago de Compostela, and abounds in ancient monasteries, the original hotels.

Catalonia, on the east coast, is more than Barcelona. The scenic and rocky north coast, called the *Costa Brava*, turns to golden sand in the south, and receives the name *Costa Dorada*. The interior is dry but fertile. Catalans are fiercely independent, speaking a language of their own related to the Provençal dialect in the proximate area of France. They are renowned for business acumen, while their art is idiosyncratic both in continuing to employ the Romanesque style later than other parts of Spain and in their avantgarde modern artists and architects: Gaudí, Sert, Miró and Dalí.

Below this belt of northern provinces, and to the west, sits the combined traditional kingdom of Old Castile and León, the largest ancient province. Beneath it, New Castile lies east, with Extremadura to its west. Valencia hugs the coast, east of New Castile and above Murcia.

The *Meseta* begins in **Old Castile and León** where horizons stretch wide despite low hills. To its east lies La Rioja, the great wine region of Spain. Elsewhere, wheat grows, sheep and cattle graze and people, concentrated in cities, are seldom seen. This is the land of medieval castles and of the first capitals of Spain during the Reconquest—León, Burgos, then Valladolid.

New Castile's Madrid is located almost exactly at the geographic center of the country, not far from medieval Toledo, massive El Escorial, Renaissance

Salamanca and Segovia with its Roman aqueduct and fairy-tale castle. New Castile's southern half is called La Mancha, possibly derived from an Arabic word meaning "parched." This is the Meseta's heart, an almost featureless half-mile-high plateau empty of humans except in widely separated cities. Infinite wheat fields can be seen today, but in the past the land was ruined by millions of migratory merino sheep who ate every growing thing. Even today, Don Quixote can almost be spied on the distant horizon, passing the castles of Spain.

Extremadura, meaning "Beyond the River Duero," is strewn with boulders which suggest Celtic dolmans at every turn. It is home to more sheep than humans, but even the sheep head for the hills during fiery summers. The land of Extremadura nurtured most of the conquistadores who, in turn, seized any opportunity to leave its inhospitable terrain. It boasts houses of the explorers, Guadalupe's holy monastery, Mérida's Roman ruins and Cáceres, a preserved Renaissance town.

Valencia and **Murcia**, on the east coast, are Extremadura's opposites. Here balmy fertile plains border a Mediterranean framed by grey mountains. Thanks to the legacy of the Moors, Valencia grows citrus trees, rice and olives. Perpetual sun shines on the white sands of the Costa Azahar in the north, and the Costa Blanca in the south. Temperatures seldom reach 90 or descend to 40 in busy Valencia, the major city. So arid is Murcia that it is a virtual desert, complete with stands of palms as if oases. The *calina*, a summer heat haze, can make activity difficult.

Andalusia, the southernmost part of the country, is everyone's ideal of Spain—the home of flamenco music and dance. The Sierra Nevada ("Snow Mountain"), capped all year in white, holds weather along the Costa del Sol to moderate Mediterranean temperatures. West, the Guadalquivir River breaks the mountains to form a wide basin that steams in summer. Further west, behind the Costa de la Luz ("Coast of Light"), rice, sugar and cotton extend on flat plains where the fighting bulls are raised. This is the fabled land of the Moors. A clear Andalusian sky reflects perpetually on Seville, Córdoba, Granada and the sherry production of Jerez de la Frontera.

Of Spain's 40 million population, about 40 percent live in the ten largest cities, following a worldwide demographic trend of migration from rural toil to urban dreams. Whether the migrants' ambitions are realized is dubious, but they spawn boring suburbs around urban centers. A happy effect of this migration, however, is that the older towns and cities have not been forced to absorb increased population, thus preserving much of their original character. The centers of most Spanish cities retain their medieval or Renaissance character of narrow, crooked streets and ancient buildings. In the context of the rest of Europe, Spain remains poor, despite enormous economic strides through the 1980s, although poverty is not evident in either the look of the cities or the stylish dress of the people. Cities and towns sparkle, with little sign of dilapidation. Throughout the vast countryside, verdant farms cover the landscape, although only one Spaniard in six is a farmer today.

The recent recession hit Spain especially hard. Unemployment has risen to an astronomical 20 percent of the eligible workforce, in part because the huge foreign investment that came into Spain during the 80s moved out once Spanish wages climbed to European standards, and in part because Spanish work laws protect employees to a degree that hampers business. Crime has increased, but prices have recently declined in efforts to increase sales. Bargains now exist both in commodities and hotel accommodations.

The physical appearance of the people ranges from small, dark-complexioned Basques in the north to slender Andalusians in the south, where one finds the startling combination of raven hair crowning fair skin and blue eyes. The modern Spaniard is a mix of more races than he generally wishes to acknowledge. Originally there was a stock of native Iberians and Celts, along with Basques of unknown origin; then Romans intermingled, followed by German Vandals and Visigoths, and finally Moors and Jews.

Most characteristically, you will see the Spanish on their evening strolls, the *paseos*, when families come together for a walk at dusk along an avenue in each town appointed long ago for the purpose. There is something touching about the familial closeness this ritual involves, and the affectionate attention the adults devote to their children. You will wonder how such gentle people can enjoy the blood of bullfights, or how they could have fought so violently against each other in the Spanish Civil War. You will find no easy answer, for the Spanish are not a simple people.

Food and Drink

The Spanish are robust in their tastes, adoring hearty food and animated conversation. Restaurants seem more like convivial meeting rooms than hallowed cathedrals of cuisine, and food portions are ample. As a result, dining customs and hours in Spain differ from our own.

Because the Spanish enjoy their leisurely main meal at two in the afternoon and follow it with an equally lengthy rest, restaurants do not reopen for dinner until eight or nine—or in Madrid, Barcelona and Andalusia at least ten at night—occasionally with restricted menus. Thus, an important consideration for visitors is not simply what to eat but when. For the most part, Americans in Spain stick to their habit of eating the main meal in the evening, causing them to search midday menus for light luncheon meals but discovering few choices among the full dinners. At night, after biding their time until the restaurants reopen, they find themselves the first arrivals, uncomfortably alone in the dining room.

Food markets, like this one, are typical throughout Spain.

Spain is relaxed about most things, including food and its availability, so it is perfectly possible to eat in Spain as you would at home. Below we explain how to find sandwiches and other light noon meals. On the other hand, it might prove interesting to try dining as the Spanish do. Take your main meal at midday, then snack on *tapas* at night. That way you'll be eating during the time many shops and sights are closed for their midday break, and you'll emerge fortified for serious sight-seeing. You will also sleep better for it.

The Spanish begin the day lightly with a *cafe completo*, a continental breakfast of delicious strong coffee and a roll or bread. Coffee is either *solo* (black), *con leche* (with milk) or *café américano*, a weaker version. Tea made from bags is available. Most hotels charge extra for breakfast, but any bar or cafe can provide it too. Those who wish more—some eggs, for example—are talking about *desayuno* (breakfast), which is generally available at hotels, often in the form of somewhat costly buffets that include cold cuts and fruit, along with ham, eggs and croissants.

At midday in any bar one can find *bocadillos* (sandwiches), consisting of rolls filled with delicious *tapas* selections, including tasty *jamón serrano* (like prosciutto). For more familiar lunch choices, stop at a cafeteria or an *auto-servicio*. Alternatively, wait until one or two o'clock to eat a full meal in a restaurant.

By early evening (seven o'clock or so) groups begin gathering in the tapas bars. The name *tapas*, which means tops or lids, derives from a time when bartenders covered a glass of wine with a small plate—to ward off flies—on which they set free appetizers. Those free days are gone; today such appetizers cost a dollar or more. In a good tapas bar, always distinguished by a large crowd, choices will be varied—slices of omelette, *chorizo* (spicy dried sausage), marinated beef, squid, clams, oysters, mussels, octopus, shrimp, *jamón York* (boiled ham), *jamón serrano* (air-cured mountain ham—like prosciutto but stronger), rice and potatoes. Most of the food will be cold, but not all, and *raciones*, larger plates, may be ordered. Pointing is an acceptable way to select. When it is time to settle up, the waiter will count the empty plates to figure your bill. These delicacies may be sampled either standing at the bar or, for higher prices, sitting at a table. The food is washed down with wine, beer or sherry—usually a dry *fino*.

Dinner, *la cena*, begins at nine or ten at night, depending on the area of Spain. However, some hotels open their restaurants earlier to accommodate our foreign habits.

Food

Spanish food is seldom spicy hot—in no way to be confused with Mexican cuisine and its generous use of chiles. What distinguishes Spanish food from northern European cooking is its use of olive oil for sautéing rather than butter. In general, Spanish cooking is based on the quality of the ingredients rather than on sauces, as in French cuisine, for the goal is to liberate fresh tastes instead of masking them with other flavors. At its best, Spanish food can be as subtle as the finest French; at its worst it can be heavy or greasy; but, in general, it provides tasty and satisfying sustenance.

Of course the quality of cooking varies, and restaurants are rated by the government through an assignment of from one through four forks, in addition to a *Lujo* (deluxe) rating. Each restaurant will have its rating posted on a plaque outside. This government assessment takes account of ambience, the variety of offerings and the elegance of service, but does not consider the quality of the cooking or the degree of graciousness with which it is placed before you. These ratings can be used as a rough measure of costs, but not of how enjoyable the dining experience will be. Our recommendations attempt to redress that lack.

Menus comprise à la carte choices, but all restaurants also offer either a *menú del día* or a *menú turistico* which provide complete meals at lower, all-encompassing prices, with a limited range of choices.

Note: serving vegetables with the main dish is not a Spanish custom. At best you can hope for a small salad, unless you specifically order a vegetable side dish.

Spanish food comprises several regional cuisines, although a famous dish from a given region will be available in most cosmopolitan centers. Common to every region is a love of seafood, rushed fresh to cities as far from the coast as Madrid. A Spaniard, on average, eats 68 pounds of fish per year. And the Spanish love garlic. If you do not sympathize, avoid dishes with names containing the words *ajillo* or *ajo*.

Andalusia is famous for its cold soup, *gazpacho*—raw vegetables, especially onion and tomatoes, blended with olive oil, vinegar and garlic. From Málaga comes the interesting white *ajo blanco*, a cold blend of garlic, ground almonds, and floating grapes. *Sopa sevillana* is a rich fish stew flavored with mayonnaise and garnished with egg. *Fritura mixta de pescados* is a mixed fry of fresh seafood. Fresh sardines *(sardinas)* can be sublime, as can trout *(trucha)*, fresh from nearby streams. A hearty casserole of lima beans and ham is called *habas con jamón*.

Valencia invented *paella*, now served all over Spain but nowhere done better than its home state. It is named for the special large skillet in which short-grained saffron rice is stewed with seafood, sausage, chicken and snails, all garnished with pimento. When seafood replaces all the meat, the name changes to *paella marinera*. Although a description of *paella's* ingredients seems to call for white wine, few whites can stand up to its rich flavors.

The center of Spain, Old and New Castile, is known for its roast meat *(asados)*. Beneath its crisp skin, *cochinillo* (suckling pig) falls off the bone, *cordero* (lamb) is memorable when roasted over wood fires called *hornos*, and *lechazo* (milk fed lamb) is a treat. A broth in which ham chunks, vegetables and eggs swim temptingly is called *sopa castellana*, while *cocido castellana* is a rich stew based on chick peas. The center for game, when it's in season, is Toledo.

Aragón and Navarre feature chicken and trout. *Pollo chilindron* is chicken in a peppery sauce, *trucha a la Navarra* is fried trout stuffed with *jamón serrano*.

The rest of Spain acknowledges that the Basque Country, where men form cooking societies, produces the finest chefs. *Pil pil*, a sort of chili sauce, is used for prawns *(gambas)* and codfish *(bacalao)*. *Bacalao a la viscaina* is stewed cod in fresh tomatoes. A specialty is *merluza a la vasca*, baked hake in a casserole of clams. Basque *nuevo cochino* (Spanish nouvelle cuisine) is one of the internationally "in" cuisines.

Galicia also merits a high reputation, not surprising given the availability of superb shellfish. *Centollos* consist of a huge local crab stuffed with its own minced meat. *Caldeirada gallega* is a heartier form of *bouillabaisse*, while *conchas de peregrino* will impress the scallop lover. *Empanada gallega* is a meat pie filled with either fish or meat.

Many dishes thought of as "Provençal," such as *bouillabaisse* and *cassoulet*, actually derive from Catalonia, where the cooking is similar to that of nearby French Provence. Mayonnaise was invented in Catalonia and brought to France in the 16th century. Pasta and snails (not in the same dish) are staples in Catalonia, though absent from menus in the rest of Spain. Fish stews are specialties—from *zarzuela de mariscos*, tomato based, to *romesco de peix*, with almonds and bread crumbs. Catalans make a delicious spicy sausage called *butifarras*. For dessert, *crema catalana* is a delectable *creme caramel*.

Drink

Wines in Spain are as various and as frequently drunk as those produced in France. They can be as good as all but the very highest level of French wines, and are available at more affordable prices. In any price category below the astronomical, a Spanish wine will beat its comparably priced French counterpart.

There are so many varieties of Spanish wine, however, that most names are unfamiliar except to specialists—a problem for the traveler who simply wants a wine to enjoy with his meal. Because its high alcohol and tannin content makes Spanish wine mature slowly, a good rule of thumb is to ignore the name and choose the oldest bottle in the price range you're considering.

Certain regions produce outstanding wines which are available all over Spain. Others make wines dispensed locally by the glass or carafe as *vino de la casa* or *del pais*, though even these generally prove enjoyable. Wine can be red *(tinto)*, white *(blanco)* or rosé *(rosado)*. Bottled wines are controlled to ensure quality by a *Denominación de Origen*, like the French "Appellation Controllée." *Reservas* are wines of good vintage, *Gran Reservas* are the best wines given bodega (winery) bottles.

Sherry is Spain's great contribution to the world of wines. Americans seldom drink it, except in its sweeter versions, yet dry sherry is a splendid aperitif, stimulating to the palate, and even serves well accompanying a meal. Sherry is manufactured by allowing the juice of grapes to ferment in contact with air, a process that normally would turn the grape juice to vinegar. But at the western tip of Spain in **Jerez de la Frontera**, the juice develops a coating of yeast, a *flor* (flower), which protects against such oxidation. A richly complex wine, high in alcohol, results. The final product is aged in a system called *solera*, in which huge casks, each containing one year's vintage, are stacked by year with the oldest on the bottom. As a bottle is filled from the lowest (thus oldest) cask, wine from the cask above replenishes what was removed, the next cask above replenishes that one, and so on. In this way, younger vintages acquire character from older ones. Sherry does not age in the bottle, only in the solera. Sherries should not be judged by cream sherry, an uncharacteristic product that develops no flor. Try *fino*, which is light and dry, if slightly bitter. *Amontillado*, a more mature *fino*, is amber in color and nutty in flavor. An old one will be an expensive treat. Though less familiar, sherry-type wines are produced in quantity in the adjoining area of **Montilla**. A montilla will generally be drier and possess greater finesse than a sherry, at least in the opinion of many.

The Spanish actually consume more brandy than sherry, though you will find Spanish brandy pales beside the French, and most popular brands taste raw indeed. Spanish beer *(cerveza)* is good, if rather light, and is ordered by the bottle *(botellin)* or draft *(caña)*. Hard, sparkling cider *(sidra)* is the drink of choice in the northwest of Spain. As to Spanish whiskey, it is best to remain silent, but liqueurs are a different matter. Many of the famous ones—such as Cointreau, Benedictine, Chartreuse and the fruit liqueurs of Marie Brizard, are produced under license in Spain at the cheapest prices anywhere.

When you are not in the mood for alcohol, bottled water *(agua con gas* or *sin gas,* water with or without carbonation) is always available, as is Coca-Cola.

History

Spain's history is both long and unfamiliar which makes it difficult to digest. Yet nothing enriches a traveler's experience more than understanding the background of what he sees. Here is an historical overview to serve as a reference for the personalities and events we discuss in descriptions of places and buildings.

Prehistory to the Visigoths (to A.D. 711)

13,000 B.C. Prehistoric people paint the cave at Altamira.

1300 B.C. Iberians inhabit Spain.

1000 B.C. Phoenicians colonize Cádiz and Málaga.

900 B.C. Celts inhabit Spain, perhaps migrating from France.

650 B.C. Greeks colonize the eastern coast of Spain.

250 B.C. Carthaginians take over the south coast.

206 B.C. The Roman general Scipio Africanus defeats the Carthaginians, beginning six centuries of Roman presence.

19 B.C. Caesar Augustus completes the Roman conquest of Spain.

A.D. 500 Visigoths conquer Spain.

A.D. 711 Muslims from Morocco conquer the Visigoths.

The regal tomb of Columbus is housed in Seville's Cathedral.

Civilization existed in the Iberian Peninsula for at least 13,000 years before the Romans arrived to impose their way of life on its inhabitants. Not only do megalithic Celtic dolmans preserved at Antequera prove the existence of a culture that spread from Brittany and Britain at the beginning of the last millennium B.C., but the haunting cave paintings in Altamira, dating from 13,000 years ago, force us to rethink our image of "primitive" caveman. Before the Celts, two different peoples inhabited the land—Iberians, perhaps originally from North Africa, and Basques, who show little affinity to any other people anywhere.

Spain had lived in splendid isolation from the rest of the world until Phoenicians landed in 1000 B.C. to mine tin for the manufacture of bronze. They established permanent trading posts at Gades (Cádiz) and Malaca (Málaga), avoiding the inland territory belonging to those they referred to as "Celtiberians," mistakenly classifying two peoples as one. Greeks followed, but kept their distance by colonizing only the east coast of Spain, where major Greek ruins still remain north of Barcelona at Empúries.

As the fortunes of Phoenicia waned in the third century B.C., its former colony of Carthage took control of the Spanish coast. This was too close to Italy for rival Rome's comfort and soon the two trading empires were at war. Just before the second century B.C. the Romans first set foot on Spanish soil when they attacked the supply lines of the Carthaginian general Hannibal. After winning, the Romans stayed in Spain and set out to do what no visitor had yet accomplished—conquer the interior.

Unlike most of Rome's opponents who fell quickly to her armies, Spain resisted for two centuries before final defeat in 19 B.C. by Caesar Augustus. The peninsula, became a province of the Roman empire, growing more Roman than Rome, with senators, Latin writers and even emperors springing from its soil. Rome embarked on major construction projects throughout Iberia, building splendid bridges (at Alcantára), huge aqueducts (still intact at Segovia) and hundreds of miles of roads throughout the peninsula. In Mérida an elegant theater still stands beside a coliseum for gladiatorial and naval battles. The common tongue throughout the peninsula became Latin, which later separately evolved into Spanish and Portuguese.

In time Rome's power declined, allowing "barbarians" to break through the Empire's border defenses. In the fourth century A.D., Franks from Germany seized present-day France. Now other German tribes were free to invade and claim what they could. By the fifth century Alans and Swabians established settlements in eastern and western Iberia, respectively. Then the Vandals came, seized the south of Spain, and gave it their name, "Andalusia" (which we corrupt from Vandal's Land). A century later, fleeing fierce Huns to their east, the mighty German tribe of the Visigoths poured into Spain. They chased the Vandals across the Gibraltar straits into Africa and conquered the other Germanic tribes, along with the indigenous people, to take command of all of Spain. With Toledo as their capital, they established an elected kingship, a caste of nobles, and a state religion (Christianity), all of which became Spanish institutions.

Moors and the Reconquest (711–1248)

711–716 Morocco conquers Spain in the name of Islam.

722 Pelayo achieves the first Christian military victory over the Moors, initiating the reconquest.

756 Led by Abd er Rahman I, Moorish Spain gains independence from Baghdad.

1072–1109 Alfonso VI conquers most of Spain for the Christians.

1090 The Almoravids reconquer Spain for the Moors.

1212 Christian forces break the Moors' hold on Spain in the decisive battle of Las Navas de Tolosa.

1236–1248 Fernando III captures two of Spain's three Moorish strongholds, Córdoba and Seville, leaving only Granada under Moorish control.

A small Moroccan army crossed the Straits of Gibraltar in 711, first routed the Visigoth army, then chased them to small enclaves in the Pyrenees and northern Asturias.

The Moors' domination of Spain would extend for 800 years—a span longer than the time that has elapsed since their final defeat in 1492. While the Dark Ages enveloped the rest of Europe, Spanish Muslims kept knowledge alive by maintaining disciplines rejected by the Christians—education, philosophy, poetry and cleanliness. Their architecture, especially in the Alhambra of **Granada** and the Mezquita of **Córdoba**, displayed a sensitivity never surpassed.

The Moors' capital of Córdoba soon became the largest city in Western Europe. But Moorish Spain remained a mere province within the Islamic empire until a dynastic change in Baghdad, the ruling center of Islam. The sole survivor of the previous dynasty, Abd er Rahman, fled to Spain where he claimed the allegiance of the Moors and forged Spain's independence. By the 10th century, under Abd er Rahman III, Moorish Spain had reached its apex, surpassing every other part of Europe in splendor, modernity and richness. This apex, however, was short-lived. The death of his grandson created problems of succession that split the Moors apart into separate weaker states.

In the meantime, Christians were attempting a reconquest of Spain from their northern confines. Tradition dates the beginning of the reconquest to 722 when Pelayo, a Visigoth noble, won the first Christian engagement against Moors. But no territory was regained in this skirmish. In fact, the Reconquest owed more to the discovery by shepherds of bones attributed to Saint James the Apostle, than to such raids. By the eighth century a church and a city—both called Santiago de Compostela—had grown around the sacred site. (Saint James in medieval Spanish was *Sant' Iago.*) It became a pilgrimage center, second only to the Holy Land and Rome, and drew Europeans by the hundreds of thousands to Christian Spain. With the pilgrims came the idea for a crusade to spread Christianity throughout the peninsula.

Over time the northern state of Asturias conquered neighboring León. By the 11th century these combined states annexed the land to their south, called "Castile" after all the defensive castles there. Castile grew dominant in the coalition and powerful in the peninsula. Meantime, a separate Christian kingdom grew in Aragón and conducted its own reconquest down the eastern side of Spain. But Castile and Aragón grew into bitter rivals who fought against each other as often as they battled separately against the Moors.

By the end of the 11th century, however, a Castilian king, Alfonso VI, was strong enough to raid as far south as the Mediterranean coast and capture Toledo, the ancient Visigoth capital. Frightened Moors called for help from their Moroccan homeland. A fanatical sect called the Almoravids heeded the call and, with the exception of Valencia which was defended by the Spanish hero El Cid, reconquered all that their brethren had lost. When the religious fervor of the Almoravids abated, another fierce fundamentalist sect, the Al-mohades, took over and regained Valencia.

This revitalization of the Moors forced the Christian rivals, Castile and Aragón, to join forces for one campaign. In 1212, the Spanish summoned crusaders from the corners of Europe, formed an army that engaged the Islamic forces south of Toledo at Las Navas de Tolosa, and inflicted a defeat from which the Moors never recovered. After this great victory, Castile and Aragón once again parted ways.

Twenty-four years later, aided by civil wars that had sapped the Moors' strength, Castile's Fernando III was able to take the Moor's capital, Córdoba. Four years after that he seized Seville, while Aragón recaptured Valencia. The Reconquest was almost complete. Granada alone held out, though more than two centuries would pass before it fell.

Ferdinand, Isabella and Columbus (1369–1516)

1454–1474	The questionable legitimacy of Enrique the Impotent's designated heir places Isabella on Castile's throne.
1469	Isabella of Castile weds Ferdinand of Aragón.
1481	The Inquisition begins.
1492	Granada surrenders, completing the Reconquest. Spain's Jews are expelled. Columbus sails for the Indies.
1502	Spain's Moors are expelled.
1504	Isabella dies.
1512	Ferdinand conquers Navarre.

The wedding of Isabella of Castile to Ferdinand of Aragón gave Christian Spain the unity it needed to complete the Reconquest. But before the wedding Castile had suffered two centuries of internecine violence and weak rulers. Foremost in this gallery of rogues was Pedro the Cruel. After Pedro killed one of his illegitimate half brothers, the other, Enrique of Trastámara, in turn murdered Pedro in 1369 and seized the throne, beginning the dynasties from which both Isabella and Ferdinand descended.

By the time Isabella's half-brother Enrique IV came to power, a century later, so much authority had been transferred to the nobles of Spain by successive kings that Castile had dissolved into virtual anarchy. Enrique IV claimed that his second wife's child was his heir, despite evidence to the contrary and his nickname of "the Impotent." To clear the succession for this "daughter" Enrique tried to marry his half-sister Isabella off to one prince after another, but Isabella defied him and, in 1469, secretly wed Ferdinand of Aragón. Enrique died in 1474, still protesting gossip about his daughter's paternity, but leaving Isabella's claim to the throne of Castile preeminent. Five years later, upon Ferdinand's ascension to his father's throne, the kingdoms of Castile and Aragón were finally united under Ferdinand and Isabella.

One of Isabella's first royal acts was to import Aragón's Inquisition to Castile. With its announced purpose of eliminating Christian heretics, the Inquisition persisted until the 19th century. What it actually accomplished was perhaps more pervasive: the esteem of "pure" bloodlines—those untainted by Jewish or Moorish ancestors.

Despite Ferdinand's generalship and Isabella's efficient organization, it required ten years of sustained warfare to subdue Granada, but, on January 2, 1492, Isabella and Ferdinand walked through the gates of Granada to conclude eight centuries of reconquest.

During that same year Isabella sent Christopher Columbus on his way to the New World and signed an order expelling all of Spain's Jews. Although Isabella lived only 12 years longer, before she died in 1504 she was to see one of her daughters marry the son of the Holy Roman Emperor—a union that would elevate Spain to the greatest power in Europe. Ferdinand survived his wife by another 12 years, during which he added Navarre to his kingdom, the territory that completes the map of modern Spain.

Habsburg Kings (1519–1700)

1519–1556 Carlos V becomes the first Habsburg king of Spain.

1519–1522 Cortéz conquers Mexico.

1532–1534 Pizarro conquers Peru.

1541–1614 The life of the painter El Greco.

1556–1598 The reign of Felipe II.

1567 Revolt against Spain begins in Holland.

1580 Felipe II gains the throne of Portugal.

1588 The Great Armada is destroyed.

1598–1621 Felipe III succeeds his father.

1599–1660 The life of the master painter Velázquez.

1621–1665 The reign of Felipe IV. Velázquez appointed court painter.

1640 Portugal regains its independence.

1665–1700 The reign of Carlos II ends the Spanish Habsburg dynasty.

The Habsburg dynasty in Spain began and ended with a Carlos, sandwiching three kings all named Felipe. Isabella and Ferdinand's daughter Juana, despite her obvious insanity, remained Spain's nominal ruler until her son Carlos V became old enough to rule. Carlos, a Habsburg on his father's side, also inherited control over Holland, Belgium, Austria and Germany along with his title of Holy Roman Emperor. Born and raised in Holland, Carlos introduced Spain to the culture and art of mainstream Europe. This opening of borders was a decidedly mixed blessing. By the time his son Felipe II succeeded him, the Low Countries, as Holland and Belgium were known, had begun a revolt that would last a hundred years and drain Spain of all its wealth from the New World.

Felipe II established a new capital at Madrid where it has remained ever since, undertook massive building projects in the capital and constructed an imposing monastery at nearby El Escorial. When, in 1580, the king of Portugal died heirless, Felipe II for a time united Portugal's throne with Spain's. In 1588, after discovering a secret alliance between England and the rebels in the Low Countries, Felipe assembled Spain's Great Armada and sent it to invade England. Only half of his ships returned. Ten years and two armadas later, Felipe died.

In 1609 his son, Felipe III, expelled all remaining Moors from Spain. In 1605 Miguel de Cervantes published *Don Quixote*, the first true novel. Felipe IV succeeded his father and lost Portugal in 1640 by violating an agreement that the Portuguese administer their own country. Although a low point in Spanish political history, the reign of Felipe IV witnessed the rise of Spain's greatest painters—Ribalta, Ribera, Murillo, Zurbarán, and, greatest of all, the court painter Velázquez.

Upon the death of Felipe IV in 1665, his son, a veritable idiot, ascended the throne. Somehow Carlos II managed to occupy his office for 35 years, but he never produced an heir and thus sealed the end of the Habsburg dynasty in Spain.

Bourbon Kings (1700–1930)

1700–1746	Felipe V becomes the first Bourbon king of Spain.
1759–1788	Carlos III brings prosperity to Spain.
1788–1808	Carlos IV rules. The weak king and his family are immortalized by Goya.
1809–1813	Britain and Portugal join Spanish guerrillas against France in the Peninsular War.
1814–1833	The absolutist Fernando VII defies the first constitution.
1833–1839	The First Carlist War brings civil war to Spain.
1874–1875	The First Republic.

1875–1885 Alfonso XII regains the throne.

1898 Spain loses Cuba, Puerto Rico and the Philippines in the Spanish-American War.

1902–1930 Alfonso XIII rules as Spain's last monarch before abdicating in favor of republican government.

The childless last Habsburg, Carlos II, named Philip of Anjou as his successor in 1700. Under the title of Felipe V, he became the first Spanish monarch from the French Bourbon line (called Borbón in Spanish). His ascension precipitated a war, appropriately called the War of Spanish Succession, with the Austrian Habsburgs. Though Felipe eventually won, the war initiated two centuries of intermittent battles that would reduce Spain from a major world power to a pawn of newer European leaders.

After Felipe V, Fernando VI negotiated a series of neutrality treaties to help Spain recover from the devastations of civil war. His policies were continued by his half-brother Carlos III, whose astute economic planning moved Spain forward into the 18th century. He was succeeded by his son Carlos IV, an amiable dolt controlled by his wife, who, in turn, was under the spell of a favorite courtier. After the French Revolution, the unrealistic Carlos went so far as to send Spanish troops into France to restore its monarchy. His army was crushed, enabling France to demand that Carlos join her in war on England and its ally, Portugal. As the 19th century dawned, Spain entered the arena of European politics as a reluctant ally of Napoléon.

In 1808 Napoléon forced Carlos IV to resign in favor of his own brother Joseph. Outraged, the Spanish people rose in rebellion on the second of May, and fought a guerilla campaign until, four years later, aided by the British under the Duke of Wellington, they expelled the French. The great artist Goya immortalized the era with unforgettable etchings of the horrors of war and with royal portraits of the fat Carlos IV, his determined wife and plump children.

After the expulsion of the French, Spain found itself without a king for the first time since before the Visigoths. A constitution was drafted, and Carlos' son was invited to return from exile to reign as Spain's first constitutional monarch. Fernando VII had other ideas, however. He repudiated the constitution and seized control as an absolute monarch. In the meantime, most of Spain's American colonies had grabbed their independence while Spain was occupied by the French.

More trouble lay ahead. Fernando left only an underage daughter when he died, prompting his brother Don Carlos to wage five years of the First Carlist War to press his own royal claims. In the end, the carnage and destruction gained nothing, and the daughter, Isabella II, ascended her father's throne.

She proved to be nothing like her namesake, preferring sexual dalliances to governing. A putsch of the army and navy ended her reign in 1868.

Since Isabella's son was too young to rule, Spain briefly enlisted two foreign relatives as king before opting for a kingless republic for a year. By 1875 Isabella's son was judged old enough to become Spain's constitutional king, but his untimely death ten years later, resulted in another regency. A rebellion in Cuba at the end of the century embroiled Spain in the Spanish-American War and cost her the last two of her American possessions—Cuba and Puerto Rico—along with the Philippines. In 1902 Alfonso XIII attained his majority and came to the throne, but the government had been so discredited in the eyes of both her citizens and her army, that only dictatorships and army revolts lay ahead.

The Spanish Civil War and After (1931–Present)

1931–1939 The Second Republic.

1936 The Spanish Civil War begins. Madrid resists.

1939 Barcelona and Madrid fall. End of the Spanish Civil War.

1975 Franco dies. Juan Carlos I is crowned.

1978 A new constitution is approved.

1989 Felipe Gonzalez is reelected prime minister.

By 1931 world depression had pushed Spain, a poor country at best, into even deeper economic decline. When Alfonso XIII called for elections, most of the large cities voted for socialists whose platform called for a kingless republican government. Lacking support, Alfonso abdicated. For the second time in Spain's history, counting the one-year experiment of 1874, Spain found herself a republic.

The 1930s were a time of radical political movements. On the left, socialists, anarchists and communists in Spain gained ground in direct proportion to the deterioration of the economy, offering their new theories in place of traditional ideas that seemed no longer effective. On the right, the fascist Spanish Falange committed political murders that caused its leader José Antonio to be jailed and martyred. One socialist government in 1931 was replaced by a different one in the election of 1933, but proved equally unable to satisfy the conflicting desires of even its own supporters. Without political direction, violence and anarchy prevailed.

In 1936 the army revolted, attempting to seize the major cities of Spain. The revolt failed in its objectives, but evolved into a civil war of army, church, royalists and fascists fighting against the government and most of the people. In the first campaign Generalissimo Francisco Franco led the army toward Madrid. There the citizens staunchly resisted, surprising the world and their own elected officials, who had previously fled for safety.

With Madrid firm against them, the Nationalists (as the army called itself) then adopted a strategy of conquering the rest of the country so Madrid would fall from lack of support. First they waged a successful campaign in Spain's northern Basque country, although the destruction of the town of Guernica by Franco's German allies cost the Nationalists much in propaganda. The next year, 1938, the Nationalists turned west and surrounded Barcelona. The Republicans tried a valiant counterattack that exhausted their remaining supplies. Ironically, although the Nationalists were abundantly provisioned by fascist Germany and Italy, the democracies of America and Europe refused to aid the Republicans. Lacking rifles for its civilian troops, Barcelona fell in 1939. Madrid tumbled three months later.

Franco ruled Spain for almost three decades thereafter. He ruthlessly imprisoned Spanish liberals, but gained a great economic advantage for Spain by maintaining the country's neutrality during World War II.

With memories of the Civil War still fresh, many feared what might follow in the wake of Franco's death in 1975, but what transpired was a peaceful transition to democracy. Juan Carlos I, the son of Alfonso XIII, returned from exile, as Franco had wished, to become the constitutional monarch. He continues to reign today with his queen, Sofia, in much the manner that Elizabeth II rules Britain. In 1979 a constitution delineating this arrangement was approved by the electorate. But in 1981 a gang of Civil Guards, a group roughly corresponding to our state troopers, attacked a session of Parliament with automatic weapons and held its members hostage. All Spain waited to hear where Juan Carlos stood—with the rightist forces, or with the Republic. When he announced his continued support of the constitution, the Civil Guards surrendered. The next year the Socialist Party won national elections by a narrow margin, and Felipe Gonzalez was named prime minister. By Spain's next election in 1989, Gonzalez had shown himself to be less a socialist than a pragmatist and won overwhelmingly.

Prime Minister Gonzalez was defeated in recent elections, but Spain now stands at the center of the European political spectrum and holds a charter membership in the European Economic Community.

Art and Architecture

The College of San Gregorio in Valladolid features an intricate cloister.

The Spanish love dramatic light in their paintings, delighting in its contrasts, but they prefer dark in their cathedrals for its mystery. Spain's architecture came to be characterized by an emphasis on solidity over openness, longitude over height and surface decoration over architectural form. Over the centuries Spanish painting, on the other hand, evolved from conveying crude emotion through contorted bodies and copious blood to the most subtle depictions of face and form.

Early Art and Architecture

Prehistoric, Celtiberian, Roman and Visigoth

Spain's oldest art does not suffer at all from comparison with the best the country would ever produce. The finest paleolithic paintings in the world, challenging those at Lascaux across the French border, adorn the ceilings of the **cave of Altamira**. The drawn animals seem to contort and breathe. The cave can hold only 15 people at a time, and admission is difficult to obtain, but **El Castillo** cave outside Puenta Viesgo near **Santillana del Mar** provides examples almost as striking without the need for prior arrangements. And no advance permission, only an admission charge to the **Museo Arqueológico Na-**

cional in **Madrid**, is required to view the artworks of the little-known Celtiberians, a people whose unique art developed in isolation from classical influences. The Celtiberian masterpiece, the lovely bust of the *Dama de Elche* with its hauntingly foreign look, captivates all who view her.

Rome's domination of the Iberian Peninsula from the second century B.C. through the third century A.D. is evidenced by its architectural legacy. Rome bequeathed an *aqueduct* at **Segovia**, which is surpassed in size only by the Pont du Gard in France. The Roman *bridge* at **Alcantara**, though much repaired, preserves its original lines. Remains of a Roman city sprawl near **Seville**; and at **Mérida**, in Extremadura, stands an intact *theater* beside the substantial remains of an *arena*. The **Museo Arqueológico Nacional** in **Madrid** displays classical sculpture, mosaics and sarcophagi collected from all over Spain.

The Museum also houses jewels of the Visigoths, especially the rare solid gold *Crown of Reccesvinthus Rex*, with its embedded emeralds and sapphires and dangling pearls. The Visigoths began as farmers, turned migratory, then settled in Spain. Little of their art or architecture remains in their Germanic homeland, and little survives in Spain, for the Visigoths enjoyed only two centuries of dominance during which to refine their art.

The Moors

No traveler to Spain should miss the 14th century **Alhambra** in **Granada**. Familiarity with western architecture does not prepare a visitor for transport to such a quiet, calm way of life. Rooms follow no prescribed plan, yet each attains an individual perfection while managing to compliment those it adjoins. Above all, the Alhambra presents a unique solution to the problem of merging the constructions of men with nature. At the Alhambra, nature is brought inside with stalactite ceilings that convey the sense of a starry sky, while nature herself waits just outside in the form of gardens and pools. The intricate decoration of tile walls surmounted by fantastic carved ceilings should seem busy and gaudy, yet serve instead as restful study pieces. And everywhere the sound of running water tranquilizes: the Moors knew secrets of peaceful architecture.

The *Mesquita* (mosque) in **Córdoba**, completed in the 10th century, shows how the Moors used their architecture to serve religion. A striped forest of pillars and double tiered horseshoe arches creates an atmosphere of mystery and awe: this mosque has no parallel in the world. The exalted aesthetic of the Moors is evident as well in the collection of the Museo Arqueologico Nacional in **Madrid**. Consider the delicate ivory jar called the *Bote de Marfil*, with its sublimely harmonious decoration.

As the Reconquest advanced, some Moors found themselves behind the lines in Christian territory. Prizing their skills, the Christians engaged them, originating a style known as *Mudéjar*—Islamic art serving Christian ends.

For examples of this fortunate collaboration, see the *Casa de Pilotes* and the *Alcázar* in **Seville**, parts of which bear comparison to the Alhambra, and the *El Tránsito* synagogue in **Toledo**.

Architecture

The Reconquest: Romanesque

So many castles were built by both Christians and Moors to defend the battleground between them that the region was given the name "Castile." Castles, in all sizes and styles, still survive in profusion today. Those with round towers were generally designed by Christians while square towers usually indicate Moorish or Mudéjar architects. The walls of **Ávila**, punctuated by round towers, form one of the most extensive medieval fortresses extant. By the 15th century the rule about round and square towers no longer held, defied by the most typical of all the world's castles, and by the fairy-like *Alcázar* (castle) at **Segovia**.

Throughout the time of the Reconquest, religious feeling was intense in the Christian parts of Spain. When, in the eighth century, bones believed to belong to Saint James were found at **Santiago de Compostela** the area blossomed into not just another pilgrimage center, but the holiest Catholic site outside of the Holy Land and Rome. By the 11th century one of the world's great churches had been erected there. Today the cathedral's splendid 18th century baroque front belies the majesty of its Romanesque interior—a towering barrel ceiling with massive ribs supported by colossal columns—whose sheer size inspires awe. The Romanesque style commands religious feeling through the power of its architecture—no filigree for these worshippers, no brightness let in by expanses of glass, no flying buttresses to permit slender columns, just awesome size. Introducing the cathedral is the *Door of Glory*, a masterpiece of Romanesque sculpture by Master Mateo, as he signed himself. At a time when other sculptors were fashioning staid statues, this genius created living beings from stone. Equally wondrous, on a smaller scale, is the *Catedral Vieja* (Old Cathedral) in **Salamanca**. The dozen Romanesque churches sprinkled around **Segovia** inspire similar feelings.

Gothic

Influenced by Abbé Suger, the French lightened their churches in the 11th century with outside, "flying," buttresses that permitted less massive interior supporting columns, walls of glass to let in light, narrow ribs supporting arched ceilings, and, in place of the rounder Romanesque, pointed arches designed to raise the eye upward. Called Gothic, the new aesthetic style spread through Europe. The Spanish built one breathtaking church, complete with glorious stained glass windows, exactly on this model—the *Cathedral* at **León**. But by the 13th century the Spanish had modified the original style to create a new version—wider in plan and lightened more by ornate decoration than by the light of windows. The cathedrals at **Burgos** and **Toledo** are masterpieces of this Spanish Gothic style, ranking among the world's outstanding churches.

Renaissance: Isabeline and Plateresque

After their modification of the Gothic, Spanish architects continued to create new styles diverging from mainstream European architecture. Fifteenth century *Isabelline* buildings add a tracery of lacy decoration to otherwise bare walls. The exuberance of the style is most evident in **Granada** in the *Capilla Real* where Ferdinand and Isabella are buried. The architect Juan Guas let his fantasies run free. There also, carved in perfection by the master sculptor Bartolome Ordoñez, is the moving mausoleum of Isabella's son-in-law and daughter, Phillip the Handsome and Juana the Mad.

In the 16th century, the Isabelline effect evolved into the famed *plateresque*. The word "plateresque" means "like silverwork"—intricate, chiseled, curving and precious. As a style, plateresque mainly refers to decoration that serves no structural function and obeys no laws of symmetry. It is an applique attracting the eye to an otherwise undistinguished wall, window or door. **Salamanca** is virtually a museum city of the plateresque—and its masterpiece is the entrance to its *university*.

Classical and Baroque

However original and striking the plateresque may have been, it survived for only a century, ending when it lost favor with its royal patrons. As early as 1526, while the plateresque was still at its height, Carlos V had ordered a pupil of Michelangelo to design a classical *Palace* in **Granada**'s Alhambra precinct. Though the formality of the structure compares badly to the ethereal adjacent Alhambra, its plan of a circular courtyard within a square exterior is simple, dignified and impressive in its way—if only it were located elsewhere.

Throughout the remainder of the 16th century, Carlos' son, Felipe II, reacted against the decorative excesses of the plateresque by originating a new style, rather than adopting an older one as his father had done. **El Escorial**, outside Madrid, was the beginning. Designed by Juan Bautista de Toledo, another pupil of Michelangelo, the monastery of El Escorial is sometimes described as a fortress. In fact it is majestic, and appears stark only when viewed from a plateresque or Gothic perspective. When Bautista died four years into the project, he was replaced by the genius of Spanish architecture—Juan de Herrera. Untrained in architecture, Herrera followed no known style, only his feeling of what was right. The church in El Escorial is all his, unique and wonderful.

Herrera's originality died with him, to be replaced by a return to the ornate. The baroque excess of the 17th century holds its own fascination, as the Spanish version, called *Churrigueresque* (after the Churreguera family who originated it), exuberantly demonstrates. The original business of the Churrigueras was designing altars—the altarpiece in the *Convento de San Esteban* in **Salamanca** shows their extravagant work. When they turned to the larger scale of architecture, they expanded the ornate, entwined curves of their altars into buildings in which the eye finds no focus or rest, only stimulation. One acknowledged masterpiece resulted, the *Plaza Mayor* in **Salamanca**. Uncharacteristically for plazas of the period, the buildings around this square are agreeably combined to form one of the finest ensembles in Spain.

Neoclassic to Art Nouveau

In the 18th century, when Bourbon rule began in Spain, Felipe V built a "little" Versailles near **Segovia** to remind him of home. The palace at *La Granja* is sumptuous, the gardens grand. Succeeding sovereigns built extensively in Madrid, favoring architects of classical, Italian bent. One of the best was Juan de Villanueva who designed the *Museo del Prado*. So successful was his design that it spawned descendents around the world, including the Metropolitan Museum in New York.

Although there was little to distinguish Spanish architecture through most of the 1800s, as the century was closing Antoni Gaudí made up for lost time. It was the era of *art nouveau*—dripping, draping, decorative appendages, and buildings abhorring sharp corners. To these expressions of art nouveau, Spain contributed its own heritage of the Gothic and plateresque to nourish its genius Gaudí. In **Barcelona** stand his fantasies, from blocks of houses— *Casa Battló* and *Casa Mila*—to the amusement park *Güell*, to the unfinished masterpiece of *Sagrada Família*, like no church in this world.

Sculpture

Romanesque sculpture in Spain followed the path of sculpture elsewhere in Europe. Figures held rigid postures, faces were caricatures, and drapery fell stiffly. In such a context, the genius of Master Mateo (previously noted) leapt out at the viewer. By the 13th century, the time of the Gothic, figures became elongated to parallel the upward thrust of Gothic cathedrals. Sculpture also began to bend and move. Drapery, though still not natural, was consciously used to add rhythm to compositions, and faces began to reflect the individuality, if not the accuracy, of portraiture.

In 15th-century Spain, during the time of the Isabelline style, genius erupted again in the person of Gil de Siloé who decorated the monastery of *Cartuja de Miraflores* in **Burgos**. His altarpiece overwhelmed the more intricate altars of his contemporaries. In the same monastery he carved a tomb that conveys for all time the sadness of the death of the *Infante* (Prince) Don Alfonso, and, finest of all, a set of tombs for Juan II and his queen Isabel of Portugal.

In the 16th and 17th centuries Siloé's lead was followed by a number of great Spanish sculptors. Berruguete, influenced by the complex movements of the Greek statue of *Laocöon*, rediscovered during his time, carved tormented figures for the cathedral in **Toledo**. Although the choir stalls of that cathedral are entirely splendid, beginning with the lower parts depicting the conquest of Granada, it is the upper stalls on the left that are by this master. At first, compared to the higher relief of the other stalls, Berruguete's carvings seem reserved, for they are infinitely more subtle. With study, they come alive.

Most characteristic of Spanish sculpture is its polychromed wood carving. Gregorio Fernández was a master of the genre. His haunting, living faces, better executed than his mannered bodies, are exhibited in the Museum of Polychrome Sculpture at **Valladolid**. The acknowledged giant of polychrome sculpture, however, is Juan Martinez Montañés who brought the art of painted wood to its summit during the 17th century. He was called *dios de la Madera*, the god of wood. His work is displayed in the Valladolid museum, but more can be seen in the churches of **Seville**, especially in the cathedral. See his *Christ of Clemency*, the *Virgin Primisima* and the *Christ Child Lifting his Arms*, all in the cathedral, and all conveying a stark and realistic dignity. Indeed, some find them too realistic to be considered art.

Painting

Romanesque and Gothic painting in Spain can best be appreciated in the superb collection of the Museo de Arte de Catalunya in **Barcelona**. Often captivating and always deeply expressive of the artist's religious feeling, early Spanish painting is remarkable for the quantity of blood it portrayed—a thinly veiled brutality.

By the time of the Renaissance, Spanish painting had advanced from concentrating on gore to enter the mainstream of European art. In fact, the greatest Spanish painters of that era all trained in Italy. Pedro Gonzalez Berruguete suggests Giotto in his *St. Dominic Before the Inquisition*. Fernando Yanez studied with Leonardo Da Vinci, but shows his own sensitivity in *Saint Catherine*, a painting remarkable for its appreciation of negative spaces. Pedro Machuca studied with Michelangelo, was greatly influenced by Caravaggio, and developed a style, especially evident in his *Madona del Suffragio*, of stark light and shadows. These paintings are included in the extraordinary Renaissance collection of the Museo del Prado in **Madrid**, a collection equally strong in both Italian and Spanish masters.

With the dawning of the 16th century, the quality of Spanish art underwent a dramatic change. Finally victorious in its long struggle against the Moors, Spain was free to turn its attentions outward to the rest of Europe. Spain's first sane monarch after Ferdinand and Isabella, Carlos V, pursued the twin goals of seeking art from all the corners of Europe and of introducing his countrymen to an array of artistic styles. Carlos V became the patron of the Venetian Titian, whose genius epitomized European art at that time. Carlos was the first of three generations of kings, from Felipe II to Felipe IV, who together acquired one of the finest art collections ever amassed—now housed in the Museo del Prado in **Madrid**. Dürer, Botticelli, Raphael, Caravaggio, Bosch, Titian and Rubens are only the best-known artists whose paintings are included in the superb royal collection that raised the standards of both art and its appreciation in Spain.

At this time the first genius of Spanish painting emerged, although he was not born Spanish. Domenico Theotocopoulos, El Greco (the Greek), after studying with Titian in Italy, came to Spain from Crete hoping to find commissions as Titian had. In 1575, at age 35, he settled in Toledo, never to leave again. El Greco had studied Byzantine icon painting in which strong outlines make thin, elongated figures emerge from their background. He introduced the device to western art, along with a palette of luminous blues and reds acquired from his Italian teachers. An ego of enormous proportions allowed him to resist pressures to make his art conform: he once told a pope that if the Sistine frescoes were removed, he could paint better ones.

El Greco first tried to sell paintings to Felipe II, who bought two. *The Martyrdom of St. Maurice* and *Adoration of the Holy Name of Jesus* still hang in Felipe's **Escorial**. In the latter work the great distance up and into the picture initially seems crude and childish, but, with study, the canvas opens up into eternity. El Greco drew from plastic models, not from life, producing angled figures and constant movement, but not realism. The Impressionists—especially Cézanne who copied El Greco's paintings repeatedly—learned much from him. But Felipe II found El Greco's paintings too radical and bought no others.

Thereafter, El Greco worked for wealthy private citizens and churches in **Toledo**. In the Hospital of Tavera, outside the city walls, two great works still hang. *The Baptism of Christ* is magnificent and the portrait of *Cardinal Tavera* haunting. The Museo Santa Cruz holds more than twenty El Grecos, including the famous *Altarpiece of the Assumption.* But the work most people call his best hangs alone inside the vestibule of the tiny church of Santo Tomé. *The Burial of Count Orgaz* is a late work (1586) and El Greco's largest. It incorporates all the original elements that this artist developed: elongated figures, drawn as if the painter were lying down looking up at his subjects; angry, living skies and raw emotion expressed as much in the mannered painting of fabric as in the faces of his subjects.

El Greco followed his own muse. In the more realistic mainstream, Spain rose to dominance in the 17th century—the Golden Age of Spanish art. It began with Francisco Ribalta (1565–1628), a Catalan, whose finest works are the *Vision of Saint Francis* and *Bernard Embracing Christ* in the Museo del Prado in **Madrid**. Then Jusepe de Ribera (1591–1652) burst upon the art world. Ribera is the only painter who can be compared with Velázquez in electing to paint ordinary people instead of idealized images. His figures are real like no others. According to most, his masterpiece is *The Martyrdom of Saint Bartholomew* hanging in the Museo del Prado. But equally engaging are *Joseph with the Christ Child*, *Saint Alexis* and, most striking, *Trinity*. Study the strong diagonals created by the two inverted triangles of the design, the look on the face of God as he holds his dead Son, and the drapery. Ribera is a consummate master.

Genius seemed to inspire genius as Francisco de Zurbarán (1598–1661) followed Ribera. Zurbarán's paintings were the most spiritual of all, not with the fire of El Greco's work, but possessed, instead, of a quiet, bare, intensely reflective, almost mystical quality. Zurbarán's solitary figures in white robes against dark, featureless backgrounds present his extraordinary ability to combine spirituality with utter realism. *The Crucifixion* in the Museo de Bellas Artes in **Seville** is a superior example. Also in the Museo de Bellas Artes in **Seville** is *Blessed Henry Suso* in which the German mystic Suso, stands, uncharacteristically for Zurbarán, against a landscape setting. The figure of Henry Suso is prime Zurbarán, and sublime. The Museo del Prado in **Madrid** displays *Saint Luke before the Crucified*, *Saint Elizabeth of Portugal*, of the luminous clothes, the striking *Virgin of the Immaculate Conception*, and the unforgettable *Saint Peter Nolasco's Vision of the Crucified Saint Peter* with Saint Peter upside down.

Contemporary with Zurbarán, though worlds apart in his career and choice of subjects, was Diego Velázquez de Silva (1599–1660), whose work represents the culmination of Spanish painting. Recognized for his genius while still a youth, Velázquez was appointed a court painter by his twenties. Two early works before his appointment—*The Adoration of the Magi* and *Mother Jerónima de la Fuente*, with her piercing, determined gaze—show him already a master. These hang with all the other paintings we discuss in the premier Velázquez collection, that of the Museo del Prado in **Madrid**.

At court, Velázquez became a royal portrait painter, entering a lifelong friendship with his patron and contemporary, the lonely Felipe IV. Velázquez' portraits of the king show his human side—a homely man with thinning hair and jutting Hapsburg jaw. The portrait of Felipe's brother *The Infante Don Carlos*, demonstrates Velázquez' mastery of the portrait genre. In 1628 Peter Paul Rubens, the most famous painter of the day visited Madrid. He had no use for any Spanish painter but Velázquez and undertook to teach him what he knew. These lessons are contained in Velázquez' disturbing *Feast of Bacchus*, in which the effete, half-naked, fair-skinned god of wine stares at us, surrounded by leathery peasants.

Velázquez was ambitious, rising in position with the years. Added responsibilities for collecting art for the king, decorating rooms in the palaces at Madrid and El Escorial, and supervising other royal painters consumed time, constricting his own artistic output. In his last phase, Velázquez determinedly painted only works that were important to him, exercised to stretch his medium. Two acknowledged masterpieces resulted. *The Fable of Arachne*, by any measure a masterpiece of complexity, depicts a weaving contest between the mortal Arachne and the goddess Minerva.

Although it would be fruitless to try to decide what painting should be called the best in the world, Velázquez' last work, *Las Meninas* (Ladies in Waiting), tempts one against reason. The picture is complex and perfect, summarizing all the painting lessons learned through the ages. Velázquez died soon after finishing *Las Meninas*, but posthumously earned the Order of Santiago he had so assiduously sought in life. A thoughtful friend—some say it was the king himself—later painted a crimson cross, the sign of the order, on Velázquez' chest in the painting.

Francisco de Goya (1746–1828) changed the direction of European painting. He first developed designs for tapestries, called "cartoons," at the royal tapestry works, before turning to portraits. By 1799 he was celebrated enough to be named painter to the king. The king happened to be a genial incompetent, dominated by his wife Maria Luisa and her lover, Godoy. Whether Goya's portraits of the royal family are the greatest art can be argued, but if art means showing the truth, these works make a case. Goya pushed his portraits toward caricature to reveal his subjects' inner character. Paintings such as *The Family of Carlos IV* in the Museo del Prado so ruthlessly display the emptiness of the king and the ambition of the queen, who takes center stage in the group, that one wonders why they allowed such a portrait to be displayed. Conversely, when Goya's subject was a person of quality, as in the case of his friend and father-in-law Bayeu, the portrait exudes character. Goya could also be sensual, as in *Maja Clothed*—more erotic than the same subject and pose in *Maja Nude*.

Still, Goya's high position in the pantheon of art depends more on his fevered imagination than on his skill at portraiture. In 1808, when the French seized Spain, Goya painted two masterworks—*The Second of May* and *The Third of May*—depicting the uprising of Spanish citizens against their invaders. The first shows a battle, fierce with violence; the second, by artificially shortening the distance from the executioners' guns to the defenseless victims, shrieks of the horrors of death. Afterwards, Goya put anguish on canvas in his "Black Paintings" (named for their dominant color)—the unforgettable *Saturn Devouring One of His Sons, Dog Half-Submerged,* and *Witches' Sabbath*. All are displayed with justifiable pride by the Prado.

Where was art to go after such geniuses? In the 20th century it became surreal or abstract, inspired by three founding fathers from Spain. The most prolific, versatile and influential modern artist surely was Pablo Ruiz Picasso (1881–1973). To those who claim modern art avoids realism because its practitioners lack talent, Picasso answered while a child by painting exceptional realistic works, but fought throughout his career to create new means of expression. Picasso, who lived in French exile most of his life, belongs to the world as much as to Spain; still, in the Museu Picasso in **Barcelona**, Spain displays a good collection of his works, stronger in early paintings than in later works. It is interesting to see the first realistic works of the teenaged Picasso and some favorite pieces from his rose and blue periods.

Picasso's most dramatic, and, most would say his finest work, the tormented *Guernica*, has finally been returned to Spain and is now displayed in Spain's new museum of modern art, the Centro de Arte Reina Sofia, in **Madrid**.

Spain does better in collecting the works of another native son, the Catalan Joan Miró (1893–1983). The Fondacio Miró in **Barcelona** presents the breadth of his work, from painting to sculpture to prints and fabrics, in a most appropriate building designed by Joseph Sert. Salvador Dalí (1904–1989), the great surrealist, has a worthy surreal gallery in the Museo-Teatro of his home town of **Figures**, northeast of Barcelona.

MADRID

Madrid's Plaza Neptuno is a pleasant stop on a walking tour.

Madrid sits almost exactly in the center of Spain. A marker at the Puerta del Sol in Madrid reads "0 kilometers," and from it are calculated distances to every village and hamlet in the country. As the surrounding territory, called New Castile, spearheaded Spain's effort to regain the country from the Moors, Castilian Spanish—the victor's language—spread from this center to become the tongue of modern Spain. Savants in the capital still rule magisterially on every attempt to alter its vocabulary.

Originally called *Majerit* by the Moors, a name that twisted off Spanish tongues as "Madrid," the city was founded as a Moorish fort to guard the northern approach to Toledo. The Spanish captured the fort in 1083, discovering a statue of the Virgin Mary in a granary (*al mudin* in Arabic) during

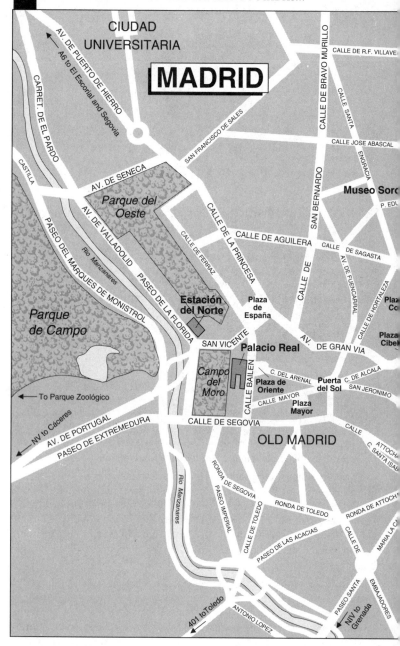

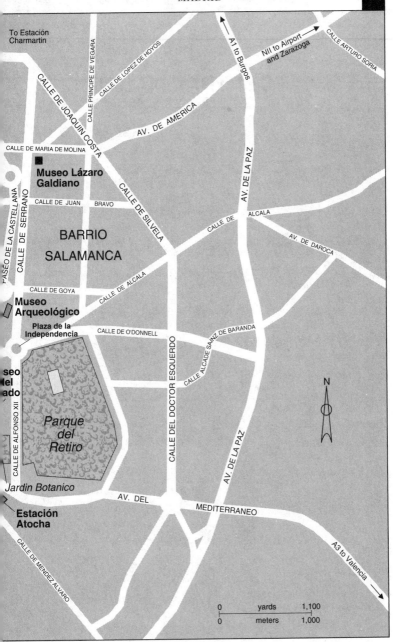

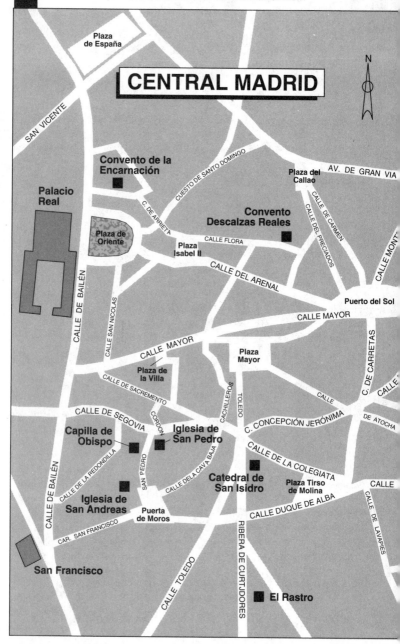

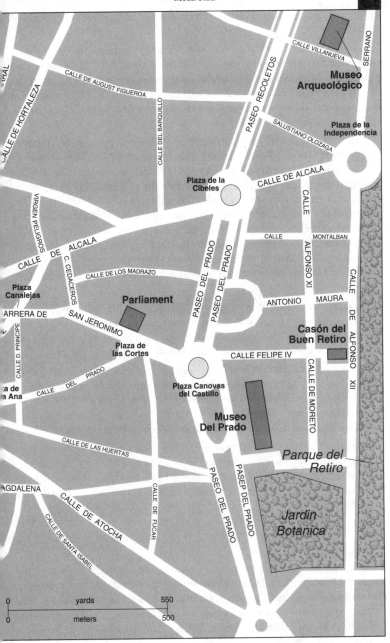

MADRID

the process. Since that time the patron saint of the city has been the Virgin of Almudina.

Although by no means a major town, Madrid's statue of the Virgin gave kings reason to visit from time to time. In the 14th century, Pedro the Cruel constructed Madrid's first castle on the site of the original Moorish fort. In the 15th century, Ferdinand and Isabella built a monastery, San Jerónimo el Real, and the following century Carlos V, their grandson, reconstructed Pedro's castle palatially.

In 1561, Carlos' son, Felipe II, decreed Madrid the permanent capital of Spain—*Real Madrid* (Royal Madrid). The reason is a subject of controversy, with most accounts attributing his decision to Madrid's central location. But Madrid is not exactly centered, and the centrality of a capital in Spain could not have mattered to a monarch whose territories extended far beyond the borders of this one domain. More likely the reason had to do with Madrid's proximity to the former capital, Valladolid. As the number of hearths in Valladolid increased, the supply of nearby trees became exhausted, making firewood scarce. But Madrid still had stands of fresh timber, pure water and few hearths. It was time to move, and Madrid was conveniently close.

With the arrival of a king and his government came tens of thousands of functionaries requiring massive public buildings to house them. Most of those original government structures, however, including the palace, burned in cataclysmic fires during the 17th century. The present palace sits on the ashes of the original and dates from the middle of the 18th century.

The majority of Madrid's grand structures, including the Prado, were erected in a late 18th-century building spurt during the peaceful reign of King Carlos III, a monarch who earned the title "King-Mayor" for his sustained effort to raise Madrid to the standards of other European capitals. Historically and architecturally, Madrid is Europe's newest capital.

Today four million people spread over miles of concrete suburbs. Happily, the original core of the city—the focus of virtually all a tourist's interest—remains relatively untouched by this growth. Most sights are an easy walk from this center, but since Madrid's original civil engineers never envisioned a city of such numbers, traffic can make traveling longer distances a problem. Streets clog, cars proceed slowly and parking in centercity is a challenge best avoided. An efficient subway system and inexpensive taxis, however, make driving unnecessary.

The Puerta del Sol is the midpoint of a line at whose eastern end stands the **Museo del Prado** with its **El Retiro Park** and at whose western end stands the **Palácio Real**. A mile and a quarter separates these monuments from each other, and between them lie most of the city's important sights. Along this axis is the Plaza Mayor, Madrid's Ciudad Antique, and the convents of Descalzas

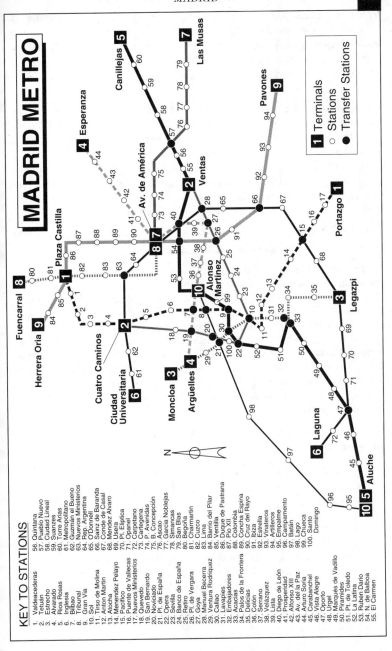

MADRID METRO

KEY TO STATIONS

1. Valdeacederas
2. Tetuán
3. Estrecho
4. Alvarado
5. Ríos Rosas
6. Inglesia
7. Bilbao
8. Tribunal
9. Gran Vía
10. Tirol
11. Tirso de Molina
12. Antón Martín
13. Atocha
14. Menéndez Pelayo
15. Pacífico
16. Puente de Vallecas
17. Nuevos Ministerios
18. Quevedo
19. San Bernardo
20. Noviciado
21. Pl. de España
22. Opera
23. Sevilla
24. Banco de España
25. Retiro
26. Pl. de Vergara
27. Goya
28. Manuel Becerra
29. Ventura Rodríguez
30. Callao
31. Lavapiés
32. Embajadores
33. Acacias
34. Palos de la Frontera
35. Delicias
36. Colón
37. Serrano
38. Velázquez
39. Lista
40. Diego de León
41. Prosperidad
42. Alfonso XIII
43. Av. de la Paz
44. Arturo Soria
45. Carabanchel
46. Vista Alegre
47. Oporto
48. Urgel
49. Marqués de Vadillo
50. Pirámides
51. Pt. de Toledo
52. La Latina
53. Rubén Darío
54. N. de Balboa
55. El Carmen
56. Quintana
57. Pueblo Nuevo
58. Ciudad Lineal
59. Suanzes
60. Torre Arias
61. Metropolitano
62. Guzmán el Bueno
63. Nuevos Ministerios
64. Rep. Argentina
65. O'Donell
66. Sáinz de Baranda
67. Conde de Casal
68. Méndez Alvaro
69. Usera
70. Pl. Elíptica
71. Opañel
72. Carpetana
73. Cartagena
74. Avenidas
75. B. Concepción
76. Ascao
77. García Noblejas
78. Simancas
79. San Blas
80. Begoña
81. Charmartín
82. Cuzco
83. Lima
84. Barrio del Pilar
85. Ventilla
86. Duque de Pastrana
87. Pío XII
88. Colombia
89. Concha Espina
90. Cruz del Rayo
91. Ibiza
92. Estrella
93. Vinateros
94. Artilleros
95. Empalme
96. Campamento
97. Batán
98. Lago
99. Chueca
100. Santo Domingo

Terminals
Stations
Transfer Stations

Plaza Castilla
Fuencarral 8
Herrera Oria 9
Cuatro Caminos
Ciudad Universitaria
Moncloa 3
Argüelles 4
Esperanza
Canillejas 5
Las Musas 7
Pavones 9
Av. de América
Ventas
Alonso Martínez
Portazgo 1
Legazpi
Laguna 6
Aluche 10 5

MADRID

Real and Encarnación. Even the Sunday-morning flea market, **El Rastro**, is located only a few blocks south. Less than a mile due north of the Prado, the **Museo Arqueológico Nacional** displays the treasures of Spain's early history amid the Barrio Salamanca's elegant shops. Including the Archaeological Museum and its surrounding shops, the sights between the Prado and Palace can abundantly fill most visitors' schedules.

Madrid has always been the most lively of capitals, exuding energy and animation. One wonders when Madrileños sleep, for drawn by 3000 restaurants and tapas bars, they fill the sidewalks until the small hours of the night. Madrid is the culinary capital of Spain, with more restaurants offering more varieties of food than anywhere else in the country. Whatever the regional specialty—Basque, Galician, Valencian or Andalusian—Madrid serves its cuisine as well or better than its home territory. A visitor can perform a complete culinary tour of Spain without ever leaving Madrid.

Population 3,084,673   **Area code: 91**   **Zip Code: 28000**

What to See and Do

The **Museo del Prado** is a high point, not simply of Madrid, but of Spain. The **Museo Arqueológico Nacional** should not be missed. To experience the atmosphere of the city, take one or more **walking tours** described below, preferably #1 and #2. The **Palácio Real** is impressive for its excesses, if not tastefulness, and almost everyone should find the associated armory and carriage museums interesting. **El Retiro** park, behind the Prado, offers an array of activities throughout the summer. Museums abound. The brand-new **Villahermosa Museum** now fills the gaps in the Prado collection. The convents of the **Encarnación** and **Descalzas Real** sumptuously house impressive furnishings. The **Centro de Arte Reina Sofia** is rapidly becoming a premier museum of modern art. And then there is shopping—elegant in the **Barrio Salamanca**, and, on Sunday mornings, fun in **El Rastro**, Madrid's flea market.

Museums

Museo del Prado   ★★★★★

> *Paseo del Prado,* ☎ *420 28 36. Subway: Banco de España or Atocha. Buses: 10, 14, 27, 37, 45, M-6.*
>
> *Hours open: Tues.–Sat. 9 a.m.–6:30 p.m., (until 7 p.m. from May 15 to Oct. 15). Open Wed. night until 9 p.m. Open Sun. 9 a.m.–2 p.m.*

In 1785, as a major component of his plan to gentrify the capital, Carlos III commissioned the building of the stately Prado on the site of the Prado de San Jerónimo, or Saint Jerome's Meadow, formerly the gardens of a monastery built by Isabella and Ferdinand. The meadow had long served as a favorite promenade for the beautiful people of Madrid, and the king hoped to edify his strolling subjects by placing natural science exhibits in their path. He gave the assignment to Juan de Villanueva, of neoclassical Italian bent, who designed a columned brick-and-stone structure with protruding end pavilions that generated countless similar museums around the world.

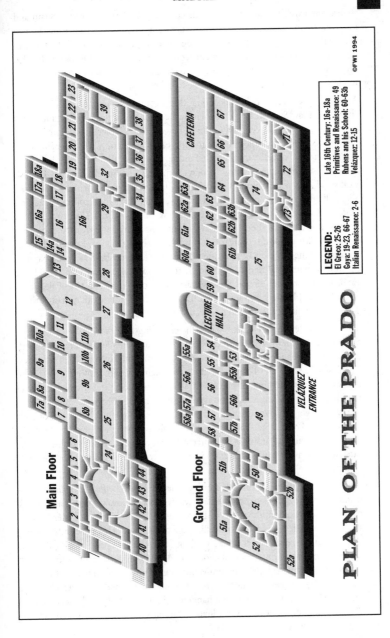

Main Floor

Ground Floor

CAFETERIA

LECTURE HALL

VELÁZQUEZ ENTRANCE

PLAN OF THE PRADO

LEGEND:
El Greco: 25-26
Goya: 19-23, 66-67
Italian Renaissance: 2-6

Late 16th Century: 16a-18a
Primitives and Renaissance: 49
Rubens and his School: 60-63b
Velázquez: 12-15

©FWI 1994

Before any exhibits could be installed, however, the French invaded Spain and lodged a troop of cavalry inside, greatly damaging the interior. When the French left, Carlos' grandson, Ferdinand VII, decided to use the abandoned building to house previously separate royal art collections under one roof. On November 19, 1817, shortly after the opening of the Louvre in Paris, the Museo del Prado first received the public.

A special aspect of the Prado collection is that, because it consists primarily of works chosen by a few Spanish kings for their own collections, it lends insight into royal tastes. Early in the 16th century, Carlos V, raised in The Netherlands before becoming Spain's king, assembled the beginning of the collection. His domains were extensive and he traveled throughout Europe, bringing a European sensibility to a Spain focused inward by its centuries of reconquest. Carlos purchased many Flemish works and, above all, paintings by the great Italian, Titian, the master he admired above all others. Carlos' son, Felipe II greatly expanded the royal collection, adding fantastic works of Hieronymus Bosch, among others. In the 17th century, his grandson, Felipe IV, became an avid collector and also patron to the great Velázquez, who he sent to Italy to select works for royal purchase. Felipe IV bought Rubens' by the score and twice offered that artist the position of court painter, though Rubens declined each time. After Cromwell ousted Charles I from England's throne and offered the royal art collection for sale, agents of Felipe IV were the main bidders, sending home Dürer's *Self Portrait* among many others. Thus was the mass of the Prado's collection assembled.

Throughout the time of Carlos V and the collecting Felipes who succeeded him, Spain governed all of Italy south of Rome, which accounts for the Prado's superb collection of Italian masterworks, especially those from the 16th and 17th centuries. Thanks to Carlos V and Felipe II, Dutch and Flemish works are well represented, including a major Rembrandt purchased later. Still, the focus of the collection is on the incomparable Spanish masters, assiduously gathered in homage—unparalleled in any other country—to its native artists. Because Spain was a political rival of both England and France, the Prado is weak in English painting and spotty in French. And, despite three great works by Albrecht Dürer, the collection must also be considered weak in German painting, for its artists were generally ignored by the royal collectors.

No one should miss the three Dürers, Raphael's *Portrait of a Cardinal*, Bosch's paintings, all the Zurbaráns, all of Velázquez' works and Goya's portraits and "black paintings." In addition, the works of Berruguette, Ribera, El Greco, Pieter Bruegel the Elder, van der Weyden, Botticelli, Fra Angelico and Titian are outstanding, although other treasures will certainly call out to you as you pass. The Prado owns more than 6000 paintings. Since it chooses to display only about 500, every one will be special. Fortunately, the museum is not huge. How much time a visit requires will depend entirely on whether you wish to cover only its highlights, which can be seen in half a day, or to view its full hanging collection, which can be seen in a full day, or better still, enjoyed over a lifetime. *Admission: 450 ptas., which includes Casón del Buen Retiro.*

Museo Arqueológico Nacional   ★★★

C. Serrano, 13, ☎ 577 79 12. Entrance in the rear on Paseo de Recoletas. Subway:
Colón or Serrano. Buses: 1, 5, 9, 14, 19, 51, 74, M-2. See "Walking Tour #3."

Hours open: Tues.–Sat. 9:30 a.m.–8:30 p.m. Open Sun. 9:30 a.m.–2:30 p.m. Closed
Mon. and holidays.

The National Archaeological Museum occupies the rear half of the large **Biblioteca Nacional**, with an entrance on C. Serrano. The building was opened in 1892 to celebrate the 400th anniversary of Columbus' discovery of America. While museums of archaeology abound throughout Spain, for the country is rich in artifacts of earlier civilizations, the very best examples have been culled for display in this national collection.

The tour begins in room one with remains from Greek, Phoenician and Carthaginian civilizations, then leads into a display in room two of artifacts from the native ancient Iberian culture. Carthaginian influence is evident in the fourth-century B.C. *Dama de Elche*, the greatest known Iberian sculpture and the centerpiece of the room. She looks somehow foreign, of a culture outside the classical tradition, for the character of an alien aesthetic seems carved in her face. Other *damas* repose around her, almost as lovely as she. Following rooms contain Roman sculpture and mosaics of some interest.

The second floor begins with Visigothic jewelry. Three crowns turned into votive hangings are the star attractions, and that of Reccesvinthus Rex from circa 670 B.C. is particularly striking. Dangling gold letters spell his name, while the crown is embedded with uncut semiprecious stones. It is the world's loss that the most splendid crown in the collection was stolen in 1921 and never recovered.

Next comes incomparable Moorish art. The small objects, including the precious ivory box called the *Bote de Marfil*, require study. Stucco work is also displayed, as are intricately coffered ceilings, all of which provide just a sample of the Moorish architecture that waits in Andalusia. Gothic sculpture comes next, and Renaissance objects and furniture follow. Higher floors display small collections of Egyptian and prehistoric art.

On the grounds by the entrance is an underground replica of Altamira cave. Although it is only a pale copy, with some quiet study the animals do begin to wriggle over your head. *Admission: 450 ptas.*

Palácio Real   ★★★

C. Bailén, ☎ 248 74 04. Subway: Opera. Buses: 3, 25, 33, 39, M-4. See "Walking Tour #2."

Hours open: Tues.–Sat. 9 a.m.–6:15 p.m. (until 5:15 p.m. in winter.) Open Sun. and holidays 9 a.m.–2 p.m. Closed Mon.

In 1764, 26 years after the former Hapsburg palace was leveled by fire, this palace was raised on the ashes of the old one. It was a new palace for a new dynasty. The final king of the Hapsburg line had been born mentally retarded and died childless, but, on his deathbed, willed the throne to a distant French relative, a cousin of the French Bourbon king. Thus did Felipe V initiate the present Bourbon line of Spanish monarchs. He ordered a palace to suit his French tastes designed by the Italian architect Sachetti.

The entrance is through its south end where tickets are purchased, followed by a huge porticoed forecourt that leads to the palace proper. In addition to the palace proper there is the Library with its numismatic and music museum, the Real Farmacia (Royal Pharmacy), the Armería (Armory) and the Museo de Carruajes Reales (Royal Carriage Museum). At least the last two museums are worth a look. Including those, it will take several hours to see the palace.

The apartments of the palace's first occupant, Carlos III, begin at the top of a grand stairway. The ceilings of two small rooms were painted by Mengs. Rooms lined with velvet, gilt and candelabras follow, and lead to a double throne room (one seat for the present King Juan Carlos, the other for his queen, Sofía) that tries hard to impress, but would be more appropriate as a Hollywood movie set—though there is that Tiepolo frescoed ceiling. The dining room sits 88 comfortably. Such rooms must be seen to be believed. Two thousand rooms fill the structure, though most are off-limits to tourists. The museum of painting, porcelain and crystal displays a Bosch, four Goyas and a Velázquez amid dinner services for scores.

Outside, in the west wing of the forecourt, is the **Real Armería** (Royal Armory), containing collections of the actual armor worn by 16th- and 17th-century kings. There is a fine tent captured from the French saint-king Francis I at the battle of Pavia, and armor for men, royalty, children, horses and dogs. The long length of the jousting lances are a surprise. The finest armor are the many suits worn by Carlos V, who needed them for a reign filled with wars. All the armor is functional and at the same time artistic, a happy blend of craft and aesthetics. Of course there are amusing excesses too, such as the plating that covers half a horse and culminates in ram's horns crowning the headpiece.

South of the palace is one of the largest churches in the world, **Nuestra Señora de la Almudena**. Construction began over 100 years ago and has not yet finished. (It is possible that disappointment with the results to date has quenched the builders' incentive.)

Outside in the Campo del Moro, the former royal park, is a modern building which houses the **Museo de Carruajes Reales** (Royal Carriage Museum). It contains elaborately decorated carriages, primarily from the late 18th century. The one in black ebony is the only carriage to have survived the fire that destroyed the former palace in the 18th century, and dates from a century earlier. Napoleon donated the one with the crown on top. The present coronation coach still bears the marks of an assassination attempt made on a former king and his bride in 1906. *By tour only, in Spanish or English. Admission: 500 ptas.*

Villahermosa Museum   ★ ★ ★

Paseo del Prado, 8, ☎ 420 39 44. Across from the Prado. Subway: Banco de España or Atocha. Buses: 10, 14, 27, 43, 37, 45, M-6.
Hours open: Tues.–Sun. 10 a.m. to 7 p.m., (until 6:30 p.m. in winter). Closed Mon.
This museum completes the Prado collection by filling its gaps. Both Baron Thyssen-Bornemisza and his son spent a fortune from Dutch mining and shipping profits

to acquire possibly the finest, and certainly the most extensive, collection of art remaining in private hands, Queen Elizabeth excepted, and decided to sell the mass of it—nearly 800 paintings, sundry furniture, jewelry and statues—to Spain thanks in no small measure to the urgings of the Baron's Spanish wife. Here these treasures will reside for our enjoyment, displayed in a tasteful palace.

The installation is arranged in reverse order. Modern art inhabited the first floor, 17th-century Dutch through 19th-century American and English on the second, and masterpieces from the Renaissance through the 17th-century the third. Here hangs the familiar, powerful *Portrait of Henry VIII* by Holbein the Younger, along with the captivating *Portrait of Giovanna Tornabuoni* by Ghirlandaio, and Caravaggio's unforgettable *St.Catherine of Alexandria.*

The second floor presents a surprising collection of great American canvases, then fine Impressionists followed by some dramatic expressionists, such as Munch. The modern art on the first floor falls below the standards of the rest, save for a fine Edward Hopper and a haunting painting of the Baron's father by Lucien Freud. *Admission: 650 ptas.*

Convento Descales Reales ★★
Pl. de las Descalzas Reales, 3, ☎ 248 74 04. Subway: Puerta del Sol (directions in "Walking Tour #2"). buses: 1, 2, 5, 20, 46, 52, 53, 74.
Hours open: Tues.–Thurs. and Sat. from 10:30 a.m.–12:30 p.m. and 4–5:15 p.m. Open Fri. 10:30 a.m.–12:30 p.m., Sun. to 1:30 p.m. Closed Mon. and all holidays.
Juana of Austria, the daughter of Carlos V, established this convent of Poor Clares in 1559 in a former Renaissance palace. The order had been founded a century before by St. Francis of Assisi, for his disciple St. Clare. After its founding, the order petitioned the pope for the "privilege of poverty," that is, for the right of its members to subsist on nothing but what they could beg.

However, there was no begging at this particular convent. It was restricted to "Poor" Clares of the highest nobility who used it as a periodic retreat from the pressures of high society. In return for their stays, they donated the sumptuous gifts now on display in buildings around the cloister.

Despite its austere exterior, the convent is a riot of decoration within. The tour passes through rooms containing fine paintings by Titian, Breugel the Elder, a splendid Zurbarán *St. Francis* and portraits of the Hapsburg royal family. Up a staircase for which "grandiose" is the only description, one enters the former dormitory hung with lovely 17th-century tapestries. The reliquary gallery displays impressive boxes and chests. This is a special museum, small but select.

The only sense of having visited a cloistered convent is by comparison—when you step outside and around the corner to the contemporary bustle of the el Corte Inglés department store. *By tour in Spanish only. Admission: 600 ptas.; free on Wed. The ticket serves also for the Convento de la Encarnación.*

Convento de la Encarnación ★
Pl. de la Encarnación, 1, ☎ 247 05 10. Subway: Opera (directions in "Walking Tour #2"), buses: 3, 25, 33, 39.

Hours open: Tues.–Thurs. 10:30 a.m.–12:30 p.m. and 4–5:15 p.m. Open Fri., Sat. and 10:30 a.m.–12:30 p.m., Sun. to 1:30 p.m. Closed Mon. and all holidays.

See "Walking Tour #2." In 1611, Margarete of Austria, wife of Felipe III, commissioned Gómez de Mora, the architect who built Madrid's Plaza Mayor, to design this convent. She and succeeding monarchs donated generously to her pet project. The art in the galleries is not up to the standards of Descalzas Reales, but there is a Ribera, a fine polychrome sculpture by Gregorio Fernandez and pleasing 17th-century Madrid paintings. The 18th-century church is severe in design and Baroque in decoration. A sumptuously frescoed ceiling canopies equally dazzling reliquaries—over 1000 of them—in the gallery. The contrast with the private rooms of the convent is marked, for they offer a taste of simple cloistered life in the 17th century. *By tour in Spanish only. Admission: 600 ptas.; free on Wed. The ticket also serves as admission to Convento Descales Reales.*

Centro de Arte Reina Sofia   ★★

C. Santa Isabel, 52, ☎ 467 50 62. Subway: Atocha, buses: 18, 59, 85, 86, C. Hours open: Wed.–Mon. 10 a.m.–9 p.m. Closed Tues. and holidays.

Located one block northwest of the Atocha train and subway station, the building began as an 18th-century hospital. Now it has been spiffed up to house the best of Spain's modern art, including Picasso's *Guernica.*

Head straight to the second floor. There in the center of Room 7 is *Guernica*, acclaimed by most experts as the masterpiece of 20th-century art. Painted entirely in shades of black and white, it expresses the horrors of war in its depiction of the devastation of the Basque capital of Guernica. The town, in no way a military target, was carpet-bombed by wave upon wave of German planes during the Spanish Civil War. Scenes of civilians and animals contorted in agony fill the canvas. Because of Franco's involvement in the attack, Picasso would not permit this painting to be exhibited in Spain until after the dictator's regime ended. Picasso's studies for the work lend insight into its composition. If you allow it to, the painting will move you to a deep sadness.

The collection of Spanish modern art is unrivaled. There are major works by Miró, Dalí and Juan Gris, in addition to many Picassos. In particular, a study of Picasso's series of drawings of Velázquez' *Las Meninas* will teach the principles of modern art. As a collection it presents a tour-de-force of modern art, reminding us how great was the contribution of Spaniards.

The museum shop is worth a stop for its prints and posters. *Admission: 450 ptas.*

Other Sights

Plaza Mayor   ★★

Subway: Puerta del Sol. Buses: 3, 25, 33, 39, M-4. From the Puerta del Sol, head west on C. Mayor for two blocks, taking the third right into the Pl. Mayor.

This huge—football field-sized—square plaza is famed for being one of the largest and most architecturally integrated plazas in Spain. Although Felipe II had commissioned his favorite architect Juan de Herrera—responsible for such neoclassical work as *El Escorial*—to design a grand square in the capital, it was not until the reign of his son that construction began, and then under the supervision of the architect

Juan Gómez de Mora. Completed over the course of just two years, the plaza officially opened in 1620 with ceremonies to celebrate the canonization of five Spanish saints: Sta. Theresa of Ávila, St. Ignatius of Loyola, St. Francis Zavier, St. Isidro, the male patron saint of Madrid, and St. Felipe Neri.

Throughout the 17th century and into the 19th, the plaza served as an arena for so many spectacles—plays, *autos-da-fé*, fireworks, royal marriage celebrations and bullfights—that the owners of the houses on the plaza's perimeter were required to lend their balconies to royalty during festivities. In the 1970s vehicles were barred from the plaza and diverted underground or around it. Thanks to the absence of traffic, today the plaza is a lively place in summer filled with crowds attending concerts and festivals, or simply milling about. In winter it is a quiet, open space useful for strolls or shortcuts. Tables spring up on Sunday mornings for a stamp fair.

On the plaza's north side is the **Casa de Panaderia**, once the home of the bakers' guild, but rebuilt in 1672 after a fire. The king often sat on its second floor to observe spectacles in the plaza. Today, **Felipe III ★** sculpted by the Italian Giovanni de Bologna, sits on horseback in the center of the plaza. With his beatific grin and baton of office held so insouciantly, his starched collar looks quite out of place, but is of no matter to the perching sparrows who love him dearly.

In the southwest corner of the plaza an archway leads to steps down to the **C. de Cuchilleros ★**, a strip of old *mesones* and *tabernas*, including the famous *Botín*. If you were to turn north, the street would become Cava de San Miguel, with more such dining places. (*Cava* was the name given to moats outside the original walls of medieval Madrid.) Instead turn right to the Pl. del Conde de Barajas, then left along its near edge down C. Lanzas to the **Plaza Puerta Cerrada**, an old city gate with a stone cross in the center, and surrounded by buildings with vegetable murals.

Plaza de la Villa ★★

Subway: Tirso de Molina. Buses: 3, 25, 33, 39, M-4. Two blocks further on C. Mayor past the Pl. Mayor.

The large street bordering the plaza is C. Mayor, which leads leftward in two blocks to the Palácio Real. The building just passed is the **Torre de Los Lujanes**, the former residence of an ancient family of Madrid grandees, in which Francis I of France was held prisoner in 1325. Of the original Gothic building one side-door remains, the first door facing the plaza. Down into the plaza, beside Los Lujanes, is the smaller **Hemeroteca**, Periodicals Library, an annex of the City Library, with a Gothic entrance and two Renaissance tombs inside the vestibule. In the center of the plaza a 19th century statue honors **Alvaro de Bazan**, one of the heroes of the naval victory over the Turks at Lepanto. The noble building across the way is the present **Ayuntamiento ★** (City Hall) designed in 1640 by de Mora, the architect of the Plaza Mayor, to serve as both the meeting place for the town council and a prison— certainly an interesting combination. The Museo Municipal inside is open Tues.– Fri. 9:30 a.m.–3 p.m.; weekends 10 a.m.–2 p.m.; admission: 450 ptas. for tours of tapestries, furniture and paintings of Madrid (☎ *522 57 32*).

Walk down the plaza to the building at the end, connected by an archway to the Ayuntamiento, but pass along its side opposite the archway. This building, called the **Casa de Cisneros** ★, was erected in 1537 for the nephew of Jimenes de Cisneros, Isabella's chief minister who became the regent of Spain after her death. Now much restored, it retains one fine 16th-century window at the back overlooking the lovely Pl. del Cordón. Inside is an interesting collection of furniture and tapestries, although it is open only on Monday evenings from 5–7 p.m. Across the Pl. del Cordón carved cording surrounding the door of the large **Casa de los Alfaro** signifies that it once served as a bishopric.

Puerto del Sol   ★

Subway: Puerta del Sol. Buses: 3, 25, 33, 39, M-4.

In every sense this plaza is the hub of Madrid, even of the country. Crowds bustle at any hour of the day or night.

North across the oval plaza is a small bronze statue of a bear and a strawberry plant, the emblem of the city of Madrid. East, at the entrance of C. Alcalá, is the imposing Treasury Building, the former royal Customs House. The tower with the clock, Madrid's Big Ben, was added to the former 17th-century post office, now reconstructed as the Governación (Ministry of the Interior). In front, on the sidewalk, a bronze plaque marks kilometer zero from which all distances in Spain are measured.

Shops of a lower caliber do their best to attract. But at the east end of the plaza, at #6, a called **La Pajareta** must be seen. It has been selling caramels here for over 150 years. A few doors east at #12 a store called **Casa de Diego** displays an astonishing number of umbrellas along with some fans. The window display is for tourists, but antique versions are stored away inside.

Head to the west end of the plaza and take the left of the forking streets there onto C. Arenal. Take the next left, C. Victoria, walking toward the el Corte Inglés department store. But just before you reach it, take the first right onto C. de San Martin. In a short block you enter the small Pl. de las Descalzas, for you just walked the width of the convent on your right.

See the description and hours of the Convento de las Descalzas ★★ under "Museums" above.

Barrio Salamanca   ★★

Subway: Serrano.

North of the Archaeology museum C. Serrano transforms into one of the main shopping streets in Madrid. One block north (left when exiting the museum), C. Goya crosses Serrano. The two streets form one corner of an area called the Barrio Salamanca, bordered by Serrano on the west, Goya on the south, Conde de Pañalver 10 short blocks east, and José Ortega four blocks north. The Barrio Salamanca contains most of the fine department, clothing, couture, antique, art and furniture shops of Madrid, with the western half, where you're standing, the most interesting.

This area, one of the first urban developments, is named for the Marqués de Salamanca who, in 1865, laid out this grid of streets which, at the time, extended beyond the walls of Madrid.

Here is the layout of the Barrio. C. Serrano runs north-south. A short block east and parallel to Serrano is C. Claudio Coello. Smaller streets run between. The first two after Goya, Calles Hermosille and Ayala, are the most interesting. Wander as you will.

Plaza de Colon and the Biblioteca Nacional are worth a visit.

Where to Stay

Madrid is an expensive place to sleep whose few inexpensive rooms go quickly. Visitors generally have to increase their budget in this city. While many factors go into choosing a hotel, proximity to the center is an asset because it permits walking to most sights and restaurants. With literally hundreds of hotels to choose from, there is little reason to stay anywhere but in the old town, near it, or in the Barrio Salamanca where Madrid's elegant shops gather. A select list covering each price range follows.

Very Expensive ($200+)

Ritz   **Deluxe ★ ★ ★ ★ ★**

Pl. de la Lealtad, 5 (1 block north of the Prado), ☎ *521 28 57, FAX 532 87 76, Telex 43986, in the U.S., 800-223-6800.*

King Alfonso XIII personally oversaw the construction of the Ritz in 1910 because he considered no existing hotel suitable for his wedding guests. César Ritz himself, the hotelier whose name connotes luxury, received the commission. Here you actually feel like a guest of royalty, with the stiffness that implies (ties must be worn in the bar and eating areas), but with service that is noble. No two pastel-colored rooms are the same, but all are carpeted with rugs handmade in the Royal Tapestry Factory and decked out in embroidered linen, fresh flowers and dangling chandeliers. Everything is lux in a *Belle Époque* style harkening to a time when the rich certainly knew how to live. Naturally the Ritz' location is special—on its own park across from the Pl. Canovas del Castillo, the Palace Hotel and the Córtez building. From it you can hit the Museo del Prado with a stone, if so inclined. Such elegance costs a king's ransom, so estimate almost $400 a night for two. But even these prices aren't enough to keep the "squares" away, as this is one of the most heavily booked hotels in Madrid. Reserve far ahead and start saving, if you want a room. 127 rooms, plus 29 suites.

Palace   Deluxe ★ ★ ★

Pl. de las Cortes, 7 (1 block north of the Prado), ☎ *429 75 51, FAX 429 82 66, Telex 23903.*

Anywhere else this would be the most elegant hotel in town, but Madrid has the Ritz too. The lobby's all-glass cupola sets the stage for its *Belle Époque* decor and trompe l'oeil paintings. However, while the Palace's public rooms are sumptuous, its bedrooms are ordinary and so numerous that, despite superb management, the special attention for each guest these prices call for is sometimes labored. Still, it has that entrance, the location is as good as the Ritz and its charges are about a quarter less—though the Palace is about that much less grand. 436 rooms, plus 20 suites.

Villa Real   1st-class ★ ★ ★

Pl. de las Cortes, 10 (1 block north of the Prado), ☎ *420 37 67, FAX 420 25 47, Telex 44 600.*

Although designed to look 19th-century, these lovely accommodations actually opened in 1989. Unlike so many fancy hotels that emphasize their lobby, this one concentrates on your room. Everything about this hotel speaks of class and good taste. The bedrooms are more comfortable and attractive than those at the Palace, and they cost a few pesetas less, at a location that is exactly as convenient. Although it certainly isn't cheap, the Villa Real gives super value for your money. 96 rooms, plus 19 suites.

Santo Mauro   Deluxe ★ ★ ★

C. Zurbano, 36 (a block north of Pl. de Becerra, 1 mile west of the Pl. Cibeles), ☎ *319 69 00, FAX 308 54 77.*

This is as distinguished a hotel as anyone is likely to find anywhere. For starters, it is lodged around a garden in a small former palace that was restored lovingly, then decorated by the finest designers. Bedrooms contain every convenience, and the restaurant is world-class. Furthermore, it is small enough for intimacy and exquisite individual service. There are two drawbacks, however. It is located in the elegant Almagro quarter which is a mile and a half from the old town, and it charges almost as much as the Ritz. Of course the first problem is easily solved by a taxi, and the second by money. 33 rooms, plus four suites.

Expensive ($100–$199)

G. H. Reina Victoria   1st-class ★ ★ ★

Pl. Santa Ana, 14 (just north of C. de San Jerónimo, two blocks west of P. del Prado), ☎ *531 45 00, FAX 522 03 07, Telex 475 47.*

The eccentric facade of this Madrid institution has been declared a historic monument. Even better, it sits beside the quiet Plaza Ana park, yet is smack in the center of town. Manolete regularly stayed here as did Hemingway and you can too at prices that are fair for Madrid. Recently it was taken over by the Tryp chain which improved the service and modernized it throughout. Comfortable, rather than fancy, rooms are bright and some include balconies overlooking the park. Now this is the place to stay in the old town (along with the Hotel Suecia, below). 195 rooms, plus six suites.

Suecia   1st-class ★ ★ ★

Marqués de Casa Ribera, 4 (Take the street going north along the west side of the Palácio Cortes on Carrera San Jerónimo. At the back, jag west, then north again, into the little square), ☎ *531 69 00, FAX 521 71 41, Telex 22313.*

The location is almost as good as that of the Victoria—in the old town, yet on a tiny quiet square. But the Suecia is new and glistening, compared to the Victoria's seasoned personality, so the choice is clear. In this category the Suecia's cleanliness and service can not be bettered in Madrid. Our only complaint is a certain lack of personality about the place. 119 rooms, plus six suites.

Tryp Ambassador   1st-class ★ ★ ★

Cuesta de Santo Domingo, 5 (near the Palácio Real, 1 block north of the Opera), ☎ *541 67 00, FAX 559 10 40, Telex 49538.*

This is a most pleasant addition to Madrid's hotel inventory. As its grand stairway attests, the Ambassador is a renovated former palace from the 19th century. Graciously sized bedrooms all include separate sitting areas and are pleasantly accessorized. Businesspeople love it. The location is quiet and convenient to sights, somewhat less so for tapas-hopping. 163 rooms, plus 18 suites.

Alcalá   1st-class ★ ★

Alcalá, 66, ☎ *435 10 60, FAX 435 11 05, Telex 48094.*

This is a modern, softly lit, executive-type hotel, located near the northeast corner of El Retiro Park. It is convenient to shopping in the Barrio Salamanca, but a bit of a walk to the Prado and old town. While walking, you can think about the prices that barely crest the expensive line. 153 rooms.

Moderate ($50–$99)

Serrano   2nd-class ★ ★ ★

Marqués de Villamejor, 8 (around the corner from Serrano, the main shopping street of the Barrio Salamanca, and half way between Pl. Colón and the park), ☎ *435 52 00, FAX 435 48 49.*

The intimate Serrano ranks as the best moderately priced hotel in expensive Madrid. It is tastefully decorated, all the rooms include TVs and are nicely appointed, and the walk to the Prado passes some of Madrid's nicest stores. 30 rooms, plus 4 suites

El Prado   2nd-class ★ ★

Prado, 11 (3 blocks along this quaint street that runs out of the Pl. Cortez), ☎ *369 02 34, FAX 429 28 29.*

Sitting on a little antique-shop street in the old town, the location of this hotel is superb for sights, tapas-hopping and restaurants. Doubly glazed windows keep the ample rooms quiet, and prices just rise into the moderate range. 47 rooms.

Regina   2nd-class ★ ★

Alcalá, 19 (one long block along this main street running west from the Pl. del Sol), ☎ *521 47 25, FAX 521 47 25, Telex 27500.*

The Regina's location is close to the Puerta del Sol and its rooms stand a clear level above most of the competition. 142 rooms.

Don Diego   HR2nd-class ★

Velázquez, 45 (on one of the nice shopping streets of the Barrio Salamanca, four blocks north of the Parque del Buen Retiro), ☎ *435 07 60, FAX 431 42 63.*

The location is more convenient for shopping than the very expensive choices above, yet closer to the Prado and old town. This is an attractive place that provides pleasant balconies with some of the rooms. At such prices in this ritzy location, don't expect a TV in your room, however. 58 rooms.

Carlos V   2nd-class ★

Maestro Vitoria, 5 (three short blocks north of the Pl. del Sol), ☎ *531 41 00, FAX 531 37 61.*

Located conveniently near the El Corte Inglés department store and the Convento de las Descalzas Reales, this venerable hotel counts as a bargain in expensive Madrid. Rooms are sufficiently comfortable and include satellite-TV, but noise can be a problem. Managed by Best-Western. 67 rooms.

Inexpensive (Less than $50)

Francisco I   Hs2nd-class ★ ★ ★

Arenal, 15 (just west of the Pl. del Sol), ☎ *548 43 14, FAX 531 01 88.*

As far as we can tell this is the only genuine hotel in Madrid that charges such low prices. It is modern, clean, recently redecorated, has air conditioning in most rooms and provides hotel services, all in a fine location. Sound too good to be true? Only slightly. In truth the prices climb into the $60 range in high summer, only sinking into the truly inexpensive the rest of the year. 58 rooms.

Hotel Residencia Lisboa   Hs2nd-class ★ ★

C. Ventura de la Vega, 17 (just off C. del Prado, near the Victoria in Pl. Santa Ana), ☎ *429 98 94.*

No frills, just a room to sleep in, but the rooms are larger than the low price would indicate and boast new private bathrooms. The location is superb. True, the hallways and public areas are low-wattage and the rooms sparsely and unfashionably furnished but, for the price, it is hard to do better in Madrid—and they accept credit cards. 23 rooms.

Residencia Santander   R2nd-class ★

Echegaray, 1 (around the corner from C. San Jerónimo, four short blocks east of the Pl. del Sol), ☎ *429 95 51.*

The location is prime, except for street noise, but don't expect anything fancy at this price. All rooms have private baths but are sparsely furnished, although, surprisingly, some have TVs. No credit cards are accepted. 38 rooms.

Mónaco   R3rd-class ★

Barbieri, 5 (Go west on Gran Via, after its start at the intersection with C. Alcalá, then take a right onto C. Hugo in one block. After two very short blocks on Hugo, jag left on C. Infantas, and take the immediate right onto Barbieri), ☎ *522 46 30, FAX 521 16 01.*

This one is a bit out of the way, located slightly north of Gran Via. The hotel is decorated in bright red, giving it an Egyptian look (or worse—in an earlier incarnation it was a brothel). Rooms are small, but include private baths. This neighborhood is replete with disco clubs and its strollers seem less amicable than those on the other side of Gran Via. 32 rooms.

Your range of choices can be expanded greatly if the requirement of sleeping within walking-distance of the sights is dropped. Near the southern Legazpi subway station, the **Hostal Auto** ★ at *Paseo de la Chopera, 69 (☎ 539 66 00; FAX 530 67 03)* is a good moderate-inexpensive choice with parking. Near the northwestern Arguelles station, the **Hotel Tirol** ★★ on *Marqués de Urquijo, 4 (☎ 548 19 00)* is a fine moderately-priced pick.

Where to Eat

You can eat in Madrid for whatever you care to spend. Of course the food generally improves as the prices rise. Specialties of Madrid are seafood, roast pig and lamb. Below we list our favorites in various price categories, but you can also do as the Madrileños do—stroll C. del Prado (which heads west from the Pl. de las Cortes) and amble up and down its adjacent side streets until a place strikes your fancy for tapas at the bar. Later, if you like what you nibbled, you can move back into the dining room for a meal.

Very Expensive ($50+)

Zalacaín   **$$$$**   ★★★★★

Álvarez de Baena, 4 (north, near the Museo de Cientas Naturales), ☎ 561 48 40, FAX 561 47 32.
Closed Saturday lunch, Sunday, Holy Week and August.
By all standards Zalacaín is the finest restaurant in Madrid, if not all of Spain. Even the Francophilic Michelin *Red Guide* once awarded this restaurant its highest rating. The decor is muted, elegant and comfortable, like a Velázquez painting, to focus all attention on what is arranged on your porcelain plate. What sits on your plate will both look and taste sublime. Try the ravioli with setas, truffles and fois gras, or *bacalao tellagom*, or duck. Or for a sampling of the best, try the *Menu Degustacion*. This is a restaurant for serious connoisseurs who don't mind spending $100 each to enjoy an exquisite dining experience. Reservations weeks in advance are essential. Credit Cards: A, V, D.

El Amparo   **$$$$**   ★★★★

Puigcerdá, 8 (one block east of Serrano, four blocks north of the park), ☎ 431 64 58, FAX 575 54 91.
Closed Sunday and August.
Catch Madrid's rising star, and look out Zalacaín! While Amparo can't match that venerable leader yet in style, it substitutes an attractive combination of rough wood amid high-tech. What is truly exceptional about Amparo, however, is the inventiveness of its Basque chef, who, breaking tradition, is a woman. Consider cold salmon with tomato sorbet, or rolled lobsters with soybean sauce. Of course, novelty without good taste is no asset, but there is discriminating sensibility to spare at this "refuge." Reservations are a must. Credit Cards: A, V, M.

Expensive ($30+)

La Trainera   **$$$**   ★★★

Lagasca, 60 (two blocks east of Serrano, six short blocks north of the park), ☎ 576 05 75, FAX 575 47 17.
Closed Sunday and August.

Forget elegance and gentile service and think about the freshest possible fish. Here it is, served in a nest of little rooms decorated with utensils of the sea. Most of the shellfish is sold by weight and eaten as appetizers by the Spanish. You can make them do for dinner or order selections from the menu, such as a delicious hake *gallega* style or salmonete (mullet) any old way. But do yourself a favor and start with the heavenly cream soup. This restaurant is very popular; reserve. Credit Cards: A, V, M.

El Pescador   **$$$**   ★★★

José Ortega y Gasset, 75 (the northern limit of the Barrio Salamanca), ☎ *402 19 90. Closed Sunday, and August.*

Seafood is expensive and this, or La Trainera above, is the best seafood restaurant in town, so its prices must be considered fair. The decor is seafaring, with checkered tablecloths, and the food incredibly fresh. The owner is from Galicia where they know how to cook a fish. Try the *crema tres eles* (if you have never tried eels) or the *salpicon*. Lobster, though delicious, will lift you into the very expensive category. Reservations are advised. Credit Cards: V, M.

El Cenador del Prado   **$$$**   ★★★

C. del Prado, 4 (just off Pl. del las Cortes), ☎ *429 15 61. Closed Saturday lunch, Sunday, and the second half of August.*

This restaurant continually improves, and is now as elegant as any in the country. Appropriately light and airy as a garden patio, this is the home of Spanish *cocina nueva*, with a menu that changes as frequently as the chef receives inspiration. If *patatas a la importancia con almajas* (potatoes with clams) is on the menu, by all means give it strong consideration. The banana ice cream is equally outstanding. Reservations are a must. Credit Cards: A, V, D, M.

Café de Oriente   **$$$**   ★★

Pl. de Oriente, 2 (facing the Palácio Real), ☎ *241 39 74. Closed Saturday for lunch, Sunday, and August.*

The decor is glittering *Belle Époque*, the building and brick ovens date to the 18th century and views of the palace from a terrace chair (aperitif in hand) are spectacular at night. Two dining rooms wait in the back, one for Castilian food, exceptionally prepared, the other for more elegant and, to our tastes, too expensive Basque cooking. Credit Cards: A, D, M, V.

Moderate ($15–$30)

Brasserie de Lista   **$$**   ★★

José Ortega y Gasset, 6 (on this fashionable street in Barrio Salamanca around the corner from Serrano, about eight short blocks north of the park), ☎ *435 28 18, FAX 576 28 17. Closed Sat. lunch and Sundays in August.*

Tasteful nouvelle Spanish dishes are served in a relaxed, turn of the century bistro atmosphere. Waiters wear appropriate long white aprons. The menu also includes continental dishes and represents a bargain for such quality in Madrid. The only problem with de Lista is that it crowds at lunch when reservations are advised. Credit Cards: A, M, V.

MADRID

Botín $$ ★★

C. Cuchilleros, 17 (out the southwest corner of the Pl. Mayor and down stairs), 366 42 17.

According to *The Guinness Book of World Records*, Botín, in continuous operation since 1725, is the oldest restaurant in the world. Its specialties are roast suckling pig *(cochinillo asado)* and roast baby lamb *(cordero asado)*, cooked in ancient wood ovens *(hornos)*. Since one or the other is always on the Menu del Día, costs can be contained. This is fortunate because Botín's prices are otherwise pushing it into the expensive category where it does not belong. The decor is rough-hewn wood beams and floors. Be warned: although the roasts are first-rate, this is a tourist favorite—we could do without the crowds and the roving musicians. Reserve, or be prepared to wait in line for up to an hour. Credit Cards: A, D, M, V.

MADRID

La Bola $$ ★★

C. de la Bola, 5 (off the Pl. de Oriente, near the Palácio Real, as explained in "Walking Tour #1"), 547 69 30.
Closed Sunday, and Saturday night in high summer.

Well over 100 years old, Bola is quiet and cozy with small dining areas for munching good Madrileño food. The specialty is *cocida Madrileño*, a stew of meat and chickpeas, served in two courses—as soup, then as meat. This dish appears only at lunch, when reservations are advised. But grills are good as well any time. Credit Cards: none.

Hylogui $$ ★

Ventura de la Vega, 3 (off C. de San Jerónimo, four blocks east of Puerta del Sol), 429 73 57.
Closed Sunday evening, and August.

This Madrid institution contains a series of dining rooms that extend on and on. The food is authentic Castilian and well prepared—the crowds would not come if the food were not first rate. This is the place to sample earthy Castilian cuisine. Credit Cards: A, M, V.

El Ingenio $$ ★

Leganitos, 10 (follow C. Bailén north from the Palace for one block to Torija going right. In four blocks it runs into Leganitos; turn left), 541 91 33, FAX 547 35 34
Closed Sun. and holidays in summer.

Sure, the Don Quixote decor is campy, but the simple food is first-rate and hugs the bottom of the moderate price range for a super value. Reservations should not be necessary. Credit Cards: A, D, M, V.

Armstrong's $$ ★

Jovellanos, 5 (opposite the Teatro de la Zarzuela, one block north of C. San Jerónimo, and three blocks east of the Pl. Cortez), ☎ 522 42 30.
There is nothing wrong with hankering for familiar food while in a foreign land. A London solicitor named Armstrong opened this attractively pink and white restaurant to answer such needs. The ambience is most pleasant and the food is familiar. Credit Cards: A, D, M, V.

Inexpensive (Less than $15)

Luarqués $ ★

C. Ventura de la Vega, 16 (off C. de San Jerónimo, four blocks east of the Puerta del Sol),
☎ *429 61 74.*
Closed Sunday, Monday and August.

This is the place for hearty, "peasant" fare. The owners are Asturians who decorate their crowded dining room with rustic farm implements from home. Good value for the money makes this a popular place, sometimes with long waits, but C. Ventura de la Vega bids to be the most interesting restaurant street in Madrid, so if the wait is too long at Luarqués, you can move to Hylogui, described above, or to Asado or Puebla, described below. No reservations accepted. Credit Cards: none.

Paellería Valenciana $ ★★

Caballero de Gracia, 12 (this little street is just west of the fork where C. de Alcalá meets A. de Gran Via), ☎ *531 17 85.*
Open weekdays for lunch only.

You have to order ahead for paella and the portion is for two persons, but it is delicious and an excellent value. If you can live without the paella, you don't have to phone ahead. Walk in and down some hearty soup, followed by a lunch special. There is a three-course menu for less than $10 that includes a carafe of wine. Credit Cards: A, M, V.

Puebla $ ★

Ventura de la Vega, 12 (off C. de San Jerónimo, four blocks east of Puerta del Sol),
☎ *429 67 13.*
Closed Sunday.

Inexpensive, well prepared food makes up for the horrendous "decor." Madrid offers no greater food bargains. No reservations accepted. Credit Cards: none.

Foster's Hollywood $

Velázquez, 80 (in Salamanca), ☎ *435 61 28.*

The name adequately suggests the decor which is bright and spare. Foster's forte is good old American hamburgers, large and in great variety. Of course, there are fries, tasty indeed, ribs and Tex-Mex, but don't neglect an order of superb onion rings. Credit Cards: A, D, M, V.

McDonald's $

Outlets are at Puerta del Sol and on Gran Via at C. Montera.

Shopping

The best buys in Madrid are leather goods, including shoes, along with antiques, and men's and women's high fashion clothing. Mammoth sales are held during the second week of January and from late July through the middle of August. Look for a sign saying *Rebajas.*

Leather

The best quality leather clothes and accessories are undoubtedly sold by the famous Spanish firm of **Loewe**. Prices are extravagant, but the quality is superb. Note that Barcelona offers similar quality for lower prices, and you do not save much at either location over the Loewe branch in New York. The firm maintains outlets in the best hotels but their most complete shops are at *C. Serrano 26* and, for men, *Serrano 34*, in the Barrio Salamanca. Less expensive and with a huge selection is **Lepanto** at *Pl. de Oriente*, 3 across from the Palácio Real. For high fashion shoes, **Farrutx** is a good bet on *C. Serrano*, *7*, just south of the Museo Arqueológico. **Gutierrez** on *C. Serrano*, *66* has moderate prices, at a step down in quality. For good luggage try **La Casa de las Maletas** on *Claudio Coello*, *45* in the Barrio Salamanca.

Antiques

Two of Madrid's finest antique establishments are located on either side of the Cortes building in the Pl. de la Cortes. **Galarias San Agustin** is at *San Agustin*, *3* which branches off from the plaza, and **Abelardo Linares** stands at *San Jerónimo 48*, just west. Prices are high, but looking is free. **C. del Prado** leading off from the Pl. de las Cortes is a street filled with antique stores, some with reasonable prices. And around the El Rastro flea market numerous stores sell old things. At *12 Ribera de Curtidores*, in the heart of the market, are **Gonzalves** for brass and **José Maria del Rey** for fine antiques. *At 15* is **Galería de Antiguedades**, an antique center, and at *27* is **Regalos Molina**, for ceramics (closed, for some reason on Sunday, the day that the market is held).

Crafts

The best *crafts* are at **El Arco de Los Cuchilleros Artesania de Hoy** in the Plaza Mayor at 9. Next best is the elegant state-owned **ArtEspaña**, which has a fine outlet at *Pl. de las Cortes*, *3*. Prices are not low, but the work from all over Spain is collected under one roof. For fans and umbrellas the place is **Casa de Diego** in *the Puerta del Sol* at 12.

The two best shops for *ceramics* are **Antiqua Casa Talavera** (☎ *247 34 17)* at *Isabel la Católica*, *2*, just north of the Pl. Santo Domingo, a subway stop two blocks northeast of the Pl. del Oriente, and **Regalos Molina** in *el Rastro at Ribera de Curtidores 27*. (Ceramics prices, however, are better in Seville and Talavera de la Reina.)

Fine *engravings* from original plates by Goya and other great artists are sold at the **Instituto de Calcografía** in the Academia de Bellas Artes de San Fernando *at Alcalá 13*.

Department Stores

Spain has two large *department store chains*, both well represented by their Madrid branches. **El Corte Inglés** is the higher in quality of the two. Its largest store is off the Puerta del Sol on C. Preciados, another branch is in the Barrio Salamanca, at the corner of Calles Goya and Alcalá. **Galarias Preciados** can cost less and has a branch near the El Corte Inglés on C. Gran Via near the Puerta del Sol. Both chains offer English interpreters. Preciados gives a 10 percent discount for tourists on every purchase made, in lieu of waiting for refunds of the IVA tax.

No Madrid shopping experience would be complete without a trip to the flea market, **El Rastro**, which takes place every Sunday. The stalls set up at about 9:30 a.m., the surrounding shops open at 11 a.m. and the whole area closes at 2 p.m. It is located along the wide street Ribera de Curtidores which runs south four blocks below the Pl. Mayor. You can take the subway to La Latina, walk a short block east, then south. The stalls in the streets mainly offer junk, but the fun is in the looking and the possibility of discovering a personal treasure. Bargaining is expected, both at the stalls and in the stores, so do not assume the price quoted is the one you must pay. Watch your wallet or purse.

Directory

Airport

Barajas Airport (☎ *305 4372*) is 13 km northeast of Madrid's center, not far removed for such a large city. A taxi into town costs about 2500 ptas. Alternatively, an airport bus, for 350 ptas., leaves every 15 minutes or so to the centrally located Pl. Colón, where taxis wait to carry you less expensively to your hotel. The bus stops under the plaza. Iberia branches dot the city, but the most convenient is in the Palace Hotel (☎ *563 99 66*, for international flights, ☎ *411 10 11*, for domestic).

City Tours

The following companies provide bus tours of the sights of Madrid: **Julia Tours**, *Gran Via, 68* (☎ *541 91 25*); **Pullmantur**, *Pl. de Oriente, 8* (☎ *541 18 07*); **Trapsatur**, *C. San Bernardo, 23* (☎ *541 63 20*). Brochures are available at most hotel desks. Pullmantur also offers excursions to nearby cities, such as Toledo, El Escorial and Segovia.

Emergencies

Police • in the Puerta del Sol (☎ *221 65 16*; emergency: *091*)

Ambulance • ☎ *061* for emergencies or *522 22 22*

English speaking doctors • (☎ *431 22 29*)

Trains

RENFE's main ticket office is at *C. Alcalá, 44;* (☎ *563 02 02*); Metro: Banco de España. Madrid has three major train stations whose service overlaps. The largest is **Chamartín** Station, located in northern Madrid (Metro: Chamartín). It serves the north and east, including France, but not Galicia (☎ *323 21 21*). **Atocha** Station is located three long blocks south of the Prado (Metro: Atocha). It primarily serves the south, but also Extremadura, Portugal, and nearby northern cities, such as Ávila and Segovia ☎ *527 31 60*). **Norte** (also called **Prícipe Pío**) Station (Metro: Norte) serves Galicia and Salamanca, but also some nearby cities to the north (☎ *247 00 00*). RENFE can be called at ☎ *563 02 02* for information on all trains, in Spanish.

Travel in Madrid

Taxis are reasonable. The meter starts at 155 pesetas, then adds 70 pesetas each kilometer, although there is a surcharge of 150 pesetas at night and on holidays. Most trips from one sight to another will cost $4 or so. Taxis are white (though some are black) with a red stripe on the side. They can be flagged on the street or found waiting at taxi stands near sights or large hotels.

Buses, though numerous and inexpensive, are slow and require exact change. The fare currently is 125 pesetas. A sign at each stop lists the numbers of those buses that pick up there.

The subway *(Metro)* is frequent, clean and quick. It does close at 1:30 a.m., however. The fare is 125 pesetas, though a 10 ride *bonos* sells for only 625 ptas. The various lines are designated by the end station on their route, and maps are available at all stations.

Excursions from Madrid

El Escorial ★★★★ and Valle de Los Caídos ★

El Escorial stands among the great monuments in Spain. For descriptions and hours, see the "El Escorial" and "Valle de los Caídos" descriptions below. Both lie about 50 km from Madrid; travel and sight-seeing will consume more than half a day.

By car, drive along C. Grand Via heading west. As it bends north it becomes first C. Princesa, then Av. Puerta de Hierro. Signs direct you to N-VI, going northwest. At 16 km exit left onto C-505 to El Escorial in 28 km, as the signs direct.

Trains leave every hour both from Atocha and Chamartin stations in Madrid. A bus meets the train in El Escorial. Incidentally, the train is on the Ávila and Segovia line, so either city can be included in the excursion.

Buses leave the Empresa Herranz station on C. Reina Victoria (near the Moncloa Metro stop) a dozen times per day. The same company runs a bus from the El Escorial stop to Valle de los Caídos at 3:15, returning at 6:15.

For directions to Valle de los Caídos, see the description of "El Escorial" in the *Central Spain* chapter.

El Pardo ★★

This country palace only 13 km outside of Madrid is a more tasteful version of Madrid's Palácio Real, but not as memorable. For a description and hours see the "El Pardo" heading below in this chapter. Travel and sights will take up almost half a day.

By car, take C. Grand Via heading west. As it bends north it becomes C. Princesa, then Av. Puerta de Hierro. Bear to the right on C-601 for 13 km as it parallels the Manzanares River through scrub woods into the village of El Pardo.

Buses from C. Martin de los Heros (near the Moncloa Metro stop) leave every quarter hour during the day.

Toledo ★★★★★

For a description and hours of the sights see "Toledo" in the *Central Spain* chapter. Travel and sights will consume a very full day.

By car, head down Paseo del Prado to the Pl. de Emperador Carlos V, where the Atocha train station is located. Drive through the plaza, past the train station, where four roads branch ahead. Take the second one from the right, which is the one directly ahead, called Paseo de Sta. Maria de la Cabeza. Signs will lead you to N 401 for Toledo, 70 km away.

Frequent trains leave Madrid's Atocha station for the 90 minute ride. Buses are a little faster and deposit you in the central Pl. de Zocodover. Continental Galiano buses (☎ 22 29 61) leave half hourly from the Estación Sur de Autobuses on C. Canarias, 17.

Segovia ★★★★★, Ávila ★★★,
Coca Castle ★★ and Salamanca ★★★★

All can be reached in two or three hours by car. See the *Central Spain* chapter.

By car, follow the directions to El Escorial, above, but continue north instead of exiting on C-505.

A dozen trains leave Madrid's Atocha station for the 2-1/2 hour trip to Segovia. Ávila trains go through El Escorial for a trip of under two hours; see the El Escorial information above. Few trains go directly from Madrid to Salamanca. The better bet is to pick up one of the eight trains per day from Ávila to Salamanca.

Buses from La Sepulveda on P. de la Florida (Norte Metro stop) are faster to Segovia, but do only five trips per day. They match the train to Ávila.

Caídos, Valle de Los (Valley of the Fallen) ★

Hours open: daily from 10 a.m.–7 p.m. (until 6 p.m. in winter). Closed all holidays.

See the directions to El Escorial. From **El Escorial** take N-601 north for 8 km to turn at the sign for Valle de los Caídos.

See the directions to El Escorial for **bus** connections.

This is Franco's memorial to the dead of the Spanish Civil War, though skeptics view it as a monument to himself. Regardless of the reason for the structure, its mountain setting is ruggedly beautiful amid granite outcrops and weathered pines. Inside a hill surmounted by a towering cross—400 feet high (with an elevator inside)—a huge underground basilica was excavated through the 1950s. Claims that this expensive basilica would exculpate the carnage and horrors of the civil war, clearing the consciences of both sides, are belied by the fact that Franco used Republican prisoners as forced labor to build the monument.

Franco wanted to awe. The nave of the underground basilica is larger than St. Peter's in Rome by a third. The cupola is huge and resplendent with bright mosaics of Spain's heroes and martyrs approaching Christ and Mary. Tapestries along the nave are 16th-century Belgian depictions of the Apocalypse, appropriately, while side chapels contain copies of famous Spanish statues of the Virgin. In a crypt behind the altar repose coffins of 40,000 unknown soldiers who died in the war, but the places of honor belong to Franco and José Antonio.

José Antonio Primo de Rivera, the son of a deposed dictatorial prime minister, led the small, quasi-fascist, Falange party during the political unrest leading up to the Spanish Civil War. Convicted of political murder, Antonio was incarcerated as the war broke out and died in prison at age 33, to be promoted to martyr status by Franco and his Nationalist sympathizers. Antonio's remains are buried at the foot of the altar. Nearby, under a white slab, the Generalissimo himself sleeps forever. *Admission: 400 ptas. per car.*

El Escorial ★★★★

Population 6192	**Area code: 91**	**Zip Code: 28280**

From **Madrid** take N-VI north for 16 km, then C-505 at the Las Rozas exit for 28 km. Well marked by signs. The total distance is 44 km.

Frequent **trains** leave Madrid's Atocha and Chamartín stations which deposit you a mile from the monument. Buses meet the trains to cover that distance.

A dozen Autocar Harranz **buses** (☎ *543 36 45*) leave the Moncloa Metro stop in Madrid for El Escorial. The same line provides afternoon service from the El Escorial stop to The Valley of the Fallen and back.

Felipe II was a complex and private monarch, deeply religious and reverential of his father, Carlos V. He wanted to build a monument to God and Carlos, and chose an insignificant village called San Lorenzo del Escorial for the site. San Lorenso attracted him because it was near enough to Madrid that Felipe could travel to watch the work progress, as he often did, and for the name of the town. In his limited personal military career, Felipe had enjoyed one major success—over the French at St. Quentin in Flanders—in a battle won on August 10, the name-day of Saint Lawrence (San Lorenzo). The fact that the area contained abundant granite for building material clinched the choice.

At the time he constructed El Escorial, Felipe was the most powerful monarch in the world and put the resources of his empire to work on this, his favored project. It occupied 1000 workmen for 21 years, and when finished contained over 1000 doors, almost 3000 windows and corridors that ran for ten miles. Felipe wept when it was finished.

Felipe's structure was a mausoleum for his father and a pantheon for himself and his descendants. A monastery was included so monks could pray perpetually for all their souls. It also contained a palace so that Felipe could work near his father's remains, and a church, of course, for services. He commissioned Juan de Toledo, who had assisted Michelangelo and Bramante on St. Peter's in Rome, to design the building, and Felipe took an active interest in its design. Four years into the project the architect Juan de Toledo died, succeeded by his assistant Juan de Herrera, who carried out most of the design. To Herrera's genius is due the elegance of the details and, most significantly, the awesome church inside.

Plan on spending at least half a day to see everything that waits inside.

Monastery of San Lorenzo del Escorial ★★★★

C. San Lorenzo de El Escorial, ☎ *890 59 02.*
Hours open: Tues.–Sun. from 10 a.m.–1 p.m., and from 3:30–6:30p.m. (until 6 p.m. in winter). Closed Mon. and all holidays.
Entrance is through the King's courtyard, named for the six grotesque statues of kings of Judea high above the church facade. Ahead is the church, to the left a former college and to the right the monastery. Back along the right side of the church stands a cloister and chapterhouse, and, on the church's left, the royal apartments, where visits begin.

Stairs lead up to the **Battle Gallery**, a long hall of charming frescos. The ceiling is elegant with Roman-style decorative tracery, a common Renaissance theme. Wall murals display various battles painted to resemble tapestry—see the top and the surrounds of the "doorways." The long wall opposite the windows shows a battle against Moors that took place in Granada in the middle of the 15th century. It is curious to find this battle depicted because the Spanish, contrary to the message of the fresco, lost. The costumes are copied from an earlier work painted during the era of the actual battle, hence providing interesting documents. Both end walls show sea battles, with accurate depictions of Spanish galleons. The window wall presents the battle of Saint Quentin, Felipe's only personal victory.

Descending to the palace proper, the first rooms are those of Felipe's favorite daughter Isabel, and rather bare except for a portable organ. In Felipe's audience hall hang two fine Brussels tapestries and drawings of various royal residences. The

MADRID

next room is fronted by splendid German marquetry doors, followed by a room with a large sundial on the floor. Next comes Felipe's bedchamber, the size of a monk's cell, where he often worked and finally died. The poor man ended his days bedridden by pain and the sores of horrendous gout. Note the door opposite which leads into the church so Felipe could attend services without moving. The throne room—with a mere stool for a throne—seems plain, especially compared to that of Felipe's successors in the Palácio Real in Madrid. Indeed, despite beautiful objects, decorations and paintings, Felipe's palace conveys the sense of a simple life. The walls, for example, are whitewashed, rather than covered in velvet as in later palaces. In an alcove rests the litter that carried the invalid king during his final years.

Stairs lead to the new **museums** where some fine paintings are displayed. There is a Bosch *Ecce Homo*, and numerous Titians and Veroneses. A recess holds charming Dürer parchment paintings of birds, animals and flowers. Five Riberas, especially *Aesop*, are symphonies of light and dark. Other rooms display *Zurbaráns*, interesting for incorporating true background scenes, instead of the monotonic fields of most of his work. The two El Grecos that Felipe purchased are also here. One in particular, the *Martyrdom of St. Maurice and the Theban Legion*, was too innovative and acerbic in color for Felipe who never ordered another from the artist, although the painting is acknowledged today as a masterpiece. Do not miss Rogier van der Weyden's monotonic *Calvary*.

The later apartments built for Bourbon Kings are sumptuously out of character with Felipe's austerity. They hold some fine tapestries and lovely furniture.

Passing behind the church, a narrow stair-tunnel, luxuriously marbled, descends to the **Panteón de los Reyes**. This pantheon was built by Felipe's successor but not finished until the reign of the following king. It has none of the feel of the rest of El Escorial, although it is moving in a different way. At the bottom of the stairs comes the double shock of the intimacy of a small round marble room combined with a seemingly infinite ceiling. All around in stacked niches are simple yet monumental porphyry sarcophagi, each identical, of the great Hapsburg and Bourbon kings of Spain—Carlos V, Felipe II, and Felipe IV, Velázquez' friend and patron. Kings lie on the left, and include Isabella II who ruled, while consorts lie opposite, including Isabella's husband, Francisco Asis. Back up the stairs stretch gallery after gallery of deceased princes and princesses, including memorials to those stillborn—a reminder of the high rate of infant mortality then. One confection contains sixty little princes and princesses. Here, too, is the tomb of Don Juan, the victor of Lepanto. At the end of the galleries stands the *Pudridero* (Rotting Place), where corpses dried for ten years before internment in sarcophagi.

Next is the **church**, the masterpiece of Juan de Herrera. It exactly suits El Escorial without duplicating the style of the rest. Monumental, simple and perfect in proportion, this church by itself constitutes an architectural movement. Looking down the nave, the pillars at first seem intrusively massive before the effect of their fluting slenderizes them. Instead of the barrel vaulting characteristic of earlier churches, these pillars support a flat vault of daring span. The effect is awe-inspiring, as intended.

If time permits, the **sacristy** to the right of the church is worth touring for its paintings, frescoed grand stairway and lovely cloister. Also interesting is the **library**, located to the right of the main entrance at the front of El Escorial, for its rich woodwork and rare books (including St. Teresa's diary and missals belonging to Ferdinand and Isabella, Carlos V and Felipe II).

In the same area as El Escorial, left and uphill, is the **Casita del Principe** ★, designed by Villanueva, the architect of Madrid's Prado Museum, for the prince who would become Carlos IV. It is situated in the new town, El Escorial de Abajo, southeast of the monastery on the road to the train station. This "Little House" is a model country cottage, resembling the Trianon at Versailles with its sumptuous interior and rich furnishings. One room is Pompeian; another is completely covered in tile. *Admission: 800 ptas.*

El Pardo ★★

From **Madrid** Gran Via heads west, bends northwest and changes its name to Calle Princesa, then changes its name again to Avenida Puerta de Hierro. Follow signs to A-6. Just past the University, a right fork onto C-601 to "El Monte de El Pardo" leads in 13 km to the palace.

This is an older, more attractive palace than those in Madrid or Aranjuez. Half a day is plenty of time to see it and the other sights of interest as well.

For centuries the woods around El Pardo formed a royal hunting preserve for Spanish kings "working" in Madrid. In fact, the original building on the site was a hunting lodge built in 1405 for Enrique III before Madrid even became the capital. After designating Madrid as his capital, Felipe II replaced that lodge with a palace and furnished it with fine art, which rather changed the hunt atmosphere. Fire, the scourge of so many palaces, later burned down half of it. Since the cataclysm occurred in 1604, however, much earlier than similar conflagrations in Madrid and Aranjuez, its latest rebuilding dates to the time of Felipe III. That makes this is a Hapsburg structure, with Bourbon additions, as compared to the Bourbon palaces of Madrid and Aranjuez, although its furnishings are to Bourbon tastes. It was Franco's favorite residence, and is still filled with his mementos and uniforms. Today, the palace is sometimes used to entertain visiting dignitaries. The residence of the present king, Juan Carlos, is nearby.

Palácio del Pardo ★★

Hours open: Mon.–Sat. 10 a.m.–1 p.m., and 4–7 p.m. (opening and closing an hour earlier winter afternoons). Closed Sun.
The "Chinese" room and those with neoclassical furniture are the most interesting. Fine Sèvres porcelain and clocks are scattered throughout. Some of the ceiling frescoes and stuccowork are notable, and a huge collection of tapestries hangs on the walls, many, including designs by Goya, from the Spanish Royal Tapestry Factory. *Admission: 400 ptas., by guided tour only.*

Casita del Principe ★★

Same hours and ticket as the palace.
This is a twin to a similar building in El Escorial. It too was designed by Villanueva, the architect of the Museo del Prado, for the same prince who would become King Carlos IV. The rooms are tiny, which only intensifies the impact of their rich deco-

ration and furniture. The dining room is a particular favorite. Some pleasing pastels by Tiepolo and some paintings by Mengs adorn the walls.

Note: The Convento de Capuchinos, on a hill to the west, contains a masterpiece of polychrome wood carving by Fernandez and two Ribera paintings.

CENTRAL SPAIN

The Alcázar rises above Segovia as in a fairy-tale.

The geographic, political and spiritual heart of Spain forms a band whose eastern end stretches from Badajoz up to Ciudad Rodrigo, near the Portuguese border, then climbs to Salamanca before flowing across to Sigüenza and Cuenca on the east. Although punctuated by occasional peaks, the mass of the area is a windswept plateau called La Mancha that covers 260 miles west to east and 100 miles north to south. Divided by mountains both from Old Castile in the north and Andalusia in the south, the terrain in between is covered with low crops reaching to distant rolling hills, the fabled land over which Cervantes, in his parable about the end of chivalry, sent Don Quixote to tilt at windmills.

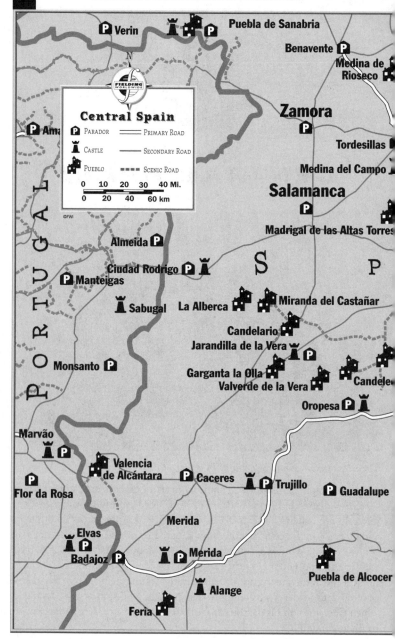

Canales de la Sierra

Ampudia

Viniegra de Arriba

Covarrubias

S. Domingo de Silos

alladolid

Peñaranda de Duero

Simancas

Berlanga de Duero

Soria

Calatañazor

San Esteban de Gormaz

Peñafiel

Maderuelo

Olmedo

Sepúlveda

Medinaceli

Pedrazza

Arevalo

Segovia

Atienza

Buitrago
de Lozoya

Siguenza

A

I

N

Avila

Las Navas del Marques

Brihuega

Madrid

Pastrana

mbeltran

arqueda

Chinchón

Cuenca

Toledo

Tembleque

Belmonte

Alarcon

Consuegra

Alcazar de S. Juan

Manzanares

Almagro

San Carlos del Valle

Despite the sweep of the land, dense communities developed, founded during the Reconquest when defense required an urban compactness that walls could encircle. Population declines since the 16th century allowed these towns to retain their character in a way that cities with expanding populations never could, and resulted in towns unrivaled for sight-seeing.

Central Spain includes three must-sees—Toledo, Segovia and Salamanca, and a score of sights that would be enjoyed if time permits.

Ciudad Rodrigo on the western border with Portugal retains its fortress character. Southeast of it, **Cáceres** and **Trujillo** are frozen in the time of the conquistadores. **Mérida**, nearby, preserves splendid Roman ruins. **Salamanca**, in the northwest, offers its ancient university, an architectural jewel of the Plateresque, and its Old Cathedral, a preserved marvel. **Zamora**, nearby, displays more Romanesque churches. **Segovia**, in the north center above Madrid, is spectacularly situated to show off its Disneyland castle. It also retains a perfect Roman aqueduct, an imposing cathedral, and a host of delicate Romanesque churches. In the 100 odd miles between Salamanca and Segovia lies **Ávila**, still surrounded by imposing medieval walls. To the east, **Sigüenza** raises an imposing cathedral and fortress upon a hill; while the aged arts-village of **Cuenca** hangs precipitously over a gorge. South of Madrid sits the quiet plaza of **Chinchón**, with a tranquil parador amid a monastery. To its west wait the glorious treasures of **Toledo**. West another 100 miles stands the mysterious mountain monastery of **Guadalupe**, and, just north of it awaits the castle-parador of **Oropesa**.

The following towns with their paradors are covered in this chapter.

Town	Parador Name	Rating	Page
Alarcón	Marqués de Villena	★★★★	*page 180*
Albacete	La Mancha	★★★	*page 178*
Ávila	Raimundo de Borgoña	★	*page 183*
Cáceres	Cáceres	★★★★	*page 131*
Chinchón	Chinchón	★★★★	*page 138*
Ciudad Rodrigo	Enrique II	★★★	*page 175*
Cuenca	Convento San Pablo	★★★★	*page 128*
Gredos	Gredos	★★	*page 146*
Guadalupe	Guadalupe	★★★★	*page 148*
Jarandilla	Carlos V	★★★★	*page 136*
Manzanares	Manzanares	★★★	*page 152*
Mérida	Via de la Plata	★★★★	*page 190*

Town	Parador Name	Rating	Page
Oropesa	Virrey Toledo	★★★★	page 172
Salamanca	Salamanca	★	page 154
Segovia	Segovia	★★★★	page 163
Sigüenza	Castillo de Sigüenza	★★★★★	page 114
Toledo	Conde de Organz	★★	page 117
Trujillo	Convento de Santa Clara	★★★★	page 141

To savor the most important sights, stay two nights at the parador in Trujillo or Cáceres, and see Trujillo, Cáceres, and Mérida; continue with three nights at Ávila, and see Salamanca and Segovia, then stay three nights at the parador in Chinchón or Toledo, to tour Toledo, Guadalupe and, perhaps, Cuenca.

PARADOR CASTILLO DE SIGÜENZA

Plaza del Castillo, s/n, Sigüenza, 19250
☎ (949) 30 01 00, FAX (949) 39 13 64
$90 per double; 81 rooms: 3 singles, 74 doubles, 4 suites

★ ★ ★ ★ ★

No hotel in the world is more imposing. Massive battlements rise loftily upon a hill above the village. It is difficult to believe that this was only a bishop's "palace." Of course it started life as a Moorish fortress (alcázar), then became a Christian fort in the early 12th-century, before remodeling in the 15th-century for Cardinal Fonseca. Here the new wife of the eccentric Pedro the Cruel was imprisoned when he fell in love with one of her attendants. The fortress has seen many battles, as recently as the last century (as bullet holes in the walls attest). Inside the walls the Bishop's palace which constitutes the parador surrounds a central plaza, though the towers and walls are off limits. The interior decor is movie-grand with soaring ceilings, vaulting lit by giant chandeliers and royal red walls. The lounge has to be seen to be believed— enormous, divided by massive pillars, with two huge fireplaces and furniture for giants. Imposing, yes; comfortable, no. Bedrooms are more human-scaled, large and simply decorated. Seven incorporate canopied beds, but may not be reserved ahead of time. All in all, the price must be considered fair, given how seldom we can sleep in a castle which imprisoned a queen.

Dining

Like the lounge, the dining room is huge, dramatic and sports heavy furniture of a medieval theme. What food could live up to such a show? What you get is underseasoned, but otherwise not notable. You might start with garlic soup *(sopa de ajo)*, graduate to cod *(bacalao)* or roast kid *(cabrito)*, then finish off with a very sweet confection of yolk of egg and sugar *(yemas)*. Skip the local Mondéjar wines for a Ribera Duero or Rioja. The bill should hover around $20, plus drinks.

Directions

Head for the Plaza Mayor and Cathedral. Take C. Mayor up to the parador as signs direct.

Paradors Nearby

Soria: 100 km	Teruel: 150 km	Cuenca: 190 km
Chinchón: 196 km	Segovia: 220 km	

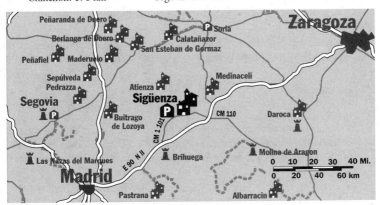

Sights

This lovely hilltop town of Renaissance houses includes a fine Cathedral, containing a masterpiece of sculpture. Calle de Medina leads uphill to the

Cathedral ★★★. Construction began on this Gothic church in 1150, although by the following century it required repairs which were not completed until the end of the 15th century. Inside, the original Romanesque shape is rather simple, while the fortresslike exterior is a mixture of all the forms that Gothic architecture passed through—but with a French feel, for the early archbishops came from there.

Down the left aisle inside is a lovely doorway surrounded by painted Renaissance pilasters and Mudejar designs. The adjoining chapel contains a 15th-century triptych. A jasper doorway leads to a marbled late Gothic cloister with intricate Plateresque doors and a collection of Flemish tapestries located in a room off the north corner. Back in the church proper, after the door to the cloister, is a side altar designed by Covarrubias for Saint Librada and her eight sisters, all born on the same day, according to legend, and all martyred together. Next comes the sepulchre of Dom Fadrique of Portugal, one of the earliest examples of the Plateresque style. As the ambulatory begins, a door on the left leads into the sacristy, also designed by Covarrubias, with an astonishing painted and sculpted ceiling of thousands of staring cherubim.

Around the south side of the ambulatory, in the Doncel Chapel, waits the star of the Cathedral. Don Martin de Arca was a page *(doncel)* to Isabella and died in the Granada wars. His queen commissioned this sepulcher in early Isabelline style of a youth relaxed and reading. It is unlike any similar work in Spain in seeming so alive. Don Martin's parents lie in a mausoleum in the center of the chapel.

Hours open: by the sacristan from 11 a.m.–2 p.m. and 4–8 p.m. (6 p.m. in winter). Apply at the Sacristy at the rear of the Cathedral. *Admission: 125 ptas.*

Diocesan Museum   ★

Hours open: Tues.–Sun. 11:30 a.m.–2 p.m., and 5–7 p.m. (During Jan. and Feb. open only Sun. and holidays).

The museum is located in a building across from the west side of the Cathedral. It contains prehistoric pieces, a collection of crucifixes, an El Greco and a superb Zurbarán of Mary floating above Seville—alone worth the price of admission. *Admission: 200 ptas.*

The Plaza Mayor ★ in front of the Cathedral is surrounded by late 15th- and early 16th-century porticos and balconies. The Ayuntamiento (city hall), from 1512, is located on the south side.

PARADOR CONDE DE ORGANZ

Cerro de Emperador, s/n, Toledo, 45000
☎ *(925) 22 18 50, FAX (925) 22 51 66*
$110 per double; 76 rooms: 4 singles, 70 doubles, 2 suites

★ ★

This is one of Spain's modern paradors, and although it provides fine views of Toledo—from a higher elevation to erase the drama—certainly the view is not spectacular enough to repay the inconvenience of being situated a long walk from town. Nor does the staff seem overly concerned with their clients' welfare. Avoid rooms 33 and 34, in which other guests' comings and goings and the elevator's rumble are clearly audible. The swimming pool, however, is welcome on a hot summer day.

Alternative Accommodations

Hostal del Cardinal

Paseo Recaredo, 24 (In the northern wall of the city. The best route is to take the circular road past Paseo de Merchan, the large square that fronts the Hospital de Tavera, where a sign will point you left to parking for the hotel), ☎ *(925) 22 49 00, FAX (925) 22 29 91. 25 rooms, plus two suites.*

Fear not, Toledo offers three better choices than the parador at substantially less money. The Hostal del Cardinal is intimate, located in a remodeled 18th-century cardinal's mansion, and encloses a luscious garden. For an additional charge—which brings the price up to only two thirds of what the parador charges—you can have a suite with a terrace.

María Cristína

Calle Marqués de Mendigorria, 1, (opposite the Hospital de Tavera, north of the walls), ☎ *(925) 21 32 02, FAX (925) 21 26 50, Telex 42827. 60 rooms, plus three suites.*

The hotel that should be the parador is the María Cristína—a historic building located in the precinct of an historic sight. It is beautiful, run like a Swiss watch, and as clean as can be, for a third less than the parador. The rooms are about as attractive as those of the Hotel Cardinal, although the location is less convenient.

Los Cigarrales

Carretera de Circunvalación, 32 (half a mile west of the parador), ☎ *(925) 22 00 53, FAX (925) 21 55 46. 36 rooms.*

Los Cigarrales offers views as nice as those from the parador at one third the cost and amid friendly service. In addition, this hotel, a remodeled country house, is more attractive. To top it off, the dining room offers decent meals for less than $15. The hotel is, however, outside of town.

Dining

The cavernous (seating 200), bright dining room is not particularly inviting. However, Toledo is a center for game, so duck paté and stuffed pheasant are often available. One good specialty is venison in raspberry sauce *(venado braseado con puré de frambuesas)*. All in all, the food is better than its surroundings though not enough so. Dinner will cost $25, plus drinks.

Alternative Dining

Asador Adolfo

La Granada, 6 (head north along the facade of the Cathedral to reach the restaurant in twenty paces or so, at the corner of Hombre do Palo), ☎ *(925) 22 73 21. Closed Sunday evening, except before holidays.*

Parts of the restaurant date to the 15th century. The food is typical of the area, but cooked with extra refinement and care. It may be the best restaurant for game in all of Spain. Which is not to disparage the stuffed peppers or the special hake in saffron sauce. Even if you don't ordinarily like marzipan, try it here. The bill will run to about $40. Reservations are recommended. Credit Cards: A, D, M, V.

Casa Aurelio and Mesón Aurelio

C. Sinagoga, 6 and 1 (a tiny street a few steps north of the Cathedral), ☎ *(925) 22 20 97, and 22 13 92. The first restaurant is closed Wednesday and July; the second is closed Monday and August.*

These neighbors are owned by the same family and serve comparable food. The food at either one should not disappoint. The decor is informal, though the patio of the Casa is just a bit nicer than the setting of the Mesón. Either should cost $30-35. Credit Cards: A, M, V.

El Emperador

Carretera del Valle, 1 (follow the Carretera de Circunvalación around Toledo to the southwest of town where this restaurant is passed), ☎ *(925) 22 46 91. Closed Monday and the first two weeks of September.*

You can walk across the lovely 14th-century Puente de San Martin west of San Juan de los Reyes, then uphill to the left for a quarter of a mile. Views along the way are

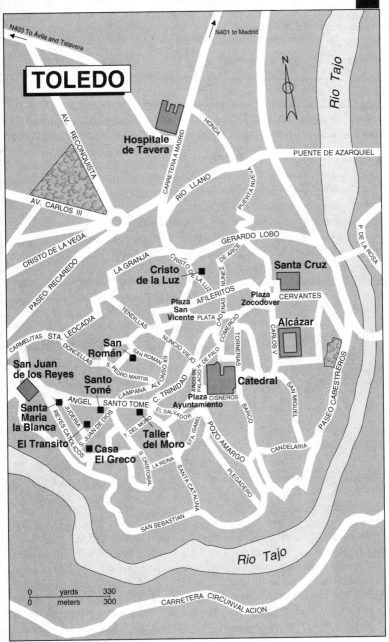

N403 To Ávila and Talavera

N401 to Madrid

TOLEDO

N

Rio Tajo

AV. RECONQUISTA

AV. CARLOS III

CARRETERA A MADRID

HONDA

**Hospitale
de Tavera**

RIO LLANO

PUENTE DE AZARQUIEL

CRISTO DE LA VEGA

PASEO RECAREDO

P. DE LA ROSA

GERARDO LOBO

DE ARCE

PUERTA NUEVA

LA GRANJA

CRISTO DE LA LUZ

NUÑEZ

**Cristo
de la Luz**

Santa Cruz

CADENAS

AFILERITOS

CERVANTES

**Plaza
Zocodover**

Plaza
San
Vicente

PLATA

COMERCIO

Alcázar

TENDILLAS

NUNCIO VIEJO

TORNERIAS

CARLOS V

CARMELITAS STA. LEOCADIA

DONCELLAS

**San
Román**

SAN ROMAN XII

ALFONSO XII

S. PEDRO MARTIR

SAN MIGUEL

PASEO CABESTREROS

**San Juan
de los Reyes**

**Santo
Tomé**

CAMPANA

C. TRINIDAD

ARCO DE PALACIO

H. DE PALO

Catedral

ANGEL

SANTO TOME

**Plaza
Ayuntamiento**

CISNEROS

**Santa
Maria
la Blanca**

JUDERIA

REYES CATOLICOS

S. JUAN DE DIOS

EL SALVADOR

BARCO

El Transito

**Casa
El Greco**

T. DEL MORO

**Taller
del Moro**

STA. ISABEL

POZO AMARGO

CANDELARIA

S. CRISTOBAL

LA REINA

SANTA CATALINA

PLEGADERO

SAN SEBASTIAN

Rio Tajo

0   yards   330
0   meters   300

CARRETERA CIRCUNVALACION

gorgeous, but a car or taxi is quicker. The best feature is terraced dining with views of Toledo. The food is simple and costs only about $15. Credit Cards: M, V.

Directions

From wherever you arrive just follow the Carretera Circunalación that circles the old town until a parador sign signals the turn.

Paradors Nearby

Chinchón: 69 km	Oropesa: 112 km	Manzanares: 123 km
Segovia: 158 km	Guadalupe: 175 km	Ávila: 184 km

Sights

Toledo rises like Gibraltar from the plains of La Mancha, its peak formed by cathedral spires and the turrets of the Alcázar. The sight is unforgettable. Over millennia the river Tagus dug a ravine around three sides of Toledo, leaving the hard bluff on which the city is situated towering above. The Romans were not the first to appreciate the importance of Toledo's site. They fought Iberians to capture it in 192 B.C. then fortified the hill and founded a town called **Toletum**, from which the present name derives. In turn, the Visigoths made Toledo their capital. When the Moors invaded in 711, they aimed straight for Toledo, and captured it in 712. It remained in Moorish hands for the next 300 years. As a result of the Moor's toleration of other religions, Toledo contained one of the largest Jewish communities in Spain, numbering about 12,000, as well as a large Christian population. But when, after centuries of harmony, the Moors attempted to extort a large sum for the defense budget primarily from the Jewish community, Jews cried for help to the Spanish Christian king. In 1085, Alfonso VI, aided by his general El Cid, attacked Toledo and captured the city.

Under subsequent Christian kings the Jewish community thrived, making important contributions to the wealth and learning of the town. This happy condition ended abruptly in pogroms in 1391 during which hundreds of Toledo Jews were murdered by Christians. Finally, in 1492, all of Spain's Jews, the sephardim, were expelled by Ferdinand and Isabella. The eviction of the Jews marked the beginning of Toledo's decline, hastened a century later by the banishment of those Moors who had evaded their own exile by converting to Christianity. Toledo had been stripped of many of its most accomplished citizens.

Toledo is remarkable enough that UNESCO designates it part of mankind's cultural heritage. No Spanish city has more to see—one frantic day barely does it justice.

The Alcázar is the place to begin. If driving from Madrid, go left on the Carretera de Circunvalación, crossing the Tagus where N-401 intersects, then going left at the circle on the opposite side. Turn right up the winding road leading to the Alcázar. Here is the largest parking place in the city, though in summer parking can be difficult even here.

Alcázar   ★

Calle Capuchinos, ☎ *(925) 22 30 38. Entrance on the north side, farthest from the parking lot.*
Hours open: Tues.–Sun. 9:30 a.m.–1:30 p.m., and 4–6:30 p.m. (to 5:30 p.m. in winter). Closed Mon.

A fortress occupied this location at least since Moorish times. Carlos V rebuilt the present edifice, using Covarrubias for his architect, but it was finished under Felipe II, Carlos's son, by Felipe's favorite architect Herrera (who designed the church at El Escorial). The north facade is Herrera's. What you see today, however, is entirely a reconstruction: the historic Alcázar was completely destroyed during the Spanish Civil War.

At the outbreak of war, the Alcázar served as an army headquarters. Since most of Toledo supported the opposition Republicans, its citizens surrounded the Alcázar and lay siege. For two months those in the building resisted artillery, mining and starvation before relief arrived at the last moment in the form of Generalissimo Franco with his army. Their stand became a symbol of determination to the Nationalists and, not surprisingly, Franco rebuilt the Alcázar after the war.

Architecturally the most interesting part of the Alcázar is its huge courtyard, which leads to entrances for various military museums. More such museums line the second floor, where the Alcázar's most moving display is also located. The office of General Moscardó, the defending Nationalist general, has been perfectly reconstructed as it was during the Civil War siege. You can see the dirt and bullet holes, the torn and hanging wallpaper, and the Spartan furnishings. Signs in all languages tell the story of how the Republicans surrounded the building and telephoned the general to inform him that his son would be killed if he did not surrender. General Moscardo asked to speak to his son and told him to prepare for death. It's a good story, but the son in question was discovered later enjoying the highlife of Madrid. *Admission: 150 ptas.*

After touring the Alcázar, the time of day determines what to see next. To the right is the **Hospital of Santa Cruz**, a museum that should be seen, but which is open throughout the day so it can be saved for midday when the other sights close for lunch. Toward the left (south) is the **Cathedral**.

To reach the Cathedral, turn left on Calle Carlos V past the Alcázar to Pascuales San Miguel which cuts across it. Turn right. The name changes to Calle Coliseo as it bends right again, then turns left as it enters the Plaza Mayor. At the end of the plaza the Cathedral can be seen. A left would take you to the modern entrance, but it is worth viewing the facade first by going right instead, then left and left again into the Plaza del Ayuntamiento. The Cathedral facade is on the left; and on the right, angling away, is the **Episcopal Palace**. Further on, beside the palace, is the **Ayuntamiento** (city hall), with a classical front designed by Herrera, finished by El Greco's son. Straight ahead are **law courts** from the 14th century.

Cathedral   ★★★★

Plaza Mayor; *(925) 22 22 41. Entrance on the north facade.*
Hours open: daily 10:30 a.m.–1 p.m., and 3:30–7 p.m. (until 6 p.m. in winter, and on Sun.).

This is Spain's most important cathedral, and, after Burgos, its grandest. Building began in 1227 on a typical French Gothic cathedral, but during its two centuries of construction the plan gradually changed to a squatter and broader version known as Spanish Gothic.

Enter on the north side, through the cloisters. The interior conveys a sense of volume and strength, rather than the lightness of the soaring French Gothic. Gradually the sumptuousness of the decoration takes effect. The stained glass is of the period, multicolored and lovely; wrought iron and marble run rampant.

The **coro** (choir) in the center of the Cathedral nave contains some of the finest wood carving in Spain. The lower row of choirstalls, carved within a decade of the event, graphically depict the Christian conquest of Granada and constitute one of the best records of the battles. The upper tier of stalls on the right, are by the sculptor Alonso Berruguete. They are masterpieces of bas-relief, subtly conveying life and movement with figures that seem to push through the wood.

Opposite the *coro* is the **sanctuary** and altar with its huge, flamboyantly-carved polychrome retable depicting the life of Christ. Royal tombs flank the altar: Alfonso VII on the left, Sancho II on the right. Behind the sanctuary, in the middle of the ambulatory, hangs a swirling Baroque *Transparante* slab by Tomé that seems out of place for all its prominence. Holes were cut in the Cathedral walls to allow the sun to illuminate it.

To the right (with your back to the Transparante), after the Chapel of San Ilde-fonso, a painted Mudejar portal leads to the **Capitular** room with its intricate 16th-century ceiling. Paintings of bishops of Toledo line the room, from the first century through the 19th, and include two painted by Goya.

Returning back around the ambulatory, the tomb of Henrique of Trastámara, ancestor of both Isabella and Ferdinand, lies adjacent to the Santiago Chapel. Next in line is the **sacristy**, which presents a gallery of art under an imposing frescoed ceiling. The first gallery contains an awesome display of El Grecos, followed by rooms with Titian's great portrait of *Pope Paul IV*, some fine Van Dykes, an unin-spired Goya, and a hauntingly "pretty" *Saint John the Baptist* by Caravaggio.

On the north side of the Cathedral front is the **tesoro** (treasury), entered through a Plateresque doorway. The Mudejar ceiling is lovely. Here you can see the 16th-cen-tury silver and gilt monstrance, weighing just under 400 pounds, which is carried through the streets during the Corpus Christi festival. A sword is displayed that belonged to Alfonso VI who conquered Toledo in 1085. Nearby is the library with richly illustrated medieval song books.

After all this splendor, the cloister disappoints. But not the **Mozarabic Chapel** that forms the front of the Cathedral on the south side. The chapel was constructed in 1504 so that those who still followed the Christian service as practiced by the Visig-oths would have a place to worship. Most of those adherents had been isolated from their brethren because they lived in Moorish territory, and were thus called Mozarabs, "almost Arabs," by the other Christians. The decor of their chapel is ele-gantly frescoed, but the chapel is open only for their special services (at 9:30 a.m.). *Admission: 350 ptas.*

Afterwards, head left through the Plaza Arco de Palácio in front of the Cathedral, bearing right along the Archbishopric. Take the second right which is Calle San Sal-vador. At the corner, Santa Tomé with its wondrous El Greco lies straight ahead in one block. If time permits, first turn left, then quickly right to reach the **Taller del Moro**, on the street of the same name.

Taller del Moro   ★

Calle Taller del Moro; ☎ *(925) 22 71 15.*
Hours open: Tues.–Sat. 10 a.m.–2 p.m., and 4–7 p.m. (until 6 p.m. in winter). Open Sun. from 10 a.m.–2 p.m. Closed Mon.
This is a museum displaying crafts and tools of the Moors, but it is most interesting as a building. The 14th-century structure was used by Moorish craftsmen as a work-shop *(taller)*, while they worked on the Cathedral. *Admission: 100 Ptas.*

From the Taller continue to the corner and turn left along Plaza del Conde. At the end turn right, then left at the cross street, for Santa Tomé.

Santa Tomé   ★ ★ ★

Plaza Conde, 1, ☎ *(925) 21 02 09.*
Hours open: daily 10:30 a.m.–1:45 p.m., and 3:30–7 p.m. (until 6 p.m. in winter).
Gonzalo Ruiz, Count of Orgaz, was a local lord of the Toledo area who donated much of the money to build this church and was buried inside in 1323. Two centu-ries later, in 1586, urged by his descendants, the church commissioned El Greco to

portray that burial. Naturally the appearance of the Count and those who attended were by then unknown, so El Greco used the faces of Toledoans of his day. A Mudejar tower stands beside the church as its annex, and in it hangs this masterpiece, so admired that a wait can be expected before admission to the small vestibule.

Tradition claimed that Sts. Stephen and Augustin attended the Count's burial to honor his charity, and El Greco shows them in rich capes supporting the deceased. El Greco's son stands in front pointing to the scene. (Inconspicuously inscribed on his handkerchief is the artist's signature.) All around in various attitudes stand citizens of Toledo, including El Greco himself, the sixth figure from the left. *Admission: 200 Ptas.*

Return to the corner where the church begins, turning right down the hill leading to the Plaza del Conde again. But go right on San Juan de Dios, instead of entering the plaza. Two alleyways later a sign directs you left to the House of El Greco.

Casa y Museo del Greco ★★

Paseo del Tránsito; ☎ *(925) 22 40 46.*

Hours open: Tues.–Sat. 10 a.m.–2 p.m., and 4–7 p.m. (until 6 p.m. in winter). Open Sun. from 10 a.m.–2 p.m. Closed Mon.

Although the actual house in which El Greco lived has long since disappeared, this one was altered 100 years ago to suggest his style of living. The structure is an interesting reconstruction of a 16th-century private dwelling and displays a most amazing collection of El Greco's paintings, so brightly restored that they do not seem authentic. *Admission: 400 ptas.; ticket good for Tránsito Synagogue.*

Return to Calle San Juan de Dios, continuing to the bottom of the street, where the Synagogue of the Tránsito stands.

Sinagoga del Tránsito ★★★

Calle Samuel Ha-Levi, ☎ *(925) 22 36 55.*

Hours open: Tues.–Sat. 10 a.m.–2 p.m., and 4–7 p.m. (until 6 p.m. in winter). Open Sun. from 10 a.m.–2 p.m. Closed Mon.

Of eight known Toledo synagogues, only this and Santa María la Blanca Synagogue remain. It was begun in 1364 with a grant from Samuel Ha-Levi, the Treasurer of Spain during the reign of King Pedro the Cruel. Unfortunately, Pedro later turned on his treasurer, seized what remained of his wealth and put him to death. After the Jews were expelled from Spain, the synagogue was transformed into a church, from which comes its present name. It fell into neglect during the 18th century, until Francisco Perez Bayer, a Hebrew scholar, undertook the work of removing Christian overlays to restore it to its former splendor as a 13th-century synagogue.

All around the upper walls, and covering the east end, run the most astonishing patterns of stuccowork inspired by the Moors. Hebrew inscriptions praise Pedro the Cruel, Samuel Ha-Levi, and God. Above the arches in the middle of the east end is a panel of delicate roses, surrounded by lovely designs. Fifty-four lacy windows are formed of stone tracery. *Admission: 400 ptas.; ticket good for Casa del Greco.*

The large street perpendicular to C. San Juan de Dios is Reyes Católicos. Go right (north), arriving in two or three blocks at the Synagogue of Santa María la Blanca on the right.

Sinagoga Santa María la Blanca   ★★

Calle Reyes Católicos, ☎ (925) 22 84 29.
Hours open: daily 10 a.m.–2 p.m., and 3:30–7 p.m. (until 6 p.m. in winter).
This was the principle synagogue of Toledo, rebuilt after a fire in 1250 on the site of its predecessor. In later years it was abandoned, then used successively as a barracks, a store and a workshop. Somehow much of the interior of the original synagogue remained intact, allowing accurate restoration.

Octagonal pillars with horseshoe arches form a main aisle with two more aisles on either side. Capitals are carved with intricate designs, relieving the whitewashed columns and walls. Above the arches sophisticated stucco designs reach to the ceiling, making the whole seem more like a mosque than a synagogue, but with a sophistication that few places of worship of any religion can claim. The incongruous sanctuary and retable were added in the middle of the 16th century. *Admission: 125 ptas.*

Continue past Santa María la Blanca on C. Reyes Católicos for one block to the monastery of San Juan de los Reyes.

San Juan de los Reyes   ★★

Calle Reyes Católicos, ☎ (925) 22 38 02.
Hours open: daily 10 a.m.–2 p.m., and 3:30–7 p.m. (until 6 p.m. in winter).
The monastery was commissioned by Ferdinand and Isabella in gratitude for their triumph over the pretender to Isabella's throne and her Portuguese allies. Ferdinand and Isabella so admired it that they planned to be buried here—before they conquered and were captivated by Granada.
The restored cloister is elaborate yet graceful and its second story is especially to be appreciated, for its gallery retains a fine Mudejar ceiling. The church interior is composed of one impressively open aisle. Where the transept crosses, openwork galleries display the entwined initials of Ferdinand and Isabella, along with a yoke and an arrow (in medieval Spanish these objects started with the first letter of the two monarchs' names), and the shields of Castile and Aragón. In no uncertain terms, the Catholic monarchs left their mark on this church. Supported by an eagle, amid statues of saints, powerful friezes of royal escutcheons line the transept walls. The heads carved beneath the arches are startling. *Admission: 125 ptas.*

Return through the C. Reyes Católicos to the first street on the left, Calle de Angel. Follow this for two blocks passing Santa Tomé. Take the narrow Calle Campaña across the intersection and left. Continue in the same direction across the next intersection where the street changes its name to Calle de Alfonso XII, which leads to the small Plaza Padre Mariana. Take the street leading from the left side of the plaza, Calle San Román, which quickly leads to the church of San Román around the corner.

Iglesia San Román   ★★

Calle San Clemente.

CENTRAL SPAIN

Hours open: Tues.–Sat. 10 a.m.–2 p.m., and 4–7 p.m. (until 6 p.m. in winter). Closed Sun. afternoon and all day Mon.

This 13th-century church demonstrates the extent to which the Moorish aesthetic dominated architecture in Toledo during its first century after passing into Christian hands. Today the church is a museum for Visigothic art, which is appropriate in the former capital of their domain. Note the jewelry especially. The lovely wall frescoes of the resurrection of the dead have been retained from the original church. *Admission: 100 ptas.*

If you have time for an act of homage, continue along C. San Román for one block to take the right fork. On the left is **Santa Domingo el Antiquo**. Inside is an early view of Toledo by El Greco as well as the genius' last remains.

Return along C. San Román, which becomes Calle Jesus y María after it crosses the intersection, then turn left at the next intersection onto Calle Trinidad. After a bend it enters the Plaza Arco de Palácio in front of the Cathedral. Continue across in the same direction, perpendicular to the Cathedral, into the large Calle Hombre de Palo. It narrows into Calle Comercio lined with shops, and in two blocks leaves you in the main square of Toledo, the Plaza Zocodover, which is lively and attractive. Here a right turn will take you to the **Museo de Santa Cruz**, or a left will lead you to **Santa Cristo del Luz** (see descriptions in this section).

Museo Santa Cruz   ★★★★

Calle Cervantes, ☎ *(925) 22 14 02.*

Hours open: Tues.–Sat. 10:30 a.m.–7 p.m. (until 6 p.m. in winter). Mon. 10 a.m. to 2 p.m. and 4:30–6:30 p.m. Closed Sun. afternoon at 2 p.m. and all day Mon.

Few museums in the world are housed in a more dramatic building. It was built by Cardinal Mendoza, private confessor to Queen Isabella, as a very sumptuous hospital, for the sick and orphaned of Toledo. In truth the outside is not special, though the statue over the main portal of Cardinal Mendoza kneeling before the cross is worth a look, but the inside is magnificent.

It is a huge barn in the shape of a cross of equal sides, and seems to extend limitlessly in four directions. Overhead runs an extraordinary wood ceiling. It would be hard to believe that paintings as spectacular as the collection in Santa Cruz would have to vie for attention against an architectural background, but architecture is seldom so dramatic.

The long entry hall is lined with fine 16th century tapestries and early furniture. At the end of the hall hangs the huge magnificent pennant from Don Juan's admiral's galley, flown during his victory over the Moors in 1571 at Lepanto. Then comes a corridor devoted to El Greco, in which over 20 canvases hang. The most famous is the *Altarpiece of the Assumption*, painted a few months before he died. The virgin in the painting holds a book containing a record of El Greco's death, a detail added by his son. On the second floor are two fine Riberas, mixed with less interesting paintings. Tapestries depicting the history of Alexander the Great are striking, if more faded than the embroideries on the lower floor. An elegant Renaissance stair by Covarrubias leads down to a Plateresque patio, which in turn leads to small rooms housing archaeological finds. *Admission: 225 ptas.*

At least one monument outside the walls of Toledo is well worth seeing, the Hospital de Tavera. The building is remarkable, as is some of the art inside.

The Hospital is due north, at the end of a large square called Paseo de Merchan. It can be walked from the Ermita del Cristo de la Luz, although it is a hike of about half a mile. To walk, head north along Cuesta del Cristo de la Luz which leads into Calle Real de Arrabal. Continuing north, pass through the Puerta Nueva de Bisagra by Covarrubias, one of the gates of Toledo. Walk along Carretera a Madrid, by the east side of the square, to the Hospital at the garden's end. Alternatively, one can drive along the perimeter road and take a right on Carretera a Madrid.

Hospital de Tavera   ★★
paseo de Madrid, ☎ *(925) 22 04 51.*
Hours open: daily 10 a.m.–1:30 p.m. and 3:30–6 p.m.
Something sad emanates from this building, perhaps because, although it was never finished, it represents the final work of three great men.

This was the last building designed by Covarrubias; its stately form is a fitting memorial. He built it for Cardinal Tavera, descended from the combined great families of Medinacelli and Lerma. A double patio inside leads to a large chapel in which lie tombs of the Medinacelli—the most elegant being the tomb of Cardinal Tavera, the last work of the great sculptor Alonso Berruguete. Off the left side of the patio is a small museum of art and furniture belonging to the Dukes of Lerma. The huge dining hall displays Titian's *Portrait of Carlos V,* and a lovely Coello. In the library hangs a fine El Greco of *The Holy Family,* and a *Virgin,* unusual for actually being pretty. Ribera's *Philosophy* is nice, but the most striking Ribera—his strange painting of a bearded lady—is stashed in a small room. On the second floor is an utterly unforgettable painting by Zurbarán of the young Duke of Medinacelli, all in orange tones. On the same floor are a Tintoretto and a number of El Grecos, including his last canvas. *The Baptism of Christ by Saint John* is huge and includes all the characteristics that make El Greco the most recognizable of artists. *Admission: 600 ptas.*

Excursions

Guadalupe, Trujillo, Cáceres, and Mérida all are near enough to visit. Simple reverse the directions above.

CENTRAL SPAIN

PARADOR CONVENTO DE SAN PABLO

Paseo Hoz del Huécar, s/n, Cuenca, 16001
☎ *(969) 23 23 20, FAX (969) 23 25 34*
$120 per double; 62 rooms: 60 doubles, 2 suites

★ ★ ★ ★

Visitors come to Cuencar for its dramatic situation over a gorge and for its modern art. This parador suits the scene perfectly. Dramatic and yet elegant, it represents one of the most recent and successful renovations of an historic building. The monastery dates from the 16th-century, and is of elegant late-gothic design. It hugs the edge of the incredible Huécar gorge opposite the "hanging" village of Cuenca for spectacular views of the town. The parador surrounds the old cloister, now garden, whose aisles serve today as a restful lounge. Fine plasterwork with lovely frescoes throughout the parador is accented by tile floors and palms. Ample spaces in all public rooms are soothing, although the bedrooms are more ordinary. Altogether, this is an unforgettable place to stay.

Alternative Accommodations

Posada de San José

Julián Romero, 4, ☎ (969) 221 13 00, FAX (969) 223 03 65. 29 rooms.
There are no more elegant accommodations than this parador's, but one hotel offers more charm. The Posada de San José in the village, opposite the parador, is a six story labyrinth going back to the 16th-century and packed with curiosities. It's spotless and charges half of the parador's fee.

Dining

Hovering above the dining room hangs a sublime paneled ceiling lit by tiered chandeliers. Below, the room is softly elegant, a fine place to enjoy rather decent food. The chef is proud of his pig´s liver paté *(morteruelo)*, garlic or gazpacho soup, cod and stuffed lamb shoulder; all of which are tasty. An interesting dessert is *alajú*, a sweet confection of breadcrumbs, walnuts and honey. Local wine choices range over Horcajo de Santiago, and Motilla del Palancar. Finish off with a devilish *resoi*, coffee with brandy, orange peel and cinnamon. A full meal will average $20–25, plus drinks.

Alternative Dining

Casa Mario   ★

Colón, 59 (outside the old section) ☎ *(969) 221 11 73.*
Inventive dishes are served in an open, though otherwise typically Castilian room. Try a stew of partridge or a mushroom tart. Desserts are equally good. A bottle of Zagarrón will complement the food. Meals cost about $25. Closed Sun. night. Credit Cards: A, V.

Directions

Follow signs for the parador which wind you around the town to the bluff opposite and parking inside the parador.

Paradors Nearby

Alarcón: 86 km   Chinchón: 130 km
Albacete: 142 km   Toledo: 238 km

CENTRAL SPAIN

Sights

Hanging over a gorge, the old city of Cuenca´s most intriguing sight is itself. And the best introduction is to walk over the pedestrian bridge, the Puente de San Pablo, from the parador. Heart in hand as you cling tightly to the narrow span, you see the remarkable tall houses that cling to every inch of space as they all but lurch over the gorge. It is quite a sight. Bearing left as you leave the bridge, you come to one of the more unusual art museums in the world. Several of the Casas Colgadas ("hanging houses") have been merged and redone inside as a museum for abstract art. The **Musea de Arte Abstracto** features Spanish artists in a setting whose window views rival anything hanging on the walls. Return to the church, then straight away from the bridge to the handsome Plaza Mayor, all but ruined by the rebuilt facade of the Cathedral. At the far end stands a pretty Town Hall from the 17th-century, whose arches constitute one entry to the square. The remainder of the old town is a compact two streets wide, made for wandering to inspect nooks and crannies.

PARADOR DE CÁCERES

Calle Ancha, 6, Cáceres, 10003
(927) 21 17 59, FAX (927) 21 17 29
$110 per double; 27 rooms: 1 single, 26 doubles

★ ★ ★ ★

Tourists flock to Cáceres to walk the streets of an almost perfectly preserved 16th-century town. They ogle all the stone mansions which form a group unparalleled for lacking a single jarring note from modern times. This parador is one of them, built in the 14th-century by a knight who won success in the wars against the Moors. But mansions aren't special in this part of town. A century ago this one became a restaurant which, in 1989, was transformed into a parador. It is stark inside, but quiet. Patios abound, as do suits of armor. Some of the bedrooms have sitting alcoves which makes them seem more spacious. Bedroom decor is mostly unimaginative, the furniture is second-rate, but the public rooms are attractive.

Alternative Accommodations

Meliá Cáceres

Pl. San Juan, 11, *(927) 21 58 00, FAX (927) 21 40 70. 86 rooms.*
The parador offers the highest priced accommodations in town, but the second best, the Meliá Cáceres, just outside the old walls one block south of the Plaza Mayor, is also renovated from a 15th-century mansion, but is more elegantly remodeled and charges 25% less than the parador.

Dining

While the dining room is simple, both the beamed ceiling and the cuisine rise a level above other paradors. Start with a competent gazpacho or a salad of roasted pimento and egg *(zorombollo)*, followed by lamb stew *(calereta de cordero)*, pheasant or, when on the menu, delicious local ham *(jamón)* flavorfully fattened on acorns. Unfortunately, local wines disappoint; look for a good Rioja, for a treat, or a Valdepeña, if watching the budget. A full meal will average a little more than $20, plus drinks.

Alternative Dining

Atrio   ★ ★ ★

Av. de España, 30 (actually the restaurant is a jag north from this main street with center island.), ☎ *(927) 24 29 28.*
Closed Sun. night.
Located in a shopping mall cul de sac, Atrio blends into the shadows in forest green. The interior is yellow and white, sleek, and surprisingly elegant for provincial Spain. The chef tries to make everything special to justify high prices, adding truffles to most dishes. Still, the service is professional and the quality of the food is astonishingly good. Pheasant is as good as it gets. Such quality is expensive. Set meals cost twice the tariff at the parador, á la carte runs more. Credit Cards: A, D, M, V.

El Figón de Eustaquio   ★ ★

Pl. San Juan, 12 (This quiet plaza is one block from the west end of the Pl. del General Mola.), ☎ *(927) 24 81 94.*
Many consider this the best restaurant in the province, forgetting the more luxurious dishes at Atrio (above). There is nothing nouvelle about the food, but local dishes are inventively and tastefully prepared. Prices will be expensive, if ordering à la carte, but moderate if one of the special menus is selected. The restaurant is attractive, consisting of a number of rooms of intimate scale. At lunchtime it is extremely busy, and reservations are required. Credit Cards: A, M, V.

Directions

From north and east you enter the city along Av. de las Delicias which curves until it reaches the bullring. There turn left along Barrio Nuevo which heads to the Plaza Mayor and the old walled section of town (following signs for **Barrio Monumental**). Turn right at the plaza, circle the church to take the first street you can going south. Take the first left onto F. Pizarro for two blocks to a fork, whose left tine enters the city walls. The parador is a short block inside, on the left.From Mérida and south you enter the city along Av. Virgen de Guadalupe. Turn right at the first large intersection onto Gil Cordero. Continue straight through two traffic circles to take the first left you can onto Ronda de San Francisco which leads to the old city walls. The parador is a short block inside, on the left.

Paradors Nearby

Trujillo: 48 km	Mérida: 68 km	Zafra: 128 km
Guadalupe: 130 km	Jarandilla: 137 km	Oropesa: 150 km

Sights

The Romans called the town *Colonia Norbensis Caesara* which the Spanish shortened to Cáceres. It was an early and persistent battleground fought over by Christians and Moors. Here the nucleus of the famed Order of Santiago, the most distinguished society in Spain, was formed in 1170 to muster knights devoted to the Reconquest. By 1229, when Christians had taken control of the city for good, Cáceres began producing company after company of soldiers—first to fight against the Moors, later to conquer the Indian civilizations in the New World. Soldiering proved lucrative for some of these men who returned from campaigns to erect houses proclaiming their wealth and status. By the end of the 16th century, when no worlds remained to conquer, Cáceres ceased raising mansions, indeed ceased to grow. The happy result for today's visitor is that the old part of the town is the most homogeneous, best preserved Renaissance quarter in Spain. What impresses most visitors is the discovery that the quarter is not particularly attractive—it is monotonous and somewhat dingy in feel— which shows that urban blight is not a 20th-century invention.

The old **walls**, although substantially restored now, rise on foundations that are part Roman, part Moorish, and the remainder date to the 15th century. Towers protrude from the walls so that defenders could shoot back at an enemy storming the town. The curving stairs and gate, called the Arco de la Estrella, were designed by a member of the Baroque Churriguera family in the 17th century. The **Office of Tourism** lies to the right, where an essential map is available.

A short block through the gate brings the 16th-century **Episcopal Palace**, on the left, with medallions of the Old and New World, interesting for depictions of geography as it was then known, flanking its portal.

We have entered the Pl. de Santa María. To the right stands the large **Mayoralgo Palace** with elegant windows and a nice patio inside. More awaits in the plaza, but first turn left down C. Conilleros to the **Casa de los Toledo-Moctezuma**, with an unusual domed tower. Now a municipal archive, the house once belonged to a lieutenant of Cortés who married the daughter of the Aztec emperor Montezuma and built this edifice with her dowry. Go south along the walls to the **Torre de los Espaderos** (Armorers) on the right at the next corner. Like most of the towers in the city this one was truncated by Isabella to prevent violent feuds among the city's families, each of which had raised a tower for defense.

Exit the walls through the Scorro Gate for a look at the church of Santiago by following C. de Godoy, which heads northwest. In one block the **Palácio de Godoy** is passed, with a fine corner balcony, to enter the **Plaza de Santiago**.

During the 12th century, in an earlier church on the site, the forerunner of the Order of Santiago was established. So prestigious did it become that 400 years later the great painter Velázquez would devote time and effort to try to gain membership in the order. The present church is 16th century, built by Rodrigo Gil de Hontañon, the last great Gothic architect. Inside, a splendid retable in high relief by Berruguete surrounds Santiago Matamore (St. James, the Slayer of Moors) with scenes from the life of Christ. Note the anguished faces and elongated bodies that are Berruguete's signature. Return through the walls again, and head directly west along C. Tiendas to return to the Pl. de Santa María.

 Passing the **Torre de Carvajal**, on the left, cross to the **Catedral de Santa María**. Sixteenth-century Gothic, the church is elegant within and without. Head along the north side of the cathedral to exit the plaza from the west and enter the Pl. de San Jorge. On the left is the **Palácio de los Golfines de Abajo**, one of two palaces in the quarter owned by this family. The façade becomes elegant through Mudejar designs, especially the windows and their

CENTRAL SPAIN

surrounds and Plateresque intricacy in the griffins along the roof edge. Its owner was permitted to display the coats of arms of Ferdinand and Isabella after they had enjoyed his hospitality.

Continue west across the plaza to pass the **Residencia de Luisa de Carvajal**, on the left, and walk around the north face of the **Iglesia de San Francisco Javier**, with an imposing 18th-century façade. Pass the **Torre del Sol**, from the 15th century, with a nicely carved family crest over the arch, to reach the rear of the church of San Mateo. Along its south side stands the 15th-century **Casa de las Ciqüeñas** (House of the Storks), now occupied by the military, retaining the only intact tower that Isabella permitted. If the guard allows, peek into the patio to see its delicate arches.

To the left is the former **Casa de las Veletas** (House of the Weathervanes). It hosts a small museum of archaeological exhibits—the costumes and utensils for everyday use are especially interesting, as is a 12th-century cistern from the original Moorish Alcázar that serves as its basement. *(Open Tues.–Sun. 9:30 a.m.–2:30 p.m. and 5–7 p.m. Closing on Sun. at 2:30. Admission: 200 ptas.)*

Return north to view the 15th-century **church of San Mateo** with its striking tower. In the austere interior rest the noble families of the city. Walk north along the church façade to the **Casa de Ulloa** and turn left (west) down the typical C. Ancha. In less than a block on the left is the **Casa do Comendador de Alcuescar**, with a Gothic tower, nice window decoration and a fine balcony. Beside it stands the former **Casa de Sanchez de Paredes**, now a parador, which may be entered for a look around.

Turn right at the walls at the end of the street, and right again at the next corner onto C. del Olmo. At the end of the block on the left is the other house of the Golfines family, the **Palácio dos Golfines de Arriba**, with an imposing tower. Both this and the **Casa Adanero** opposite have lovely patios. Go left around the Palácio dos Golfines to reach the walls and turn right to come to the **Casa de la Generala** in one more block. Another block brings a return to the Arco de la Estrella from which the tour began.

Excursions

From Cáceres, **Trujillo**, **Mérida** and **Guadalupe** each are an hour or two away. See the descriptions under these respective paradors in this chapter. **Lisbon** is 335 km west, by going south on N-630 to Mérida, then west on N-V (N-4 across the border).

CENTRAL SPAIN

PARADOR DE CARLOS V

Av. Garcia Prieto, 1, Jarandilla, 10450
☎ *(927) 56 01 17, FAX (927) 56 00 88*
$105 per double; 53 rooms: 10 singles, 43 doubles

★ ★ ★ ★

If you like your palaces fortified, old, rather small, and eccentric enough to be "cute," you've found your place. Begun in the late 15th-century, this castle comes complete with fortified walls and drawbridge. Towers, all different, guard the four corners of the grounds, a fine patio lies in the center. Despite all the fortifications and heavy stone, however, the complex is too small for all the fuss and thus the "cuteness." Yes, there is a cloister as well. Inside, everything is appropriately castlelike, especially the lounge with baronial fireplace and aged wood ceiling. Opt for one of the 16 rooms in the old building, rather than the new annex—you came to stay in a castle. These contain high ceilings and lovely old floors. To gild the lily, tennis courts and a pool are included.

Dining

The elegantly appointed dining room overlooks the courtyard through graceful arches. Antiques are set off by the white walls. The chairs are upholstered and the tables set with linen, to make you feel like a noble while you dine. Start with a tomato soup that tastes like tomatoes, follow with lamb stew or kid, then ice cream or a selection of cheeses. The featured wine is a strong Tierra de Barros. A full meal will average a little more than $20, plus drinks.

Directions

From **Madrid** take N-5 for 176 km to Navalmoral de la Mata, then go north for 33 km to Jarandilla de la Vera. From **Trujillo** take N-V north for 62 km Navalmoral de la Mata, then go north for 33 km to Jarandilla de la Vera. From **Toledo** take N-403 west for 47 km to Santa Olalla, then N-V west for 90 km to Navalmoral de la Mata. A leg north for 33 km reaches Jarandilla de la Vera.

Paradors Nearby

Oropesa: 60 km	Guadalupe: 90 km	Trujillo: 105 km
Gredos: 120 km	Salamanca: 135 km	Cáceres: 150 km

Excursions

A pleasant pilgrimage can be made to the **Monastery of Yuste**, 11 km west on C-501, then look for a sign to the monastery and a right turn of 2 km. This is the place that one of the most powerful rulers the world has ever seen chose to spend his final years. Carlos V was the Holy Roman Emperor, the king of Spain, of Holland and Belgium, of the Americas, and of various parts of France. He fought continually during all of his thirty odd year reign, then retired to this monastery to contemplate and eat. Unfortunately the monastery was the site of a great battle between the Duke of Wellington and the French in the 19th-century when it was substantially destroyed. But you can see the small palace where this mighty monarch ended his days and the two lovely courtyards where he passed his time thinking about what might have been. Perhaps you will even understand why, with all the world to choose from, he chose this spot.

PARADOR DE CHINCHÓN

Av. del Generalissimo, 1, Chinchón, 28370
☎ *(91) 894 08 36, FAX (91) 894 09 08*
$120 per double; 38 rooms: 36 doubles, 2 suites

★ ★ ★ ★

Amble past terraced gardens graced by calming fountains, settle into a bench on a well-worn patio and you'll never know you are enjoying a former prison. True, the buildings were constructed in the 17th-century as an Augustinian convent to induce tranquil contemplation and study, until, in the last century, it was seized by the government during an anticlerical reaction. The government turned the convent over to the village which promptly housed its court and jails inside. Fear not, since the government again got hold of the property and performed tasteful renovations to make this parador one of its most restful. Delicate old blue "azulejo" tiles covering white walls helped, aged terra cotta floors assisted, and the frescoed arched ceiling at the top of the main stairs made its irreplaceable contribution. The bedrooms now are starkly white, clean and crisp. Their furniture is sparse, but includes beds covered in white, headed by golden garlands on the bedsteads. All around, quiet patios call, and the garden in the rear tastefully embraces a swimming pool. If you can't relax here, get professional help.

Alternative Accommodations

There are no more restful, tranquil accommodations for miles around than this parador.

Dining

Those wonderful blue "azulejo" tiles make happy elegance of the dining room. A bar in bright blue jars only slightly. Featured is a hearty soup *(sopa castellana)* and venison *(ciervo)* in season. Look also for *pisto manchego*, a Spanish version of ratatouille. At meal's end the usual sweet egg yolks are available, but this time with truffles *(yemas y trufas)*, along with a most unusual garlic sorbet. The chef here thinks more creatively than those at most paradors. For an aperitif, try the specialty of the village, anisette. Chinchón's wines, though few have heard of them, are much appreciated by those who know. A full meal will average $20, plus drinks.

Alternative Dining

Mesón Cuevas del Viño   ★

Benito Hortelano, 13, ☎ *(91) 894 02 06.*
A fine collection of wine, virtually a museum of the grape, appropriately inhabits an ancient mill. Tasty chicken fricassee is offered, along with roasts from perfuming wood fires to enhance the wine. Meals will cost about the same $20 as at the parador. Closed Mon. and Aug. Credit Cards: None

Mesón de la Virreina   ★

Pl. Mayor, 21, ☎ *(91) 894 00 15.*
Installed in a 17th-century mansion on the lovely main square, here you dine more elegantly, though without as choice accompaniments to the food. Roast meats are the feature and hearty Sopa Castellana. Ask for a table by the balcony *(balconada)* over the square. Prices are a peseta or two higher than the "Wine Cave" above. Credit Cards: A, D, M, V.

Directions

From wherever you arrive, make your way up to the main Plaza Mayor, then follow signs.

Paradors Nearby

Toledo: 69 km	Cuenca: 130 km	Segovia: 133 km
Alarcón: 153 km	Ávila: 159 km	

Sights

Stroll to the truly lovely Plaza Mayor, picturesquely surrounded by arcaded buildings with attractive balconies. Relax in any of the cafes around the square and sip an anisette, the drink for which the village is famous.

Excursions

For **Cuenca's** "hanging" houses head 5 k south to Colmenar de Oreja, then 12 k east to Villarejo de Salvares and N-III south for 32 k to Taracón. Here N-400 reaches Cuenca to the east in 82 k more, then take N-400 to Cuenca for 82 km. For **Toledo's** treasures head 5 k south to Colmenar de Oreja, then 21 k to Aranjuez. A final 42 k on N-400 west brings your destination.

Castillo de Santa Catalina in Jaén features spectacular views of the Sierra Morena.

Aiguablava in Girona features pine trees, coves and gardens.

Some of Setenil's streets are lined with rock overhangs.

PARADOR DE CONVENTO DE SANTA CLARA

Beatriz de Silva, s/n, Trujillo, 10200
☎ *(927) 32 13 50, FAX (927) 32 13 66*
$90 per double; 46 rooms: 45 doubles, 1 suite

★ ★ ★ ★

This time the parador is installed in a former 16th-century convent, hidden behind a massive outer wall. Befitting its convent heritage, it is less formal than many paradors and correspondingly more relaxed. Half of the rooms are in the convent and focus on a simple central cloister planted with orange and lemon trees; the other half are in a new wing surrounding an attractive pool. Antiques are spread around. The bedrooms are simple, white and severe, befitting their heritage. Also, befitting the heritage, the air is still and serene.

Alternative Accommodations

Mesón Cadena

Pl. Mayor, 8, ☎ *(927) 32 14 63. Eight rooms*

Nothing in this town is as comfortable and serene as the parador, but one hotel is more quirky yet costs only $30. Mesón Cadena is housed in a 16th-century mansion with rooms above the mesón that are pleasant and comfortable. It also offers views of the plaza and town walls.

Dining

The dining room in the former refractory is roofed by a dramatic barrel vault and bright with a modern azulejo tiled picture at one end, providing a happy feeling throughout. Food is exceptionally good for a parador. Start with light anchovies *(anchoas)* or a savory tomato with basil soup *(tomate al tomillo)*, followed by whatever truffle dish is on the menu or a local fish called *tencas*. Desserts are very sweet, but fruit is always an alternative. Enhance the meal with a nice bottle of the local Herguijuela de la Sierra. For such food a tariff of $25, plus drinks is most reasonable.

Alternative Dining

Hostal Pizarro   ★★

Pl. Mayor, 13, ☎ (927) 32 02 55.

This restaurant is an institution, not only of Trujillo, but of all Extremadura. The chef and waitress are two sisters who inherited this place long ago from their father. Together, they serve the most authentic Extremaduran home cooking. Partridge casserole is delicious and the roast lamb is quite good. The prices, the same or less than the parador, will please you almost as much as the food does. Credit Cards: M, V.

Mesón la Troya   ★★

Pl. Mayor, 10, ☎ (927) 32 13 64.

Over a hundred years ago this was a stable, but now humans chow down some of the best tasting food for the money in Spain. Every dish is authentic, hearty and good. An omelette and salad arrive to keep you happy while you peruse the short menu. Give the *prueba de cerdo*, a heavily garlicked pork casserole, serious consideration. $15 should cover the tab. Credit Card: V.

Directions

From wherever you arrive follow signs to the Plaza Mayor, then go right (or left, if arriving from the north on C-524) on Domingo Ramos for three short blocks.

Paradors Nearby

Mérida: 90 km	Oropesa: 100 km
Guadalupe: 100 km	Jarandilla:105 km

Sights

Trujillo is said to have spawned 20 American nations. While that is an exaggeration, this village contributed far more than its share to the conquest of the Americas, for it was the home of Francisco Pizarro. Pizarro, an illegitimate son of a noble family, left his dead-end job as a swineherd to seek a fortune in the New World. When he reached Peru, he followed the strategy that Cortés had employed in Mexico. Under the protection of a truce, he captured the Inca Atahualpa, and ruled his empire through him until he was strong enough to grab the reins himself. Thereby he accumulated riches that are incalculable in modern terms. However, rivalry with a lieutenant led Pizarro to kill him, only to be murdered in turn by the dead man's friends. Pizarro's half-brother Hernando and various compatriots from Trujillo survived the death to return with sufficient treasures to make their hometown wealthy for a while.

Trujillo had been an unimportant village before the Conquistadores left to seek their fortunes. When they returned, each built a mansion as impressive as his booty would allow. However, this new wealth provided only a one-time injection into the economy of the town, which settled back into obscurity after its building boom in the 16th and 17th centuries. Today Trujillo offers mansions similar to those of Cáceres, though less densely and—thanks to their whitewashed facades—less austerely. They surround one of the most pleasant, expansive plaza mayors in Spain. Above the plaza, majestic ruins of a 12th-century Moorish fortress look down. Trujillo is an engaging village.

From **Madrid** and **Guadalupe** the road funnels into the Pl. del General Mola. Go straight through onto C. San António, which enters the Pl. San Miquel in one block. Continue through to C. Sofrago, which changes its name to C. Silleria, then enters the Pl. Mayor, where parking should be available. From **Mérida** Trujillo is entered along Carretera de Badajoz. Continue across the large Av. de la Encarnación, following the side of a park along C. Pardos. Continue straight through the small Pl. de Aragon along C. Romanos, which is named C. Parra when it bends right, and leads into the Pl. Mayor for parking. From **Cáceres** the town is entered along Av. Ramon y Cajal. Bear left at the park onto C. Ruiz de Mendoza. Angle left at the small Pl. de Aragón onto C. Romanos, which is named C. Parra when it bends right, and leads to Pl. Mayor for parking.

Begin in the lovely **Plaza Mayor ★**. The plaza is irregular in shape, although almost forming a triangle. Varying levels are linked by broad flights of stairs for variety. At the north center strides a powerful bronze **statue of Francisco Pizarro**, sculpted in 1927 by two American artists. Its twin resides in Lima, Peru, the city Pizarro founded. To the left (west), in an arcade, is the **Office of Tourism** which provides a map.

At the northeast side of the plaza stands the 16th-century Gothic church of **San Martín**, with a soaring nave and numerous Renaissance tombs. An arcade on its south side once served as a communal meeting place. Opposite is the **Palacio de San Carlos**, from the early 17th century, now a convent. The bell at the door will bring a nun (if rung at any normal Spanish museum hour) to show off an arched inner court storing Visigothic fragments, and interesting vaults of the basement. (A donation is in order.)

South around the plaza is the mansion of the **Marquesa de Piedras Alba**. At the southwest corner of the plaza stands the **Palácio de la Conquista**. De la Conquista was the Marquis' title conferred on Francisco Pizarro's brother Hernando, who returned wealthy from Peru. Once home, he built this mansion with an extraordinary number of grilled windows. At the corner balcony is a series of busts of the family. On the left are Francisco with his wife, Yupanqui Huaynas, daughter of the Inca. On the right are Hernando and his bride, Francisca (Francisco's daughter).

Proceeding west by the mansion, you reach the former **ayuntamiento** (town hall), from the 16th century, with an old reconstructed triple arcade. Passing the front (south), follow C. Almenas due west to the restored town walls and one of the original seven gates, the **Gate of San Andres**. Once through and past San Andres Church, the remains of **Moorish baths**, now a stagnant reservoir, are faced. Turn right into the quiet, almost abandoned old town, then left along C. de la Paloma going north, and prepare for a climb.

In two blocks you arrive at the Gothic **Santa María**, restored in the 15th century. The bell tower remains from the original Romanesque structure. (If closed, apply at the house to the right of the steps.) Inside, the church is pristine Gothic, with lovely vaulting. The retable at the altar is a Spanish master-piece by the great Fernando Gallego from Salamanca. A hundred peseta coin is necessary to illuminate it. All around are the tombs of the great families of the city. The upper choir is fronted by an elaborate balustrade with coats of arms of Ferdinand and Isabella at each end to indicate their seats, should they be in residence.

Follow the church facade to the east side, and walk north to its rear, across from which is the **Pizarro Museum**. Although it was closed for repairs at our visit, it should be reopened for yours. (Open daily 10 a.m.–2 p.m. and 4–6 p.m.; closed on holidays; admission: 250 ptas.). This is the former home of Francisco Pizarro's father. It is unlikely that the illegitimate Francisco was born here, though he did spend some of his childhood playing with his legitimate brothers in this place. Some of the rooms are nice, although the so-called museum has little to show.

The steep lane continues up to the top of the hill to massive twelfth-century crenulated walls of the **Castillo** (Castle). So far only the Moorish curtain-wall with its square towers has been restored. The area is a peaceful place to wander, watch the birds and look over the countryside.

Excursions

Guadalupe, Toledo, Trujillo, Cáceres, Ávila and Mérida all are near enough to visit. Simply reverse the directions above.

PARADOR DE GREDOS

Carretera Barraco-Béjar, km 43, Gredos, 05132
☎ *(920) 34 80 48, FAX (920) 34 82 05*
$75 per double; 77 rooms: 4 singles, 72 doubles, 1 suite

★ ★

This was the first of all the paradors, built in 1928, so it has some age about it. It was commissioned as a hunting lodge and retains that feeling. The Sierra de Gredos in which it sits now is a game preserve—so much for the hunting. But the mountains are relatively unspoiled, lush with pines and rise in massive peaks over 8000 feet high—views from the terrace of the parador extend for twenty miles on a clear day. Abundant trails for a walk or a canter on horseback ring the area, while a castle or two provide the excuse for an outing (the management provides maps). The parador is not a flimsy chalet. Constructed of solid stone, with ample rooms and surfaced with rich wide-board floors, it has been around for half a century and should last at least that much longer. The decor holds some interest for its 30s design. Bedrooms are gracious in size and sparsely furnished, but those wood floors can be cold in the morning.

Dining

Let us call the dining room comfortable, and note that the colorful ceramic plates add interest, but during daylight hours, the view overwhelms what any decorator can offer. Stick to simple basic food and you should be satisfied. Mashed potatoes and green beans can accompany a steak or some roast pork. A full meal will average $18, plus drinks.

Directions

From **Ávila** take N-110 toward El Barco, but take the fork in 6 km toward Arenas de San Pedro on N-502. Continue for a total of 44 km to a right turn along the scenic, but slow-going, C-500 which reaches the parador in about 10 km. From **Madrid** go to Ávila and follow the directions above.

Paradors Nearby

Ávila: 60 km	Oropesa: 103 km	Segovia: 130 km
Jarandilla: 137 km	Salamanca: 162 km	Ciudad Rodrigo: 171 km

Parador de Guadalupe

Marqués de la Romana, 12, Guadalupe, 10140
☎ *(927) 36 70 75, FAX (927) 36 70 76*
$75 per double; 40 rooms: 40 doubles

★ ★ ★ ★

Pilgrims have slept here since the 15th century. Isabella stayed too, signing her contract with Columbus in these rooms. The surviving Mudejar decorations are lovely, as is the patio. Bedrooms were decorated more recently in a restful Moorish style after a two-story modern wing was added to double the number of rooms. The hotel is a quiet whitewashed hacienda that provides fine views of surrounding mountains and valley, and offers a tasteful pool amid Moorish gardens. There is a choice to be made, however. Bedrooms in the old part retain some charm and some even sport fireplaces, but are smallish; those in the new wing are more spacious and annex balconies for mountain and monastery views, but lack character. In whichever room you choose, it's only a short stroll to the monastery.

Alternative Accommodations

Hospedería del Real Monasterio

Pl. Juan Carlos I, ☎ *(927) 36 70 00, FAX (927) 36 71 77. 46 rooms.*

For something a bit different, sleep in the monastery. The brothers run the Hospedería del Real Monasterio at the rear of the monastery, around the cloisters. Public rooms are art objects, the cloisters are sublime, but the bedrooms were monk cells, and tiny. The cost is tiny too—under $40.

CENTRAL SPAIN

Dining

The dining room looks out on lovely gardens, whose terrace serves as an addition to the restaurant when weather permits. Azulejo tiles and ceramic plates are the decoration. Here we recommend simple tomato soup that tastes nothing like the Campbell's we grew up on. But in general the food is not adventuresome. Roast kid, soupy rice, codfish, lamb on a spit, and chicken about cover the menu. For a treat, look for chestnut pudding *(pudding de castañas)*, which sometimes is available. A full meal should come in at about $15, plus drinks.

Alternative Dining

Cerezo   ★

> *Gregorio López, 20 (about a block east and uphill from the monastery),* ☎ *(927) 15 41 77.* For food this hearty and tasty, the price of $15 or less is a true bargain. Soups are especially good, as are the stews. Credit Cards: A, D, V.

Directions

You arrive at the plaza in front of the Monastery where signs direct a short distance to the parador.

Paradors Nearby

Trujillo: 80 km	Oropesa: 90 km	Jarandilla: 120 km
Cáceres: 130 km	Mérida 130 km	Zafra: 190 km

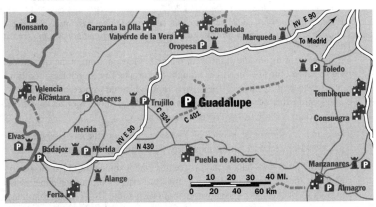

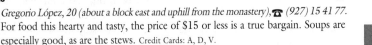

Sights

Legend has it that a shepherd found a cow, apparently dead, in the mountains beside the Guadalupe River at the beginning of the 13th-century. As he knelt to examine the beast, Mary suddenly appeared exhorting him to summon the priest, for a sacred image of herself lay buried beneath the animal. The cow revived, and a blackened three-feet-high image of the Virgin Mary holding Jesus soon was unearthed—the Black Virgin of Guadalupe.

Alfonso XI invoked the aid of this icon during a crucial engagement with the Moors 50 years later. After victory, he built a grand monastery for her sanctuary which became a famous pilgrimage center. Here Isabella and Ferdinand signed the documents authorizing Columbus' explorations, and Columbus brought Indians from the Americas to be baptized in the fountain in front of the church. In gratitude for their successes, the Conquistadores heaped riches on the church of this Virgin to make it the most richly adorned in Spain. Yet, by the 19th century the monastery was abandoned by the monks who had inhabited it, and it fell into disrepair. Franciscan friars took it over at the start of the present century to restore its former glory. Once again it has become a center of pilgrimages as the symbol of **hispanidad**, the cultural ties linking Spain with Latin America.

Though there are no monuments to see other than the monastery and its church, the village surrounding the monastery has been famed for copperwork for centuries. Products are on sale in numerous little shops.

Monasterio Guadalupe   ★★★

Pl. de Santa Mará de Guadalupe, ☎ *(927) 36 70 0.*
Hours open: daily 9:30 a.m.–1 p.m. and 3:30–7 p.m.
Although the core of the building is late 14th-century, additions were made though the 18th. The complex is a jumble because geography crowded each addition within a limited perimeter.

The **fountain** in the middle of the picturesque Pl. Mayor in front of the church was used to baptize the first Americans brought to Europe. The church facade is flamboyant 15th-century Gothic. Two towers in rough stone with crenuled battlements guard either side, and fortress walls surround the whole. Bronze doors from the 15th century illustrate the events of Mary's life.

The church may be toured on one's own for free; the tour of the monastery requires a guide and fee. Entrance for the monastery tour is through the arcade to the left.

The **church** proper was built in the 14th century and is among the oldest monastery churches in the country. The interior retains its original proportions and dimensions, almost hidden under later decorative additions such as the 18th-century balustrade

at the top of the nave and 16th-century wrought iron grille fac
classical retable is 17th-century work by El Greco's son and anoth

In a splendid dress (changed daily), the Black Virgin, the reason for all
looks down from on high, illuminated by spotlights.

The tour of the **monastery** comes first to a 15th-century Mudejar-style cloister with two stories of horseshoe arches. A tiled brick fountain in the center wears a complex spire. The former rectory displays a collection of extravagant church vestments, all sewn by the former Hieronymite monks with exquisitely rich and ornate handwork. A fine Gothic cloister lies beyond. Although not normally included in the tour, it can be seen from the hotel Hospedería next door.

The Chapterhouse, with fine artesonado ceiling, stores medieval choirbooks, some with delicate illustrations. Paintings are displayed as well, including small panels by Zurbarán. The tour passes through the church next, along the second floor choir (note the organ cases), to enter a splendid 17th-century sacristy.

Here is the only series of Zurbarán's paintings remaining in the place for which they were designed—a truly remarkable group of eight works. The room itself is sumptuous with mirrors and gilt and shows the simplicity of these paintings in a far different way than would the plain walls of a museum.

The tour then wends through a series of chapels, each more ornate than the last. In the first is another fine Zurbarán, after the next comes an octagonal room with ornate reliquaries. Rich jasper stairs lead up to a room with interesting full length paintings of Biblical figures by the 17th-century Neapolitan, Luca Giorano. Finally the tour enters the closet-sized 17th-century *Camarin*. A garish marble dais spins, and the Virgin herself is there. *Admission: 300 ptas., for the guided tour in Spanish of approximately one hour.*

Excursions

Trujillo, **Cáceres** and **Mérida** are easily reached from Guadalupe. See directions and a description under the appropriate paradors in this chapter. **Toledo** is less than 200 km away on C-401.

151

PARADOR DE MANZANARES

Autovia N-IV, km 174, Manzanares, 13200
☎ *(926) 61 04 00, FAX (926) 61 09 35*
$75 per double; 50 rooms: 50 doubles

★ ★ ★

CENTRAL SPAIN

T his pleasant modern hacienda-style hotel, the Spanish equivalent of our motels, beckons travelers on their way to Andalusia. It provides a comfortable overnight stop to break the long drive. Although attractively white, clean and crisp, you will find nothing memorable, which is as it should be given the purpose. It does offer a pool encased in a well-manicured lawn.

Dining

The dining room is not memorable either, though tasteful. The food is pleasant thanks to good local vegetables, but the menu covers only the usual parador fare. What is different is lower prices—less than $20, plus drinks.

Directions

From **Madrid** take N-IV south 176 km. From **Toledo** take C-400 south to Madriodejos in 68 km to join N-IV south for 57 km.

Paradors Nearby

Almagro: 32 km	Toledo: 123 km	Chinchón: 146 km
Albacete: 154 km	Jaén: 159 km	Úbeda: 161 km

PARADOR DE SALAMANCA

Teso de la Feria, 2, Salamanca, 37008
☎ *(923) 26 87 00, FAX (923) 21 54 08*
$100 per double; 108 rooms: 10 singles, 94 doubles, 4 suites

★ ★

Although the city of Salamanca is one of our favorites, its parador is not. It is a modern building; in fact, it is one of the first of the modern paradors, and beginning to show its age. It looks rather like an office building, and is too far outside of town for walking. However, the reception is very professional and helpful, and the spacious rooms include enclosed balconies with views of the city. So, it is a not a bad place to stay if you don't mind a mile walk or taxi ride to town. On its behalf we should add that the reception area consists of soaring spaces and the parador provides a pool and tennis courts.

Alternative Accommodations

Hotel Residencia Rector

Paseo del Rector Esperabe, 10, ☎ *(923) 21 84 82, FAX (923) 21 40 08. 13 rooms, plus one suite.*

The Hotel Residencia Rector is one of our favorite hotels in all Spain; its only problem is that others have discovered it and it accepts only a few guests. Before1990 it was a private mansion, when its owners decided to open the lower floors to the public. As it happens, the Ferran family and their architect have utterly exquisite taste. They planned rooms in which you can stay, but so beautiful and comfortable that it demeans them to apply hotel standards. Bedrooms are huge and decorated in perfect taste with no thought to saving costs anywhere. For this the charge is no more than at the parador. However, since the establishment is small and family-run it does not offer the services of larger hotels, and is thus called a *residencia*.

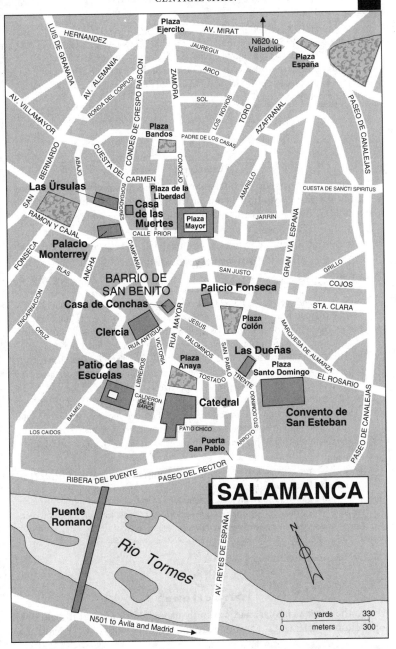

Amefa

Pozo Amarillo, 8 (two blocks northeast of the Pl. Mayor on the street parallel to C. Azafranal), ☎ *(923) 21 81 89, FAX (923) 26 02 00. 33 rooms.*

For half the price you can enjoy a modest sized, clean room close to the sights at the Amefa, another family-owned hotel. You cannot do better in Salamanca for anything close to this low price. Service is willing and friendly, though English-speaking staff are not always available.

Dining

The dining room is also modern, and large, as it must be for so many guests. Softly lit in pastels, it is not unattractive. But since it is so large, it must cater to the tastes of the masses, which means generally bland food. Stick to plain fish or meat. One nice aspect of this parador is a decent list of fine wines from Ribera de Duero. A full meal will average $20, plus drinks.

Alternative Dining

Chez Victor   ★★★★

Espoz y Mina, 26 (Pl. de la Libertad is a small park north of Pl. Mayor, at whose west end is the restaurant), ☎ *(923) 21 31 23. Closed Sunday night, Monday, and August.*

Chef Victoriano learned his craft in France and brought the lessons home to produce some of the most sublime cooking in Spain. The restaurant itself is just a rectangle leaving all focus on ample tables set attractively with fine linen and china. The final decoration is food as exquisite to the eye as to the palate. Entrees change with the season, but if rape (skate of lovely chewy texture), or magrite of duck are available, they deserve serious consideration. Appetizers are constant and both the *hojaldre de verduras y foie-gras con salsa de trufas* and *crab crepe* are outstanding. Desserts can be sublime and include exquisite chocolate mousse, sinful chocolate tart and delicate ice creams and sherbets. Reservations are strongly recommended. Costs will approach $50 per person, and will be worth it. Credit Cards: A, D, M, V.

Rio de la Plata   ★★

Pl. del Peso, 1 (just south of the Pl. Mayor, across from the Gran Hotel), ☎ *(923) 21 90 05. Closed Monday, and July.*

Cozy with dark wood and a fireplace, and usually crowded—a good sign—the menu ranges over Castilian dishes but excels in seafood. Ordering sea creatures, however, can push your bill into the expensive range. Credit Cards: M, V.

Directions

From the **north** a circular road, variously named, leads around the old hilltop section of Salamanca. Continue around the hilled city until arriving at a bridge over the Tormes River. Take the bridge, proceed to the traffic circle, and turn left. Make your first right into the drive for the parador. From **any other direction** you arrive on N-501 which reaches a large traffic circle. Take the road heading south to take the first right into the drive for the parador.

Paradors Nearby

Zamora: 65 km   Tordesillas: 85 km   Ciudad Rodrigo: 88 km
Ávila: 97 km   Gredos: 162 km

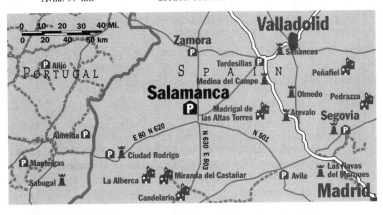

Sights

In 1215 Alfonso IX founded the second university in Spain here, which soon swallowed up the first in nearby Palencia, and Salamanca flourished as a university town. From this center Europe received the fruits of Arab science, which awakened it from the Dark Ages.

Salamanca became a kind of company town with the university as its prime employer and builder. It grew quickly, with most construction occurring from the 15th through the 16th century so it presents a remarkably homogeneous face. Indeed, it is a museum of Plateresque architecture, that curious Spanish appliqué of stone on plain facades, all heightened by the warm tones of the local sandstone.

During the 18th century, Salamanca fell on hard times. The university suffered as Spain grew paranoid about the dangers of Protestantism, demanding orthodoxy above inquiry which subverted educational standards. More recently, Salamanca served as the headquarters of the Nationalists during the early years of the Civil War. One night the university faculty was harangued by the Nationalist General Millán Astry about the necessity for blood and violence to purify the soul. After this diatribe, Miguel de Unamuno, rector of the university and renowned philosopher of religion, rose uninvited to rebut Millán's views as contrary to the principles of western civilization. The audience, with Generalissimo Franco in attendance, was offended by Unamuno's disagreement with a Nationalist hero. Soon after, Unamuno was fired from his position and placed under house-arrest for life. Today his spirit infuses the revitalized university, for it thrives, numbering 16,000 students, about twice its Renaissance complement.

With its golden buildings amid the unhurried pace of academe, Salamanca is a most inviting city. UNESCO considers it a world treasure.

Begin in the Patio de Las Escuelas for a lesson in the Plateresque. If climbing the hill from the river, this plaza is off the left side of C. Libros, which is the second true street—excluding an alley—going left.

The University   ★ ★ ★ ★

Patio de Las Escuelas, ☎ *(923) 29 44 00.*
Hours open: Mon.–Sat. 9:30 a.m.–1:30 p.m. and 4–7 p.m. Open Sun. and holidays 10 a.m.–1 p.m.

This patio dates from the dawn of the 16th century, a gift of Ferdinand and Isabella by unknown architects. On first entering the plaza the larger **Escuelas Mayores** is right, and the smaller **Escuelas Menores**, a kind of preparatory school for the main university, is to the left rear.

Above the double doors of the Mayores rises a great Plateresque work. The central medallion in the first register shows the benefactors, the Catholic Monarchs, with Isabella's face unidealized enough to be a genuine portrait. The middle register makes much of the double eagle crest of Carlos V, who reigned when the carving was finished, flanked by visages of the Emperor and his wife. From the top peer early founders and teachers of the university, flanked by Venus, Hercules and the Virtues. The carving deepens as it goes up to compensate for its greater distance from the viewer. The whole is a brilliant composition almost hidden by all the detail.

The slightly later frieze above the portal to the Menores school is simpler and more elegant, though not so daring or seminal. On the bare walls next to the Menores, red-painted names can still be discerned. These are the graffiti of Renaissance graduates, said to be written in bull's blood.

Through the portal of the Mayores, where the ticket of admission to both schools is purchased, one penetrates the sixth oldest university in the Western World. The Copernican system was taught first at this university, and Isabella sent Columbus here when she wanted scholarly judgment about his proposed trip. (Incidentally, the professors concluded that Columbus' ideas were based on faulty assumptions, as indeed they were.)

Salamanca employed the first known woman professor—Beatriz de Galindo—who taught Queen Isabella Latin. Famous students included the son of Isabella and Ferdinand, and the son of Felipe II, who suffered a concussion from falling down stairs in pursuit of a maid. Hernán Cortéz attended for one year before quitting to conquer Mexico. St. Ignatius Loyola, founder of the Jesuits, and Lope de Vega, one of Spain's greatest writers, both received degrees from Salamanca, and many say that Cervantes attended. At its height in the 16th century the university consisted of 25 departments and about 7000 students.

Enter the 15th-century cloisters covered by an original wooden ceiling of Mudejar work. Around the arcade ancient classrooms lead off. Next is the **paraninfo**, or assembly hall, still used for solemn ceremonies such as the opening of the academic term and the conferring of doctorates. The next hall is a 19th-century meeting room. One passes a doorway with a lovely Moorish ceiling above, then three rooms of little interest, followed by the **chapel**. Most arresting is its splendid ceiling, despite the fact that a large part of the original has been removed to a museum in the Menores School. Next comes a wonderful Plateresque **staircase** with elegant "star" vaulting above. Scenes carved on the balustrade change at each flight—from pages, knights and jesters, to matrimonial scenes, to, at the top, jousts and bull baiting. The second floor gallery retains a fine ceiling and lets into an old **library** with a rich frieze high up.

At the nearby **Escuelas Menores**, after passing through a Plateresque-topped portal, you enter a lovely, quiet patio, the small forerunner of every modern university's Quad. The scalloped arches, called **Salamancine**, that seem to reverse the expected figure and ground, are unattractive enough to be a style peculiar to this one town in Spain. To the right is a library with the finest Mudejar ceiling left in the university complex. Across the patio a modern building serves as a sort of **museum**. It houses the remainder of the ceiling from the Mayores' chapel, along with some nice primitive paintings, sophisticated works by Francisco Gallego, and, at the far end, part of a magnificent 15th-century frescoed ceiling of the *Zodiac*, a grand Renaissance work by native son Fernando Gallego. *Admission: 200 ptas.*

By retracing a few steps back up the C. Libreros to the first street going left, in one block is reached the Old Cathedral, right, and the New Cathedral adjoining, left. Along the way, note the walls topped with merlons, whether to keep students in or out is unclear.

New Cathedral and Old Cathedral ★★★★

Pl. Juan XXII, ☎ (923) 21 74 76. The entrance to the New Cathedral is on its northern face. The entrance to the Old Cathedral is from the first bay on the south inside the New Cathedral.
Hours open: daily 9:30 a.m.–1:30 p.m. and 3:30–6:30 p.m. (the Old Cathedral closes at 6 p.m. in winter).

Before rounding the **New Cathedral** to enter from the north side, it is impossible to avoid admiring the front, which is as extravagant a piece of late Gothic carving as ever you'll see. The foundation for the church was laid in 1513, and work finished 50 years later, though some additions were made as late as the 18th century after an earthquake weakened the cupola.

Inside, a narrow, lofty nave accompanies sweeping aisles on either side, divided by piers carved into delicate columns that rise to an elegant vaulted ceiling. Atop arches joining the piers runs a lovely balustrade punctuated by delicate medallions. The

coro contains flamboyant choirstalls designed by one of the Churriguera brothers, while the **trascoro** was designed by another. But the main monument to the Churriguera family, the **cupola** and its drum with baroque painted scenes of the life of the Virgin, is the work of both brothers together. A chapel in the apse at the right side displays a beautiful painted **Pieta** by Salvador Carmona.

A door from the first chapel on the south side leads to stairs descending to the **Old Cathedral**. Consecrated in 1160, it remains a museum of the Romanesque. The contrast with the New Cathedral is extreme. Undeniable elegance in the New Cathedral pales beside that of the Old, which had no need for the device of a narrow, high nave impossible, in any case, at such an early date. Subtly pointed arches on simple columns, with higher columns dividing each, rise to equally simple groining in the ceiling. And how lovely is the execution—see the charming, unobtrusive carvings on and above the capitals.

At the altar stands a sublime early 15th-century **retable** of 53 paintings, each in a frame. Above, in a half dome, a fresco of the Final Judgement leaps out of a striking black background. The statue of the Virgin on the altar is from the 12th century. Look up to the unusual lantern with its tiers of windows and flamboyant ribbing, an artwork on its own.

From the south transept a door leads to the **cloister**, largely reconstructed, from which chapels radiate. These were used as classrooms until the University Mayores was built in the 15th century. On the east side is the **Chapel de Talavera**, for those who still followed the church rites practiced in the time of the Visigoths. The Mudejar dome is admirable as is the altarpiece by Alonso Berruguete.

Next comes the **Santa Barbara Chapel** in which theology students took their final examinations, one at a time. The chair is original and much squirmed upon. Tradition had the students place their hands on the effigy of Bishop Lucero for inspiration and luck. What a dandy the Bishop is, with rings on every finger and fancy shoes.

The Council of Castile once met in the **Santa Catalina Chapel**, which now displays lovely paintings. The original **chapterhouse** contains a Diocesan museum and more paintings. Note the **Santa Catalina altar** by Gallego, a lovely small gold picture of *San Pedro y San Pablo*, and the *Virgin with a Rose* tryptic. On the second floor is a fine **altar** for St. Michael by Juan de Flanders, among other works.

The **Anaya Chapel** on the south side of the cloister is dedicated to San Bartolome. Here are founders' tombs of the finest 15th-century carving and a remarkable ceiling. Also in this chapel is an organ from the 14th century that may well be the oldest such surviving instrument, with lovely Mudejar inlay. *Admission: 200 ptas., to the Old Cathedral.*

Exit from the churches is into the peaceful Pl. de Anaya. The street going left, C. Tostado, downhill, leads to the wide C. San Pablo. Continuing straight on C. Concilio de Trento and passing the end of a large building on the left, the Las Dueñas Convent is reached.

Convento de las Dueñas   ★ ★

Pl. del Concilio de Trento, ☎ *(923) 21 54 42.*

Hours open: daily 10 a.m.–1 p.m. and 4–8 p.m. (until 7 p.m. in winter.)

The building was a palace donated to house a nunnery for women of the highest rank, hence the name Dueñas (Ladies). The convent church is faced with a nice Plateresque doorway, through which one enters the cloister, the only part of the convent open to the public. But this is no ordinary cloister. Constructed in the 16th century in the form of an irregular pentagon, the capitals of the second story gallery are carved with a profusion of grotesques from Dante's hell to excite our imagination and admiration. *Admission: 100 ptas.*

The large Convento de San Esteban, across the plaza, rises above a flight of stairs. Its facade is oddly shaped and luxuriantly carved.

Convento de San Esteban   ★ ★

Pl. del Concilio de Trento, *(923) 21 50 00.*
Hours open: daily 9 a.m.–1 p.m. and 4:30–8 p.m. (until 6 p.m. in winter.)

The original church was assigned to the Dominicans in 1524 when a flood destroyed their previous home. One of the brothers, Fra Alava, designed the present church at the height of the Plateresque movement. Planned to present its elaborate front as dramatically as possible, it lacks towers which might distract and leaves the sides bare. Above the portal is a round arch framing the stoning of St. Stephan, all contained in a huge recessed curved arch, with Christ on the cross at the top. Note the delicate upper frieze of children and horses. The portico to the right of the facade is elegant Renaissance.

Entrance to the church is through a door at the end of the portico which lets onto a cloister, then the church. The interior dates to the 17th century and is unusually simple, heavy and dark. The one note of brightness and the center of attention is the high altar by the most famous of the Churriguera family, José. Massive gilt circling vines with grapes twist their way up wood columns, so massive that they almost hide figures of prophets and angels. On high is a painting by Claudio Coello of the Martyrdom of St. Stephen. It is said that 4000 pine trees died for this altar. Nothing is easier to criticize today than such a riotous excess of gilt, but it must be admitted that from a distance the altar makes a dramatic statement. *Admission: 150 ptas.*

Return by C. Concilio de Trento on which you came for one block to the large straight C. San Pablo. A right turn brings you in five blocks to the **Plaza Mayor**.

Plaza Mayor   ★ ★

Designed in part by the Churriguera brothers, who created the churrigueresque, Spanish baroque, style, and finished in 1733 (though the most imposing building, the Ayuntamiento on the north side, was added in 1755), many people consider this the most beautiful plaza in Spain. One wonders whether they have ever been to Santiago de Compostela. In any case, the plaza is more harmonious than most, with a unity of design that offers a reasonable solution to the problem of placing three stories of building above an arched arcade. Attractive cafes and shops ring the plaza.

Mansion Walk   ★ ★

C. Prior lies outside the southwest corner of the Plaza Mayor. At the second crossing street turn right onto C. de Bordadores, in a few steps reaching the **Casa de las**

Muertes ★ on your right. Here is one of the earliest examples of what came to be called Plateresque, attributed to the great architect Gil de Siloé. The house belonged to the Archbishop Alonso de Fonseca whose portrait is carved over the window. When he died, his nephew had tiny skulls carved just under the top window jambs, lending the present name "Death" to the house.

Across the street and a few steps farther along is a statue to the philosopher **Unamuno** in front of the house, now a museum, in which he died under Franco's house arrest. Directly opposite the Casa de las Muertes, set back in a square is the **Convent of Las Ursulas** ★, with an octagonal turret topped by an elaborate balustrade. The convent was founded by the same Archbishop Fonseca who owned the Casa de las Muertes. He is buried inside in an elegant tomb by Gil de Siloé.

Back up the C. Prior is the **Monterrey Palace** ★. Turn right to see the elegant facade framed by two corner towers and topped by an openwork balustrade. The palace (now owned by the Duke of Alba) was built for the Count of Monterrey, who through marriage was connected to all the best families, including the Fonsecas of the Casa de las Muertes. The Count displayed the coats of arms of all these connections on his home. Across the street is the **Iglesia de la Purisima Concepcion** ★, founded by the same Count of Monterrey. Inside is a wonderful Ribera *Immaculate Conception* over the altar, and the tomb of the Count.

Back on C. de la Compañia one block further is the famed **Casa de las Conchas** ★ (House of the Shells). After the owner was appointed Chancellor of the Order of Santiago he was so proud that he placed 400 scallop shells, the symbol of the order, on the walls of his house. The main door is surmounted by a Salamancine arch in which lions hold a shield with a fleur-de-lis field, the crest of the owner. The shield is repeated at the house corner. On the opposite side of the street is the **Pontifical University**, also known as the Clerecia. This is a Jesuit College begun in 1617 and finished a century and a half later in a fine baroque design.

Return around the side of the Casa de las Conchas to enter the large Rua Mayor going northeast to the Pl. del Corralillo in two blocks that contains the **Iglesia San Martin** ★. The building was erected in the 12th century, though many additions were appended later, such as the Plateresque front. Inside is some lovely vaulting and nice Gothic tombs.

Excursions

Beside the Portuguese border, **Ciudad Rodrigo** ★ is a town full of history with a nice cathedral and castle. Not far north, **Zamora** ★ ★ has Romanesque churches reminiscent of the Old Cathedral in Salamanca, and a castle besides. Nearer to hand are both **Ávila** of the wondrous walls and **Segovia** of the Disneyland castle.

PARADOR DE SEGOVIA

Carretera N-601, s/n, Segovia, 40003
☎ *(921) 44 37 37, FAX (921) 43 73 62*
$110 per double 113 rooms: 5 singles, 100 doubles, 8 suites

★ ★ ★ ★

T his is one of the modern paradors. It tries to impress with design by looking like an oversided Swiss chalet, and actually succeeds in the attempt. Smooth, polished stone floors contrast oddly and well with exposed brick and unexpected spaciousness. Public areas are landscaped with contemporary sculpture and crafts, and the staff is efficient, organized and helpful. Everything is clean, if somehow institutional. Ample bedrooms all overlook aged Segovia for postcard views. This parador offers every facility from indoor swimming pool to new tennis courts and gym, but is situated in nowhere'sville, a mile from the old town.

Alternative Accommodations

Los Linajes

C. Dr. Velasco, 9 (follow the street to the right, when facing the Alcázar), ☎ *(921) 43 04 75, FAX (921) 46 04 79. 55 rooms.*

You can do better for less at Los Linajes, and stay on the hill where you sightsee. The facade is 11th-century, a former palace of nobles named Falconis. Inside, attractively decorated, it has the cozy feel of small spaces. All rooms present glorious views, and the staff could not be more helpful. This is the best place to stay in town, at half the parador's cost. Parking is provided for a fee at the foot of the hotel outside the city walls, but hard to find.

Las Sirenas

Juan Bravo, 30 (opposite Pl. San Martin, a few doors past Juan Bravo's purported house),
☎ *(921) 43 40 11, FAX (921) 43 06 33. 39 rooms.*
Without the history or views, Las Sirenas offers faded luxury at a rock bottom $50.
Attractiveness starts with a spacious lobby and continues to a lounge with a fireplace. Bedrooms are comfortable, if unmemorable, and include TVs.

Dining

The dining room has architectural interest and presents lovely views over Segovia. The intelligent chef keeps things simple and succeeds better than the average parador. Start with hearty soup *(sopa castellana)*, graduate to piglet cooked over a wood fire *(cochinillo asado al horno de leña)*, the signature dish of Segovia. Save room for some sweet desserts. In summer the menu grows more varied with added local delicacies. There is a good selection of nice Rivera del Duero wines, but for a treat try the little known local wine, Rueda. The tariff should not pass $25, minus wine.

Alternative Dining

Mesón de Cándido   ★★

Pl. Azoguejo, 5, ☎ *(921) 42 59 11.*
Thanks to the showmanship of its former owner, this is one of the most famous restaurants in Spain. Lodged in an old inn, parts of which go back to the 15th-century, it consists of small timbered rooms with fireplaces, displaying the memorabilia of years. The specialty is Castilian roasts of piglet or milk-lamb whose tenderness is proved by slicing the carcass with a dinner plate. The meat is truly flavorful, but it could only be so tender if overcooked. Trout is tasty, as is garlic soup, and the house wine is quite good. Expect to pay a little more than at the parador. Reserve on weekends. Credit Cards: A, D, M, V.

José María   ★★

C. Cronista Lecea, 11 (a short block on the street leading east out of the Pl. Mayor),
☎ *(921) 43 44 84.*
This time the restaurant is modern, but it still does a mean suckling pig cut with a dinner plate as at Cándido. The difference is that the chef here does other dishes well too. Frogs' legs and fish are good, as are the blood sausage, or the special eggs as appetizer. The house red wine is delicious, the white more ordinary. For dessert order an orange and watch the waiter cut it artfully before you are transported by the taste. Raspberry cream with walnuts isn't bad either. You will pay the same prices as at Cándito. Reservations recommended. Credit Cards: A, D, M, V.

La Taurina   ★

Pl. Mayor, 8, ☎ *(921) 43 05 77.*

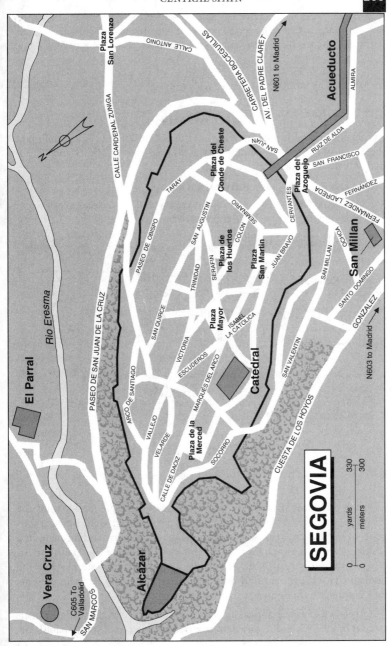

SEGOVIA

yards 330
meters 300
0 0

Acueducto

N601 to Madrid
AV. DEL PADRE CLARET
CARRETERA BOCEGUILLAS
CALLE ANTONIO
Plaza San Lorenzo
ALMIRA

SAN JUAN
RUIZ DE ALDA
Plaza del Azoguejo
SAN FRANCISCO
Plaza del Conde de Cheste
CALLE CARDENAL ZUNIGA
TARAY
FERNANDEZ LADREDA
FERNANDEZ
CERVANTES
SEMINARIO
SAN AUGUSTIN
Plaza de los Huertos
COLON
Plaza San Martín
San Millán
SAN MILLAN
OCHOA
PASEO DE OBISPO
SERAFIN
TRINIDAD
JUAN BRAVO
SANTO DOMINGO
GONZALEZ
PASEO DE SAN JUAN DE LA CRUZ
SAN QUIRCE
Plaza Mayor
ISABEL LA CATOLICA
N603 to Madrid
Rio Eresma
VICTORIA
ESCUDEROS
Catedral
SAN VALENTIN
ARCO DE SANTIAGO
MARQUES DEL ARCO
El Parral
VALLEJO
VELARDE
Plaza de la Merced
SOCORRO
CUESTA DE LOS HOYOS
CALLE DE DAOIZ
Vera Cruz
C605 To Valladolid
SAN MARCOS
Alcázar

Yes, this is yet another place for roasts like the preceding, with an attempt at the same ambience, though at even lower prices. Ordering from the special menu can make this an inexpensive meal, and the food can be very good. Credit Cards: A, D, M, V.

Directions

From the central Pl. del Azoguejo at the bottom of the old city hill, take the center of three roads fanning east, following signs to N-601 and Valladolid. Then watch for the parador sign.

Paradors Nearby

Ávila: 65 km   Tordesillas: 116 km   Toledo: 158 km
Salamanca: 162 km   Sigüenza: 218 km

Sights

Take a ride around Segovia's perimeter following signs designating the "Ruta Panorámica" before entering the town to appreciate the unusual situation of the old city, thrust precipitously above the surrounding plain in a slender ellipse. Its appearance has often been likened to a ship, with the Alcázar at the prow and the towers of the Cathedral at the stern, while the original city walls run around most of its length. No city in Spain presents such a dramatic appearance, not even Toledo.

Segovia began as Sogobriga, a major town of the Celts. The Romans captured it in 80 B.C. and it grew into one of their most important Spanish cities which they favored with a great engineering feat by constructing an aqueduct two thirds of a mile long to lift water up from the Rio Riofrio. What is remarkable is that the elevation of the city required the aqueduct to rise 95 feet (ten stories) above the ground. Miraculously, the aqueduct remains in perfect condition 2000 years later and could still be used today to supply the city's water.

After reconquest from the Moors, Segovia became the royal capital for a brief period. Its greatest moment occurred when the grandees of Spain met in the Alcázar to designate Isabella the monarch after her half-brother Enrique IV died, passing over his heir, La Beltraneja, as illegitimate. By this time the Alcázar was centuries old, stretching back to Moorish times if not to the age of the Romans.

Segovia is a city that once was important but could not find continued reasons to remain so. Though by no means poor, its population today is less by 20 percent than at its height in Renaissance times. Tourism is the main revenue producer.

Parking is an unsolved problem, especially in summer when hordes descend. Little space is available on the hill, and none at all in the main plaza below, Pl. Azoguejo (with the aqueduct). All we can suggest is to keep eyes peeled for any spot as you near the hill and to be prepared to walk some distance. Our tour of the old city starts in the Pl. Azoguejo, so we direct you there.

From **Madrid** turn right onto Carretera de San Rafael at the major intersection where four large avenues converge. After passing the bullring, go left onto Av. del Padre Claret, which brings you to the large Pl. Azoguejo with the aqueduct in a few blocks. From **Ávila** and **Salamanca** no changes of road are necessary. Unless you turn away, you will end up in the Pl. Azoguejo. From **Burgos** or **Valladolid** no changes of road are necessary either; unless you intentionally deviate, you will end up in the Pl. Azoguejo.

Outside the Walls: Vera Cruz, San Millán, El Parral

Go southwest from Pl. Azoguejo on Av. Fernández Ladreda, following signs to N-110 and Ávila. In three blocks the small church of **San Millán** with a side porch, set back in its tiny square, is passed. After San Millán continue on Av. Ladreda to the second street going right, Paseo Ezequiel González, which runs beside the elevated old town and provides lovely views. When it crosses the river, turn right for a moment onto C-605 heading to Segovia, and take the second left to **La Vera Cruz** sitting atop a hill. Return to C-605 again toward Segovia, which is named Paseo de San Juan after it crosses the river. The first left across the river takes you to **El Parral** Monastery.

San Millán   ★★

    Av. Fernández Ladreda, ☎ *(921) 43 43 88.*
    Hours open: daily 11 a.m.–1 p.m. (only for services in winter).

San Millán is the oldest (perhaps 11th century), purest Romanesque church in Segovia and one of the more charming designs in Spain. The porch outside was a place where important meetings were held; the Mudejar tower is an 11th century addition. Instead of thicker walls, external columns supporting the bays of the apse become architectural features—a local peculiarity of other Romanesque churches in Segovia. Inside, massive columns are topped with capitals carved in lively Biblical scenes. Newer baroque decoration has just been removed, uncovering marvelous Romanesque frescoes.

Vera Cruz Chapel   ★★

Carretera de Zamarramala, ☎ *(921) 43 14 75.*
Hours open: Tues.–Sun. 10:30 a.m.–1:30 p.m. and 3–7 p.m. (until 6 p.m. in winter). Closed Mon. and holidays.

From the outside one can see that this is an unusual church—a polygon instead of the expected rectangle or cruciform shape. It was erected by the Knights Templar in the 13th century as a place for their rites, many of which were secret. In 1226 Pope Honore gave the church a piece of the True Cross, so the name was changed to La Vera Cruz. Inside, one finds a central chamber, circular in shape and two stories tall. Stairs lead up to the second story in which novice knights performed vigils while overlooking the altar. The surrounding nave is plain, except for faded 13th-century frescoes. The place has a lovely feel of age. Stairs beside the altar lead up the tower for nice views of Segovia. *Admission: 150 ptas.*

El Parrel Monastery   ★

C. de Marqués de Villena, ☎ *(921) 43 12 98.*
Hours open: Tues.–Sun. 10 a.m.–1 p.m. and 3–6:30 p.m. (until 6 p.m. in winter.) Closed Mon. and holidays.

The facade, never completed, shows two unusual soaring columns with clustered niches at the bottom still waiting to be filled by statues. The church was built in the middle 15th century by Juan Pacheco in homage to the Virgin for her help in winning a duel. The Plateresque interior contains a sensitive reredo of Juan Pacheco praying on one side, his wife on the other. In the transept rests a Gothic effigy of his illegitimate sister beside a lovely flamboyant door to the sacristy.

Aqueduct   ★★

A channel in the Sierra de Fuenfria, over 11 miles away, starts water on its way to Segovia. But the land descends into a valley as it approaches the heights of the old town, so the Romans raised the water with an aqueduct to carry it up to the hill. The structure of massive granite blocks secured by physics, not mortar, was completed in the first century B.C., during the reign of the Emperor Trajan (who was born in Spain). Each block contains indentations for gripping by pincers to raise them into place. The aqueduct runs for two-thirds of a mile, reaching its greatest height of 95 feet in the Pl. del Azoguejo. It no longer functions, despite claims by the tourist authorities, but looks as if it could.

Inside the Walls

From the Pl. del Azoquejo ascend the hill by the pedestrian walk C. Cervantes, running northwest. As it goes slightly right at the top entering C. Juan Bravo, the strange

Casa de los Picos lies left. This 14th-century fortified mansion was studded profusely with faceted protrusions a century later to produce an armored effect. C. Juan Bravo continues past the 14th-century palace of the **Condes de Alpuente**, set back left, with nice windows and plaster decoration, then past a restored former public granary down stairs to the left, before entering the well-preserved **Pl. San Martin** ★.

Facing the plaza, opposite his statue in the center, is a Gothic house reputed to be that of **Juan Bravo** who led the uprising of the Comuneros in the 16th century. Other mansions surround the square, most interesting for their entrances. The house of the **Marqués de Moya** places intricate stucco designs around an utterly plain Romanesque door of massive stones; the Palace of the **Marqués of Lozoya** presents a Romanesque arched doorway fit for a church; and the **Palace of Quintanar** has an arched door surmounted by a row of curious helmets. In the center stands the 12th-century Romanesque **San Martin** ★, framed by a fine porch, and with nice carving on the front portal toward the west.

Continue on Juan Bravo pass the 18th-century prison, now the archives for the city. One block later pass the 16th-century church of **San Miguel** to the left, then take the right fork into the **Plaza Mayor** (a.k.a. Plaza José Antonio), lined with cafes. On its west side stands the Cathedral.

CENTRAL SPAIN

Cathedral ★★

Pl. Mayor, ☎ *(921) 43 53 25.*
Hours open: weekdays 9:30 a.m.–1 p.m. and 3–6 p.m. Open weekends and holidays 9:30 a.m.–6 p.m. Open in summer daily 9 a.m.–7 p.m.
When their old Cathedral near the Alcázar burned in the 16th century, the city fathers hired the Hontañons, father and son, who had achieved success with their neoclassical New Cathedral in Salamanca, but instructed them to design a Gothic

building. This the architects did with flair, producing the last great Gothic church but with occasional Plateresque gestures. The entrance to the Cathedral is from the Plaza Mayor into the north transept.

The Cathedral impresses with soaring spaces, perfect lines, nice vaulting and light, though the trascoro is nothing but a distraction. Moreover, the flamboyantly decorated chapels are not of great merit, with the exception of a nice retablo by Juan de Juni and a triptych in the La Piedad chapel, first off the south aisle.

A door in the south transept leads to the cloister, reconstructed stone by stone from the cloister of the former cathedral. As you enter, step over the tombs of the Hontañons who designed the Cathedral. The chapterhouse off the cloister has a late Mudejar ceiling in striking white and gold. Dramatic 17th-century Brussels tapestries are displayed, most of them designed by Rubens. *Admission: 200 ptas., for the cloister and museum.*

Facing the front of the church, head right down c. Daoiz, lined with souvenir shops, to number 9.

Museo de Holográfica   ★

C. Daoiz, 9.
Hours open: Tues.–Sun. 10:30 a.m.–2 p.m. and 4–7:30 p.m. Closed Mon. and holidays.
Three-dimensional holographs of scary creatures are appropriately presented in a 15th-century cellar. Kids enjoy the experience almost as much as their parents. *Admission: 220 ptas.*

Follow c. Daoiz to its end, then right past **San Andres** along R. Socorro which brings the gardens of the Alcázar 4 blocks with the castle itself ahead.

Alcázar   ★★★

Pl. de La Reina Victoria Eugenia, ☎ (921) 43 01 76.
Hours open: Daily 10 a.m.–7 p.m. (until 6 p.m. in winter.) Closed holidays.
Though it appears to be the archetypal medieval castle, the interior today is mainly artifice. In the 14th century a former Moorish Alcázar, was made into a Christian castle. Here Princess Isabella was first proclaimed queen of Spain. Most of Spain's medieval kings stayed at least a while; Prince Charles of England, later King Charles I, enjoyed a visit; and the fourth marriage of Felipe II was celebrated inside. But in 1862, after Carlos III turned the old palace into an artillery school, a fire gutted the interior. Today, except for the entrance tower, the inside is a fanciful 19th-century reconstruction. If taken with a grain of salt, it remains fun to wander through.

Inside, furniture of the period, much armor, and some nice frescoes of medieval themes are displayed. The "King's Bedroom" is evocative and gives a sense of how tapestries were used to insulate cold stone walls, showing the profusion of colors in a medieval castle. The throne room is a 19th-century fantasy of how state rooms should look. *Admission: 350 ptas.*

From the Alcázar gardens go straight for a few steps, then follow C. de Velarde, the left fork, which wends for three blocks before changing its name to C. Pozuelo as it bends left to enter the Pl. de San Esteban. **San Esteban** ★ is yet another lovely Segovian Romanesque church with a beautiful side gallery. It is the latest (13th century) of Segovia's Romanesque churches, and perhaps the most harmonious of all, prefaced by an elegantly thin front tower. The **Bishop's Palace** opposite is covered with curious reliefs.

Continue across the plaza to pick up C. Vitoria heading east, passing the **Casa de los Hierro**, with an intricate 16th-century entrance and grotesques, in one block on the left. The street changes its name to C. Valdelaguila as, on the left, it passes the **Casa de Hercules**, a Dominican convent named for the mighty figure on its tower. A block later the street changes its name to C. Trinidad as it passes the open and austere **San Trinidad**, yet another Romanesque church. One block later the street passes through the Pl. de Guevara, merging in another block with C. San Augustin. Then it passes a 16th-century mansion housing the **Museo Provincial del Bellas Artes**, before entering, two blocks later, the **Pl. del Conde de Cheste ★**, surrounded by mansions, past which is the aqueduct's end and stairs descending back to the Pl. Azoguejo.

Excursions

Guadalupe, Toledo, Trujillo, Cáceres, Ávila and Mérida all are near enough to visit. Simply reverse the directions above. Nearer at hand is a 17th-century palace—**La Granja ★★★**, with lovely gardens and extravagant fountains.

From Pl. Azoguejo take the southernmost of the two streets forking east, Av. del Padre Claret, following signs to N-601 and Madrid. As the bullring comes into view, stay left. After 11 km, signs lead you to San Ildefonso and La Granja.

La Granja Palace

Hours open: daily 10 a.m.–1 p.m. and 3–5:30 p.m. (Sun. closes at 2 p.m.) Gardens: open daily from 10 a.m. to sunset. Check with the Segovia Office of Tourism for the time of the fountain show (in summer, usually at 5:30 p.m.).

When, at the beginning of the 18th century, Felipe V, cousin to the King of France, received the Spanish throne, he built this reminder of home, his Versailles. With classic Gallic understatement, he named it La Granja, "the farm." Name aside, it looks very much the French palace, especially from the back, and overlooks splendid gardens, both formal and wild, that stretch to the horizon past a series of fountains that provide about the best waterworks display you'll ever see.

Unfortunately the interior of the palace suffered from fire at the beginning of our century. The reconstructed results are still worth a look for their Versailles-like vistas through room after room and for the vast tapestry collection. In the chapel lie the tombs of Felipe V and his queen, Isabel Farnese. *Admission: 500 ptas.*

But the main attraction is the gardens and, in summer, the incredible sunset display when the fountains go on, one by one, until Fuente La Fama, the last, shoots water 130 feet in the air. *Admission: 300ptas.*

CENTRAL SPAIN

PARADOR DE VIRREY TOLEDO

Plaza del Palacio, 1, Oropesa, 45460
☎ *(925) 43 00 00, FAX (925) 43 07 77*
$90 per double; 48 rooms: 2 singles, 42 doubles, 4 suites
★ ★ ★ ★

An unusually homogeneous fortified residence was raised here in the 14th-century by the Counts of Toledo. A century later one of the Counts became the Viceroy of Peru, hence the parador's name (*Virrey* means Viceroy). In 1930 this became the first of the historical paradors, though a recent refurbishment brought it up to modern comfort standards. Monolithically square in plan but flanked by one round and one square tower for relief, the place feels solid indeed. You can visit remains of a small renaissance palace on the grounds. The patio served as a bullring in former times. The interior is more authentic than most historical paradors because the remodeling gutted less of the original architecture. Most of the floors are 500-years-old and the spaces generally retain their original detail and character. You can sense how pleasant it was to be a count in those days. Fine views extend over the unspoiled Gredos Valley from many of the rooms. The bedrooms that do not overlook the valley, look over the patio, which is no great sacrifice. There is even a pool for a dip.

Dining

The dining room is dramatic and Renaissance in feeling, presided over by a wonderful towering peaked wood ceiling and generously sized tables spread around a white rectangular space. The old tile floors glow. What is truly special about this parador restaurant, however, is that it serves as a restaurant school for the others. Understandably, therefore, the food here is probably the best of any of the paradors. Wonderful things happen to game at this place, as well as to more familiar pork, lamb and goat. Go with any specials on the menu, but pheasant *(perdiz)* Oropesana or steak *(solomillo)* Virrey should always be available. The tart *(tarta del Beato Alonso)* is delectable. Enhance the meal with a nice bottle of Valdepeñas. For such food a tariff of $25, plus drinks is most reasonable.

Directions

From **Madrid** take N-V west to Legartera in 132 km. Oropesa lies 2 km east of this town. From **Toledo** take C-502 west for 81 km to join N-V west for 32 km to Legartera and Oropesa just outside the town. From **Guadalupe** take the road north for 71 km to Mavalmoral de la Mata, where N-V is joined going east to Legartera for 31 km and the parador. From **Trujillo** take N-V east to Legartera in 107 km. Oropesa lies 2 km east of this town. From **Cáceres** and **Mérida** follow directions to Trujillo, then onward as above.

Paradors Nearby

Guadalupe: 90 km	Toledo: 102 km	Trujillo: 102 km
Gredos: 103 km	Ávila: 145 km	Jarandilla: 200 km

Sights

The sights here are the castle you are staying in. The little town of Oropesa does have two nice old churches, however, and attractive pottery is sold at various stores. Lagartera, 2 km away, is famed for its women's embroidery. Each cottage contains a display, from napkins to tablecloths to skirts.

Excursions

Guadalupe, Toledo, Trujillo, Cáceres, Ávila and Mérida all are near enough to visit. Simply reverse the directions above.

CENTRAL SPAIN

PARADOR ENRIQUE II

Plaza del Castillo, 2, Ciudad Rodrigo, 37500
☎ *(923) 46 01 50, FAX (923) 46 04 04*
$95 per double; 27 rooms: 26 doubles, 1suite

★ ★ ★

This parador provides a pleasant stopover for travelers on their way to Portugal. The fortress housing this parador was built in the 13th century by Enrique Trastámara, ancestor of both Queen Isabella and King Ferdinand. One original imposing tower remains inside the walls along with a low-slung building with a modern addition that houses the present parador. Pleasantly covered by ivy, the old and modern parts of the parador blend smoothly. Much of the ancient character was lost in the renovation but replaced by a tasteful and warm decor. Room 10 in the old part, the more expensive suite, sports a dramatic domed roof. Four bedrooms in the new part include pleasant views over lovely terraced gardens in the rear of the parador.

Dining

Spacious in feeling, crowned by timbered ceiling and graced by a sweeping arch, the dining room is very comfortable, and, in this case, serves the best food in town. Featured is a special six course menu that promotes regional dishes, ends with a sampling of desserts and includes aperitif and coffee. Á la carte choices begin with oxtail soup or marinated salmon, followed by a lovely stuffed shoulder of lamb *(paletilla de cordero relleno)* or a fish dish, such as halibut *(mero)* or turbot *(rodaballo)*. For dessert order a sampling of homemade cookies. A Pesquera or Mauro will top off the meal, which will average $20, plus drinks.

Directions

Parador signs will direct you to the parador near the Plaza Mayor, but you can simply head for the medieval tower of the parador atop its hill.

Paradors Nearby

Salamanca: 88 km	Zamora: 150 km	Cáceres: 158 km
Gredos: 171 km	Ávila: 185 km	Jarandilla: 230 km

Sights

Atop its hill, the city still looks like the frontier outpost it always was, with circling ramparts and a square-towered castle. Its name "Rodrigo City" comes from Count Rodrigo Gonzalez Giron who repopulated the town in the 12th-century after defeating the Moors who had held it for centuries.

A grand **Cathedral** ★ begun in the late 12th century received its last addition, the apse, in the 16th. The fine west portal contains quaint carvings of the Last Supper. Pleasant sculpture and strikingly grotesque choir stalls decorate the solid interior. The cloister off the north side consists of columns whose capitals represent fine Romanesque work. A pure Plateresque door opens at the east.

The **Plaza Mayor** is picturesque, with a former 15th-century mansion, now the Ayuntamiento, using towers to anchor its arcade. Near the northern rampart is the long 15th-century **Palace of Los Castros** ★, faced by Plateresque twisted columns. The 18th-century city **ramparts** ★ near the parador can be climbed. These were the latest design in military architecture, featuring a star-shaped wall to concentrate attackers for artillery barrages.

Excursions

For **Guarda** with its surrounding fortress in Portugal take n-620 west for 27 k to the border, then N-16 to Guarda in 80 km. **Salamanca** is 89 k east on N-620.

CENTRAL SPAIN

PARADOR LA MANCHA

Carretera Nacional, Km 251, 1, Albacete, 02000
☎ *(967) 22 94 50, FAX (967) 435 98 69*
$102 per double; 70 rooms: 3 singles, 67 doubles

★

This parador serves as a gateway to the south, a place to break a long drive. Relatively new (1970), it is designed for relaxing around a pool. With its low white walls and orange tile roof, the building suggests a hacienda on the plains of Andalusia circling a central courtyard. Comfortably large bedrooms (overdue for repainting) overlook the pool, each with a terrace outside. Two tennis courts, unfortunately, have been around for a while. The parador serves its purpose, but is nothing more than a convenient place to spend a night—with a pool for a quick dip—before continuing onward.

Dining

The dining room is functional and bright, but the sporting decor is no asset. The cuisine combines Castilian roasted meats with Andalusian dishes. *Pisto* (like ratatouille) or flavorful *gazpacho manchego* make tasty appetizers, followed by pheasant *(perdiz)* or rabbit *(conejo)* for a treat. Desserts include pears *(higos)* and custard *(natillas)*. La Mancha wines, which are enjoyable when young, are featured. A full meal will average $20, plus drinks.

Directions

On N-301, 5 k east of Albacete.

Paradors Nearby

Alarcón: 90 km   Cuenca: 142 km

PARADOR MARQUÉS DE VILLENA

Av. Amigos de los Castillos, 3, Alarcón, 16213
☎ *(969) 33 13 50, FAX (969) 33 11 07*
$120 per double; 13 rooms: 1 single, 12 doubles

★ ★ ★ ★

This is the hotel people dream of. Perched atop a massive crag stands a veritable 13th-century fortress, complete with tower. A tiny village clusters around it, girded by crenulated walls, all circled by a river. Fish or hike at huge Lake Alarcón, only three miles away.

The castle exudes history. It was built soon after the Christians stormed a Moorish fortress here at the end of the 12th century. By the 15th century the territory had come into the hands of the Marqués de Villena. When Queen Isabella decided she wanted to be more than a feudal lord relying on policy approval from her nobles, the lords of the realm rebelled against her, led by the marqués. This fortress saw battle after battle between the fabled Queen and her disloyal subject. Yet it remains one of the best preserved fortresses from that hoary era, fitted out appropriately to accommodate modern guests.

It feels just right inside. The lounge presents a huge tapestry, suits of armor, throne-like chairs and a fireplace, presided over by a towering beamed ceiling. Guest rooms in the tower (the keep of the fortress) retain the original arrow-slit windows cut through massively thick walls. Elsewhere, each room is an individual solution to the question of how to create a bedroom and bath out of medieval chambers. Room 105 remains a favorite for its vaulted ceiling and parapet overlooking the valley. Understand, this is no castle; it is a former fortress, so don't expect elegance. Come for the fantasy.

Dining

A vaulted ceiling makes the dining room appropriately baronial. Specialties include pig´s liver paté, lamb tripe and mashed peas—medieval meals are reconstructed in winter. Go for the lamb chops *(chuletilla de cordero)* or somewhat bland garliced cod *(ajo mortero)*. The wine list includes some special bottles. End the meal with a *Resolí*, a seductive combination of coffee, brandy, oranges and cinnamon. A full meal will average $20, plus drinks.

Alternative Dining

Seto   ★

On N-III east for 16 km, just past Montillade Palancar, ☎ *(969) 33 32 28.*
The ambiance cannot compare with the parador but the food clearly outdoes the competition. Hearty, savory roasts and chops satisfy at this local favorite. In addition, meals will cost a few dollars less than at the parador. Closed Mon. and Aug.
Credit Cards: A, D, M, V

Directions

From wherever you arrive, make your way up to the main Plaza Mayor, then follow signs.

Paradors Nearby

Cuenca: 86 km   Albacete: 90 km   Chinchón: 153 km

CENTRAL SPAIN

Sights

This village is old. It was originally founded in the 6th-century by the son of the Visigoth king Alaric, from whence the name derives. Wander to look at medieval houses, then make your way to the 15th-century church of Santa María with an elegant Isabelline door and impressive gothic interior. The main Plaza of Don Juan Manuel contains a charmingly porticoed town hall.

Excursions

For **Cuenca**, with its art and "hanging" houses, take N-III south to Motilla del Palencar for 15 km, then N-320 north for 68 km. For **Toledo's** treasures take N-III north, toward Madrid, for 93 k to Taracón, switching to N-400 for 49 k to Ocaña, then continuing for 59 k more to Toledo. For **Albacete** take N-III south to Montilla del Palancar, then N-320 south to La Gineta in 57 km, then N-301 south for 20 k to the city of Albacete then a final 5 k past the city.

PARADOR RAIMUNDO DE BORGOÑAS

Marqués Canales de Chozas, 2, Ávila, 05001
☎ *(920) 21 13 40, FAX (920) 22 61 66*
$100 per double; 62 rooms: 3 singles, 58 doubles, 1 suite

★ ★ ★

Although named to honor the man who oversaw the construction of Ávila's walls, this parador originally was a 15th-century mansion of the Benavides family. Sited away from the tourists, just a small park distant from the grand city walls, this is a good place to absorb the atmosphere of a medieval walled city. If truth be told, however, only one tower of the parador remains from the ancient mansion. The mass of the place is new, crafted in a style and of a stone that harmonizes with the old tower. Twelve of the rooms are located in the old part, and they are somewhat cramped; the rest are more spaciously housed in a modern addition, but provide no special charm. Most of the furniture in the public areas is antique, in the dark, heavy style of Castile. The nearby park is restful and harbors a stairway that leads up to the city walls. Follow it and take a walk back through time.

Alternative Accommodations

Meliá Palacio do Los Velada

Pl. de la Catedral, 10, ☎ *(920) 25 51 00, FAX (920) 25 49 00. 84 rooms, plus one suite.* In this city the parador is the third or fourth choice. For a few pesetas more you can stay at the more luxurious, more atmospheric, equally aged, Meliá Palacio do Los Velada.

Palacio de Valderrábanos

Pl. de la Catedral, 9, ☎ *(920) 21 10 23, FAX (920) 25 16 91, Telex 22481).*

For a few pesetas less than the parador you can stay at an even more aged mansion on the cathedral square at the Palacio de Valderrábanos, though the decor can be a bit harsh.

Hostería de Bracamonte

☎ *(920) 25 12 80. 16 rooms, plus two suites.*

For one third less, enjoy the same venerable stone ambiance at the equally historic Hostería de Bracamonte with a homier atmosphere. Bracamonte, 6, one block north of Pl. de Victoria, the market square within the walls.

El Rastro

☎ *(920) 21 12 18, FAX 25 16 26. 10 rooms.*

For under $50, El Rastro offers small, comfortable rooms. Pl. del Rastro, 1, halfway along the inside of the south city wall.

Dining

Cozy in stone and wood, the large dining room offers specialties of Castile— roasts and chops of veal, lamb and pork. Such cooking does not require great subtlety and is done adequately here. Featured is a hearty casserole of beans with chorizo, called *judías de Barco,* a beef stew *(pucherete teresiano),* and roast pig *(cochinillo asado).* The true specialty of the town, and of this restaurant, is a dessert of egg yolks beaten with sugar, called *yemas de Ávila.* It is sweet indeed. A full meal will average $20, with a refreshing glass of local wine.

Alternative Dining

Hostería de Bracamonte   ★ ★

Bracamonte, 6, ☎ *(920) 25 12 80.*

The setting in a 16th-century mansion is cozy and softly lit, for a change, and the attractive dining room presents the best values in town. Here Castilian cuisine is served, as elsewhere, but lightened by *nueva* touches. Full-course set meals can be had for 2000 ptas., though á la carte runs more. Closed Tues. and Nov. Credit Cards: M, V.

El Rastro   ★

Pl. del Rastro, 1, ☎ *(920) 21 31 43.*

Halfway along the inside of the south wall of Ávila stands this noted restaurant, housed in a former palace, though the decor is more rustic than elegant. Succulent roasts are the specialties. When the restaurant is crowded, as it is frequently, service can be slow. Prices are about the same as the Bracamonte. Credit Cards: A, D, M, V.

A number of inexpensive restaurants surround the large Pl. de la Victoria, three short blocks west of the cathedral. All serve reasonably prepared food.

Directions

If arriving from **Madrid** or **Segovia**, on N501 west, you are funneled along Av. San Pedro Bautista inside the city limits. Continue as you pass the Basilica of San Vincente on your left with its park and the street becomes Av. de Madrid. In about a third of a mile, look for the first right which takes you through the city walls in two blocks. The parador is a stone's throw straight ahead, on the left side of the street. From **Salamanca** by N 501 east, cross the Adaja bridge then turn left along Av. de Madrid as it circles the town walls. Take the first right, then a hard right which takes you to the city walls. The parador is a stone's throw ahead, on the left side of the street. From **Toledo** on N 403, you are funneled along Carret. de Burgohondo which becomes Av. de Madrid when it reaches the city walls. From there follow the Salamanca directions above.

Paradors Nearby

Gredos: 60 km   Segovia: 65 km   Salamanca: 97 km

Map showing: Salamanca, Madrigal de las Altas Torres, Olmedo, Arevalo, Pedraza, Segovia, Atienza, Ciudad Rodrigo, Buitrago de Lozoya, La Alberca, Miranda del Castañar, Ávila, Las Navas del Marques, Brihuega, Madrid, Candelario, Jarandilla de la Vera, Mombeltran, Pastrana, Garganta la Olla, Candeleda, Valverde de la Vera, Marqueda, Oropesa, Chinchón, Toledo. Scales: 0 10 20 30 40 MI.; 0 20 40 60 km.

Sights

The most striking feature of Ávila is its walls. No other city in Spain and few in the world can rival its imposing picture of strength and age.

In the 11th century, when Alfonso VI drove south to take Toledo in a major early campaign of the reconquest from the Moors, the center of his power shifted. He moved his fortifications southward below Ávila, ordering the city to be fortified. Count Raymond of Burgundy, his son-in-law, completed the project in three years, in 1091. Two thousand citizens did the work of enclosing a rectangle almost 3000 by 1500 yards with walls 10 feet thick, over 40 feet high, punctuated by 88 round towers.

During the late stages of the Reconquest, the Knights of Ávila helped conquer Zaragoza, Córdoba and Seville, and their spoils fueled the desire for a commemorating cathedral. Work in the earliest Gothic style began in 1157 in the form of a fortress-church stuck into the town walls. But Ávila began to decline with the end of the Reconquest. Decline accelerated when its gentry followed the Spanish court to Madrid. The expulsion of the Moors from Spain, in 1609, sealed Ávila's fate by depriving it of most of its craftsmen.

In 1515 Teresa Sanchez de Cepeda y Ahumanda was born and, as Saint Theresa, brought fame again to Ávila. She must have been an unusual little girl for, at the age of seven, she attempted to run to the Moors, hoping to be martyred by them. Theresa's background was nobility tainted, from the Spanish point of view, by the blood of a Jewish grandfather. At puberty she began to experience mystical visions and religious dreams, all of which she wrote about exquisitely in diaries. At 19, she took the veil as a Carmelite nun. Led by visions to reform the Church, which had relaxed its views as it grew rich, she founded her own stricter version of the order, the Descalced (Barefoot) Carmelites. By the time she died in 1582, she had been interviewed by kings and earned a reputation as holy. This was confirmed by sainthood conferred only 40 years after her death. In 1975 she was named a Doctor of the Church, which put her in the company of Sts. Augustine and Thomas Aquinas.

If arriving from **Madrid** or **Segovia**, turn left off of N-501, called Av. de Madrid, after passing the Basilica of San Vincente. At the park turn left and make the first right onto C. San Segundo which takes you past the town walls and Cathedral into the Pl. Sta. Teresa, for parking. If arriving from **Salamanca** turn left at the city walls onto Av. de Madrid. Circle the walls until the large basilica of San Vincente. Turn right. At the park turn left and take the first right onto C. San Segundo which follows the town walls, past the Cathedral, and into the Pl. Sta. Teresa for parking.

Walls   ★★★★

These imposing barricades are almost 1000 years old, yet complete. Of course, some reconstruction has been necessary, but overall their character remains original. Scan these walls from a distance to gather their extent, view them from the base to appreciate their height, and walk along the top (entrance in the park beside the parador) to appreciate their massiveness and sense what it would be like to defend a medieval city.

Pass from Pl. Sta. Teresa through the gate into the old city. Once through, turn onto the second right, following the street as it bends left and right again until it reaches the Pl. de la Catedral. Ahead, on the right, is the front of the Cathedral; on the left is the 14th-century palace of a nobleman named Valderrabános, now a hotel.

Cathedral   ★★

Pl. Catedral, ☎ *(920) 21 16 41.*

Hours open: daily 9 a.m.–1 p.m. and 3–7 p.m. (Opens at 10 a.m. in winter.)

The outside of massive grey granite is a curious architectural mishmash, punctuated by rows of balls. The center portal, more animatedly carved than the others, was added in the 18th century. Most dramatic is the back of the church, so fortresslike that it is incorporated into the town walls.

The interior is surprising, after the dull fortress exterior. The nave soars and looks up to stones surprisingly patterned in red and yellow. Best of all, the clerestory stretches high, letting enough light inside to see the art clearly, a pleasant change from most Spanish churches. The altar is by the great Berruguete and others. At the center of the ambulatory reposes a lovely alabaster tomb of Cardinal Madrigal, a 15th-century bishop of Ávila who is depicted sitting and reading. In the south (left-hand) aisle, the sacristy still wears enough original paint to suggest what a church of the period would look like when new—all colorful and bright. Its rear serves as a museum, containing an El Greco portrait and a huge monstrans (portable reliquary). A Romanesque doorway farther on leads to a delicate cloister. *Admission: 200 ptas., to the Sanctuary.*

C. Reyes Católicos runs behind the Palácio Valderrábanos hotel (opposite the Cathedral) west into the Pl. de la Victoria. The street going left across the plaza runs to the Pl. General Mola and the **Palace of Onates**, sporting a tower complete with battlements. A gentle right along the palace leads into the Pl. la Santa where the church of the **Convent of Sta. Teresa** is located.

Convento de Sta. Teresa   ★

Pl. de al Santa, ☎ *(920) 21 10 30.*

Hours open: daily 9 a.m.–1 p.m. and from 4–7 p.m.

The present Baroque edifice, dating from the late 17th century, is built on land once owned by Saint Theresa's father, where she was born and raised. Off the north transept an ornate chapel marks the place of her birth. Pieces of the saint lie beside the gift shop. *Admission: free.*

West of the church front is the Renaissance **Palace de Nuñez Vela** ★ with lovely windows and an elegant patio. Back at the Cathedral, a street along its north side leads through the main gate of the walls. Outside, straight ahead, a left from the Pl. de Italia leads to the **Casa de los Deanes**.

Casa de los Deanes   ★

Pl de Navillos.

Hours open: Tues.–Sun. 10 a.m.–2 p.m. and 4–7 p.m. Open Sun. 11 a.m. to 1:30 p.m. Closed Mon.

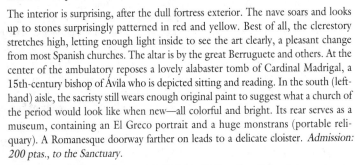

CENTRAL SPAIN

This 16th-century palace, once the deanery of the Cathedral, is now the local museum. It contains a fine triptych attributed to Memling along with early furniture and attractive ceramics. *Admission: 200 ptas.*

Past the Deanery, the first left runs to a park. A left turn along its far end, brings a first right which leads to the **Basilica of San Vicente**.

San Vicente   ★★

Pl. de San Vicente, ☎ *(920) 25 5230. Access is from the south side.*
Hours open: Tues.–Sun. 10 a.m.–1 p.m. and 4–7 p.m. (until 6 p.m. in winter and Sun.) Closed Mon.

The church commemorates the martyrdom in 303 of the child-saint Vincent and his sisters. The basilica was begun in the 12th century, but took 200 years to complete, so it is mainly Romanesque but incorporates early Gothic elements, such as ceiling ribs. Inside, beneath a fine lantern tower, rests the 12th-century tomb of the Saint. The canopy is a later addition, but the carving on the tomb is of the period and depicts the martyrdom in an evocative and accomplished manner. *Admission: 100 ptas.*

The walls lead south to the parking in the Pl. Sta. Teresa, which at its east end presents the church of **San Pedro** ★ , a fine Romanesque edifice, with an impressive lantern and rose windows. Pass along the north (left) side of the church to take the C. Duque de Alba, which heads left, for three blocks to the **Convento of San José**.

Convento San José   ★

Pl. de Las Madres, ☎ *(920) 22 21 27.*
Hours open: daily 10 a.m.–1 p.m. and 4–7 p.m.

Saint Theresa began her reform of the Church with this convent in 1562 by offering the inhabitants a simple life of worship. Inside are tombs of the early adherents, including that of Lorenzo de Cepeda, the Saint's brother. A small museum displays mementos of the Saint and musical instruments that the first nuns played. It seems that Theresa handled percussion. *Admission: 30 ptas.*

From the Pl. Sta. Teresa parking lot, past the front of San Pedro Church, then along its south face, the Av. de Alverez Provisional is entered. In a few blocks it passes the **Monesterio San Tomás**.

Monesterio San Tomás   ★★★

Pl. Granada, ☎ *(920) 22 21 27.*
Hours open: daily 10:30 a.m.–1 p.m. and 4–7 p.m.

For a time this monastery was the favorite residence of Ferdinand and Isabella. Isabella's former confessor, Tomás de Torquemada, the first and most infamous Inquisitor General of the Inquisition, often joined them, and chose to be buried at this spot. Then tragedy struck when Ferdinand and Isabella's son, Don Juan, suddenly died. They buried him in this beloved monastery, but thereafter could not bear to pass their summers here.

Inside, at the crossing of the transept, is the mausoleum of the only son of Ferdinand and Isabella, who died at 19. The delicate tomb is a Renaissance marvel by the Florentine Domenico Fancelli, who years later carved another in Granada for the parents of the boy. The altar retablo depicting the life of Saint Thomas in high relief is a masterpiece by Berruguete. A plain slab in the sacristy marks the final resting place (until he goes elsewhere) of Torquemada, the infamous Inquisitor General.

Three cloisters gird the church. The first is relatively unadorned, the second is the "Silent Cloister," intimate and richly decorated on the upper gallery. Beyond the Silent Cloister is the third, larger, solemn "Cloister of the Catholic Monarchs." It displays a collection of oriental objects gathered by missionary brothers. Stairs lead up to a gallery in which Isabella and Ferdinand sat in virtual thrones. Notice their coats of arms on the balustrade. *Admission: 100 ptas., to the cloisters.*

Excursions

Segovia waits 65 k away by N-501 east to Villacastin, then N-110. **Salamanca** is a straight 99 k drive along N-501 west. A lovely, if slow, mountain drive along N-403 south toward Barraco, then through El Tiempo, San Martin, to Maqueda, and Torrijos arrives in **Toledo** in 134 km. **Cáceres** is best reached by looping up to Salamanca then taking N-630 south toward Béjar to reach your destination in 308 k. The more direct N-110 involves slow mountain driving. Fortress **Ciudad Rodrigo**, with parador, is reached by N-501 west to Salamanca, then N-620 west for 269 km. The mountain lodge parador of **Gredos** is 48 k southwest along C-502.

PARADOR VIA DE LA PLATA

Plaza de la Constitución, 3, Mérida, 06800
☎ *(924) 31 38 00, FAX (924) 31 92 08*
$105 per double; 82 rooms: 1 single, 79 doubles, 2 suites

★ ★ ★ ★

This is a favorite parador because, while it is not the most elegant, it is one of the prettiest. It was renovated from a 15th century monastery. During renovations artifacts were unearthed (many now spread around the parador as decoration) that showed the monastery stood upon a much earlier temple to Augustus. While paradors often surround a central patio, this one ranks among the loveliest. While other paradors tout their lounges, this one, a former chapel, ranks with the most splendid. Many bedrooms are graced with domed ceilings, and the large doubles in the back offer balconies overlooking attractive gardens. Most incorporate commodious bathrooms lined with stone.

Dining

The dining room is spacious and contains some elegant columns. Here you can sample the hearty cuisine of Extremadura province. Specialties include game, such as pheasant, venison and wild boar, along with a local fish named *trencha*, besides the standby lamb stew *(caldereta de cordero)*. The chef is proud of his dessert tart. Local wines come from Matanegra and Tierra de Barros and tend to be full-bodied. A full meal will average $30, plus drinks.

Alternative Dining

Nicholás ★★

Félix Valverde Lillo, 13 (this street runs parallel to, and to the west of, the main shopping street, C. Santa Eulalia), ☎ *(924) 31 96 10.*
Closed Sun. night, and the middle three weeks in Sept.
In its own townhouse, this is easily the prettiest and the most elegant restaurant in town. The cuisine is that of the region—partridge with truffles and good pork. The fixed-price menus usually include good choices at moderate prices, otherwise figure $40 per person. Credit Cards: A, D, V.

Briz ★★

C. Félix Valverde Lillo, 5 (near Nicholás), ☎ *(924) 31 93 07.*
This is an unassuming place that serves very good food at very reasonable prices. Hearty food is the point here—either lamb or partridge stew, for example, or tasty sausage. The house wine is hearty as well. About $15 will cover the tab. Credit Cards: A, D, V.

Directions

Arrivals from the **north** should bear right after crossing the small Albarregas river (more a stream), which puts them on Av. Extremadura, though it changes its name to Almendralejo. At the second church on your right, turn left then left again at the post office for the parador. From the **south** you cross the Guadiana river to drive along Av. Almendralejo. At a church in about four blocks turn right, then left in one block at the post office for the parador. From **Trujillo** comes an interchange at the outskirts of town. Take Av. Juan Carlos I, heading southwest. In about five blocks (passing faint remains of the Roman racecourse on the left) this ends. Go right on Av. de Extremadura, which changes its name to C. de Almendralejo, then follow the directions from the north above.

Paradors Nearby

Zafra: 60 km	Cáceres: 70 km	Trujillo: 90 km
Guadalupe: 125 km	Jarandilla: 200 km	Oropesa: 200 km

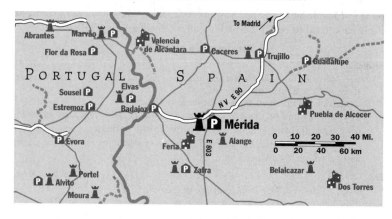

Sights

Mérida was founded as a retirement village by soldiers from Caesar Augustus' Spanish campaigns in 23 B.C. They called it Emerita Augusta (Augustus' Veterans), from whose first half the present name evolved. Augustus' son-in-law donated a theater to the new town that seated 6000, and the citizens added two aqueducts and a racecourse plus an arena for chariot races and sea battles that could hold 14,000 cheering spectators. Mérida prospered at the crossroads linking Salamanca to Seville, and Toledo to Lisbon. It also administered the large Roman territory of Lusitania, which encompassed latter-day Portugal, but lost that importance when Portugal broke away from Spain. Indeed, one of Mérida's claims to fame is that it is one of the few cities in Spain that Isabella and Ferdinand never visited.

Today Mérida seems more a large village—albeit with a certain vitality—than a city. All seems ordinary until one reaches the top of the hill and looks on the remains of ancient Rome. The Roman **theater** ★★ is probably the most elegant anywhere and the **arena** ★ is imposing. In addition, Mérida has just completed a lovely **museum** ★ to house some of the finest Roman art in Spain. Ruins of Mérida's Moorish **alcazaba** are evocative. From its walls you look over a still-functioning **Roman bridge**.

Alcazaba

Pl. de España, ☎ *(924) 31 73 30. Walk downstream along the river (south) for approximately one block. The entrance is on the north side, away from the river.*

Hours open: Mon.–Fri. 9 a.m.–2 p.m. and 4–7 p.m. (closes an hour earlier in winter). Open Sat. 9 a.m.–2 p.m.

The Romans built a substantial fortress here, constructed so stoutly that successive Visigoths and Moors had only to repair and maintain it. After the Moors, it fell into disrepair and suffers now from 1000 years of neglect exacerbated by a French gutting in 1808. What you see today is the fortress walls and the cistern, the rest being mainly a dusty field. A walk on the walls gives nice views of the river—often with sheep and cattle gently grazing nearby—and of the long Roman bridge with 64 arches. *Admission: 200 ptas.; ticket good for the Roman precinct as well.*

Walk left from the Alcazaba entrance to the Pl. de España at the corner, the main square of the town surrounded by shops and restaurants. Here, at the west end of the plaza is the **Hotel Emperatriz**, a former 16th-century palace with a huge interior patio. Walk along the near side (south) of the plaza to C. Santa Eulalia, the major shopping street. In two and a half blocks, turn right on C. Francisco to see the Roman **Temple of Diana**, with a nice Corinthian peristyle. Continue for two more blocks up C. Santa Eulalia, turning right onto C. José Ramon Melida, where stores are passed that sell local red incised pottery and handsome reproductions of Roman blue and green glass. The attractively modern brick building in two blocks is the **Museo Nacional de Arte Romano**. At its end lies the precinct of the **Roman ruins**.

Museo Nacional de Arte Romano ★

C. José Ramón Melida, ☎ *(924) 31 16 90.*
Hours open: Tues.–Sat. 10 a.m.–2 p.m. and 4–6 p.m. Open Sun. 10 a.m.–2 p.m. Closed Mon., and holidays.
This is a daringly modern building in which to display ancient art, and it suits almost perfectly one of the best Roman collections in the country, all excavated from this area. The ground floor shows statues, including a lovely Ceres taken from the Roman theater (a copy stands there now in place of this original). The next floor is for less interesting ceramics, glassware and coins. The top floor houses some nice mosaics and several fine busts. In the basement are original Roman *thermae* (steam-baths). *Admission: 200 ptas.*

Monumentos Romanos ★★

C. José Ramón Melida, ☎ *(924) 31 25 30.*
Hours open: Same hours as the Roman Museum above.
The theater is surely Spain's most beautiful remembrance of Rome. Most of it dates to A.D. 23, including the seats for 6000, the entranceways formed of stones so carefully fitted that they required no mortar, and a pit in the front for the chorus. The elegant towering stage wall was added in the second century A.D. Beyond the stage reposes a garden and portico where the audience could stroll during intermission. It all seems so civilized.

North of the theater stands a large arena that held 14,000 spectators at chariot races, gladiatorial combats and mock sea battles (for which the floor was flooded). A low wall protected the spectators in the front row, the most expensive seats, from wild animals sometimes employed as contestants during gladiatorial bouts. The cavern in the center of the arena floor presumably held the machinery for producing such shows. *Admission: 200 ptas., valid for Alcázar as well.*

CENTRAL SPAIN

Directory

Shopping

Mérida sells inexpensive reproductions of blue and green Roman glass goblets and vases. On the street leading to the Roman precinct, C. José Ramon, **Reproduciones Romanes** at #40 and **Copias Romanes** at #20, both provide nice selections, especially the latter. They also sell the local incised brown-red pottery. **Greylop #24** has the best pottery selection. Across the street at number 13, **Mascara** sells endearing puppets and other high quality crafts.

Excursions

For **Cáceres** Renaissance old town see the Cáceres directions. For **Trujillo** of the Conquistadores, see the Trujillo direction. Both can be reached in an hour. **Seville** and Andalusia lies three hours south.

SOUTHERN SPAIN

A typical Andalusian lane in San Roque.

Southern Spain is what the world imagines all of Spain to be—flamenco, guitars, caballeros, beaches and romance. Not surprisingly, it attracts most of Spain's tourists. The light is stark and bright, the weather warm—it has it all, including elegant whitewashed houses surrounding lovely flowered court-yards that constitute the southern style. This is one of the legacies of the Moors, for they remained longer in the south than the rest of Spain. They also left one of the world's great edifices here, their mosque at Córdoba, along with suites of surpassing elegance in the Alhambra, and their zest for life in Seville. Here you can dutifully visit sights, then reward yourself with indolent beach basking, until, rested, you awake to imbibe and dance the night away.

195

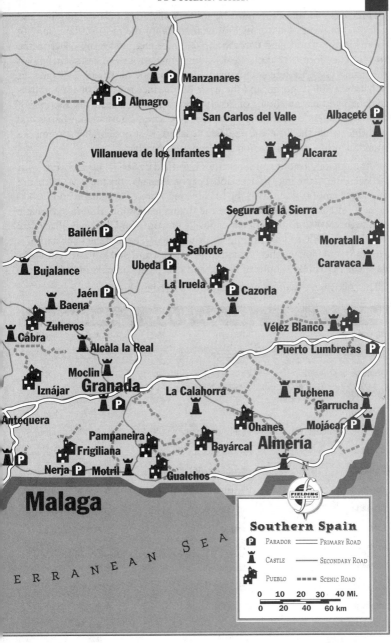

Manzanares
Almagro
San Carlos del Valle
Albacete
Villanueva de los Infantes
Alcaraz
Segura de la Sierra
Bailén
Moratalla
Bujalance
Sabiote
Caravaca
Ubeda
La Iruela
Cazorla
Jaén
Baena
Zuheros
Vélez Blanco
Cábra
Puerto Lumbreras
Alcala la Real
Moclin
Granada
La Calahorra
Puchena
Iznájar
Garrucha
Antequera
Ohanes
Mojácar
Pampaneira
Bayárcal
Almería
Frigiliana
Nerja
Motril
Gualchos

Malaga

ERRANEAN SEA

Southern Spain

🅿 PARADOR	══════	PRIMARY ROAD
♜ CASTLE	──────	SECONDARY ROAD
🏠 PUEBLO	▬ ▬ ▬ ▬	SCENIC ROAD

0   10   20   30   40 Mi.
0   20   40   60 km

FIELDING
WORLDWIDE

Three cities in the south must be seen—**Seville** for a host of churches and palaces, but most of all for its beauty; **Granada** for the most sublime suite of rooms in the world; and **Córdoba** for one mosque, unlike any other in the world. They form a triangle small enough that a tour can easily encompass them all. Lesser, though still dramatic sights include the **Ronda**, a village split in half by a 300 ft. gorge, and the sister Renaissance towns of **Úbeda** and **Baeza**. Then you have a choice of beach areas. The famed **Costa del Sol**, east of Gibraltar, offers overdevelopment, stone beaches, international flavor and nightlife, while the little known **Costa de la Luz**, west of Gibraltar, promises a more Spanish experience, more rest and sand beaches.

A triangle of glorious southern cities is formed by **Seville**, on the west, with its awesome cathedral, palaces and beauty; **Granada**, on the east, with the famed Alhambra, along with the final resting place of Ferdinand and Isabella; and, in between, **Córdoba**, with the dramatic mosque. Ronda's dramatic site lies just 100 km south of either Seville of Córdoba. Úbeda and Baeza are 100 km east of Córdoba and north of Granada. The **Costa del Sol** starts 75 km south of Granada, then extends 200 km west and 300 km east. The **Costa de la Luz** lies 100 km south of Seville and sweeps 50 km east and west.

The following towns and paradors are covered in this chapter.

Town	Parador Name	Rating	Page
Almagro	Almagro	★★★★	*page 217*
Antequera	Antequera	★	*page 219*
Arcos de la Frontera	Casa del Corregidor	★★★	*page 204*
Ayamonte	Costa de la Luz	★	*page 214*
Bailén	Bailén	★★★	*page 221*
Cádiz	Hotel Atlántico	★★	*page 258*
Carmona	Alcázar del Rey Don Pedro	☆☆☆☆	*page 202*
Cazorla	El Adelantado	★★★	*page 200*
Córdoba	El Arruzafa	★★★★	*page 247*
Granada	San Francisco	★★★★★	*page 233*
Jaén	Castillo de Santa Catalina	★★★★	*page 207*
Málaga	Málaga-Gibralfaro	★★★★	*page 263*
Málaga	Málaga-Golf	★★★★	*page 268*
Mazagón	Cristóbal Colón	★★★★★	*page 215*
Mojácar	Reyes Católicos	★★★★	*page 270*
Nerja	Nerja	★★★★	*page 223*

Town	Parador Name	Rating	Page
Puerto Lumbreras	Puerto Lumbreras	★	page 226
Ronda	Ronda	★★★★	page 228
Seville	None		page 272
Úbeda	Condestable Davalos	★★★★	page 209
Zafra	Hernán Cortéz	★★★★	page 256

If possible stay at least one night in both Seville and Granada. Add an extra night in Seville for Ronda and Córdoba, and an extra night in Granada for Úbeda and Baeza. For beaches choose among Mazagón for utter seclusion, Málaga-Golf for sports, Mojacar for resort life or Nerja for beach and charming village.

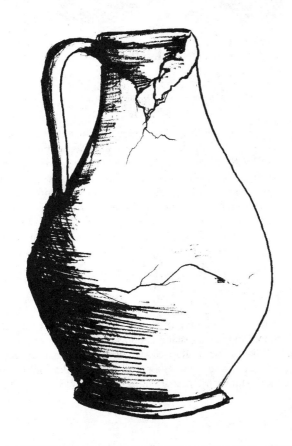

El Andelantado

El Sacejo, Sierra de Cazorla, Cazorla, 23470
☎ *(953) 72 10 75, FAX (953) 72 13 03*
$70 per double; 33 rooms: 33 doubles

★ ★ ★

Want to get away from it all? Like the mountains? Here is your place. It looks not at all like a hunting lodge, more a huge house, but the interior is open and simple with inviting fireplaces to warm the bones. Luxury would be out of place, so the guest rooms are plain, though certainly adequate. One with a splendid view of trees and mountains will be appreciated. There is a pool in a grass terrace in front of the hotel, but the point is to walk mountain trails to spot wild sheep, mountain goats, golden eagles and vultures. Or drive to Cazorla for a spectacularly situated medieval castle.

Dining

The dining room is comfortable, thanks to large upholstered chairs, but the food is simple and basic, making good use of mountain game. Start with gazpacho, this is the south, after all. Follow with venison cooked over a wood fire, or with a fresh trout. Chocolate pudding, that old favorite, will top off the meal. Dinner will cost about $20, plus drinks.

Directions

25 km past Cazorla by a steep, but well posted road.

Parados Nearby

Úbeda: 75 km   Jaén: 138 km   Córdoba: 220 km
Granada: 224 km   Málaga: 330 km

PARADOR ALCÁZAR DEL REY
DON PEDRO

Alcázar, s/n, Carmona, 41410
☎ *(95) 414 10 10, FAX (95) 414 17 12*
$110 per double; 63 rooms: 3 singles, 60 doubles

T he good news is that this is one of the two or three most glamorous and romantic paradors in all the land; the bad news is that it is sinking and, therefore closed for the foreseeable future. Too bad. It began life in the 12th century as a Moorish fort (alcázar). In the 14th century King Pedro the Cruel employed the same Moorish architects who designed a spectacular palace in Seville to convert the old fort into a spectacular palace here. More than six centuries later the parador people accomplished one of their most sensitive renovations to produce the present hotel. Through a massive gateway an elegant patio is formed of Moorish columns and sublime arches, while a fountain gurgles restfully. What an introduction! Lovely geometrical tiles of a Moorish style decorate the walls throughout. Bedrooms are large and present glorious views over the plains. That is what you are missing.

Alternative Accommodations

Casa de Carmona

Pl. de Lasso, 1, ☎ *(95) 414 33 00; FAX 414 37 52. 29 rooms.*

Fear not, a wonderful hotel serves handsomely until the parador reopens. The Casa de Carmona is a 16th century mansion dotted with fine antiques that features a lovely patio of its own and guest rooms of charm. True, it costs 25% more than the parador, but it is well worth the price.

Directions

From Seville you drive through the Puerta de Sevilla along San Felipe which becomes Pedro I before depositing you at the parador.

Paradors Nearby

Córdoba: 100 km	Arcos: 120 km	Cádiz: 154 km
Mazagón: 154 km	Antequera: 180 km	Ayamonte: 180 km

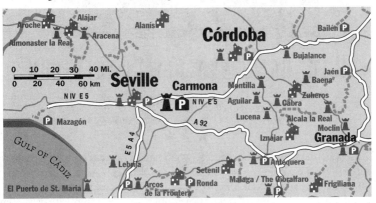

Sights

Wander the old town, within Moorish town walls that stand on Roman foundations. Here are assorted mudéjar mansions and Renaissance churches, including a town hall in the main Pl. de San Francisco with a fine Roman mosaic in its courtyard. Just outside the town, on the road to Seville a sign points to the Necrópolis Romana with more than 800 tombs, some ornate indeed. (*Tues.–Sun. 10 a.m. to 2 p.m. and 4–6 p.m. Closed Aug. Admission: 400 ptas.*)

PARADOR CASA DEL CORREGIDOR

Plaza del Cabildo, s/n, Arcos de la Frontera, 11630
☎ *(956) 70 05 00, FAX (956) 70 11 16*
$100 per double; 24 rooms: 4 singles, 20 doubles

★ ★ ★

Located in one of the loveliest "white cities" of Andalusia, this parador forms a good base to explore the others, as well as Jerez, where sherry is produced, and Ronda, with its dramatic location. The parador's situation is special, high above the pretty town it overlooks, with an exterior that has the look of a venerable mansion (although it was constructed just thirty years ago). Once quite garish inside, a recent renovation tastefully redid the rooms, making the enclosed patio off the dining room a special place to sit. Now, too, the service is first-rate. Bedrooms are comfortable, although red bedspreads are not our favorites. You should request a room with a terrace overlooking the countryside and pay the small supplement.

Dining

"Very Spanish" is the phrase for the arched, wood-beamed dining room, which altogether feels comfortable because of roomy tables and a fireplace at one end. Views are splendid. Enjoy the cuisine of Andalusia—gazpacho or ajo blanco soups to start, delicately fried fish to continue, and special desserts such as *los alfajores* and *el turrón* to finish. The cooking rises above that at most paradors and here you have the rare chance to sample the wines of Arcos, seldom available elsewhere, which nicely complement the food. Tierra Blanca is a nice white, Lucía is a nice red. A full meal will average $20, with a refreshing glass of local wine.

Alternative Dining

El Convento ★

Marqués de Torresoto, 7, *(956) 70 32 33.*

Dine on a sunny, flower-bedecked patio or in one of two intimate rooms for one of the area's best values in food, all produced from the freshest local produce. The garlic soup is special, as is the lamb with aromatic herbs. End with rice pudding like nothing mother ever made. You will pay no more than at the parador. Credit Cards: A, M, V.

Directions

The parador, standing high above the town, is hard to miss. Angle right along C. Nueva to take a steep right turn after the Plaza del Cabilido.

Paradors Nearby

Cádiz: 45 km	Ronda: 90 km	Carmona: 130 km
Málaga: 195 km	Mazagón: 215 km	

Sights

Wander the village of Arcos and, if you like what you see, there is more. This is one of a string of similar "white towns" that can be explored in a leisurely outing. North on N-342 comes **Bornos** in 10 km beside a reservoir. In 38 km, near Algondonales, the silhouette of **Zahara** and its castle ruins hover over the valley. Head east for 21 km to **Olvera** on a ridge decorated by olive trees. Back at Algondonales, take C-339 south for 28 km for **Ronda** (see the description under its parador below) or turn south on N-339 for 9 km to take N-344 west to **Grazalema** surrounded by pines. It is a pretty village known for hand-woven blankets. Continue on N-344 west to Arcos again in 55 km. Alternatively, a quick trip is possible to taste the sherries of **Jerez**. See the description under the parador of Cádiz "Excursion."

PARADOR CASTILLO DE SANTA CATALINA

Castillo de Santa Catalina, s/n, Jaén, 23001
☎ *(953) 23 00 00, FAX (953) 23 09 30*
$100 per double; 45 rooms: 9 singles, 36 doubles

★ ★ ★ ★

On the grounds of a grand Moorish fortress high above the plains stands this "modern" parador. Equally monolithic, also all in stone, its architecture marvelously suits the historic fortress it adjoins. The fortress was the stronghold of the Nasrid caliphs. When it fell to the Christians in 1246, the family fled to Granada where they built the Alhambra. The parador is grand too, with a fortresslike entrance. Inside stone walls rise to soaring arched ceilings. Museum quality tapestries and paintings decorate the public spaces, equipped with dowdy furniture. Guest rooms feature high ceilings and terraces with magnificent views. Their decor is rustic, with brick floors brightened by rugs and bedspreads. There is a pool for relaxing.

Dining

Long, with peaked arches rising up to a wood ceiling, the dining room feels like a cathedral, although with large windows letting in light and allowing views over the plain. After a complimentary class of local amontillado, cucumbers and tomatoes form a kind of gazpacho salad *(pipirrana)* for a refreshing beginning to the meal. Game is the local specialty, although good fish is usually an alternative. A special almond dessert *(almendrados de Jaén)* is pleasant. The local wines are Bailén and a surprisingly good Torreperogil. A full meal will average $20, plus drinks.

Directions

The parador is located 5 km outside the city. Circle the city along Av. del Ejército Español and Carretera de Córdoba to reach Carretera de Circunvalación. Look for a parador sign to Carretera al Castillo to the right which circles to the parador.

Paradors Nearby

Úbeda: 60 km	Córdoba: 100 km
Granada: 100 km	Cazorla: 125 km

PARADOR CONDESTABLE DAVALOS

Plaza Vázquez de Molina, 1, Úbeda, 22400
☎ *(953) 75 03 45, FAX (953) 75 12 59*
$110 per double; 31 rooms: 30 doubles, 1 suite

★ ★ ★ ★

This parador, installed in the 16th-century palace of the commander-in-chief of Castile's army, is one of the loveliest small ones, and situated on an unusual square. The facade is original, simple Renaissance. Inside one sees a 17th century renovation, which is glorious in its different way. A lovely central patio is ringed by guest rooms on its second story, another patio is now a garden. Inside rises a granite staircase lit by one of the world's great lamps in the form of a soaring eagle. Suits of armor dot halls enhanced by lovely azulejo tiles, while homier common spaces incorporate working fireplaces, making an altogether lovely place to stay. Two sorts of guest rooms are available. Those in the old building offer elegant artesonado ceilings, tile floors and history; those in the new wing are larger. All have commodious baths.

Alternative Accommodations

Palacio de la Rambla

Pl. del Marqués, 1 (head south from the Pl. de Andalucia for 2 blocks, then a left)
☎ *(953) 75 01 96, FAX 75 02 67. 8 rooms.*
For a hotel as historic as the parador for a third less, try the Palacio de la Rambla. The Marquesa de la Rambla lets a few charming rooms in her 16th century mansion. The patio is lovely, rooms are decorated with antiques, but the service is not that of a hotel.

SOUTHERN SPAIN

Dining

The dining room is new, pleasantly styled with elegant chandeliers. For a treat, ask to be shown the original wine cellar below. The food is a good cut above the average parador, with original dishes. Take the shrimp and vegetable soup *(andrajos)*, for example. Sausage and red pepper pie *(morcilla en caldera con ochios)*, pheasant salad *(ensalada de perdiz)* or roast lamb with pinenuts *(cabrito guisado con piñones)* might be taken with a squash *(carruécano)* or spinach side. Puff pastry custard *(suspiros de monja)* is an unusual dessert. The local wine is a light Torreperogil. For all this, a full meal will average $25, plus drinks.

Directions

You arrive in town on Obispo Cobos which soon deposits you into the large Pl. de Andalucia. At the far end turn right, then take the first left into Dr. Quesada which soon jags right. Go left which becomes C. Real and deposits you in 7 blocks in the large Pl. Ayuntamiento at whose southern end and left is the Pl. Molina and the parador. Throughout, follow signs for **Zona Monumental**.

Paradors Nearby

Jaén: 57 km   Cazorla: 70 km   Córdoba: 144 km
Granada: 174 km   Almagro: 271 km

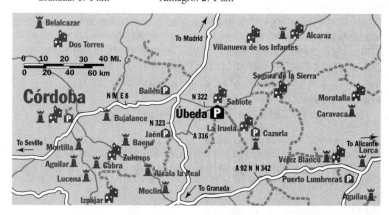

Sights

Like its sister city Baeza, Úbeda was taken early by the Christians during their Reconquest and became wealthy as a staging post for the battles farther south. In the 16th century, it invested those profits on monuments and palaces, unfortunately just as a new road to thriving Jaén was about to turn Úbeda into a backwater. These lovely buildings are spread around, but one perfect concentration in the Pl. Vázquez de Molina constitutes one of the finest single assemblages of Renaissance architecture in Spain.

The city does its part to accommodate tourists by clear signs directing traffic to the *Zona Monumental*, the major sights within the old city walls. Úbeda also offers crafts in a Gypsy quarter nearby. All can be seen in two hours.

The place to begin is the harmonious open Pl. Vázquez de Molina. Due north is the **Casa de las Cadenas**, now the city hall, named for the chains around the forecourt, and built for a secretary to Felipe II. Its front is imposing with classical columns and surprising, out of place, caryatids. Wander around the back for a look at its lovely patio and a stop at the **tourist office** next door for a fine brochure and map.

In the Pl. Molina again, the mansion next to the Casa de las Cadenas is the **Palacio del Condestable Dávalos** ★, a 17th-century renovation of a structure a century older. Its long, restrained front is made harmonious by two elegant lines of windows. This is one of the first historic buildings made into a parador, in 1930, and is still splendid inside. Opposite, to the south of the plaza, is the church of **Santa Maria de los Reales Alcázares**. Behind it are remains of the Moorish **Alcázar** for which it is named, but the church is mainly 16th-century inside with notable painted ironwork and unusual ceilings of arabesques painted blue.

At the east end of the plaza stands the unusual **Capilla del Salvador**. (If closed, apply to the first door on the right.) This church once formed part of a great palace designed for Carlos V, but only it and some ruins behind remain. The front is a truly original design by the architect Vandelvira from plans by Gil de Siloé. Two round towers at the corners seem much too low, until the eye rises to the triangular pediment above, and grasps the triangular design. The portal is styled as a Roman arch with scenes carved around and above. The inside suffered great damage during anticlerical raids at the outbreak of the Spanish Civil War, including the destruction of most of the church treasures and art, but has been reconstructed to its original neoclassical look. A theatrical high altar behind fine ornamental ironwork contains what remains of Berruguete's original retable, and the sacristy is a glorious Italianate masterpiece of coffered ceiling, medallions, graceful caryatids and atlantes.

Walk north from the front of the chapel up C. Horno Contador passing the **Casa de los Salvajes** on the left in one block. The reason for the name is evident in the men dressed in animal skins holding the coat of arms of a local bishop. A short block further brings the Pl. Primero de Mayo, the main square. Across, well displayed, sits the church of **San Pablo ★** . The west front portal is accomplished 13th-century work; the south portal is a lovely Isabelline design. Inside, the chapels command attention with fine iron grillwork, stucco vaults and doorways.

Continue from the rear of the church northeast along C. Rosal. The **Casa Canastero**, in a short block, was a bishop's mansion, with two carved soldiers bearing the owner's coat of arms. More mansions line the previous street, C. Montiel. Ahead stand the city walls and a 14th-century **Mudejar gate**. Outside the walls the street is renamed Cuesta de la Merced, and changes its name again after going through a square to C. Valencia. Here is the Gypsy quarter and crafts of pottery, ironwork and esparto grass.

Excursions

The natural excursion is to Baeza. Granada, Córdoba and even Seville are an hour or two away. See the respective descriptions under separate headings in this chapter. Take N-321 west for nine km to Baeza. After Baeza, N-321 wends to Jaén in 48 km, just before which N-323 heads south to Granada in 93 km. N-IV heads west to Córdoba in 108 km.

Baeza

For two centuries it served as the base from which the Christians pushed their Reconquest south, supplying shelter for royalty and the nobles of the army of Castile and growing rich off them. After the Reconquest was complete, Baeza sat astride the main southern route, enjoying trade and prosperity. Wealthy citizens put up grand mansions in the 16th and 17th centuries, and the city added a university in 1595. But when the town of Jaén to the southwest developed into a major city, the road moved to head directly into Jaén, bypassing Baeza and turning it into the quiet town it remains today.

From **Úbeda** you travel on C. José Burell. In two blocks comes another fork. Take the right hand road, C. San Pablo, which lets onto the Paseo de la Constitución and parking.

Go southwest through the large arcaded Paseo de la Constitución, noting the early 18th-century **Casas Consistoriales Bajas** on the north side, providing comfortable seating for officials during ceremonies in the square.

A few steps after the southwest end of the Paseo comes the attractive **Plaza de los Leones** on the left, named for the **fountain ★** in its center. The fountain is composed of genuine antiques—the lions seem to be Roman, and the female atop the pillar is either Celtiberian or Carthaginian, bearing a likeness, according to some, of Hannibal's wife. The imposing building to the east is the 16th-century **Antigua Carnicería ★** (Old Butcher's Shop), with a lovely coat of arms for Carlos V. Moving south through the plaza we come to an arch, the **Jaén Gate**, erected in 1526 to mark the passage of Carlos V on his way to marry in Seville. Then comes the **Casa de Pópulo**, the former courthouse, with elegant Plateresque windows and medallions. Its six doors formerly led to six notaries' offices, but now it serves as the **Office of Tourism** and can provide a worthwhile map.

Exit from the south end of the plaza along Cuesta de San Gil, taking the first left onto C. Callejon to enter the Pl. Santa María. The walls of the former 17th-century **seminary** on the left are covered with faint red names of graduates painted with bull's blood. Right (south), across the plaza, is an unusual late **Gothic fountain ★** in the form of a small arch, with the former **Cathedral** beyond. Before entering the Cathedral, notice the **Casas Consistoriales Altas** with an imposing pair of coats of arms—of Juana the Mad, Ferdinand and Isabella's daughter, and her husband, Philip the Handsome, the parents of Carlos V.

Cathedral

Pl. de la Fuente de Santa María.
Hours open: daily 10:30 a.m.–1 p.m. and 4–6 p.m.

Technically this is not a cathedral since, after 60 years as a bishopric, the prelate left for Jaén. The building is the same, however, as when the bishop presided. Fernando III, who first conquered the city, raised the present church on the site of a former mosque. In the 16th century the interior was extensively remodeled and redecorated, but the main portal on the west front, the Puerta de la Luna with a horseshoe arch, remains from the early church. Inside are flamboyant chapels, and arches from the former mosque in the cloisters.

Head north along Cuestra San Felipe, arriving after one block at the remarkable Renaissance **Palacio del Marqueses de Jabalquinto ★**. The golden facade is covered with Isabelline decoration—every feature seems to sprout something. Though impressive, it is more admirable in detail than overall conception. Inside what today is a seminary stands a more somber patio with two charming lions guarding a grand baroque stairway. Opposite the palace is the attractive Romanesque church of **Santa Cruz ★**, the only complete church dating to the time of Baeza's liberation in the early 13th century. It remains a gem, still with some frescoes inside. North of the church stands the former **university**, dating from the late 16th century. A fine patio hides behind the plain facade, and a lovely Mudejar ceiling crowns the amphitheater.

By heading along the long west face of the university, then across its front, and turning left for a few feet then right along C. San Pablo, in half a block you pass the 16th century **Alhondiga** (grain exchange), with an arched portico. Next turn left across the Pl. del Constitutión to round the arcaded Paseo for a closer look at the **Casas Consistoriales Bajas** to the north. Continue along its east face on C. Gaspar Becerra for one block to the **Ayuntamiento** (city hall), a former prison, transformed in the 16th century into a sample of everything Plateresque. The arms of Felipe II are proudly displayed.

SOUTHERN SPAIN

PARADOR COSTA DE LA LUZ

El Castillito, s/n, Ayamonte, 21400
☎ *(959) 32 07 00, FAX (959) 32 07 00*
$90 per double; 54 rooms: 1 single, 50 doubles, 3 suites

★

The sole purpose of this parador is to provide a stop for visitors from Portugal or for those about to leave Spain. This modern, low-slung motel serves the use intended. As a bonus it offers nice views of the town below, the mouth of the Guadiana River, and the bridge to Portugal. There is a pool with quite a view, too, for relaxing. Bedrooms are adequate. In any case, no one spends more than one night.

Dining

The dining room feels a bit cold with a dark ceiling pressing down overhead, but the views make up for this chill. Fish is the dish to order, from the lovely texture of anglerfish *(rape)* to skate *(raya)* and squid *(almendrilla)*. A special cocoa tart ends the meal, which will come to about $20, plus drinks.

Directions

At the highest point north of town.

Paradors Nearby

Mazagón: 99 km   Sagres: 166 km   Cádiz: 200 km

Parador Cristóbal Colón

Carretera Huelva-Matalascañas, km 24, Mazagón, 21130
☎ *(959) 53 63 00, FAX (959) 53 62 28*
$110 per double, 43 rooms: 42 doubles, 1 suite

★ ★ ★ ★ ★

For pure beach and natural beauty, this is the best parador in the land. Lying at the edge of a huge coastal wildlife sanctuary, a pine forest behind and a long golden beach in front isolate the parador from all signs of human occupation. Of course there will be a few score of our fellow creatures staying with you at the parador, but that is it, unless you travel east along the coast for 10 km to a budding development at Matalascañas. The parador is sprawling modern, consisting of a guest wing and a public wing angled around a pool. The complex sits on a bluff above the sea, so a room with a view will prove special. Tennis, windsurfing and horses are available. Relax and enjoy.

Dining

A large dining room sports a wall of windows over the pine forest. Fish, of course, are the specialties. A simply done porgy with onions *(pargo encebollado)* is delectable, as is stewed anglerfish *(rape a la marinero)*. There is also an invertebrate we do not know here, called *choco*, which looks like octopus, but tastes like fish. Try it. If tired of food of the sea, the ham is delicious and chocolate pudding isn't bad. A full meal will average $25, plus drinks.

Directions

From **Seville** take N-431 west to exit 13 at San Juan del Puerto in 74 km. Go south through Moguer and Palos de la Frontera to Mazagón on C-442 for an additional 25 km.

Paradors Nearby

Ayamonte: 86 km	Carmona: 147 km	Arcos de la Frontera: 209 km
Cádiz: 243 km	Córdoba: 256 km	Zafra: 258 km

Excursions

Coto Doñana National Park is Spain's finest bird sanctuary. It is a vast wetland consisting of almost 200,000 acres, which receives migratory birds going to and from Europe and Africa. Visitors include flamingos and storks, herons, ducks and coots. The native population consists of predatory imperial eagles and vultures, along with rare European lynx, wild boars and deer. If interested, check at the desk about the availability of Land Rover tours conducted by the rangers. The station lies 12 km east between Matalascañas and El Rocío.

PARADOR DE ALMAGRO

Ronda de San Francisco, 31, Almagro, 13270
☎ *(926) 86 01 00, FAX (926) 86 01 50*
$100 per double; Rooms (55): 6 singles, 48 doubles, 1 suite

★ ★ ★ ★

Almost exactly half way from Madrid to either Granada or Córdoba in the south, this parador provides a restful stop along the way. Indeed, it is one of the most restful of all the paradors with just enough attentiveness to allow anyone to sigh once and then let the tension fade away. After all, it started out in the early 16th century as a convent. Today, although most of the hotel is only 20 years old, it blends well with an original vine-clad entrance-lobby and old church—all that remain of the convent. Intelligent design of the additions left 16 patios spread around, one containing the pool, cozy sitting areas (with fireplaces), painted ceilings and tapestries on the walls. Guest rooms are white and ample, containing lovely windows and often lace bedspreads (the local art). This is more than your average hotel.

Dining

The sedate dining room is installed in the ancient refractory. It impresses with lovely wood ceiling, arches and tapestry. Here decent meals are served that feature the hearty food of La Mancha. This means a sort of ratatouille *(pisto manchego)* and a lamb tripe *(el tiznao)*, plus cold gazpacho soups. Roasts are featured, and pheasant *(perdiz)* in season. Cheeses of the region top off the meal. The local wines are mild, but others from around Spain are available, including Rioja and Duero. Expect a bill of about $20, plus drinks.

Alternative Dining

La Cuerda   ★

Ronda de Santo Domingo, 29 (near the old university), ☎ *(926) 88 28 05.*
The unattractive ambience cannot compare with the parador but the food surpasses it. In addition, meals will cost a few dollars less. Closed Mon. and Aug. Credit Cards: A, M, V.

Directions

Ronda de San Francisco is two blocks south of the Plaza Mayor, then a right turn. At the end of the street, turn left for the parador.

Paradors Nearby

Manzanares: 35 km   Toledo: 130 km   Jaén: 165 km
Úbeda: 165 km   Albacete: 180 km

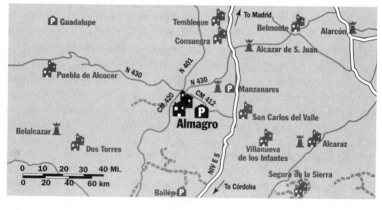

Sights

Walk two blocks north to an unusual **Plaza Mayor**, bound on two sides by stone colonnades with rows of windows above. In earlier times bull fights took place in this square, and jousts before that. At number 17 stands one of the oldest **theaters** in the world, dating to Shakespeare's day. South of the plaza is a square of attractive **mansions**, and more dot surrounding streets. You will pass houses selling hand-made **lace** on the way, the local craft.

Parador de Antequera

Paseo Garcia del Olmo, s/n, Antequera, 29200
☎ *(95) 284 09 01, FAX (95) 284 13 12*
$70 per double; 55 rooms: 55 doubles

★

There is nothing wrong with this parador; the question is why it is here. In the midst of so many wonderful sights in Andalusia, with nice beaches an hour away, why stay at a modern hotel overlooking an ordinary city and plain? Of course you could base here for excursions to Granada, Seville and beaches, but more interesting accommodations exist for that. In any case, this is an ordinary looking hotel, with mismatched furniture and boxy bedrooms that are indistinguishable from one another. There is a pool surrounded by grass for relaxing and wondering why you are here.

Dining

A split level dining room shares a cathedral ceiling and contemporary furniture with the lounge. Food is of the south which means gazpacho or *ajo blanco* (a garlic and almond cold soup) to start, better than the local specialty, gravy soaked fritters (pío). Follow with either fried fish or the special fish. A full meal will average $20, plus drinks.

SOUTHERN SPAIN

Directions

Located just north of the bull ring.

Paradors Nearby

Málaga: 50 km	Nerja: 80 km	Ronda: 96 km
Granada: 99 km	Córdoba: 122 km	

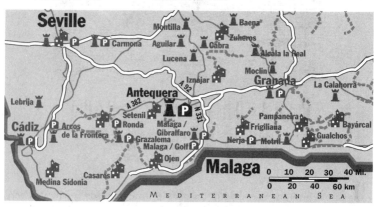

PARADOR DE BAILÉN

Avenida de Málaga, s/n, Bailén, 23710
☎ *(953) 67 01 00/(953) 67 25 30*
$50 per double; 86 rooms: 4 singles, 82 doubles

★ ★ ★

Bailén sits almost halfway between Madrid and Seville, so it breaks a long drive into two convenient legs. That is the reason for a low, modern hotel waiting here. The garden is pleasant; there is a pool; rooms serve their purpose; and prices are rock-bottom. All in all, not a bad combination. Still, we would travel 36 km further to Úbeda for more atmosphere and things to see and do.

Dining

Views of the garden add the best decoration to the dining room, though the interior is clean and crisp. During high season a buffet allows tastes of everything. The cooking is regional, with venison steak and pheasant often available. Otherwise, bull's tail stew and cod are always on the menu. Only here will the opportunity present itself of trying a bottle of white Santa Gertrudis or a red Torreperogil. Not bad. A full meal will average $30, plus drinks.

Directions

Located on the old route N-IV just north of Linares.

Paradors Nearby

Úbeda: 38 km	Granada: 99 km	Córdoba: 104 km
Manzanares: 122 km	Granada: 136 km	Albacete: 247 km

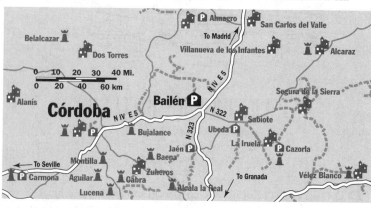

PARADOR DE NERJA

Almuñécar, 8, Nerja, 29780
☎ *(95) 252 00 50, FAX (95) 252 19 97*
$110 per double; 73 rooms: 3 singles, 57 doubles, 13 with jacuzzi

★ ★ ★ ★

Nerja is the least overdeveloped and most attractive of the resorts that comprise the Costa del Sol. Development there is, but kept outside of the village which thereby manages to retain its charm. The parador sits on a bluff above the best beach in the area. It resembles a modern resort style hotel outside, but inside wait exposed wood beams and traditional tile floors. A lush surrounding garden provides views almost as fabulous as those from the Balcón de Europa in the village. A few of the rooms partake of this view, but most overlook a central patio and pool. An elevator descends to the sandy beach, and tennis courts are available.

Alternative Accommodations

Balcón de Europa

> *Paseo Balcón de Europa, 1,* ☎ *(95) 252 08 00, FAX (95) 252 44 90, Telex 79503. 105 rooms.*
> The most interesting of the local hotels is the Balcón de Europa, named for the spectacular vantage point of the village, called the Balcony of Europe. Bedrooms take advantage of the views and there is a private beach below, otherwise this is just a modern businessperson-type establishment.

Dining

A dining room that is too large atones with views across the garden to the sea. Good soups start the meal. There is traditional gazpacho, of course, but also a richer version (*gazpachuelo*) with egg and lemon, also *ajo blanco*, made from garlic and almond paste. Fried fresh fish are always light and tasty, but a featured goat stew is savory indeed. Rice pudding clears the palate. The wine list covers Riojas and lighter Valdepeñas. A full meal will average $25, plus drinks.

Alternative Dining

Casa Luque   ★★

     Pl. Cavana, 2 (the main square behind the church), ☎ *(95) 252 10 04. Closed Monday.*
The house is charming and the decor is elegant, although the dining room is small. The food is authentic elevated Spanish with a Basque touch and runs to meats more than fish, although the fish is fresh and delicious. For the style of the place and savory cooking, prices are more than fair at $30. Reserve. Credit Cards: A, M, V.

Portofino   ★

     Puerta del Mar, 4 (directly below the Balcón de Europa, down stairs), ☎ *(95) 252 01 60. Dinners only; closed in Winter.*
The views alone would make this restaurant worth a visit, but it adds good, traditional Spanish food (including paella) to make itself irresistible at a price of only $20. Credit Cards: M, V.

Directions

The parador sits above Burriana-Tablazo beach, west of town.

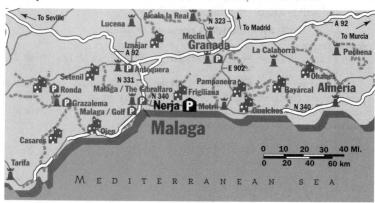

Paradors Nearby

Málaga: 55 km	Granada: 110 km
Antequera: 120 km	Ronda: 160 km

Sights

Nerja is most famous for its **Balcón de Europa**, a clifftop promenade above the sea dubbed by King Alfonso XII when he paused to admire the view. Four kilometers east is a series of remarkable stalactite decorated caves, the **Cuevas de Nerja**, large enough to hold summer concerts inside. (Open 9:30 a.m. to 6 p.m. in summer; from 10 a.m. to 1:30 p.m. and from 3–6 p.m. the rest of the year. Admission: 400 ptas.)

PARADOR DE PUERTO LUMBRERAS

Avenida Juan Carlos I, 77, Puerto Lumbreras, 13650
☎ *(956) 40 20 25, FAX (956) 40 28 36*
$70 per double; 60 rooms: 8 singles, 52 doubles

This is one of those stopover paradors situated to provide a logical break in a long journey. There is little reason otherwise to stop here. The problem with this one is that it is close enough to other paradors in more interesting places that there is no reason not to spend a half hour more driving to Mojácar, on the beach, or an hour more driving to marvelous Granada. If interested, this is a purely functional place to lay your head, modern but plain. There is a pool.

Dining

Besides being too bright by half, the dining room is merely a place to sit while eating. Fish soup *(caldero)*, more a stew, is featured. Vegetables are the local pride, with creamed eggplant *(berenjenas a la crema)* and salads standing out. Green pepper steak and the local rabbit are filling, so save room for a very good almond mousse *(mousse de almendras)*. A full meal will average $20, plus drinks.

Directions

From **Madrid** take N-IV south for 62 km to Ocaña where N-301 goes south through Albacete then to Murcia in 391 km. Take N-340 west for an additional 74 km. From **Granada** take N-342 east for 59 km to Guadix, then N-342 east for 146 km.

Paradors Nearby

Mojácar: 60 km   Jávea: 190 km
Granada: 202 km   Albacete: 230 km

PARADOR DE RONDA

Plaza de España, s/n, Ronda, 29400
☎ *(95) 287 75 00, FAX (95) 287 81 88*
$110 per double; 70 rooms: 69 doubles, 1 suite

★ ★ ★ ★

Ronda's old market and much of the 18th-century Ayuntamiento (City Hall) has just been made over as one of the newest paradors. The building is attractively neo-classic, crisp with some character. Best of all, it provides the best views over Ronda's awesome gorge and countryside. And that is the main reason to visit Ronda. The hotel forms a virtual compound at the edge of the, so-called, "new city," adjoining the bull ring. Public spaces are architecturally interesting, subtly lit and comfortable. Guest rooms continue the good taste with ample size. There is a pool as well. Though not a place for anyone with vertigo, most will enjoy their stay. The problem is a dizzying walk from the hotel over the gorge to see the sights of the "old town." Service is more attentive and thoughtful than at the average parador.

Alternative Accommodations

Reina Victoria

Av. Dr. Fleming, 25 (on entering town take the first right to the hotel), ☎ *(95) 287 12 40, FAX (95) 287 10 75.89 rooms.*

Sorry, parador, as long as it stands there will only be one place to stay in Ronda. The Reina Victoria, built in 1906 by an English company for British guests, is the most charmingly colonial hotel in Spain. It truly does seem Victorian, with the grace, charm and decor of that era. Today it is run by the Husa chain, caters to tour groups and has recently been completely renovated, but it still retains its old feeling. The gardens are lovely, with views that are wonderful, even though second to the parador's. Try very hard to get a room at the back with a balcony overlooking the valley. One more plus—it costs less than $100.

Dining

Although tastefully decorated, the dining room seems more formal than the food served in it. The cuisine consists of typically Andalusian fare modified by the more earthy people of these mountains. So look for *salmorejo*, a richer gazpacho, rabbit *(conejo)* and partridge *(perdice)*. Desserts range over almond custard *(sopa de almendras)* and a sweet egg yolk confection *(yemas)*. Local wines are cloying, choose a Ribera del Deuro or Valdepeñas instead. Diner will cost $25, without drinks.

Alternative Dining

Don Miguel   ★★

> *Pl. de España, 3 (at the Puente Nuevo),* ☎ *(95) 287 10 90.*
> *Two terraces offer such spectacular views of the Tajo Gorge that they may be too much for vertigo prone diners. If bothered, feast your eyes on the milk-fed baby lamb on your plate and all will be well, for it is good. The tariff will rise a few dollars above that at the parador. Reservations are advised on weekends. Closed Sun., and the middle two weeks in Jan.* Credit Cards: A, D, M, V.

Pedro Romero   ★

> *Virgen de la Paz, 18 (opposite the Pl. de Toros),* ☎ *(95) 287 11 10.*
> Named after the founder of modern bullfighting, naturally the restaurant is decorated with memorabilia of the bullring. Somehow it is attractive and homey (if you can ignore the stares of dead bulls). Of course you should try the *rabo de toro* here, and for dessert there is a special caramel custard *al coco* (with coconut) that should not be missed. A meal will cost about the same as at the parador. Credit Cards: A, D, M, V.

Directions

Drive the length of the Mercadillo (new town) up to the Puente Nuevo bridge to the Ciudad (old town). The parador compound is to the right of the bridge.

Paradors Nearby

Arcos: 90 km	Antequera: 92 km	Málaga: 125 km
Carmona: 140 km	Seville: 147 km	Cádiz: 162 km

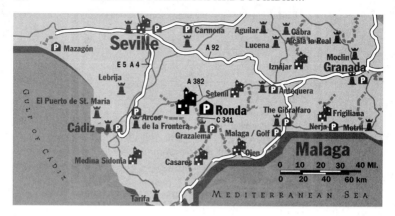

Sights

Ronda could hardly be more unusual in its situation. The old city stands on a bluff with precipitous drops on three sides, and the fourth side is separated from the newer part of town (post-Reconquest) by an incredible slice of 300-feet-deep gorge. From this aerie, views over the valley and distant hills are nothing short of stupendous.

Everyone, beginning with the Celts, made a stronghold of the impregnable old city, but it was the Moors who left the most lasting remains. Only surprise and the use of the first metal cannonballs in Spain allowed Ferdinand to capture it in 1485. Still, Ronda served as the center of a revolt by the Moors against forced conversions to Christianity a decade after the fall of Granada. The insurrection was put down with great difficulty and loss of life. When the Moors were expelled to quell such threats in Ronda, the remaining citizens turned to banditry, safe in their fortress fastness, causing two centuries of problems for the police.

Little Ronda had a seminal impact on the sport of bullfighting. Until the beginning of the 18th century, bulls were fought by men on horseback. The local Romero family invented a new way to fight—on foot using capes, a team of assistants, and killing the bull at the end with a sword thrust. The modern, stylized form of bullfighting was thus invented in Ronda. At first corridas were held in Ronda's Pl. de la Ciudad by sealing off the streets, then a special ring for the purpose was built in 1785, the second oldest in Spain (after Seville).

Being close to Gibraltar and enjoying cool summer breezes, Ronda has always been a favorite of the English. Hence, the very British hotel Reina Victoria was built here in 1906 for officers vacationing with their families. Here Rainer Maria Rilke, the great German poet, stayed for several months in 1912 recovering from an illness, and began his *Spanish Elegies*. Hemingway visited frequently, and the substantial ashes of Orson Welles are buried on a bull farm outside of town. Today, tourists throng on weekends, but weekdays remain serene.

The town is entered on C. de Sevilla. To cross the Puente Nuevo into the old town a turn must be made at some time to the parallel street to the right, C. Jerez, which changes its name to San Carlos. Across the bridge the name again changes to C. Armiñan. Parking is where you find it. If all else fails, city parking is just to the right of the Puente Nuevo on the Mercadillo, or new town, side.

The old town, called the Ciudad, is less than half a mile long by a quarter wide, so no one can get lost by too much. On the other hand, it conforms to a Moorish layout of winding streets and alleys so everyone gets lost at least a little. That is to say, it's a place for wandering. Start at the far (southern) end of the Ciudad, at the **Alcazaba**.

Not that there is much to see of the old Moorish fort, for the French demolished it in 1809, but it is a romantic site with nice views. Follow the main street, called C. Nuñez at this point, back in the direction of the new town for two blocks. As the street bends right go left into the main square, the **Pl. de la Ciudad ★**. It was here that the modern form of bullfighting was first practiced. At the north end of the plaza stands the church of **Santa María la Mayor ★** (open at the caretaker's whim; 100 ptas. donation). This is a mosque done over with the trappings of a 17th-century Christian church, as the recently uncovered mihrab in the vestibule shows (now with a statue of the Virgin inside). The church tower originally was the minaret. Inside, a Gothic nave hovers above a gilded baroque high altar.

Leave by a small street running from the east side of the church. Go east to a "T" where C. Ruedi de Gameros goes north for one block to the **Mondragon Palace ★**, imposing with twin graceful turrets. This is a Renaissance rebuilding on the site of the former Moorish palace in which Ferdinand and Isabella stayed while Isabella gave birth to a daughter. Today it houses exhibitions, so you can enter to admire its two handsome patios with glazed tiles and Mudejar stucco tracery. Do not miss the gallery in the rear with lovely artesonado ceiling and dramatic views of the valley. (Open weekdays 9 a.m.–2 p.m.; admission: 200 ptas.)

Retrace steps back to the church and go east to the main street, here called C. Armiñan, but take the first right into a pretty square with a striking little

minaret standing alone to show that there once was a mosque nearby. Take C. Marqués de Salvatierra from the northeast corner of this plaza for two blocks to the **Casa del Marqués de Salvatierra** on the right. The Renaissance facade displays "savages" over the portal and may be visited (open daily, except Thurs., 10 a.m.–1 p.m. and 4–7 p.m.; admission: 200 ptas., for guided tour).

Downhill to the right one passes two bridges, the first on Roman foundations, the second claimed to be Moorish. Further down the ravine are some of the finest **Moorish baths** ★ remaining in Spain (open Tues.–Sat. 10 a.m.–1 p.m. and 4–7 p.m.; open Sun. 10 a.m.–1 p.m.; admission: free). On the return up the hill, continue past the Casa del Marqués de Salvatierra toward the Puente Nuevo, and pass the **Casa del Rey Moro**. Although called the House of the Moorish king, it obviously dates from the early 18th century.

Continue to the Mercadillo (new town) over the Puente Nuevo, a spectacular 18th-century bridge, then along C. San Carlos to the **Pl. de Toros** ★, the bullring, in two blocks. It was completed in 1785, and surely is the most charming in Spain—which is why it has so often been featured in movies (open daily 10 a.m.–6 p.m.; admission to the museum: 200 ptas.). One block farther on C. San Carlos brings the lovely gardens of the **Alamenda Tajo** on the left. From here a dramatic walk along the cliffs leads to the Victorian hotel with the apt name of **Hotel Reina Victoria**, worth looking in and walking through the gardens in the rear.

PARADOR DE SAN FRANCISCO

Alhambra de Granada, s/n, Granada, 18009,
☎ *(958) 22 14 40, FAX (958) 22 22 64*
$180 per double; 39 rooms: 4 singles, 35 doubles

★ ★ ★ ★ ★

The Alhambra is one of the great buildings in the world and surrounded by lovely gardens. Imagine spending the night in these gardens, in the place where Queen Isabella herself rested (after her death) while priests prayed for her soul. Well, you won't be the only one who thinks this might be a special treat. The San Francisco is the most heavily booked of all paradors, reserved a year in advance by many, and six months is the minimum advance reservation for high season. It is also, as popular things tend to be, overrated. True, parts of the hotel date to the early 16th century, and include the chapel where Isabella was first interred before permanent disposition in her Granada chapel. So there are some wonderful architectural details—a blend of Moor and Christian. Extra special are the religious objects, paintings, sculpture and tapestries dotting the public rooms. The garden is undeniably lovely, while there is no more splendid building to be near than the Alhambra. But these compliments apply to the public spaces, and not even to all of them. You won't be sleeping in such beauty, for the bedrooms are housed in a modern addition which is ordinary at best. Then too, when a hotel is booked far beyond its available rooms, there is no need to coddle guests, so the service can be quite uncaring. What then is the conclusion? Stay if you can, it is a special place and provides the chance to wander the gardens without the tourists; but don't expect perfection.

Alternative Accommodations

Alhambra Palace

Peña Partida, 2 (continue on the main road through the Alhambra hill to the circle where signs direct you left for the Alhambra, but turn right), ☎ *(958) 22 14 68, FAX (958) 22 64 04, Telex 78400. 132 rooms.*

The parador is not the only treat in this city. The Alhambra Palace, located a stone's throw from the Alhambra, was done at the turn of the century in Moorish style with arches, bright tiles, and wooden ceilings that make it a fantasy appropriate to its location. The terrace bar faces the Sierra Nevadas and rooms overlook either the town or the same sublime mountains. Rooms are large and comfortably designed, although the public spaces are showing signs of wear. Indeed deterioration has reached the point where the only acceptable accommodations are those on the top floor, which provide spectacular views as well. We have also heard complaints about sloppy service and mis-additions on the bill. This is *not* a deluxe hotel, but it can be great fun and costs half the price of the parador.

América

Real de la Alhambra, 53 (fifty feet south of the Parador), ☎ *(958) 22 74 71, FAX (958) 22 74 70. Open Mar.–Nov. 9. 11 rooms, plus one suite.*

Want something cheaper? The hotel América is also near the gardens, is a flower-bedecked gem that beats the location of the parador by 50 feet and costs about $60. It is an utterly charming place to stay, but already discovered, so its few rooms must be booked months in advance.

Princesa Ana

Av. de la Constitución, 37 (on the main street into the city, opposite the bullring and just before the train station, about one mile northwest of the Cathedral), ☎ *(958) 28 74 47, FAX (958) 27 39 54. 57 rooms, plus 2 suites.*

If nothing is available near the Alhambra, taxi from the city below. Princesa Ana, although modern (built in 1989), combines white marble and peachy pink decorative tones to make it the most elegant hostelry downtown. Bedrooms are lovely, and the cost is very reasonable, at less than $100.

Inglaterra

Cetti Meriem, 4 (this street is directly behind the rear of the Cathedral, off C. Gran Via de Colón), ☎ *(958) 22 15 58, FAX (958) 22 71 00. 36 rooms.*

If full, or if you want a better location, try the Inglaterrra. New in 1992, the place sparkles with good taste. Bedrooms are comfortable and sufficiently large.

Parador Dining

Unfortunately, except for having a most intricate plaster ceiling, the small dining room is not otherwise memorable and cramped. Still, it's worth ordering a meal just for the extra chance to look out on the gardens. Gazpacho is featured, along with excellent cold cuts, including tasty local ham. Too

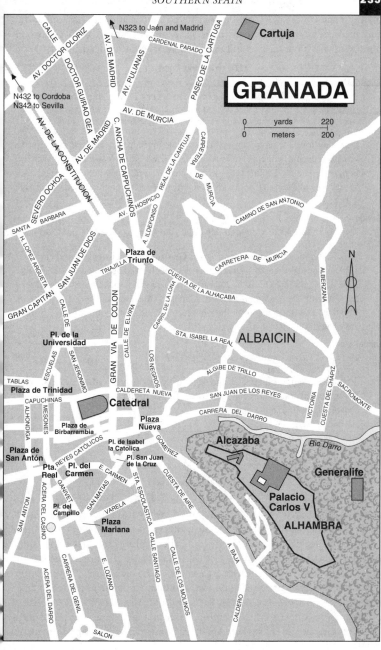

SOUTHERN SPAIN

many of the dishes can only be considered "international," for our tastes, and the prices are higher than the food justifies. Truth be told, Granada is not a gourmet's paradise. A full meal will average $40, plus drinks.

Alternative Dining

Ruta del Veleta ★★

Carretera de Sierra Nevada, 50; six km southeast of Granada (from the Pl. Real head south along Carrera del Genil, left on Paseo del Salón, then continue on Paseo de la Bomba following signs to "Pico del Veleta and Sierra Nevada"), ☎ *(958) 48 61 34. Closed Sun. evening.*

Granada's loveliest restaurant is this large one, outside the city. The dining room spreads blue and white ceramics around and overhead to lend both elegance and hominess. The food is first rate—from grilled meat to fish—the wines superb, and the service polished, all for about $35. Reservations are strongly advised. Credit Cards: A, D, M, V.

Sevilla ★

Oficios, 12 (in the alley opposite the Capilla Real), ☎ *(958) 22 88 62. Closed Sun. evening.*

This is the most famous restaurant in Granada, as celebrity pictures indicate, although not particularly touristy. It is charmingly decorated with tiles lining intimate dining rooms. This is the place to try Andalusian specialties, such as *sopa sevillana* (with fish), *cordero al la pastoril* (spicy lamb stew) and *rape a la granadina* (monkfish in a shrimp and mushroom sauce). It will cost about $35. Reservations are advised. Credit Cards: A, D, M, V.

Cunini ★

Pescaderia, 9 (two short blocks south of the Cathedral front, in the Alcaicería), ☎ *(958) 25 07 77. Closed Mon.*

The decor is simple but precise, and seafood is perfectly prepared. Without question this is the best seafood restaurant in town. Try the fritura to prove it. Prices are reasonable at about $25 per person. Credit Cards: A, D, M, V.

Directions

From **Madrid** and north, Granada is entered on Av. de Madrid, which arrives at a traffic circle just after passing the University on the left. Take Av. de la Constitución to the left. At the next intersection, in one very long block past a park, go left on Av. del Hospicio, then right at the first opportunity onto Av. Andaluces. Round the circle at Pl. del Triunfo to continue out the opposite end on C. Elvira. Elvira ends in about ten blocks at C. Reyes Católicos. Turn left here into the Pl. Nueva, and take the first right onto the narrow Cuesta de Gomerez, which leads through the gate to the Alhambra precinct. Signs direct to the Alhambra Palace and the parador. From **Córdoba** and west Granada is entered on Av. de la Constitución. After passing a large park on the left, follow the directions from Madrid above. From the **Costa del Sol** and south, traffic funnels into Acara del Casino which ends at the large Pl. Puerta Real. Take the large street right, Reyos Católicos, for about eight blocks to the Pl. Nueva. The right at the far end of the plaza, the narrow Cuesta de Gomerez, leads in six blocks through the gate to the Alhambra Precinct. Signs direct to the Alhambra Palace and parador.

Paradors Nearby

Antequera: 98 km	Jaén: 100 km	Nerja: 110 km
Málaga: 127 km	Úbeda: 130 km	

Sights

Granada did not stand among the major cities of the Moors during most of their 700-year reign in Spain, but as their last capital it constituted the culmination of an artistry so impressive that Christian conquerors could not bear to destroy it. For this reason the last palace of the Moors, the Alhambra, remains standing today.

Granada first attained prominence when Jaén was captured by the Spanish in 1246, forcing the Moorish ruler of the principality to move his capital southward. He chose Granada, which thus became the final capital of the dynasty of Nasrids, for his family name was Ibn el Ahmar Nasir. He learned from his defeat to make treaties with Christians rather than fight them. His successors used diplomacy to stave off the Christians, even allying with them to capture Seville, and by doing so prospered. But the Christians seized piece after piece of the rest of the Moorish empire, until Granada stood alone. Swollen with refugees from lost domains, Granada grew to 200,000 souls by the 14th century, about four times the London of those times, and construction began on the Alhambra Palace.

Toward the end of the 15th-century a revolt weakened Granada. Caliph Muley Hassan fell in love with a Christian woman named *Zoraya* (Morning Star), who had converted to Islam. This love affair threatened the position of his principal wife who fled with her young son before the caliph could repudiate her. She marshalled supporters, then returned to depose the old caliph and placed her son Abu Abdallah, known to the Christians as Boabdil, on the throne. Granada's rule had fallen to a child-king who reigned over subjects divided into those supporting the young new caliph and those favoring the previous one. It was a perfect time to attack; Isabella and Ferdinand declared war. Twice Boabdil sallied forth with his army, and each time was captured and forced to cede territory. After the second loss, he vowed never to leave Granada again.

By 1491 the Christians had cut Granada off from the sea and all other avenues of supply, and settled in for a siege. Eight months later, on January 2, 1492, the city surrendered and Boabdil marched away forever with tears in his eyes. The Catholic monarchs entered the city dressed in Moorish clothes to seal the end of 781 years of Moorish domination.

Within decades the Christians expelled the Moors from Spain and burned most of Granada, including all its mosques. Only the Alhambra remained untouched, for its beauty lent it a sanctity. Although Ferdinand and Isabella chose this city as their final resting place, decline continued. The last blow was the expulsion in 1609 of the Moroscos, people of Moorish descent, depleting Granada of most of its population. By the 18th century the city numbered less than 50,000 citizens. But through good times and bad, the stream of visitors never abated. The most famous tourist was Washington Irving, who lived for three months in the ruins of the Alhambra Palace and there began his evocative *Tales of the Alhambra*.

Note: Granada also retains a significant Gypsy population, as visitors discover. The women sell flowers, while the men hover around. They can be very insistent; and valuables should be carefully watched.

Parking is available on the Alhambra hill, but parking in the city below is far from the sights. The best course is to begin at the Alhambra, walk or taxi down, then taxi back up to your car.

Alhambra Precinct

Puerta de las Granadas, ☎ *(958) 22 75 27.*
Hours open: Mon.–Sat. 9 a.m.–8 p.m. (closes at 6 p.m. in winter). Open Sun. 9:30 a.m.–6 p.m. Illuminated in the summer on Tues., Thurs. and Sat. nights from 10 p.m.–midnight (in winter on Sat. 8–10 p.m.), for a separate charge of 625 ptas.
A steep climb begins before passing through the entry gate to the precinct. This gate, the *Puerta Las Granadas* (Pomegranates' Gate) was erected by Carlos V in

1536 on the site of a former Moorish portal. Past this entrance waits an enchanted forest where everything suddenly quiets in stands of stately elms, planted by the duke of Wellington in the 19th century. Signs direct pedestrians to the **Puerta de la Justicia**, their entrance, and cars to the **Puerta de Coches**, by a roundabout but scenic route. One combined ticket serves all the sights, but the proper order in which to visit the various sights is an issue. The best course is to see the palace of Carlos V first, for it pales after the Alhambra, and the same point holds for the Alcazaba. Then see the Alhambra, followed by the lovely walk to the gardens of the Generalife. However, this timing is made difficult by the fact that tickets now prescribe set times of entry to the Alhambra and palácio. Do not miss your appointed time, for the ticket is invalid thereafter. If possible, go early in the day before the crowd collects. *Admission: 625 ptas. for the Alhambra Palace, Alcazaba, Generalife and palace of Carlos V; free after 3 p.m. on Sun.*

Note: The number of visitors per day is limited. Go early to ensure admission.

The palace of Carlos V lies directly ahead, if entering from the Puerta de la Justicia, or to the left, if entering from the Puerta de Coches.

Palácio de Carlos V   ★ ★

Because he so loved the site, Carlos V wanted a palace of his own adjoining the Alhambra, though his love was not so pure that it prevented him from destroying about a third of the Alhambra Palace—all the private royal rooms—to gain space. As his architect he used the Italian Machuca, who had trained with Michelangelo, to plan a severely neoclassical structure. The design is wholly elegant, so much that it seems too austere to inhabit, although it delights as pure design.

The plan is a circle inside a square. The outer face emphasizes two stories with rows of regular windows distinguished by alternating piedmonts and circles above, and separated by Ionic pilasters on the upper story. Inside comes the shock of a huge open circular patio formed of simple Doric columns below and Ionic columns above, with recesses intended for statues. On at least one occasion a bullfight was held in this patio. The original plan included a huge dome to cover the central patio, but the building was never finished and seems never to have been inhabited, by Carlos V or by anyone else.

To the left, on the ground floor, is the **Museo de Art Hispano-Musulman** *(open Mon.–Fri. 10 a.m. to 2 p.m.; admission: 250 ptas.)*. It contains objects found in the Alhambra area, including pieces of original decoration, a cistern with lions attacking gazelles and a huge blue 14th-century pitcher almost as tall as a person. On the second floor is the **Museo de Bellas Artes** *(open Tues.–Sun. 10 a.m. to 2 p.m.; admission: 250 ptas.)*. It displays works by Granada artists, including paintings by Cano, but also a fine Limoges enamel triptych of the Crucifixion from the early 16th century.

Alcazaba   ★

To the left (west) of the Palácio de Carlos V is an open area known as the Pl. de los Aljibes (cisterns). The reservoir beneath was constructed by the Catholic monarchs to collect water, for the Christians did not know how to work the existing Moorish water system. The Alcazaba stands to the left (west) of this plaza.

A fortress *(alcazaba)* has existed on this eminently defensible site since the 10th century, though the present structure dates from the 13th. The fortress adds a 12-foot thickness of wall to that surrounding the entire Alhambra precinct. Sturdy square towers gave defenders secure places from which to fire down on attackers. The one in the northwest corner, called the **Torre de le Vela**, was that from which Cardinal Mendoza, sent ahead to ascertain that the town was safe, raised the flag of Christian Spain to signal that the city was theirs at last. Today it offers splendid views over the city and the Alhambra Palace, with the Sierra Nevada behind. A plaque nearby quotes the haunting lament of a Moorish poet: Nothing is sadder than to be blind in Granada.

Alhambra Palace   ★★★★

Ibn el Ahmar Nasir (a.k.a. Muhammad I), founder of the Nasrid dynasty, began a palace on this site in the 13th century, but little of the original remains. Of what survives, the Court of Myrtles was built for Yusuf I in the middle of the 14th century, the Court of the Lions for Muhammad V near the end of that century and the Tower of the Infantas for Muhammad VII at the close of the 14th century.

The facade is of no architectural interest, for Islamic palaces are intended as private places, and hide all luxury from public view. Further, tradition called for each new ruler to add rooms of his own, rather than occupy his predecessor's quarters, thus, the palace is a compound consisting of numerous rooms, rather than a unified structure. However, the Alhambra did separate into three distinct areas. One contained the living accommodations for the caliph. That part was destroyed to build Carlos V's palace. Another consisted of public rooms for ceremonies—such as audiences with the caliph or his ministers—and for music, or other entertainments. Several of these survive—the Mexuar, Hall of the Ambassadors, Kings' Chamber, Hall of the Two Sisters and Abencerrajes Gallery. A final part sheltered the close staff of the caliph, most importantly his harem. Note that the names today applied to the rooms are generally fanciful and give little indication of original names or uses.

No consideration was given to permanence or future generations in designing these rooms, they served only for the enjoyment of one owner. Construction was of brick, wood and, especially, stucco, molded and carved into the most intricate designs then painted and gilded, but eminently perishable. In 1591 gunpowder exploded outside the walls near the Court of the Lions, causing great damage. In the 19th century French troops left explosives when they retreated from bivouac here, which fortunately did not go off. But in general, centuries of neglect exacted a heavy toll on such fragile materials.

Reconstruction has been under way for almost a century. If what you see looks too new to be original, that is because it is, but all has been restored with the greatest authenticity to suggest the original.

Still, the feeling of these rooms would have been quite different from what you see today, for they would have been furnished, Persian carpets would have lined the floors, metal and glass lanterns would have spread soft light on brightly painted decorative wood and stucco. The miracle of the Alhambra is that despite reconstruction and the loss of furniture and paint it still captivates as few other buildings can. Very likely its appeal is for the way of life this architecture presents, so different from anything Western. There is no attempt to awe with size, only with beauty. No room is farther than a few feet from an outdoor patio playing water for both its sight and sound, and gardens are never more than a step away. Nature and artifice cohabit more intimately than in our western buildings.

Entrance is into the **Mexuar**, from the Arabic *Mashwar*, "audience chamber." Its balcony was added when Isabella and Ferdinand remodeled this room as a chapel and still bears traces of 15th-century painted design. At the end of the room Isabella and Ferdinand added an oratory which involved lowering the original floor. Christians preferred to stand to look out of windows, while Moors sat. The exit door on the left was cut through the walls for tourists.

That doorway leads to the **Patio de Cuarto Dorado**, redecorated in Mudejar style after the Reconquest but with an elegant low fountain. Across the patio is the facade of the **Palace of Comares**, from 1370, which serves as a fine sample of the Alhambra aesthetic. Simple rectangular portals are surrounded by the most refined carved stucco designs. Windows above are fitted with intricate wooden screens, *mashrabia*, to allow the ladies of the court to look out without being seen. The left portal leads to royal apartments; the right once opened to administrative offices, no longer existing.

Take the left portal into a small room then go left again into the glorious **Patio de Los Arrayanes** (Court of the Myrtles). A central reflecting pool is lined by Myrtle bushes. By reflection the pool doubles the arcades at both ends to emphasize the harmony of simple arches and ornate decoration. The center arch is higher than the others to display a more ornate arch behind it that leads into an end room. Around the sides of the pool repose four sets of chambers for wives, with alcoves for their divans, but little surviving decoration. The room at the far end (south) was destroyed to construct the palace of Carlos V.

Before entering the near end, notice the fine carved design of its original doors. They lead into the apartment for the caliph, the **Sala de la Barca**, with alcoves on either end for divans showing that it served as a bedroom. A lovely wood ceiling above places a half dome on either end so the caliph could see "stars" as he closed his eyes. At the rear is the magnificent **Solón de Embajadores** (Room of the Ambassadors), the audience chamber of the palace. Here the caliph would sit in the recess of the center window, framed and made dazzling by its light, to receive embassies. Decoration on the walls of amazing complexity would have been even more startling with original paint, and almost prevents the eyes from rising to an astonishing ceiling that ascends to a dome symbolizing heaven.

Return to the Patio de los Arrayanes and follow the left side to the next to last portal, the open one. Before going though to one of the great wonders of the Alhambra, enter the end arcade for a look at the basement of the palace of Carlos V, just to remember how cold Christian architecture became two centuries after the Alhambra. It seems altogether inhuman after a taste of the Moors.

Through the portal, after a small chamber for a caliph's wife, comes the **Sala de los Mozárabes**, whose ceiling was once highly praised before it suffered great damage from an explosion.

But it is difficult to concentrate on this room when the **Patio de los Leones** beckons. The hall opens to a pavilion of slender columns with unique capitals supporting stalactite arches and domes. Across the way, past the fountain, is the pavilion's twin. The fountain rests on the backs of twelve charming lions who give the patio its name. Various state apartments ring the patio with entrances off a columned arcade.

In the center of the right side is the **Sala de los Abencerrajes**, named for a clan who supported Boabdil and his mother in their rebellion against the reigning caliph. Tradition says the former caliph murdered the leaders of this family before ceding his throne and sees remains of that blood in stains on the floor. The doors are lovely and the stalactite ceiling is a wonder.

At the far end of the patio is the **Sala de los Reyes**, three rooms in a row named for the painting of ten seated Moors over the central room. (The Christians believed that Moors had kings.) Given Islamic strictures against painted figures, these 14th-century paintings on leather probably were executed by Christians.

Off to the left side of the patio is the **Sala de las Dos Hermanas** (Two Sisters), fancifully named for two marble slabs in the pavement, although the room may indeed once have formed part of the harem. It has the most amazing of the surviving stalactite, or honeycombed, domed ceilings said to contain 5000 individual cells. How it manages to be beautiful amid the incredible detail is one of art's mysteries. The walls too are rich in decoration. The Arabic inscription that looks so elegant actually commemorates the circumcision of a caliph's son. Opposite the entrance, a window retains the only surviving Moorish shutter in the palace, although most windows originally had them.

A portal at the rear lets into the **Sala de los Ajimeces**, named for the windows of its porch that give a lovely view of the **Patio de Lindaraja** below, originally with a reflecting pool like the other patios. Once more the ceilings are worth admiring.

A corridor at the end leads across the patio to rooms remodeled by Carlos V. It was here that Washington Irving stayed to study the beauties and myths of the Alhambra. At the far end of these apartments a modern corridor runs to the **Tocador de la Reina** (queen's dressing room) in a tower, remodeled by Elizabeth of Parma, wife of Felipe V, and hung with paintings.

Stairs descend to a patio with four cypresses where a sign points to **baños** (baths). These were the original *hamman*, or bath, of the palace, today in the form of a remodeling by Carlos V.

Cross the Patio de Lindaraja to enter the main gardens of the Alhambra. Ahead and to the left is the **Torre de las Damas**, the oldest surviving part of the palace—dating from the beginning of the 14th century—and not in the best condition. The pool is watched over by two Moorish lions rescued from a hospital in the city below. The pavilion now is simple, since columns have replaced the original carved stucco piers in the rear wall, but the tower retains some fine workmanship inside.

Several other towers in the Alhambra walls are worth visiting, especially the **Torre de la Captiva** (Imprisoned Woman), a miniature palace three towers farther along the walls, and the **Torre del las Infantas** (Princesses), next in line and late in period but sumptuously decadent.

From the Torre de las Infantas, it is worth a minute to return in the direction of the palace to visit the **Parador de San Francisco** in the center of the gardens. Once this was a convent in whose chapel the bodies of Isabella and Ferdinand rested while waiting completion of their tombs in the lower town. Return to the Torre de las Infantas where a gate, a little farther along the wall, lets out to a cypress-lined walk up to the Generalife.

Generalife   ★ ★ ★

Its present name is a distortion of the Arabic *Jennat al Arife*, "Garden of the Architect." This was a summer retreat for the caliph and his court, placed higher on the Alhambra hill to capture breezes. Originally, it would have been rustic and a working farm, though today it has been reconstructed into formal gardens. The building is arranged around a central court in which, as usual for the Moors, water flows. Both short sides of the building contain graceful pavilions. A gallery for views over the Alhambra Palace runs along the near long side. On the far side were apartments for the caliph and his entourage, but compared to the luxuries of the palace, the Generalife is simple and fresh.

The Lower City

While a taxi back to the city is not expensive, it is pleasant to walk from the Alhambra hill if feet are not too tired. Simply head downhill. After a couple of hundred yards to the gate of Puerta las Granada, Cuesta de Gomerez leads to the Pl. Nueva in about five blocks. A left turn onto the large C. Reyes Católicos brings the busy Pl. de Isabel la Católica in five blocks more. Head right along Gran Via de Colón to take the second left down C. de los Oficios. The **Palácio Madraza** is passed on the left, with painted 18th-century facade. It was Granada's university under the Moors. Inside is an octagonal Mudejar room with nice decoration and dome, and the Sala de Babildos with a fine ceiling. (Open 9 a.m. to 2 p.m.; admission is free.) On the right, a little farther along the alley, is the entrance to the **Capilla Real**, and still farther along is the **Cathedral**.

Capilla Real   ★★★

C. de los Oficios, ☎ *(958) 22 92 39.*
Hours open: daily 10:30 a.m.–1 p.m. and 4–7 p.m. (until 6 p.m. in winter).

In her will Isabella asked to be buried with Ferdinand at whichever place he chose. Ferdinand selected Granada, the site of his greatest victory. In 1506, two years after Isabella's death, a mausoleum was begun by Enrique de Egas under Ferdinand's direction and finished in 1521, five years after Ferdinand's death. The art this chapel contains, the beauty of the tombs and their historical importance makes this one of the most moving sights in Spain.

Behind an uninspired facade lies an interior composed of every element of the developed Isabelline style. Emblems of the Catholic monarchs are everywhere, including their well-known arrow and yoke motif (the first letter of the Spanish word for arrow and for yoke was the same as the first letter in Ferdinand and Isabella's name). Entry is through the sacristy—two simple rooms made splendid by the art inside them.

The paintings are the original collection of Isabella and demonstrate both her deep religious devotion and surprisingly refined aesthetic sense. Here are some masterpieces, seldom reproduced, from the 15th century and earlier. Paintings include a wonderful *Cristo Muerto* by Roger van der Weyden, a very interesting Botticelli, a fine *San Juan Evangelista* by Berruguete, and four spectacular Memlings, among others. Also on display are Isabella's crown and scepter, some needlework by her own hand, and the sword of Ferdinand. Adorning the walls are banners flown by the Christian army during the conquest of Granada.

The adjoining chapel seems surprisingly small for figures that loom so large in history. Near the entrance, in the finest Italian marble, are the effigies of Ferdinand and Isabella. Farther back and standing slightly higher are effigies of their daughter, Juana the Mad, and her husband, Philip the Handsome—the parents of Carlos V. The carvings of Ferdinand and Isabella hold the greatest interest for the personages represented, and suggest true if idealized likenesses of that famed pair. However, the faces are difficult to see without a ladder—climb the pulpit for the best look. Nonetheless, the other pair of carvings—of Juana and Philip—are artistically superior, the masterpiece of Bartolome Ordoñez. In the crypt below lie the actual lead coffins, unadorned, each under its corresponding effigy. The small fifth casket holds a niece of Juana's.

The retable at the altar is among the first in the Plateresque style, and its panels depict the capture of Granada and conversion of the infidels. Kneeling painted statues of Ferdinand and Isabella that seem to be true portraits, by the great Diego de Siloé, flank the retable. *Admission: 200 ptas.; Sun. free.*

Cathedral ★

Gran Via de Colón, ☎ *(958) 22 29 59.*
Hours open: same hours and ticket as the Capilla Real; Sun. free.

After finishing the Capilla Real, its architect Egas was commissioned by Carlos V to design an adjoining cathedral. To Carlos the chapel was not sufficiently impressive to memorialize his illustrious grandparents. Seven years later the great architect Diego de Siloé took over the job, though the Cathedral was not finished until 1714. Given its purpose and the talent that worked on it, the Cathedral should be wonderful. Unfortunately, it is not a success, although interesting in its parts.

The main facade is due to Granada's great artist, Alonso Cano (buried inside). It is simple in design but heavy in feeling. Inside, soaring ceilings seem to bear down on too massive piers. What is original about the interior is the main altar, set in a huge circular niche with arches cut through to a circling ambulatory. The effect, though interesting, detracts from the importance of the altar. The upper gallery in the rotunda above the altar contains some fine paintings by Cano, and the stained glass higher up is the finest 16th century work. But the loveliest part of the Cathedral is the doorway in the south transept. This was the original door to the Capilla Real and is harmonious Isabelline work.

The streets south of the Cathedral are known as the **Alcaicería**. They formed the silk bazaar under the Moors, but it burned in 1843. Today it is reconstructed as a warren of souvenir shops. The baroque church of **San Juan de Dios** is nearby, and the charming quarter of the **Albaicín** is not far. For the church, follow C. San Jerónimo that goes north from the middle of the north face of the Cathedral. In about eight short blocks, turn right on the large C. San Juan de Dios for two blocks to the church on the left.

San Juan de Dios ★

C. San Juan de Dios, ☎ *(958) 27 57 00.*
Hours open: daily 10 a.m.–1 p.m. and 2–6 p.m.

Juan de Robles was a Portuguese of Jewish descent who devoted his life to the sick and needy. He was canonized for founding the Order of the Knights Hospitallers and the adjoining hospital was established in his memory in 1552, two years after his death. The church was added in the 18th century. Its facade is admirable and the inside is a glittering baroque fantasy, culminating in the churrigueresque high altar. Behind the altar is Juan's tomb. The patio of the still-functioning hospital that precedes the church is a painted Renaissance beauty. *Admission: 150 ptas.*

La Cartuja is two km north of the center of town and reached by driving west from the Pl. Nueva along Carrera del Darro. After the street changes its name to Passeo del Padre Manion, it turns north and changes its name again to Cuesta del Chapiz. It turns right and changes its name, for the last time, to C. Pages, before ending at a "T." Go left on Carretera de Murcia as it winds up the hill to the monastery.

La Cartuja ★

Añfácar, ☎ *(958) 20 19 32. Bus number 8 from the front of the Cathedral goes here.*
Hours open: daily 10 a.m.–1 p.m. and 4–7 p.m. (closes at 6 p.m. in winter).

This church was redecorated in 1662 at the height of the baroque period and stands as one of the finest examples of that exuberant style, a constant surprise to the eye. In a way it brings you back to Europe after a visit to the Moorish Alhambra. The altar is a swirl of brown and white marble, frosted by molded stucco, beneath a painted dome. The sacristy is admirable for its marquetry doors, vestment chests and walls inlaid with silver, tortoiseshell and ivory. In the monastery proper hangs a series of paintings by a former monk—martyrdoms that luxuriate in blood. *Admission: 250 ptas.*

Shopping

The Alcaicería is a warren of souvenir shops where you will see examples of the local blue and white ceramic. However, the top quality is sold at *Ceramica Arabe (☎ (958) 20 12 27)* in the *Pl. San Isidro, 5.* This square is located a half mile north of the Cathedral, past the Hospital Real, a block east of Av. de la Constitución.

Excursions

Granada is a good base from which to visit **Úbeda** and **Baeza**, both described in this chapter. The natural tour is to visit **Córdoba**, less than two hours northwest, and/or **Seville**, three hours due west. The scenic town of **Ronda** is another good trip. The **Costa del Sol** is also near.

PARADOR EL ARRUZAFA

Avenida de la Arruzafa, 33, Córdoba, 14012
☎ (957) 27 59 00, FAX (957) 28 04 09
$100 per double; 94 rooms: 2 singles, 86 doubles, 4 suites

In a sort of suburb two miles from center city stands this modern hotel, looking like a thousand others. Yet it is spacious, open and surrounded by palms. Here you can relax at the pool before and after a speedy 15 minute ride to Córdoba's glorious mosque. In fact the interior of the hotel is rather grand with soaring ceilings and plenty of space to spread out. A striped motif echoes the coloring of the mosque, a bit too cutely for our taste. Bedrooms are generous in size and tasteful without stamping much on the memory. Tennis courts are provided. The question is whether you want the quiet of the suburbs or the feel of the old city; and whether you want a pleasant hotel or something special.

Alternative Accommodations

El Conquistador´s

Magistral González Francés, 15 (facing the east wall of the mosque), ☎ *(957) 48 11 02, FAX (957) 47 46 77. 103 rooms.*

All white in the style of a new Moorish villa, El Conquistador´s elegance of decor and the beauty of its patio make it unrivaled in Códoba. In addition, the hotel sits across the street from the mosque. However, it demands that guests solve the difficult problem of choosing between a room facing the lovely interior patio and one facing the mosque. Since this area is brightly lit at night, sleep will be more restful in an interior room. Parking is available for a fee.

Amistad Córdoba

Pl. de Maimónides, 3 (beside the synagogue in the Judería), ☎ *(957) 42 03 35, FAX (957) 42 03 65.69 rooms.*

Also special is the Amistad Córdoba. Newly opened, a stone's throw from the mosque, the Amistad is constructed from two 18th-century townhouses to provide the most pleasant stay in the Judería. A mudéjar decorated patio sets a lovely tone. Prices at either hotel are a few dollars less than the parador's.

Dining

The dining room is also spacious and modern with pleasing views over grass to downtown Córdoba. Since this is the south, there is gazpacho, of course, but also a somewhat thicker, more garlicky version called *salmorejo* in which ham and eggs are included. The other specialty is *rabo de toro*—oxtail stewed in heavy tomato sauce—which no one should disparage without first trying. You seldom go wrong with lightly fried fish, however. Montilla and Moriles are the local wines. A full meal will average $20, plus drinks.

Alternative Dining

El Caballo Rojo   ★★

Cardenal herrero, 28 (opposite the northwest corner of the mosque), ☎ *(957) 47 53 75.* Dining is upstairs in a huge fifties kind of place that is noisy because hordes of people are enjoying themselves. The menu claims dishes based on ancient recipes, some of which are tasty indeed, such as *rape mozárabe*. A complimentary sherry aperitif settles you in, and ordering from a special menu can hold prices down, which otherwise approach $40. Reservations are strongly advised. Credit Cards: A, D, M, V.

El Blasón   ★★

José Zorrilla, 11 (near the hotel Andalucia), ☎ *(957) 48 06 25.*

Upstairs, past an inviting patio, silks and candelabra produce a Belle Époche feeling of quiet luxury. Service is excellent and the dishes are innovative. There is a reasonably-priced special menu, plus a more expensive *menu de degustación* to put the chef through his paces. Figure $35 per person. Credit Cards: A, D, M, V.

El Churrasco   ★★

Romero, 16 (the street heading northwest from the northwest corner of the mosque), ☎ *(957) 29 08 19. Closed August.*

Again, white walls with brick arches characterize this restaurant, this time with iron chairs and an indoor garden under a skylight. Upstairs is a more formal room. The specialty after which the restaurant is named is a spicy barbecued pork that, along with other grilled dishes, draws a crowd even at about $35 each. The *salmorejo* soup is delicious as well. Reservations are strongly recommended. Credit Cards: A, D, M, V.

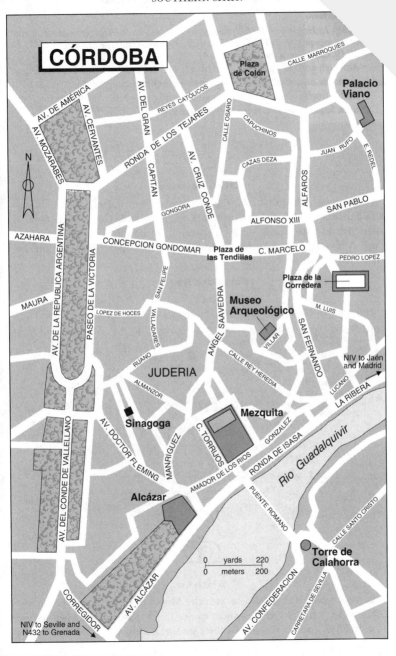

...guera, 5 *(this alley angles of C. Deanes, which leaves the northwest corner ...e; or, walk through El Caballo Rojo restaurant, cited above),* ☎ *(957) 47 ...d the second half of Nov.*

...od inexpensive food is hard to find in Córdoba, here it is served either ...a small patio or indoors on checkered tablecloths surrounded by ...ies. For the price of about $15, there is no better, more authentic food ...in the city. Credit Cards: A, D, M, V.

Directions

Cross the Guadalquivir over the first bridge (San Rafael), then continue straight along Passeo de la Victoria, beside a long park. Turn right at the first traffic island onto Ronda de los Tejares. Take the third left, again along a park. After crossing tracks this becomes Av. de Brillante where signs indicate the parador in 4 km.

Paradors Nearby

Jaén: 104 km	Bailén: 105 km	Carmona: 109 km
Antequera: 127 km	Granada: 166 km	Málaga: 178 km

Sights

As their capital, Córdoba rose with the Moors to glory, but it was an important city long before the Moors came. Eight hundred years before, the Romans had made it the seat of their southern province. Córdoba became

SOUTHERN SPAIN

the largest city in Roman Spain, and here the great Latin writer Seneca the Elder was born. Later, its archbishop Hosius presided over the Church Council of Nicea, from which emanated the famous creed.

Under the Moors Córdoba glowed as the shining light of medieval Europe. By the 10th century its population had reached half a million—double its size today—at a time when neither London nor Paris approached 100,000. The streets were paved and lighted, public baths were open to all, 50 hospitals served the sick, and a third of a million mansions, houses and stores filled the city. Nor was Córdoba merely large and modern for the times. While the Dark Ages eclipsed science in the rest of Europe, Córdoba served as its reservoir of learning. Córdoba's library housed a quarter of a million volumes at a time when books elsewhere in Europe were rare as hen's teeth and only one Christian in a hundred could read. Of course the Moors had an advantage—they knew how to make paper while the rest of Europe wrote on costly sheepskin—and Córdoba sent its children to one of 29 public schools. The great Jewish philosopher Moses Maimonides was born and lived in Córdoba, as did the great Aristotelian scholar Ibn Rushd, known to the West as Averröes. Later his works were translated into Latin to produce the scholastic thought which Abelard, Duns Scotus and Thomas Aquinas developed to lift Europe into the Renaissance. Even algebra and Arabic numbers were disseminated from Andalusia to the rest of the continent. Without the Moorish culture in Andalusia—indeed, without Córdoba—the west would have remained in its Dark Ages for centuries longer, with unpredictable results.

Christians captured Córdoba in 1236, ending its preeminence. Even after the reconquest, Córdoba retained fame for its tooled, embossed and colored leatherwork, so desired throughout Europe that "cordovan" became a common noun in English for special leather. But never again would the city shine as it had once.

Arriving from **Madrid** or from the direction of **Jaén**, travel along Paseo de la Rivera beside the Guadalquivir River. After passing the gardens of the Alcázar you arrive at a "T." Continue right onto Av. de Conde de Vallallano. Stay along the boulevard gardens on Paseo de la Victoria, though if a spot for parking presents itself, as it usually does, take it. Otherwise continue to the circle, taking Ronda de los Tejares northeast. At the third right, turn onto C. Cruz Conde, whose second right onto C. de Robledo leads to parking. From both **Seville** and **Granada** you arrive at a large traffic circle and proceed northwest to cross the bridge over the Guadalquivir River, which funnels into Av. de Conde de Vallallano. Then follow the directions above.

The best approach to the mosque is through the medieval quarters, the Judería, to acquire some feel for life as it was then. Make your way to the grand boulevard of Córdoba, the gardened Paseo de la Victoria. Head a few blocks south to reach the beginning of the reconstructed town walls. Follow these walls to their gate, the **Puerta de Almodovar**, watched over by a statue of Seneca.

Judería   ★★

Turn immediately right through the town gate to hug the walls along C. Maimonides. Whitewashed houses, many with lovely interior patios and flowers, line the lanes. In one long block is the **Synagogue ★**, on the right (open Tues.–Sat. 10 a.m. to 2 p.m. and 3:30–5:30 p.m., opening and closing an hour earlier in winter; closed Mon. as well as Sun. afternoons; admission: 75 ptas.). Along with the two in Toledo, this is one of the last surviving synagogues in Spain. It dates to the 14th century and is tiny, though with attractive Mudejar stuccowork along the upper walls and balcony.

Across from the synagogue is a touristy, reconstructed **Zoco** (souk, "market"), interesting only for a look at the building with craftsmen working around an open patio, which contains a museum of bullfighting (dedicated to locally born Manolete). Turn east across its southern face, first passing a statue of Maimonides and then the **Capilla de San Bartolome** on the right, with vaulting and Mudejar work inside. At the end of C. Cardenal Salazar, C. Almanzor Romero leads southeast to the corner of the **Mezquita** (mosque). Along its northern face, beside the bell tower, is its normal entrance. See the description below.

After the Mezquita, head east along its north face to take the alley going left, just before the corner of the walls, called C. Velázquez Bosco. Almost immediately take the right that leads past beautiful **flowered patios ★** on either side and into an alley heading south, called the Calleja de las Flores. Córdoba takes great pride in its patios, holding a contest during the first two weeks of May. The alley lets into C. Encarnación which goes east for a block to C. Rey Heredia. Jag right, then left onto Calle Horno de Cristo which leads to the **archaeological museum ★**, also described below.

Mezquita   ★★★★★

C. Cardenal Herrero, ☎ *(957) 47 05 12.*
Hours open: daily 10 a.m.–7 p.m. (in winter 10 a.m.–1:30 p.m. and 3:30–5:30 p.m.).
Approximately one-third of the present structure was completed by Abd er Rahman I in 785, after he purchased a Christian church on the site and razed it to erect a mosque in one year. This earliest stage covered half of a football field—75 yards by 25 wide—and employed the innovation of creating aisles by superimposing two tiers of arches for height and spaciousness. Over the next 200 years three additions were made, each incorporating the idea of superimposed arches, to quadruple the original size to 200 yards long (counting 50 yards of courtyard) by 130 wide.

When finished, Córdoba had one of the largest mosques in the world and one of the finest, not excepting those in Cairo, Istanbul or Mecca. The plan, however, is typical of mosques the world over. First comes a courtyard with a basin for ritual ablution, followed by the mosque proper—a rectangular building with a special niche, called a *mihrab*, in its far wall that indicates the direction of Mecca. Toward this niche the congregation bows in prayer. What is unique about this mosque is the addition, made in the 16th century, of a cathedral inside. At that time, all aisles of the mosque but two were sealed off, destroying its original open feeling, and the flat, carved and painted wooden ceiling was replaced by vaulting. (A portion of this original ceiling has been restored near the mihrab.) Today the building is the most incongruous of structures—an Oriental mosque encasing a Gothic cathedral. Upon seeing the intrusive cathedral, Carlos V, who initially had authorized its construction, berated the city fathers saying, "You have built here what you might have built anywhere else, but you destroyed what was unique in the world." (Ironically, this same king destroyed sections of the Alhambra to make room for his own palace there.)

The Puerta del Perdón entrance was added to the enclosing walls in the 14th century, though in a style—except for the coats of arms of Córdoba and Spain high on the outer side—suitable to the mosque. The side facing the courtyard is wholly Moorish in flavor and lovely. The courtyard itself, with rows of shading orange trees and a large ablution basin near the long wall, looks much as it would have in the 10th century. (Incidentally, the oranges are as bitter as can be.) Directly across from the Pardon Gate is the entrance to the mosque proper.

Inside stands a magical forest. Pillars like trees stretch in every forward direction into the distance. Originally 850 of them, all different—of marble, jasper, porphyry and breccia—supported arches that alternated limestone and brick to form red and white stripes. About half the pillars—the rest were displaced by the Cathedral—remain, enough to produce an effect like no other building in the world. They came mainly from looted older buildings in Spain, but some were shipped from Carthage in North Africa and a few from as far as Constantinople. Since they were appropriated from different buildings, the pillars varied in height and required bases of individual elevations to even them out. The vast majority of the capitals are concrete replicas, with a few marble originals bearing traces of gilt near the mihrab.

The route to the mihrab is straight ahead against the south wall of the mosque, although it involves passing the Cathedral (as quickly as possible). The **Villavicosa Chapel** is situated just in front of the mihrab. This chamber was remodeled in a Mudejar style in the 14th century as a Christian chapel with a lovely dome reminiscent of that prefacing the mihrab. Adjoining, on the left, is the **Capilla Real**, again a 14th-century chapel addition of harmonious Mudejar work. Directly ahead is the **mihrab**.

The mihrab was constructed in 965 using Byzantine craftsmen, probably from Greece, hence the glittering mosaics. The mihrab proper is the tiny closet through the horseshoe arch. Preceding it are three bays forming an enclosure for the caliph and his family. The wooden ceiling prefacing this enclosure is the only remainder of the tenth-century original that once covered the whole mosque. Three domes above the caliph's enclosure are original designs of intersecting arcs that form an octagonal center, all inlaid with mosaics to present arabesques on a gold field. Brilliant mosaics make the walls rich, but the most splendid are the arabesques framing the archway to the mihrab. That octagonal chamber, which you cannot enter, consists of carved marble walls and a dome formed by an elegant plaster shell. So successful was the design of this mihrab that it became the standard throughout the Muslim world.

The **Cathedral**, insistently placed in the midst of this oriental splendor, cannot be entirely ignored. It is a mishmash of every ornate style from Gothic to baroque, as if competing with the elegance of the mosque by overwhelming the viewer. On its own it is impressive, if overblown, with fine workmanship throughout. Ignoring the gilded stucco roof, the coro encloses fine baroque choir stalls, and the pulpits are baroque masterpieces in mahogany—note the bull who cranes to hear the sermon. But nothing can excuse the travesty of placing this florid Christian structure inside one of the world's greatest works of architecture. Some say that the mosque is large enough and sufficiently grand to absorb the Cathedral without loss, but most will find the Cathedral so disturbing that the experience of the mosque is undermined. Carlos V's assessment is sadly accurate. *Admission: 800 ptas.*

Walk due south to the river and the so-called **Roman bridge**. The bridge does rest on Roman foundations, though its present form derives from Moorish construction in the eighth century, much restored since. On the opposite bank is the **Torre de Calahorro**, from the 14th century. It was recently taken over by an artist into a museum of models of ancient Córdoba with inane verbal descriptions. (It closes at 7 p.m. in summer, 6 p.m. in winter, all day Sun. and Mon., and costs 350 ptas.) A model of the mosque when new almost makes a visit worthwhile. Downstream in two blocks is the Alcázar.

Alcázar   ★

Amador de los Rios, ☎ *(957) 47 20 00.*
Hours open: Tues.–Sat. 9:30 a.m.–1:30 p.m. and 5–8 p.m. (until 7 p.m. in winter). Open Sun. 9:30 a.m.–1:30 p.m.

The original alcázar of the Moors stood east of the present structure—where the present bishopric faces the mosque. In the 13th century Alfonso X the Wise built a palace in the gardens of the original alcázar, which was substantially modified in the succeeding century to what exists today. Later the building served as the office of the local Inquisition and its prison until the 19th century. Although the interior is not of great interest, there are some nice mosaics inside and Moorish baths. The gardens with pools, flowers and cypresses make for peaceful strolling. *Admission: 300 ptas.*

Palácio de Viana   ★★★

Pl. Jerónimo Páez, ☎ *(957) 48 22 75.*
Hours open: Mon., Tues., Thurs., and Fri. 9 a.m.–2 p.m. and 4–6 p.m. (Opens and closes an hour earlier winter afternoons). Closed Wed.

The simplest course is to take a taxi, which should not cost more than $3 for the mile ride from the mosque. Normally one hardly bothers with an 18th-century palace in Spain, unless it was built by a king, but the reason for seeing this one is its dozen patios, in some ways the loveliest in this city of fine patios. In addition, there are nearly 50 rooms open to the public to show how the very rich once lived. *Admission: 300 ptas.*

Excursions

Medina Azahara, located about 11 km from Córdoba, is an excavated pleasure city built by the first caliph of al Andalus, Abd er Rahman III. It is atmospheric and contains some lovely buildings reconstructed from the ruins.

From the hotel Meliá Córdoba, make a circuit around the north end of the Victoria garden heading south. Take the first right on Av. Medina Azahara, which becomes C-431. In eight km, bear right as a sign directs to reach the ruins in three km more.

Medinet Azahara ★★★

Carretera Palma de Río, ☎ *(957) 32 91 30.*
Hours open: Tues.–Sat. 10 a.m.–2 p.m. and 6–8 p.m. (opening and closing two hours earlier on winter afternoons). Open Sun. and holidays 10 a.m.–1:30 p.m. Closed Mon.
Caliph Abd er Rahman III, mightiest of the Moors, began work in 936 on a city terraced on a hill to afford beautiful views. He named it for his favorite wife, az Zahara. Records tell of construction crews numbering in the tens of thousands, of a garrison to lodge a 12,000-man army, and lovely gardens with a zoo. It must have been an Arabian Nights place, perhaps rivalling the Alhambra, and certainly surpassing it in size and age. Yet it endured for less than a century because Berbers who felt betrayed by one of Abd er Rahman III's successors razed it. Over the ensuing centuries the site was looted for building materials by Christian kings and aristocracy for their own building projects.

Excavations began in 1944, and reconstruction—still underway—commenced a decade later. The area contains a small city, and the Spanish government is in no hurry. The grand gate to the town and **plaza** inside have been reconstructed enough to give a sense of their design, but most impressive is the **Salon Rico**. Its walls have been re-erected, some of the original carved stones replaced, and the floor reconstructed. It is an imposing structure. The carved designs in stone are interesting for their more realistic portrayal of nature, compared to the abstraction of later Alhambra stucco. The **mosque** nearby is also worth a look. The site is a place to wander through and dream of other times and worlds. *Admission: 250 ptas.*

SOUTHERN SPAIN

PARADOR HERNÁN CORTÉS

Plaza Corazón María, 7, Zafra, 06300
☎ *(924) 55 45 40, FAX (924) 55 10 18*
$90 per double; 45 rooms: 45 doubles

SOUTHERN SPAIN

You can experience a bit of history on the way to or from Portugal by staying where Cortes stayed a while. He was the protégé of the Duke of Feria whose ancestors constructed this fortress in the 15th century. Although smaller than the one in our fantasies, this castle otherwise looks suitably robust with high crenulated walls, anchored by solid towers, fronted by a massive keep. It is very well preserved. Inside, a graceful patio leads to the lobby. Do not miss the Sala Dorada with stunning artesonado ceiling or the golden dome of the elegant chapel. Guest rooms all are different, many with furniture of the region. Although welcome on a hot summer day, the pool rather spoils the Renaissance feeling.

Dining

The classical dining room is inviting, a place for hearty food. Gazpacho or garlic soup will start a meal that features either lamb stew (caldereta de cordero), roast sirloin with cream sauce or a fresh trout. A full meal will average $25, plus drinks.

Directions

You enter along Carretera de los Santos. Take the second right after the start of Triunfo Park. Take the first left after passing the park, which brings you into Pl. Corazón de María and the parador.

Paradors Nearby

Mérida: 60 km	Cáceres: 128 km	Trujillo: 150 km
Seville: 151 km	Carmona: 169 km	Guadalupe: 195 km

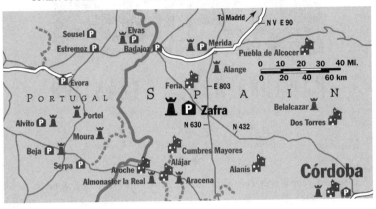

PARADOR HOTEL ATLÁNTICO

Duque de Najera, 9, Cádiz, 11002
☎ *(956) 22 69 0501, FAX (956) 21 45 82*
$90 per double; 153 rooms: 147 doubles, 6 suites

★ ★

You will consider it a nice, modern beachfront hotel and wonder, as we do, why it rates parador status. Whatever the reason, it is a decent enough hotel, especially for the price, providing sea views from the ocean side that are spectacular (request such a room). The hotel occupies the grounds of a lovely seaside park, dampening the sounds of this noisy seaport. There is a monumental pool, and tennis can be arranged. The interior features greys and blacks against stark white walls. Bedrooms feel warmer with natural wood floors, though they are somewhat cramped for our taste.

Dining

The too large dining room tries for elegance with flimsy chandeliers, marble floors and drapes, not making it by half. Still the mood is festive and the seafood fresh. Shrimp are a specialty, including a shrimp omelette (tortilla), as are a mixture of lovely fried fish. Fried sardines are delectable. The thing to drink, both before the meal and along with it is a dry sherry or similar manzanilla. A full meal will average $25, plus drinks.

Alternative Dining

It is hard to better Cádiz fried sardines, whether from stalls along the harbor in the southeast corner of the old town or in almost any local restaurant. But two establishments stand out.

El Faro   ★ ★

C. San Félix, 15 (at the southwest tip of the old town, a block before the sea wall), ☎ *(956) 21 10 68.*

The owner hangs hams in an Andalusian decor to let you know he is serious about food. Here you do not need to stick to plain seafood; sauces and marinades are tastefully done, and the chef knows meat as well. Dinner will run about $25. This is a popular place, so reservations are advised. Credit Cards: A, D and V.

El Sardinero   ★

Pl. San Juan de Dios (this large plaza is two blocks east of the Pl. de la Catedral along C. Pelota), ☎ *(956) 28 25 05. Closed Sun. dinner.*

A number of decent seafood restaurants line this square, so it is fun to walk around and choose, though el Sardinero's Basque chef elevates it above the rest. This is the proverbial simple place where good food is served for $20 or less. Credit Cards: A, D, V.

Directions

Located in the Park Genovés at the farthest end of the peninsula.

Paradors Nearby

Arcos: 60 km	Mazagón: 160 km
Ronda: 166 km	Málaga: 260 km

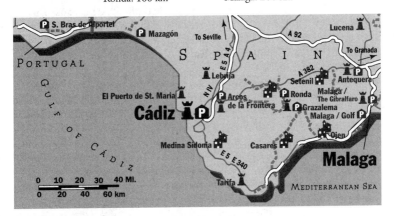

Sights

Although Cádiz belongs to the Costa de la Luz, its city beaches are best left undescribed. There are fine sands a ferry-ride away across the bay, however, and more inland on the isthmus. Spain's largest port retains a romantic feeling and offers sights to see, so it is not a bad place to settle for a day or two.

Cádiz is truly old. It was founded as a port named Gadir by the Phoenicians, and has remained a port for 3000 years (it is situated on an isthmus that carries the city three miles out into a fine bay). In time it became the main depot for treasure ships from the mines of the New World, and it prospered, although prosperity also made for temptations. Barbary corsairs raided, as did Francis Drake during preparations for the Great Armada. In Napoléon's time, the French fleet was bottled up in Cádiz by Admiral Nelson. The fleet broke through the gauntlet of English ships only to sail to defeat off the Cape of Trafalgar a few miles south.

Cádiz defies most expectations of a port. It is not grey, dirty, seedy or frightening. This is the Andalusian version—whitewashed houses, with turrets, lining narrow streets that let into lovely squares. Along the sea, north and east, gardens invite promenades. While none of the sights in Cádiz are remarkable, the walking is most pleasant.

From whichever direction you set out for Cádiz, the narrow isthmus funnels all roads to the old town at the tip. Parking is a challenge, but when N-IV ends at the large Pl. de la Constitución, go through the city walls and turn right onto Cuesta de las Calasas, which becomes Av. Ramon de Carranza in three blocks at the train station and parking.

Walk north along Av. Carranza for half a mile to the Pl. de España. Take C. Antonio Lopez going left, just past the Disputacion, which, in four short blocks, brings you to the palms of the lovely **Plaza de Mina**, the former garden of a convent. The **Office of Tourism** is located at the north corner of the plaza at C. Calderon de la Barca, 1 (open Mon.-Sat. 9 to 2 p.m.) where a map is available for navigating the maze of Cádiz' streets. Head northwest along C. Calderon de la Barca for two blocks to the ramparts and gardens for lovely views. Return to the east side of the plaza for the **Museo del Bellas Artes y Arqueológico**.

Museo del Bellas Artes y Arqueológico   ★

Pl. de Mini, ☎ *(956) 21 43 00.*
Hours open: Mon.–Fri. 9 a.m.–p.m. and 5:30–7:30 p.m. Open Sat. 9 a.m.–1:30 p.m.
As its name describes, this building combines two separate museums. The archaeological collection, consisting of local finds, is not outstanding; it is the paintings in

the fine arts section that make a visit worthwhile. There are canvases by Rubens, Cano, Murillo and Ribera, and an extraordinary collection of Zurbaráns. The Zurbaráns come from a group of saints he painted for the Monastery at Jerez, and form one of his few remaining intact series. In all 21 hang there, some are sublime. *Admission: 250 ptas., to both museums.*

Leaving from the west end of the Pl. de Mina, C. San José goes southwest to the Pl. San Antonio in one block and a jag right. The main shopping street, C. Ancha, heads southeast. Southwest on C. San José is the **Church of San Felipe Neri** (open only during services). It was in this church that the First Republic was proclaimed, although King Fernando VII promptly renounced its constitution when he returned to the throne. On the east side, adjacent to the church, is the **Museo Historico Municipal ★** with an admirable ivory and mahogany model of Cádiz as it looked at the end of the 18th century. The city presents much the same appearance as today, if more battered by time and weather (open Tues.-Fri. 9 a.m.–1 p.m. and 4–7 p.m.; open weekends 9 a.m.–1 p.m.; admission: free).

Take C. Sacramento southeast for five blocks into the Pl. Castelar. Across the plaza, at the southeast corner, C. de Santiago leads past the baroque **Iglesia Santiago** and into the Pl. de la Catedral, after two blocks more. To the west of the Cathedral with its golden dome stands a medieval town gate.

Cathedral ★

Pl. Catedral, ☎ *(956) 28 6154. Entrance on C. Acero.*
Hours open: Mon.–Sat. 10 a.m.–1 p.m.
The mass of the Cathedral was in place by the middle of the 18th century, though it was not finished until a century later. Its baroque facade leads to an interior of lovely proportions. Manuel de Falla, whose music incorporated so much Andalusian folklore and songs, is buried in the crypt. The museum contains about as much silver and gold as one is ever likely to see, and a monstrance (portable reliquary) that may outdo all the rest in Spain, which is saying a great deal. *Admission: 250 ptas., to the Cathedral museum.*

Excursions

For the sherry tastes take N-IV north for 24 km to Jerez de la Frontera, home of sherry.

Arrival is along Av. Alcalde Álvaro Domecq, though at C. Guadalete one-way signs force a right onto C. Beato Juan Grande, which becomes Alameda Cristina in one block. Continue one block more before turning slightly left. Then one-way signs again force a right fork onto C. Larga. Again comes a fork and a right on C. Lanceria to the garden of the Pl. del Arenal. Turn right then left around the garden, taking the first right into the Pl. Monti. Turn left at the end of the plaza past the gardens of the Alcázar. At their end waits parking beside the Alcázar.

NOTE... Almost all bodegas close Aug., and on weekends.

The Arabs corrupted the Roman name *Caesaris* to *Xerex*, which the Spanish in turn corrupted to Jerez. Then an English corruption gave us "sherry." Jerez is a rather quiet and pleasant town, a place to see a nice Alcázar, some mansions, a sherry bodega or two, and even some elegant dressage similar to the Viennese Lippizaners. As to the bodegas, most open only weekday mornings between 10 a.m. and 1 p.m., close all of August, and charge an admission of between 250 and 400 ptas. For this you get a tour of almost an hour and samples. Most of the tours are in English.

After a look at the restored **Alcázar**, a stop can be made at the oldest bodega in Jerez, **Gonzalez Byass** (needs a reservation), at *C. Manuel Maria Gonzalez, 12* (☎ *(956) 34 00 00*), the street west of the Alcázar. Return to C. Manuel Maria Gonzalez and follow it north. As it bends east around the gardens, take the first left to the **Colegiata church ★** with a fine baroque stair and portal. In the sacristy hangs Zurbarán's *Sleeping Girl*, a worthwhile work seldom seen or reproduced. North of the church we arrive in the Pl. del Arroyo, a.k.a. Pl. de Domencq. At its west end C. San Ildefonso runs north to the bodega of **Pedro Domencq**, one of the largest shippers. In this instance reservations are required (☎ *(956) 33 19 00*), but the visit is free. At the east end of the Pl. Arroyo is the huge **Palacio de Marquesse de Bertemati**. Following its south side for a block brings the charming **Pl. del Asunción**. At its south end is the **Casa del Cabildo Vieja**, late 16th-century with an ornate facade. A small archaeological museum is housed inside. On the east side of the plaza is **San Dionisio**, a redone Moorish-Gothic church, still with a nice Mudejar tower and fine artesonado ceiling above the nave. Four or five blocks northeast of the plaza is the house of the discoverer of Florida, **Ponce de León** (1537), with a pretty patio.

For more bodegas stop by the **office of tourism** for a map and information. It is located two blocks north of the Pl. Arenal gardens at *C. Alameda Cristina, 7* (☎ *(956) 33 11 50*).

You need a cab to get to the **Real Escuela de Andaluza de Arte Equestre** on *Av. de Duque de Abrantes, 11* (☎ *(956) 31 11 11*) to see Lippizaner-like dressage. Shows are Thurs. from noon to 1:30 p.m. and tickets are available at the box office, which opens at 11 a.m., for 1800–2300 ptas., depending on seas (children pay less). Dress rehearsals happen on Mon., Wed. and Fri. at 11 a.m. for less than half the full-dress charge.

PARADOR MÁLAGA-GIBRALFARO

Castillo de Gibralfaro, s/n, Málaga, 29000,
☎ *(95) 222 19 02, FAX (95) 222 19 04*
$110 per double; 38 rooms: 5 singles, 33 doubles

★ ★ ★ ★

Málaga is a gateway to the Costa del Sol, and this is the nicest place to stay in the city. It isn't fancy, but it is quiet with lovely views of sea and city while offering some history. Atop the mount over the city, the parador abuts a fort of the Moors on which stood a light to guide ships to the harbor, thus the name (*gibral*, mountain, plus *faro*, lighthouse). Rustic stone outside, plain inside, though just renovated, the best feature of the parador is the lush gardens surrounding it. Each plain room comes with a terrace on which you will spend your time looking over the eternal sea below.

Alternative Accommodations

Málaga Palacio

Corina del Muelle, 1 (off the northeast corner of the Pl. de la Marina), ☎ *(95) 221 51 85, FAX (95) 221 51 85.205 rooms, plus 16 suites.*

The parador is the nicest place to stay, but there are second choices. Although the glitter has faded from the Málaga Palacio, it still retains its fine location and views of the park and harbor from the rooms that face it. Rooms start at the parador's charges, then go up.

Los Naranjos

Paseo de Sancha, 35 (about one half mile due east of the Paseo del Parque), ☎ *(95) 222 43 19, FAX (95) 222 59 75, Telex 77030. 41 rooms.*

A more charming choice is Los Naranjos, whose name comes from the small orange grove in front, a nice touch that heralds the attention given throughout this admirably run little hotel. There is a decent beach nearby.

Dining

The dining room is plain enough to be called severe, though it does have sea views through large windows. Demand a window table. Follow the compulsory and always good gazpacho with assorted lightly fried fish, or just go for the fried anchovies *(boquerones)*. A full meal will average $20, plus drinks.

Alternative Dining

Think fried fish and walk to the east end of the Paseo del Parque, then a block further for the area known as Pedragalejos. Here unassuming places serve delectable fried fish for a pittance.

Café de Paris   ★★

C. Vélez Málaga, 8 (east of the Paseo del Parque and a soft right onto Paseo Canovas del Castillo), ☎ *(95) 222 50 43. Closed Sun and the first half of Sept.*
No question that this elegant establishment serves the best food in town. It is owned by a former chef at some of Spain's finest restaurants. Try the *menu de degustación* to sample his wares. Seafood is the star, of course, and prepared with care. The bill should be under $40. Reservations and jacket and tie are required. Credit Cards: A, D, M, V.

Antonio Martín

Paseo Marítimo, 4 (a block south of the Cafe de Paris), ☎ *(95) 222 21 13. Closed Sun. eve.*
The ocean view from the terrace makes this old institution a pleasure. Fish simply prepared is your best choice, for the kitchen can be erratic with sauces. Prices are a reasonable $20. Reservations are strongly advised. Credit Cards: A, D, M, V.

Directions

Aim for the center of the city. When you pass the bull ring, at the Largo del Paseo de Reding, follow signs up to the parador.

Paradors Nearby

Málaga-Golf: 14 km	Nerja: 50 km
Ronda: 92 km	Granada: 135 km

Sights

Málaga's cloudless skies had made it a garden lauded by Arab poets. Wine, apricots, oranges and later sugarcane, helped keep Málaga rich. But those who tended the garden were Moors, so when they were expelled in the 16th century Málaga fell on hard times. In the 18th century demand for Málaga's sweet wine helped it recover, though the city suffered again when tastes in the next century turned to drier French vintages. Tourism in recent days has helped, but Málaga remains a poor city with a high crime rate for Spain.

Málaga also claims of a famous native son, Pablo Picasso, although his family moved away when he was ten.

Málaga is the major city of the Costa del Sol. Since it has no beaches to speak of, most people use it as a transit hub without bothering to look at the town. The city may not be attractive overall but it contains handsome sights, certainly worth part of a day to explore. Be alert in the evening, however, because street robberies are too prevalent.

From the **Airport** and from the **western Costa del Sol** watch for signs to Av. de Andalucia as you approach one of the rare clover leafs in Spain. Head east to the Pl. de la Marina and parking. From **Granada and north** one-way streets complicate matters. The city is entered on Av. de Jorge Silvela along the Guadalmedina. At the second bridge one-way streets force the crossing of the river. Take the first left to parallel the river, but at the next bridge, go right for one block on C. Marmoles, taking the next left to a large traffic circle. Go left again along Av. de Andalucia, which enters the Pl. de la Marina and parking. From the **eastern Costa del Sol** the city is entered on Paseo de

Marítimo which reaches a large traffic circle after passing the hospital. Head left along the Paseo del Parque, at the end of which is the Pl. de la Marina and parking.

Additional parking lies two blocks north along Cortina del Muelle which runs east.

From the Pl. de la Marina walk north to the edge of the park. There C. Molina continues north for two blocks to the Cathedral. Or take the next main street to the east, C. Marqués de Larios, which also heads due north. This is the main shopping street of Málaga, bordered by interesting stores. The **office of tourism** is on the right in about three blocks. An alley going right, just past the office of tourism, leads to the Cathedral.

Cathedral ★

Pl. Obispo, ☎ *(95) 221 59 17.*
Hours open: daily 10 a.m.–1 p.m. and 4–5:30 p.m.
Original designs for the Cathedral were drawn by the famed Diego de Siloé in 1528 in a neoclassical style, but the single completed tower shows that it is not finished yet. Some would say that funds were cut off when the church elders saw what it looked like, for, although interesting enough for a peek, this is not the most attractive of cathedrals,. The various chapels and altar hold little of interest, but the choir is quite another story. The stalls consist of the finest wood carving by masters of that genre—by Pedro de Mena (buried nearby) and Alonso Cano, among others—admirable for exquisite details. *Admission: 100 ptas., to the choir and treasury.*

From the front of the Cathedral walk due north beside the baroque **Bishopric**. At the end of the Pl. turn right (east) along C. Cister by the **Sagradio**, formerly the site of the city mosque, now with a nice Isabelline north face. At its west end C. San Agustin heads northeast for two blocks to the Museo de Bellas Artes.

Museo de Bellas Artes ★

San Augustín, 6, ☎ *(95) 221 83 82.*
Hours open: Tues.–Sat. 10 a.m.–1:30 p.m. and 5–8 p.m. (closes an hour earlier in winter). Open Sun. 10 a.m.–1:30 p.m. Closed Mon.
The building itself is interesting—the former palace of Buenavista. Inside waits a varied collection, from Roman mosaics, to paintings by Zurbarán and Ribera. The paintings are on loan from the Prado, and thus not of the first class, but childhood drawings by Picasso are simply wonderful. *Admission: 250 ptas.*

Turn right after the museum for two blocks to the **Pl. de la Merced**, passing the church of **Santiago** with a Mudejar tower on the way. The buildings around the plaza with peeling shutters harken to the turn of the century. A plaque at number 15 on the north edge of the plaza marks the house where **Picasso** was born. Go south from the plaza along C. Alcazabilla, passing remains of a **Roman theater** on the right. At the end of the street stands the large **Aduaña**, from the end of the 18th century. To the left is the **alcazaba**.

Alcazaba ★

Pl. de la Aduana, ☎ *(95) 221 60 05.*

Hours open: Mon.–Sat. 11 a.m.–2 p.m. and 5–8 p.m. (closes an hour earlier in winter). Open Sun. 10 a.m.–2 p.m.

Although restored from the foundations up, the buildings and, especially the gates and fortifications, are evocative, a kind of second-rate Alhambra. The walls were built in the 11th century and show clever tactics to concentrate attackers in a winding entrance. Inside, a small inner palace, built over the course of the 11th-14th centuries, remains admirable in reconstruction. It contains a museum of material from the Visigothic era through the Moorish, including fine ceramics. The double fortress wall leads steeply up to the **Gibralfaro** (mountain lighthouse), actually ruins of a castle from the 14th century. The parador stands beside it amid lovely gardens and striking views of the town. *Admission: 100 ptas.*

Airport

Ten flights (☎ *(95) 224 00 00*) arrive daily from Madrid and there are four daily flights to Barcelona. No carriers from the U.S. land here, but a changeover can be made at Madrid. Electric trains (Ferriocarril) go the 10 km to and from the airport every half hour. The best stop is the Centro/Alameda station, located a block north and slightly west of the Pl. de la Marina. Buses also make the trip on the same schedule, leaving from the Cathedral. The Iberia office is at *Molina Lario, 13* (☎ *(95) 221 82 04*).

PARADOR MÁLAGA-GOLF

Cruze de Churriana, s/n, Málaga, 29080,
☎ *(95) 238 12 55, FAX (95) 238 21 41*
$90 per double; 60 rooms: 55 doubles, 4 suites

★ ★ ★ ★

Sun, sea, and golf itemize the reasons for staying here. This is a golf re-sort, as the name says, formed of a comfortable, nicely designed two-story "u" enveloping a circular pool. Guest rooms all have terraces; four supply Jacuzzis. The 18 hole course, designed by Tom Simpson, was the site of the Spanish Masters a few years ago. The sport is free for guests from November through June, at other times they pay. Putting greens and instruction are available, as are tennis courts, horses and bicycles. Mother nature supplies the beach and the warm weather that makes outdoor sports enjoyable.

Dining

A spacious dining room looks out on the pool. Decoration is minimal. In keeping with all the sports activities, an informal buffet is the featured meal. So don't expect gourmet dishes. Gazpacho soup and fried fish are about the level here. A full meal will average $20, plus drinks.

Hondarribia combines medieval decor with modern comforts.

Mojacar is situated on the sunny coast of Almería.

Trujillo's parador incorporates part of a 16th-century convent's cloister.

Santo Domingo de la Calzada's lounge is enhanced by arches and a curved ceiling.

Alternative Dining

Casa Guaquín ★

In Torremolinos, 4 km west along N-340. Carmen, 37 (along the beach at Carihuela) ☎ *(95) 238 45 30.*

In this area chock-full of seafood restaurants, Guaquín is the best and far from the most expensive, as the crowds indicate. Just look around and choose or go for the fritura malagueñña. Your meal will cost no more than the bland food at the parador. Closed Thurs. and from middle Dec. through middle Jan. Credit Cards: A, M, V.

La Hacienda ★★★

Seventeen km west along N-340, ten km before Marbella, look for a sign pointing to an additional one and one-half km north, ☎ *(95) 283 12 67.*

The restaurant is housed in an elegant villa overlooking the sea. The food is sublime. The chef is Belgian, and his lamb matches the best we ever tasted. Finish with a sublime sherbet. In all, figure about $40. Reservations are required. Closed Mon. (except in Aug.), Tues. (except in July and Aug.), and from the third week of Nov. to the last week of Dec. Credit Cards: A, D, M, V.

Directions

From **Málaga** take N-340 west for 9 km to a sign for the parador along C-344 in 3 km.

Paradors Nearby

Málaga-Gibralfaro: 14 km	Antequera: 55 km	Nerja: 62 km
Ronda: 102 km	Granada: 137 km	Córdoba: 167 km

Excursions

Try the activity of Torremolinos, the packaged tour capital of Spain, 4 km west along N-340 for international excitement and bodies wall-to-wall on the beach. 25 km further is Marbella, its opposite. This is the playground of the wealthy, deluxe hotels and yachts.

PARADOR REYES CATÓLICOS

Playa de Mojácar, s/n, Mojácar, 04638
☎ *(951) 47 82 50, FAX (951) 47 81 83*
$90 per double; 98 rooms: 9 singles, 89 doubles

★ ★ ★ ★

This is not at all the expected parador; it is a resort complex on the beach. It is modern, bustling and like other luxury beach resorts the world over. But its prices are lower than most and there is nothing wrong with staying at a nice beach resort with a sand beach across the road, a pool if that distance is too far, cabanas, etc. Best of all, this corner of Spain enjoys the warmest weather in the continent, so swimming is pleasant for eight months of the year.

Dining

Flowers on the table and the sea outside decorate a large dining room to which the freshest fish are whisked from the little fishing village of Garrucha nearby. But start with a lovely fish soup made of dorado, then choose your sea creature or order the special fish stew, almost a paella *(arroz a la garruchera)*. A full meal will average $25, plus drinks.

Directions

The parador lies 2.5 km along the road to Carboneras east of Mojácar on the coast.

Parados Nearby

Puerto Lumbreras: 60 km   Nerja: 250 km
Jávea: 300 km   Málaga: 300 km

Sights

High above the plains below, the village of Mojácar is worth a walk through. Houses are so cubical that it has been called a cubist village. Strange stick symbols painted near house doors to ward off evil may descend from prehistoric times.

SOUTHERN SPAIN

SEVILLE

★ ★ ★ ★ ★

Accommodations

Seville lacks a parador because it doesn't need one. Interesting accommodations exist for every taste. If there is a lack it is rooms at lower price points.

Alfonso XIII

San Fernando, 2, Seville 41000 (on its own grounds opposite the rear of the Alcázar gardens), ☎ *(95) 422 28 50, FAX (95) 421 60 33, Telex 72725. 122 rooms, plus 19 suites.*
For splendor, try the Alfonso XIII. Utterly deluxe and among the most atmospheric hotel in Spain, the Alfonso was built so that aristocrats would have a place to stay while visiting the 1929 World's Fair. The style is Mudejar with elegant glazed tiles, marble and mahogany everywhere, surrounding a central patio that offers as lovely a spot for a drink as anyone could wish for. Of course the hotel location is perfect. It is, however, very expensive, approaching 40,000 pesetas for a double (though handsome discounts are given for stays of two nights or more).

Hacienda Benazuza

Virgén de las Nieves, Sanlúcar la Mayor, Seville 41000 (take exit 6 off A-49 to Huelva to N-431 to Sanlúcar for signs), ☎ *(95) 570 33 44, FAX (95) 570 34 10. Closed from the middle of July through Aug. 26 rooms, plus 18 suites.*
If you prefer a luxury hacienda, travel 30 km west to Hacienda Benazuza in Sanlúcar la Mayor. Be a caballero for a night or two in this luxury ranch, parts of which date to the 10th century. It's majestic, evocative and supplies every luxury including elevated food. Chef Eric Del Gallo of the hotel's La Alqueria Restaurant is French trained, but composes his own dishes, such as hot shrimp salad, saffron potatoes and

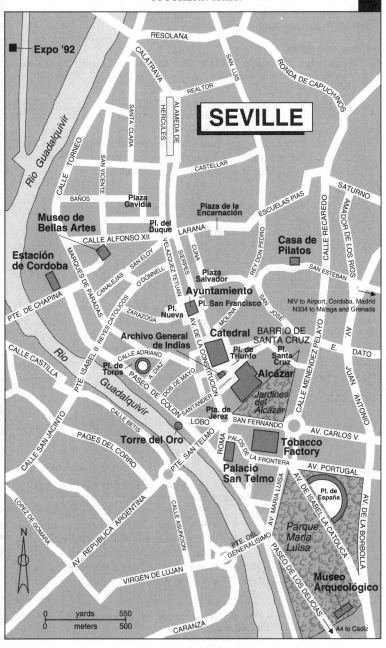

SEVILLE

Expo '92

Río Guadalquivir

RESOLANA
CALATRAVA
SAN LUIS
RONDA DE CAPUCHINOS
REALTOR
SANTA CLARA
ALAMEDA DE HERCULES
SAN VICENTE
CALLE TORNEO
CASTELLAR
SATURNO
AMADOR DE LOS RIOS
BAÑOS
CALLE RECAREDO

Plaza Gavidia
Plaza de la Encarnación
ESCUELAS PIAS

Museo de Bellas Artes
Pl. del Duque
LARANA
REY DON PEDRO
Casa de Pilatos

Estación de Cordoba
CALLE ALFONSO XII
CUNA
SAN ESTEBAN
MARQUES DE PARADAS
SAN ELOY
VELAZQUEZ TETUAN
SIERPES

Plaza Salvador
O'DONNELL
CANALEJAS
REYES CATOLICOS
ZARAZOGA
Ayuntamiento
NIV to Airport, Cordoba, Madrid
N334 to Málaga and Grenada

PTE. DE CHAPINA
Pl. Nueva
AV. DE LA CONSTITUCION
MOLINA
SAN JOSÉ
AV.

Archivo General de Indias
CALLE ADRIANO
A. DIAZ
Catedral
Pl. de Triunfo
Pl. Santa Cruz
BARRIO DE SANTA CRUZ
E.
DATO

CALLE CASTILLA
Río
PTE. ISABEL II
Pl. de Toros
PASEO DE COLON
DOS DE MAYO
Alcázar
CALLE MENENDEZ PELAYO
JUAN

Guadalquivir
SANTANDER
Jardines del Alcázar
ANTONIO

CALLE BETIS
Pta. de Jerez
LOBO
SAN FERNANDO
AV. CARLOS V

CALLE SAN JACINTO
PAGES DEL CORRO
Torre del Oro
PTE. SAN TELMO
ROMA
PALOS DE LA FRONTERA
Tobacco Factory

Palacio San Telmo
AV. PORTUGAL
Pl. de España

LOPEZ DE GOMARA
AV. REPUBLICA ARGENTINA
CALLE ASUNCION
AV. DE ISABEL LA CATOLICA
AV. MARIA LUISA
AV. DE LA BORBOLLA

N

VIRGEN DE LUJAN
PTE. DEL GENERALISIMO
PASEO DE LOS DELICIAS
Parque Maria Luisa
Museo Arqueológico

| 0 | yards | 550 |
| 0 | meters | 500 |

CARANZA
A4 to Cádiz

squab with truffles and cabbage. This special stay costs $250 per night, and a sumptuous dinner will cross the $50 line.

Las Casas de la Judería

Pl. Santa Maria la Blanca, Seville 41000 (This plaza runs north-south at the eastern end of the Barrio Santa Cruz. The hotel is a block north.), ☎ *(95) 441 51 50, FAX (95) 442 21 70. 31 suites.*

Want all the comforts of home including washer-dryer and kitchen? Try Las Casas de la Judería. Four houses near the Barrio Santa Cruz were combined and gutted to produce a small number of comfortable apartment suites. The furniture includes fine antique reproductions, and many rooms overlook lovely internal patios. For a party of travelers who would need more than one hotel room, a suite with two or three bedrooms could prove a bargain. Prices start at $80.

Tryp Colón

Canalejas, 1 (two blocks south of the Museo Bellas Artes), Seville 41000, ☎ *(95) 422 29 00, FAX (95) 422 09 38, Telex 72726. 211 rooms, plus seven suites.*

The other grand old hotel of Seville is the Tryp Colón, also built for the 1929 World's Fair. The lobby is dramatically lit by a stained glass dome and the hotel has been recently remodeled to maintain its place near the top. However, it is not the Alfonso XIII either in luxury, location or romance, although it does save half the pesetas.

For under $100 you can reserve at a charmer, run by a Marquesa, and as conveniently located as a hotel can be—you can hit the Cathedral with a rock. The decor is lux and homey at the same time and each bedroom is different, which means that some are better than others. This is a most pleasant change from big hotel monotony. *Don Remondo, 16 (head to the east end of the Cathedral and go northeast along C. Don Remondo for less than half a block), 5* ☎ *(95) 422 49 90, FAX (95) 422 97 65. nine rooms, plus two suites.*

Dining

Egaña Oriza ★★★★

San Fernando, 41, Seville 41000 (at the southeast tip of the Alcázar Garden), ☎ *(95) 422 72 11. Closed Saturday at lunch, Sunday, and August.*

This restaurant is the most innovative and acclaimed in Seville. The bar at the entrance serves sublime tapas. The dining room is comfortably large, modern and tan, brightened by light from a two-story glass wall. The food is Basque nueva, unique and subtle. How does quenelles of duck on a potato nest sound? Game is a specialty. Here you are in the chef's hands and they are good hands indeed. Reservations are essential and prices pass $50, but worth it. Credit Cards: A, D, M, V.

Taberna del Albardero ★★★

Zaragoza, 20, Seville 41000 (the large street that leaves the west end of the Pl. Nueva), ☎ *(95) 456 06 37. Closed August.*

More elegantly situated in a mansion, this is the new challenger to Egaña Oriza. Although it is less inventive, this newcomer shines in subtlety and simple good taste. The thought of the steak with liver paste and green pepper still makes my mouth water. The tab reaches Oriza's height, but a fabulous value in lunch is served for $10 in the cafe. Credit Cards: A, D, M, V.

La Albahaca ★★

Pl. Santa Cruz, 12, Seville 41000 (in the Barrio Santa Cruz, one block north of the eastern end of the Alcázar Gardens), ☎ *(95) 422 07 14. Closed Sunday.*

This is the intimate, romantic place people imagine in Seville, all tiles and greens in an elegant small mansion. The food and service will not disappoint. Sea bass with fennel and bonito are just two specialties, and how does tangerine mousse sound for dessert? $35 will cover the bill. Credit Cards: A, D, M, V.

La Isla ★★

C. Arfe, 25, Seville 41000 (cross Av. de la Constitución at the southern end of the Cathedral and take the first right down C. Arfe, little more than an alley), ☎ *(95) 421 26 31. Closed Monday, and from the middle of August to the middle of September.*

In an ancient building but newly decorated in salmon and white with black lacquer furniture, this is the best pure seafood restaurant in Seville and not expensive, as such food goes, at $35. Start with the house paella, followed by the fish of your choice, and you will hardly notice that the service lacks a certain graciousness. Credit Cards: A, D, M, V.

Modesto ★

C. Cano y Cueto, 5, Seville 41000 (C. Santa Maria la Blanca forms the eastern border of the Barrio Santa Cruz. The restaurant's street runs east from its southern end), ☎ *(95) 441 68 11. Closed Wednesday.*

For a lot less, but excellent tapas, try this popular, unassuming place. If you're in the mood for a full meal, the dining room upstairs is pleasant with white walls and blue-and-white tiles, more intimate than the tables outside. Fried fish is delectable, as are the specials. Credit Cards: A, D, M, V.

Directions

From **Madrid** aim either for Córdoba or Granada and follow the directions from there. From **Granada** take N-342 west for 92 km past Antequera, then take N-334 northwest for 159 km to Seville. From **Córdoba** take N-IV (E-5) southwest for Seville in 142 km.

Paradors Nearby

Córdoba: 138 km	Ronda: 153 km	Zafra: 157 km
Málaga: 217 km	Granada: 258 km	

Sights

Seville does not boast the best art museum, cathedral or Moorish architecture, but it is second best in all these arenas and, thus, places high on total points. Since it is a beautiful city replete with lovely vistas, a cosmopolitan city where orange and palm trees line streets punctuated by quiet parks, it is a tourist's delight. For better or worse, it is also, however, the hottest city in Spain.

Seville has been important since the time of the Iberians, thanks to its safe situation inland along the Guadalquivir River that provided an easy road to the sea. Julius Caesar himself fortified it in 45 B.C. and it grew into one of the most important Roman towns in Spain, as still impressive ruins at nearby Italica attest. In fact, it bred two Roman Emperors—Trajan and Hadrian. Seville was the first capital of the Visigoths, before Toledo took over that position. Under the Moors, Seville stood second behind Córdoba until 1023, when the kingdom split into principalities and Seville's independence left it free to surpass the former capital. For two centuries her prosperity was unrivaled, then, in 1248, Seville was conquered by the great Christian warrior Fernando III, later sainted for his accomplishments and buried here in 1252.

In the early 14th century, Seville was favored by the notorious king Pedro the Cruel, who remodeled the palace of the Moors into the striking Alcázar we see today. Later, riches from the New World brought great prosperity to Seville, for this was the port to which the treasure ships sailed to unload their silver, gold and tobacco, much of which remained in local pockets. Carlos V came to Seville to meet and marry his bride, Isabel of Portugal, remodeling rooms in the Alcázar for his honeymoon suite. But, in 1647, a plague broke out, ran rampant for five years and reduced the population by one third. This, combined with declining trade from the New World, began a slide that was climaxed by the silting up of the Guadalquivir River, handing preeminence thereafter to Cádiz as Spain's New World port.

Nonetheless, life continued in Seville. Spain's finest artist, Velázquez, was born here in 1599, as was Murillo in 1618. Zurbarán became an adopted son. The French writer Beaumarchais visited in 1764, and wrote a story about a Seville roué named Don Juan that inspired Mozart's *Don Giovanni.* Mozart followed with *The Marriage of Figaro,* inspiring Rossini's *Barber of Seville.* Later Prosper Merimée wrote a story about a Gypsy in Seville who enchanted a soldier, which became Bizet's *Carmen.* Seville's Tobacco Factory served as the model for Carmen's place of employment. In the present century, textiles and metallurgy have returned prosperity to Seville.

Seville is famed in Spain for its Easter festivities, when nightly processions of hooded and robed penitents march behind floats of bejeweled and flower-bedecked Saints and Virgins. Bands and bystanders break out into song as the processions pass. This is followed two weeks later by the April Fair, a week of celebrations. Tents are set up outside the town to which Sevillanos ride on horseback in costumes like those in *Carmen* and celebrate with food, wine and parties throughout the night. In association with these festivities are a month of bullfights involving the finest matadors, as well as impromptu nightly dancing, including flamenco and the local dance called the Sevillano. It is a festive and memorable time to visit, but a period when all hotels are booked full at prices twice their usual charges.

Seville also hosted the World's Fair of 1992, Expo'92. In fact this was the city's second World's Fair. Its first, celebrated in 1929 as the Ibero-America Exposition, was rather a dud because of the world financial collapse that year. The recent fair occupied the island of La Cartuja, just north of the city-center. Some pavilions and rides remain.

Arriving from the north or east on **N-IV**, or from the **Airport**, one travels along Av. Aeropuerto which becomes Av. de Kansas City as it goes through the city. When it ends in a "T," go left along Av. Luis Morales which changes its name to Av. San Francisco Javier near the university on the right. Take the next right along C. Enramadilla, which narrows, then widens, and is called Av. Carlos V. As it passes the bus park, parking is available to the right.

Arriving from **Málaga** on **N-334** enter the city along Av. de Andalucía, passing through one huge, clover-leafed intersection and then two other major intersections. At the third intersection, with the Soccer Stadium visible to the right, turn right along Av. Luis Morales, and follow the rest of the directions above.

Arriving from **Cádiz** or **Jerez** on N-IV from the south along Av. de Jerez, the corner of the large Parque de Maria Luisa is soon reached. Turn right at the park onto C. Muñoz León, which follows the edge of the park under the new name of C. Borbolla. Continue for one block past the park's end, make a left onto Av. Carlos V, and parking to the left in two blocks.

Proceed west along Av. de Carlos V from the parking lot to cross the Pl. de Juan de Austria. Across the plaza the still westward street is renamed C. San Francisco. Pass the gardens at the rear of the Alcázar on the right by the huge building on the left. This was the former **tobacco factory**, famed as the model for Carmen's place of employment. At one time 10,000 workers rolled Cuban cigars here, but now it constitutes a part of the University of Seville and only the carving of the story of tobacco around the main door betrays its former function. At the end of the street stands the grand **Hotel Alfonso XIII**. Turn right along C. San Gregoro into the **Pl. de Contratación**, the hub of numerous sights. The **Office of Tourism** is down the alley to the right. The square building to the left is the **Archivo General de Indias**, and ahead is the **Cathedral** with the **Giralda Tower** visible above its west side. To its right is the **Alcázar**, and between the Cathedral and Alcázar is the entrance to the **Barrio Santa Cruz**.

The Cathedral Area

Cathedral and Giralda Tower   ★★★

Pl. del Triunfo, ☎ *(95) 421 28 00.*

Hours open: Mon.–Sat. 11 a.m.–5 p.m., Sun. 2–4 p.m. Closed Jan. 1 and 6, May 30, Aug. 15, Dec. 8 and 25.

After conquering Seville, the Christians first used the mosque of the Moors for religious services, but in 1401 decided to build a cathedral of their own, and finished the project in the remarkably quick time of a century. A member of the original building committee is said to have exclaimed: "Let us build a cathedral so immense that everyone who sees it will take us for madmen." What they constructed was the largest Gothic cathedral in the world, save perhaps the still unfinished Saint John the Divine in New York, and the fourth largest cathedral of any sort. They razed the mosque to build it, though left its Patio of Oranges for a cathedral cloister and its minaret for a bell tower. The main portal of the present facade is modern, surrounded by two others of the period.

On the east face of the Cathedral, to the rear, rises the **Torre Giralda ★★** (Weathervane Tower). Beside it waits the entrance to the Cathedral and the ticket counter.

The tower is actually the minaret from the mosque of 1198. When the Cathedral went up, a bell tower was added to the top of the minaret surmounted by a statue which turned in the wind and symbolized Faith. Altogether, the tower stands over 300 feet high, as handsome and harmonious a structure as can be imagined up to the place where the arcade of the belfry begins. (Use a hand to block the top and its harmony becomes apparent.)

The tower may be climbed by walking up interior sloping ramps for the best view of the Cathedral and surrounding city. Note that each bell in the clarion is named.

When the Cathedral is entered, its vast size is not initially apparent. The light is dusky because the stained glass windows are unusually high, the piers seem less massive because they are formed into smaller columns, and the doubling of the aisles on each side of the nave is not evident at first. Further, as with so many Spanish cathedrals, the central coro blocks any grand view down the nave. Nonetheless, the cathedral is a football field long, almost equally wide and the vaulting above the nave soars 135 feet into the air.

Entering by the south transept one confronts the impressive **tomb of Christopher Columbus**. The coffin is carried by four figures representing the original four kingdoms of Spain—Castile, Aragón, Navarre and León. The work was cast in the 19th century. However, whether Columbus' body actually lies in the coffin is a subject of controversy. It is known that he died in Valladolid and that his body was carried to the island of Santo Domingo for burial. The Spanish say that the corpse was disinterred, taken to Havana, then returned here to prevent capture during the Spanish-American War. In Santo Domingo they claim that Columbus' remains never left.

The **high altar** is fronted by an ornate Plateresque gilt screen which seems to double the gilt of the awesome Gothic retable, the largest in Spain. Its details are difficult to study from a distance. In the apse behind the high altar is the large **Capilla Real**, a Plateresque marvel. High up Fernando III, the conqueror of Seville, is shown receiving the keys to the city. On the chapel altar stands a silver and bronze shrine for the king's remains. His body proved incorruptible, so Fernando was declared a saint and is still carried in processions during Easter week. Above the shrine stands a small Virgin, said to be a gift from Louis IX of France that Fernando carried with him in battle. To the left is the effigy of King Alfonso X, the Wise, Fernando's son, and opposite is Fernando's wife, Beatrice of Swabia. The striking dome above radiates heads of martyrs spiralling to the apex.

Stairs in the chapel lead to a vault below (generally closed) in which coffins hold Pedro the Cruel and his "wife" Maria de Padilla. Ironically, resting beside Pedro is his half-brother Fadrique Trastámara, who Pedro killed, and whose brother avenged the death by killing Pedro before founding the dynasty that bred both Isabella and Ferdinand.

To the left, facing the Capilla Real is a chapel with a retable by Zurbarán. To the right, in the corner, is a lovely oval room with a fine frescoed ceiling, the **Chapterhouse**. Church vestments are displayed adjoining. Further along is a neoclassical **Sacristy** with a painting by Zurbarán, and an adjacent **treasury** displaying numerous relics, including the actual keys to the city presented to St. Fernando—silver gilt by the Moors, iron gilt by the Jewish community.

In the center of the nave stands an ornate **coro** with fine Gothic choirstalls. Between the coro and the front door to the Cathedral lies a **tombstone for Columbus' son Hernando**.

Before one finishes with the Cathedral, a quiet treat awaits through a door on the right side that gives access to the **Patio de los Naranjos**, the courtyard for the former mosque. Inside is the original basin for the mosque, perhaps appropriated from a Visigothic fountain. The chapel to **Our Lady of Granada** carries a fine Mudejar ceiling, and up red marble stairs is stored the **Columbus Archives** of books owned by the discoverer, many annotated in his hand, which were donated to the Cathedral by his son Hernando. *Admission: 550 ptas., to the Cathedral and Giralda Tower.*

Alcázar   ★★★★

> Pl. del Triunfo, ☎ (95) 422 71 63.
> Hours open: Tues.–Sat. 10 a.m.–5 p.m. Open Sun. 10 a.m.–1 p.m. Closed Mon.

Across the Pl. de Triunfo south from the Cathedral, past square battlement towers and through an unassuming gateway with a tiled lion above, is the entrance to the Alcázar. These walls are all that remain of a Moorish palace from 1176. In 1366 Pedro the Cruel replaced that palace with a smaller one of his own. But he so admired the Moorish aesthetic that he borrowed artisans from the Caliph of Granada to construct it. Here Pedro lived with his "wife" Maria de Padilla. And here he murdered Fadrique of Trastámara, his half-brother. On another occasion he invited the emir from Granada to dinner and killed him for his jewels, one of which, a giant uncut ruby, found its way into the British royal crown. Later Isabella gave birth to her only son while she and Ferdinand resided here. Carlos V, their grandson, married his wife in the Hall of the Ambassadors. A hundred years later, Velázquez' patron Felipe IV, restored the Alcázar, although an earthquake and fire in the 18th century did substantial damage and restoration has been crude at times. Nonetheless, this is the oldest continually occupied palace in Europe (the present king and queen often stay), and the finest surviving example of Mudejar architecture.

Through the gate one enters the **Patio de Montería**. On the left is the **Sala de Justicia** with plaster coats of arms around the walls, and a remarkable wooden ceiling above. Farther left, though presently closed, is the lovely **Patio de Yeso**, one of the few remaining parts of the original Moorish palace. From the Patio de Montería, three **stone arches** (possibly Roman) straight ahead lead to the **Patio de Leones**, with patterned pavement and the handsome **Palace of Pedro the Cruel** across the way.

The main façade, with its arcaded wings on two sides, presents an almost Byzantine look due to a deep overhanging eave above the entrance. Below the eave, blue tiles bear an Arabic inscription saying that there is no conqueror but God, a kind of putdown by the Moorish craftsmen of their Christian master who could not read Arabic. The right-hand wing was built by Ferdinand and Isabella as a center to deal with matters concerning the New World.

Starting in this Isabelline wing, a vestibule hung with nice tapestries leads to a room for audiences and finally a small **chapel** with ornate coffered ceiling. The picture above the altar shows Mary protecting dim figures of Native Americans under her cloak. The blond-haired figure beside her on the right is thought to be Columbus.

Outside, at the far end, a grand stair leads to **royal apartments** on the second floor. Left of the landing is the intimate **Oratory of Isabella** with a remarkable tile depiction of Mary visiting her cousin St. Isabella. Rooms of varying styles and age follow, including the **banquet hall** with a lovely ceiling, built by Carlos V for his wedding feast. But the finest of the rooms is **Pedro the Cruel's bedroom** with intricate carving in perfect Mudejar style, and an alcove for his bed.

The treasure of the Alcázar is Pedro's palace. Enter through the main portal into a **vestibule** that presents an elegant vista of horseshoe arches. Bright tiles (unfortunately modern) line the walls halfway up, intricate painted stucco runs along the high walls and through the arches, and a complex coffered ceiling hangs overhead.

Turn left from the vestibule into the **Patio de las Doncellas** (Maids of Honor), the center of the palace. If only Carlos V had not added the classical second story to the patio it would be a perfect jewel. Ignore that second story and enjoy the multilobed arches, brilliant tiles and the rhythm of the arches, not ignoring the ancient original doors. Of course there is a fountain in the center for the sound of water, and vistas through the patio sides of surrounding rooms.

Cross to the right side to see the so-called **Salón de los Reyes Moros**, which of course was intended for Christian, not Moorish kings. In any case it displays nice woodwork, fine wooden doors and alcoves for beds.

Cross to the far side to enter the **Salón de Carlos V**, with a fine coffered ceiling that replaced the original Mudejar one. This is followed by a long room that ends at the triple arches of the **Peacocks**, named for the tiled birds above the arches, a fantasy of pattern on pattern.

Through the peacock arches waits the most splendid room in the Alcázar, the **Salón de Embajadores**, in which Carlos V is said to have held his wedding. The room seems more a jeweler's work than that of tilers or plasterers, for the complexity of the intricate designs stretches belief. Above is a dome that has no equal in the world. Throughout there is the surprise of western motifs—seashells over the arches, castles and lions above portraits of the kings of Spain around the ceiling—that makes sense in a room designed for Christians by the Moors.

Off this room and through another for Felipe II, the small **Patio de las Muñecas** (dolls) is entered, named for two tiny faces on the capital of one of the columns. For many this is the favorite of all the Alcázar rooms, because of its human scale, despite the intricacy of designs which seem to rise to the heavens. On one side is a room called **Isabella's bedroom**, on another, the bedroom for her new baby, **Don Juan**.

Return through the vestibule to the Patio de Leons. Turn right along a gallery to the **Patio de María de Padilla**, the site of a Gothic palace older than Pedro's, though much remodeled. Here are a suite of rooms known as the **Palace of Carlos V**.

The **Emperor's Room** with non-Moorish tiles halfway up the walls and groined vaulting above seems rather a mishmash, but the **Tapestry Room** displays an amazing series of tapestries depicting a battle that Carlos fought in Tunis. Two hundred years later Felipe V ordered copies made of all the tapestries, which is our good fortune, because the originals disappeared and today you see these perfect copies.

What would a Moorish palace be without gardens? The Alcázar has its own in the rear planted with exotic trees and dotted with ornamental waterways. Directly behind the Alcázar, first passing the aptly named **Grotesque Gallery** to the left, is the beautifully tiled **Carlos V Pavilion**. After the gardens, the Alcázar is exited through a garage in which two 17th-century carriages are parked. Note the use of leather straps as shock absorbers. *Admission: 600 ptas., exact change.*

Archivo General de Indias

Pl. Archivo de Indias, ☎ (95) 421 12 34.
Hours open: Mon.–Sat. 10 a.m.–1 p.m. Closed Sun.
On its own square between the Cathedral and Alcázar, this impressive building was designed in 1572 by Herrera, the architect of the Escorial. Originally it was an exchange where merchants conducted business, but it was remodeled in the 18th century into an archive for the masses of material relating to the discovery, administration and trade of New World. Almost 40,000 files, going back to Columbus' time, are stored on the second floor, along with changing exhibits of maps and documents of general historical interest. It is worth the climb for a look. *Admission: free.*

Barrio Santa Cruz ★

This quarter is what remains of the Moorish layout of Seville, crowding houses along meandering alleys. Located next to the Alcázar and the mosque, this would have been the most densely populated part of the city during the time of the Moors. Long after the Moors and Jews who lived here had been expelled, this area again became a desirable place to live. Today the quarter's real estate is expensive and the glistening whitewashed houses are perfectly maintained. The barrio is a place for strolling past cafes, artisans' shops and lovely patios to come unexpectedly into charming squares. The whole area can be explored in a half hour's leisurely ramble.

The barrio begins alongside the east face of the Alcázar complex, extending in a rectangle for about five blocks east and north. Exit from the Alcázar to the right around the building, following its east face, to arrive in one block at the **Pl. Elvira**, with fountain and benches. Continue along the Alcázar side, turning right at the wall that borders the Alcázar gardens to follow Callejon del Agua past some of the nicest houses in the barrio. A short left turn at the end of the wall brings the attractive **Pl. Alfaro**. This is where Figaro supposedly serenaded Rosina on her balcony (a dozen other houses, however, claim that honor as well). To the right of the plaza a short street lets into the attractive **Pl. Santa Cruz**. From here you can wander north and west again to see more of the barrio, or retrace your steps to the Alcázar for the next sight.

West of the Cathedral

Covering about four blocks to the west of the Cathedral are a few nice things to see—the **Hospital de la Caridad**, the **Torre del Oro**, and the **Pl. de Toros**.

The wide Av. de la Constitución runs along the west side of the Cathedral. Head south along it, turning right on C. Santander just after passing the Archivo de Indias. Turn right at the next corner on C. Temprado to view the **Hospital de la Caridad** on the right. It was founded in 1674 by Don Miguel de Manara who decided, after spending the first part of his life in pleasure and debauchery, to devote his remaining time to helping the poor. Some claim he was a model for the character Don Juan. The building is subdued baroque in style and its church contains a series of paintings by Murillo, along with two gruesome canvases by Leal. Manara is buried in front of the altar of the church. *(Open Mon.–Sat. 10 a.m.–1 p.m. and 3:30–6 p.m.; Sun. 10 a.m.–1 p.m.; admission: 200 ptas.)*. On the opposite side of the street is the **Teatro de la Maestranza**, Seville's new opera house.

Back on C. Santander continue for one block to its end at Paseo de Cristobal Colón and the river. Left is the impressive **Torre del Oro**, so named for gold hued tiles that used to decorate its sides. It was built in 1220, along with a twin across the river (no longer standing), to control river traffic. At night a chain between the two towers could be raised to close the river. The smaller tower on top and steeple are later additions. Today the structure functions as a naval museum *(open Tues.–Fri. 10 a.m.–2 p.m.; weekends to 1 p.m.; closed Mon.; admission 100 ptas.)*.

Two blocks north along Paseo Cristobal Colón is the **Pl. de Toros de la Maestranza ★**, Seville's bullring. Built in 1763, it is the oldest and most beautiful in Spain. Across the river C. Betis, a riverfront street with the feeling of a resort, is festive with cafes, restaurants and shops.

North of the Cathedral

Two worthwhile sights lie north of the Cathedral area. Each is eminently walkable—at a distance of roughly half a mile—though the **Museo de Bellas Artes** is west and the **Casa de Pilatos** is east, which makes the combined trip closer to a mile. If the walk sounds too long, take a taxi for one leg of it. We describe the entire walk from the Cathedral but it can be followed in the reverse direction, of course.

From the northern face of the Cathedral either Av. de constitución or the smaller C. Hernando Colón leads due north for one block into the Pl. San Francisco. Running along the left side of the plaza is the most unusual **Ayuntamiento ★**, completed in 1564. The façade is a riot of Plateresque decoration, so much adorned that the building seems too slight to bear it. The surprise is the other side, barely embellished at all. That side was redone in the 19th century when styles had changed.

Running away from the north end of the plaza is the pedestrian shopping street of C. Sierpes, lined with attractive stores. Where it begins, a bust of Cervantes marks the spot of the former debtors' prison in which the writer began *Don Quixote*.

One block along C. Sierpes, down an alley to the left, is the church of **San José** (1766), a gaudy little structure with the most baroque of altars. Returning to Sierpes and continuing across it on C. Sagasta for a block to the west, the attractive plaza and church of **San Salvador** presents itself. The church was completed in 1712 on the site of the first great mosque of Seville. Its bell tower is the former minaret from 1079, and the facade incorporates original arches of the mosque. Only a foot or two of the arch columns show, demonstrating how much the ground has risen in 900 years.

For the **Casa de Pilatos** (see the description that follows) continue across the plaza and due west for five blocks.

Return to C. Sierpes and continue north for two blocks to the **Palacio de la Condesa de Lebrija**, on the right. The interior is not of the first order, but it has three patios with mosaics from nearby Roman Italica and a rather nice artesonado ceiling over the stairs. C. Sierpes ends in one block more when it reaches the busy C. Martín Villa. Slightly right is the department store el Corte Inglés. The **Museo de Bellas Artes** (see description that follows) is left along Martín Villa, which becomes C. Campaña for a block, then becomes C. Alfonso XII before reaching the museum three blocks later.

Casa de Pilatos   ★★★

Pl. Pilatos, 1, ☎ *(95) 422 50 55.*
Hours open: daily 9 a.m.–6 p.m.

On the right day, when the crowds are small and the mood is right, this can be one of the most memorable sights in Spain. But it should not be measured by the aesthetics of the Moors. Theirs was an ornate look of patterns heaped upon patterns but always with lightness and elegance. This palace for the Marqués of Tarifa was completed in 1540, and partially modeled on the House of Pontius Pilate which the Marqués had visited in Jerusalem. You will not notice any Roman or near-Eastern features, but you will see a riot of Mudejar design. Here are the elements of Moorish architecture—vibrant patterned tiles, carved stucco filigree and textured wood ceilings—all taken to their extreme. The result is brash compared to the Moor's delicacy, but wonderful on its own terms.

Past a Plateresque portal and entrance courtyard, the drama begins with the central patio—Moorish arches on the lower level, Gothic balustrade and arches above, bright tiles on the walls and Roman statues inhabiting the corners. In the center stands a fountain, not a low, unassuming water trickling device, but a strong architectural statement. The fantasy continues in rooms leading from this patio, culminating in the southwest corner in the stairway to the upper floor with its remarkable ceiling. The second floor is more prosaic, with rooms of varying later periods and some antiques. Only part can be visited, because the present owner, the Duque de Medinaceli, still lives in one wing. *Admission: 10000 ptas.*

Museo de Bellas Artes   ★★★

Pl. del Museo, ☎ *(95) 422 18 29.*
Hours open: Tues.–Fri. 10 a.m.–2 p.m. and 4–7 p.m.; Sun. 10 a.m.–2 p.m. Closed Mon.
This is the second best art museum in Spain, which still leaves it far removed from the Prado. The art is housed in a former convent with three delicate patios constructed in 1612, but thoroughly restored in the early 19th century. Its collection of works was rescued from nearby convents during the 19th century when many religious orders were suppressed in Spain. Extensive remodeling was still underway at our last visit with no end in sight.

The collection is weighted heavily toward artists from Seville, including some of the finest work of her adopted son Zurbarán. Room IV displays a fine El Greco portrait of his son Jorge Manuel. In the same room a canvas by Pacheco, teacher and father-in-law of Velázquez, of a man and woman praying is worth a look. Pacheco is universally condemned as a journeyman artist, with good reason, but this work is inspired.

The Zurbarán collection, in Rooms V-VII, rivals that of the Prado. *Saint Hugh and the Carthusian Monks at Table* is interesting, *The Apotheosis of Saint Thomas Aquinas* is a miracle of perspective and design (with Zurbarán himself peering at the viewer, behind the kneeling Carlos V), and the *Virgin of the Caves*, in which those magical white Zurbarán monks kneel to a Virgin with astonishing pink roses at her feet, is unforgettable.

Upstairs in Room X are the two Velázquez works owned by the museum, and one, *The Portrait of Cristobal Suarez de Ribera*, by itself repays the admission charge. It is among the most profound portraits ever painted.

Subsequent rooms display a nice Goya *Portrait of José Duarzo*, and a fine statue of *Saint Bruno* by Montañes, as lifelike as wood can be. There are some charming 19th- and early 20th-century works by local artists as well. The museum owns an extensive collection of Murillo (in Room VIII) and of Valdés Leal (in Room IX), a Sevillano taken with Ruben's historical style. *Admission: 250 ptas.*

South of the Cathedral

South of the Cathedral past the baroque **Palacio de San Telmo** an imposing arc of buildings borders a canal at the **Pl. España**, built for the aborted 1929 Seville World's Fair. The lovely **Parque de Maria Luisa** harbors the **Museo Arqueológico**, **Museo de Atres y Costumbres Populares** and the **Pabillon Real**.

Av. de la Constitución runs south from the west side of the Cathedral and ends in the traffic circle of Puerta de Jerez. Continuing south past the Hotel Alfonso XIII, Av. de Roma arrives in one block at the **Palacio de San Telmo** whose churrigueresque portal is admirable. This was the residence of the dukes of Montpensier who donated their palace grounds—now the Parque de María Luisa—to the city. They also donated this palace, although the city has not yet decided what to do with it.

Around the end of the palace, head southeast along its remaining gardens to Av. del Peru. In two blocks after passing the **Teatro Lope de Vega**, one of the buildings of the 1929 World's Fair, you arrive at Av. María Luisa, across which is the **Parque de María Luisa**. Walk south through the park, part wild, part formally arranged, to the south end past attractive villas left over from the 1929 World's Fair. Just before the end, comes the **Museo de Artes y Costumbres Populares** ★ with interesting exhibits of crafts, furniture and costumes *(open Tues.–Sun. 10 a.m.–2 p.m.; admission: 250 ptas.)*. In a few yards more the park ends, facing the **Museo Arqueológico** across the street.

Museo Arqueológico   ★

Pl. de América, ☎ *(95) 423 24 01.*
Hours open: Tues.–Sun. 10 a.m.–2 p.m. Closed Mon.
In the basement reside artifacts from pre-Roman cultures, including a famous hoard of sixth century B.C. gold found at Carambola, fine Phoenician statues and ceramics. The ground floor displays Celtiberian statuary, although none as wonderful as in Madrid, with the exception of some charming bulls and lions. Here too are lovely Roman mosaics and statuary from nearby Italica. *Admission: 250 ptas.*

Head east then north along the eastern edge of the park on Av. de Isabel la Católica, to pass the monumental **Pl. de España**. This was Spain's pavilion for the 1929 World's Fair, and is a fantasy worth viewing. By continuing along Av. de Isabel la Católica, you return to the huge university building (the former tobacco factory), past which are the gardens of the Alcázar and the Cathedral area again.

Discovery Park, Isla de la Cartuja ★

Isla de la Caruja, ☎ *(95) 446 16 16. This island is in the Guadalquivir north of the Cathedral square, opposite the Museo de Bellas Artes.*

Hours open: in summer and during holidays Tues.–Thurs. 8 p.m.–2 a.m., Fri.–Sun. noon–1 a. m. (pavilions close at midnight, or 8 p.m. on Sun. Open in winter Fri.-Sun. noon-midnight (pavilions close at 8 p.m., or midnight on Sun.).

Here are remains of the 1st-Class World's Fair of 1992 in case you missed it. The fair commemorated the 500th anniversary of Columbus' discovery of the New World, and its theme was "The Age of Discovery." For this mammoth event, a lake was dug on the island to provide natural air conditioning. Now it is all a huge theme park that can be fun and educational for children of all ages.

The exhibition centers on the 15th-century monastery of **Santa Maria las Cuevas**, where Columbus reputedly explained his theories to the monks. From here begins the Way of Discovery, that includes a **Pavilion of the 15th Century** to show what life was like in Columbus' time in various parts of the world. The **Discovery Pavilion** presents the great inventions and discoveries that formed the modern world, including an audiovisual presentation in which the seats move. The **Navigation Pavilion** traces the history of maritime exploration, and lets you "walk on water." The **Puerto de Indias** reconstructs a 15th-century port with shops, taverns and crafts of the era. There are miles of nature sights and cable cars, catamarans and a circus, ending with an impressive fireworks and laser show at night. *Admission: 500 ptas. for entry; 4000 ptas. for adults or 3000 ptas. for children and senior citizens for all pavilions.*

Evenings Out

Seville is the best place to see flamenco and maintains three permanent *tablas* for the art. Each is a small place, seating an audience of 50 or fewer, so reservations are always a good idea and can be arranged by most hotels.

Los Gallos

Pl. Santa Cruz, 11, ☎ *(95) 421 69 81.*

Too intimate for comfort, Gallos puts on the most authentic flamenco, and prides itself on the best performers.

El Arenal

Dos de Mayo, 26, ☎ *(95) 421 64 92.*

Will serve you dinner, or not, as you wish, and the show is often good.

El Patio Sevillano

Paseo de Colón, 11, ☎ *(95) 421 41 20.*

Mixes other kinds of folk dance and songs with flamenco for mainly tour groups.

Understand that pure flamenco can be very intense. The aim is to throw one's soul to the audience; performers are judged by the depth of their feelings. It is part dance, part guitar music, part singing and part rhythmic clapping. The dancing should be familiar, but the singing is strangely guttural and as earthy as the human voice can become. Guitarists can be amazing virtuosos, and the clapping incredible. Given a good group of performers, the experience will be unforgettable. Current prices are 3000 ptas., which includes one free drink. In summer there usually are three shows, one at about 7:30 p.m., another at 10 p.m., the last at midnight, but check. In winter the second and final performance will be at around 10 p.m.

Airport

Seville's **San Pablo Airport** (☎ *(95) 451 61 11)* connects with major European cities and most Spanish airports, but few overseas destinations. It is located 12 km east along N-IV. A taxi should cost about 2000 ptas. Currently, seven flights per day travel to Madrid and five to Barcelona. Iberia is located at *Almirante Lobo, 3* (☎ *(95) 422 89 01)*. This street runs to the river from Puerta de Jerez, the plaza at the western corner of the Alcázar gardens. Buses connect from there with flights.

Trains

The train station is **Santa Justa** (☎ *(95) 454 02 02)* at the intersection of José Laguillo and Av. Kansas City, about one mile northeast of the Cathedral. Six high speed AVE trains connect with Madrid in under three hours (6000–9000 ptas.), half the time and twice the price of other types of trains. The AVE also goes to Córdoba 10 times per day in under an hour (about 3000 ptas.). Slower trains double the time and halve the price. Only three trains go to Granada per day for a trip of almost five hours. Málaga is also served three times per day. Four trains daily take the 10–13 hour trip to Barcelona for 9000 to 7000 ptas. The RENFE office is on *C. Zaragoza, 29*, about three blocks north of the Pl. de Toros (☎ *(95) 421 79 98)*.

Shopping

Among the best buys in Spain are ceramics made in Seville, partly because their prices are low, partly because the quality of work and design is high. You can get a taste of the wares by walking along the pedestrian mall of C. Sierpes. At #30 is **Cerámica Sevillano**, with fine designs, and at #66 **Sevillarte**, equally good. **Martian** at #6 sells thicker, more folk-like pieces. If you like what you see, there is a larger selection at **Cerámicas Sevilla** on Pemiento, #9, which runs beside the wall to the Alcázar Gardens in the Barrio Santa Cruz. This outlet continues around the corner, at Gloria, #5. The wares are part gold-rimmed which are Moorish-inspired and part Renaissance blues on white and blues and greens on white. The supply is so large this shop seems to be a factory, but it is not. For the true factories and their outlets, you have to cross the river over Puente Isabel II, the bridge just north of the Pl. de Toros. Directly off the bridge you come to C. San Jorge and the heart of the ceramic outlets. Prices are incredibly low, and most companies will ship. Try **Cerámica Santa Ana** at #31, **Cerámica Ruiz** at #27, and **Cerámica Montalvan**, especially for tiles, around the corner at Alfareria #21.

Interesting too are the fans, including some very expensive hand-painted antiques, at **Casa Rubio** on C. Sierpes, #56. Farther down Sierpes at #73 is a leather shop named **Bolsos Casal** with copies of expensive name bags for women at modest prices. For the horsey set there is a superb leather store, **El Caballo**, on *C. Antonio Diaz, #7,* at the end of the street on the east side of the Pl. de Toros. You can also get those flat brimmed Spanish riding hats. A nice branch of **Artespaña** displays well-made furniture and accessories in the Pl. de la Gavidia, just north of the **el Corte Inglés** department store at the end of C. Sierpes.

Yes, there is a **flea market**. It opens every Sunday morning along C. Alameda de Hercules, which is north of the Museo de Bellas Artes.

Excursions

Roman remains at **Itálica** lie nine km north, for a half day of exploring. **Jerez de la Frontera**, the home of sherry, waits an hour south for a pleasant half day of free or inexpensive samples. See the description under Arcos de la Frontera. Of course, magical **Córdoba** and **Granada** are within a few hours east, and described under their respective headings in this chapter. Also, the Portuguese border and beginning of the Algarve beaches are 175 km to the west; Lisbon is 417 km distant.

For **Itálica** cross the river on the Puente de Chapina, the third bridge north of the Cathedral area, to travel west along C. Ordiel on the west bank. Follow signs to Santiponce and Mérida. About three km outside of town turn north on N-630. Follow signs one km past Santiponce for Itálica.

For the **Algarve** follow the directions for Itálica but do not turn north on N-630. Continue west instead on A-49 (E-1). After three km, switch to N-431, just before Huelva in 92 km, and a farther journey of 63 km to Portuguese border.

For **Lisbon** follow the directions to Itálica and continue past it along N-630. Just before Zafra in 134 km turn west on N-432 (E-102) to Badajoz in 79 km at the border. West from Badajoz on N-4 (E-90) brings you to Cruzamento de Pagoes in 152 km. There go south on N-10 (still E-90) to Setubal in 35 km and the highway E-1 to Lisbon 50 km away.

For **Jerez** follow Av. de la Palmera leading south from the southern end of the Parque de Maria Luisa. You are given the choices of the toll road A-4 or the free N-IV toward Cádiz, reaching Jerez in about 70 km.

Itálica ★

Satiponce, ☎ *(95) 439 27 84.*
Hours open: Tues.–Sat. 9 a.m.–5:30 p.m., Sun. 10 a.m.–4 p.m.
This Roman town was among the earliest in Spain for it was founded in 206 B.C. by Scipio Africanus as a place of retirement for his veterans who defeated Hannibal. By the second century A.D. it had grown to 10,000 and stood among the most important towns in Spain. Two emperors were born here—Trajan and Hadrian. Prosperity ended with the arrival of the Visigoths who favored nearby Seville. Itálica then became a quarry for marble and stone materials, even for mosaics, for use as decoration in later Christian mansions. The surprise is that anything remains, and quite a bit does, though only a quarter of the site has been excavated so far.

There is a huge amphitheater that once seated 40,000, a theater, two baths, a forum and a network of streets. Here and there some remaining mosaics fenced off, but the major works and all the statuary continue to be carted off to museums in Madrid and Seville whenever they are uncovered. *Admission: 250 ptas.*

SOUTHERN SPAIN

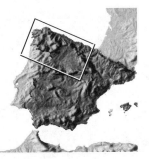

NORTHERN SPAIN

The Plaza Obradoiro, Santiago de Compostela, invites contemplation.

Northern Spain presents soaring Gothic cathedrals (in León), massive Romanesque edifices (in Santiago de Compostela), craggy mountains, rugged coast and lovely beaches. It is the Spain least visited by tourists, hence the most Spanish part of the country. Covering the northern third of Spain, it ranges across the old territories of Galicia and Asturias through the Basque provinces, west to east, then continues down to the province of León and most of Old Castile. That is to say, it runs 400 miles west to east and 300 miles in depth. Included are the two most regal paradors, the Hotel Reyes Católicos in Santiago de Compostela and the San Marcos in León, among some of the most charming.

CANTÁB

San Andrés de Teixido
Barqueiro
Ferrol
Ribadeo
La Coruña
Mondoñedo
Villalba

Santiago

O Cebreiro
Mosteiro
Pontevedra
Villafranca del Bierzo
Combarro
Ponferrada
Pazos de Arenteiro
Vilanova dos Infantes
Peñalba de Santiago
Castro Caldelas
Biona
As Ermitas
Tui
Allariz
Valença de Minho
Vila Nova de Cerveira
Verin
Puebla de Sanabria
Viana do Castelo

ATLANTIC OCEAN

Porto
Amarante
Alijó

Ria
Serem
Caramulo
Almeida

Northern Spain

P PARADOR	═══ PRIMARY ROAD	
Castle CASTLE	─── SECONDARY ROAD	
Pueblo PUEBLO	▬▬▬ SCENIC ROAD	

```
0    10   20   30   40 Mi.
0      20     40     60 km
```

N

RICO SEA

Cudillero

Gijón **P**

Oviedo

Santander

Sandujo

Santillana del Mar **P**

Espinaredo

Carmona

Llanuces

Rénedo

Bárcena Mayor

P Cervera de Pisuerga

Frias

Bembibre

León

Poza de la Sal

Castrillo de los Polvazares

Burgos **P**

Benavente **P**

Ampudia

Medina de Rioseco

Covarrubias
S. Domingo de Silos

Valladolid

Peñaranda de Duero

Zamora **P**

Berlanga de Duero

Simancas

Tordesillas **P**

Peñafiel   Maderuelo

Medina del Campo

Salamanca **P**

Olmedo

Sepúlveda
Pedrazza

Madrigal de
las Altas Torres

Arevalo Segovia **P**

Buitrago
de Lozoya

In general the sights of Northern Spain are a quieter sort than those of the center or the south—a contemplative ancient abbey here, or a beach for luxuriating there. The exceptions are two of the great churches of the world: Santiago de Compostela and the Cathedral of Burgos.

To the west waits **Santiago de Compostela** with its awesome cathedral and plaza, along with ruggedly beautiful Atlantic coastline, called the **Rias**. In the center stands **Burgos**, with the most moving Spanish Gothic cathedral and two ancient monasteries on its outskirts. **León**, with a most regal parador, adds a lovely cathedral in the airy French Gothic style. Then relax in the charming beach town of **Santillana del Mar**.

The following towns and paradors are covered in this chapter.

Town	Parador Name	Rating	Page
Bayona	Conde de Gondomar	★★★★	page 321
Bentavente	Fernando II de León	★★★★	page 343
Burgos	None		page 296
Cambados	El Albariño	★★★	page 341
Cerva de Pisuerga	Cervera de Pisuerga	★★★	page 326
Ferrol	Ferrol	★★★	page 328
Fuente Dé	Rio Deva	★★★	page 352
Gujón	Molino Vejo	★★★★	page 348
León	Hotel San Marcos	★★★★★	page 354
Pontevedra	Casa del Barón	★★★	page 318
Puebla de Sanabria	Puebla de Sanabria	★	page 330
Ribadeo	Ribadeo	★★	page 332
Santiago de Compostela	Hotel Reyes Católicos	★★★★★	page 308
Santillana del Mar	Gil Blas	★★★	page 345
Tordesillas	Tordesillas	★★★	page 334
Túy	San Telmo	★★	page 363
Verín	Monterrey	★★	page 350
Villafranca del Bierzo	Villafranca del Bierzo	★	page 337
Villalba	Conde de Villalba	★★★★★	page 339
Zamora	Condes de Alba y Aliste	★★★★	page 323

To savor the region, you want two nights in western Galicia. Break the long drive from Madrid with an overnight at the parador in Benavente, from which you could also base for León and Burgos before continuing on. Or, for a special experience, break the drive at the Villalba parador. Then stay two nights at the parador in Bayona, Pontevedra or Cambados, while you visit Santiago de Compostela and the rias of Galicia; or luxuriate for one night in Santiago's wonderful parador, then take another night at one of the foregoing on the rias. You want two nights for León and Burgo, which can be managed from Benavente or more regally by staying in León's splendid parador. If possible add a stay at either Ribadeo or, especially, Santillana, near the northern beaches. And, if you like mountains, book into the parador of Cervera de Pisuerga or Fuente Dé.

BURGOS

★ ★ ★

Accommodations

Palacio Landa

Carretera Madrid-Irun, at kilometer 236, Burgos, 09000, ☎ *(947) 20 63 43, FAX (947) 26 46 76. 39 rooms, plus three suites.*

There are no wonderful hotels in the city, but one lies two miles outside. The Palacio Landa is one of the most dramatic hotels in Spain, with an over-the-top elegance surpassed by few others, and its prices are improbably reasonable at $100 (luxurious suites go for under $200). Located 3.5 km south of Burgos on N-1, it can be reached by going south on Calle Madrid, which leads away from the Santa María pedestrian bridge. The hotel is built around a 14th-century castle which was carted here stone by stone. You see, the hotel is a fantasy of the owner's imagination. The Palacio Landa provides whatever the heart desires, including swimming. It is affiliated with the top-notch French Relais & Chateux chain (U.S. ☎ 800-677-3524).

Choices in the city are more ordinary. Two similar hotels stand a short walk from the cathedral. Each charges $100 per night.

Condestable

C. Vitoria, 8, Burgos, 09000, ☎ *(947) 26 71 25, FAX (947) 20 46 45, Telex 395 72. 85 rooms.*

The Condestable is four blocks from the cathedral, a modern, efficient hotel. Rooms are small but sleekly designed.

Almirante Bonfaz

C. Vitoria, 22, Burgos, 09000, ☎ *(947) 20 69 43, FAX (947) 20 29 19, Telex 39430. 79 rooms.*

The Almirante Bonfaz lies on the same street, two blocks further away.

BURGOS

N623 to Santander

CAMPEADOR

SANZ PASTOR

Plaza General
Santocildes

Plaza
Alonso
Martinez

CALLE DE SANTANDER

SAN JUAN

Casa del
Cordon

PUEBLA

Plaza
Calvo Satelo

Plaza
Primo de
Rivera

Museo
Marceliano
Santa Maria

Plaza de
San Juan

GARCIA

CALLE DE VITORIA

CALLE DE SANTA CLARA

AV. GENERAL SANJURJO

AV. CONDE DE VALLELLANO

To Cartuja de Miraflores →

yards   0   220
meters 0   200

MONEDA

ALMIRANTE BONITAZ

Plaza
Santo
Domingo

SAN LORENZO

LAIN CALVO

DEL REY

GONZALEZ

SEGURA

Plaza
José Antonio

PASEO DEL ESPOLÓN

Río Arlanzón

Plaza Conde
de Castro

BURGENSE

CALLE DE GENERAL MOLA

Plaza Conde
de Castro

CALERA

Casa de
Miranda

CALLE DE MIRANDA

ESTABAN

PALENCIA

PALOMA

Catedral

Plaza Rey
San Fernando

CALLE DE VALLADOLID

CALLE DE MADRID

Plaza de
Vega

SAN COSME

NI to Madrid →

CALLE DE LA CONCEPCION

Castillo

Plaza Santa
Maria

San Nicolas

Arco de
Santa Maria

NUÑO RASURA

EDWARDO MARTINEZ DEL CAMPO

AV. DEL GENERALISIMO FRANCO

AV. DE LA MERCED

CALLE DEL CARMEN

P. DE LOS CUBOS

BARRANTOS

APARICIO Y RUIZ

Plaza de
Castilla

N20 to Valladolid

PASEO DEL EMPECINADO

C. GUADALHORCE

To Las
Huelgas
Reales

N

NORTHERN SPAIN

Del Cid

Pl. Santa María, 8, Burgos, 09000, *(947) 20 87 15, FAX (947) 26 94 60. 25 rooms, plus three suites.*

More interesting, ten percent cheaper and directly across the street from the cathedral is the Del Cid. Part of the building is a 15th-century house, rambling and full of curiosities. Recently it became affiliated with the Best Western hotel chain, and we will have to see what that does to the service. Associated with the hotel is a good restaurant.

Cordón

La Puebla, 6, Burgos, 09000, *(947) 26 50 00, FAX (947) 20 02 69. 35 rooms.*

For $90 you can stay one block north of the Condestable at the Cordón whose small size allows greater attention to each guest, but whose staff does not speak English.

Dining

The best food, in the most elegant surroundings, is served at the Palacio Landa outside of town (see under hotels). In town the choices are:

Fernán Gonzáles   ★ ★

C. Calera, 19 (across the river from the old town, left from the Santa María pedestrian bridge), Burgos, 09000, *(947) 20 94 42.*

Located beside the hotel of the same name, this restaurant is elegant, yet more adventuresome than most in town. In addition to the usual roasts, there are *nueva cocina* specialties such as sole with shrimp sauce and green beans with foie gras and truffles. The owner knows wines—in fact he owns several vineyards—so his selection is exemplary. A meal should cost $25. Credit Cards: A, D, V.

Mesón del Cid   ★

Pl. Santa María, 8 (to the west of the Cathedral square), Burgos, 09000, *(947) 20 87 15. Closed Sunday evening.*

Two ancient dining rooms on the second and third floors framed by hand-hewn wood present views of the Cathedral. Or try the pleasant terrace for fresh-air dining. The *sopa de Doña Jimena*, its version of garlic soup, is yummy, as is the baby lamb with mushrooms. It costs about the same as the Fernán Gonzáles. Credit Cards: A, D, M, V.

Casa Ojeda   ★

C. Vitoria, 5 (opposite the Casa Cordón), Burgos, 09000, *(947) 20 90 52. Closed Sunday night.*

This well-known Burgos institution, with an elegant gourmet store adjacent and a fine upstairs dining room decorated in typical Castilian style, serves classical regional cooking. The cheeses are special. The bill may reach $30. Credit Cards: A, D, M, V.

Directions

From **Madrid** A-1 (E-5) becomes N-1, reaching Burgos in 235 km. From **Segovia** take N-110 for 57 km to Cerezo de Abajo where N-1 is picked up going north for a total of 194 km. From **León** take N-601 south towards Valladolid for 67 km to Becilla de Valderaduey where you change to N-610 to Palencia for 61 km. There pick up N-620 (E-80) for a total of 216 km. From **Valladolid** N-620 north reaches Burgos in 117 km, but be careful not to turn off into Palencia. From **Santander** N-623 goes south to Burgos in 93 km. From **Pamplona** N-III heads west to Logrono in 92 km. There you take N-120 for 113 km further west.

Paradors Nearby

Sta. Domingo de Calzada: 69 km   Santillana: 130 km   Soria: 131 km
León: 211 km   Fuente Dé: km

Sights

Burgos began as a military outpost to fend off Moors, but gained prominence when Count Fernán González briefly united Castile in 950 and made Burgos his seat. The city's importance was enhanced by Fernando I, the first king of a united Castile and León, who appointed it his capital in 1037. Fifty years later, however, Alfonso VI captured Toledo and moved the capital there. Over the next 400 years, these two cities vied for the honor of being Christian Spain's primary city. In 1221 Burgos commenced a great cathedral, in part to meet the "cathedral challenge" from Toledo. The rivalry became moot, however, after the conquest of Granada in 1492, when Ferdinand and Isabella chose still another city, Valladolid, as their capital. Burgos did not really need the status of a capital to be important, however, because it was situated at the crossroads of the main routes both to Santiago de Compostela and to southern Spain. It was and remains a commercial and military center, even to serving as the seat of Franco's government throughout Spain's Civil War.

Burgos claims El Cid as its most famous son, though, as Rodrigo Diaz, he was actually born in Vivar, six miles away. When Alfonso VI came to the throne after the suspicious death of his brother, the nobles appointed Diaz to extract a public oath from Alfonso that he bore no complicity in the death. Alfonso never forgave his vassal for this and soon found an excuse to expel him. Homeless, Rodrigo became a mercenary soldier who enjoyed outstanding success, campaigning both against and also for the Moors. Soon he was known by the Arabic title of El Sidi, "The Commander," which the Christians mispronounced as El Cid. El Cid's greatest feat was the conquest of a huge area around Valencia, which he held until he was defeated and killed by the Moors five years later. His wife, Doña Jimena, brought his body home, and today it lies in the Burgos Cathedral.

The Cathedral and old town lie along the Arlanzón River, which is lined on the north side with trees and flowered promenades. The old town, hemmed on its other side by a forested hill and ruined castle, is relatively small. The newer city spreads east and west and across the river, but offers little of historic or scenic interest. Unlike the typical medieval hill town with a maze of cobblestoned alleys, old Burgos seems green and light, a place to relax as well as to enjoy the sights.

Arriving from **Valladolid** you enter the western part of Burgos and follow the Arlanzón River on Paseo del Empecinado as far as a pedestrian bridge opposite the Cathedral. Turn right here, away from the bridge, into the Pl. de Vega for parking. More parking is available at the next bridge after a right at the Pl. de Conde de Castro, where a large lot stands at the next left. From **Madrid** and **Segovia** on N-1, follow the opposite bank of the river and pass the lovely Pl. Miguel Primo de Riveira and bridge. Turn left and cross the river, then take the second left into a large parking lot. From the **north** you enter eastern Burgos. Cross, if necessary, to the southern side of the Arlanzón River and follow it until opposite the Cathedral. Turn left into the Pl. de Vega for parking.

Cathedral   ★★★★★

Pl. de Santa María, ☎ (947) 20 4712.
Hours open: daily 10 a.m.–1 p.m. and 4–7 p.m.

This is Spain's third largest cathedral, after Toledo and Seville, but its most imposing. It is variegated yet uniform, solidly standing as if for eternity—the finest example of the Spanish Gothic. The foundation was laid in 1221 by Fernando II, under
the supervision of Bishop Mauricio. The mass of the Cathedral was completed by
the end of that century. In the 15th century a second stage of construction took
place. Tall spires were added to the front, the huge Condestable Chapel was
appended to the rear, a cloister built on the side, and the interior chapels decorated
anew. All this was effected by some of the great artists of the time who gathered in
Burgos for the purpose. Slightly later, grand ramped stairways were added around
the Cathedral so that a walk to the Cathedral would also involve a tour of its exterior.

Appreciation of the Cathedral starts outside with its front in the **Pl. Santa María**.
Intricate openwork spires soar 300 feet into the sky, reminiscent of the Cathedral of
Cologne. In fact, their architect was from Cologne and surely imported the design.
Above the **rose window** in the center is a row of **statues** of kings of Castile and bish-
ops of Burgos. Over the door an incongruous classical pediment separates a bishop
leading a king on the right side and a queen on the left, each holding real spears.

Inside, the nave rises to vaulting made elegant with 15th-century ribs, though the
view down the Cathedral is unfortunately obstructed by the choir. Atop a clock high
on the left is the 16th-century *Papamosca*, "Flycatcher," a bird who opens his
mouth each time the clock chimes. Proceed left.

The first chapel presents a riotously overblown 18th-century retablo dedicated to
Saint Tecla. It is the work of a member of the Churriguera family who helped create
the baroque churrigueresque style of architecture. Next is a chapel for Saint Ana,
built a century and a half earlier. It contains a lovely retable by Gil de Siloé. The two
chapels demonstrate, respectively, ornateness as opposed to art. At the transept,
look left to a glorious diamond flight of **renaissance stairs**, all gilded and lovely,
that merely lead to the outside.

Enter the nave to view the altar and choir, but look up first to see a Plateresque elegant lantern where the transept crosses the nave. Under the lantern, a plain copper
slab marks the place where El Cid rests beside his wife Jimena. The 16th-century
reredos behind the high altar effectively place Biblical figures in classical niches.
Though ornate, the choirstalls in the coro are well done and are unusual for having
inlays. In the center of the coro is the 13th-century coffin of the founding Archbishop, named Mauricio. His wood effigy is covered with embossed copper and
Limoge enameling.

Continue around the left side of the apse to come to the chapel of Saint Nicolas,
which contains a portable organ from the 16th century. Next is a 16th-century
chapel with an **elliptical dome**, followed by two 13th-century chapels.

In the left rear is the outstanding **Chapel of the Condestable**. This addition to the
Cathedral, a medley of the Isabelline, was fashioned in 1482 for the Constable of
Castile and worked on by all the great artists in Burgos. Elegant vaulting meets in a
star unexpectedly filled by glass. The pillars are carved with figures of the Apostles,

rendered by the Renaissance master, Gil de Siloé. Compared with the usual busy altar retablo, this one is bold and dramatic, carved by Gil de Siloé's son Diego. The peaceful Constable and his wife, carved by an unknown artist, face the altar. Done in lovely Carrara marble, the artist obviously took delight in fabric folds. Shields on the rear wall and the balustrade record the families of the Constable and his wife. To the right rear, a door leads to a sacristy in which hangs a Da Vinci-like painting of Mary Magdaline.

The Santiago Chapel next along in the apse carries a ceiling of delicate ribs. Continuing around to the right transept, a magnificent Gothic paneled door on the left leads into 14th-century cloisters, with statues everywhere and more chapels along the left side. The first of these chapels stores clerical vestments, plates and manuscripts, including the marriage contract of El Cid. The next room, the Chapterhouse, has a lovely Mudejar ceiling and displays a graceful Memling *Virgin and Child*, along with a Van Eyke. The *"Coffer of El Cid"* is bolted to the wall. This chest, purportedly El Cid's security for a loan worth far less than the gold that filled it, was found to hold sand when it was opened after repayment of the loan. In the adjoining Sacristy is a masterpiece of sculpture by Diego de Siloé of *Christ at the Column*.

Back in the Cathedral proper, return to the front along the right side of the nave. The large chapel of the Visitation contains a carved tomb of the Bishop of Lerma, a Renaissance masterpiece of a dour faced personage. Also in that chapel hangs a delicate painting of the Madonna and Child. Notice the beautiful vaulting above. In the front chapel on the far right is a gruesome crucifixion constructed with a figure made of buffalo hide that looks for all the world like human skin. *Admission: 350 ptas., for the treasury and cloister.*

Outside, take a look at the curious figures that make up the fountain in the plaza. Mary and her son wear real gilt crowns, while grotesques below ride fish with ears. Go up the ramped stair again, this time for a view of the **Church of San Nicolás**, directly ahead. Look opposite the church front at the engaging Renaissance **Palace of Castrofuerte** with a lovely patio.

Iglesia de San Nicolás   ★

C. Fernán González.
Hours open: daily 9 a.m.–1:30 p.m. and from 4:30–6:30 p.m.
Although the architecture of this late Gothic church is not special, some of the art inside is. The retablo by Francisco de Colonia is huge and ornate, containing more than 400 stone figures depicting the life of Saint Nicholas. At the base of the altar are two fine pairs of tombs of the church's patrons, Alfonso and Gonzalo Polanco, and their wives.

Walking directly along past the face of the Cathedral brings the Arch of Santa María.

Arco de Santa María   ★

Pl. Rey San Fernando.
At this spot once stood a gate through 11th-century walls that girded the town. Today only a few stones on either side of the arch remain, inscribed here and there with Arabic writing. Past the gate looking back in the direction of the Cathedral is

the facade of the arch that, despite a more modern appearance, dates to 1550. Just before its construction citizens throughout Spain had risen against their new king, Carlos V, to protest his preference for foreign advisors and foreign affairs. This was the Comuneros Revolt which forced the king to accept many of the rebel's demands. After the king agreed to the will of the people, loyal citizens of Burgos raised this monument to atone for their participation in the uprising.

The center figure on the top register is Count Fernán González, the first man to unite Castile. On his left is Carlos V; on his right, El Cid. Below, two legendary early judges flank Diego Porcelos, the alleged founder of the city of Burgos. He was called Porcelos (Pig) because he was one of seven siblings, which is the size of a normal pig litter. With its tiny turrets evoking a castle, the arch seems a bit of fantasy.

Stretching west is the lovely Paseo del Espolan, lined with sycamores, flowers and topiary, where the citizens of Burgos stroll. The second left leads to the **Plaza Mayor ★**, a.k.a. **Plaza José Antonio**. Unusual in its oval shape, the arcaded plaza presents an attractive appearance; it houses stores and numerous cafes. On the south side stands the Ayuntamiento (City Hall), opened in 1791. Leave the east side of the Plaza, opposite the Cathedral, to pass through the Pl. Santo Domingo. Take the next left onto the wide pedestrian walk, C. Santander. Turn right into the attractive Pl. de Calvo Sotelo for the *Casa del Cordón*, with the arresting carving of a rope forming a triangle over the door.

Casa del Cordón   ★

Pl. de Calvo Sotelo.

Although it is now a bank, this handsome structure was once the palace of the Constables of Castile, at which the sovereigns of the time often stopped for extended visits. Here Ferdinand and Isabella met Columbus to learn about his second voyage. Here, too, Philip the Handsome, the young husband of their daughter Juana the Mad and father of Carlos V, died from a chill caught while playing ball with a retainer. Its popular name "House of the Rope," obviously comes from the carved Franciscan cord serving as a kind of tympanum to frame the coats-of-arms of the Constables of Castile. The animals in the top door corners are a whimsical touch.

Across the river, three streets back and midway between the pedestrian bridge which leads to the Arco Santa María and the vehicular bridge upstream, stands the **Casa de Miranda** on C. Miranda.

Casa de Miranda (Museo Arqueológico)   ★★

C. Miranda, 13, ☎ *(947) 26 58 75.*
Hours open: Tues.–Fri. 10 a.m.–2 p.m. and 4–7 p.m. Open Sat. and Sun. 11 a.m. to 1 p.m. Closed Mon.

The building, a 16th-century palace, is elegant with an unusual Plateresque patio containing columns that evoke the classical. Its grand staircase is imposing. The art collection is small but unusual too. The tomb of Juan de Padilla, a page of Isabella's killed during the siege of Granada, is a masterwork by Gil de Siloé. On the first floor is a collection of Visigothic sarcophagi, and also Gothic and Renaissance tombs. On the second floor are some extraordinary Moorish pieces, including a 10th-century ivory case for balls (perhaps for some sort of bowling), and an ivory casket from the

11th century with Limoges plaques for Christian use later affixed to the ends. There is also an interesting altar of beaten and enameled copper images of saints from the 12th century. The paintings vary in quality, but a weeping, Flemish-style Christ is riveting. *Admission: 200 ptas.*

A convent and a monastery in opposite suburbs should not be missed. **Las Huelgas Reales Convent** is 1.5 km west of the center. Take the river road on the bank opposite the Cathedral (signs point to N-630) until you see signs directing you to the convent. **Cartuja de Miraflores Monastery** is 4 km east of the city. Follow the river road east on the side opposite the Cathedral until signs direct you to the monastery.

Buses leave Pl. de Calvo Sotelo (where the Casa del Cordón is) several times per day for each monastery, marked "Barrio de Pilar" and "Fuentes Blancas," respectively.

Convento Las Huelgas Reales   ★★★★

C. Compás de Adentro, ☎ *(947) 20 16 30. 1.5k. west of Burgos.*
Hours open: Tues.–Sat. 10:30 a.m.–2 p.m. and 4–6:30 p.m. Open Sun. and holidays 11 a.m. to 3 p.m. Closed Mon.

The convent originally was a summer residence (*huelgas* means "repose") for the first kings of Castile. In 1187 this masculine lodge was converted to a convent by the queen of Alfonso VIII. She was Eleanor of Aquitaine, Richard the Lionheart's sister. The convent eventually controlled 50 manors and towns whose revenues supported the nunnery nicely enough that often queens would arrive to spend periods of retreat.

The convent grew in size over the centuries, accruing various architectural styles, and served as a royal pantheon for the first kings and queens of Castile. Napoléon's soldiers desecrated most of those tombs during their occupation in the 19th century, but fortunately missed a few early coffers that contained clothing miraculously preserved from the 12th and 13th centuries, now on display in the convent's **Museo de Talas**.

Past a Gothic arch and along the cloister, the church tower, with model castles on its top, beckons. The church is entered from a porch on which four early ornate sarcophagi still rest. The church is early 13th-century and its simple Cistercian style allows artworks clear display. Kneeling statues of the founders, Eleanor (Leonor in Spanish) of Aquitaine and Alfonso VIII, flank the altar. Royal tombs line the aisles, while the simple and moving tombs of the founders and their children are housed in the separate nun's choir. Here magnificent tapestries line the walls, and the wood floors seem too old to walk on.

The "Gothic" cloister retains enough intricate Mudejar stuccowork and wood ceiling to convey a sense of its original delicate appearance. Exquisite doors lead to the sacristy. The large chapterhouse with nine bays displays what is said to be the standard of the Moorish commander from the battle of Las Navas de Tolosa. If only one battle turned the tide for the Christians it was this victory in 1212 when they defeated a large army of fierce Almohad Moors. Although the "standard" is more likely a flap from a tent, it is still lovely and rich with history. This hall has seen its own history as well. It was here that Franco assembled his first government during the Spanish Civil War.

In the **Museo de Ricas Telas** (Clothing Museum), the former sewing room of the convent, clothing, jewelry and swords from the 12th and 13th century are simply displayed. Most remarkable is the equipment found with Infante Don Fernando de la Cerda, displayed in cases eight-11. But all of the clothing is striking for its intricacy and beauty. Don't miss the dress of María Almenar from 1196.

The Romanesque Cloister from the 12th century, the earlier of two, is simple with rounded arches. Rooms off this cloister constitute the royal apartments of the convent, with fine Mudejar decoration still intact in places. Across the garden stands the Chapel of Santiago, looking entirely Moorish, with fine wood paneling inside. A lifesize statue of Saint James sits on a throne. His articulated right arm holds a sword that can be lowered through a series of counterbalances. It was used to dub new knights, usually princes, in the early 13th century. Tradition has it that it was built so the later Fernando III would not suffer the indignity of being knighted by an inferior. *Admission: 400 ptas., for guided tour in Spanish. Free Wed.*

Cartuja de Miraflores ★★★

C. de Valladolid. Four km west of Burgos.
Hours open: Mon.–Sat. 10:30 a.m–3 p.m. and 4–6 p.m. Open Sun. and holidays 11:20 a.m.–12:30 and 1–3 p.m, then 4–7 p.m.
In 1442 King Juan II decided to erect a monastery on the site of one of his father's palaces to hold his family tomb. When the king died in 1454, the unfinished project was completed by his loving daughter Isabella the Catholic. She called on Juan de Colonia who worked on the second stage of the Burgos Cathedral to help her finish the memorial to her parents. He designed a plain exterior with only a florid Gothic doorway surmounted by the founder's lion-held shields to break the monotony, making the rich interior all the more impressive.

The superb altar and marble tombs are perhaps the finest works of Gil de Siloé, a rare instance of plan and execution by the same artist. Instead of the standard rectangular design, the gilt retable presents a great circle enclosing a crucifixion. At its bottom, left and right, figures of the king and queen kneel beneath their coats of arms. But in front of the altar is the reason for the entire edifice—the paired tomb of Juan II and his wife, Doña Isabel of Portugal. Its base forms a star on which countless tiny figures, mostly characters from the New Testament, adore and watch over the recumbent king and queen above. The openwork carving is so intricate it is difficult to believe it could be fashioned from marble. The inscription reads: "It does not have an equal in the world and constitutes the principle adornment and glory of this church."

In a niche to the left is a tomb that almost rivals this one. It was made for the Infante Don Alfonso—Isabella's brother who would have been king instead of Isabella had he lived. But at age 14, he fell to his death from the walls of the Alcázar in Segovia, thereby allowing Isabella to ascend the throne. His tomb is masterful, if somewhat ornate, but the artistry of Gil de Siloé saves it from prettiness. The spectacled figure in the left bottom register is said to be the artist himself. In the chapel, to the left of the altar, usually hangs a splendid *Annunciation* by Pedro Berruguete, though it was not there on our last visit. *Admission: free.*

Excursions

On the route southeast to **Santo Domingo de Silos** ★, (which has a treasured cloister) famous today for its top-10 hit of Gregorian chant, a stop can be made at charming **Covarrubias** ★. **Peñaranda de Duero** ★ due south, contains an elegant Renaissance palace in a pretty square.

Covarrubias   ★

Leave Burgos on Av. Madrid heading due south from the Santa María pedestrian bridge, following signs to N-1. At 9.5 km fork left onto N-234 toward Soria. In 33.5 km at Hortiguela turn right onto C110 toward Covarrubias and Lerma. In 13 km you arrive.

Still partly girded by medieval ramparts, the town is guarded by the **Doña Urraca Tower** (a.k.a. **Fernán González Tower**). It rises with an extreme batter, in the shape of a truncated pyramid. A Renaissance palace leads to a picturesque old quarter with many restored, half-timbered house facades. The **Colegiata** church is crammed with attractive tombs, including that of Fernán González, who first united Castile, and his wife, Doña Sancha. The associated museum (open 10 a.m. to 2 p.m. and 4–7 p.m.; closed Tues.) contains some nice works, including a Berruguete, a Van Eyck and several fine primitives.

Santo Domingo de Silos   ★

From Covarrubias take BU-903 south for 11.5 km, turning left past Santibañez del Val to Silos in seven km more.

All that remains of a monastery built in the 12th century is this Romanesque cloister. But what a cloister! Called the most beautiful in the world, its elegant shape and the animation of its carvings make it undeniably special. Apply at the porter's lodge; enter through the 18th-century church and descend to the lower cloister level. Take time to study the wondrous Romanesque carving on the columns, especially at the cloister corners, bases and capitals. The 14th-century painted Mudejar ceiling, though restored in large part, is still exquisite. On the north side, a sarcophagus lid in high relief supported by three lions, stands over Saint Dominic, who reconstructed the convent early in the 12th century and added the upper story. The small museum at the northwest corner holds an 11th-century chalice, a 10th-century manuscript, a gilt and enamel copper chest, and lovely ivories.

The associated church presents little of architectural interest but at 7 p.m. vespers one can hear the very best of Gregorian Chant by the monks, who improbably had a hit album a few years ago.

Peñaranda de Duero   ★

Leave Burgos on Av. Madrid leading due south from the Santa María pedestrian bridge, and follow signs to N-1. From N-1 exit at Aranda de Duero in 79 km to take C-111 east for 21 km to Peñaranda de Duero, a total trip of 100 km.

This walled village is dominated by a square medieval keep. But it is the **Plaza Mayor** and the palace fronting it that merits the trip. The plaza is a harmonious composition of half-timbered houses on massive stone pillars. In the center stands a stone pillory from the 15th century, unusual to see in Spain today. On the west side of the plaza stands the large **Palacio de los Condes de Miranda** with a noble facade (open 10 a.m.–1:30 p.m. and 4–7 p.m., until 6 p.m. in winter; closed Sun.). This is one of the great Renaissance palaces of Spain, and it combines architectural styles from Gothic to Mudejar to Plateresque. Inside is a lovely patio with surrounding gallery, a grand staircase and rooms with intricate wood ceilings.

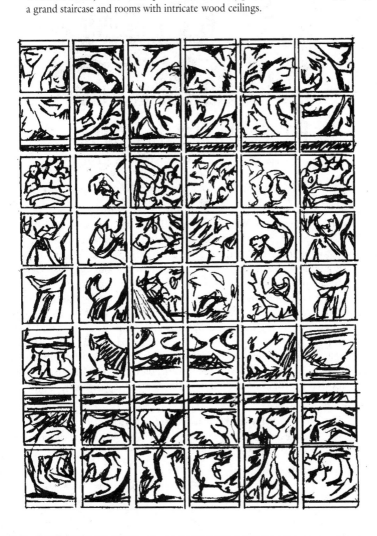

HOTEL REYES CATÓLICOS

Plaza del Obradoiro, 1, Santiago de Compostela, 15705
☎ *(981) 58 22 00, FAX (981) 56 30 94*
$140 per double; 133 rooms: 12 singles, 120 doubles, 1 suite

★ ★ ★ ★ ★

If you stay at only one parador, it should be this, the most deluxe of them all. As the sixteenth century dawned, Ferdinand and Isabella constructed this hospice for pilgrims to Santiago. It was their most magnificent building project, and now one of the world's great hotels. The building plan is the result of religious symbolism—surround four interior patios (for Mathew, Mark, Luke and John) by buildings—but it is successful by the highest aesthetic standards. Everywhere you walk or look there is some wonderful sight. If you are lucky enough to get a room overlooking the plaza, you'll never want to leave. But if you are among the less fortunate, your room will look onto one of the four lovely patios, which requires no sympathy from anyone. All guest rooms include luxurious marble bathrooms, with heated towel racks for that lux touch. Although it is expensive, it is worth every centavo—simply wandering the halls and patios is a thrilling excursion.

Alternative Accommodations

The parador is the only choice for anyone who can foot its bill; second choices cannot approach a memorable stay there.

Hogar San Francisco

Campillo de San Francisco, 3 (follow C. San Francisco, the street along the east side of Los Reyes Católicos, for one long block north), ☎ *(981) 58 16 00, FAX (981) 57 19 16. 71 rooms.*

The only competition in town for historic atmosphere is Hogar San Francisco, and what could be more appropriate than staying in a convent in Santiago? This hotel is installed in the Convent of San Francisco, although the cells have been modernized into comfortable, if small and spartan, rooms. The public rooms, however, retain some of their rich 18th-century decoration. This is a special hotel, for $65, but not deluxe.

Windsor

República de El Salvador, 16-A, (directly behind the Hotel Araguaney, a block further south), ☎ *(981) 59 29 39. 50 rooms.*

The Windsor is even cheaper at $60 per room. It is not historic, but it is an inviting little hotel. True, it is located on a busy shopping street and caters to tour groups, but the service is considerate, and prices are low compared to others in this category.

Dining

It is amusing to imagine how the dining room was a stable as it was when the Reyes Católicos was a pilgrim hospice, for it is grand now in its restaurant incarnation. Furnishings are posh, tapestries and paintings are the genuine article and the food presentation is an artwork that stands up to the standards of the room. The truth is that the food does not have to be spectacular when presented in such a room. Shall we then call the high standards of the cooking a bonus? Intelligently, the chef strives for fine ingredients, then cooks them simply. Steak with fries can be delicious. But the sea provides the stars. Order any broiled fish or invertebrate. To accompany, treat yourself to a fine Albariño. Dinner will cost a most fair $25.

Alternative Dining

Toñi Vicente ★★★

Av. Rosalia de Castro, 24 (this artery is a kind of continuation of C. Franco),. ☎ *(981) 59 41 00, FAX (981) 59 35 54. Closed Sun., the first three weeks of Jan.*

This comet just landed on the restaurant scene in Santiago. It is as elegant as anyone could wish and the food is truly spectacular. Baked sea brill is sublime and the desserts are memorable. Seafood is the specialty, so prices of $35 must be considered bargains for such sublime food. Credit Cards: A, D, M, V.

Anexo Vilas ★★

Av. Villagarcia, 21 (C. Marinez Anido runs along the south side of the Herradura park in the new town. It changes its name to C. Rosalia de Castro before coming to a large intersection. The right-hand road, Av. Romero Donallo, arrives at this restaurant at its first left), ☎ *(981) 59 86 37. Closed Mon.*

The second best food in town is served at this Santiago institution. Sr. Vilas, the owner, tirelessly promotes the cooking of Galicia. After you try the sardines *Mama Sueiro* (sardines with peppers and garlic), you may well become a promoter too. Prices run to about $30. Credit Cards: A, D, V.

NORTHERN SPAIN

Fielding   **ESTELLA TO SANTIAGO DE COMPOSTELA**

ROUTE OF THE PILGRIMAGE OF SANTIAGO DE COMPOSTELA

HISTORY OF THE PILGRIMAGE-Founded on the belief that the final resting place of St. James is the altar in the Cathedral of Santiago de Compostela, the city became a destination for pilgrims from all over the world. The pilgrimage took on its most important historical and political significance during the reconquest of Spain from the Islamic moors during which good Christians were encouraged to take up the pilgrimage and follow the example of their pious king. The defense of the Christian homeland of Spain and the final resting place of St. James became a rallying point of the reconquest. Although Santiago de Compostela can be reached in many different ways, the most famous route (and the one shown here) is called the

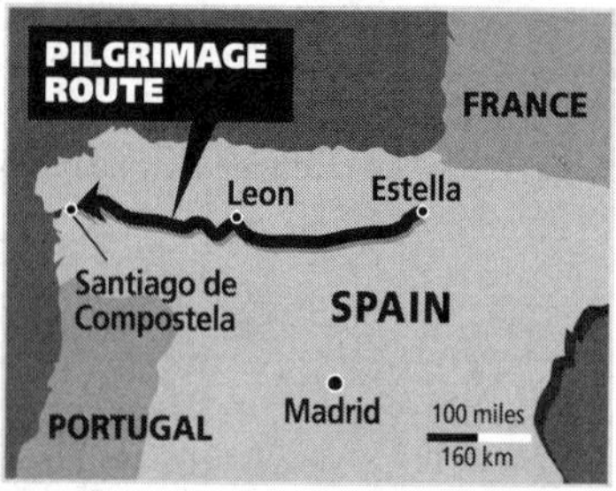

PILGRIMAGE ROUTE

FRANCE

Leon   Estella

Santiago de Compostela   SPAIN

PORTUGAL   Madrid   100 miles
                              160 km

French route. For centuries, towns along the route have catered to the needs of pilgrims as hospitals, chapels and lodgings sprang up. Today few of the hospitals remain but it is impossible to look over your shoulder and not see a church.

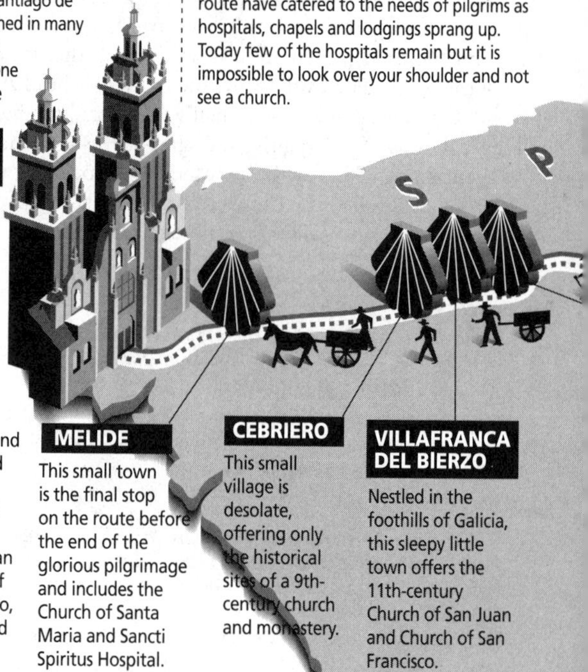

SANTIAGO DE COMPOSTELA

Considered the third city of Christendom after Jerusalem and Rome, Santiago de Compostela lives up to this reputation with an impressive array of churches and religious shrines including the 12th-century Romanesque and Baroque Cathedral and University, Church of Santa Maria la Real del Sar, Church of San Dominico, Church of San Francisco, Monestary of San Lorenzo of Trasouto, Archbishop's Palace and Royal Hospital Chapel.

MELIDE

This small town is the final stop on the route before the end of the glorious pilgrimage and includes the Church of Santa Maria and Sancti Spiritus Hospital.

CEBRIERO

This small village is desolate, offering only the historical sites of a 9th-century church and monastery.

VILLAFRANCA DEL BIERZO

Nestled in the foothills of Galicia, this sleepy little town offers the 11th-century Church of San Juan and Church of San Francisco.

Bustling with life, this university town reflects what days must have been like during the peak of the pilgrimage. Sites include 11th century city walls, a 13th-century Gothic Cathedral, Royal Basilica of San Isidoro, 15th-century Renaissance Convent of San Marcos and 12th-century Santa Maria del Mercado Church.

Like many of the towns along the route, Fromista has lost much of its population and offers only fading memories of the days when it was a busy crossroads along the route. Sites include Jacobean Romanesque Church of San Martin, Church of Santa Maria of the Castle, Church of San Pedro and Hermitage of Santiago.

A small quiet town that sprang up as a way station on the pilgrimage route, this town offer the 14th-century city walls and Gothic Cathedral of the Savior.

The first town in the Spanish portion of the French route of Santiago de Compostela includes the l3th-century Romanesque Church of San Miguel and the l2th-century Romanesque Monastery of San Juan de la Pena.

SANTO DOMINGO DE LA CALZADA

ESTELLA

FROMISTA

LEON

LOGRONO

One of the larger cities on the route, Logrono is also more modern than many of the other towns. Sitting on the crossroads between the Basque country, Navarre and Old Castille, it offers the historical sights of the Church of San Bartolome, Church of Santa Maria del Palacio, and the 1 5th-century Gothic and Baroque Cathedral of Santa Maria la Redonda.

BURGOS

Historically the capital of Old Castille, Burgos still maintains a solemn dignity reflected in the monuments found there including the Gothic cathedral, 15th-century Churches of St. Nicolas, St. Agueda, St. Lesmes, St. Gil, St. Stephen, and El Alcazar fortress.

SAHAGUN

While Moorish influence is strong in this town, the majority of sights are Christian in nature including the Romanesque Church of San Tirso and Church of San Lorenzo, 1 3th-century Church of San Juan and Church of Los Peregrinos and ruins of the 1 2th-century Benedictine monastery.

PONFERRADA

Industrial as well as historical, Ponferrada exhibits an interesting balance between the old and the new with 15th-century Queen's Hospital and 1Oth-century Mozarabic San Tomas de las Ollas Church.

Nova Gallihea ★

> *C. Franco, 56,* ☎ *(981) 58 27 99.*

This is a restaurant for locals, with no concessions to tourists. The decor is nothing much, the restaurant tiny, but the food is authentic home cooking if your home is in Galicia. Ordering one of the special menus will keep costs under $30.

San Clemente ★

> *Pl. San Clemente, 6 (this little plaza is downstairs at the south end of the ayuntamiento from the Pl. Obradoiro),* ☎ *(981) 58 08 82. Closed Sun. eve.*

Seafood is what makes this restaurant special and seafood is not inexpensive, but the crowds here demonstrate that the quality is good and the prices are fair at $30.

Credit Cards: A, D, M, V.

Directions

From **Lugo**, the **airport** and **east** the city is entered on C. Concheiros which is soon renamed San Pedro. At Puerto de Camino turn left onto C. Virgen de la Cerca. As it bends right the street receives the name C. Fuente de San Antonio and reaches the Pl. de Gelmirez Galicia on the right in three blocks. Continue straight, though the street changes its name to C. Mola. In two blocks a park is reached. Go right, then left along its border on C. Pombal. Take the first right which forks off from Pombal. When the street bends right continue for one block more into the Pl. Obradoiro.

Parados Nearby

Cambados: 54 km	Pontevedra: 59 km	Ferrol: 95 km
Túy:108 km	Bayona: 113 km	Villalba: 120 km

Sights

Legend tells of a sea voyage by the Apostle Saint James whose boat was driven by storms to the mouth of the Ulla river. He anchored in the present city of Padrón and began preaching to the heathen locals. Seven years later he returned to Jerusalem where he was killed by Herod. According to the legend, however, disciples brought James' body back to Spain and buried it near the place where his ship had originally landed. The troubled times of invasions by Visigoths and Moors caused the location of the body to be forgotten, until 813 when a shining light drew shepherds to the spot. A cult grew around the venerated remains. Thirty years later, during an engagement between a band of Christians and Moors, a knight mysteriously appeared whose standard bore a red cross on a white field. He routed the infidels, then disappeared as mysteriously as he had come, but several knights claimed to recognize him as Saint James—Santiago. This event fixed the epithet *Matamoro*, "Slayer of Moors," to Saint James, and made him the patron saint of the Reconquest.

By the 11th century, pilgrims by the hundreds of thousands (two million, in the record year) from all corners of Europe walked as far as 1000 miles to visit those sacred remains. They came to atone for some sin or to receive help with a personal problem, and wore a kind of uniform. Enclosed by long hooded cloaks, they carried a stave taller than a man, tied a gourd for water to the stave and sported a broad hat with three scallop shells attached. Such shells were the symbols of the saint, so the pilgrims were referred to as those who "took the cockleshell." The route was hard and unfamiliar, monasteries and hospices sprang up along the route to offer simple accommodations for weary pilgrims. Among the famous pilgrims were Charlemagne, el Cid and Saint Francis of Assisi.

In the 16th century because of Spanish wars against France, Holland and England, the number of pilgrims declined drastically. In 1589 Francis Drake raided La Coruña, 50 miles from Santiago, frightening the Bishop of Santiago so much that he hid the sacred relics for safety. Incredibly, afterward no one could remember where. It was not until 1879 that they turned up again, were duly certified as authentic by the pope, and the pilgrimages began again. In any year when the Feast of Saint James (July 25) falls on a Sunday, special indulgences are granted to pilgrims. At that time, they arrive in numbers that pass one million.

The entire area around the Cathedral of Santiago is a national monument. A newer town surrounds it, heavily populated by university students. On weekends, as a kind of initiation rite, male students in ancient capes roam the plazas serenading women. If a woman is pleased, she contributes a bright ribbon the student pins to his cape; if displeased, she douses him with water. All the sights lie in a radius of a few blocks of the Cathedral.

Parking is an unsolved problem in Santiago, compounded by one-way streets, unmarked dead-ends and a lack of direction signs.

From **Lugo**, the **airport** and **east** the city is entered on C. Concheiros which is soon renamed San Pedro. At Puerto de Camino turn left onto C. Virgen de la Cerca. As it bends right the street receives the name C. Fuente de San Antonio and reaches parking in the Pl. de Gelmirez Galicia on the right in three blocks. The lot is four blocks due south of the Cathedral. For additional parking closer to the Cathedral, continue straight, though the street changes its name to C. Mola. In two blocks a park is reached. Go right, then left along its border, C. Pombal. Take the first right which forks off from Pombal. When the street bends right, parking lies both left and right in one block.

From **Portugal** and **south** N-550 continues straight on Av. Rosalia de Castro until reaching the end of a park. Turn left and left again to follow the park, now on C. Pombal. Take the first street that forks right from Pombal. When this street bends right, parking lies to both on the left and the right in one block.

Cathedral of Santiago ★★★★★

Pl. de Obradoiro, ☎ *(981) 58 35 48.*
Hours open: Mon.–Sat. 10 a.m.–1 p.m. and 4–7 p.m. Open Sun. 10 a.m.–1:30 p.m.
A church was erected to protect the remains of Saint James immediately after their discovery in 813. It was enlarged a hundred years later, only to be destroyed during a raid by the Moors in 997. The present edifice was begun in the 11th century and finished by the 13th, although a new front was added in the 18th century. Plazas surround the front, back and most of both sides to show off this cathedral better than any other in Spain.

No plaza in Spain can match the spacious **Pl. de Obradoiro** (Work of Gold) ★★★★ in front of the cathedral. Opposite the cathedral stands the ornate former **Palacio de Rajoy** from 1772, now the ayuntamiento. To the west is the imposing façade of the **Hospital Real** ★★, a pilgrim hostelry from 1511, now Spain's grandest parador. Its Plateresque façade was added in 1687. To the East is the **Colegio de San Jerónimo**, in the Romanesque style but from the 17th century. And to the north is the cathedral, rising two flights above the Plaza to dominate everything else. In between, a vast field space keeps these magnificent buildings at a slight distance, both in space and time.

The so-called Obradoiro façade of the cathedral is perhaps the most successful example of the churrigueresque style. Though replete with twistings, intricate knobs, spikes and vines, as the style dictates, the strong thrust of the two towers' rising, creates an effect like flames shooting up to the sky. The façade was added to the original front of the cathedral by Ferdinand Casas y Novoa in 1750. Fortunately, the original front was not torn down to make way for the new. It remains inside, protected from the elements as any great work of art should be.

A 12th-century Romanesque cathedral resides beyond the facade. Inside the entrance is the original front of the Cathedral, one of the masterpieces of Western art. It is known as the **Door of Glory** and consists of a series of statues and scenes by a sculptor named Mateo who died in 1217. The central shaft which presents the figure of Santiago above the Tree of Life, shows Mateo himself kneeling at the base. Centuries of pilgrims, thankful to have completed their pilgrimage, wore away the impress of five fingers in this central pillar. Above the main door is *Christ in His Glory*, surrounded by an orchestra of church elders. The arches are supported by Apostles, and the columns rest on monsters. (Traces of painting, visible here and there, are newer—16th century.) The left door presents the tribes of Israel, and the right, the Last Judgement.

The interior is surprisingly plain and dark to those used to Gothic and later cathedrals. The Romanesque order lacks the gallery of windows known as the clerestory which let light into later churches. Nor does it employ pointed arches and rising ribs in the vaulting to carry the eye upwards, or carved columns or balustrades to add variety. It takes but a moment, however, for the utter simplicity and huge scale of this Cathedral (300 feet long, 100 feet high at the dome) to work its magic.

A portal to the right leads to the Plateresque **Reliquary Chapel**, with effigies of the earliest kings and queens of Spain. To its right is the **Treasury**. Amid countless crucifixes, the bejeweled bust of Santiago Alfeo stands out. But the reason for the church lies ahead at the end of the nave. The high **altar** is lit by a dome added in the 15th century from which a huge silver censer, called the **botafumeiro**, is swung on special days through the energies of eight men. The 18th-century altar contains a 13th century seated statue of Saint James, elaborately attired. Ascending stairs on the right side allow the faithful to kiss the hem of his gown. Descending stairs on the right side lead to a plain **crypt** in which rests the body of Saint James and two of his disciples. This crypt actually is part of the foundation of the original ninth century basilica. Excavations have shown that beneath it lies an ancient Roman and Swabian necropolis, which suggests that the name Compostela, instead of being a corruption of *campus stella* (field of stars), comes directly from the Roman *compostela* (cemetery).

In the right hand transept is the entrance to the cloister. But first study the tenth-century depiction of Santiago Matamoro to its right above a door leading to the sacristy. This is the earliest portrayal of Santiago as the Slayer of Moors. The plain **cloister** is late Gothic by Gil de Hotañton. Across it waits the entrance to the Cathedral **museum**. Its library displays the huge Botafumeiro, a censer swung by ten men on holidays, while the chapterhouse shows 17th-century and earlier Spanish tapestries, and allows fine views of the plaza and its buildings. There too is the papal letter certifying that the remains in the crypt indeed are those of Saint James. In the basement are various archaeological bits, some excavated from earlier churches on the site. *Admission:300 ptas., to the museum and cloisters.*

Exit from the south transept through the **Puerta de las Platerias** (Goldsmith's Door) ★. This too is an early 11th-century Romanesque work, without the elegance of the Door of Glory but with exuberance to take its place. Unfortunately some of the carving is obscured by additions on either side of the portal. Ahead and slightly left is the **Casa de la Canonica** (Canon's House), now a monastery. Rounding the rear of the Cathedral we come to the **Puerta Santa**, a door added in the 17th century which incorporates far older sculpture by Mateo originally intended for the Cathedral choir. We now are in another lovely square, the **Pl. de la Quintana**. Stairs lead up to a baroque 17th-century mansion on the right, the **Casa de la Parra**, now a gallery rotating exhibits of modern art.

Ahead, across the Pl. de la Inmaculada, stands the **Convento de San Marin Pinario** ★. The facade facing the plaza, completed in the 18th century, sends massive classical columns to the roof. Further north, its church is more ornate. A decaying interior remains dramatic with a wide nave covered by a daring coffered vault. The churrigueresque retable is by the architect of the Cathedral facade, Casas y Novoa. The choirstalls are lovely 17th-century work.

Continuing the circuit of the Cathedral, pass along the alley of the Passaje Gelmirez, which goes under an archway to return to the Pl. Obradoiro. To the left of the arch is the **Palacio Gelmírez** ★, the former Bishop's Palace. Parts are as old as the 12th century. Several rooms may be visited, including the kitchen, Salon de Fiestas, and the huge Salon de Synod. A visit is most worthwhile. (Open daily through the summer Mon.–Sat. 10 a.m.–1 p.m. and 4–7 p.m.; admission: 100 ptas.)

In the plaza, the huge building forming the north side is the **Hotel de los Reyes Católicos** ★ ★, a former hospice for pilgrims built by Ferdinand and Isabella in gratitude for their victory over the Moors. The design of the building is a cross within a square which affords four lovely patios, each different from the other. A nice chapel sits decorously in the center. The Plateresque facade with stunning doorway and harmonious window moldings was added in 1678. Today it is the most luxurious of all the paradors. (Free tours available daily 10 a.m.–1 p.m. and 4–6 p.m.)

Calle Franco ★ heads south between the cloisters of the Cathedral and the San Jerónimo College across the plaza. Old buildings and new shops and restaurants run for six blocks down to the pleasant Pl. del Toral, with its fountain. A return to the Pl. Obradoiro can be made along **Rua del Villar**, which runs parallel to C. Franco, also with old houses and interesting shops.

Santa María del Sar   ★

R. do Castrón d'Ouro. The church is located about one and one-half km southeast of the old town. South of the circular road, Av. Fuente de San Antonio, C. Castrón d'Ouro becomes C. de Sar. As it passes beneath the bypass road, the church lies to the right. Hours open: Mon.–Sat. 10 a.m.–1 p.m. and 4–6 p.m. Closed Sun.

This is a church of the same 12th-century era as the Cathedral. Incongruous buttresses were added in the 12th century, for reasons that become evident as soon as you step inside. Before doing so, however, look at the remaining cloister gallery with elegant carved small paired arches. There reside the tombs of priors through the 15th century.

The inside startles, because the pillars of the nave all lean inward. The reason is that this ground near a river could not support the burden the pillars carried, hence the need for outside buttresses. The effect is strange indeed. *Admission: 100 ptas.*

Trains and Buses

The train station is at R. Gen. Franco, just south of the main circular road, Av. de Lugo, a 15 minute walk south of the Cathedral. (☎ *(981) 52 02 02)*. Two trains per day travel to Madrid in eight hours, others cover most destinations in the area.

Airport

Santiago Airport (☎ *(981) 59 74 00)* is 11 km east of town on N-547, the road to Lugo. There are direct flights to European capitals, and good connections with all of Spain. Buses to Santiago meet the flights. The Iberia office is located on C. General Pardiñas at 36, which is west of C. Horno, the main street of the new town. Buses leave here for the airport. ☎ *(981) 57 20 24.*

PARADOR CASA DEL BARÓN

Calle Maceda, s/n, Pontevedra, 36002
☎ *(986) 85 58 00, FAX (986) 85 21 95*
$90 per double; 47 rooms: 3 singles, 42 doubles, 2 suites

★ ★ ★

This parador is housed in the ancestral home of the Counts of Maceda, a solid granite mansion erected in the 16th century then redone in the 18th. Outside it is square, yet houselike; inside it is all manorial. Witness the massive granite stair off the lobby and the former fireplace large enough to contain four chairs comfortably. Curiously, the parador lounge served as the kitchen of the original structure, hence the huge fireplace. Everything is quite grand, down to old paintings and antiques on walls and on every surface. Bedrooms continue the grandeur and make one agree that it is good to be a count, if only for a night or two.

Dining

The elegant restaurant is hung with tapestries, mirrors, chandeliers and paintings. It looks out through French doors onto a lovely garden with a fountain. Specialties are from the sea, naturally, but emphasize the local production of crustaceans. Octopus is served either fresh or dried, lamprey is featured for you to try, but best are the scallops, spider crabs, clams and mussels, done several ways including with mayonnaise sauce, and, of course, lobster. *Caldo gallego* soup is special. The wine treat is the locally grown Albariños, a fruity dry white of international reputation. All this will cost a very fair $20, unless you spring for the lobster.

Alternative Dining

Doña Antonia   ★★★★

> *Soportales de la Herreria, 9 (the second floor),* ☎ *(986) 84 72 74.*
> *Closed Sun.*
> This restaurant is a gourmet's dream. Oh, that lamb coated in honey cooked over a wood fire! All the food is superb and served with elegance for an eminently fair $30.
> Credit Cards: V, D, M, A.

Casa Solla   ★★★

> *Carretera de La Toya (2 km west of town),* ☎ *(986) 85 60 29.*
> *Closed Sun. eve, Thurs. eve, and Christmas week.*
> Pity the person who must choose between this restaurant and Doña Antonia. This one is more sylvan, with a lovely garden, but the food is no less spectacular. Want proof? Try the creamed oysters. Nor will you suffer if you order the lamb here. Figure about $35 for a full meal. Credit Cards: A, V, M.

Directions

From wherever you enter town, follow signs for the "Zona Monumental." The parador is smack in the center, at the intersection of C. Baron and C. Princesa, by the Pl. del Teucro.

Paradors Nearby

Cambados: 23 km   Bayona: 50 km
Túy: 50 km   Santiago: 55 km

Sights

Pontevedra is a sleepy town of some size that can serve as a base for exploring the rias. It preserves an old section in a small area opposite the Burgo Bridge. Here is **Santa María la Mayor**, a late 15th-century Plateresque church for fishermen. (Note the reliefs at the rear of the west end.) The **Museo Provincial**, five blocks southeast on the Pl. de Lena consists of two elegant former mansions tied together by an arch. The pre-Roman—especially the Celtic—material is most worthwhile. This museum tries hard to interest by reconstructing parts of famous ships, and modeling antique kitchens *(open daily 11 a.m. to 1:30 p.m. and 5–8 p.m.; admission: 200 ptas.).* Near the northeast edge of the Jardines Vincenti are romantic ruins of the 14th-century convent of **Santo Domingo**.

While there is no beach in Pontevedra, there are plenty close by. Take N-550 southwest to circle the Ria Pontevedra, a 45 km circuit, and you will see. After Marin comes miles of beaches stretching to the cape, near which **Hio** presents a fine Romanesque church.

Parador Conde de Gondamar

Carretera de Bayona, km 1.6 (Monterreal), Bayona, 36300
☎ (986) 35 50 00, FAX (986) 35 50 76
$115 per double; 124 rooms: 12 single, 110 doubles, 2 singles

★ ★ ★ ★

Here is a place for getting away from it all. The parador occupies the knoll of a tiny peninsula, Monte Real, overlooking wild coastline and an ocean that extends forever. 16th century fortress walls seal off the peninsula, the parador and its guests. The reception area, once the governor's residence, is solidly grand and leads to modern buildings for the guests. Rooms with beamed ceilings and wood floors are ample. Be sure to request one with a seaview. You have arrived at a resort hotel with three dining rooms and all amenities, so you never have to leave. There is a pool, a beach, a sauna and tennis courts. Stroll through lovely pines, walk the fortress walls, then relax at the pool or beach. But should you miss the bustle of modern life, one mile away waits the active beach town of Bayona, with a charming old quarter and beach throngs.

Dining

An elegant dining room adjoins the lobby, though a more informal tavern, "La Pinta" sits on the peninsula's edge. Of course, seafood is the thing to order, fresh and nicely done, especially the shellfish. Galicia's spider crabs *(cen-*

NORTHERN SPAIN

tollas) are famed, as are smaller fiddler crabs (nécoras). *Cangrejo real* are delicious large crayfish, clams *(almejas)* and mussels *(mejillones)* are delectable, scallops *(vieiras)* are delicate, and fish soup will blend all the flavors of the sea in one dish. Not in the mood? Try an empanada, filled pastry. The perfect wine to accompany the delicate flavor of fish is the local pride Albariño. This is a mild, slightly sparkling white wine. Otherwise the wine list includes nice bottles from Rioja and Duero. Shellfish are not cheap anywhere; expect a bill of almost $30, plus drinks, unless you order meat.

Alternative Dining

El Moscón   ★

C. Alferez Barreiro, 2 (in Bayona), ☎ *(986) 35 50 08.*

The ambiance cannot compare with the parador but the fish is fresh as can be, perfectly done, and there are more interesting local dishes than at the parador. Try *Bogavante con Arroz*, or a cascade of *pescados y mariscos de la ria*. You will not be disappointed, for this is one of the finest restaurants in the area. In addition, meals will cost a few dollars less than at the parador. Credit Cards: A, D, M, V

Directions

From **Madrid** take A-6 (or N-VI to avoids the tolls) to N-VI at Villacastin in 84 km, which reaches Benavente in 170 km. C-620 reaches Orense in 258 km, where N-120 arrives at Vigo in 102 km and C-550 gets to the parador in 23 km more, 1.5 km southwest of Bayona. From **Santiago de Compostela** take N-550 south to Vigo in 102 km, then C-550 to the parador in 23 km. From Portugal's **Porto** take N-13 north for 124 km to the border at Valença do Minho where Spain's N-550 arrives at Porriño in 14 km and a west turn through Pamallosa arrives at the parador in 27 km.

Paradors Nearby

Túy: 22 km	Pontevedra: 50 km	Cambados: 78 km
Santiago: 125 km	Verín: 170 km	

Excursions

For **Santiago de Compostela**, with its awesome cathedral and square, take C-550 back to Vigo in 23 km, then join N-550 north to Santiago in 102 km.

PARADOR CONDES DE ALBA Y ALISTE

P.aza de Viriato, 5, Zamora, 49001
☎ *(980) 51 44 97, FAX (980) 53 00 63*
$115 per double; 27 rooms: 25 doubles, 2 suites

★ ★ ★ ★

T his hotel is a genuine treat. The facade is plain, elegant 15th century, the interior was remodeled after a fire in the 16th. Inside has as much Renaissance feeling as any hotel can offer. Most dramatic is the central courtyard, now with windowed arches to allow all-weather comfort. Doorways often have carved surrounds, tapestries and banners hang on the walls, and, instead of a suit of armor at the stair landing, there is an entire horse and rider in armor. One special feature is that this largish building allows fewer than thirty visitors, so you can roam the halls by yourself and feel you own the place. There is a pool in the back, which the locals can use as well as the guests. Guest rooms are simply furnished, but more than ample. However, if you can find a few extra pesetas, book one of the lovely suites with large canopied bed and sitting area.

Dining

The dining room suits the elegance of the rest of the parador, graced with a beam ceiling, paintings and a view of the garden. Here you can sample the specialties of Castile—roasts and chops of veal, lamb and pork, or some spe-

cial attractions from nearby Galicia—octopus and broiled cod. Sample one of the local wines of Toro, nearby. Dinner will cost less than $25.

Alternative Dining

Valderrrey   ★

Benavente, 9 (behind Santiago del Burgo church) ☎ *(980) 53 02 40.*
Here is the best food value in town served in an attractive room. Hearty roasts and stews are the thing and cost no more than the parador. Credit Cards: A, D, M, V.

Directions

The parador is located almost exactly in the center of the old city, along the central Rua de los Francos.

Paradors Nearby

Benavente: 65 km	Salamanca: 65 km	Tordesillas: 65 km
Puebla de Sanabria: 120 km	León: 136 km	C. Rodrigo: 235 km

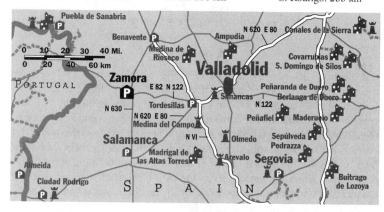

Sights

Turn left immediately upon crossing the Duero River on Av. del Mengue. Parking is available after the road curves north by the ruins of a castle surrounded by imposing ramparts.

The **castle** ★ last belonged to Urraca, daughter of Fernando I. It seems she lured one brother, who had succeeded his father to the throne, here to kill him so that another, whom she favored, could rule instead.

The gem of Zamora lies across the park—the **Cathedral** ★★★. Do not be misled by the neoclassic north front; this is a 12th-century Romanesque beauty. Travel to the south end to see its original appearance. Inside the nave rises on characteristic massive piers, but uncharacteristic light streams onto the altar from a lantern at the transept crossing, an idea borrowed from the Old Cathedral in Salamanca. Also interesting are the choir stalls, from the 15th century. Though expected Biblical scenes cover the backs, the arms and misericords contain burlesques of cloistered life and fantastic animals. Stairs from the neoclassic cloister lead up to a museum with fine tapestries.

If you like the Cathedral, there is more of the same. Head northwest along C. Notarios leading away from the rear of the Cathedral. In three blocks you come to **Santa Magdalena** ★ church on the left, noted particularly for its *south portal* with elaborately decorated recessed arches.

Returning to the street by which we came, continue on it until it becomes C. Ramos. One block later brings a park with a lovely Renaissance palace on its right side. Today it is the city's parador, but it was a **palace for the Dukes of Alba** ★ in the 15th century. A lovely courtyard is decorated with medallions and coats of arms. One short block farther lies the **Plaza Mayor**. One block northeast is the **Casa de los Momos** with attractive windows, and the next right brings you to **Santiago del Burgos** ★, another lovely Romanesque church. Two more—**Santa Maria de la Horta** and **Santo Tomé**, lie due south.

Nearby **Toro** (33 km west on N-122) is also full of Romanesque churches, most built of brick. One in particular is noteworthy, the limestone **Iglesia del Colegiata** ★★, which boasts a glorious and almost perfectly preserved *Gothic west portal*, repainted in the 18th century to suggest its original appearance. (Open daily 10:30 a.m. to 1:30 p.m. and 5–7 p.m., until 8 p.m. in summer.) The figures of the Celestial Court and those in the Last Judgment scene are expressive as only the stiff Romanesque can be. Inside is another wondrous lantern, plus nice polychrome statuary at the nave end. The sacristy contains a painting of *The Virgin of the Fly*. Note the realistic fly on the Virgin's robe.

PARADOR DE CERVERA DE PISUERGA

Carretera de Reseba, km 2.5, Cervera de Pisuerga, 34840
☎ *(979) 87 00 75, FAX (979) 87 01 05*
$90 per double; 80 rooms: 80 doubles

★ ★ ★

This is an elegant but masculine mountain lodge high in the Picos de Europa range, above a glacier lake. If you enjoy mountain views, it will be hard to move you off your terrace which looks over the lake to peak after peak marching into the distance. The modern parador looks a bit like a midwestern granary outside, but inside it is all warm woods—floors, ceilings and panelled walls—lit by chandeliers. It seems rather too grand for a hunting lodge, but few complain if a hotel is *too* grand. Guest rooms are spacious, topped by beamed ceiling, but this time with tile floors. What to do besides look at nature? Bikes and horses are available, as well as kayaks. There are also one's own feet.

Dining

Cozily paneled, as is the ceiling, with warm wood floors, the dining room presents paintings of food to whet the appetite, as if mountain air needed assistance. What goes well? Marinated quail, roast baby lamb, local ham or partridge suits the site. For dessert try a cheese pudding. The local wine is Ribera del Cea, and disappointing, but there are the usual standards available as well. A complete dinner should cost about $20.

Directions

2 km west of Cervera de Pisuerga.

Paradors Nearby

Fuente Dé: 80 km   Santillana: 112 km   León: 133 km
Santo Domingo: 179 km   Tordesillas: 189 km   Benavente: 203 km

PARADOR DE FERROL

Almirante Fernándz Martín, s/n, Ferrol, 15401
☎ *(981) 35 67 20, FAX (981) 35 67 20*
$90 per double; 39 rooms: 11 singles, 27 doubles, 1 suite

★ ★ ★

Ferrol is the town where Generalissimo Franco was born. To no one's surprise, he commanded that a parador be built here. That is the reason for it, the only reason for it. Not that anything is wrong with the town. It preserves a medieval core and a 16th century quarter as well, but essentially it lives as a naval harbor. The question is why visit a naval harbor, since there are a hundred towns in Spain that preserve equally old, equally attractive sections? Well, if interested in ships, this is a fine place to stay. Nautica is the theme of the 60-year-old building, incorporating yards of paned windows to take in the sight of the shipyards. Inside it seems a men's club, with leather chairs, palms and nautical prints. Not surprisingly, the guest rooms are spartan and cold-feeling.

Dining

Bentwood chairs, not the most comfortable, circle round tables that look out through two walls of windows on the shipyards. Franco, the son of a naval officer would love it, and you are likely to see a captain or two dining here. Fish is featured—what else?—and actually quite nicely prepared. The fish soup is good, as is any fish simply done. Hake casserole, shellfish gratiné and salted pork with turnips are less successful. If fish do not appeal, try a meat empanada. Wash it all down with a fresh Albariños. Dinner should cost about $20.

Directions

The parador is at the tip of the town, one street back from the yards, in front of Rena Sofia Park. Take the Carretera del Puerto.

Paradors Nearby

Villalba: 68 km	Santiago: 95 km	Ribadeo: 142 km
Cambados: 149 km	Pontevedra: 154 km	

PARADOR DE PUEBLA DE SANABRIA

Carretera del Lago, 18, Puebla de Sanabria, 49300
☎ *(980) 62 00 01, FAX (980) 62 03 51*
$70 per double; 44 rooms: 5 singles, 39 doubles

★

This parador combines a stopping place on the way to Portugal or to Santiago de Compostella with a lovely natural setting near a lake and wildlife park. The parador itself is nothing to remember, just a sort of large house, but the views are very pleasant. Inside it rates as about the most boring and tasteless of all the paradors, but it will do for a stop-over. **Note**: closed during December and January.

Dining

Dining is in a glass walled addition that looks like, well, about a thousand mom-and-pop Spanish roadside restaurants. The surprise is that the food is pretty good. A la carte specials are a delicate trout, broiled cod, octopus or pork. But the more interesting option is a buffet for sampling everything. The featured wines are strong Toros. Dinner counts as a good value at about $20.

Directions

From **Madrid** take A-6/N-VI north for 254 km to Benavente where C-620/N-525 reaches Sanabria in 83 km. From **Salamanca** take N-630 north for 125 km to Benavente and follow the Madrid directions from there. From **Santiago** take N-550 south for 91 km to skirt Vigo and join N120 east for 103 km to Orense where N-525 south reaches Sanabria in 72 km.

Paradors Nearby

Benavente: 84 km	Verín: 100 km	Zamora: 111 km
León: 153 km	Tordesillas: 158 km	Salamanca: 173 km

PARADOR DE RIBADEO

Amador Fernández, 7, Ribadeo, 27700
☎ *(982) 11 08 25, FAX (982) 11 03 46*
$90 per double; 47 rooms: 6 singles, 40 doubles, 1 suite

Ribadeo is a more substantial town than its population of under 10,000 would suggest. It offers a quaint fisherman's quarter, a lighthouse, a castle and an attractive beach, with truly spectacular beaches nearby. On a hill two km outside the town is the Hermitage of Santa Cruz and fine views of the coast. Northwest of Ribadeo range miles of fine beach and few tourists. The parador does not impress, however. Outside it's a box, although there's a lot of wood paneling inside to suggest it is more than just another resort hotel of the middling sort. But it all shows signs of wear and the bedrooms are characterless. The best feature is views of the harbor from most guest rooms.

Alternative Accommodations

Eo

Av. de Asturias, 5, ☎ *(982) 10 07 50, FAX 10 00 21. (Open only in summer.) 24 rooms.* Although the paradors has views, it lacks charm. Consider saving 50% by staying at Eo, a restful, well-managed place in town.

Palacete Pañalba

C. El Cotarelo, in Figueras, two km from Casariego, ☎ *(982) 563 61 25, FAX (982) 563 62 47. 10 rooms, plus two suites.*
Better still, travel 12 km east to Figueres and stay at a luxurious *modernista* mansion, the Palacete Pañalba of delicate proportions, made into a hotel that is tasteful, reserved, quiet and costs an unbelievable $65. In fact, it is more a museum than a hotel, having been declared a national artistic monument. One more enticement is its lovely restaurant that serves the best food for miles around.

Dining

The dining room is furnished with chairs that can only be explained by bad taste or graft, so keep your face to the window and attention on the harbor. Stick to the seafood, which is fresh and delicious, if simply done. Ribadeo is near some good lobster beds, so splurge, if the budget allows. The fish soup and scallops in their shells can be quite good, as can the anglerfish *(rape)*. The perfect wine is a good Albariños, such as a Martin Codax. The bill should run about $20.

Alternative Dining

O Xardin ★

C. Reinante, 20, ☎ (982) 10 02 22.
Closed Mon. in winter, and from Christmas through Jan.
Aptly named "The Garden," this is a relaxed, bistro place that serves inventive, well-prepared food for less than the parador. Credit Cards: D, M, V.

Directions

The parador sits above the ria, about one kilometer north of the village center.

Paradors Nearby

Villalba: 74 km	Ferrol: 142 km	Gijón: 170 km
Villafranca: 189 km	Santiago: 194 km	León: 286 km

Sights

From Ribadeo N-634 meets N-642 going north in 19 km toward Foz. In about three km signs direct to **San Martin de Mondoñedo** ★★, a church from the beginning of the 12th century. It is all that remains of a former monastery. The style is the earliest form of Romanesque, with a timber roof, and outer buttresses. The capitals inside are carved in charming scenes and the stone retable is endearing. **Foz** ★, in 20 km, is a busy little port with two fine beaches separated by a headland. More white sand beaches, this time amid scenery, lie 40 km north around the town of Vivero.

PARADOR DE TORDESILLAS

Car. Salamanca, 5, Tordesillas, 47100
☎ *(983) 77 00 51, FAX (983) 77 10 13*
$90 per double; 71 rooms: 6 singles, 65 doubles

★ ★ ★

When you first sight this parador, you'll know everything will be all right. Its front lawn is covered with pine trees to create a secluded feeling, and, even better, is the lovely garden in the rear. Otherwise, this parador does not look special. It was built in 1958 to look like a large country house, but inside it spreads out, though made cozy with tapestries, antiques and paintings. Bedrooms incorporate nice parquet floors accented with area rugs; the furniture is solidly comfortable. Everything is well maintained for a pleasant rest on your journey. A large pool waits in the back.

Dining

The dining room continues the good taste of the rest of the parador, with a wall of windows looking over a lovely pine forest and another wall filled with a large tapestry depicting the discovery of the Americas. The food is hearty, well thought out and good. Start with a selection of sausages *(embutidos ibéricos)* for hors d'oeuvres. The special garlic soup adds eggs and ham to the basic version. Then choose between stuffed quails *(codornices rellenas)*, suckling pig *(cochinillo)* and roast baby lamb *(lechazo asado)*. For the wine, choose among a variety of Ribera de Dueros. The bill should come in at about $25.

Directions

The parador is one km west of Tordesillas on N-620.

Paradors Nearby

Zamora: 66 km	Benavente: 82 km	Salamanca: 85 km
Ávila: 110 km	Segovia: 116 km	León: 152 km

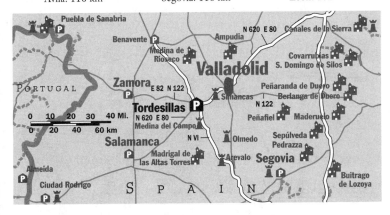

Sights

Tordesillas began as a town surrounding a palace built by the father of Pedro the Cruel in the 14th century. Pedro changed his father's palace by adding buildings and creating a convent. Here Pedro installed his mistress, María de Padilla. The idea caught on, for Emperor Carlos V incarcerated his mother, the aptly named Juanna the Mad, here until she died. The oldest parts of **Santa Clara Convent** are simple lovely. The patio is surrounded by graceful arches and tiles. Inside the Gilded Chapel contains relics of Spain's great personages below a magnificent cupola. The church, a remodeling of the throne room of the original palace, still bears a wonderful ceiling above

NORTHERN SPAIN

the choir. *(Open daily except Mon., 10:30 a. m. to 1:30 and 3:30-7 p. m. Sun. only in the morning. Admission: 400 ptas.)*

The **Plaza Mayor** is nicely arcaded; **San Atolín** contains a fine Plateresque tomb and nice retablo.

Excursions

Tordesillas is perfectly centered for trips that allow exploring and a return to the parador in the evening. **Zamora** lies 66 km west on N-122. **Salamanca** lies 84 km southwest on N-620. **Burgos** lies 122 km northeast on N-620. **León** lies a 72 km leg north to Benavente on N-VI, then a 76 km leg further north on N-630. Both **Ávila** and **Segovia** lie 98 km south on N-VI to Villacastin, then a turn west of 28 km to Ávila on N-501, or a turn east of 37 km to Segovia on N-110. All are described in this chapter, except Salamanca, Ávila and Segovia, which are described in the "Central Spain" chapter.

Parador de Villafranca del Bierzo

Avenida Calvo Sotelo, s/n, Villafranca del Bierzo, 24500
☎ *(987) 54 01 75, FAX (987) 54 00 10*
$80 per double; 40 rooms: 10 singles, 29 doubles, 1 suite

★

The good news is its location—in an old, quaint town stuffed with ancient religious buildings surrounded by two rivers, in a valley ringed by mountains. The bad news is the parador. From the outside it looks like a motel, inside it is just plain dowdy and decorated with no taste at all. On a brighter note, the landscaping is attractive. Bedrooms are cells, but at least have balconies, and there is nothing like a mountain view.

Dining

Brick dividers do not make the dining room less institutional; they just look out of place. So, let us get to the food. Most of the specials are tasty but heavy, such as the pork empanada and the stuffed peppers. The onion soup is interesting, however, and simple roast veal has flavor. Bierzo's wines are worth a try. The meal should cost $20.

Directions

From **Madrid** take A-6/N-VI north for 415 km. From **Salamanca** take N-630 north for 125 km to Caserio del Puente where N-VI is joined for the final 162 km. From **Segovia** take N-110 west for 37 km to Villacastin, then N-VI north for 335 km. From **León** take N-120 west for 47 km to Astorga where N-VI northwest travels the final 93 km.

Paradors Nearby

León: 123 km	Villalba: 135 km	Benavente: 145 km
Verín: 148 km	Ribadeo: 189 km	Zamora: 210 km

Sights

At the high part of town stands a 16th century castle and a 12th century Romanesque church. Also elevated is the Plaza Mayor with the **Church of San Francisco** which contains a fine mudjar ceiling. 3 km south of Cacabelos (which is 8 km east on N-VI) stands the splendidly isolated, incredibly old monastery of **Santa María de Carracedo**, founded in the tenth century, with a little palace from the 14th.

Parador de Villalba

Calle Valeriano Valdesuso, s/n, Villalba, 27800
☎ *(982) 51 00 11, FAX (982) 51 00 90*
$105 per double; 6 rooms: 6 doubles

★ ★ ★ ★ ★

For the most unique parador experience, book into this one (although with only six rooms that isn't easy). The parador occupies all that remains of the medieval fortification of the town. It is just one tower, probably the original castle keep, octagonal in shape, crenulated on top, formed of ten feet thick walls broken by slit windows for shooting. Of course you enter over an appropriately small drawbridge.

Inside it is wonderfully medieval, with soaring ceilings, huge arched doorways, granite stairs and huge chandeliers. A massive reception area takes up the second floor (the restaurant is on the first), leaving the remaining three floors for guest rooms, two spacious rooms to a floor. There is an elevator, of course, but the fun is to wind your way up ancient stairs and look down on the floors below. If you are fortunate enough to secure a room here, you'll remember it for years.

Dining

The dining room occupies the old cellar and holds only ten tables, but is not intimate, not with the massive fireplace, the stone and the high wood ceiling swinging massive chandeliers. After *caldo gallego* soup, try either the stuffed scallops in their shells *(vieiras)*, fish stew *(caldeirada de pescados)*, pigs' knuckles with truffles *(lacón)* or veal brochette *(ternera)*. End with a selection of the notable local cheeses. The meal should run about $20.

Directions

The parador sits beside the main church of the town.

Paradors Nearby

Ferrol: 70 km	Ribadeo: 74 km	Santiago: 105 km
Villafranca: 137 km	Cambados: 174 km	Pontevedra: 179 km

Parador del Albariño

Paseo de la Calzada, s/n, Cambados, 36630
☎ *(986) 54 22 50, FAX (986) 54 20 68*
$90 per double, 63 rooms: 12 singles, 51 doubles

★ ★ ★

T he parador's name does homage to the great wine of the region, a refreshing white that marries perfectly with seafood. It is located in an elegant little town sitting on a *ria* (rugged coast). Since there are no beaches in town, the village has avoided vacationing throngs to retain its character. However, a lovely beach not 10 miles away makes Cambados a pleasant place to while away a day or two. The parador is lodged in a noble house almost a century old that fronts a pretty garden dotted with palm trees. It is a Thirties kind of place, filled with gracious spaces. Bedrooms have balconies and floor-to-ceiling windows that look over the garden and lend an open feeling to the rooms.

Dining

The dining room, like the rest of the hotel, feels spacious. It sports a fancy beam ceiling and stone floor. Informally furnished, it is just the place for a seafood meal. But start with the hearty local white bean soup, *caldo gallego*. One of the more unusual entrees is an empanada filled with scallops *(berberechos)*. Local lobster *(cigalas)* is sweet, hake *(merluza)* broiled over wood is delicate, and the simple mixed grill of fish and crustaceans is delectable. Save room for seductive desserts, from puff pastry with whipped cream *(milhojas)* to a flan melba. Of course, sip a fruity Albariño with the meal. Two of the best bodegas are Gran Bazán and Bouzas do Rei. The tab will run to about $20, minus the drinks, unless you order lobster.

Alternative Dining

Loliña ★★★

Pl. del Muelle, Carril (this tiny town lies 20 km north on C-550), *(986) 50 12 81.*
Simple and attractively rustic, this establishment serves superb fish. Try the beans with lobster *(habas con bogavante)* or the special angler fish *(rape Loliña)* and we bet you will agree. A full meal will cost $30 or more, but is worth every peseta. Closed Sun. night, Mon. and Nov. Credit Cards: A, D, M, V.

La Taberna de Rotillo ★★★

Av. del Puerto, Sanxenxo (on the beach in Sanxenxo, 12 km south on C-550), *(986) 72 02 00.*
This is a delightful restaurant, serving some of the most inventive food in Galicia for deservedly expensive prices. What about lobster cake *(pastil de bogavante)*, or fried oysters with crunchy greens *(ostras fritas en verduritas crujentes)*, for a meal that runs $30? Closed Sun. night and Mon, our of season. Credit Cards: A, D, M, V.

Directions

Once in the village, signs direct you.

Paradors Nearby

Pontevedra: 22 km	Santiago: 54 km	Bayona: 70 km
Túy: 74 km	Villalba: 174 km	Verín: 200 km

Sights

Cambados is quite a lovely town with an unforgettable square, two sides of which are formed by the 16th-century palace of Fefiñanes, the third by an attractive 17th century church and the fourth by arcaded houses. The problem is that the town lacks true beaches. This matter is taken care of 15 km south along C-550 at O Grova (El Grove) ★, and the gorgeous pine island of **A Toxa** (La Toja) ★, off its coast. Grand sand beaches are plentiful in this resort area, although the island of A Toxa has recently been subjected to large-scale hotel development, even a casino.

Parador Fernando II de León

Paseo Ramón y Cajal, s/n, Benavente, 49600
☎ *(980) 63 03 00, FAX (980) 63 03 03*
$105 per double; 30 rooms: two singles, 26 doubles, two suites

★ ★ ★ ★

This parador can break the long drive from Madrid to Santiago in a most pleasant way. The original building that houses the public rooms of the parador goes back to the 12th-century King Ferdinand II. While he didn't build it or live in it, he was the first Spanish monarch to summon a parliament, and thus earns a parador named in his honor. When you arrive you will think you have reached the most romantic hotel in the world. You enter the original keep of the castle to look up to an astounding artesonado ceiling soaring three stories above (actually moved here from a church in the neighborhood). Worn stone stairs ascend, huge tapestries surround you—it's love at first sight. Then comes the disappointment. You leave this medieval romance to walk to a modern addition that houses the guest rooms and another modern addition for the restaurant. As it happens, the rest of the castle was destroyed during some war or other. Oh, well! The tower is extraordinary and you can roam about and descend to the bar down stone stairs worn over centuries by those who came before you while imagining a sword at your side and chain mail attire. And the bedrooms are perfectly adequate with nice views of the countryside. Lovely formal gardens abut the new wing.

Dining

The dining room is long and narrow with arches dividing the space. It is a modern interpretation of a medieval dining hall. The cooking is nicely spicy. Main dishes range over cod, trout and veal, with onion soup to begin. The local wine is a Benavente Campos and not bad. A full meal will average $24, plus drinks.

Directions

You arrive at the Pl. de Solidad where a left, if coming from León, or the road straight ahead, if coming from Madrid, will take you to C. de Venezuela. At its end turn left onto C. del Perú which becomes C. de Portugal, then signs will direct you.

Paradors Nearby

Zamora: 65 km	León: 70 km	Tordesillas: 82 km
Puebla de Sanabria: 84 km	Salamanca: 130 km	Villafranca del Bierzo: 147 km

PARADOR GIL BLAS

Plaza Ramón Pelayo, 8, Santillana del Mar, 39330
☎ *(942) 81 80 00, FAX (942) 81 83 91*
$105 per double; 56 rooms: 5 singles, 47 doubles, 4 suites

★ ★ ★

Both the village and the parador are quaint. The 17th century parador is situated among country style Renaissance mansions. Baronially rustic in every way, it oozes atmosphere. Prices barely crest the expensive range, which is one reason the rooms are heavily booked. After a plain stone exterior waits a pleasing cobbled courtyard. Inside, every door and window wears a stone surround, and floors reek of centuries of being walked on, whether antique tile or parquet. Bedrooms are whitewashed and carry beamed ceilings. Note that the hotel has a modern annex across the way that offers none of the character you came for. Demand a room in the manor house, or go elsewhere.

Alternative Accommodations

The parador is the best choice, but other possibilities are similar and almost as good.

Altamira

C. Cantón, 1, ☎ *(942) 81 80 25, FAX (942) 84 01 03. 32 rooms.*
At the Altamira you also get to stay in a baronial mansion, from the 17th century, but at the lower price of $65 that makes up for the fact that this mansion is a little smaller and the service not as grand as at the parador.

Los Infantes

Av. Le Dorat, 1, ☎ *(942) 81 81 00, FAX (942) 81 01 03. 50 rooms.*
Similar is Los Infantes, although a few dollars more and a tad less medieval.

Dining

Good taste designed the dining room. It is nicely proportioned, looks through arched windows onto a pretty garden and supports a timbered ceiling. We could quibble about the chairs, however, and the food is not special. There are meats—ham, sirloin and magritte of duck, but the sea provides better selections. Clams, stuffed salmon, cod and stuffed hake can be quite pleasant. The selection of cheese is good. An Albariños goes smoothly with seafood. The tab should be about $20.

Alternative Dining

El Capricho de Gaudí   ★

Barrio de Sobrellano, (in Camillas 19 km west) ☎ *(942) 72 03 65.*

Closed Mon. (except in summer), and from the 2nd week in Jan. through the 2nd week in Feb.

To be frank, the food is not extraordinary and on the expensive side, but the building is a treat, the service is elegant and the food looks beautiful. The building was designed by Gaudí in 1885 as a summer pavilion in a style composed of Moorish elements carried to their extremes. You can peek in, of course, without dining. If you eat, the bill should run about $30. Credit Cards: A, D, M, V.

El Molino   ★★★

In Puente Arce, 13 km west on N-611, ☎ *(942) 57 50 55.*

Closed Sun. night, and Mon. except in summer.

Though installed in a 17th-century mill in gardens beside a stream, the renovation is utterly elegant. The food is of the first order and expensive ($35 per), but worth every peseta. Oh, that sea bream braised with thyme! Credit Cards: A, D, M, V.

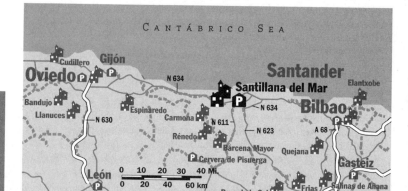

Directions

There are only two streets in the village and both lead to the main square with the parador.

Paradors Nearby

Fuente Dé: 101 km	Argómaniz: 109 km	Cervera: 112 km
Gijón: 163 km	Hondarribia: 273 km	León: 292 km

Sights

Santillana has been called the prettiest village in Spain, which does not quite capture what is special about it. It is small, real (except on weekends when the tourists descend) and oozes a medieval atmosphere. Whatever the description, it is a special place to visit. Exception must be taken to its name however, for it is several kilometers from the sea.

At the northern end of the main street stands the late 12th-century **Collegiate Church of Santa Julliana** (whose corrupted name denominates the village). The façade is elegant Romanesque on the east end, and the interior contains interesting vaulting. In the choir four lovely Romanesque statues hide inside a 17th-century Mexican silver altarfront. The cloisters are quietly moving. Throughout the length of the village stand **mansions** from the 15th-17th centuries. Half a mile to the south is a **zoo** which presents several European bison exactly like those depicted on the ceiling of **Altamira Cave**. That cave lies two km southwest, but can be entered only with official permission that takes months to secure.

Excursions

Camillas ★ has long been a resort attracting visitors of the ilk of King Alfonso XII. The town is attractive with a charming Plaza Mayor and fishing port. It also contains a set of neo-Gothic buildings from the end of the 19th century, including a Moorish style **pavilion by Gaudí** (now a restaurant). To all this it adds miles of beaches to the west, five km outside of town, that atones for Santillana´s lack. **Santander ★★**, 27 km east on N-611, is one of Spain's most elegant resorts, with a palace from the 30s and a casino.

PARADOR MOLINO VIEJO

Parque Isabel la Católica, s/n, Gijón, 33203
☎ *(98) 537 05 11, FAX (98) 537 02 33*
$110 per double; 40 rooms: 1 single, 39 doubles

★ ★ ★ ★

Gijón is an industrial city, so it attracts few tourists, which is a pity because it has good beaches and a charming parador. Both seem wasted on the town. The parador sits quietly in a large pretty park. It consists of an old mill, hence its name, so it strides a little stream and overlooks a swan pond. Surrounded by trees and quiet, there is no nicer place to sleep in this bustling city. Lots of wood inside makes a former mill quite elegant. We especially like the understated decor of the guest rooms. While there is no pool, the beach and ocean wait a ten-minute stroll away. The problem is that Gijón is not situated near other sights of interest.

Dining

Dining is on a long veranda, decorated with cane furniture and attractive linen. Here you can sample the special cuisine of Asturias, although the starter is a soup from neighboring Galicia *(caldos gallegos)*. Beans are a favorite Asturian dish, served here with clams or without. The shellfish stew *(caldereta de pescado de roca y marisco)* is luscious. Cheese is notable in the region, although there is a refreshing rice pudding alternative to end the meal. The drink of choice in Asturias is sparkling cider. The bill should not exceed $20.

Alternative Dining

Casa Victor ★

C. Carmen, 11 (near the train station, by the port), ☎ *(98) 534 83 10.*
Closed Sun. and Nov.
The restaurant looks like many a mesón in the area but serves the best seafood in town. Victor, the owner and something of a culinary legend, is a thoughtful restaurateur who modifies the traditional fare of the region with his nueva touches. Credit Cards: A, D, M, V.

Directions

You enter the huge traffic circle of Pl. Humeda. Go left then bear right along the wide José las Clotas. After it angles left, your intent is to continue straight, but one-ways force a jag right then left to put you on Av. Pablo Iglesias for ten blocks to the bull ring. Turn left to enter Isabel La Católica Park and the parador.

Paradors Nearby

León: 145 km   Santillana: 163 km   Ribadeo: 170 km
Fuente Dé: 186 km   Benavente: 215 km   Cervera: 220 km

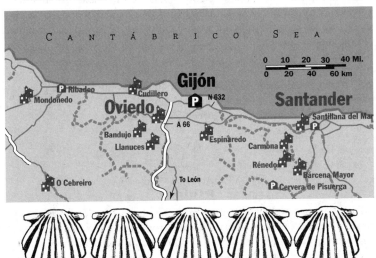

PARADOR MONTERREY

Verín, 32600
☎ *(988) 41 00 75, (988) 41 20 17*
$80 per double; 23 rooms: 1 single, 21 doubles, 1 suite

★ ★

Spain's northwestern tip, near Portugal, is rife with paradors. Here is yet another. What it offers is sylvan views from atop a hill of vineyards beside a marvelous old castle in ruins. Otherwise this parador is not special. It is new, although configured as a large Galacian manor house, all granite and complete with corner tower. The best feature is the views. Inside, it is rather pleasant with nice wood ceilings and floors. Guest rooms, however are boxes. Turned wood furniture adds the only interest, outside of the gorgeous views. We like to look over the old castle in rooms 102, 104, 106 or 107. There is a pool prettily set in the tree bedecked lawn.

Dining

The dining room is intelligently arranged with pillars to lend a sense of intimacy. Pictures on the walls make it stately too. Start with a hearty *caldo gallego* soup (with beans and cabbage). Follow with a juicy veal chop, creamed shellfish or cod in one of several styles. The local Monterrey wine is high in alcohol: a Ribera would be smoother. The bill will be about $20.

Directions

The parador is 5 km west of Verín along N-525; look for a sign.

Paradors Nearby

Puebla de Sanabria: 85 km	Villafranca: 148 km	Pontevedra: 175 km
Túy: 178 km	Benavente: 180 km	Bayona: 199 km

Sights

The castle of Monterrey incorporated a hospital and a village inside its walls until abandonment in the 19th century. So it is rather eerie to wander through this ghost fortress. As you pass through successive walls, you go back in time. The outermost date from the 17th century, enclosing an innermost 14th and 15th century core. The church is 13th century with a finely carved period doorway.

PARADOR RIO DEVA

Carretera de Fuent Dé, s/n, Fuente Dé, 39588
☎ *(942) 73 00 01, FAX (942) 73 02 12*
$70 per double; 78 rooms: 6 singles, 72 doubles

★ ★ ★

The Spanish love their mountains. This parador is an homage to nature's majesty, sitting in a meadow at the foot of awesome peaks, called the Picos de Europa. A nearby cable-car whisks you up to the Mirador del Cable, over a mile high. The hotel looks like a factory outside because it wants no walls without windows to cover the views. Inside it is more a huge hunting lodge with bare wood floors, throw rugs and guns and trophies on the walls. Bedrooms too are bare, although of a nice size. Bikes and four-wheeled vehicles may be hired.

Dining

The dining room is bare with a cold stone floor and furnished with clunky wood chairs. Hearty stews and roasts are called for and supplied. Try the *pucherete montañes* (a stew), the baby lamb, sirloin with cheese, or a salmon. Mountain cheeses make a fine finish. You are not far from Riojas, so the wine choice must be from that region. The bill should not be more than $20.

Directions

From **Gijón** take the Autovia south to Oviedo in 29 km where N-634 runs to Unquera in 126 km. There take N-621 south to Potes in 39 km and a final leg of 25 km west. From **León** take N-601 south to Mansilla de las Mulas in 18 km where N-621 winds north through Cisterna to Potes in 132 km. Head west on N-621 to Fuente Dé in 25 km. From **Santillana** join N-634 west to Unquera in 41 km, then follow the Gijón directions.

Parados Nearby

Cervera: 80 km   Santillana: 101 km
León: 175 km   Benavente: 245 km

PARADOR SAN MARCOS

Plaza de San Marcos, 7, León, 24001
☎ *(987) 23 73 00, FAX (987) 23 34 58*
$130 per double; 229 rooms: 214 doubles, 15 suites

★ ★ ★ ★ ★

Grand, stately and splendid are the only words for this magnificent building. You will not believe that you can actually spend a night inside, but it only takes money. The entrance to the San Marcos is a sumptuous Plateresque façade stretching forever, opening to an entrance hall crowned by a 16th-century grand staircase and lined with antiques and tapestries. The hall is presided over by a chandelier that must be 10 feet tall. There is a unique feeling to walking into such a place and heading for your room, even if it is yours for only a night. Here you actually sleep inside one of the city's sights. (For more on the building see the entry under "Sights" below.) Only 30 of the rooms are situated in the old monastery (some sumptuous with exposed stone and two story ceilings) and are well worth their higher cost, with the rest forming a modern wing added to the back. Even the modern rooms are large and pleasant, with ample marble bathrooms. Need we mention that a swimming pool is provided? The hotel is not faultless—service, although friendly, is not always a model of efficiency—but the entrance could not be more dramatic or the public areas more grand.

Alternative Accommodations

Consider another option only if the budget is tight or the San Marcos is full.

Quindós

Av. José Antonio, 24, ☎ *(987) 23 62 00, FAX (987) 24 22 01. 96 rooms.*

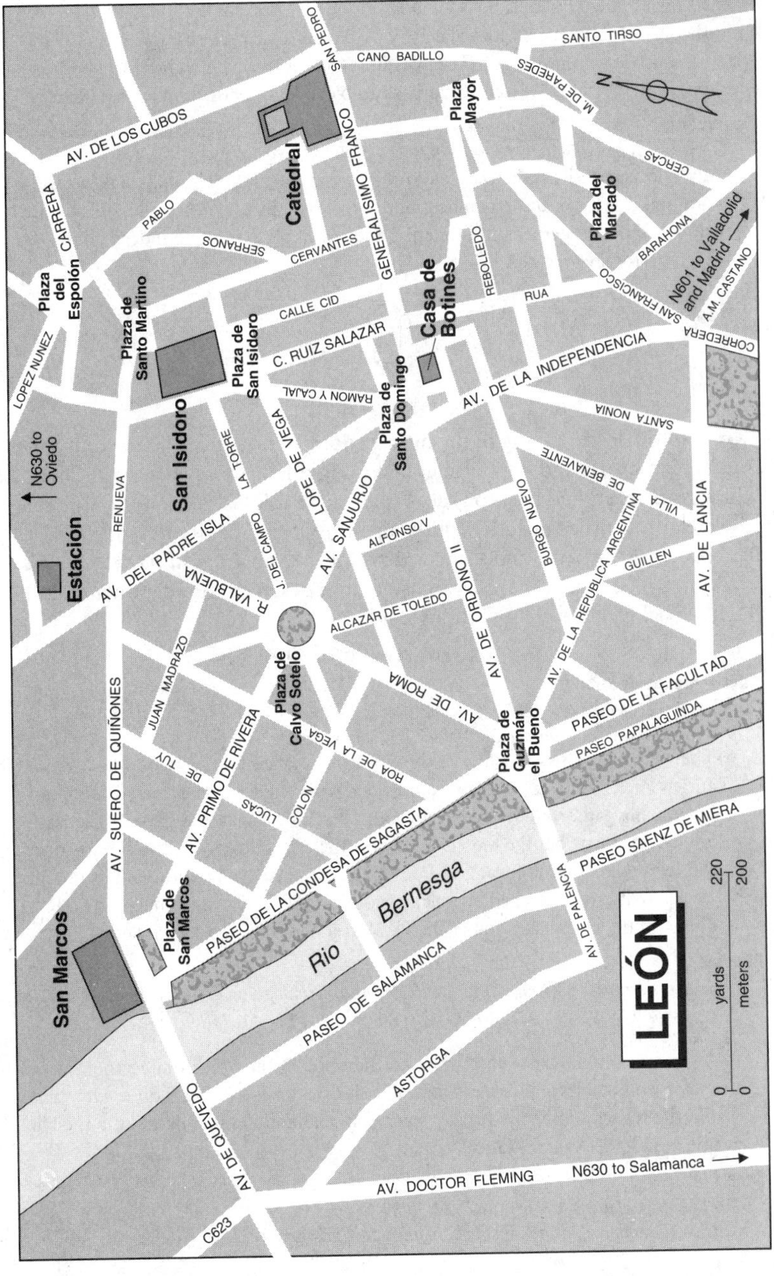

LEÓN

San Marcos

Plaza de San Marcos

Estación

Plaza del Espolón

Plaza de Santo Martino

San Isidoro

Plaza de San Isidoro

Catedral

Plaza Mayor

Plaza del Marcado

Casa de Botines

Plaza de Santo Domingo

Plaza de Calvo Sotelo

Plaza de Guzmán el Bueno

Rio Bernesga

AV. DE LOS CUBOS
CARRERA
SAN PEDRO
CANO BADILLO
SANTO TIRSO
M. DE PAREDES
GENERALISIMO FRANCO
PABLO
SERRANOS
CERVANTES
CALLE CID
C. RUIZ SALAZAR
RAMON Y CAJAL
LOPEZ NUNEZ
RENUEVA
LA TORRE
LOPE DE VEGA
J. DEL CAMPO
R. VALBUENA
AV. DEL PADRE ISLA
AV. SANJURJO
ALFONSO V
AV. DE ORDONO II
ALCAZAR DE TOLEDO
AV. DE ROMA
RODA DE LA VEGA
JUAN MADRAZO
LUCAS
DE TUY
COLON
AV. PRIMO DE RIVERA
AV. SUERO DE QUIÑONES
PASEO DE LA CONDESA DE SAGASTA
PASEO DE SALAMANCA
ASTORGA
AV. DE QUEVEDO
C623
AV. DOCTOR FLEMING
REBOLLEDO
RUA
CORREDERA SAN FRANCISCO
A.M. CASTANO
BARAHONA
CERCAS
SANTA NONIA
VILLA DE BENAVENTE
BURGO NUEVO
AV. DE LA REPUBLICA ARGENTINA
GUILLEN
AV. DE LANCIA
AV. DE LA INDEPENDENCIA
PASEO DE LA FACULTAD
PASEO PAPALAGUINDA
PASEO SAENZ DE MIERA
AV. DE PALENCIA

N630 to Oviedo ←

N601 to Valladolid and Madrid →

N630 to Salamanca →

yards 0 — 220
meters 0 — 200

At lower prices, there is the Quindós, a modern hotel that provides what a hotel should—clean comfort with willing service. What makes it special is that it does all this for much less than what others charge, just $65. It is located in a quiet neighborhood one block north of Av. Gen. Sanjurjo and a block south of the Parador San Marcos.

Don Suero

Av. Suero de Quiñones, 15, ☎ *(987) 23 06 00. 106 rooms.*

Even less expensive is the Don Suero. When you see this hotel you'll think we made a mistake; it looks and acts much more expensive than it is. Actually, its rates are under $50. Altogether this modern professional place is a find indeed. **Note**: no credit cards are accepted.

Dining

Grand, too, is the feeling of the dining room, although red walls seem a bit much. The chairs and appointments are dignified, more so than the food which features stuffed beef tongue. Fish include sole, salmon and conger eel. More elegant dishes include trout soup, cured veal *(cecina de vaca)*, frogs' legs *(las ancas de rana)* and stuffed partridge *(perdiz del páramo estofada con verduras)*. The local wine, Bierzo, is gaining deserved international repute. Such a meal will cost $25, without drink.

Alternative Dining

Nuevo Racimo de Oro   ★★

Pl. San Martin, 8, ☎ *(987) 21 47 67.*
Closed Sunday in summer and Wednesday the rest of the year.

The restaurant looks as a mesón should. It is installed on the second floor of an ancient tavern, and serves roasts from a wood fire oven, following a mandatory bowl of steaming garlic soup (served in a wooden bowl with a wooden spoon). The place is a mite touristy, but the food is good nonetheless, and a few dollars cheaper than the restaurants that follow at $20 per diner. Located at the north end of the Pl. Mercado, it can be reached by walking east from Pl. de Santo Domingo to C. Rua going south, which takes you to the Pl. Mercado in three blocks. Credit Cards: A, V.

Adonías   ★★

C. Santa Nonia, 16, (south from the Pl. de Santo Domingo on C. Independencia for one block until it forks, with C. Santa Nonia going right) ☎ *(987) 20 67 68.*
Closed Sunday.

A pleasant dining experience waits up the stairs in the green dining room with sturdy wood tables and ceramics on the walls. Regional cooking is done with care, and the service is friendly. It takes some consideration in ordering to keep the bill under $25. Credit Cards: A, D, M, V.

Casa Pozo   ★★

Pl. de San Marcelo, 15, ☎ *(987) 22 30 39.*
Closed Sunday night, the first half of July and Christmas week.

Owned by the brother of the proprietor of Adonías, there are those who consider this better and those who consider it not as good as Adonías. We find each different—this one is less formal and the food a touch more earthy—but hard to choose between. The bread is terrific as is the trout. Special menus are available for $20. Located directly opposite the Casa Botines. Credit Cards: A, D, M, V.

Directions

If arriving from the **south**, just follow the Bernesga River and you will arrive in the Pl. San Marcos with the parador. From the **north** you arrive at a sort of "T," which is Av. Álvaro López Nuñes. Turn right for four blocks, then take the left on the wide Los Reyes de León. When it arrives in a square, turn right for the parador in two blocks.

Paradors Nearby

Benavente: 70 km	Villafranca: 131 km	Cervera: 133 km
Zamora: 135 km	Gijón: 145 km	Tordesillas: 152 km

Sights

Despite a Leonese fixation with lions, the name of their city derives from the Latin *Legio Septima*, because the site was first settled by the Seventh Legion under Caesar Augustus. After conquest by first Visigoths, then Moors, Christians from Asturias in the north recaptured León in 850. But the Moors took it back in 996 and burned the town. In 1002 it was retaken by the Christians—this time for good—and made the capital of a province of the same name. With such status, the city became a haven for Christian refugees from Moorish territory and thus the Mozarabic center of Spain during the 11th and 12th centuries. The wonder is that there is not more fine Mozarabic architecture and art surviving. The present walls date to 1324, replacing an earlier construction that in turn replaced Roman walls. Parts remain standing in the old town along with a collection of houses from the 12th and 13th centuries. Still in use, the houses' exterior plaster sometimes flakes off to reveal their original half-timbered brick.

As the Reconquest gained territory, the capital of Christian Spain followed its armies further south and León languished. For centuries the town lay under the dust of decay. Then the citizens undertook a great cathedral, perhaps in memory of other times, incredibly raising a rival to those across the Pyrenees in France. In the 20th century rich deposits of iron and coal were discovered in the mountains north of León so today the city thrives again.

León is a city of modern buildings, wide avenues and fountains, yet maintains an old quarter from a different age.

Arriving from **Salamanca** and **Zamora** on **N-630** travel on Av. Dr. Fleming past the northern train station. After the station turn acutely right onto C. Astorga. Astorga ends forcing a left onto Av. de Palencia which crosses the Bernesga River and empties into a large traffic circle (Guzman el Bueno). Continue through the circle to Ordoño II opposite, which leads in a few blocks to another circle, Pl. de Santo Domingo, with underground parking to the right. From **N-601** (**Madrid**, **Valladolid** and **Burgos**) drive down Alcalde Miguel Castana which soon ends at a confluence of large streets. Continue for a few blocks on the right street, Av. Independencia, until it lets into the circle of the Pl. de Santo Domingo with underground parking to the right. From the north on **N-630** (**Oviedo**) enter an intersection from which a right turn leads along Av. Asturia. In about two blocks, take the first left onto Av. del Padre Isla which in several blocks goes into the circle of the Pl. de Santo Domingo, with parking across the plaza.

León's grand avenues all funnel into the large Plaza de Santo Domingo, a center from which the sights radiate. Walking east on Generalissimo Franco brings you to the Pl. de Regla and, three blocks later, the **Cathedral**. Walking north on C. Ramon y Caja brings **San Isidoro** in two blocks. Northwest along Av. de General Sanjurjo lies the **Monastery of San Marcos** nine blocks away.

Plaza de Santo Domingo ★

San Marcelo church ★, rebuilt in the 16th century, stands at the east end of the plaza. It contains a moving wood sculpture by Gregorio Fernandez. Facing the church's south side is the **Ayuntamiento ★** (city hall) from 1585 with the arms of León emblazoned on its facade. Across the plaza, opposite the Ayuntamiento, is the former **Casa de los Guzmanes**, now the Diputación, with a fine 16th-century patio and grillwork. Next to it, west, is the **Casa de Botines ★** set back on its own lot.

Now a bank, it was designed at the end of the 19th century by Antoni Gaudí as a small palace. Built to look Gothic, it shows Gaudí's mastery of that aesthetic, for it almost seems period though not exactly like any structure of that time. A walk east along Calle Generalissimo Franco past the Casa de los Guzmanes brings you to the Cathedral three blocks later.

Cathedral ★★★

Pl. de Regla, ☎ *(987) 23 00 60.*
Hours open: weekdays 9:30 a.m.–1:30 p.m. and 4–7 p.m. Sat. 9:30–1:30 p.m. Closed Sun.

Begun in the middle of the 13th century and finished 150 years later, it is surprising that this church reflects so little of the Spanish interpretation of Gothic that turned most of her churches into wider, less lofty, darker structures than those north of the Pyrenees. This Cathedral would suit any French town and bring glory to most.

Two equal but dissimilar towers frame the facade containing three portals beneath a great rose window. The central **portal** houses a vivid depiction of the fate of the damned; the left portal holds two fine depictions of prophets. A triple portal along the southern face is surmounted by a statue of Saint Froilan, the Bishop of León in the 10th century, and has lovely carvings decorating the door jambs. Continue around to the rear for a view of **buttresses** flying as they support the high nave.

Inside one is struck first by soaring height, then by all the glass. Even by Gothic standards the nave is narrow, which serves to emphasize its loftiness. Graceful piers carved to resemble bundled columns rise to an elegant ceiling traced with ribs. All around and behind in the rainbow's colors are a literal third of an acre of stained glass, the glory of the Cathedral. The front rose window and that in the chapels of the apse are the oldest; those in the nave are Renaissance and later, depicting flora and minerals beneath historic personages and their crests, surmounted by the blessed. The sun transforms the interior with heavenly colors.

Carved with painted alabaster reliefs, the trascoro in the center of the nave frames a central arch which gives the best view of the length of the Cathedral. The altar is later, 15th century, containing a nice depiction of the Entombment on the left side. Farther left is a *Pieta* by Rodger van der Weyden.

Both windows in the transepts are early. The one in the south wing is especially striking. Chapels in the apse behind the altar hold tombs of early bishops. The east chapel contains the tomb of **Condesa Sancha** that shows horses tearing her nephew and heir to pieces in punishment for having killed her.

From the north end of the Cathedral (left) a fine Plateresque doorway lets into the **cloisters** adorned with fine frescoes. Museums are installed off the left and far sides, and display a 10th-century Visigothic Bible and a crucifix by Juan de Juni, among other miscellanies. *Admission: 300 ptas. for the museum and cloisters.*

Return to Pl. de Santo Domingo for the simplest route to San Isidoro. Take C. Ramon y Cajal north for two blocks to the basilica, still attached to the city walls.

San Isidoro el Real ★★

Pl. San Isidoro, 4, ☎ *(987) 22 96 08.*

Hours open: Tues.–Sat. 10 a.m.–2 p.m. and 4–8 p.m. (until 6 p.m. in winter). Open Sun. 10 a.m.–1:30 p.m. Closed Mon.

Fernando I, the first king of a united Castile and León, built a church here in the 11th century dedicated to St. Isidoro. This saint from Seville, not to be confused with Madrid's St. Isidro Labrador, was a seventh-century archbishop whose organization of church councils did much to define Catholic orthodoxy. Fernando I transferred the saint's bones here, before dying himself the next week. Building continued under the supervision of, at first, Fernando's daughter, then his son and in turn his grandson. By then the structure had been rededicated to serve as a pantheon for the kings of Asturias, León and those of the united Castile and León.

Of Fernando's church, only the narthex survives, housing its royal pantheon. The mass of the basilica was built about a century later by his successors. The look of the front was much altered by Gothic and Plateresque additions in the 16th century, including an equestrian statue of St. Isidoro. The **portals**, however, are original and the depiction of the sacrifice of Abraham in the **tympanum** is vivid. To the east a lovely early portal depicts Christ's descent from the cross.

The uncharacteristic height of the clerestory makes the small and almost square Romanesque interior unusually light. Yet it seems claustrophobic, almost subterranean, after the light of the soaring Cathedral. Huge pillars are surmounted by richly-sculpted capitals, while arches at the beginning of the nave and in the transepts show Mudejar influence. The retablo is late, early 16th-century, and overlooks a reliquary containing the bones of St. Isidoro. The north transept contains a 12th-century chapel retaining faded, but lively, **frescos**.

A doorway at the front of the basilica, left, leads to the **Pantheon of the Kings**. Carvings on the interior side of the portal and on the capitals of the columns are some of the earliest depictions of figures in all Spain. Two cryptlike rooms comprise the 11th-century structure raised by Fernando I, probably the first Spanish building in the Romanesque style. Here rested the remains of Alfonso V of León, Fernando I, Urrica, his daughter, and almost 20 other Infantes and Infantas until the French desecrated the building in the 19th century.

But they did not destroy the 12th-century frescoes—still vibrant today thanks to the dry, airtight construction of the building. The vault ceilings depict New Testament episodes involving Christ, evangelists (with animal heads), saints and angels, and the **first Spanish nativity scene**. A charming calendar covers one archway, showing which farming tasks should be performed each month.

The adjoining Treasury contains 10th- and 11th-century pieces, including an enamel casket, another with ivory plaques and a chalice of two Roman agate cups mounted together in gold. *Admission: 300 ptas., for a guided tour of the Royal Pantheon.*

Old Town   ★

The basilica of **St. Isidoro** is in the area of the old walls which enclose a warren of streets, ending southeast at the Cathedral. Modern houses abut ancient buildings from the 13th century, which show their age by the half timbered brick exposed where plaster coatings have flaked off. Another concentration of ancient houses lies in the area between the arcaded Pl. Mayor, directly south of the Cathedral, and the Pl. del Mercado, to its southwest.

For a visit to the Monastery of San Marcos take the broad Av. General Sanjurjo that leads northwest out of the Pl. de Santo Domingo for 10 blocks. The walk provides lovely views of the facade as you proceed.

Antiguo Monasterio de San Marcos ★★★

Pl. San Marcos, 7, ☎ (987) 23 73 00.
Hours open: (museum) Tues.–Sat. 10 a.m.–1 p.m. and 4–6pm. Open Sun. 10 a.m.–1 p.m. Closed Mon.
In the 12th century this was the mother house of the Order of Santiago, established to protect pilgrims on their way to Santiago de Compostela. Three centuries later Ferdinand the Catholic, as the order's Master, drew plans to embellish the monastery to proclaim the order's Reconquest accomplishments. The plan was finally carried out between 1513 and 1549 under the supervision of Ferdinand's successor Carlos V, in a style that was not his favorite.

The present imposing facade is the result—a sumptuous Plateresque monument stretching larger than a football field. A baroque pediment added in the 18th century does not unduly disturb the original two-story design of regular windows, friezes, engaged columns and pilasters. Santiago (St. James) on horseback strides over the elaborate main door to the left, which includes scenes from his life. The right-hand door to the church is incomplete but covered with scallop shells, Santiago's symbol. All along, a row of medallions depicts assorted Biblical, Roman and Spanish personages, including Isabella the Catholic supported by Lucretia and Judith, and Carlos V supported by Trajan and Augustus.

Today most of the former monastery is given over to one of Spain's most deluxe paradors, though the church inside with its beautiful choir stalls remains open to all. Anyone can enter the hotel to look at the magnificent stone staircase leading from the lobby. The Chapterhouse, which now contains an archaeological museum under a splendid carved wood roof, and the sumptuously decorated sacristy, to the right, may be toured for a fee. Roman statuary and mosaics in the museum hold some interest, but the main treasures are the medieval works. Included are textiles and clothing, arms and religious articles, with one outstanding 11th-century Romanesque ivory, the Carrizo Crucifix, tiny, elongated and haunting. *Admission: 200 ptas.*

Trains

Five trains a day connect Madrid with León for a trip of 4–5 hours and a cost of about 2000 ptas. Connections between León and Burgos (a two and one-half-hour ride), Valladolid (two hours), Oviedo (two hours), and Barcelona (10–11 hours) are also convenient. One train per day goes to Salamanca. The station is located at *Av. Astorga, 2.* This is about five blocks west of the Pl. Santo Domingo along Av. Ordoño II, which changes its name to Av. de Palencia after it crosses the river and runs into Av. Astorga, perpendicular to it. (☎ *(987) 22 02 02).*

Excursions

Burgos, Zamora, Salamanca and Santiago de Compostella, would all make logical next stops. Or, there is beach at Ribadeo.

PARADOR SAN TELMO

Avenida de Portugal, s/n, Túy, 36700
☎ *(986) 60 03 00, FAX (986) 60 21 63*
$80 per double; 22 rooms: 1 singles, 20 doubles, 1 suite

★ ★

Smack above the River Miño, the Spanish border, this parador lets you inspect Portugal before a visit. However, the parador does not win any prize for its exterior. It's an austere, concrete bunker. Terraced gardens spilling down to the river redeem the appearance somewhat, indeed an elegant pair of stairs in the garden atone for almost anything. Inside, the best feature is the views of the outside scenery of river and Portugal across the way. The interior is spare, hard walls and hard floor, a theme carried over to the bedrooms. So, spend your time outside on the back terrace and garden with a pool and tennis court above a river eternally flowing by.

Dining

Long and thin to allow a row of windows with lovely views, the dining room is otherwise rather cafeterialike. Surprisingly creative food is served, however. For example, consider an empanada stuffed with cod and currants, or conch with shellfish sauce, or turbot in a sauce of clams and shrimp. For meat, the specialty is a veal chop topped with delicate peppers. Incidentally, you are near the largest clam bed in the county, so those little critters are certain to be fresh. Wash the meal down with an elegant Albariños. The bill should come to $20, plus the wine.

Alternative Dining

O Novo cabalo Furado   ★

Pl. del Generalissimo, ☎ *(986) 60 12 15.*

Just a few steps from the cathedral, this homey place serves true home cooking (if your home is in Galicia). Try any of the seafood that appeals and your bill should be a few pesetas less than at the parador. Closed Sun. dinner and Mon. Credit Cards: A, V.

Directions

Just continue toward the river for one km after entering Túy.

Paradors Nearby

Bayona: 25 km	Pontevedra: 49 km	Cambados: 74 km
Santiago: 108 km	Verín: 178 km	Ferrol: 203 km

Sights

Túy, a granite village spilling down the steep bank of the Miño, is picturesque. It boasts of one great church, a cathedral that goes back to the thirteenth century, and has served as church, castle and fortress since that time.

As to beaches, there are riverine ones near town, but miles of the real thing require a trip to the mouth of the river and a turn north up the coast. The distance is about 25 km to the tip on N-550.

Pontevedra is an elegant manor complete with antiques.

Ponte de Lima, Costa Verde, is located near the coast and picturesque villages.

Palmela pousada is in the heart of the sierra of Arrábida.

Pousada do Castelo is found within Obidos' ramparts.

EASTERN SPAIN

Casa Batlló in Barcelona is Gaudi's exercise in blue-green tiles.

Eastern Spain comprises a large slice of the country—about a third of it—250 miles wide by 500 miles long. It includes Aragón with its Rioja wines, Navarre with its ski and mountain resorts, Catalonia with cosmopolitan Barcelona amid the ruggedly beautiful Costa Brava, and Valencia with inviting beaches. That is to say, it is high on variety. You can soak up culture in Barcelona one day and swim at the beach at Aiguablava or ski in the mountains at Bielsa or El Saler the next. Or, you can spend the night in Olite's castle, then travel to Hondarribia's palace for a dip in the sea before dining at an extraordinary restaurant nearby. Then visit Rioja's famous vineyards. Valencia waits in the south with plenty of beach nearby.

CANTÁBRICO SEA

Elantxobe

Bilbao

Etxalar

Quejana

Zerain

Zugarramurdi

Gasteiz

Ochagavia

Ansó

Frias

Salinas de Añana

Sajazarra

Sanguesa

Domingo de la Calzada

Olite

Sos del Rey Católico

Calahorra

Canales de la Sierra

Uncastillo

Viniegra de Arriba

Sadaba

Zaragoza

Soria

Calatañazor

San Esteban de Gormaz

Atienza

Medinaceli

Daroca

Alcañiz

Siguenza

Brihuega

Molina de Aragon

Pastrana

Albarracin

Teruel

Rubielos de Mora

Peñiscol

FRANCE

Eastern Spain

P PARADOR	PRIMARY ROAD
Castle CASTLE	SECONDARY ROAD
Pueblo PUEBLO	SCENIC ROAD

0   10   20   30   40 Mi.
0   20   40   60 km

Vielha Arties
Monte Perdido
Durro
Ainsa   Os de Civís   Toloriu
Alquézar   La Seu d'Urgell   Camprodón   Beget   Roses
                                                              Figueres
Monzon   Rupit   Pals
          Balaguer   Cardona   Vic
Lerida   Tossa
          Prades   Barcelona
     Vilanova i la Geltrú   Castelldefels
Miravet
          L' Ametlla de Mar
     Tortosa
Morella   MEDITERRANEAN SEA
     Benicarló

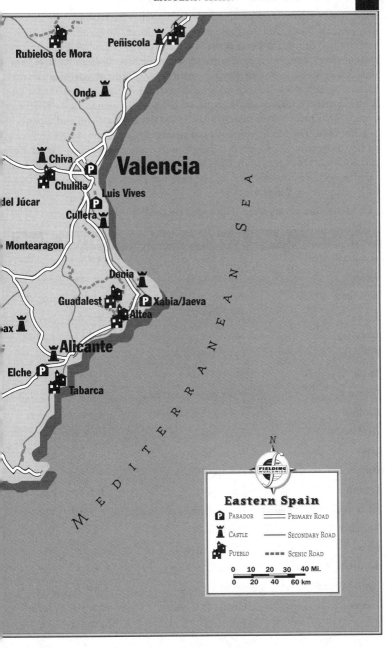

Rubielos de Mora

Peñiscola

Onda

Chiva

Chulilla

del Júcar

Valencia

Luis Vives

Cullera

Montearagon

Denia

Guadalest

Xabia/Jaeva

Altea

ax

Alicante

Elche

Tabarca

MEDITERRANEAN SEA

N

FIELDING
WORLDWIDE

Eastern Spain

P PARADOR		PRIMARY ROAD
CASTLE		SECONDARY ROAD
PUEBLO		SCENIC ROAD

0	10	20	30	40 Mi.
0	20	40	60 km	

The major city of eastern Spain is cosmopolitan **Barcelona**, with elegant shopping, art nouveau buildings and fabulous food. Ruggedly scenic Mediterranean coastline, the **Costa Brava**, lies to its north, including **Empuries**, an ancient Greek city. Northwest stand the Pyrenees with **Ordessa National Park** and skiing. On the bay of Biscay, further west, waits **Hondarribia** on the French border, a lovely town with great restaurants nearby. South of it are the vineyards of **Rioja** near the parador at Santo Domingo de la Calzada, along with a preserved medieval town at **Sos del Rey Católico**, and a perfect castle at **Olite**. The Mediterranean coast stretches south from Barcelona, bordering the renowned Costa del Azahar and Costa Blanca. Another castle-parador awaits for a rest along the way at **Alcañiz**. Attractive **Benicarló** offers a parador on the Costa del Azahar, **Jávea** does the same on the Costa Blanca, with proximity to **Valencia** as a plus.

The following towns and paradors are covered in this chapter.

Town	Parador Name	Rating	Page
Vielha	Valle de Arán	★★★	*page 450*

To savor the region, stay two nights in Barcelona, then consider a rest at the parador of Aiguablave on the coast or at one of three mountain paradors at Arties, Bielsa or Vielha. Travel west to stay one or two nights at paradors either at Santo Domingo de la Calzada, Olite or Hondarribia, all special hotels with sights nearby. For more beach stay at Benicarló or Jávea, near Valencia, perhaps overnighting in Alcañiz on the way.

BARCELONA
★★★★

Accommodations

When it hosted the 1992 Olympics, Barcelona built 12 major new hotels which increased rooms in the city by a third, easing some of the hotel pressure. Still, costs in Barcelona stand with Marbella as the highest in Spain. The premier location would be on or near the Ramblas, convenient to both sights and shopping. But given that Barcelona provides a subway system, it is possible to stay outside of this center if near a subway stop,. Such a location is a decided second best, however, to the Ramblas area with its opportunity for serendipitous walks.

Ritz

Gran Via de les Corts Catalanes, 668, Barcelona, 08000, ☎ *(93) 318 52 00, FAX (93) 318 01 48, Telex 52739. 148 rooms, plus 13 suites.*

If you want the best, the Ritz ranks with the finest hotels in the world. It was built in the belle époque style of 1919, and a recent facelift has made it dazzle again. The entrance—all chandeliers, gilded mirrors and flowers—is as grand as can be, but this hotel is not merely a lobby. Its rooms are among the most spacious and beautiful in Spain. Many contain marble fireplaces (though not lit these days), and huge baths in bathrooms the size of some other hotels' bedrooms. Even if its accommodations were merely ordinary, the Ritz would still be worth a stay for the service—you will find no more attentive staff or knowledgeable concierges anywhere. Of course it costs in the $250 range, but that is only money.

Claris

Pau Claris, 150, Barcelona, 08000, ☎ (93) 487 62 62, FAX (93) 215 79 11. 106 rooms, plus 18 suites.

Also outstanding and fun is the Claris, a lovely 19th-century neoclassic building, done post-modern inside. Antiques abound; and a Japanese garden adds just the touch for this eclectic mix. Don't worry, the bedrooms are tastefully new. As a bonus, prices of under $200 drop almost 30 percent on weekends.

Regente

Rambla de Catalunya, 76 (five blocks west of Pl. de Catalunya), Barcelona, 08000, ☎ (93) 487 59 89, FAX (93) 487 32 27, Telex 51939. 78 rooms.

For rooms at $100–150, a good choice is the Regente. Its townhouse-intimacy, modernista front, tastefully decorated rooms and lovely roof terrace all deserve raves. Now that it has reduced its prices to just over $100, so does its value. Hooray as well for its location, but service and accessories are not quite first-class.

Gran Derby

C. Loreto, 28 (Follow Av. Diagonal northwest to Pl. Francisco Macia, a circle with fountain. Take the left onto Av. J. Tarradellas, then the first right onto Av. de Sarria for a short block to C. Loreto.), Barcelona, 08000, ☎ (93) 322 20 62, FAX (93) 410 08 62, Telex 9742931. 31 rooms, plus 12 suites.

The Gran Derby costs about $100 and, although situated in a quiet neighborhood, is both three miles from the center of town and a fair distance from the nearest subway stop. It is worth considering because the rooms are tasteful and huge. All include a separate sitting room, and two-bedroom suites are available. For two couples traveling together, or for a family, such an arrangement could prove cost-effective. (Don't confuse it with its more ordinary annex, called the Derby, a few doors down.)

Colón

Av. de Catedral, 7 (across the plaza fronting the Cathedral), Barcelona, 08000, ☎ (93) 301 14 04, FAX (93) 317 29 15, Telex 52654. 138 rooms, plus nine suites.

For about $150 the Colón offers comfort and some style, although we feel nostalgic for the eccentric, if threadbare, former look. Its location is most convenient (although the bells of the Cathedral chime outside the windows). Sixth-floor rooms with balconies over the plaza are preferred.

España

C. Sant Pau 9-11 (just south of the Ramblas by the Teatre del Liceu), Barcelona, 08000, ☎ (93) 315 22 11, FAX (93) 317 11 34. 84 rooms.

At under $100, the España stands out. The location of this old Barcelona standard is terrific, with the Ramblas just around the corner. The elegant inside, designed by the great modernista architect Domènech i Montaner, is a treat and the rooms were thoroughly remodeled and upgraded for the Olympics. This is one special hotel for the price.

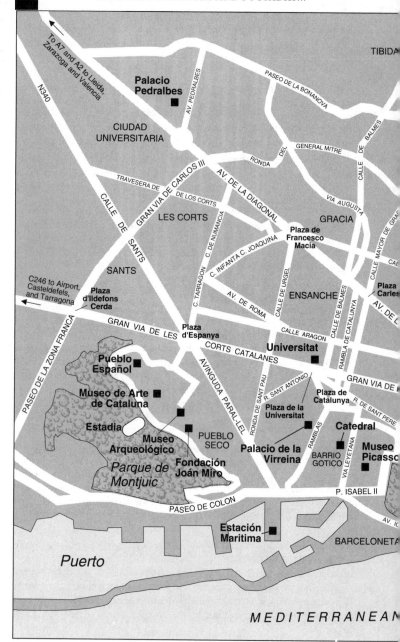

BARCELONA

PASEO DEL VALLE HEBRON

VIA FAVENCIA

VIA JULIA

Parque Grüell

SERA DE DALT

SAN ANDRES

To A7 and Girona

AV. DE LA MERIDIANA

C. CAMELIAS VIRGEN DE MONTSERRAT

CALLE SAN ANDRES

PASEO DE FABRA Y PUIG

CALLE DE FELIPE II

E GRACIA

CONGRESO

AV. GAUDI

agrada Familia

CALLE DE SAGRERA

za de ros

CALLE ARAGON

AV. DE LA MERIDIANA

ATALANES

Plaza de les Glories Catalanes

SAN MARTIN

CALLE GUIPUZCOA

P. CARLOS II

Río Besós

Río

CALLLE ALMOGAVARES

CALLE PEDRO IV

A19

rque de la udadela

SAN ANDRIA DE BESOS

To Mataró and Costa Bravo

seo de e Moderno

PUEBLO NUEVO

BADALONA

SEA

| 0 | yards | 1,100 |
| 0 | meters | 1,000 |

Montecarlo

Rambla dels Estudis, 124, Barcelona, 08000, ☎ *(93) 317 58 00, FAX (93) 317 57 50, Telex 93345. 80 rooms.*

Next best is the Montecarlo whose marble entrance and wooded reception area is the way we think of Barcelona, and location on the Ramblas is a great plus. Accommodations are sufficiently comfortable, and the prices, for a change, are fair.

Suizo

Pl. del Angel, 12 (this plaza is two blocks behind the back of the Cathedral and north beside Via Laietana), Barcelona, 08000, ☎ *(93) 315 41 11, FAX (93) 315 38 19, Telex 97206. 48 rooms.*

For a terrific location, go for the Suizo. The decor is charming, and the service respectful. Go for one of the attic rooms with skylights and parquet floors.

Nouvel

C. Santa Ana 18-20 (the street goes north from the western end of Rambla Estudis), Barcelona, 08000, ☎ *(93) 301 82 74, FAX (93) 301 83 70. 55 rooms.*

There are a few choices at $50 or less. The Nouvel is attractively decorated in a modernista style, its rooms have just been renovated and are ample for the price. Best of all, the service is conscientious.

Lausanne

Av. Portal de l'Angel, 24 (just east of the southern end of the Pl. Catalunya), Barcelona, 08000, ☎ *(93) 302 11 39. 17 rooms, half with showers.*

At the hotel Lausanne you get a room with some size and style, and the management is most professional. The location is good, if a few blocks from the sights.

Dining

By mingling French ideas with Spanish, Barcelona serves some of the best food in Spain. *Suquet de peix,* the French fish stew bouillabaisse, is available, along with the less elegant *sarsuela,* a "comic opera" of seafood. Since the south of France influences Catalan cuisine, Italian-style dishes have migrate to Barcelona menus. *Pa amb tomàquet,* bread soaked with olive oil and spread with tomato, is the usual appetizer; and pasta, such as macaroni, will often be seen. Catalans dine very late. The normal dinner hour is 10 p.m., and restaurants do not open in the evening much before that time.

Neichel   ★★★★★

Av. de Pedralbes, 16bis (Av. Pedralbes heads northwest from Pl. Pius XII, which is at the southern end of Diagonal. The restaurant is in the third alley on the right.), Barcelona, 08000, ☎ *(93) 203 84 08, FAX (93) 205 63 69.*
Closed Saturday for lunch, Sunday, Christmas week, Holy Week and August.

To cite one restaurant as the best in Barcelona is certain to provoke argument. With some trepidation we offer this one. True, it is not as beautiful as some others, since it is installed in a modern housing complex. Also, the cooking is as much French as

Spanish, since its owner hails from Alsace. But no chef in Spain is more thoughtful about his food. The *menu de degustació* will set you back about $60, but presents the best the restaurant offers which is exceptional indeed. Save room for extraordinary cheeses and desserts. Our only complaint is that the atmosphere is so serious and formal that it is hard to lose oneself in the pure joys of the food. Reservations are required. Credit Cards: A, D, M, V.

Can Gaig ★ ★ ★ ★

Pas. de Maragall, 402 (located in the far west of the city, a 15-minute taxi ride is simplest, although the Maragall subway stop from either the 4 or 5 line brings you to within six blocks), Barcelona, 08000, ☎ *(93) 429 10 17.*
Closed Mon., holiday evenings, Holy Week and August.

If you want the best of pure Catalan cooking, here it is. Not prettified, not served in dramatic or romantic surroundings, just food that brings the pleasure of good taste. The beautiful people will be at El Dorado Petit or Via Veneto, the gourmets will be at Neichel, or here if they are Catalans. Gaig's version of *suquet* is sublime, lobster ravioli is a delight and the pigeon roasted in its own juices is unrivaled. The chef is talented, imaginative and serious about his craft. True, the loveliness of surroundings that can add so much to the total dining experience is not offered here, but the food ranks above what those pretty places serve, at a value of about $40. Reservations are imperative. Credit Cards: A, D, M, V.

Botafumeiro ★ ★ ★

C. Mayor de Gràcia, 81 (Mayor de Gràcia is the continuation of Pas. de Gràcia, after it crosses Diagonal. The restaurant is located four blocks farther along the street.), Barcelona, 08000, ☎ *(93) 218 42 30, FAX (93) 415 58 48.*

The restaurant is named after the giant censor in the Cathedral of Santiago de Compostela, for the owner migrated from Galicia. He flies his fish daily to Barcelona. Need we mention that this is the best pure seafood restaurant in the city, and some say the country? The decor is functional white and light wood, for this is a no-nonsense restaurant. Order *mariscos Botafumeiro*, a cascade of shellfish of every variety, and we think you will agree. Prices easily reach $45, and reservations are advised. Credit Cards: A, D, M, V.

La Dama ★ ★ ★

Avinguda Diagonal, 423 (three blocks south of the intersection of Diagonal with Pas. de Gràcia), Barcelona, 08000, ☎ *(93) 202 06 86, FAX (93) 200 72 99.*
Convenient to the boutiques of Passeig de Gràcia, this is a most elegant restaurant housed in an architectural statement—an art nouveau building that contributes to the experience. The food is first rate, getting better all the time, and *nueva* to the core—witness cream of potato soup with caviar, or roast potatoes stuffed with crayfish or crayfish flavored with orange vinegar. A set-price dinner is offered for $35.

Via Veneto ★ ★ ★

C. Ganduxer, 10 (heading southwest along Diagonal, turn right at the second street past the traffic circle Pl. Francisco March), Barcelona, 08000, ☎ *(93) 200 72 44.*
Closed Saturday lunch, Sunday and the first three weeks in August.

Via Veneto ranks among the most dramatic Barcelona restaurants—with its Belle Époque decor—and stands with the best for the caliber of its food. Despite the res-

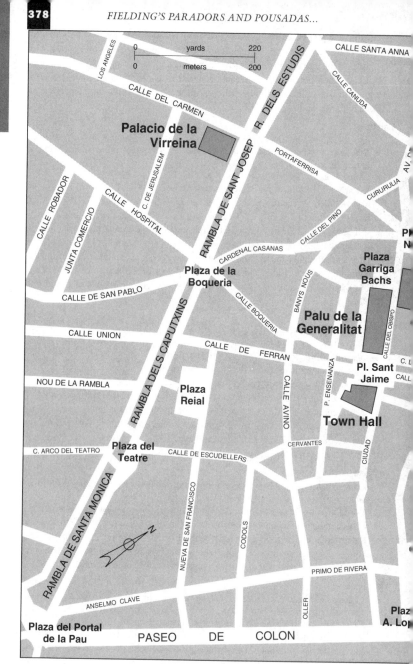

CALLE CONDAL

TENSION

JUNQUERAS

C. ORTIGOSA

CALLE

DE TRAFALGAR

RONDA DE SANT PEDRO

CARRER DE PAU CLARIS

C. ALTA DE SAN PEDRO

CENTRAL BARCELONA

C. DR. J. POU

CALLE BAJA DE SAN PEDRO

V. DE LA ATEDRAL

Plaza d'Antoni Maura

AV. F. CAMBO

atedral

Museo F. Marés

GIRALT PELLICER

C. J. GIRALT

Pl. Berenguer el Gran

Barcelona Museum

CALLE CARDERS

COMERCIO

ME I

laza de l'Angel

CALLE DE LA PRINCESA

TANTARANTANA

DEL

NAVARRO

VIA LAIETANA

CALLE PLATERIA

CALLE DE MONTCADA

Museo Picasso

CALLE RECH

CALLE FUSSINAS

PASSEIG DE PICASSO

Plaza Comercial

PASEO DEL BORN

ERAS

RIBERA

C. CONSULADO DEL MAR

Parque de la Ciudadela

AS. ISABEL II

Plaza del Palau

AV. ARGENTERIA

taurant name, the cuisine is Catalan of the *nueva cocina* sort. Food is elegant to the eye, sublime on the palate and comes in at about $45. Reservations are required. Credit Cards: A, D, M, V.

Agut d'Avinyó

C. Trinitat, 3 (From the Rambla de Caputxins go north along C. Ferrán, bordering the Pl. Reial. One block after the plaza turn right onto C. d'Avinyó to find this restaurant a few steps later in a cul-de-sac on the right.), Barcelona, 08000, ☎ *(93) 302 60 34. Closed Holy Week and Christmas week.*

Dark wood, rush-caned chairs and white walls create the first impression of a mesón. A closer look at the venerable antiques shows the restaurant to be more elegant than that. Seating is on five intimate levels. The cuisine is traditional Catalan compared to the *nueva cocina* in vogue elsewhere. Mussels in garlic cream sauce are delectable; meat and game generally are combined with some fruit sauce. The food is good, although not at the outstanding level of some others, but a convenient Barri Gòtic location and comfortable surroundings, along with a bill that will run about $30, entitle it consideration. Reservations are advised. Credit Cards: A, D, M, V.

Moderate ($15–$30)

Siete Portas

Passeig Isabel II, 14 (in the port, two blocks left of the end of Via Laietana), Barcelona, 08000, ☎ *(93) 319 30 33.*

Seven doors do indeed front the street, opening onto a large mirrored, marble-floored dining area. The specialty is seafood which is amazingly reasonable for the quality and quantity. Fish paella and the house version of *sarsuela* are excellent and bountiful enough to share. Dinner will run about $30. Note that this area is not safe at night, so commuting by taxi is recommended. Reservations are advised. Credit Cards: A, D, M, V.

Senyor Parellada

C. Argentería, 37 (the street leads northeast from Via Laietana, just north of the Pl. Jaume), Barcelona, 08000, ☎ *(93) 315 50 94. Closed Sunday and holidays.*

The restaurant is dignified without being stuffy, surrounding a leafy atrium, and well-prepared Catalan dishes at fair prices, about $25, are an excellent value all around. Credit Cards: A, D, M, V.

El Cangrejo Loco

Moll del Gregal, 29-30 (along the new beach esplanade just north of the port), Barcelona, 08000, ☎ *(93) 221 17 48.*

This is a convivial and popular place that serves good, moderately priced seafood. Blow the budget on a menu degustació for about $20. and you should end both full and happy. Credit Cards: A, D, V.

Los Caracoles ★

P. Escudellers, 14 (the street runs east from the Pl. Reial at the end of Rambla Caputxins), Barcelona, 08000, ☎ *(93) 302 31 85.*

This venerable Barcelona institution is much favored by tourists. Despite its popularity, the rustic surroundings are relaxed and it serves hearty Catalan food prepared well. Of course, try the snails *(caracoles)*, but fried fish, roast chicken, mussels and paella are tasty too. Reserve, but there still may be long waits. Credit Cards: A, D, M, V.

Inexpensive (Less than $15)

Agut   ★★

C. Gignas, 16 (follow C. Ciutat from the north side of the Ajuntament in Pl. Jaume in the Barri Gòtic to C. Ample just before reaching the port. Jag left then right.), Barcelona, 08000, ☎ (93) 315 17 09.
Closed Sunday evening, Monday, and the month of July.
This one is almost too good to be true. It offers fantastic value for food that is genuinely well prepared—and has done so for 75 years. It looks as it should, incorporating a kind of fifties decor in a place that is older. Of course nothing is perfect. The neighborhood should be walked with caution at night. No reservations. Credit Cards: A, M, V.

Egipte   ★

C. Jerusalem, 12 (directly behind the Boquería market off Rambla Sant Josep), Barcelona, 08000, ☎ (93) 317 74 80.
Closed Sunday.
No frills here, just good food of the homey Catalan variety, although the reason for the Egyptian motif is anyone's guess. There are crowds at lunch, but also numerous low-priced special menus. Things grow quieter in the evening. Being practically a part of the market, the fish are always fresh. Prices are fair, and no reservations are taken. Credit Cards: none.

Raim D'or Can Maxim   ★

C. Bonsucces, 8 (Bonsucces goes south from the west end of Rambla Etudis), Barcelona, 08000, ☎ (93) 302 02 34.
Closed Sunday.
This place is always crowded because the food is good and the prices low. The gazpacho is heavenly, although only served at lunchtime. Credit Cards: A, M, V.

Les Corts Catalanes

Gran Via de les Corts Catalanes. 630 (a block west of the P. Catalunya), Barcelona, 08000, ☎ (93) 301 03 76.
This is the place for the vegetarians among us, but the food is good enough for carnivores to enjoy too. The empanadas in particular are tasty. Credit Cards: V.

Directions

From **Perpignan** in France both the toll A-9, and the free N-9, reach the Spanish border at La Jonquera in 20 km. There they continue in Spain under the new names of A-7 and N-II and reach Barcelona after 160 km. From **Zaragoza** the toll road A-2 east joins A-7 in 137 km for a further trip of 62 km. Alternatively, there is the free N-II which reaches **Llerida** (Lérida) in 142 km and Barcelona in a further 156 km. From **Madrid** and west, follow direc-

EASTERN SPAIN

tions to Zaragoza. From **Valencia** the best routes are the parallel coast roads A-7 (toll) and N-340. They reach Barcelona in 331 km. Note that N-340 can be slow going when beach towns are crowded in summer.

Paradors Nearby

Túy: 22 km	Pontevedra: 50 km	Cambados: 78 km
Santiago: 125 km	Verín: 170 km	

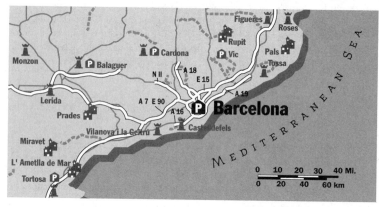

Sights

The city descends from a Roman colony established in the time of Augustus, named Faventia Julia Augusta Paterna Barcino. Shortened to Barcino, the name transmogrified over time into "Barcelona." The original town comprised a low hill just inland from the sea—the present Barri Gòtic—as it would for almost 1000 years. Franks captured Barcelona from the Romans in A.D. 263, and when the Romans reconquered it they surrounded the hill by a cyclopian wall that still exists in scattered pieces. In 874, after the French had expelled the Moors and annexed Catalonia in the process, Wilfredo el Velloso (the Hairy) was named the Count of Barcelona and granted independence by the ironically named French king, Charles the Bald. From that time forth, Barcelona maintained preeminence in Catalonia.

In both the middle of the 18th and the middle of the 19th centuries Barcelona undertook imposing urban renewals. The first entailed razing most of the ancient Roman walls to construct a wide thoroughfare along the western edge of the Barri Gòtic, primarily for promenades. The thoroughfare followed a sometime stream and permanent sewer and was named the Ramblas, perhaps from the Arabic *raml*, meaning "stream." The second project pro-

duced a great addition to the city north of the Barri Gòtic. Called the Eixample (Extension), it was a marvel of rational city planning that more than
doubled the city's size. Today, Barcelona spreads both north and south of
this extension, following the coastline.

Visitors will spend most of their time in the center of this sprawling metropolis, anchored by the port of Barcelona midway between the north and
south halves of the city. Immediately south of the port rises the abrupt hill of
Montjuïc. Here are several fine museums and arenas from the 1992 Olympic
Games. Two blocks inland from the port and running for ten blocks further
west is the original heart of Barcelona, the **Barri Gòtic**, containing the Cathedral and other medieval buildings. Its border consists of the lovely Ramblas,
which changes names every few blocks. South of the Ramblas, leading to
Montjüic, is a maze of streets called the **Barri Xines** (Chinese Quarter), the
former red-light district, now much toned down, although still not the safest
place after dark. North of the Barri Gòtic a park called the **Ciudadela** blooms
where an 18th-century fortress once stood, providing space for a **zoo** and the
Museum of Modern Art. Extending west from the Barri Gòtic, beginning at
the landmark Plaça Catalunya, runs the 19th-century urban development
Eixample, with boulevards, elegant stores and buildings by Gaudí.

Convenient underground parking is generally available in a large lot under
the square behind the Boquería, the main food market. It is one block west
of the Rambla St. Josep, and thus near the Barri Gòtic.

From the **Airport** 22 km south of the city, C-246 feeds into the expressway
Ronda del Litoral. Take exit 21, Pl. Colom/Pl. de la Pau and head west
along the wide Ramblas divided by a center strip for about six blocks, until
passing the Teatre del Liceu on the left. Take the next left, C. Hospital, and
the first true right off it to parking.

From **France** and north, exit to either A-17 or A-18. Both intersect with
Ronda del Besòs which becomes the Ronda del Litoral in about one mile.
Take exit 21, Pl. Colom/Pl. de la Pau and head west along the wide Ramblas
divided by a center strip for about six blocks, until passing the Teatre del
Liceu on the left. Take the next left, C. Hospital, and the first true right off it
to parking.

From **Madrid**, **Zaragoza** and west Barcelona stay on A-7 as it becomes the
Ronda del Litoral. Take exit 21, Pl. Colom/Pl. de la Pau and head west
along the wide Ramblas divided by a center strip for about six blocks, until
passing the Teatre del Liceu on the left. Take the next left, C. Hospital, and
the first true right off it to parking.

Note: the **Bus Turístic Cien (100)** provides convenient transport to most of
Barcelona's sights, leaving from outside the el Corte Inglés department store
in the Pl. Catalunya at the west end of the Ramblas every half hour starting at

9 a.m., from mid-June until the middle of September. The bus stops at fifteen sights around the city, at any one of which passengers may get off to board again half an hour later for the next circuit. Multilingual members of the Tourist Board ride along to answer questions. The cost for a full day's ride is 1000 ptas., or 700 ptas. for half a day, payable on boarding.

Barri Gòtic

This quarter is named for the dense concentration of Gothic buildings creating more of a medieval atmosphere than survives in any other city in the world. It encompasses the original city of Barcelona before its expansion, and includes traces from as far back as Roman times, pedestrian walks and a charming square.

At the corner of C. Hospital at the end of Rambla Sant Josep stands the small Pl. de la Boquería on the north side of the street. C. Boquería, more a shopping arcade than a street, heads north for a bit more than three blocks before changing its name to C. Coll and entering the charming Plaça Sant Jaume.

Plaça Sant Jaume   ★

Two Gothic buildings form the east and west borders of the plaza. On the east is the much restored **Ajuntament** (City Hall), generally with banners hanging from second-story windows of its 19th-century facade. Its northern face along C. de la Ciutat is from the 15th-century. A dramatic black and gold mural by the 20th-century artist and architect Josep Sert resides inside, along with an impressive Gothic hall where the Consell de Cent, the ruling body of Barcelona, once met. *(Open Mon.–Sat. 9:30 a.m.–1:30 p.m. and 4:30–7:30 p.m.)* On the west side of the plaza stands the **Palau de la Géneralitat ★**, a grand 15th-century palace and, until recently, the seat of Catalonia's government. Walk west from the plaza along the north face of the palace to its entrance on C. Bisbe Irurita. Inside is an elegant Renaissance patio, an imposing 16th-century hall, and a lovely chapel dedicated to Saint George, the dragon-slayer—who is a patron saint of Barcelona as well as of Britain. A weathered 15th-century medallion of that saint on C. Bisbe Irurita marks the outside entrance to the patio. You can't enter without special permission.

The narrow C. Bisbe Irurita is bordered on the right side by the **Casa de los Canonigos** (Canons), connected to the Palau de la Géneralitat by a covered passageway overhead that looks eminently medieval, although constructed in 1926. At the end of Bisbe the plaza of the Cathedral opens, **Plaça Nova**. Turning back to face the Cathedral, the **Palacio de Bisbe** on the right contains two soaring plain towers of a more weathered stone than the rest, grizzled because they remain from the fourth-century Roman walls of the town. The open plaza before the Cathedral is the place to see the local folk dance, the Sardana, danced to the accompaniment of fife and drum by parishioners after mass on Sundays.

Cathedral   ★ ★

Pl. de la Seu, *(93) 315 15 54.*
Hours open: daily 7:30 a.m.–1:30 p.m. and 4–7:30 p.m. Cloister Museum open daily 11 a.m.–1 p.m.

Although the Cathedral was constructed in the 14th century, its facade is more recent—late 19th-century—designed to suit the Gothic interior. Inside, the church is harmonious in proportion, though wider in feeling than even normally wide Spanish Gothic churches. The whole is unfortunately dulled by blackened stone and a less spacious clerestory than eyes would wish.

In the center a trascoro in marble carved after designs by the great Bartolomé Ordoñez illustrates the martyrdom of Saint Eulalia by Romans in the 4th century. She was a native of Barcelona and is the patron saint of the Cathedral. The coro of two tiers of high stalls surmounted by individual spires is admirable. Upper tiers are emblazoned with the coats of arms of France, England, Portugal, Hungary, Poland, Sweden and The Netherlands, for here Carlos V convened kings to join his exclusive club—the Knights of the Golden Fleece.

Stairs at the foot of the altar descend to a crypt preserving remains of Saint Eulalia in a fine 14th-century marble sarcophagus attributed to Giovanni Pisano, but more likely by an unknown north Italian. The Gothic door to the sacristy and museum leads to 11th century wooden coffins of the founders of the original church on this site, Ramón Berenguer I and his wife.

Off the south transept stands an unusual cloister. Magnolias and palm trees surround a pond in which geese play in memory of their Capitoline ancestors. A small museum in the chapter house on the west side exhibits a collection of paintings. The most striking is the composition and faces of *Pieta* by Bartolomé Bermijo, with a most human-looking bespectacled priest. *Admission: 50 ptas.*

Pass around to the north side of the Cathedral to follow the narrow C. dels Contes de Barcelona along its flank. At number 10 on the left is the Frederic Marès Museum.

Museu Frederic Marès   ★

Pl. De Sant Iù, 5-6, *(93) 310 58 00.*
Hours open: Tues.–Sat. 10 a.m.–2 p.m. and 4–7 p.m. Open Sun. 10 a.m.–2 p.m. Closed Mon.
The top floor of the museum displays a melange of everyday objects and advertisements that capture the spirit of design in the early part of this century. Displayed in the basement are early stone sculptures, including Roman, Moorish, Romanesque and Gothic pieces, gathered by this inveterate collector. On floors in between, beneath lovely ceilings, is a singular collection of polychromed wood sculpture—mostly from Catalonia, but also from elsewhere in Spain. *Admission: 250 ptas.*

Continue along C. dels Contes de Barcelona to take the first left into the Pl. del Rei.

Plaça del Rei   ★

Hours open: Tues.–Sat. 10 a.m.–2 p.m. and 4–7 p.m. Open Sun. 10 a.m.–2 p.m. Closed Mon.
The plaza is named for the 14th-century royal **palace** of the Kings of Aragón that occupies its far left, down a flight of stairs. One enters an immense arched Gothic audience hall, the Saló del Tinell, with a reconstructed wood ceiling. Among other rooms that may be visited is one with splendid murals of the Catholic Monarchs attending Columbus, for somewhere in this palace, perhaps in the Saló del Tinell, the

Catholic Monarchs received Columbus after his first trip to the New World to hear the news of his amazing discoveries and weep together with joy. *Admission: free.*

Next to the palace stands its **Capilla de Santa Agata**, spare and moving with a fine altar and splendid painted wood ceiling. Its stained glass displays medieval coats-of-arms. Enter the chapel from the building on the right side of the plaza, the 15th-century Casa Padillàs, now the **Museu d'Història de la Ciutat**. The purpose of the museum is to show models of early buildings and various stages of Barcelona's growth, but, in the course of moving the building from its original site in the Eixample and digging a new foundation, Roman and Visigoth structures were discovered. So the most interesting sights reside in the basement where these ancient remains are displayed. *(Hours for the Museu are the same as for the palace; admission: 250 ptas.)*

The building on the near left side of the plaza is the 16th-century **Palau del Lloctinant**, now housing an astonishing collection of medieval records. For the average person a look in the courtyard at the grand stairway with its lovely ceiling will suffice.

Continue along C. dels Contes de Barcelona to the second left onto C. Libreteria. Take the second left again to enter the grassy Pl. Berenguer el Gran. Here is the best look at the remaining **Roman walls**, for the Chapel of Saint Agatha was built into them, and would have lost an outer wall if this part of the Roman fortification had been torn down along with the rest. The walls were 27 feet thick in parts and 60 feet high, though not quite so elevated here. Return to the Pl. del Rei and go away from it along the apse of the Cathedral. At the end of the apse, tiny C. Paradis turns left. Where it bends right, the CEC Mountaineering Club stands at number 10. Walk inside to see the four pillars remaining from the Roman **Temple of Augustus**.

Montjuïc

Commanding both city and sea, this steep hill seems to call for a fortress. In more peaceful times its abundant land provides space for museums and athletic stadiums. The best entrance, if driving, is from the Pl. Espanya. Head down the Ramblas to the sea. Turn right at the statue to Columbus and right again in one short block onto Av. del Parral-lel, which ends in about 15 blocks in the Pl. Espanya. A grand vista to the left leads up an equally grand stairway to the Palau Nacional.

If you are not renting a car, Montjuïc is best reached by the funicular that runs from 11 a.m.–9:30 p.m. in summer, only on weekends in winter, and costs 165 ptas. Walk toward the sea along Rambla Caputxins for two blocks. Turn right on C. Nou de la Rambla for seven short blocks to Av. del Paral-lel and the funicular station. You exit on the hill near the Fundació Miró. Follow the directions below in reverse.

Palau Nacional, Museo de Arte de Catalunya   ★ ★ ★

Parc de Montjüic, ☎ *(93) 423 71 99.*
Hours open: Tues.–Sun. 9 a.m.–2 p.m. Closed Mon.

The grand boulevard leading from the Pl. Espanya, the fountains, the van der Rohe German Pavilion, and the palace itself all were built for a world's fair hosted by Barcelona in 1929. Today the palace houses the Museu d'Arte de Catalunya, one of the world's great assemblages of medieval art. Its collection of Romanesque painting is unsurpassed.

The reason for the excellence of the collection is that its works were appropriated by the government during the early 1900s from Romanesque and Gothic churches throughout Catalonia to protect the art both from thieves and natural deterioration. Although one way to amass a great collection, this seizure denuded parish churches throughout Catalunya.

Romanesque paintings alone fill 34 rooms. Special notice should be paid to the charming 12th- and 13th-century works, such as frescoes from Pedret, Bohi and Santa María, and especially to the *Pantocrator* fresco from Sant Clemint de Taull, with a precocious use of foreshortening and a haunting gaze. Note the Byzantine feeling combined with attempts at portraiture. The Gothic period blossoms with the *Nativity* of Lluis Borrassa, and the precision of Bernat Martorell, then ascends to genius in Lluis Dalmau's *Verge dels Consellers*, and culminates in the retablos of Jaume Huguet. Although weakest in artworks from periods after the Gothic, the museum features paintings by Ribalta, Velázquez and Zurbarán, a fine Ribera, and lesser works by el Greco and Tintoretto. *Admission: 500 ptas.*

Museu Arqueològic ★

Passeig de Santa madrona, 39-41, ☎ *(93) 423 21 49. Go east from the palace, taking the left fork along Passeig de Santa Madrona.*
Hours open: Tues.–Sat. 9 a.m.–1 p.m. and 4–7 p.m. Open Sun. 9:30 a.m.–1 p.m. Closed Mon.
This museum displays notable and rare Carthaginian jewelry discovered in the Balearic Islands, along with a fine selection of Celtiberian pieces. The collection is strong in Roman and Greek artifacts, mainly from excavations at nearby Empüries—note the bronze panther head and the *Venus of Empüries*. Interesting too are reconstructions of a Roman kitchen and atrium. The fittings of an actual Roman catapult are also on view. *Admission: 250 ptas., free on Sun.*

Fundació Miró ★

Pl. de Neptú, ☎ *(93) 329 19 08. Return along Santa Madrona back to the fork to curve around left. Turn left at Av. de Miramar for a few yards.*
Hours open: Tues.–Sat. 11 a.m.–7 p.m. Open Sun. 10:30 a.m.–2:30 p.m. Open Thurs. evening to 9:30 p.m. Closed Mon.
The all-white building designed by Josep Sert provides part of the pleasure, for it is perfectly suited to the bright colors of the art on its walls. Joan Miró was born in Barcelona, but lived in France in self-imposed exile during Franco's years. It was he who donated most of the artworks and the money to house them. The collection spans the breadth of his work, from sculptures, to tapestries, to mobiles, to precisely designed colorful paintings. The building is bright and airy, and the art makes one smile. *Admission: 500 ptas.*

Return along Av. de Miramar for the 70,000 seat Olympic Stadium, swimming pool, and other stadia. Note the covered Sant Jordi stadium of impressive Japanese design. Ahead on Av. de Miramar is the teleferique (cable car) that, for 325 ptas., rides up to the **Parc d'Atracciones**, a rather tame amusement park, then continues up to the **castle** at the summit of Montjuïc for 100 ptas. more. (The cable car runs weekdays from noon to 3 p.m. and from 4–8:30 p.m.; weekends from 11:30 a.m. to 8:30 p.m. In the winter it opens only on weekends.)

Castell de Montjuïc

Parc de Montjüic, ☎ *(93) 412 00 00.*
Hours open: Tues.–Sat. 10 a.m.–2 p.m. and 4–7 p.m. Open Sun. 10 a.m.–8 p.m., or to 2 p.m. in winter. Closed Mon.
The fortress was built in 1640 by the citizens of Barcelona during one of their rebellions against the rest of Spain. Although the English stormed it, followed later by the French and by Franco, it presents an imposing front. Unrivaled views over the city and sea are presented from the roof, but housed inside is the usual collection of military museums. *Admission: 150 ptas.*

The Ramblas ★★

The Ramblas consists of a wide pedestrian island bordered by two narrow streets that run for just under one mile. Citizens and visitors alike love to *Paseo* past kiosks selling newspapers, magazines, books and erotic comics, flower stalls, bird sellers, and impromptu entertainers. Every block or two the Ramblas change their name and character. None of the sights along the way are spectacular, but the walk continually presents precious surprises, and for many this will be the Barcelona remembered longest. Note that the Ramblas turn more seedy at night when they function as the city drug center. We start from the beginning of the Rambla Sant Josep, one long block west of the C. de l'Hospital, or three blocks east of the Pl. Catalunya.

On the southwest corner at number 99 stands the 18th-century **Palau de la Virreina**. Although named for his widow, it was built by a viceroy to Peru who skimmed a fortune from Peruvian silver. Today revolving exhibitions are presented, with a choice display of canvas treasures by Raphael, Van Dyke and Zurbarán on the second floor and a stamp collection on the top floor. *(Open Tues.–Sat. 10 a.m.–2 p.m. and 4:30–8:30 p.m.; open Sun. 10 a.m.–2 p.m., Mon. 4:30–9 p.m. Admission: 500 ptas.)*

Continue down Rambla Sant Josep toward the sea. On the right, half way along the block, is the entrance to a huge covered food market, called the **Boquería ★**, roofed in 1870's girdered ironwork. Walk through the market and out the rear entrance to see the 18th-century **Antic Hospital de la Santa Creu** across the parking lot. No longer a hospital, its patios are tranquil. Returning to the Rambla, a sidewalk mosaic by Miró is located near the corner.

Crossing C. de l'Hospital and the next street, C. de Sant Pau, brings the remains of the opera house of Barcelona at the next corner—the **Gran Teatre del Liceu**, one of the few buildings for true opera in Spain. A horrible fire consumed it in 1994. It had a rocky beginning too. On opening night in 1892, an anarchist threw two bombs into the audience, though performances were more ordinary afterward. Reconstruction is under way.

Now following Rambla del Caputxins, cross C. la Unio. On the left side of the street C. Colom leads into the **Plaça Reial ★**. This is a rare true plaza in Barcelona, surrounded by an arcade of homogeneous buildings. Palm trees wave and a fountain of the three graces decorates the center, whose street lamps were designed by Gaudí. Today the square is slightly seedy with bars all around, but on Sundays it comes to life with a philatelic and numismatic market.

Continuing a few feet down the Rambla, turn right onto C. Nou de la Rambla. At number 3 is the **Palau Güell ★ ★**, an early building by Gaudí. Since it now functions as a museum (for theater memorabilia), it is the rare civil building by this eccentric architect open to the public. Don't miss it! *(Open weekdays 11 a.m.–2 p.m. and 5 p.m.–8 p.m., weekend 4–8 p.m. Admission: 200 ptas.)*

The Rambla grows less attractive from this point on. At its end stands a solemn statue of Columbus pointing over the wrong sea. To his left, the first street north, C. Banca, holds the **Museu de Cera de Barcelona**, one of those wax museums that every large European city seems to have. *(Open Mon.–Sat. 11 a.m.–2 p.m. and 5–8 p.m. Admission: 750 ptas.)*

To Columbus' right, in a barn of an old building, is the **Museu Maritim ★**. The building, called the *Drassens Reials*, is worth the visit. Dating from the 14th century, it is the only surviving medieval shipyard in Europe. The collection inside features an exact model of the galley *La Real*, flagship of Prince Don Juan during the great battle of Lepanto against the Turks in 1571. *(Open Tues.–Sat. 10 a.m.–2 p.m. and 4–7 p.m. Open Sun. 10 a.m.–2 p.m. Admission: 200 ptas.)* Floating in the harbor opposite the far side of the Maritime Museum is a replica of Columbus' flagship, the caravel ***Santa Maria ★***. Its tiny size is a shock that evokes appreciation for the courage of those who sailed so insubstantially past the end of the known world. The ship may be toured, using the ticket from the Maritime Museum. *(Open daily 9 a.m.–2 p.m. and 3 p.m.–sunset.)*

Along the water, north of the port, stands Barcelona's latest example of urban development, constructed to serve as the 1992 Olympic village, and then to be sold for expensive condominiums. Beside the ocean stretches a wide ocean promenade and beach, yacht clubs, bars and restaurants. Here is where Barcelona's hip crowd takes a pleasant but lively Paseo in the evening. Tapas tend to be good and fresh seafood is available (for suggestions, look for Moll del Gregal addresses in the restaurant reviews following).

The Eixample

The area known as the Eixample was constructed above the western end of the Barri Gòtic in the middle of the 19th century to proclaim a modern age for Barcelona. Streets run straight as arrows, intersecting at right angles to form the clean lines of a grid. Its design represented both the rationality and egalitarianism of the time through orderly homogeneity. By the original plan, each block would be a square of the same size, every 200 squares would contain a hospital, every 25 a school. However, the program was only haphazardly carried through.

The buildings raised along these streets were separately commissioned by individuals and companies, but most aimed to incorporate the latest ideas in architecture—to express the spirit of the modern. Hence, the young Gaudí found several commissions here, along other noted Catalan architects of his era. Most of their buildings no longer remain, as changing ideas of what was contemporary led to replacement by later models, but enough survive to give this area the most extensive collection of art nouveau architecture in the world.

Guided tours of *Modernista* architecture are given Tuesday, Wednesday and Thursday at 3 p.m. by the **Guide Bureau** at *54 Via Laietana* (☎ *310 77 78*), just east of the Picasso Museum. The tours take about two hours and cost about $7. The Bureau will arrange individual tours at other times.

Passeig de Gràcia remains the most elegant street of the Eixample. It is lined with stylish shops, banks and fancy apartments, but one side of a single block of Passeig de Gràcia retains enough early 20th-century buildings to earn the playful name "Manzana de la Discordia" ★—the Block of Discord.

Pas. de Gràcia begins at the Pl. de Catalunya with its fountains. The plaza lies four blocks west of the Pl. Nova, fronting the Cathedral. It is also the western terminus of the Ramblas, about three blocks west of the Rambla Sant José. Pas. de Gràcia leaves the northwest corner of the plaza and heads west beside the el Corte Inglés department store.

Three blocks west along Passeig de Gràcia, bordered by street lamps designed by Gaudí, C. del Consell de Cent is crossed. Here begins the "Block of Discord." Stay on the north side of Pas. de Gràcia for the full view of the buildings opposite, then cross over to inspect their details.

The principle of this early modern movement was the opposite of what governed later 20th-century design. Clean lines, smooth, even-textured materials, the simplest and straightest shapes all characterize architecture in our time, but the *modernista* movement from the late 19th-century found inspiration in the curves and irregularities of nature, not in mathematical precision. To our eyes such buildings seem playful, full of unexpected turns and details, and serve as an antidote for the uniform simplicity whose familiarity has bred, if not contempt, at least a kind of boredom. The proof that we hardly look at contemporary buildings lies in how arresting these earlier fantasies are.

First, at number 35, is the **Casa Lleó Morera**, designed by a famed Gaudí contemporary named Domènech i Montaner. Only the upper two floors remain from his design, but grow enough flowers and beasts to give a sense of how exotic and Gothic in feel it must once have been. The interior is more elegant than what the exterior leads one to expect and incorporates the finest craftsmanship.

At number 41 stands the pyramid-topped medieval-looking **Casa Amatller**, designed by another Gaudí contemporary—Puig i Cadafalch. The interior is again elegant, though not open to the public. However, the art institute on the second floor often responds to sincere inquiries to show visitors around their office. The **Casa Batlló** next door at number 43, is Gaudí's exercise in blue-green tiles. This was his interpretation of the cave of St. George's dragon, with balconies suggesting skulls, beneath the sinuous dragon of a roof. The front doors seem to undulate as if made of soft material—understandably Salvador Dali admired them. Admission requires advance permission, but a quick peek from outside is allowed.

Two blocks farther west, occupying the corner of the south side of the street at number 92, is Gaudí's most imposing building, an apartment complex named **Casa Milà**, though known familiarly as "La Pedrera" (The Stone Quarry). The exterior looks like a massive fortress melting. Ironwork balconies are intricate assemblages of matted vegetablelike matter, each unique. Chimneys on the roof remind of the shapes children produce by dripping wet sand. In this case a free tour, at least of the roof, is available to the public. *(Tours on Tues.–Sat. at 10 a.m., 11 a.m., noon and 1 p.m. by calling ☎ 487 36 13 in advance.)*

Turn left in one block for a few steps along C. d'Aranyó to number 255. Here is the **Fundació Antoni Tàpies**, another building by Domènech i Montaner in an Islamic-influenced style. Towering over its roof is metal sculpture by the artist Antoni Tàpies, whose works the building now exhibits. *(Open Tues.–Sun. 11 a.m.–8 p.m.; Admission: 400 ptas.)*

North in 11 blocks along C. de Provence waits the incomparable Gaudí church of Sagrada Família, but a slight detour along the way presents two more *modernista* buildings. Continue along Pas. de Gràcia to turn right in three blocks to reach the **Pilau Quadras** at *Av. Diagonal 373.* This is another building by Puig i Cadafalch, whose interior with its sculpture and mosaics is stunning, and entrance is both allowed and free, for it is now a museum of musical instruments. *(Open Tues.–Sun. 9 a.m.–2 p.m.)* One block further north along the Diagonal on the opposite side of the street at 416 stands the huge **Casa de les Punxes**, like a Gothic castle.

Continue one block farther on Diagonal to take C. Provenca that forks off to the left. It leads in six blocks to Sagrada Família.

Sagrada Família   ★ ★ ★

C. Mallorca, 401, ☎ (93) 455 02 47.
Hours open: daily 9 a.m.–8 p.m. (closes at 7 p.m. in winter).

Work began on a rather ordinary neo-Gothic church in 1882. Two years later the architect resigned and Gaudí won the commission to complete it. It remained his favorite project until he died in 1926. Work proceeded slowly, since funds were inadequate, and private commissions would take Gaudí away from his work on the church for years at a time. For the last ten years of his life Gaudí lived in a small room on the church grounds, for the project consumed him, and he spoke of it as needing two centuries to complete. In 1926, absentmindedly crossing a street, he was struck by a trolley and killed. Since then the issue has been whether or not to finish the church. Gaudí left an awesome, but roofless structure, too incomplete to function as a church and of a design so personal that no one could complete it as he would have. Anarchists burned all of Gaudí's plans during the Civil War. Nonetheless, work, financed in large part by admission fees, has been under way since 1979 to finish the church with an intent to be as faithful to Gaudí's conception as possible. The problem is that Gaudí himself worked from the inspiration of the moment as much as from blueprints.

Only the west façade of three envisioned by Gaudí was finished by the time of his death, but what an awesome facade it is, of a spirit recognizably Gothic translated into modern idioms. The façade represents Christ's birth in carved scenes that seem to grow from the stone around the portals. Study the fine details and wonder at the overall conception. Fear of the power of an unrestrained imagination causes some people to feel a strong aversion to the building, but most agree that the building is spiritual, awesome and playful, providing a wholly unforgettable experience. *Admission: 600 ptas.; 150 ptas. more to ride to the tower top.*

North of the Barri Gòtic

Via Laietana forms the north border of the Barri Gòtic. It can be reached either by going north one block from the Pl. Nova in front of the Cathedral, or by continuing through the Pl. Sant Jaume along C. Jaume I for four very short blocks. At Pl. de l'Angel where Via Laietana intersects with C. Jaume I, take C. de la Princesa north (straight).

Turn down the fourth right along C. de Montcada onto **C. Montcada** ★ , a street declared a national monument for all the mansions that line it. At number 15, on the right is the **Palau Berenguer d'Aguilar**, a 15th-century mansion that houses the **Picasso Museum**. Opposite is the 14th-century **Palau dels Marques de Lleó**, at number 12, displaying an extensive collection of Spanish clothing and other apparel (open Tues.–Sat. from 10 a.m. until 2 p.m. and from 4:30 p.m. until 7 p.m.; admission: 200 ptas.). More 15th-century mansions stand at numbers 14, 23 and 25 (home of a branch of the French Galería Maeght run by the founder's children), ending with the baroque, forbidding **Palau Dalmases** at number 20.

Museo Picasso   ★

> *C. Montcada, 15-17, ☎ (93) 319 63 10.*
> *Hours open: Tues.–Sun. 10 a.m.–7:30 p.m. Open Sun. 10 a.m.–3 p.m.*
>
> Two things make this an interesting museum. Of course the first is the artworks displayed. While this is far from the finest assemblage of Picassos, and does not contain many of the artist's familiar works, the collection is the largest in the world, strong in childhood drawings and paintings of the seminal "Blue Period." The second note of interest is that the building is composed of two 14th-century mansions remodeled and joined. Against all expectations they provide a fine setting for the modern art on their walls. *Admission: 500 ptas.*

At the end of C. Montcada, on the right, stands the rear of the church of **Santa Maria del Mar**.

Santa María del Mar   ★ ★

> *Pl. de Santa María.*
> *Hours open: Mon.–Fri. 9 a.m.–1 p.m. and 5–8 p.m.*
>
> Barcelona's most dramatic church was finished in the 14th century to epitomize the Gothic style as interpreted in Catalonia. Although the west octagonal tower was not added until five centuries later, the remainder of the outside is early, and celebrated for its west portal. Note the solid buttresses surrounding the church, so different from the "flying" French versions. The interior was gutted of its baroque decoration during the Spanish Civil War, which restored its original Gothic lines. The nave is high, the vaulting unusually wide, and the adjoining aisles narrow to emphasize spaciousness. Pillars are set more widely than in any other Gothic church in order to carry the eye to the apse behind. Instead of a solid wall, the high altar is formed of soaring columns connected by narrow arches. Chapels along the aisles seem denuded, although fine stained-glass windows provide their own decoration. *Admission: free.*

Return to C. Montcada and continue across on Passeig del Born to reach the beginning of the **Parc de la Ciutadella** in four blocks.

Parc de la Ciutadella

At the beginning of the 18th-century, after Barcelona had taken arms against the national government yet one more time, an angry Felipe V razed blocks of houses to build a fortress for cowing the citizens. A century and a half later the citizens got their revenge by razing his fortress to turn it into a lovely city park, and placed museums and a zoo within its ample confines.

The layout is as follows. Ahead on the left is the **Geology Museum**, of interest to those who know about such things. A short distance to its left stands the **Castell del Tre Dragons**, originally a modernista cafe erected by Domènech for the 1888 Exhibition held in the park, but now a museum displaying almost every kind of dead animal. The building is most interesting architecturally as a harbinger of the *modernista* movement. *(Open Tues.–Sun. 9 a.m.–2 p.m. Closed Sun. Admission: 250 ptas.)*

To the right of the Geology Museum is the **Umbraculo**, a lovely conservatory of tropical plants. Straight ahead in about two blocks' distance are the gardens and lakes of the park, including the **Font de Aurora**, a work on which Gaudí assisted. To the right of the lakes and fountains stands the **Palau de la Ciudadela**, what remains of the fortress of Felipe V after the rest was torn down. Today the palace houses the Catalan Parliament and the **Museum of Modern Art**. Pre-modern would be a more accurate name, for, despite an occasional Picasso or Miró, most of the works are by earlier Catalans. Some of the modernista furniture is appealing. *(Open Tues.–Sat. 9 a.m.–7 p.m. Open Sun. 9 a.m.–3 p.m., and Mon. 3–7 p.m. Admission: 400 ptas.)*

Continuing south (right), is the **Parc Zoológic**. While there may be larger collections of animals elsewhere, only this zoo offers an albino gorilla. His name is *Copito de Nieve* (Snowflake). The dolphin and orca show enchants everyone. *(Open daily 9:30 a.m.–7:30 p.m.; closes at 5 p.m. in winter; admission: 900 ptas.)*

Shopping

Fine **boutiques** for clothing, leather, jewelry and shoes, many on the cutting edge, are concentrated in a rectangle bordered by Pas. de Gràcia on the east, Rambla de Catalunya to the south, Pl. Catalunya to the north and Diagonal nine blocks west. It is perfectly possible to cover the whole area in a leisurely late afternoon and early evening.

The area begins with a branch of **El Corte Inglés** department store, for moderate-priced clothing, at the Pl. Catalunya. **Loewe's** extravagant leather stands at *Pas. de Gràcia, 35.* At *53-55* a mall, called **Boulevard Rosa**, contains over 100 fine boutiques. Also at *55* is **Centre Permanent D'Artesana**, displaying works by artisans from around Catalunya. **Rodier** is at *66,* **Fiorucci** at *76.* **Adolfo Domíngues,** the designer who gave Don Johnson his look on *Miami Vice,* has a shop at *89,* with clothes for women as well.

Turn west (left) on C. Mallorca for some special stores. At the corner of Rambla de Catalunya, at *100,* is **Groc**, an outstanding designer for men. Across the street at *C. Mallorca 242* stands **José Tomas**, another fine men's designer. Turning left down Ramblas de Catalunya brings **Artespaña** *at 75*, a government store for superior craft furniture and accessories, and they ship.

Returning to C. Mallorca, further along is an extraordinary showplace of houseware and furniture design. **B.D. Ediciones de Diseno**, at *291*, is run by architects who sell museum-quality designs by the greats, living and deceased, such as chairs and furniture fittings by Gaudí. The building that houses the store is a monument too, designed by the *modernista* architect Domènech i Montaner. At number *258 on C. Còrsega*, which is the last street along Passeig de Gràcia going south before Diagonal, is a shop named **Urbana** which stocks fixtures reclaimed and restored from *modernista* buildings. It sells everything from light fixtures to mantels, armoirs and door knobs, each an artwork. Return to *Pas. de Gràcia at 96* for **Vincón**, another superior furniture and houseware vendor.

Different goods can be found in other areas. For **trimmings and costume jewelry** at great prices, walk from the Rambla Sant Josep to the Pl. Jaume along C. Boquería, which changes its name to C. Call. This is the wholesale trimmings and accessories area with store after store, though only a few sell to retail buyers.

There are two areas for **antiques**. One is in the Barri Gòtic in the area just south of the Cathedral along the tiny streets of C. Banys Nous and C. del la Palla. Art nouveau jewelry can be surprisingly affordable in some of these tiny shops. For fine **lace**, try **L'Arca de l'Avia** at *Banys Nous, 20*. Behind the Cathedral on C. Franseria is **Grafiques el Tinell**, for **prints** from old woodblocks and etchings, some handcolored. *On Baixada de la Libreteria, 2*, the next street to the east, is **Papirum** which sells antique and handcolored **paper** and end-papers.

The second antique area is just west of the Barri Gòtic on C. Montcada. From the Pl. Jaume in the heart of the Barri Gòtic go north through the Pl. Angel to follow C. Princesa. The fourth right is C. Montcada, with the **Picasso Museum** selling a large selection of **prints**, **shirts**, etc., on the corner. For four short blocks antique shops line both sides of Montcada going south. Also on this street is a fine shop for **handcrafts** called **1741** *at number 2*, and an outlet of **Fondacion Maeght**, the great French **art gallery**, *at 25*. Lastly, an **antiques market** is held in the Pl. del Pi, just west of the Pl. de la Boqueia, on Thurs. from about 10 a.m. until 2 p.m. or so.

Espadrilles, the traditional rope-soled canvas shoes of Catalonia, can be purchased at **La Manual Lapargalera** on C. d'Avinyó, just after it turns east from C. Ferrán on the way to the Pl. Jaume in the Barri Gòtic.

Yes, there is a large **flea market** in Barcelona. It consists of more junk than jewels, but you never know. It is called **Els Encants**, and takes place in the Pl. de les Glòries Catalanes which is on Gran Via Corts Catalanes about 15 blocks north and one block west of the Pl. Catalunya. The red line 1 metro from Pl. Catalunya toward Santa Coloma stops at the Glòries station right at the spot. Markets take place Mon., Wed., Fri. and Sat. beginning at dawn. Note: there has been talk recently of moving this market. Check at the tourist office before making the trip.

All day Thursday (except in Aug.) the **Mercado Gòtic de Antiquedes** takes over the Pl. Nova (in front of the Cathedral) for antiques and personal treasures galore.

Directory

City Tours

Both **Julià Tours** at *Ronda Universitat, 5* (☎ *(93) 317 64 54)* and **Pullmantur** at *Gran Via, 635* (☎ *(93) 318 12 97)* offer half-day tours of Barcelona for about 3500 ptas. The **Palau de la Virreina** at *Rambla 99* rents cassettes for walking tours of the city.

Airport

International and domestic flights all arrive at **El Prat de Llobregat Airport**, 14 km south of the city (☎ *(93) 478 50 00)*. A taxi will cost about 2500 ptas. and take half an hour. An **Aerobús** outside the door from customs travels to the central Pl. Catalunya every 15 minutes or so for 450 ptas. Trains leave to and from the airport every 30 minutes for a 20-minute trip that costs 300 ptas. The Barcelona terminus is **Estació Central De Sants**, well-connected by metro. Iberia has an office at *Pas. Gràcia, 30* (☎ *(93) 401 33 84)*. An airport shuttle bus leaves from there every hour or so.

PARADOR ANTONIO MACHADO

Parque del Castillo, Soria, 42005
☎ *(975) 21 34 45, FAX (975) 21 28 49*
$90 per double; 34 rooms: 4 singles, 28 doubles, 2 suites

★ ★ ★

 Situated on top of a picturesque wooded hill in a park, this starkly modern parador makes no references at all to the past. Everything is rectangular and hard-edged, which make noise a problem and does not induce comfort. In this case, the best feature of the parador is its guest rooms which are attractively wooded and enjoy almost a wall of window. The parador has four levels; the top two floors provide the best views.

Dining

The dining room is so bright and colorful it seems more like an ice cream parlor than a restaurant. Bentwood-style chairs are flimsy and uncomfortable. The food is not bad, however. Start with hearty garlic soup, then graduate to either beans and sausage *(alubias con chorizo)* or, better, to local roast lamb *(cordero de la tierra addado)*. Milk pudding *(costrada)* makes a delicate dessert. Enjoy a good Ribera de Duero with your meal. The bill will be about $20.

Directions

If arriving from the **south**, you come into town on Av. Mariano Vicén. At the main Mariano Granados Square continue straight out the opposite end along Campo which soon reaches a "T." Turn right along Tejera Santo Tome until it bends, where the first left is Carr. Logroño. Its first left is Paseo del Mirón which reaches the parador. From the **east** you arrive on Carr. de Agreda which crosses the river and becomes Agustin. After it does an "S," take the first right which is Carr. Logrono. Its first left is Paseo del Mirón which goes to the parador. From the **west** you reach a traffic circle, at whose opposite end the left fork should be taken. This is San Benito which becomes Tejera Santo Tome after the bull ring. From here follow the south directions.

Paradors Nearby

Siguenza: 100 km	Calahora: 116 km	Olite: 142 km
Santo Domingo: 174 km	Segovia: 194 km	Argómaniz: 205 km

Sights

Though its charm lauded by poets has been obscured by modern buildings, Soria retains a pretty center with interesting sights.

Once in Soria, drive along Passeo Espolón by Alameda de Cervantes Park until the postmodern Museo Numantia appears on the left.

The **Numantia Museum** ★ ★ *(open 10 a.m. to 2 p.m. and 4:30–9 p.m.; closed Sun. afternoon and Mon.; admission: 200 ptas.)* spaciously houses a good collection of Roman and Iberian pieces, especially those on the second floor from excavations at nearby Numantia.

Cross C. Ferial to enter the Pl. Ramon Benito Acona. A right and quick left brings you past the Diputacion into the Pl. San Esteban with a Romanesque church of harmonious lines. **San Juan de Rabanera** ★ has Byzantine-style vaulting, and a stunning Romanesque crucifix over the altar.

Outside, turn left at the back of the church to enter the Pl. San Blas y el Rosel. Directly ahead, across the plaza, is the long facade of the **Palace of the Counts of Gomara** ★. The two-story patio inside is elegant. On the west end of the palace, the street heading north leads in one block to **Santo Domingo** ★, which has one of the finest Romanesque facades in Spain. The central portal is covered with carving that well repays study. The interior, however, was redone in the 16th century.

Cross to the side of the plaza opposite Santo Domingo and go left down C. de la Aduana Vieja, passing the 18th-century **Casa de los Castejones** ★, with Baroque doorway, after which a right onto C. Ferial returns again to the Pl. Ramon y Cajal.

Parador Castillo de la Zuda

Castillo de la Zuda, s/n, Tortosa, 43500
☎ *(977) 44 44 50, FAX (977) 44 44 58*
$95 per double; 82 rooms: 9 single, 70 doubles, 3 suites

★ ★ ★ ★

Here is a case of a fine parador saddled with a not so pleasant city. Tortosa is large, unappealing and lacking in worthwhile sights. The parador, on the other hand, sits magisterially atop a hill commanding fine views of the city and countryside. It occupies a fortress that dates back to the time of the greatest calif, Abd er Rahman III. Later it became a Templar fort. Although the parador is 90% new building, it incorporates what remains of the older structures behind original fortress walls. Its style harmonizes well with the old remains. Best is the pool, against the old fortress walls, with panoramic views. With the exception of the dining room, the inside is modern. This allows guest rooms with balconies and views. They are decorated in simple patterns of some charm.

Dining

The dining room incorporates what remains of the Templar castle in the form of four lovely windows and three fireplaces below a beamed ceiling. It all feels medieval. The cooking combines Catalan and Valencian dishes. From the north comes a Spanish version of spaghetti with clams *(fedeo con almejas)*, from the south a *paella de mariscos* (shellfish). From Tortosa comes elvers in sauce *(menu)* and frogs' legs, along with fresh local fish, such as dorado and swordfish. The local wine is not memorable; a fixed-price menu of $20 is available.

Directions

From **Barcelona** take A-7 north then southwest for 171 km. From **Zaragoza** take N-232 southeast for 233 km to Vinarós, then N-340 north for 36 km. From **Valencia** take N-7 northeast for 137 km.

Paradors Nearby

Benicarló: 52 km	Alcañiz: 100 km
Cardona: 230 km	Vic: 262 km

PARADOR COSTA BLANCA

Avenida El Arenal, 2, Jávea, 03730
☎ *(96) 579 02 00, FAX (96) 579 03 08*
$125 per double; 65 rooms: 65 doubles

★ ★

The "White Coast" is named for its fine sand. Since good sand attracts humans like picnics attract ants, most of the Costa Blanca is overbuilt. In this context, Jávea fares better than most. An elevated old town still rings a 14th century fortified church while the new development clings to the harbor. Away on its own little peninsula, the parador is able to provide a feeling of isolation and naturalness. It lies at one end of a crescent beach, just across a waterway, on its own enclave. As a building the parador looks like a thousand other beach hotels, but a pleasant terrace and garden elevate it above many of the others. Rather spacious guest rooms provide all necessities and almost all have terraces over the sea. For all that, they remain just hotel rooms.

Dining

The dining room is large enough for 250 people, not an intimate place to say the least. A wall of sea windows provides the only interesting sight. But you are near Valencia, so the seafood will be a delight. Combinations with rice are the norm, from *arroz con costra* (with various meats and chick peas), to octopus cooked in its ink *(negre)* to familiar *paella*. Fish abound, but also a tasty meat cake *(pasteles de carne)*. Expect a bill of almost $20, plus drinks.

Alternative Dining

El Girasol   ★★★★

Drive back to Jávea, then south to Moraira in 15 km, continue 1.5 km past on the road to Calpe, ☎ *(96) 574 43 73.*

Save up for this one, it's a memorable experience. In the cozy dining room of this elegantly restored villa are served the best meals along the Costa Blanca, food that need not bow to any in the country. Fish are the stars, served with a French touch—expensive, but memorable. Try the shrimp with basil vinaigrette, or lamb chop with balsamic vinegar. What bowls us over, however, are the desserts, including sinful chocolate soufflé. It is not difficult to spend $60 per person. Closed off season and Nov. Credit Cards: A, D, M, V.

Monte Molar   ★★★

Get back to N-332 and go south for 26 km to just before Altea, where a sign directs a 1 km turn. ☎ *(96) 584 15 81.*

The restaurant is absolutely gorgeous and elegant, with a pretty terrace overlooking the sea. The food matches its surroundings—as memorable, though of course more expensive. For seafood, try the timbale of fish with asparagus; for meat, the magret of duck with mushrooms; and for fun, the snails with rice. Such elegance will cost about $50. Reservations are strongly advised. Closed Wed. off season, and from Dec. to Apr. 1. Credit Cards: A, D, M, V.

Directions

From **Madrid** take N-III east for 164 km to Honrubia, where A-31 speeds you to La Roda in 98 km and N-301 reaches the outskirts of Albacete in 37 km. From here N-430 branches in 81 km to put you on N-330 to **Alacant** in 90 km. Don't enter the city. Take A-7 east to exit 63 in 72 km where 11 km northeast to Sata on N-332, then 11 km east past Jávea brings the parador on its cape. From **Valencia** take A-7 south to exit 62 in 97 km, where a turn east through Denia, then around the cape brings the parador in 20 km. From **Barcelona** take A-16 southwest which becomes A-7 and reaches Valencia in 287 km. See the Valencia directions above. From **Granada** take A-90/ N-342 east for 192 km to Puerto Lumbreras, where N-15 goes northeast to **Murcia** in 85 km. Join A-7 which reaches exit 63 in 147 km. 11 km east to Sato on N-332, then 11 km east past Jávea brings the parador on its cape.

Paradors Nearby

El Saler: 92 km	Benicarló: 245 km	Teruel: 255 km
Albacete: 262 km	Alarcón: 278 km	

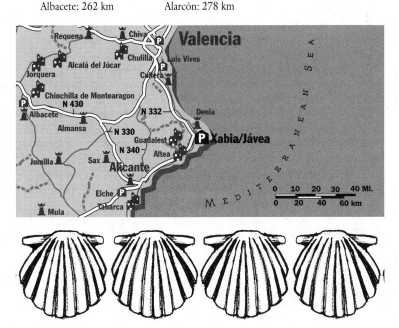

PARADOR COSTA BRAVA

Cala de Aiguablave, Aiguablave, 17255
☎ *(972) 62 21 62, FAX (972) 62 21 66*
$150 per double; 87 rooms: 18 single, 69 doubles

★ ★ ★ ★

This parador is set on as pretty a stretch of coast as there is—atop a densely wooded peninsula that separates a turquoise bay from the sea. As a building, the hotel is a long box that is light and spacious inside, defined with pastels. It takes every advantage of its situation with abundant windows to show off sea and iridescent bay. Guest rooms are larger than most and comfortable. Each offers a good view, but, for a few pesetas more, you can book one of six larger rooms with glorious bathrooms and exercise equipment in your own room. Other guests have to go downstairs to the gym. A path descends to a small beach on the bay, but a pool on the premises saves even that trouble.

Alternative Accommodations

Hotel Aigua Blava

Playa de Fornells, ☎ *(972) 62 20 58, FAX (972) 62 21 12. 85 rooms.*
The view is almost as lovely from the nearby Hotel Aigua Blava, situated on the bay. It's less luxurious but more charming and costs under $100.

Dining

The best architectural feature of the restaurant is a wall of windows presenting a glorious seascape. Since you've come for the sea, sample its products. Start with Catalan fish soup *(suquet de peix)*, graduate to either rice with octopus cooked in its ink *(arroz negro)* or a decent paella. Fresh fish, either lightly fried or broiled, can be delicate. For the wine, try a local Ampurdán and think about how the grapes were brought here by ancient Greeks over two millennia ago. A set-course meal is available for about $25, plus drinks.

Alternative Dining

Can Toni ★★★

C. Sant Martiria, 29 (in San Feliu, 29 km south on the coast road; well back from the beach, near the bus station), ☎ *(972) 32 10 26.*
Closed Mon. from Oct.–May.

Though the restaurant lacks grand style, the chef here is exceptionally talented and creative. For informality and superb food at reasonable prices, this is one of our favorites. Credit Cards: A, D, M, V.

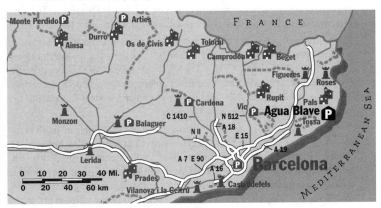

Directions

From **Barcelona** take A-17 north for 66 km to exit at Vidreres for a 53 km coastal run on C-253 through Palmos and Palafrugell. From **France** take A-17 south from the La Junquera crossing for 50 km to Gerona where C-252 east goes to La Bisbal in 27 km and C-255 goes further east to Aiguablava in 21 km.

Paradors Nearby

Vic: 177 km   Cardona: 233 km   Seo de Urgel: 245 km
Tortosa: 327 km   Benicarló: 360 km

Excursions

Begur offers a medieval castle. A 50 minute walk from Calella, 10 km south along the coast, brings the **Castell i Jardins de Cap Roig**, a fine botanical garden formed of a maze of flowers and tropical plants. (Open daily Mar.–Dec. 9 a.m.–9 p.m.; admission: 200 ptas.) Good ceramics are produced in **La Bisbal**, 12 km along C-255 on the way back toward Girona. The most unusual outing is to an ancient Greek town at **Empúries** 26 km up the coast to L'Escala, where a sign points along a paved road.

Empuries   ★

Hours open: Tues.–Sun. 10 a.m.–2 p.m. and 3–7 p.m. From the middle of Sept.–May open from Tues.–Sun. 10 a.m.–1 p.m. and 3–5 p.m. Closed Mon.

While the ruins are not extensive, neither are they abundant in Greece itself. The experience is heightened by the fact that the site, having drastically declined by the third century A.D. and abandoned since the eighth century, is not surrounded by modern buildings—thus freeing the imagination to humanize the stones. There are also remains of a Roman city, beaches and guides in togas to show you around.

Phoenicians settled first on this spot in the sixth century B.C. on what was then an offshore island, now joined to the mainland. Greeks arrived in the fourth century B.C. and built their *Neapolis* ("New Town") about an eighth of a mile south of that first settlement. It became the major Greek colony on the peninsula, from which both the grape and olive were introduced to Spain and western Europe. But the Greeks faded as upstart Rome grew aggressive.

The Greek city, lowest on the hill, is entered through a cyclopian gate south of the Museum. Immediately to the left stands its sacred precinct with remains of the Temple of Aesculapeus, the god of medicine. A tall watchtower rises, just north, from which lookouts could scan the sea. At its feet lie remains of the town cisterns, including a reconstructed water filter. Directly to the right of the gate run the colonnades of the Temple of Zeus Serapis, a combined Greek and Egyptian god of the sun and fertility. The town meeting place—*agora*—stands 100 yards north of this gate. Behind it is a reconstruction of the *stoa*, or roofed market. Ruins of a very early Christian basilica lie just to the north.

The extensive Roman town spreads up the hill and across a road. Much remains to be excavated, though two houses with mosaics have been cleared and are interesting studies as early versions of the typical patioed Spanish houses of today. The forum, lined by porticos, lies to the south of these houses. Temples and shops would have surrounded this plaza. An amphitheater can be discerned 100 yards further on. *Admission: 400 ptas. A helpful guidebook in English costs 500 ptas.*

PARADOR COSTA DEL AZAHAR

Avenida del Papa Luna,5, Benicarló, 12580
☎ *(964) 47 01 00, FAX (964) 47 09 34*
$95 per double; 108 rooms: 15 singles, 93 doubles

★ ★

Perfumed by acres of orange groves, the resorts of the Costa del Azahar begin 175 km south of Barcelona and stretch south past Valencia to the Cabo de la Nao, covering a distance of 260 km. These resorts are a mixed lot—some charming, some overdeveloped—but their sand beaches are the finest in Spain. Once attractive, Benicarló now is overbuilt, although it still retains a small port and decent beaches. The parador is modern and of no special distinction, but its gardens run down to the sea to produce a feeling of peaceful quiet. Tennis, billiards and a pool are provided along with palm trees that make most of us immediately relax.

Alternative Accommodations

Hostería del Mar

Carretera de Benicarló, Peñiscola (on the road to Benicarló, one km north of the peninsula), ☎ *(964) 48 06 00, FAX (964) 48 13 63. 85 rooms, plus one suite.*

Peñiscola is a more interesting village, only 7 km south on the coastal road, with better beaches and a more memorable place to stay in the Hostería del Mar. This hotel is affiliated with the national paradors and outdoes most of the modern ones in style. It's located inside castle grounds, so it's perched high with fabulous views. Inside, white wall and dark wood lend a pleasant Castilian look. Tennis is available.

Dining

Although the decor of the dining room makes no impression, a buffet table heaped with products of the sea soon gains attention. On the sea, near Valencia, the kitchen focuses on grilled shrimp, mullet either roasted or in mariniere sauce, and rice in multiple incarnations, not a bad lot for about $20, plus drinks.

Directions

Head to the water, next to the port beside the sea wall.

Paradors Nearby

Tortosa: 52 km	Alcañiz: 145 km	Valencia: 153 km
Teruel: 234 km	Jávea: 245 km	Cardona: 264 km

Excursions

Peñiscola, on a small peninsula (which is what the town's name means) off the coastal road 7 km south, snuggles tiny whitewashed houses against a solemn castle on a hill. Cars are not allowed in the narrow twisting streets. The village is charming, and the castle, which was the home of the antipope Luna during his exile in the 15th century, is worth a look. What is less charming is the stretch of high-rises that line the beach on either side of the peninsula. However, finer, whiter sand beaches do not exist elsewhere in Europe and run for miles.

PARADOR DE ARGÓMANIZ

Carretera N-1, km 363, Argómaniz, 01192
☎ *(945) 28 22 00, FAX (945) 28 28 22*
$90 per double; 54 rooms: 54 doubles
★ ★ ★

This parador is a find indeed. It was good enough for Napoleón to spend a night, on his way to capture Vitoria, so it will probably do for most of us. It started as a little 17th century palace built by the prime minister of Felipe IV (Valázquez benefactor). Now it is a parador full of pleasant surprises you wouldn't expect from the plain oblong exterior, lightened only by a fancy family crest of the Larrea's. On entering you are faced with as grand a columned doorway as you will ever see, followed by a spacious lobby and equally spacious sitting rooms. Guest rooms wait in the back in two modern wings. They are large, with sitting areas by windows that take advantage of nice views. True, the place needs sprucing up, but it provides a worn charm even in its less than perfect state that no modern buildings can offer, along with the knowledge that you've made a real discovery.

Dining

You will love the dining room, too. It's in the attic of the palace, but some clever person thought to expose the timbering that supports the roof to create more grandeur than the usual attic. The only complaint is that it is too large. Food ranges over specialties from both Navarre and the Basques, which means that it is innovative and very good. Here you can try snails in tomato sauce *(caracoles)*, potatoes with *chorizo* (sausage), beans with ham *(habas)*, peppers stuffed with baby squid *(pimientos del chipirones)*, angler-fish in green sauce with clams and shrimp *(rape en salsa verde)*, in addition to a nice trout or roast lamb. Local cheese is excellent. For the wine, since you are near Rioja, treat yourself to a Salceda or Arana reserve. A set-course meal is offered for under $25, plus drinks.

Directions

From **Madrid** take N-1 north for 238 km to just short of Burgos where A-1, for speed, or N-1 for price, goes east for 86 km. At this point N-1 is your only option for the final 26 km to Gasteiz/Vitoria and for the remaining 12 km east to Km 363 where a sign points to the parador, 1 km away. From **Burgos** take N-1 or A-1 east for 86 km, where only N-1 continues the final 38 km to Gasteiz/Vitoria and beyond to Km 363 where a sign points to the parador, 1 km away. From **Zaragoza** take A-68 or N-232 northwest for 86 km where A-68 forks to A-15 and N-232 forks to N-121. Continue for 71 km to Irunea/Pamplona and follow the Pamplona directions. From **Pamplona**/Irunea take A-15 north west for 19 km to exit 6 where N-1 west reaches Km 363 and a sign for the parador in 57 km.

Paradors Nearby

Sto. Domingo: 75 km	Santillana: 85 km	Olite: 120 km
Hondarribia: 125 km	Sos del Rey: 140 km	Calahorra: 150 km

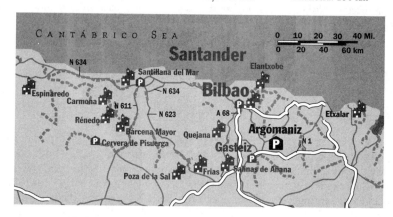

Excursions

You are well situated to tour a variety of sights. Haro, the capital of **Rioja**'s vineyards lies 54 km away, by a leg west along N-1 to Gasteiz/Vitoria, then south along N-232. See the description under Sto. Domingo de la Calzada in this chapter. Pamplona of the running of the bulls waits 77 km east along N-1, though it offers little to see when the bulls aren't there. The elegant ancient monastery of **Olite ★★**, however, is nice all year. It lies 75 km east to Pamplona along N-1 then 48 km south along N-121, and is described under its parador below in this chapter. Lovely renaissance **Santillana del Mar ★** is west on N-1, skirting Gasteiz/Vitoria to join N-68 north in 36 km and reach the outskirts of Bilbao in 42 km, where A-8 goes west to Santander in 100 km for a final leg west of 22 km on A-87 and a signed connecting road. It is described in the Northern Spain chapter. The splendid sights of **Burgos ★★★** (also described in the Northern Spain chapter) lie 135 km west along N-1.

PARADOR DE LA SEU D'URGELL

Santo Domingo, s/n, Seu d'Urgell, 25700
☎ (973) 35 20 00, FAX (973) 35 23 09
$95 per double; 78 rooms: 6 singles, 71 doubles, 1 suite

★ ★ ★

Although this parador is special, it is located in a part of Spain difficult to reach, and without sights spectacular enough to make a trip worthwhile. The best reason to stay here is to break a trip from France after stopping at the duty-free shops of Andorra, or, simply to get away from it all in mountain surroundings. Although modern outside, the hotel makes clever use of the remains of a 14th-century convent on its site by building itself around and over it. The ancient cloister was restored and a roof put on it which acts as a skylight. All that light allows bedecking the elegant arches of the cloister with hanging vines to create a warm, historic glow. This is some lounge! The rest of the hotel is similarly innovative, and dedicated to bringing the outdoors inside, including a Spanish rarity—an indoor pool. Guest rooms are full of wood to give them warm glows.

Dining

Continuing the motif of the hotel, the dining room is covered with a pyramidal skylight as a ceiling. Again, this encourages the arranging of plants for color, so the room echoes the older lounge with crisp modern arches and

Bauhaus chairs. The cuisine is Catalan and special. How about a snail casserole with fresh mint, or pickled fresh trout, or stew of wild boar? A set-price menu of $20 is available. The wine list ranges from Catalans, to Riojas to French.

Alternative Accommodations and Dining

El Castell   ★★

In Castellciutat, at km 129, 1 km south on N-260, ☎ *(973) 36 05 12.*

Although the food here is outstanding, there are rooms for rent as well in sumptuous, modern guest rooms with balcony views at $100. Either way, try this kitchen. A sauce of tomatoes, mozzarella and olives livens a fresh red mullet. Wood roasted sea bass is served with vegetables, and baby lamb chops with a purée of potatoes. A set-course menu runs about $45. Credit Cards: A, D, M, V.

Directions

From **Barcelona** take A-18 north, which becomes C-7411 and reaches Puigcerdà in 154 km. Take N-260 west for 51 km. (25 km can be saved by cutting straight to Bellver de Cerdanaya immediately after the Super-Molina tunnel.) From **Zaragoza** take A-2 east for 144 km to ring the north of **Lérida** and pick up C-1313 north for 132 km. From **Perpignan** in France take N-116 west for 102 km to Bourg-Madame at the border, then N-260 east in Spain for 51 km.

Paradors Nearby

Cardona: 95 km	Artíes: 125 km	Vielha: 135 km
Vic: 170 km	Aiguablava: 245 km	Alcañiz: 270 km

Sights

Across the plaza from the parador is the **Cathedral of Santa Maria**, the oldest in Catalan. Finished by the 12th century, it is a remarkable relic from olden times. The cloisters are reverential and open into an even older, 11th century church of Sant Miquel.

Excursions

Andorra for duty-free shopping stands 10 km north on N-145.

PARADOR DE TERUEL

Carretera de Zaragoza, s/n, Teruel, 44080
☎ *(978) 60 25 53, FAX (978) 60 86 12*
$80 per double; 60 rooms: 58 doubles, 2 suites

★ ★ ★

Come if you crave Mudéjar art, a complex blend of pattern on pattern created by Moorish craftsmen in the service of Spanish patrons. That is the chief treasure of the city. The parador is a modern interpretation of that same aesthetic and pleasantly situated a mile from town amid gardens with tennis courts, pool and quiet. The tone is set in the ornate lobby with carved ceiling. An enclosed terrace invites leisurely drinks. Guest rooms are bare, done in ochres and browns, with attractive bedspreads. It's a pleasant place to stay, but nothing special.

Dining

The dining room is attractively done in muted colors with soft lighting for a change. *Chicken chilindrón* (with red peppers and tomatos) is featured, along with a tasty veal stew *(el castellar)*. Local ham is good, as is the cheese, along with always tasty chorizo sausage. There are no local wines, however, of merit. A set-course meal can be had for under $25.

Directions

From **Madrid** take N-111 southeast for 81 km to join N-400 east for 84 km to **Cuenca**, where it turns south and changes designation to N-420. Continue for 151 km to Torrebaja, where N-330 north reaches Teruel in 34 km. The parador is 2 km north on N-234. From **Zaragoza** take N-330 southwest for 86 km to Daroca, then N-234 south for 96 km to see the parador 2 km before the city of Teruel. From **Valencia** take either N-340 or A-7 north for 23 km to the interchange before Sagunto where N-234 goes north for 124 km to Teruel. Continue on N-234 for 2 km past the town.

Paradors Nearby

Cuenca: 153 km	Alcañiz: 162 km	Saler: 163 km
Siguenza: 185 km	Alarcón: 208 km	Benicarló: 234 km

Sights

Teruel is blessed by its old Mudéjar towers because Christians and Moors lived together here longer than in most of Spain.

Parking is available against the bay of hills that cradles the eastern end of town off Ronda de Ambeles

The cathedral sits smack in the center of town, fronted by a long plaza. Although remodeling has ruined most of the 13th century original, one original treasure was recently revealed inside. A 13th century ceiling of artesonado painted wood is now stripped of late Gothic frou frou. A retable from three centuries later is notable for its lively portraits. *(Open daily 9 a.m.–2 p.m. and 5–10 p.m.)*

The Museo Provincial, in back of the cathedral, is worth a visit for its Renaissance façade as much as for the local ceramics displayed. *(Open Tues.–Fri. from 10 a.m. to 2 p.m. and from 4–7 p.m. Open weekends 10 a.m.–2 p.m.)*

At the end of the long cathedral plaza, go two blocks right, after which retrace your steps two blocks left of the cathedral plaza and one more right for two of Teruel's Mudéjar towers. Both date from the 13th century, are festooned with patterned bricks and ceramic applique. Each contains a belfry at the top, for that was their function.

PARADOR DE VIC

Junto al pantano de Sau, s/n, Vic, 08500
☎ *(93) 888 72 11, FAX (93) 888 73 11*
$95, double; 36 rooms: 6 singles, 30 doubles

★ ★ ★ ★

T his parador allows communing with nature a short distance from bustling Barcelona. It sits on a bluff above a large lake created by a reservoir. Mountains in the distance, forests all around, blue lake below—all contribute to the serenity, although the parador itself is hewn of massive stone—functional but not aesthetic. Inside, a stained-glass skylight covers the lobby to cast blue and orange light and create an eerie rather than a restful mood. More successful is a sitting room with cozy fireplace and a bar overlooking the lake. In this parador the best feature is the front guest rooms with terraces over the lawn, pool and lake. There are tennis courts amid a pleasant lawn and garden.

Dining

The dining room is someone's idea of grand, but not ours. Large, with lots of marble, chandeliers and modern murals, it would do well for a Long Island wedding reception, but not for dining. The specialty is *olla*, a stew of garbanzo beans, cold cuts and beef. It's hearty. Also hearty is the smoked pork. Otherwise the offerings are a familiar list of lamb and chicken. But look for fresh trout. Wines cover Rioja and more local Catalans, such as the always enjoyable Penedes. A set-course menu costs under $20.

Directions

From **Barcelona** take N-152 north to Vic in 67 km. In town, stay on N-152 until 1 km after crossing the river Mèder where an interchange enables an exit onto La Sagrada Familia. Continue straight through the impending traffic circle, where the street now is named first, Ronda de Francisco Camprodon, then Av. de Sant Bernat Calbó before finally feeding into C-153 toward Roda de Ter and Olot. Look for signs in 5 km for the pantano de Sau and the parador, 10 km east.

Paradors Nearby

Cardona: 101 km   Seo de Urgel: 166 km   Aiguablava: 177 km
Tortosa: 262 km   Arties: 290 km   Benicarló: 295 km

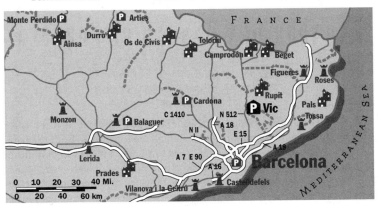

Sights

Vic is worth a visit. All its sights are concentrated in a central core of the city around the **cathedral**. What remains of the 11th-century original cathedral is an elegant belfry. But inside, the modern replacement walls are covered by are a series of dramatic paintings by the Catalan artist José María Sert. The original set was destroyed in the Civil War but Sert repainted them in 1945. The retable, however, is 15th-century fine. (*Open Tues.-Sun. from 10 a.m.–3 p.m. Admission: 200 ptas.*)

Opposite the cathedral is the **Episcopal Museum**, displaying one of the finest collections of Romanesque and Gothic art. It is not to be missed. (*Open Mon.– Sat. from 10 a.m.–3 p.m. In summer also open 4–6 p.m. Admission: 200 ptas.*)

PARADOR DON GASPAR DE PORTOLÁ

Carretera Baqueira, s/n, Arties, 25599
☎ *(973) 64 08 01, FAX (973) 64 10 01*
$95 per double; 40 rooms: 38 doubles, 2 suites

★ ★ ★ ★

Three paradors congregate in a 50 mile radius. The one at Bielsa is for lovers of mountains and nature. It's in a huge national park. Both the parador here at Arties and one nearby in Vielha sit in mountains too, but meant for skiers. How to choose between those two? Vielha is a high-tech, largish, modern place, Arties is older, in part, and smaller. It's your pick. (See descriptions of the other two paradors below under their own headings.) Arties is a quiet old town, mostly given over to skiing, but with mountains nearby for walking and spotting wild goats, chamois and boars. The village contains a parador that looks like a Swiss chalet, although it's actually built around the 18th century house of the man who founded Mission San Diego in California. Most of the parador, however is a modern addition whose inside feels spacious and clean, with occasional antique touches. Guest rooms are similarly spare, though roomy.

Dining

The dining room is bright and features a mural we could do without. The room connotes an appropriate light wood feeling. You can begin with a refreshing clear broth *(olla aranesa)*. We recommend the oh-so-fresh mountain trout. Otherwise, there is quite a selection, from octopus and rice cooked in the ink, a stew or soup (depending on your definition) of anglerfish and shellfish *(suquet de rape y marisco)*, an interesting rabbit with snails *(conejo con caracoles)*, pheasant, venison, or special patés. Try chocolate truffle or local flan for dessert. A nice selection of Catalan wines are available. The food is good and reasonable at $20.

Alternative Dining

Casa Irene   ★★

Hotel Valartiés, Plaza Mayor, 3 ☎ *(973) 64 43 64.*

This little village contains a genuine treasure of cuisine. Although the parador does a good job, it does not attain the subtlety or inventiveness of Irene. Try the foie gras or the beef with foie gras sauce. And how does bass with sweet onion and vinegar sound? You will pay more than at the parador—expect a bill of $30+. Closed Mon.

Credit Cards: A, D, M, V

Directions

From **Barcelona** take A-7 west for 22 km to join N-II. Go west for 162 km to Lérida where N-230 goes north for 162 km to Vielha, and a jag 8 km east reaches Arties. From **Zaragoza** take N-330 north for 70 km to Huesca, then N-240 east for 51 km to Barbastro, N-123 northeast for 38 km to Benabarre where N-230 goes east then north for 98 km to Vielha and a 8 km jag east reaches Arties.

Paradors Nearby

Vielha: 7 km	Seo de Urgel: 124 km	Bielsa: 170 km
Cardona: 205 km	Hondarribia: 306 km	Sos del Rey: 347 km

Sights

This is ski country. **Val d'Aran** is international and sophisticated, a magnificent glacier-ringed valley. **Tuca-Betrèn** is the older and smaller of the area's two resorts, offering 18 slopes and trails. Modern **Baqueiria-Beret** is huge, with 41 slopes and trails, 19 lifts and helicopter skiing available. The French love it, and they have some nice slopes of their own; King Juan Carlos does too.

PARADOR DUQUES DE CARDONA

Castillo de Cardona, Cardona, 08261
☎ *(93) 869 12 75, FAX (93) 869 16 36*
$110, double; 60 rooms: 7 singles, 52 doubles, 1 suite

★ ★ ★ ★

Atop a steep hill, surrounded by massive walls, sits a monolithic, almost cubical fortress heaping building on top of building. It's an impressive sight. Parts are as old as the 11th century, although most date to the 18th. When you pass through the walls, you're faced with a courtyard containing an elegant little romanesque porch. Then you go inside to the more "ordinary" 18th century. Actually the interior is rather nicely restored with some genuine feeling for the original aesthetic. Guest rooms vary from spectacular suites to still pleasant rooms. More antiques are spread around this parador than most, including some wonderful old headboards and fourposters. Some of the rooms, however, feel cramped.

Dining

The restaurant is formed of a long vaulted tunnel that makes for soft lighting and intimacy, while enjoying cooking that surpasses the average parador. Veggie fanciers will relish *escudella*, a stew of legumes and greens. Fish fanciers will sop up every drop of *suquet*, a fish stew similar to bouillabaisse. Also on the menu is an interesting rabbit with snails *(conejo con caracoles)*. For dessert savor a smooth creme caramel *(crema catalana)*. Catalan wines are featured; consider a Penares or even a champagne. Set-course meals cost $20, plus drinks.

Directions

From **Barcelona** take A-18 north for 37 km to the exit for Manresa, where C-1410 toward Solsona reaches Cardona in 25 km. From **Zaragoza** take A-2 east for 144 km to exit 6 and Lérida, where C-1313 goes northeast toward Balaguer and beyond for 70 km to Ponts. C-1410 east toward Solsona is picked up 19 km further for the final 52 km. From **Madrid** take N-II for 316 km to Zaragoza and follow the directions above. From **France** get to the tiny Pyrenees country of **Andorra** where N-145 for south 20 km to Seu d'Urgell allows a turn onto C-1313 for 49 km to just past Oliana and a final leg east on C-1410 toward Solsona reaches Cardona in 52 km.

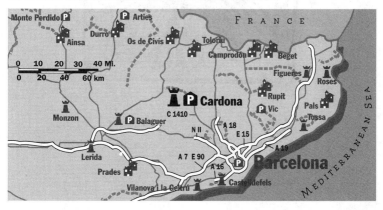

Paradors Nearby

Vic: 96 km	Seo de Urgel: 100 km	Artíes: 205 km
Vielha: 212 km	Tortosa: 231 km	Aiguablava: 233 km

Sights

As the arriving tourists demonstrate, you are staying in the most interesting sight in Cardona. Roam the castle grounds to find a tower from the 2nd century and an 11th century church. Its inside is elegant. The castle overlooks a hill of salt still mined as it was in Roman times.

Excursions

Barcelona, only 80 km away, is too close to miss. Reverse the directions to Cardona above, and see its description above under its own heading.

PARADOR EL EMPERADOR

Plaza de Armas, Hondarribia, 20280
☎ *(943) 64 55 00, FAX (943) 64 21 53*
$115 per double; 36 rooms: 6 singles, 30 doubles
★ ★ ★ ★ ★

Hondarribia, called *Fuentarrabia* in Spanish, has it all. There are stately mansions, colorfully painted houses, a charming yet serious port and a lovely stretch of beach. A fine restaurant stands in the town and the best restaurants in Spain lie close enough for lunch or dinner. And since this is the border with France, you can eat French in Hendaye, St. Jean de Luz or Biarritz as well. The parador is wonderful. It's a small castle that goes back to the 10th century, although its present form was due to Emperor Carlos V in the 16th. Carlos slept here, as did Ferdinand and Isabella, so it should prove suitable. You'll agree as soon as you pass the severe facade through a small doorway to step into a stunning lobby lined with arches, presided over by a ceiling 50 feet above, and cozily furnished with elegant wicker. There are suits of armor, tapestries and a cannon. In fact everything is massive and magisterial. The walls are nine feet thick, which is why the window in guest rooms lies behind an alcove. Ceilings are stone, the floors polished wood, and the spaces are grand. Abundant taste was exercised in the choice of both decoration and furniture. This is one of the great paradors!

Alternative Accommodations
Wonderful though it is, the parador is not the only special hotel in this village.

Obispo
It is located in the Pl. del Obispo, ☎ *(943) 64 54 00, FAX (943) 64 23 86. 14 rooms.*

Similar in massiveness, but two centuries older, is the Obispo, and it costs $20 less.

Pampinot

Pl. Mayor, 5, ☎ (943) 64 06 00, FAX (943) 64 51 29. 8 rooms.

For elegance galore, there is the Pampinot, a mansion from the 18th century. Marie Teresa stayed here the night before she married the King of France. Extravagant "French" decor is the theme. Bedrooms are more tasteful than at the other choices, although bathrooms are spartan.

Dining

The bad news concerning the dining room is that only breakfast is served. That's a pity, because it is a lovely room with views of the dramatic lobby. So, enjoy your breakfast, then savor the abundant options below for lunch or dinner.

Alternative Dining

Ramón Roteta   ★ ★ ★

In Irun, 3 km south of town, ☎ (943) 64 16 63.

Lodged in an elegant mansion, this restaurant serves food elevated both in style and price. Poached eggs with truffles are sublime, and rice with vegetables and clams is simply outstanding. A fixed-price menu holds the cost to about $30, but a la carte is more. Closed Sun. night and Tues., and the second half of both Feb. and Nov. Credit Cards: A, D, M, V

Arraunlauri   ★

Paseo Butrón, 6, ☎ (943) 64 15 81.

The ambiance is relaxed, the seafood first rate, and the price about $20. No, it's not a cathedral to cuisine, like the other options, but it's mighty good. Credit Cards: A, D, M, V.

20 km west lies the culinary center of the country, Donostia. Here you can choose among the finest cooking offered by Spain.

Arzak   ★ ★ ★ ★ ★

Kalea Alto de Miracruz, 21 (east of the city, on the way to Hondarribia), ☎ (943) 27 84 65, FAX (943) 27 27 53.

The only question about this restaurant is whether it's the first or second best in all Spain. When you eat here, however, the issue seems settled in Arzak's favor. It was Chef Jean Arzak who created Basque *nueva cucina*, and he presents a menu of dishes every one of which is innovative and perfect in its way. To start, blow the budget on crayfish or save a little with fish soup that will spoil you for this dish forever. Chef Arzak's renowned favorites are listed on the back menu. Save room for orange flavored flan. Considering the succulence of the food and the elegance of service, prices are correct, though, of course, very expensive in the $60 range (without drinks). Reservations at least weeks in advance are a must. Closed Sun. night, Mon., the last half of June and the first 3 weeks of Nov. Credit Cards: A, D, M, V.

Akelarre ★ ★ ★ ★

Paseo del Padre Orcolaga, 56, in the barrio de Iqueldo (east of the city on the slopes of Mount Iqueldo), ☎ *(943) 21 20 52, FAX (943) 21 92 68.*

Anywhere else this restaurant would stand above all others, but Donostia has Arzak too. Views are exceptional from the slope of Mount Igueldo and the food is sublime. Start with mushrooms and asparagus spears. Some justly rave about the *lubina* (sea bass with green peppers), but the *salmonetes* (red mullet) create a choice between two utterly wonderful options. Prices are in the expensive range, but 15% below those at Arzak. Reservations are absolutely required. Closed Sun. night, Mon., Feb. and the first week of Oct. Credit Cards: A, D, M, V.

Panier Fleuri ★ ★ ★

Paseo de Salamanca, 1 (at the mouth of the Urumea River), ☎ *(943) 42 42 05, FAX (943) 42 42 05.*

Since the chef was recently named the best in the country, this restaurant would be a standout in any part of Spain, but here the competition keeps every establishment on its toes. There is a definite French accent to the Basque food here, but every dish is utterly delectable. We still can taste the sole with spinach. That, along with tuna tartar and a splendid mullet, make it difficult to save room for an exquisite pear dessert. As with the preceding, prices climb over $40 and reservations are required. Closed Sun. night, Wed. and the first two weeks in June. Credit Cards: A, D, M, V.

Directions

The fastest route from **Madrid** is to take N-I north for 238 km to **Burgos**, then A-1 east for 83 km to the intersection with A-86, which intersects with A-8 in 70 km and reaches Hondarribia/Fuentarrabia in a final 110 km. From **Zaragoza** take A-68 northwest for 86 km to the intersection with A-15 which passes **Pamplona** in 71 km. At exit 5 join N-1214, which first heads east, then north to Hondarribia/Fuentarrabia in 97 km.

Parados Nearby

Argómaniz: 129 km	Olite: 156 km	Sos del Rey: 173 km
Sto. Domingo: 204 km	Calahora: 226 km	Santillana: 273 km

Sights

The Plaza de Armas fronting the parador is lined with colorful houses. Walk the cobbled stones of Calle Mayor to the sea. The lighthouse at Cabo Higuer, 4 km north, provides glorious sunset views.

Excursions

Take a splendid 17 km drive to elegant **Donostia/San Sebastián** along the Jaizkibel Road heading west of town, passing pretty little ports and offering spectacular views of the bay.

Donostia ★★★ (*San Sebastián*, in Spanish) nestles between two small mountains that face a bay of elegant proportions, looking something like a scallop shell. It is a *Belle Époque* resort, much frequented by the French. Resting atop a hill at the foot of Mount Igueldo, the **Miramar Palace** is under renovation today, but its fine gardens are open for strolling. The palace faces the mile-long curve of **La Concha beach** that must be counted among the most beautiful in the world. At the west end of the beach towers Monte Igueldo, with splendid views from the summit. At the east end stands Monte Urgull, at the tip of a peninsula. A lovely promenade lines the length of the beach for pleasant walks. Most sights, however, cluster near Monte Urgull.

Where La Concha beach ends on the east, a garden grows around the present **Ayuntamiento**. The building was formerly the city casino, built before the turn of the century. But, during the time of Franco when games of chance were banned, the unused structure was taken over by the city. Inside it is a glittering mass of marble and glass. At the end of the gardens of this Parque Alderdi Eder, the elegant shopping street of **Av. de la Libertad** runs east-west. Two blocks north of the park, and one block east, is the main square of the town, the **Pl. de la Constitución**. It is a friendly place, busy with groups of strollers. Some balconies still retain numbers from the days when bullfights were held in the plaza and balconies were rented to fans. Three blocks north of the Pl. de la Constitución is the city museum—**Museo San**

Telmo ★. Formerly it was a monastery; now it houses a nice collection of Basque art through the ages, along with paintings by El Greco, Goya and others. *(Open in summer Mon.–Sat. 9 a.m.–9 p.m.; Sun. 9 a.m.–1 p.m. Other seasons, 10 a.m.–1 p.m. and 3:30–7 p.m.; Sun. 10 a.m.–1 p.m. Admission: free.)*

Beside the museum stands the 18th-century church of **Santa María**, with a sober interior and fanciful chapels. A steep path northwest of the church leads upwards to the fortress of **Castillo de Santa Cruz del la Mota**, which guards the summit of Monte Urgull. The castle, from the 16th century, illustrates how buildings changed from secure places of lodging for important persons to fortresses designed to withstand heavy bombardment by cannon. A military museum inside provides little of interest.

Proceeding east, then north, from the Museo San Telmo brings the **Paseo Nuevo**, an attractive promenade around the peninsula of Urgull. At its end is the **Palacio del Mar**, an oceanographic museum. *(Open daily 10 a.m.–1:30 p.m. and 3:30–7:30 p.m., to 8 p.m. in summer; closed Mon. from the middle of Sept. to the middle of May. Admission: 300 ptas.)* East of the museum, in three short blocks, is the Urumea River, spanned by four ornate **art deco bridges** from the turn of the century. Near the first of these, the Puente de Kursaal, a park surrounds the **Victoria Eugenia Theater** and the **María Cristina Hotel**, both Victorian palace-like structures from early in our century.

PARADOR FERNANDO DE ARAGÓN

Arquitecto Sáinz de Vicuña, 1, Sos del Rey Católico, 50680
 (948) 88 80 110, FAX (948) 88 81 00
$95 per double; 65 rooms: 6 singles, 57 doubles, 2 suites

★ ★ ★

Those who make this trip are generally glad they did. This is a sleepy little village of under 1000 that had one early moment in the sun, then remained medieval so completely that the entire village has been declared a national monument. Its moment in the sun? It was the birthplace of Ferdinand who married Isabella. Sos is an almost holy site for the Spanish, so when it came to placing a parador there was a large problem. As an historic village, no old buildings could be altered, yet a new building would ruin the unique homogeneity. One of the great architects of the country thus designed a completely modern building in 1979 so perfectly in the style of the others that it could almost be mistaken for an original. Care was lavished on the choice of materials and their workmanship. Nothing fancy, just good taste. Guest rooms are terra-cotta tiled, with lovely "folk" bedspreads covering iron and brass beds, an antique touch in a modern hotel. Those on the second floor have sitting areas, while those on the third incorporate balconies. Opt for the view.

Dining

The restaurant sits on the top floor for views. Otherwise it is cozy and comfortable with nice linen and leather chairs. Here you sample the food of

Aragón. You can have either chicken or lamb *chilindrón* (with red pepper, onion and tomato), rabbit with snails *(conejo con caracoles)* or roast veal *(ternaco asado)*. For a vegetable side dish, try the fennel *(hinojos)*. Wines range over local Aragonese bottles, such as Cariñena and Campo de Borja, and Riojas. A fixed-price dinner is offered for under $20.

Directions

From **Madrid** take N-II northeast for 153 km to Meninaceli where N-111 goes to Soria in 75 km more. At **Soria** take N-122 east for 55 km to Ágreda where N-113 reaches N-15 north in 41 km. At exit 4 take N-240 southeast for 28 km to A-127 south for 19 km. From **Barcelona** take A-2 north then west for 296 km to circle **Zaragoza** and pick up A-68 north to fork onto A-15 in 86 km and continue to exit 4 in 71 km. Take N-240 southeast for 28 km to A-127 south for 19 km. From **Burgos** take N-1 east for 86 km to join N-124 north for 16 km where it forks to N-I to circle **Gasteiz/Vitoria** and heads east for 82 km to A-15 south. Fork onto N-240 southeast at exit 4 in 33 km. In 33 km take A-127 south for 24 km.

Paradors Nearby

Olite: 15 km	Calahorra: 121 km	Argómaniz: 139 km
Hondarribia: 173 km	Sto. Domingo: 192 km	Bielsa: 304 km

Sights

In 1452 Ferdinand the Catholic was born in Sos, the second son of a second son of the King of Aragón. He stood two removed from any chance at the throne. Through implausible circumstances he became king soon after marrying the young Isabella, who, equally improbably, inherited a throne from which she was twice removed. The rest is familiar history.

Wander the village filled with houses so old they are sunken, noting family crests on doorways. Cobbled streets and alleys lead to the **Palacio de los Sade**, where Ferdinand was born. Mementos of the King are inside. In the small Plaza Mayor stands an imposing **town hall** from the 16th century, with sweeping wood eaves. The **Loja** (bourse) incorporates wide arches to shelter commercial dealings. Through a vaulted passageway Romanesque **San Esteban** is reached, with fine statues around the door. Inside are frescoes from the 14th century, lovely carved capitals, a Renaissance gallery and a haunting 12th century figure of Christ.

PARADOR LA CONCORDIA

Castillo de los Calatravos, s/n, Alcañiz, 44600
☎ *(978) 83 04 00, FAX (978) 83 03 66*
$110 per double; 12 rooms: 2 singles, 10 doubles

★ ★ ★

Far from the madding crowd, this ancient castle overlooks a rolling plain and quaint village. Its castle tower goes back to the 12th century, the chapel to the 14th, which makes the prince's palace in which the parador is lodged the new kid on the block, for it was added in the 18th century. What is truly special about this historic parador is that the remodeling did not try to cram as many guests as possible inside, so the halls, the lobby, in fact all areas, are grand in spaciousness as well as in style. Here you can, as they say, feel like royalty for a night. This is a special place to stay. Guest rooms are unusually large, and although not particularly palatial, tastefully decorated.

Note: the parador closes from December 18 through January.

Dining

A lovely beamed ceiling contributes to the intimacy of the rich dining room. Here you can taste the cuisine of Aragón, which means a lot of meat. The chicken can be stewed, as in *pollo al chilindrón,* although roast birds are available. Stews include lamb, as in *Cordero a la pastora* or *ternasco asado a lo pobre. Arroz a la Aragonesa* features rabbit cooked with the rice. A set-course dinner is offered for $25, plus drinks.

Directions

From **Madrid** take A-2/N-II east for 240 km to just past Calatayud where C-221 goes east for 117 km through Cariña, Belchite and Azalla, from which N-252 reaches Alcañiz in 32 km. From **Barcelona** take A-7/A-2 southwest for 180 km to Tortosa where C-235 goes north, then west for 67 km to Valderrobres from which C-231 reaches Alcañiz in 38 km.

Parados Nearby

Tortosa: 100 km	Benicarló: 160 km	Teruel: 169 km
Calahorra: 227 km	Olite: 244 km	Soria: 250 km

PARADOR LUIS VIVES

El Saler, 46012
☎ *(96) 161 11 86, FAX (96) 162 70 16*
$125, double; 58 rooms: 57 doubles, 1 suite

★ ★ ★ ★

This one is for golfers and/or those who want miles of windswept beach all to themselves (well, with about 100 other guests). The hotel sits on a thin spit of land that divides the ocean from a huge fresh water lagoon. Around the hotel flows one of Spain's prettiest and most challenging 18-hole courses (those sea breezes don't help the golf though). The parador itself is modern, in an almost Bauhaus style, a self-contained resort with a pool, tennis courts and soccer field. The ocean is a stone's throw away lined by a beach that stretches to infinity. Guest rooms are large, attractive and all have views.

Dining

The dining room leaves something to be desired, however, both in appearance and food. Best is the local specialty—rice dishes in great variety. There is rice with saffron and shellfish *(paella marinara)*, with shellfish and chicken *(paella)*, with octopus cooked in its own ink *(negre)*, with fish *(pescados)*, and with hosts of vegetables. Set-course meals run $20, plus drinks.

Alternative Dining

Óscar Torrijos ★ ★ ★

In Valencia: Dr. Sumsi, 4 (6 blocks west and 4 blocks south of the train station) ☎ *(96) 373 29 49.*

This is our pick for Valencia's best. Dignified, almost "English" in feel, the decor sets the tone for precisely orchestrated food. This is the place to sample Valencian rice dishes at their best. Here, too, you can try some inventive combinations, such as rice with anglerfish and artichokes (arroz de rape y alcachofas). For dessert go for warmed raspberries with ice cream. The wine list is choice. Closed Sun. and from the middle of Aug. to the middle of Sept. Credit Cards: A, D, M, V.

Directions

From **Madrid** take N-III southeast for 332 km to Valencia. After the airport comes a traffic interchange along the Rio Tuia canal; take V-30 heading toward the port. Take the last exit before the port south on V-15 which arrives at the parador in 19 km. From **Barcelona** take A-7, which first heads north, then consistently southwest for 353 km to Valencia. In Valencia a major interchange allows you to take Av. Cardinal Benlloch, which leads to an exit for V-15 in a few blocks. V-15 arrives at the parador in about 20 km.

Paradors Nearby

Jávea: 92 km	Bemocarçó: 153 km	Teruel: 163 km
Alarcón: 186 km	Tortosa: 205 km	Albacete: 209 km

Excursions

Valencia ★ is near and worth a visit. Follow signs for "Centro" to the Pl. De la Reina and the Cathedral.

Cathedral ★

Pl. de la Reina, ☎ *(96) 391 81 27.*

Hours open: daily 10 a.m.–1 p.m. and 4–6 p.m. (in winter for the morning hours only).
Most of the cathedral was built in the 14th and 15th centuries, the Gothic era. Plateresque and baroque decorations that were applied later to the interior as in so many Spanish churches, have been removed to leave the simpler Gothic original. The main facade is a strange bird—remodeled in the early 18th century in a Gothic style to blend with the interior. More striking is the adjoining octagonal Gothic tower, called the Miguelete, with a pierced upper story lined with tracery. It is unique.

Inside, stripped of decoration, the revealed Gothic superstructure seems plain. The first chapel on the right with elegant vaulting is the original chapterhouse. On its altar stands a small purple agate cup surrounded by alabaster reliefs. According to legend, this is the Holy Grail used by Christ at the Last Supper. Indeed it is an old cup, certainly dating to Roman times, that had been venerated for centuries in northern Catalonia before its donation to the cathedral. The chains nearby were captured by an Aragonese fleet in the 15th century from the port of Marseilles, though why they should be displayed in a church is a puzzle. The museum off this chapel contains a number of early Valencian polychromed sculptures, a dark Zurbarán, a lovely Caravaggio *Virgin* and two special large Goyas of St. Francisco Borja, the saintly member of that otherwise venal Borge family. *Admission: 100 ptas. to the museum.*

Proceed around the Cathedral to view the outside. The earliest part, the south facade, is Romanesque, while the north facade is badly weathered Gothic. A huge **Archbishop's Palace** is connected to the south face. Off the north side stretches the lovely **Pl. de la Virgin** with a neoclassic fountain of a reclining colossus in the center. To the right, connected to the Cathedral by an arcade, is the **Basilica de Nuestra Señora de los Desamparados** (Our lady of the Forsaken), with a venerated gilt statue of the Virgin inside. This building, completed in 1667, was the first Spanish lunatic asylum, and possibly the first in the world.

To the right of the plaza, fronted by orange trees, is the Gothic **Palau de la Géneralitat** ★. In this 15th-century building the Cortés of Valencia sat to impose the "general" tax, for which the building was named. The façade is elegant, though the second tower is 20th century. Inside is a fine patio, a splendid hall with lovely tiles, 16th-century murals, an artesonado ceiling, and two tower rooms with wondrous gilt and painted ceilings. (Open weekdays 9 a.m.–2 p.m. Admission: free, but by advance permission only. ☎ *(96) 332 02 06.*)

Continue along the street fronting the palace, **C. Caballeros**. The door-knockers of many mansions lining this street are high so a horseman could reach them without dismounting. Some Gothic patios (such as numbers 22 and 23) are visible through doorways. After number 41, turn left down the tiny C. Abadadia San Nicholas to **Iglesia San Nicolás**. Although this was one of the oldest churches in the city, during the 16th century it was redecorated inside and out in the most flamboyant churrigueresque style. The interior is a baroque extravaganza.

Return to C. Caballeros, to take C. Bolseria, the third left. It leads downhill in three blocks to the Pl. del Mercado. The **Mercado Central**, after which the plaza is named, is on the right—a *modernista* production of tiles and glass from 1928. Inside is a collection of over a thousand stalls, divided into two sections, one for meat and produce and another for fish.

Across from the Mercado is the Gothic Lonja de la Seda.

Lonja de la Seda   ★★

Pl. del Mercado, ☎(96) 391 36 08.
Hours open: Tues.–Sat. 10 a.m.–2 p.m. and 4–8 p.m. Open Sun. 10 a.m.–2 p.m. Closed Mon.
Valencia became the center for the silk the Moors introduced into Spain. Late in the 15th century, to proclaim their prosperous status, silk merchants erected this building as a bourse to manage and trade their goods. The richly decorated result is one of the finest surviving examples of Gothic civil architecture. A center tower divides the façade into halves, one side with the arms of Aragón and elaborate tracery, the other with an ornate upper gallery. The large Salon de Contratación inside, where contracts were bought and sold, supports a lofty ceiling on unusual Gothic twisted columns. A stairway from the Orange Tree Courtyard leads up to the Salon de Consular del Mar (Maritime Court), covered with a wonderful carved gargoyle ceiling of the period, brought here from the former town hall. *Admission: free.*

Continue along the plaza, which lets into Av. Maria Cristina at the end, and leads in four blocks to the bustling garden Pl. del Pais Valenciano (a.k.a. Pl. de Ayuntamiento), with the **Ayuntamiento** on the right. Although its facade is early 20th-century, the interior is 18th. An elegant Salo de Festes is left of the entrance. There is a small museum containing miscellany along with some fine ceramics. (Open Sun.–Fri. 9 a.m.–1:30 p.m.; Admission: free.) The **Office of Tourism** with a worthwhile map is located in this building.

Two blocks ahead the imposing **Estación del Norte** can be seen, a modernista marvel worth the walk for a closer look.

From the north end of the Pl. Valenciano take C. Barcas going right. Turn left at the old theater building onto C. Poeta Querol. The second left at a church on C. Salva brings the 19th-century university complex. To its north stands **Colegio del Patriarca**, a former 16th-century seminary. Inside, around an elegantly simple patio, are rooms with fine tiles. The second floor consists of a choice museum with charming Valencian primitives, a superb Van der Weyden triptych, a Caravaggio, Ribaltas and an El Greco. (Open daily 11 a.m. to 1:30 pm, but only on weekends in winter; admission: 100 ptas.)

Return to C. Querol, continuing north to the next corner after the church. Here, on the left around the corner, is an unforgettable building—the Palacio Marqués de Dos Aguas.

Museo de Cerámica/ Palacio Marqués de Dos Aguas   ★★

Poeta Querol, 2, ☎ (96) 351 63 92.
Hours open: Tues.–Sat. 10 a.m.–2 p.m. and 4–6 p.m. Open Sun. 10 a.m.–2 p.m. Closed Mon.
Erected in the 18th century, this is the most baroque civil building in Spain. The main portal is surrounded by an incredible assemblage, including two alabaster atlantes pouring water in an obvious pun on the Marqués' name. Originally, the façade was covered in murals as well. Inside is an exceptional ceramics museum, with over 5000 pieces on display, the best collection in a country famous for that art. It must be admitted, however, that it is difficult to concentrate on ceramics amid the extravagance of gilt, marble and murals in the palace rooms. Such bad taste has seldom been surpassed, and the opportunity to see it is special. *Admission: 300 ptas.*

Continue to the end of the street, and right around the Gothic church of **San Martín**, coated in baroque decoration although sporting a 15th-century bronze equestrian statue of the saint over the door. Head toward the cathedral and along its right (south) side, this time rounding the right side of the Archbishop's Palace to view the **Almudín** at its rear. This was the public granary from the 16th century and now houses a museum of paleontology.

Walk north to the Puente Trinadad, crossing the riverbed. On the other side, to the right on C. San Pio V is the Fine Arts Museum.

Museo San Pío/Provincial de Bellas Artes   ★

San Pio V, 9, ☎ (96) 360 57 93.
Hours open: Tues.–Sat. 10 a.m.–2 p.m. and 4–6 p.m. Open Sun. 10 a.m.–2 p.m. Closed Mon.
For the scope and quality of its paintings this museum ranks as the third best in Spain. For the art of Valencia it is first-rate. The ground floor, however, is dedicated to sculpture and mosaics of a secondary sort. It is the second floor that shines, beginning with rooms emphasizing medieval primitive paintings from the area surrounding Valencia. The paintings are unrestrained in their graphic depictions of blood and gore, yet refreshingly innocent. The contrast with the rampant imagination displayed by Bosch's *Los Improperios* (The Mockers) in gallery 30, drawn by a more tutored hand, is instructive. (The centerpiece of this triptych hangs in El Escorial.)

Juan Macip and Juan de Juanes represent the Renaissance well. Extraordinary canvases by Ribalta in gallery 37 lead the way to Ribera in gallery 40. One gallery is devoted to Goya, and another to a single painting—a haunting Velázquez self-portrait. *Admission: free.*

PARADOR MARCO FABIO QUINTILIANO

Era Alta, s/n, Calahorra, 26500
☎ *(941) 13 03 58, (941) 13 51 39*
$95 per double; 63 rooms: 6 singles, 57 doubles

★ ★ ★

This parador is not historic or in a village full of sights. Olite's parador lies less than 50 miles away and is both. You could base at Quintiliano parador for a tour of Rioja's vineyards, for it is located in the Rioja Baja area, but the more famous Rioja wineries (Rioja Alta) are some distance away and well served by the closer parador of Santo Domingo de la Calzada. So it's is hard to think of any good reason for staying here, although nothing at all is wrong with the parador. It is new, built in 1973, but of a weathered brick that makes it feel more venerable. It looks like, well, an older hotel. In an attempt at history it is named for Calahorra's most famous citizen, the Roman orator Quintilian. Behind sits a pleasant terrace, in front a flowering park. Inside, nice tile floors glisten and more brick picks out architectural details. Guest rooms, although sparsely furnished and cold with wood floors, are amply sized.

Dining

Potted palms and comfortable chairs help settle guests in. This area is famous for its vegetables—for a sample try *menestra* (a vegetable stew) or stuffed peppers *(pimientos rellenos)*. Cod or lamb are tasty specialties. While you are not in the Rioja Alta, you are close enough to sample a fine, vanilla-

Directions

From **Madrid** take N-II east for 153 km to Medinacelli, where N-111 goes to Soria in 92 km. Take C-115 north for 73 km to Arnedo, just past which a road goes to Calahorra in 12 km. From **Burgos** take N-120 east for 113 km to Logroño where N-68 goes east to Calahorra in 46 km at exit 15. From **Barcelona** take A-7 west for 22 km to join N-II. Go west for 162 km to Lérida, just past which A-2 whisks you to **Zaragoza** in 144 km and A-68 goes 120 km northwest to exit 15 and Calahorra.

Paradors Nearby

Olite: 44 km	Sos del Rey: 80 km	Santo Domingo: 90 km
Soria: 95 km	Argómaniz: 120 km	Hondarribia: 170 km

Sights

Calahorra contains an old, interesting **cathedral**, whose 18th century facade hides a graceful interior. The treasury contains some interesting curios.

Excursions

For **Olite** ★★, with a graceful palace, take N-232 south for 12 km to Soto, then the road through Peralta to Olite in 44 km, and see the description under its parador below. For the wines of **Rioja** ★, take A-68 north for 86 km to exit 9 and Haro. See the description under the parador at Santo Domingo de la Calzada below.

PARADOR MONTE PERDIDO

Valle de Pineta, Bielsa, 22350
☎ *(974) 50 10 88, FAX (974) 50 11 88*
$105 per double; 24 rooms: 24 doubles

★ ★

This modern parador wins no design awards, but the point is not to offend the spectacular scenery. All in mountain stone, this parador nestles in the pines beside a pretty stream. Inside, there is wood all around to lend warmth to the stone. The furniture can only be described as tacky, but the fireplace comfortably heats up the lounge. What is special is the conviviality of the guests. They share a common cause in their love of nature and hiking, and this is Spain's largest and best national park, tucked below the highest peak of the Pyrenees, at over a mile in altitude. Bedrooms are spare and camplike, which encourage the guests to gather in the lounge.

Dining

In this hotel an otherwise ordinary dining room counts as the prettiest space with its soft wood pillars and ceiling. Here you should think hearty rather than subtleness. A nice stew combining chicken and lamb with onions, garlic, peppers and tomato is available *(a la chilindrón)*, along with lamb served with potatoes and peppers. Most renowned is the local trout.

Otherwise, there is steak or roast kid. A full-course dinner is available for about $20, plus drinks.

Directions

From **Madrid** take N-II east for 316 km to Zaragoza, then follow the directions from Zaragoza. From **Zaragoza** take N-130 north for 70 km to Huesca, then N-240 east for 51 km to Barbastro; finally N-123 east for 10 km to join N-138 to Bielsa in 77 km. The parador lies 9 km west along a marked road. From **Barcelona** take A-7 west for 22 km to join N-II. Go west for 162 km to Lérida where N-240 north reaches Barbastro in 68 km. Take N-123 east for 10 km to join N-138 to Bielsa in 77 km. The parador lies 9 km west along a marked road. From **Pamplona** take N-121 south toward Zaragoza by following Av. de Zaragoza as it leaves the large hub of the Pl. del Principe de Viana. Five km outside the city take N-240 heading east. In 113 km Jaca is reached. Continue east on N-330 for 18 km to Sabinanigo. Go north on N-260 for 15 km to Biescas, staying on N-260 as it turns east for 23 km to Torla and the entrance to the park.

Paradors Nearby

Vielha: 163 km   Arties: 170 km   Sos del Rey: 304 km

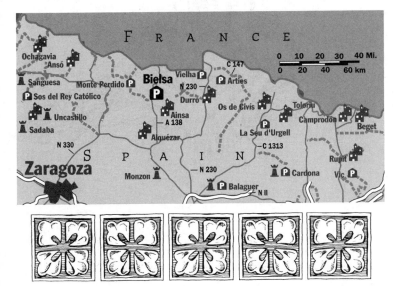

Sights

Although Spain maintains a number of parks and wildlife preserves, Ordessa is its most dramatic, recognized since 1918 as a natural treasure. The park cannot be driven through; it consists of a number of well-marked hiking trails that cover its most attractive sights. These trails range from easy walks to demanding hikes, though most lie within the abilities of the average person. The scenery is breathtaking—waterfalls, gorges, caves, precipitous peaks, mountain meadows and stands of fir and beech. Chamois, boar and mountain goats share the beauties. The park includes a restaurant serving inexpensive meals, and a tourist office nearby (open July and Aug.).

The Circo Soaso walk covers most of the dramatic scenery. Hiking is not difficult, though the complete circle covers 28 miles. It begins at the Cadiera refuge.

NOTE...*The trails are passable only from May through Sept., with the first and last of these months unpredictable. Check with the Oficina de Turismo de Huesca* ☎ *(974) 22 57 78).*

PARADOR PRINCIPE DE VIANA

Plaza de los Teobaldos, 2, Olite, 31390
☎ *(948) 74 00 00, FAX (948) 74 02 01*
$110 per double; 43 rooms: 1 single, 35 doubles, 7 suites

★ ★ ★ ★

This one is exactly what most people hope a parador will be. It's a pretty little castle that looks like the one in our fantasies, and welcomes you to spend a while. To get there you pass through fortified village walls, then pull into a lovely little square, and there it is—a very proper castle, not *too* large, and, if anything, a bit more artfully designed than we expect. Inside wait grand halls, hidden stairways, parapets, tapestries, suits of armor, and, yes, a dungeon—all a great deal of fun. Demand one of the sixteen rooms in the original castle. They have canopied beds, exposed castle walls, and antiques. Two contain large fireplaces (#106 and #107). The other rooms are housed in a modern addition. While they may be larger, they are not what you came here for.

Dining

The light is dim and romantic thanks in part to large leaded windows. The room is more elegant than the one Robin Hood made a mess of with his Merry Men and the food surpasses the animal haunches he kicked off the table. Here you may have fresh trout, delicately done, or steak with duck paté *(solomillo de cabón)*, or partridge, (perdiz), or rabbit with snails *(conejo con caracoles)*, and, as anywhere in Spain, lamb chops *(costillas de cordero asadas)*. You dine near Rioja here, so the wine list is choice. A set-course meal costs $20, plus drinks.

Alternative Dining

In Tafalla, 5 km north of Olite on N-121:

Tubal   ★★

In Tafalla, 5 km north on N-121, Pl. de Navarra, 2 (on the second floor), ☎ *(948) 70 08 52.*

This unassuming restaurant may be the best in Navarre, and is unquestionably the best for the price. Every dish is prepared with exquisite taste, and served in a lovely garden atmosphere. If the cod with garlic and crab does not make your mouth water, the partridge salad should. Save some room for fresh ice cream. Closed Sun. night, Mon. and from the last week of Aug. through the first week of Sept. Credit Cards: A, D, M, V.

Directions

From **Madrid** take N-I north for 104 km to Cerexo de Abajo, exit 100, where N-110 goes northeast to San Esteban de Gormaz in 76 km, then switches to N-122 to Soria in 66 km. Go east at the fork on N-234 just for 8km to fork again onto N-122 east. In 55 km take N-113, which becomes N-121 and reaches Olite in 94 km. From **Burgos** take N-120 due east for 113 km to **Logroño**, then N-111 for 68 km to Puente la Reina for a 14 km skip east to Campanas. The final leg is south on N-121 for 26 km. From **Pamplona** go south on N-121 for 37 km. From **Barcelona** go north then east on A-2 for 320 km to **Zaragoza**, then northwest on A-68 for 86 km to the fork onto A-15. Exit at exit 3 in 42 km to backtrack on N-121 for 7 km.

Paradors Nearby

Sos del Rey: 51 km
Santo Domingo: 130 km

Calahorra: 70 km
Soria: 142 km

Argómaniz: 122 km
Hondarribia: 156 km

Sights

Charles III, king of Navarre, ordered a castle built here in 1406. Charles was also the count of Evreux in France, so he employed French architects. What arose was a fantasy that blended solid stone walls with the elegant apartments of a palace. From that time until Ferdinand conquered Navarre in the 16th century, Olite was the main fortress of the Navarrese kings. Dominated by this castle, the entire village today retains a medieval atmosphere, not yet spoiled by crowds of tourists.

The village is entered through an arched gateway; then the turrets of the **castle ★** come into view. Fifteen towers mark the perimeter walls. Originally the castle inside contained a roof garden, a lions' den, an aviary and a small courtyard used for bullfights. It has been much remodeled over the centuries and today houses a parador for which some original stuccowork and painted marquetry ceilings have been restored. *(Open Mon.–Sat. 10 a.m.–2 p.m. and 4 p.m.–7 p.m., closes an hour earlier in winter; open Sun. 10 a.m.–2 p.m.; admission: 100 ptas.)*

The Gothic **Santa María la Real**, formerly the royal chapel, stands beside the castle with a fine 14th-century facade. Nearby **San Pedro**, in many ways artistically superior to Santa María, although in the Romanesque style, has a richly carved 12th-century portal.

Excursions

17 km southeast on N-533, then C-124 stands the **Monastery of Oliva ★**. It was built by French followers of St. Bernard in the eleventh century in an austere Cistercian style. The church is majestic and the cloisters add Gothic elements to instill solemnity.

PARADOR SANTO DOMINGO DE LA CALZADA

Plaza del Santo, 3, Santo Domingo de la Calzada, 26250
☎ *(941) 34 03 00, FAX (941) 34 01 25*
$110, double; 61 rooms: 59 doubles, 2 suites

★ ★ ★ ★

Today the greatest attraction of Santo Domingo's parador is its proximity to Haro, capital of the finest of Rioja's wineries. In olden days, however, the building was a hospice for pilgrims on their arduous way to Santiago de Compostela. In fact it was built by a saint, Saint Dominic—not the famous one, but a man who devoted his life to building accommodations for pilgrims. So the austere exterior covers dramatic sweeps of 11th century multiple arches inside. The lounge is truly memorable, rising to an old wooden ceiling punctuated by a stained glass skylight. Plain guest rooms are appropriate to the original hospice purpose, but ample in size, and some of the wood furniture is gracefully simple. The best rooms are those on the second floor front with terraces over a pretty square.

Alternative Accommodations

Los Augustinos

> *San Agustin, 2, Haro,* ☎ *(941) 31 13 08, FAX (941) 30 31 48, Telex 37161. 60 rooms.* In Haro waits Los Augustinos, which looks like a parador—it is housed in a reconstructed convent from the 14th century—though it is owned by a private chain. The hotel was renovated in 1990 and is top-grade throughout. Public spaces are nicely decorated with real and reproduction antiques, and the bedrooms are spotlessly

modern. The sitting room is so grand as to be slightly uncomfortable, bedrooms are less memorable. What we don't understand is why it charges only $75 per room.

Dining

Soft patina of old wood beams and pillars playing against the glow of old floor tiles make romance of the dining room. Rioja is famous for vegetables (try *menestra de verduras*, a stew), in general, and stuffed peppers *(pimientos rellenos)*, in particular. The restaurant does a nice hake *(merluza)*, potatoes with *chorizo* (spicy sausage) and baby lamb chops *(chuletillas)*. For a change of pace, you could try *zurracapote*, the local version of sangría, with the meal, however, a decent selection of Rioja's is available. A set-course meal is available for $23, about what you will pay à la carte.

Alternative Dining

Terete ★★★

In Haro: Lucrecia Arana, 17 (west of the plaza), ☎ *(941) 31 00 23.*
This is the outstanding Haro restaurant, over 100 years old. Nothing fancy—white picnic tables upstairs—but roasts are perfectly seasoned and cooked in an ancient *horno* (wood fireplace), a bargain at $20. Naturally the selection of wines is exemplary. Closed Mon., the first half of July and last half of Oct. Credit Cards: M, V.

Directions

From **Madrid** take N-I north for 238 km to circle **Burgos** and join N-120 east for 74 km. From **Pamplona** take N-111 west for 92 km to circle **Logroño** and join N-232 for 8 km until it lets you onto N-120 for a final 42 km. From **Zaragoza** take A-68 northwest for 166 km to feed into N-232 for a short leg west until it lets you onto N-120 for a final 42 km.

Paradors Nearby

Argómaniz: 75 km	Calahorra: 95 km	Olite: 136 km
Soria: 151 km	Sos del Rey: 192 km	

Sights

The village **cathedral** combines Romanesque and Gothic elements behind an 18th century facade. The interior is lavish, with a fine retable, but most notable for a rooster and hen in their little house. It seems that a condemned prisoner claimed the judge's roast rooster supper would arise to proclaim his innocence. When it did, he was set free and the miracle commemorated ever after. It's a nice story, so nice that Barcelos in Portugal tells exactly the same tale.

Excursions

Haro ★ is a prosperous, attractive town that serves as the capital of Rioja Alta, the finest wine region in Spain. It lies 16 km north on the old LR-111, and is a pleasant place to explore the great bodegas (wineries). Old Haro covers a hill rising from the Plaza de la Paz, circled by an arcade of glass-balconied houses surrounding an old bandstand. Dating from 1769, the stately Ayuntamiento (city hall) across the plaza is a source of information about the area. **Santo Tomás** ★, a pretty 16th-century church, sits atop the hill. The south portal is a sumptuous with Plateresque carving; the interior is nicely Gothic.

But it is wine that brings most people to Haro. Bodegas proliferate down the hill to the north, near the railway station from which they ship their wares. There the stream called Rio Oja, which gave its name to this region, enters the larger River Ebro. Bodega tours are given on an ad hoc basis, waiting for four or more tourists to assemble. Check with the tourist office for what is open and to make reservations. The best bodegas are **Lopez de Heredia, CVNE** (☎ *(941) 31 02 76)*, **La Rioja Alta** (☎ *(941) 31 03 46)*, **Muga** (☎ *(941) 31 04 98)*, and **Bilbaiñas**.

NOTE ... *Most bodegas close from Aug. through the first half of Sept., and most allow tours only in the morning.*

Other good bodegas require a drive, although a pleasant one. Leave Haro east from the area of the bodegas, following signs to Labastida, four km northeast. From there follow signs to Logrono and N-232 (confusingly with the same designation as the different N-232 that passes south by Haro). On the right, in 10 km, pass by the picturesque hilltop village of **San Vicente de la Sonsierra** ★, surrounded by vineyards. Past Samaniego in seven km a sign points to the road for Puerto de Herrera, which in three km leads into the mountains for the **Balcon de la Rioja** ★ and its panoramic views over the Rioja area. Seven km farther, back on N-232, brings beautiful **Laguardia** ★ (Biasteri, in Basque).

Laguardia retains its medieval village walls, gates, towers and grace. The town has ruins of a 10th-century castle, a Romanesque and a Gothic church, along with old mansions and the Bodegas Palacio, one of Spain's best. (**Marixa** ★★, just outside the walls, is a nice restaurant with moderate prices, and has 10 clean rooms for inexpensive rates. ☎ *(941) 10 01 65.*)

From Laguardia head south toward Elciego and Cenicero. **Elciego** ★, in four km, is another picturesque village that hosts the bodega of Marqués de Riscal, one of Spain's premier crus—and its oldest. Across the Ebro is Cenicero, the location of Bodegas Marqués de Cáceres, producer of a modest-quality wine. From here, the better highway N-232 leads northwest back to Haro.

PARADOR VALLE DE ARÁN

Carretara del Túnel, s/n, Vielha, 25530
☎ *(973) 64 01 00, FAX (973) 64 11 00*
$95 per double; 135 rooms: 19 singles, 113 doubles, 3 suites

★ ★ ★

This and the parador at Arties are Spain's ski paradors. Both sit a snow-ball throw from the majestic slopes at Vall d'Aran. This modern structure sits on a knoll for fine valley and mountain views. It is a large, bustling hotel with merely functional bedrooms, but each owns a balcony for a view of one's own. A pool surrounded by grass and lawn chairs waits for the sun.

Dining

Architecturally, the most interesting design of the building is the circular dining room. From outside it looks as if a giant chef had placed his equally gigantic funnel upside down to create the roof. The effect inside is of a soaringly high ceiling. Windows surround the dining room for tranquil vistas. Start with fish soup *(suquet de pescado)*, then gorge yourself on an Aragonese specialty, *olla aranesa*, a casserole of beans, sausage, vegetables and veal. Rabbit and skate are available as well. Wines cover Rioja and more local Catalans. A set-course menu costs under $20.

Directions

From **Barcelona** take A-2 west for 155 km to Lérida then N-230 north for 143 km. From **Toulouse**, in France, take N-117 south for 52 km, the last bit on A-64 west to the border at Saint Gaudens. Take N-125 for 18 km through the Pyrenees where it joins N-230 south for the final 20 km.

Paradors Nearby

Arties: 5 km	Bielsa: 118 km	Seu d'Urgell: 134 km
Cardona: 232 km	Vic: 300 km	

Sights

Interspersed with high-rises, ski shops and bars, lovely **Iglesia de San Miguel** still reposes. It is a 12th century Romanesque church of simple beauty that retains a remarkable 12th century Christ figure. (*Open daily from 11 a.m.-8 p.m.*)

Otherwise, there is skiing, hiking and hunting.

PORTUGAL

BACKGROUND FOR PORTUGAL

The children of Portugal are warm and friendly.

The Land and People

As countries go, Portugal is tiny, occupying the western fifth of the Iberian Peninsula in a rectangle 137 miles wide (at its widest) by 350 miles long—it would just about cover the state of Indiana. You could drive from the northern border to the southern coast in one day. Yet Portugal manages to fit geographic variety into its small package. Forests, mountains and rolling hills contrast with the generally more ascetic landscape of its larger neighbor, Spain.

Between the Minho River that forms the northern border with Spain and the parallel Douro river 200 km south of it, the land rises in mountainous granite covered in dense vegetation. This plateau is known as Trás-o-Montes, "beyond the mountains," where the lifestyle isn't that different from a hundred years ago. Small villages nestle in warmer valleys where lyre-horned oxen still pull wooden-wheeled carts. The Douro River slices through this granite plateau on its way to the sea, growing the grapes for port wine along its banks, before shipping west down the river to the aptly named Porto, and the sea.

South of the Douro dense mountains continue in the east, but the land drops low along the coast. Castles and fortified walls in the eastern mountains still defend villages from the Spanish as they have for eight centuries, while sheep graze and farmers raise grapes for the fine wines of the Dão region. Rice paddies on the low western coast stretch for uninterrupted miles, protected from sea salt by dunes anchored by pines.

The substantial river Tagus (*Tejo*, in Portuguese) cuts the country roughly in half lengthwise, widening into an estuary beside Lisbon before it empties into the sea. Its alluvial banks raise olives, grapes, vegetables and wheat. Rice grows on spreading plains where horses and black fighting bulls roam. On the coast, both north and south of Lisbon, cliffs surround sand beaches and quaint fishing villages.

South of the Tejo spreads the vast department of the *Alentejo*, constituting almost a third of Portugal. Flat and poorly watered by nature, artificial irrigation has transformed it into the granary of Portugal. Geological plainness is broken by clustered stands of eucalyptus and cork oaks—one-third of all those in the world—from which Portugal sells more cork products than any other country. Away from these isolated forests, rolling hills cradle houses dazzlingly whitewashed, topped by orange tile roofs that grow ornate, eccentric chimneys. Occasional windmills turn in the breeze.

The southernmost part of Portugal is called the *Algarve*, named from the Arabic word for west, for this was the western extremity of the Moors' territory. The ancient volcanos of the Monchique mountains separate the Algarve from the southern Alentejo, and are tall enough to constitute a barrier that allows the Atlantic waters to temper weather and produce a semitropical climate along the coast. Vegetation is lush with camellias and citrus groves. Rolling sand beaches and sandbars on the eastern coast turn to spectacular cliffs on the west framing smaller beaches. The Algarve ends in the sheer windswept bluffs of Capo de São Vicente, the southwestern extremity of Europe. Not surprisingly, tourists have discovered the mild climate, beautiful beaches and crystal ocean and arrive in droves each summer.

By virtue of occupying the southwest corner of Europe, Portugal owns 520 miles of coastline, most of it in beaches bathed by a mild climate, thanks to the warmth of the Atlantic's Gulf Stream that passes by. These tepid waters produce mild winters but summer temperatures of over 100 on the coast, though subdued by continual sea breezes, while the inland plains of the Alentejo grow stifling and airless in midsummer when temperatures of 120 are known. Hence, palms and agave can be spotted almost anywhere along the coastline, except in the extreme north.

Indeed, Portugal appears to be a Mediterranean country, akin in climate and flora to Italy or Greece, despite the fact that this sea never touches its shore. More than France and even Spain, Portugal exudes the warm languor that the Mediterranean calls to mind.

The census in 1981 gave Portugal a population of just under 10 million, including the islands of Madeira and the Azores. Today the population probably approaches 11 million. This number incorporates almost a million expatriates from the African colonies of Angola, Guinea and Mozambique who returned in 1975 to raise the country's population by 10 percent in six months. Portugal boasts only one metropolis—Lisbon, in which one Portuguese in 10 lives, and one additional true city—Porto, with a population of a third of a million. In Portugal a family of visiting tourists can raise the population of towns by percentage points.

Despite major efforts to industrialize, Portugal remains a country of farmers. One in five still earns his living from the land. Sixty percent of Portugal's industry concentrates in Lisbon and Porto, leaving the majority of the country either empty or in farms. Fishing remains a major industry, with sailors routinely harvesting catches off the Newfoundland Banks in North America as they have since time immemorial, as well as from local seas. Portugal is one of the largest producers of tungsten and mines significant quantities of uranium, but must import all its petroleum, and has built the usual ugly refineries outside Porto and Sines.

Despite great economic advances through the '70s and '80s, Portugal is a poor country with many of its people still making do without indoor plumbing. None of this will be apparent to the visitor, however, as he passes scattered old houses of indeterminate age and inescapable charm throughout the countryside, separated by gleaming new buildings owned by Portuguese who left the country to find their fortune and proclaimed it in their real estate when they returned. In particular, most visitors from the United States are impressed by all the new cars they see in Portugal. When we asked a native how so many can afford them, he answered in perfect English "Have you ever heard of leasing?"

The Portuguese tend to be short and stocky, but seldom fat, with black hair and olive complexions. Yet occasional taller, blue-eyed and sometimes red-haired Portuguese probably descend from some Viking raider or passing northern European crusader from long ago.

As a people the Portuguese seem surprisingly quiet, always dignified in contrast to southern Spanish exuberance. A streak of melancholy lies just beneath the surface, and emerges in their music, the plaintive *Fado*. Their outstanding trait is an extreme courtesy—*Disculpe*, "excuse me" is likely to be the Portuguese word most often heard. You will seldom see a Portuguese display anger (other than when he changes into another creature behind the wheel of his car), even in the midst of chaotic and frustrating circumstances (usually when dealing with uncomprehending tourists). The Portuguese go far out of their way to help anyone who asks for help, seem to love all dogs and children, and may be the sweetest people on earth.

But even they realize that their language seems like Greek to everyone else, and strive hard to understand a visitor in his own tongue. All have studied a second language, and the chances are that anyone under 40 will understand English, for this has been taught in the schools for three decades. Older citizens will know some French. All Portuguese understand Spanish, though many become offended when a Spaniard speaks to them in his language while a guest in their land. Centuries of conflict are not readily forgotten. Of course they do not take the same offense when a tourist tries Spanish, should English fail.

The Portuguese work so hard that it is difficult to find one at rest, outside of old men in local bars in the evening. In particular, women in the countryside seem always on the move, often with heavy bundles on their heads. Both sexes show the depths of their feelings when they cry during *fado* songs. But most outstanding is their simple sincerity, plain on their faces and in their eyes.

Food and Drink

Visitors will find lots to like about Portuguese food and much that is familiar. Meals are served at the times we are used to, as opposed to the late hours of neighbor Spain, and encompass expected fish, meat, starches and vegetables. Seafood can be relied on to be wonderful; simple grilled chicken will be a treat; and all the breads are guaranteed to be delicious.

Most Portuguese restaurants bill what moderate dining establishments charge at home. All are government-rated by a system of graphic "forks" indicating a price, service level and range of offerings, with four and five forks signifying the high end. A plaque outside the establishment displays its rating. Note that this governmental evaluation does not take into account how good the food tastes, while our stars most assuredly do.

Bread lovers will find delectable varieties in Portugal.

Like the Spanish, the Portuguese sauté in olive oil, rather than Northern Europeans' butter, and use garlic generously. (Say *sem alho* to request no garlic.) In general, seasonings lean to the bland (spicy *piri piri* sauce excepted). In most restaurants simply prepared dishes, broiled meats and fish, will surpass those in sauces.

Breakfast *(pequeno almoço)* is a light meal, consisting of bread or a roll *(bolo)*, tea *(chá)* or coffee—*café solo* (black), or *café com leite* (with milk).

A full, three- or four-course lunch *(almoço)* may be eaten in any restaurant. But for those not so hungry or looking to save escudos, there are other options. Sandwiches *(pregos* or *sandes)* and simple platters can be munched in a *cervejaria* (beer hall) or most local bars. In addition to sweets, *Pastelarias* (pastry shops) also serve sandwiches, along with fried envelopes of meat or seafood *(rissóis)* and a sort of small pizza. And, still for pre-dinner, there are tapas-type bars, called *tascas*, serving delectables after work.

Restaurants open for dinner *(jantar)* at 7 p.m. and close at 10, later in Lisbon. A *menu do dia* will offer a multicourse meal at a set price lower than the à la carte regular menu. The *Prato do dia* is the daily special, and always fresh.

Food

Bread lovers will think they've reached heaven in Portuguese restaurants. Corn bread *(pão de milho)* is not sweet or coarse, but fragrant with the aroma of corn. If you have never had barley bread *(pão do centeio)*, here is your chance. *Pão de broa* is a rye bread beyond compare. There are scores of other varieties of bread, some regional, some available nationally, and every one is delectable.

The bread will be served before you order your meal along with some side-dishes to nibble. These are part of a cover-charge *(couvert)* imposed by almost all Portuguese restaurants that can range from a dollar, at inexpensive establishments, up to seven or eight dollars at the most expensive.

Vegetables, even salads, are not a Portuguese staple. You cannot assume your main course will be so garnished. Construct your own by searching for the few vegetable or salad choices.

The menu *(lista* or *ementa)* will start with appetizers—either individual choices, such as *presunto* (proscuitto-type cured ham), or a combination *(acepipes* or *entrada)* that includes more wonderful bread. Soups *(sopas)* are prepared in a great variety and can be hearty enough for a light meal. The most famous is *caldo verde*, a potato soup containing spiced sausage and lightly cooked kale. Tomato soup is a delicate combination of stock with chunks of tomato, rather than the creamed version produced in the United States. *Sopa a alentejana* is the most garlicky of garlic soups, usually arriving with an egg poaching in the broth. *Sopa de mariscos* is a seafood bisque; *caldeirada*, a seafood chowder. Hearty bean soup is *sopa de feijões.* The Portuguese also make their own version of *gazpacho*, and if it is *a alentejana*, it will have ham or sausage added. For something lighter, try *canja de galenha*, chicken and rice soup.

In most restaurants fish *(peixe)* is the best entree choice. Broiled or fried, its freshness makes the taste a revelation. *Sardinhas assadas* are the world's best grilled sardines. Just sprinkle with lemon, or add oil and vinegar. Equally delectable is red mullet *(salmonette)*, sea bass *(robalo)* or mackerel *(cavala)*. Less assertive, but still tastier than what we are used to, are hake *(pescada)* and sole *(lenguado)*. Shellfish are wonderful, although more expensive. If your budget allows, splurge on a big plate of *camarãoes* (large shrimp). Baby clams *(amêijoas)* can be spectacular.

Incredibly, the fish that appears most often on the menu is dried *bacalhau*, or codfish. Why, with some of the best fresh fish in the world, do the Portuguese pine for salted cod? In the store it looks like an animal flattened by a truck. So dry it has to be cut with a saw, it is soaked in water overnight before it can be eaten, which does not exactly infuse it with flavor. Yet the Portuguese love their bacalhau and have found hundreds of ways to prepare it, although just about every recipe is as bland as the fish it incorporates. Baked cod with potatoes could attract only the Portuguese, though *bacalhau dourado*, in a tomato, onion and garlic sauce, or *lisbonense*, in a cream sauce, are tastier. *Bacalhau á Bras*, which also goes by a score of other names, is a famous specialty that scrambles the cod with egg and onion to produce a bland but not unpleasant combination. Most people who visit Portugal feel an obligation to try its national dish, but remember there is no requirement that you order it more than once. And spiced codfish cakes (*pastéis de bacalhau*) can be extraordinary.

Another seafood combination is *cataplana*, clams stewed with sausage and bacon in a sort of double wok. This one is certainly flavorful, though the delicate taste of the clams is overwhelmed by the stronger pork products.

Meat *(carne)* and poultry *(ave)* can be interesting. The flavor of a simple grilled chicken *(frango assado)* is quite unlike the taste of our own mass-produced fowl. Try one *piri-piri*, with a peppery red sauce that kicks. Portuguese pork *(porco)*, is famed throughout Europe for it comes from pigs fed on flavorful chestnuts—simply done it can be delicious. Suckling pig *(leitao)* is invariably good. Lamb *(cordiero)* or kid *(cabrito)* cooked over wood is well worth seeking out. Portugal's *chouriço* is a tasty smoked sausage similar to the Spanish chorizo. On the other hand, beef is generally better avoided. It does not form a regular part of the Portuguese diet, so they neither produce nor prepare it well.

In local restaurants, the more ambitious the dish the less successful it generally proves to be. For example, a national specialty is *porco a alentejana*—pork marinated in wine and spices to which clams are added. As with clams cataplana, while the flavor is tasty, the delicate bivalves cannot stand up to the pork and spices.

Portuguese cheese *(queijo)* is delicious, especially milky goat *serra*, mild *Castelo Branco*, and *alentejo*, made from sheep's milk. *Cabreiro* is a goat cheese—*beja* means it is salty, *serpa* that it is sharp. *Flamengo* is similar to Gouda.

Desserts *(sobremesas)* include Europe's universal flan *(flã)*; others tend to cloying sweetness. If such is your fancy, try *pudim Molotov*, a moist meringue with caramelized sugar topping. Another unusual dessert is clotted egg yolks swimming in a sugar sauce called *trouxas de ovos*, although it goes by other regional names. *Arroz doce*, rice pudding is generally available and good. Fruit *(fruta)*, especially oranges or peaches in season, will generally prove an excellent choice.

Finish your meal with a cup of the best coffee *(café)* in the world, as flavorful as, but avoiding the bitter taste of, espresso.

Drink

Do not judge Portuguese wine by Mateus—those omnipresent flagons of semisparkling, slightly sweet rosé wine—or by Lancers in the pottery bottle. Portugal can do much better, and at prices that will gratify.

In the center of the country, around the city of Viseu, the large production area of **Dão** bottles superior reds and whites in quantity. Here wine is aged for five to seven years in oak to create smooth vintages of great body, similar to burgundy. These are good, modestly priced wines. Allow at least five years for the reds, but make sure the whites are no older than five years. The largest bottler is *SOGRAPE* whose "*Grão Vasco*" is reliable, but J.M. Da Fonseca's "*Terras Altas*" ranks a level higher. **Pinhel**, nearby, produces wines of similar character but with more finesse. A good Pinhel can stand up to a second-growth French wine at a third or even a quarter of its price.

Portugal's best wine comes from the coast just north of Lisbon. **Colares**, near Sintra, grows grapes on vines anchored in 20 feet of sand dunes. At the turn of the century this sand warded off the attack of *phylloxera* mites that destroyed all vines throughout Europe, forcing a grafting of traditional European vines to American roots resistant to the plague. In all of Europe, only the wines of Colares still grow from native root stock. The reds of Colares are dry and rich in tannin. Unfortunately, the vineyards are rapidly giving way to seaside bungalows, causing supplies to dwindle and prices to rise.

The best whites come from **Buçelas** and **Carcavelos**, whose territory is unfortunately small. They are light, dry and fruity.

South of Lisbon near the city of **Setubal**, J.M. da Fonseca produces two reds, "*Periquita*" and "*Palmela*." There are wine connoisseurs who dismiss "Periquita" as ordinary, but we have found it satisfactorily smooth, if light, and an exceptional buy. "Palmela," a lighter bordeaux type wine despite its burgundy bottle, also counts as a good value.

East of Lisbon the Alentejo produces a great deal of wine, generally high in alcohol content. For a treat try a fine old **Redondo** red.

Of all the affordable Portuguese wines, the best value in a red is **Esporão** from the Alentejo; and for whites our favorite is a complex young **Bairrada**. The one wine to be avoided at all costs is a **Convento Tomar** white, unless you appreciate the taste of petroleum.

For a different experience, try one of Portugal's **green wines** *(vinhos verdes)*. These are grown in the extreme north where cool temperatures shorten the growing season. Grapes are picked young— "green"—hence the name. A chilled white will be light and dry, even astringent; the reds, also chilled, are an acquired taste. *Monção* holds first place among the regions producing such wine.

Portugal's most famous wine is **port**, named for Porto, the place from which it has been shipped since the 18th century. Port is an intensely rich, fortified wine—brandy is added to arrest grape fermentation and raise the alcohol content to 20 percent. At their best and oldest they enter the mouth with a smooth sweet taste, then fill the palate with a most delicate aroma for savoring. They are best sipped after dinner like a brandy, or before as an aperitif. A vintage port (on average only one year in five produces such a beverage) is not ready for drinking until 10 years old, and becomes special and a characteristic tawny color only as it approaches 20 years. People either love its mix of rich flavors or find them cloying. *Graham's* is an outstanding bottler. Crusted port is a blend of different years; lighter than vintage port and ready for drinking in five years or so. The most accessible of the ports is called tawny. It is matured in casks rather than bottles until it is delicate and pale maroon in color. A 20-year-old tawny will be a treat. Try *Fereira* for the best. Darker-colored ruby port is a younger, cheaper version. White ports are gaining in popularity; dry and chilled they make a nice aperitif. *Taylor, Cockburn* and *Sandeman* each bottles acceptably dry versions.

The other famous Portuguese fortified wine is **Madeira**, from the island of that name, so rich it suggests a syrup.

Most of the wine in Portugal is sold as *vinho da casa*, house wine, or *vinho da região*, regional wine, and will be better than it costs. It can be red *(tinto)*, white *(branco)* or rose. Beer *(cerveja)* can be excellent; try Sagres brand. Water is *água*.

History

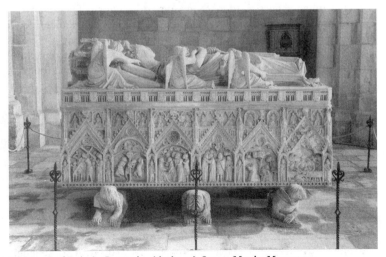

The tomb of Inês de Castro in Alcobaça's Santa Maria Monastery

Prehistory Through the Birth of Portugal (20,000 B.C.–A.D. 1139)

c. 20,000 B.C. Neolithic Era.

c. 1300 B.C. Iberians inhabit the peninsula.

c. 1000 B.C. Phoenician traders and settlements.

206 B.C. Rome invades Iberia.

19 B.C. Augustus completes the conquest of the peninsula.

c. A.D. 400 German Swabians migrate to Portugal.

A.D. 711 Muslims invade from Morocco.

A.D. 1095 Henri of Burgundy is named Count of Portucale.

A.D. 1139 Afonso Henrique, Henri's son, titles himself King of Portugal.

Portugal has been inhabited for at least 100,000 years, down through "Stone Age" cultures of about 10,000 B.C., although, until 1995, nothing as splendid as the cave paintings done by their kin in Spain or France had been uncovered. Then the world learned of a magnificent prehistoric art gallery along the rock cliffs of the Douro River near Vila Nova de Fozcoa. Dating to 20,000 years ago, these chiseled images of bison, horses, ibexes and deer constitute the finest outdoor Stone Age art in Europe, if not the world. The fact that such early art lay out of doors has changed the thinking about our early ancestors, thought previously to hide their art deep inside dark caves. Still, it is not until the third century B.C. when Romans encountered a people they dubbed Iberians that the historical record of the Portuguese may be said to begin.

Iberians had settled throughout the peninsula at least seven or eight hundred years before the Romans arrived to name them. It was believed at one time that they migrated from North Africa, for archeologists assumed that all civilizations spread outward from a common Middle-East origin. However, the experts have revised those opinions today, and now maintain that Iberians were a race indigenous to the Iberian peninsula who borrowed certain ideas and practices from people across the Straits of Gibraltar.

The Romans found a second tribe sharing the peninsula with the Iberians—Celts. Originally they may have migrated south from Brittany, though it is more likely that an indigenous people borrowed burial and building practices from these northern neighbors. Origins aside, archaeologists have so much trouble distinguishing Celts from Iberians that they coined the term "Celtiberian" to apply equally to both.

Phoenicians had also visited Portugal before the Romans came, searching for tin to manufacture bronze. They established a trading post to conduct their business on a hill overlooking the mouth of the Tejo (Tagus) River, the forerunner of Lisbon. In due course they were followed by people from Carthage, originally a colony of Phoenicia, then successors of that trading empire. When the Carthaginians' general Hannibal attacked Rome, Romans came to the Iberian Peninsula to return the favor.

The Romans confronted a particularly warlike bunch of Celtiberians living in the south of Portugal who called themselves Lusitanians, after which the Romans named a province, "Lusitania"—which became Portugal's original name. The Lusitanian chief Virianthus defeated every Roman army sent against him for three decades until three of his own soldiers, bribed by the Romans, murdered him as he slept. Indeed it took Rome longer to subdue Iberia than any of its territories except Britain. She finally prevailed only after 200 years of struggle in 19 B.C., then set out to civilize the peninsula with roads and buildings. When the Romans left, 400 years later, their Latin language began a slow evolution into Spanish and Portuguese.

Roman decline, by the dawn of the fifth century A.D., allowed German tribes to divide up its empire. Swabians grabbed latter-day Portugal. Visigoths swept into Spain 40 years later, subduing or evicting all the other German tribes who had arrived ahead of them, except for those Swabians entrenched in Portugal. The Swabians resisted for a century and a half before the Visigoths incorporated them into a Germanic state comprising all Iberia.

The Germans enjoyed their conquest for only two centuries, although long enough to plant their new religion of Christianity ineradicably throughout Iberia. Their undoing was Moroccans from across the Straits of Gibraltar who eyed Portugal and Spain voraciously. In 711 a small army of well disciplined Muslims landed on the Spanish coast, then swept through the peninsula. Only scattered enclaves of Swabians and Visigoths remained unsubdued in the extreme north of latter-day Spain, but from these confines they launched a stubborn reconquest that persisted for five centuries.

During their half-millennium of control, the Moors, as the Spanish called them, introduced a civilization superior in science and culture to that of any country in Europe. They prized literacy and art, and encouraged the cultivation of olives, rice and citrus fruits. Not only did the Moors build in a sophisticated style, they introduced the techniques of paper-making from China, resurrected the secret of making glass, and taught advanced glazing techniques for pottery. They also brought their tolerance for any "people of the Bible," that is, for Muslim, Christian and Jew. Above all else, this Islamic influence distinguishes Spain and Portugal from other European nations.

The natives bided their time in northern enclaves throughout the Islamic domination of the rest of the peninsula. Their reconquest advanced at a snail's pace until Alfonso VI came to the throne of Spanish Castile. Alfonso managed to capture Toledo as well as Lisbon, raiding as far as the southern coast of Spain. His victories so frightened the Moors that they called on Morocco for assistance. Alfonso, in turn, cried to France for help to beat back the so-called infidel. A division of knights answered the call, including Henri, a younger son of the Count of Burgundy. Henri helped turn the tide and was rewarded with the hand of one of Alfonso's illegitimate daughters, plus the dowry of a large northwestern territory then known as *Portucale*, from which the modern name of Portugal derives.

Being a feudal state, Portucale was ruled by Henri on behalf of the King of Castile. Henry struggled to gain his independence but died young, leaving a three-year-old son and a widow under 30 who moved in with a new man, then refused to render feudal homage to the King of Castile until compelled by force. But Henri's young son had become estranged from his mother, not least by her new living arrangements, so he claimed that his mother's fealty did not include his. In time that son, Afonso Henrique, came of age, assumed his father's title, fought his mother in battle and continued to refuse the traditional homage until defeated by the next king of Castile. Then another invasion by Moroccans pressed hard on Castile, although Afonso Henrique stemmed their advance in his territory. That success and the continued distraction by the Moors, enabled the Count to title himself Afonso I, the King of Portugal in 1139. From that moment on, with only a 60-year hiatus, Portugal has been independent of Spain, thanks to a royal house bred of a French noble and an illegitimate Spanish princess.

The Burgundian Dynasty (1107–1385)

1107–1185 The lifespan of Afonso Henrique.

1185–1211 Sancho I completes most of the reconquest of Portugal.

1277–1325 Dinis I revitalizes agriculture and founds the University of Coimbra.

1357–1367 Pedro I, the Cruel, breeds an illegitimate son from whom the succeeding House of Avís descends.

1385 João, Master of the House of Avís, seizes the throne.

Initially Afonso's kingdom consisted only of the northern third of modern Portugal; the rest was controlled by Moors. But Afonso managed to retake Lisbon, already a major city because of its harbor. He also recaptured much of the south, although he could not hold it all. After his death in 1185, his son and grandson carried on the campaign, regaining all of modern-day Portugal except for scattered pockets of Moors, mopped up by 1249. Thus did Portugal become the first unified country in Europe, three and a half centuries before Spain managed the same feat. Afonso Henrique had founded the first of Portugal's dynasties, and illegitimate children of his descendents would establish the rest. No wonder Afonso Henrique is known as the father of his country.

The first king after the pacification was Dinis I. He granted land to the common farmer, who previously had subsisted as a serf, thus earning the sobriquet *Dom Dinis Labrador* (Lord Dinis the Farmer). In addition, he founded Portugal's first university, originally in Lisbon but later moved to Coimbra, where it remains. During his reign the majority of the great Portuguese fortresses were completed that still guard the eastern border heroically against Spain. He married a woman later canonized as Saint Isabel. With all this he had time to write respectable poetry, and proved to be the best monarch of this original Burgundian line.

Two reigns later Pedro I, the Cruel, occupied the throne. He came honestly to his cruelty for his father had ordered the murder of the woman Pedro loved. In revenge, Pedro personally killed the assassins, then buried the body of his beloved in the greatest Portuguese tomb, inside the church of Alcobaça, north of Lisbon. Between murders Pedro found time to sire a number of illegitimate children, one of whom he installed as the abbot of the religio-military order of *Avís*, an organization something like the Knights Templar. That abbot would one day seize the crown.

Fernando I succeeded Pedro. His early death left his heiress daughter Beatrice under the control of his widow, Leonor Teles. Leonor openly took up residence with a courtier, then married off Beatrice to the King of Castile. Many were upset, both at Leonor's morals and politics, especially when she sent heralds through the land announcing that the King of rival Castile now ruled Portugal. This prompted the Master of the House of Avís to hie to the palace and kill Leonor's paramour. Then he incited a crowd to proclaim him Regent and, finally, King. Thus did João I, formerly the abbot Master of the Order of Avís, become King of Portugal in 1385, and the founder of its second dynasty.

The House of Avís (1385–1580)

1385–1433 The reign of João I.

1394–1460 The life of Prince Henry the Navigator.

1419 Discovery of the Madeira Islands.

1431 Discovery of the Azores.

1487 Bartolemeu Dias rounds the Cape of Good Hope.

1495–1512	The reign of Manuel I, the Fortunate.
1497–1498	Vasco de Gama reaches India.
1500	Pedro Álvares Cabral discovers Brazil.
1519–1521	Magellan circles the globe.
1580	The last king of the Avís line dies.

It was one thing for João to declare himself king, quite another to convince the mighty King of Castile to give up his own, rightful claim to Portugal. The two met in a decisive battle on the plains of Abjubarrota north of Lisbon where João miraculously won the day. In celebration he constructed the great monastery at Batalha nearby.

João I was fortunate to marry a special woman, the English Philippa of Lancaster, who raised four exceptional boys. When old enough they joined in an invasion of Ceuta on the Moroccan coast. Most of the credit for their successful conquest was paid to one son—Dom Henrique, who devoted the remainder of his life to encouraging maritime exploration. For such enterprises he became known to the English-speaking world as "Prince Henry the Navigator." He financed expeditions that discovered Madeira and the Azore Islands, still territories of Portugal today, and voyages that made their way down most of the African coast. The reason for these explorations was that European tastes for eastern spices had drained the continent of gold; Henry was pursuing more of both.

His older brother succeeded their father as king in 1433, but died five years later mourning yet a third brother who had been captured in Morocco. The fourth, and last, brother traveled to the corners of Europe, something seldom done in those times.

Two reigns later, João II received Columbus to hear his plan to sail west to India, but declined to back him when Bartolemeu Dias rounded the Cape of Good Hope, giving Portugal its own route to India.

João II died without heirs, bringing the throne to the son of an adopted child of Prince Henry the Navigator. Manuel I, called the Fortunate, presided over many of the great Portuguese discoveries. Vasco de Gama reached India, establishing Portuguese colonies, and Pedro Cabral discovered Brazil. Portugal grew rich, allowing Manuel to build extensively in a flamboyant style named "Manueline" for himself. Splendid examples survive in the Belém Tower and the Hieronymite Monastery, both in Lisbon's suburb, as well as at the Convent at Tomar and parts of the great monastery at Batalha. Intricate designs displayed the exotic flora and fauna discovered by the Portuguese on their explorations.

For a brief moment, tiny Portugal had become the richest country in Europe, thanks to its overseas colonies. It manned outposts throughout Africa, in India and in the Far East from which it imported the spices, tea and coffee that Europeans soon found indispensable. For a time money flowed into Portugal like the waves of the sea. But, one by one, these outposts were seized by more powerful nations. The inexhaustible funds were soon drained.

Manuel married the daughter of the Spanish monarchs Ferdinand and Isabella, hoping that a son would grow up to rule a united peninsula, but he paid a terrible price. The Spanish required that Portugal expel her Jews and institute an inquisition like their own, thus ending the history of Jews in Portugal. As it happened, Manuel's scheme came to naught, for his bride died in childbirth and the infant son expired soon after. Manuel remarried, producing an heir who continued the practice of marrying Spanish royalty and sent his sister to marry the new King of Spain. This exchange gave Spain a future claim on the Portuguese throne. When the next Portuguese monarch, Don Sebastião, died heirless pursuing chivalric fantasies in Morocco, the only remaining Portuguese in line for the throne was his uncle, a cardinal, who died in 1580 childless.

Spain and the House of Bragança (1580–1910)

1580–1640	Spain rules Portugal.
1640–1656	The Duke of Bragança recaptures the throne.
1706–1750	Architecture flowers under João V.
1750–1777	The indolent José I cedes governing to Prime Minister Pombal.
1755	Lisbon is razed by the Great Earthquake.
1808–1812	The Peninsular War.
1808–1821	The court goes into exile in Brazil.
1908	King Carlos I and his heir are assassinated.
1910	Manuel II abdicates, ending the monarchy.

As a result of all the Portuguese and Spanish royal intermarriages, when the last Avís died childless, Felipe II of Spain gained the throne of Portugal. To ensure popular acceptance, he agreed that the Portuguese government would be run solely by Portuguese. While this arrangement lasted, Spain ruled Portugal, but 60 years later one of Felipe's descendents appointed Spaniards to government positions, inciting the Portuguese.

The most powerful Portuguese of the time was the Duke of Bragança, who the Spanish feared as a rallying point for rebellion. They foolishly tried to seduce him with power by giving him control of the Portuguese army. He turned his troops against the Spanish in 1640, conquering all of Portugal in a matter of weeks. Thus did João IV found the Bragança dynasty, Portugal's last.

Half a century later, after independence had been consolidated, João V came to the throne. Supported by gold and diamonds mined in the colony of Brazil, he built ostentatiously throughout Portugal. Especially splendid is the palace at Mafra, near Lisbon, and the library at Coimbra, an ideal of its type. His son, José I, lacking all ambition, trifled while a favorite minister named Pombal ruled the country. In 1755, Lisbon was leveled by a cataclysmic earthquake. Pombal stepped forward to resurrect the city, which still bears his orderly stamp.

Since 1386 Portugal had been tied by treaty in a "strong, perpetual and true league of friendship" with England. When Napoléon declared war on England, this treaty embroiled Portugal in a conflict that otherwise did not affect her. Napoléon's troops invaded in 1808 to deprive the English of Portuguese bases, and England sent the future Duke of Wellington to drive them out. By this time there was no royal court in Portugal, for all the blue-bloods had run as fast as silk slippers could take them to ships bound for Brazil. Wellington chased the French from Portugal by 1811, and from Spain two years later, but the royal court had found the weather and society of Rio de Janeiro more congenial than Lisbon, and remained abroad for another decade.

By the time a king returned to Portugal in 1821 he found a constitution had been drafted in his absence that rejected absolute rule. By this time monarchies through most of Europe had been replaced by republics, and many voices in Portugal shouted for the political freedoms enjoyed elsewhere. They fell on deaf royal ears. In 1908 the king and his heir were assassinated. The king who followed would be the last—an uprising by the navy sent him into exile in 1910, making Portugal at last a republic.

The Republic (1910–1976)

1910–1926	Liberal governments replace one another.
1932	Salazar becomes prime minister.
1968	Incapacitated, Salazar is replaced.
1974	The flower revolution brings socialism.
1975	The African colonies are given independence.
1976	A new constitution is enacted.

With no tradition of democratic rule, Portugal had a stormy time with republican government, switching ministers and parties several times a year. At the same time the economic situation deteriorated, exacerbated by the cost of joining the Allies in World War I. The situation had grown desperate by the 1920s. In 1925 three separate military coups were attempted; in 1926 one succeeded.

The military government drafted a civilian economics professor, António de Oliveira Salazar, to solve crushing economic problems. At first he succeeded brilliantly, so much so that he became prime minister by 1932. He then promulgated a new constitution in which only his party could field candidates, becoming a dictator in fact, if not in title. Although he kept Portugal out of World War II, from which it profited greatly, by the 1960s, economic troubles stewed again. At the same time, independence movements in Portugal's African colonies of Angola, Mozambique and Guinea, all residues of Portugal's early explorations, could not be quelled. During this crisis, Salazar suffered an incapacitating stroke from which he never recovered, and finally died in 1970. His replacement was a party faithful, Marcelo Caetano, who tried to hold on to the African colonies with 50,000 Portuguese troops, a huge drain for a small country. Still it was too few to silence the African independence movements. Before long almost everyone except the government could see that the expensive military enterprise was not working.

It was the army who finally revolted, in 1974, filling the streets of Lisbon with flower-draped tanks in the so-called "Flower Revolution." A realistic general who recognized the futility of military colonization in Africa became president, freeing the African colonies as his first official act. Much strife remained before Portugal could settle into orderly political processes—a communist government that had to be ousted by a popular uprising, and governments that changed themselves capriciously. During the 1970s Portugal seemed the most politicized of countries, but now appears set on a moderate socialist course.

Art and Architecture

The outstanding Portuguese art form is architecture, exemplified in modest homes as well as grand palaces. Every southern village is filled with tiny houses, brilliantly whitewashed, whose doorways and windows wear playful cerulean blue or ochre outlines. In northern towns you will be drawn to that one house in an ordinary row covered in wildly patterned tiles. Called *azulejos*, these bold glazed tiles reveal the passionate side of the Portuguese.

The nave of the church at Batalha Monastery is 14th-century Gothic.

The same love of display can be observed in more august edifices, such as palaces and cathedrals. Like all European countries, Portugal spared no expense to create grand palaces of the finest materials, and erected splendid cathedrals of imposing size, sumptuous with marble and gilt. However, grand Portuguese buildings differ from their French and Italian counterparts in managing to be inviting despite all their grandeur. You can (almost) imagine living in a Portuguese palace, for there is an engaging quality about its human scale that survives the beauty.

The best Portuguese architecture adds distinctive touches to styles common throughout Europe. Especially characteristic is the 16th-century Manueline, a lightening of formal Gothic frameworks with intricate carved decoration of flora, fauna and instruments of the sea. And, hardly a city or town fails to provide at least one plaster building of pleasing proportions whose details are picked out by darker stone—the Portuguese translation of the Baroque style. Portuguese architecture, like her people, is little known but always appealing.

Roman to Romanesque

Various influences came together to form the Portuguese aesthetic. First were the Romans, who left a special souvenir of their occupation—a lovely second-century temple in the center of **Évora**. In fact, an entire Roman city has been excavated at **Conímbriga,** which contains the largest private houses so far discovered from Roman times, and fine mosaics.

Although the Moors controlled Portugal from the eighth through the 12th centuries, few of their buildings survive. This does not mean their presence had no impact on the Portuguese. Brightly colored tiles in a profusion of patterns *(azulejos)*, and elegant paired windows separated by a slender column *(ajimeses)*, are both the Moors' aesthetic remains.

The 12th century ushered in the Romanesque architectural style, with an emphasis on imposing, barrel-vaulted ceilings supported by round Roman arches. Portugal has two exceptional examples. *Sé Velha* (Old Cathedral) in **Coimbra** was designed in the middle of the 12th century as a fortress church, since it was wartime and Coimbra defended the front. A monolithic facade with a single window is topped by triangular merlons to protect rooftop defenders shooting at attackers. Massive piers support the ceiling while Byzantine columns define the galleries (the impressive altar and cloisters, however, were added a century later). This church "in armor" epitomizes medieval times.

Tomar retains the magnificent *Convento do Cristo* surrounded by sturdy Medieval walls. All of the convent is wonderful, but the centerpiece is the oldest part, the 12th-century *Charola*, a 16-sided church of the Knights Templar modeled on the Mosque of the Rock in Jerusalem. Inside, an octagon rises an impressive two stories to a dome resting on the polygon of the building walls.

In **Bragança**, miraculously, a civil building remains from the 12th century—the *Domus Municipalis,* City Hall. Its five sides are pierced by multiple Romanesque round arches, playing against circular medallions that ring the roof. Since the interior of the structure is composed of one huge room, the wonder is how the city government could function.

Castles survive from the hoary times of warfare with the Moors. The oldest is the castle in **Guimarães**, whose 10th-century perpendicular towers precede the founding of Portugal. But the most romantic castle is **Almourol**, perfectly situated on an island in the Tagus River near Tomar. Approachable only by boat, it looks as a fairy castle should, with stout walls and soaring towers. High on a hill in **Leiria**, Afonso Henriques, the first King of Portugal, constructed another castle in the early 12th century. Although sticklers point out that the castle was modified later, it looks magical from a distance nonetheless.

These early fortresses, designed to protect territory captured from the Moors, were followed by more once Portugal became embroiled with neighboring Spain. In the 13th and 14th centuries, Portugal walled itself in with an immense number of fortified keeps. Always placed high to command the surrounding countryside, they generally consisted of a double outer wall enclosing a square massive tower topped with merlons. A fantastic line of 20 still watch over the Estrela mountains on the eastern border with Spain.

By the 16th century, Portugal was using the ideas of the French architect Vauban to create fortresses in a star shape, whose rays would concentrate attackers at the center into massed targets hard to miss. Dramatic examples survive at **Almeida** in the Estrela mountains and at **Elvas** near Évora. In fact, Portugal retains so many imposing castles (more than 50), that by rights the world should refer to "castles in Portugal," rather to those in Spain.

Gothic and Manueline

Toward the end of the 12th century, the new Gothic aesthetic for churches began its sweep through Europe. Round arches grew points to reach up to ever-higher ribbed vaults resting on thin supports—lending a heavenly upward thrust to buildings.

To see what the Portuguese did with this Gothic style visit 14th-century *Santa Maria de Vitoria* in the monastery at **Batalha**. The monastery was commissioned by João I, the founder of the house of Avís, in gratitude for God's help in defeating the Spanish. Complete with rose window, buttresses, pinnacles and mammoth outside door (unfortunately, except for the central *Christ in Majesty*, surrounded only by copies of the original statues), the plain interior sweeps upward to a forest of ribs in the vaulting. This is flamboyant Gothic at its most harmonious.

The other buildings of the monastery are magnificent Gothic structures as well, though decorated in a new style. As Portugal grew rich from her overseas colonies during the reign of Manuel I, "the Fortunate," an original Portuguese style developed celebrating the sea and the foreign flora and fauna that Portugal had discovered. The term *Manueline* refers not to building plans or structures, but to the profusion of the decoration, and the representation of ropes, knots, ship's masts, palm trees, acorns, leaves and flowers, or even playful designs. Decoration became a wonder of its own, a feature on which light could leap and gambol.

The very first Manueline building is the *Church of Jesus* at **Setúbal**. Inside, huge pillars unexpectedly twist in spirals to support a flamboyantly ribbed ceiling. The *Royal Palace* at **Sintra** shows off Manueline wings against a rich mudjar center. But the stately *Hieronymite Monastery* at **Belém**, outside Lisbon, presents the culmination of the style. The church interior is a grotto of tapering columns rising to webs of crossed vaulting. The cloister outside is a study-piece of sophisticated decoration.

For a harmonious mix of Gothic structure and Manueline decor see *Santa Maria de Vitoria* monastery at **Batalha**, noted before, whose *Claustro Real* (Royal Cloister) and the *Capelas Imperfeitas* (Unfinished Chapels) employ rich decoration that plays well against a simple Gothic structure. Yet the most famous example of the Manueline is the often-pictured window surround of the nave in the *Convent of Christ* at **Tomar**. Amid the masts, knots, seaweed and chains, a window can barely be discerned. This was the apex of Manueline exuberance.

Neoclassic and Baroque

The Manueline style lasted only 100 years. A neoclassical reaction against extravagant decoration took over by the late 16th century. *São Vencente de Fora* in **Lisbon** is simple and classically perfect in its coffered ceiling. Lovely *azulejos* (painted tiles) cover the walls, some depicting the capture of Lisbon from the Moors. At **Coimbra** *Santa Clara a Nova* suggests the Parthenon of Rome. Although harmonious, it shows tastes moving again toward profuse adornment.

In the beginning of the 18th century, King João V promised to build a monastery if God would grant him an heir. When God fulfilled His part of the bargain, João erected the sumptuous palace/monastery at **Mafra**. Availing himself of huge deposits of gold and emeralds discovered in Brazil, João lavished millions on this palace. He ordered a German architect, to design a Baroque masterpiece whose walls run two miles in circumference, and whose every interior inch is covered with marble.

But this change of style again produced a reaction. After an earthquake leveled much of **Lisbon** in 1755, Prime Minister Pombal took up the challenge of restoring the city. Classically simple open squares and boulevards created a style named after its producer—*Pombaline*—and survive to this day. The epitome of the style is Lisbon's grand square, the *Praça do Comércio*, elegantly lined with buildings that frame a statue of the king.

By the end of the century, a busier Baroque style became dominant, exemplified by the Baroque *Royal Palace* at **Queluz**, 10 miles outside Lisbon. Although inspired by Versailles, its feel is different, thanks to a rose stucco facade and the delicacy of an interior decorated for a queen, rather than a king. Yet the crowning achievement of the Portuguese Baroque is a single flight of stairs. But what a flight it is! Built to bring penitents to the church of *Bom Jesus*, in the outskirts of **Braga**, this staircase is perfectly harmonious despite splitting into two and folding back upon itself. One doubts that it has an equal in the world.

In the 19th century, Portugal—as did many other countries—adopted the Victorian style, but did so in an unusual way. In 1836 the Queen of Portugal married the Duke of Saxe-Coburg-Gotha, a German, while another cousin, Albert, married Queen Victoria of Britain. Although little known, it was Victoria's cousin-in-law Fernando of Portugal who first built in the style that would become so closely associated with Victoria as to be called by her name. For an afternoon of pure fun visit the original Victorian building, the *National Palace of Pena* at **Sintra**. No other decor attempts to mix such varied patterns within a structure combining Moorish elements, Gothic additions and oriental motifs.

Then, at the turn of the present century, Portugal developed its own version of the art deco style that would also travel through Europe and the Americas. Unfortunately, very little of it has been preserved. What remains may be stumbled upon and enjoyed—as in the case of a little house along the main canal in the city of **Aveiro**.

Portugal also supports a thriving modern architectural community today. Two especially interesting examples are the post-modern shopping mall called *Amoreis* in **Lisbon**, as well as the clever modern glass addition to the top of a 19th-century building at the corner of Castilho and Herculano streets.

Sculpture

Sculpture in Portugal pops up everywhere, although seldom of first quality. The surprise lies in its delicacy, a refinement stemming from French aesthetics rather than the robustness of perennial enemy Spain.

Of the early sculpture, everyone's favorite are the tombs of Pedro I and his beloved Inês de Castro in the monastery in **Alcobaça**. The story behind them adds some spice. While still a prince, Pedro fell in love with the Spanish Inês, but his father had her murdered because he mistrusted her foreign connections. When Pedro came to the throne, he viciously killed her assassins, then moved Inês' body to Alcobaça where he constructed his own tomb facing hers so she would be his first sight on resurrection. Thus, these tombs lie foot-to-foot in opposite transepts of the church. Inês' effigy, borne by six angels, looks beautiful enough to explain Pedro's passion. The carving of the Last Judgment at Inês' feet is sublime. Pedro's tomb is emblazoned with an intricately designed wheel of fortune at his head and scenes of his last moments at his feet. The tombs are not to be missed.

The place to study the range of Portuguese sculpture is in the *Museu Machado de Castro* in **Coimbra**. The wing to the right on the ground floor traces the art of sculpture up to the Renaissance. Take a close look at an early limestone knight. Only two feet high, the man in heavy armor sits astride his equally sturdy steed. In the left wing is displayed the genius of Nicolas Chanterene. A Walloon by birth, Chanterene's French aesthetic made him the great sculptor of the Manueline period. His *Virgin Reading*, and *Entombment of Eight Personages* provide a foretaste of the exceptional sensitivity he exhibited in such masterpieces as the tombs in **Coimbra's** *Monastery of Santa Cruz* of Afonso Henriques and Sancho I, the first two kings of Portugal. Unretouched, they still exude strength in restful sleep. Chanterene is largely responsible for the imposing west door of the church at the *Hieronymite Monastery* at **Belém** in the outskirts of Lisbon, which includes a statue of Prince Henry the Navigator and effigies of Manuel I and his queen. The overall harmony of conception is remarkable for a time when the placement of statues was dictated by architecture.

Chanterene aside, sculptors are largely unsung in Portugal and attributions to individuals remain dubious because most pieces were products of workshops. Here and there, however, an exceptional artist can be picked out. In the late 16th century two Portuguese brothers Gaspar and Domingos Coelho produced a lovely work in **Portalegre**. They placed rectangular panels in an arched frame in the high altar of the *Cathedral* to produce a pleasing classical aberration during a time of gilded excess.

By the 18th century, rococo gilded wood ran riot through churches. *São Francisco* in **Porto** is the outstanding example, although the tiny chapel of *São Lourenço* in the Algarve's **Almansil** will do as well. Both look as if carvers covered every inch with gilded wood and were not satisfied, so they topped their gilding with even more gilding. And, in **Aveiro**, near Porto, the chancel of the church of *Convento de Jesus das Barrocas*, now a museum, includes a remarkable marble mosaic, only outdone by the astonishing marble chapel of São Baptista in *São Roque* in **Lisbon**.

One last sculpture deserves mention because every visitor to **Lisbon** sees it— the statue of José I in *Terreiro do Paço* square. Construction of the grand monastery at Mafra, discussed above, required so much carving that a school was established to train sculptors. Joaquim Machado de Castro emerged as its most gifted pupil. To ensure that his rebuilding of Lisbon would receive royal commendation, Prime Minister Pombal wanted a statue of his King centrally displayed and called upon de Castro to set this "pretty" king atop a small horse. The bronze work is of the highest order, amazingly intricate in detail. However, to say the least, the conception does not seem flattering; yet José was apparently pleased to see himself portrayed as a chubby boy on a pony.

Painting

Paintings in Portugal, little known or reproduced, come as fresh surprises. Portugal bred scores of competent artists whose work is admirable, and, in the 15th century it produced one certified genius—Nuno Gonçalves.

To explore the scope of this small nation's painters, proceed directly to the *Museu Nacional de Arte Antiga* in **Lisbon**, which exhibits both native and foreign works. The second floor displays great works by foreign artists, including a fine *Temptation of Saint Antony* by Bosch, the splendid *Saint Jerome* by Dürer, and the magnificent *Twelve Apostles* by Zurbáran.

Portuguese paintings take up the third floor. The star is a huge six-panel polyptych called *The Adoration of Saint Vincent* by Gonçalves, from the middle of the 15th century. Saint Vincent, the patron saint of Lisbon, is portrayed full-figure in the middle of both center panels as he receives homage from princes and peasants alike. In the left center panel Alonso V kneels with his son beside him, the future João II, while Prince Henry the Navigator hovers behind. Queen Isabel kneels opposite, the king's mother behind her, and standing in the rear left is probably the artist himself. The crowded composition presents wondrous faces of almost startling realism. Sadly, this is the only known work of Gonçalves' genius.

Gonçalves' talent soars above his contemporaries whose works are displayed on the same floor. In fact, aside from this outstanding artist, most 15th-century painting in Portugal slavishly imitated the Flemish artist Jan van Eyck (who visited Portugal in 1428). The other exceptions are works by untrained painters who substituted personal feeling for academic instruction to produce delightful primitives.

By the next century, however, Portugal found its stride. The great Manueline painter Jorge Afonso (died 1540) painted *Christ Appearing to the Virgin* for the church *Madre de Deus* in **Lisbon** as a balanced portrayal of peaceful faces. In the ambulatory of the *Templars' church* in **Tomar** hangs his *Resurrection*, with Christ floating above the city of Lisbon.

Gregorio Lopes (died 1550) is famed for his backgrounds, which make intricate frames for unexceptional figures. The *Museu Nacional de Arte Antiga* in **Lisbon** displays his striking *Virgin and Child with Angels*. Another artist, Cristovão Figueiredo (c. 1500–1555) painted faces as well as anyone, as his *Entombment* in the same museum proves. But perhaps the most haunting painting in the museum is by an unknown artist—*Portrait of a Lady with a Rosary*, worthy of Zurbarán.

"The Grand Vasco," Vasco Fernandes, was born about 1542 and practiced in Viseu, the best place to see and appreciate his work. *Museu Grão Vasco* holds his masterpieces—five altars from the cathedral. *Saint Peter on his Throne* is a tour-de-force of spatial illusion, while *Calvary* crowds peasants and German soldiers in an assemblage for the eye to wander over and the mind to contemplate.

Domingos António de Sequieira (1768–1837) was Portugal's Goya, and like Goya, an exile because of his liberal political views. He won a gold medal in Paris by besting Delacroix and Gericault, among other luminaries. Much of his finest work is displayed in the *Museu Nacional de Arte Antiga* in **Lisbon**. *Saint Bruno at Prayer*, simple and intense, employs bold foreshortening. *Count do Farrobo* is perceptive and forceful. The *Portrait of the Viscount of Santarem and Family* is complex, subtle in tone, and arresting. His charcoals are luminous. Sequieira indeed was a master, and a fitting culmination for Portuguese art.

In 1955 Portugal received one of the greatest gifts of art ever donated. Calouste Gulbenkian, an Armenian from Turkey, brokered oil for Iraq to become one of the wealthiest men in the world. He was an avid collector who spent his last 15 years in Portugal, and left a museum in **Lisbon** to house his treasures when he died in 1955. The *Calouste Gulbenkian Museum* ranks with the major museums of the world, constituting the finest collection amassed by a single person. Oriental carpets and ceramics, European paintings from the 12th through the 20th century and art nouveau Lalique glass all make this a museum to savor.

Azulejos

Portugal's most eye-catching contribution to the world of art is the glazed-tile scenes that cover church and palace walls, and even house facades. The Portuguese acquired a taste for such tiles after conquering northern Morocco early in the 15th century. At first, the tiles were imported both from Morocco and Moorish Spain, but by the late 16th century the Portuguese were manufacturing their own versions. The original tiles were drawn in deep blue tones on white, causing them to be named *azulejos,* from *azul,* meaning "blue."

A national craze for the tiled scenes soon developed, and by the 17th century yellows and greens had joined the original blues. Biblical themes gave way to classical scenes, sylvan pictures and even landscapes. Churches, palaces and manor houses all were covered in the latest style. This huge demand ultimately led to the mass production of azulejos, causing an inevitable decline both in quality and panache. As a result, the artform fell out of favor, until recently when the Portuguese learned all over again to appreciate the old tiles, bidding them up in auctions or in antique shops.

Sixteenth- and 17th-century originals remain in churches and palaces around the country, adorning otherwise bare walls. The unsuspecting visitor, coming upon a room or church nave covered with naive scenes in cheery blue, feels the irresistible delight of this Portuguese specialty.

The best of azulejos include the 16th-century tiles from Spain that cover the walls of the *Palácio Real* in **Sintra**. The tiles in the *Church of the Convento dos Lólos* in **Évora** from 1711 were done by António de Oliveira Bernardes, one of the great practitioners of the craft. For the apex of sumptuous tile art, see *São Francisco* in **Porto**. But for a special treat, spend a night or two in the grand azulejo corridors of *Pousada Santa Marinha* in **Guimarães** or in the more intimate halls of the *Hotel Convento São Paulo* near **Évora**. You'll be glad you did.

LISBON AND SURROUNDINGS

Pena Palace in Sintra is a castle with Moorish/Gothic influences complete with minarets, turrets and drawbridges.

Lisbon dwarfs all other Portuguese cities in size and number of visitors. Not surprisingly, it houses fine museums and offers great food, but it is also fortunate in its surroundings. Elegant Batalha, the greatest religious complex of Portugal, waits 120 kilometers north, only 20 kilometers from Alcobaça, with its own dignified cathedral and two storied tombs. Near, as well, is the charming little village of Óbidos, with appropriately cute castle. Fátima of the miracles occupies the same area. Magical Sintra, only 23 kilometers from Lisbon, presents not one, but three palaces amid romantic scenery. Even closer stand the elegant royal palace at Queluz and a huge, sumptuous one at Mafra. There is beach near Lisbon—wild and long at Cabo do Guincho, small, amid elegance at adjoining Cascais and Escoril. Setúbal is less than fifty kilometers south of Lisbon with one fascinating church, a fortress at Pamela and more beaches nearby.

Lisbon holds the two best museums of Portugal, three or four churches worth a look, a magnificent Gothic monastery and provides walks amid the cosmopolitan hustle and bustle only a capital can provide. **Sintra** becomes the favorite of all who visit for its magical forest and one Medieval castle, one Moorish castle and a Victorian extravaganza. In **Batalha** resides the architectural glory of the country, close to the lovely tombs of two lovers in **Alcobaça**. **Óbidos** is a cute town with a cute castle. **Mafra**, only 43 km from Lisbon, presents as baroque a palace as you will ever see. Even closer, **Queluz** offers a pretty palace of a queen. Across the Tagus, south of Lisbon, lie **Setubal** with an interesting church and pretty **Palmela** with a fine old fortress/castle. (Alcobaça and Fátima are discussed as excursions from Batalha, Mafra as an excursion from Queluz.)

The following towns and pousadas are covered in this chapter.

Town	Pousada Name	Rating	Page
Batalha	Mestre Afonso Dominges	★★★	*page 527*
Lisboa	None		*page 484*
Óbidos	de Castilo	★★★	*page 523*
Palmela	Palmela	★★★★	*page 517*
Queluz	Donha Maria I	★★★★	*page 512*
Setúbal	São Filipe	★★★★	*page 520*
Sintra	None		*page 534*

To savor the region, you can stay six nights in Lisbon and take day-trips all around. You will experience much more, however, by leaving Lisbon after three nights to spend a night at the pousadas in Óbidos, Batalha or Queluz. For an unforgettable treat, spend a night or two at the beautiful Palácio de Seteais in Sintra, even if it is not a pousada.

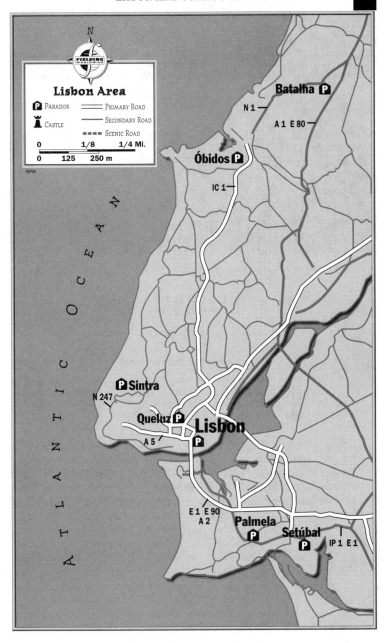

A Lisbon streetcar is a fun mode of sightseeing.

LISBON

★★★★

Accommodations

Da Lapa ★★★★★

R. do Pau de Bandeira, 4 (in the section called Lapa, two blocks north of the Museum of Ancient Art; take a cab), Lisbon, 1100, *(01) 395 00 05, FAX (01) 395 06 65. 76 rooms, plus 8 suites.*

If willing to pay for the best, the most intimate, elegant and welcoming hotel in town is the **Da Lapa** located in the embassy section, one mile from city-center. Housed in a renovated 19th-century *palacita* formerly owned by the Count of Valenças, the Lapa has been renovated throughout with unerring good taste. Public spaces flow gently into each other to permit guests to wander as if through a private home and choose atmospheres suited to their mood. Every detail is perfect in the original mansion, including bedrooms and suites each decorated in a different style. From top-floor suites the views of Lisbon and the Tagus are spectacular. As recompense, the lower floors and a modern wing overlook a lush tropical park below a cascading two-story waterfall. If all this were not sufficient reason to stay at the Lapa, the attentive yet never intrusive staff would be. Perfection extends to its Embaixada restaurant, which serves the finest food of any hotel in Lisbon. Even with a new full-facility health club, so far prices hit $225 only from April through June and after the middle of September. In July and August they fall below.

Ritz ★★★★

R. Rodrigo da Fonseca, 88 (one block east of the Parque Eduardo VII), Lisbon, 1100, ☎ (01) 69 20 20, FAX (01) 69 17 83, Telex 12589. 265 rooms.

We prefer the Da Lapa to the more famous Ritz, which has coasted on its laurels since a takeover by the huge Intercontinental Hotel Corporation. It had always been too large to provide individual service, while its location beyond the edge of tourist interests left it out of things. But it had no serious competition for luxury before the Hotel da Lapa came along. Modern outside, its elegance is all within, consisting of furniture and appointments. It may have the finest bathrooms in Europe. Although all the suites are utterly elegant, many of the simple bedrooms remain ordinary. A suite with a park view is well worth the additional escudos. However, ordinary bedrooms cost $200 in season. Ask for a room at the back, overlooking the park.

York House ★★★★

Rua das Janelas Verdes, 32, Lisbon, 1100, ☎ (01) 396 25 44, FAX (01) 397 27 93. 31 rooms, plus 3 suites.

The York House stands out at the $100-$200 level. That overused word "charming" is its perfect description, and a word you'll exclaim again and again if you stay there. This *residencial* is remodeled from a 16th-century convent including closing off the city and its noise with a high enclosing wall. All furnishings are lovely; floors are homey old wood or tile. Its location is far enough from the heart of the city for relative quiet, despite its location on a busy street, and close enough to taxi to in minutes. The best rooms are those overlooking the beautiful courtyard. Classed as a residencial, primarily because it lacks such extras as an elevator, its service is good, but not that of the Ritz or Da Lapa. Prices dip below $150 for a double through the end of April, but approach $200 in July and August. This one is very popular, so should be booked well in advance.

Veneza ★★

Av. da Liberdade, 189, Lisbon, 1100, ☎ (01) 352 26 18, FAX (01) 352 66 78. 36 rooms.

A charmer in the heart of town is the Veneza. This 19th-century mansion has just opened as one of Lisbon's most stylish hotels. Although there is an odd contrast between elegant marble stairs in the lobby and bedrooms done in a homey green with white wicker, the former impresses and the latter welcomes. This hotel combines elegance, homeyness and a fine location in one intimate package. Surprisingly, the cost is just $125.

As Janelas Verdes ★★

R. das Janelas Verdes, 47 (down the street from the York House, near the Museum of Ancient Art in Lapa), Lisbon, 1100, ☎ (01) 396 81 43 (or 44), FAX (01) 396 81 44. 17 rooms.

Another fine choice is the As Janelas Verdes, near the York House. This was the annex of the York House; now it has reopened separately owned and nicely redone. The building is a late 18th-century mansion, decorated more formally than the York to provide a stately but less-charming option up the street. Bedrooms are larger, but the ones fronting the street can be noisy. For this reason and for the view, ask for a back room over the quiet patio.

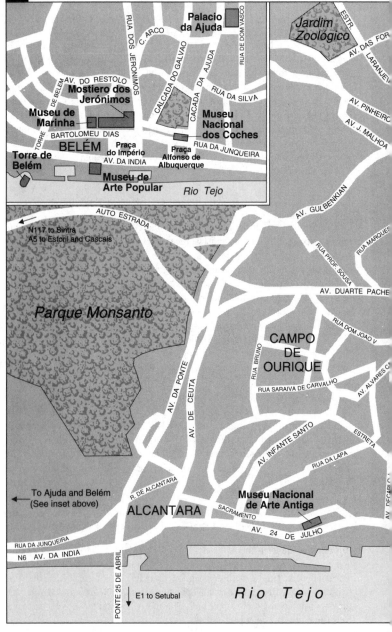

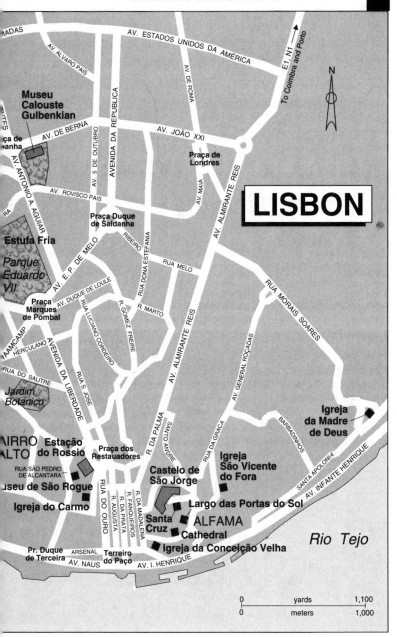

Albergaria da Senhora do Monte

Calçada do Monte, 39 (on a hilltop just north of the São Jorge hill), Lisbon, 1100,
☎ *(01) 886 60 02, FAX (01) 887 77 83. 28 rooms.*

At $100 or less the Albergaria da Senhora do Monte makes the category only is you
factor in the free breakfast. Views of the castle, city and river are perhaps the best
available, and this special hotel is pleasantly decorated. Bedrooms are comfortable
and all incorporate terraces. Those at the back provide the views worth coming for.
While the bedrooms are not air-conditioned, they seldom need it. Admittedly, the
location is not central, but the modest price saves enough for plenty of taxi rides.

Dom Carlos

*Av. Duque de Loule, 121 (fronting its own park two blocks east of the Pr. de Pombal),
Lisbon, 1100,* ☎ *(01) 353 90 71, FAX (01) 352 07 28, Telex 16468. 73 rooms, plus 17
suites.*

The recently remodeled Dom Carlos uses yards of glass to take advantage of a garden outside. Bedrooms are Scandinavian and wood panelled, with Portuguese
touches. This is a comfortable and efficient hotel that charges a quarter of the fee of
most of its neighbors.

Hotel Metropole

Pr. do Rossío, 30, Lisbon, 1100, ☎ *(01) 346 91 64, FAX (01) 346 91 66. 36 rooms.*
The location of the Hotel Metropole could not be better, right in the heart of the
city. This is a 75-year-old hotel that has just been spruced up with every convenience, while preserving art deco details. It glistens and presents fine views from the
higher floors.

Residential Florescente

*R. Portas de Santo Antão, 99 (one short block west of the Pr. Restauradores), Lisbon,
1100,* ☎ *(01) 342 66 09, FAX (01) 342 77 33. 100 rooms, half with bath or shower.*
There are reasonable options for $50 as well. The uniformed desk staff of the Resi-
dential Florescente, its great location and airy rooms with TVs all suggest high-
priced territory. On the other hand, there is no elevator and the rooms without
bathing facilities can be dreary, presenting quite a different impression. This is a
truly paranoid hotel—half terrific value, the rest rather seedy—which is why the
hotel's official rating and prices are so low that its good rooms emerge as truly outstanding values. You must ask to see a room before booking and it must be one of
the more "expensive" for it to please. Here, too, you are smack in the low-priced
restaurant section of the city.

Imperador

*Av. 5 de Outubro, 55 (a quarter of a mile north of the northeast corner of Parque Edu-
ardo VII, one block west and north of the Saldanha metro stop), Lisbon, 1100,* ☎ *(01)
352 48 84, FAX (01) 352 65 37. 43 rooms.*

Past a claustrophobic entrance wait spotless rooms at the Imperador, comfortably
decorated in muted colors. Front rooms overlook a small garden. Even at its low
prices it provides a free breakfast.

Dining

While only a few truly exceptional restaurants exist in Portugal, about half grace the capital. At these you will pay $70 or more for dinner for two, be treated like royalty, surrounded by elegance and relish an extraordinary meal. But fear not, there are also enough modest restaurants serving tasty dishes made from fresh ingredients for diners to enjoy a different one every night for a year.

Expensive ($30+)

Conventual ★★★★★

Pr. das Flores, 45 (in a little green square just west of the Bairro Alto. From R. da Escola Politecnica, which is a continuation of R. Dom Pedro V in the Bairro Alto, take a left on R. San Marcal at the Botanical Gardens, then the third right. Better still, take a cab, Lisbon, 1100, ☎ *(01) 60 91 96. Closed Sat. lunch, Sun. and for lunch on holidays.*

Our hearts cry that this is the best restaurant in Lisbon; our wallets agree since this one charges about 30 percent less than its competition. While most elegant Lisbon restaurants earn their excellence by incorporating French recipes, Sra. Marques is a true original. Her coriander soup is sublime, monkfish with creamy herb sauce is delectable, and the sole with shellfish sauce a delight. Every dish is prepared with taste, and most succeed memorably. The restaurant is more comfortable than formal—a former convent with old stone walls and ancient terra cotta floors decorated by the owner's eclectic collection of antiques. Reservations are necessary. Credit Cards: A, D, MC,V.

Casa da Comida ★★★★★

Travessa das Amoreiras, 1 (just off the Pr. de Amoreiras, 4 blocks west and 3 south of Parque Eduardo VII), Lisbon, 1100, ☎ *(01) 388 53 76; FAX (01) 387 51 32. Closed Sat. lunch, Sun. and Aug.*

We wrestle mightily about whether Conventual (above) or Comida is the best restaurant in Lisbon. Let us just say they are different, and each is a treasure. Comida adds a French touch to traditional Portuguese cuisine and serves it in a grander style than does Conventual, although at almost twice the price. The restaurant is housed in a most discrete townhouse with a roaring fire in winter or a beautiful planted patio in summer. The decor is elegant, the bar inviting, and tables are decorated with style. In general the food is slightly nouveau, with the delicate portions of that genre. Special dishes include savory clam soup or a succulent cascade of shellfish. Mention the turbot with green pepper and we salivate. The extensive menu includes a number of standard dishes as well, although we confess to prefer Tágide's version of roast baby kid with herbs. Prices are high, and will easily pass $100 for a couple, but no one complains. Reservations are absolutely necessary. Credit Cards: A, D, MC, V.

Tágide ★★★★

Largo da Academia Nacional de Belas Artes, 18 (two blocks south of the R. Garrett in Chiado), Lisbon, 1100, ☎ *(01) 342 07 20; FAX (01) 347 18 80. Closed Sat. night and Sun.*

The spacious windows of this former townhouse look over the port and reflect the crystal chandeliers of its elegant off-white dining room. (Request a window table.) Service is discrete, and the dishes, if anything, surpass expectations. Start with salmon pâté, clams in broth with coriander and garlic or cold stuffed crab. Graduate to grilled baby goat with herbs or supreme of halibut. Either the soufflé with hot chocolate sauce, dessert crepes or a superb creme caramel will cap a fine meal. A couple will spend about 20.000$with wine, which is a bargain for such exquisitely prepared food. Reservations are necessary. Credit Cards: A, D, MC, V.

Gambrinus

R. das Portas de Santo Antão, 25 (on a tiny square behind the east side of the Teatro Nacional a few steps north of Pr. Rossío), Lisbon, 1100, ☎ (01) 342 14 66; FAX (01) 346 50 32.

There is no question that this is the best seafood restaurant in Lisbon, nor that it is the most expensive restaurant in Portugal. A dinner can cost a third more than at Tágide. Fish and shellfish are invariably fresh and done to a turn as they should be at these prices. Reservations are advised. Credit Cards: A, V.

Embaixada

R. Pau de Bandeira, 4 (in the Hotel da Lapa near the Museum of Ancient Art; take a taxi), Lisbon, 1100, ☎ (01) 395 00 05.

The dining room is divided by a kind of gazebo to create intimate seating arrangements, just one example of the thought invested in this establishment. Large windows overlook a tropical garden complete with waterfall, while all Lisbon spreads beyond. The nouvelle-style food is characterized by attention to detail and the finest ingredients. Lunch is a $25 menu that counts among the great bargains in Portugal. Dinner prices rise to about $40 for an excellent five-course *menu de dégustation*, or there are intriguing à la carte choices. Credit Cards: MC, V.

Moderate ($15–$30)

Sua Excelencia

R. do Conde, 42 (In Lapa, 1 block due north of the National Museum of Ancient Art), Lisbon, 1100, ☎ (01) 60 36 14. Closed Sat. and Sun. lunch, Wed.in Sept.

This restaurant is entirely the child of its owner, Francisco Queiroz. Only a discrete awning announces it. When the doorbell is rung, the owner greets you, escorts you to a table in a colorful room with tile floor, then recites the menu of the day. Selections depend on what is fresh in the market. Sr. Queiroz speaks enough English to convey what is necessary and, although it will push this price category to the limit, be assured that whatever is selected will be carefully prepared. Reservations are necessary. Credit Cards: A, D, MC, V.

Pap'Açorda

R. da Atalaya, 57 (from the church of São Roque in the Bairro Alto head west along Trav. da Queimada to take the fifth left), Lisbon, 1100, ☎ (01) 346 48 11. Closed Sun. and Mon. lunch, and the first half of July and Oct.

This restaurant, housed in an old bakery, specializes in the hearty food of the Alentejo. Naturally the favored dish is *açorda*, a delicious stew of fish, bread and eggs seasoned with coriander. For the quality and authenticity of the food, it is a bargain. Mário Soures, the president of Portugal, loves this place, and it is very popular with locals, so reservations are necessary on weekends. Credit Cards: A, D, MC, V.

Sancho ★★

Travessa da Gloria, 14 (just off Av. de Liberdade, 1 long block north of the Pr. Restauradores), Lisbon, 1100, ☎ (01) 346 97 80. Closed Sun. and holidays.
Cozy with stucco walls, fireplace, leather furniture and wood-beamed ceiling, this restaurant provides relaxed, enjoyable meals. Shellfish are specialties, and expensive, but moderately priced meat courses are offered as well. Credit Cards: A, MC, V.

Cervajaria Portugális ★

Av. Almirante Reis, 117 (at the north end of the Baixa the large R. da Palma bears northeast and becomes Almirante Reis in half a mile, for another half mile to this restaurant), Lisbon, 1100, ☎ (01) 52 00 02.
Although slightly out of the way, this busy beer-hall is worth a trip for the best seafood values in the city. There is no atmosphere unless you count the bustle and noise of a lot of people enjoying their food. Open until 1:30 a.m. Credit Cards: MC, V.

Inexpensive (Less than $15)

On the east side of Pr. Restauradores, and parallel to it, the small street of *R. Portas de Santo Antão*, and surrounding alleys collect a large number of inexpensive dining establishments. Wander and choose for yourself or use one of our recommendations below.

Bota Alta ★★

Travessa da Queimada, 35 (the street heads west from the church of São Roque in the Bairro Alto), Lisbon, 1100, ☎ (01) 32 79 59. Closed Sunday.
The only problem with this place is that it is well known for tasty food and good value, so waiting in line can be expected. It is a small bistro with a smoke-stained ceiling. The *caldo verde* is delicious. Of course cod is present in many varieties, but there are also daily specials. No reservations are taken.

Cervajaria da Trindade ★

R. Nova de Trindade, 20-B (off R. Garrett in the Chiado), Lisbon, 1100, ☎ (01) 342 35 06.
The room once formed part of a convent and then a brewery, although now it is a beer hall owned by the Sagres beer company. Even if prawns are ordered, the meal should be inexpensive, filling and tasty. A tourist menu is offered for $10. Wash it down with a *mista*, a mixture of light and dark beer. Credit Cards: A, D, MC, V.

Pastelaria Bénard ★

R. Garrett, 104 (the main street of the Chiado in the Bairro Alto), Lisbon, 1100, ☎ (01) 347 31 33. Closed Sunday.
This is the most fashionable of the dozen tea houses in Lisbon. Tea and cakes are the specialties, but there is a small selection of heartier foods. Best for lunch. Credit Cards: None.

Xêlê Bananas ★

Pr. des Flores, 29 (from R. da Escola Politecnica, which is a continuation of R. Dom Pedro V in the Bairro Alto, take a left on R. San Marcal at the Botanical Gardens, then the third right), Lisbon, 1100, ☎ (01) 395 25 15. Closed Saturday lunch and Sunday.

The pretty square opposite adds to the pleasure of the dining experience. The restaurant looks more expensive than it is, and Lisboetas know that well. Credit Cards: A, D, MC, V.

Bonjardim ★

Traversa de Santo Antão, 11 (a narrow street beside the post office building behind (east of) Pr. dos Restauradores), Lisbon, 1100, ☎ (01) 342 43 89.

Noted for perfectly done, roast chicken served with salad and fries, this plain-and-simple eatery is sufficiently successful to support two additional outlets on the same street. Fish soup and the pork *alentejana* aren't bad either. But don't expect atmosphere. Credit Cards: A, D, MC, V.

Directions

From the Airport: A taxi to the center should cost about 2000$00, plus a surcharge for luggage. Aero-express buses leave every 20 minutes or so, until 9 p.m., for center city stops at a cost of 400$00. Save the ticket, for it is good all that day for any other city transport.

By Train: International trains stop at Santa Apolónia Station, a 15-minute walk to the center of the city, but an Aero-express bus covers that distance for 400$00, and its ticket is good for any other city transport. Trains from southern Portugal stop across the river, but include a ferry ride to the Praça do Comércio in the fare. Other trains disgorge in the centrally located Praça Rossío.

By Car: The autoestrada A-1 from **Porto** and **Coimbra** also rings the **airport**, 7 km north of the city. It bends west along the southern edge of the airport where it is called Av. Craveiro Lopes. Just before the racetrack, turn right at the large interchange to travel along Av. Campo Grande with a center island. At the second traffic circle (the Pr. Duque de Saldanha) bear rightward along the wide Pereira de Melo for three blocks until it enters the circle of the Pr. Marquês de Pombal, with a park to the right. Turn south (left) along Av. de Liberdad, lined with flowers, to skirt the Pr. dos Restauradores and enter the Pr. Rossío. Take the rightmost of the parallel streets heading south toward the river, R. do Aurea, which ends in six blocks in the huge plaza of Praça do Comércio with the best chance for parking.

From **Setúbal** and **south**, the soaring span of the Ponte 25 da Abril is crossed to become Av. de Ponte in the city. Exit at the first opportunity. Follow the river east along Av. 24 de Julho, which leads in three miles to the huge Praça do Comércio with parking.

From **Cascais** and **Estoril** by the coastal N-6, Belém is entered along Av. Marginal, which changes its name to Av. de India and finally to Av. 24 de

Julho as it follows the river. In a few miles it deposits traffic in the huge Praça do Comércio with parking.

By the inland road and from **Sintra** along N-7, the autoestrada becomes Av. Duarte Pacheco, then changes its name to Av. Joaquim de Aguiar before reaching the large traffic circle of Pr. Marquês de Pombal. From there follow the Porto directions.

Pousadas Nearby

Queluz: 12 km	Palmela: 43 km	Setúbal: 55 km
Óbidos: 92 km	Batalha: 120 km	

Sights

Lisbon forms a canyon emptying into the wide Tagus (*Tejo* in Portuguese) River. A valley called the **Baixa** (slang for "lowland"), beginning at the river with Pombal's **Praça do Comércio**, leads north over an orderly grid of avenues for seven short blocks to the **Praça Rossío**, the heart of town. On either side hills rise. To the east (right, if facing inland) stands the steep bluff of **São Jorge** crowned by a castle of the same name. As the bluff descends southward toward the river, the most characteristic quarter of the city, the **Alfama**, spills down its sides. To the west (left) of the Baixa, another hill rises to the **Bairro Alto** (the High Quarter), an area of shops and restaurants. Lisbon's better stores perch on its southern slopes in a quarter named **Chiado**. Farther inland, past the Rossío, the grand avenue of **Liberdade** parades to the plaza of the **Marquês de Pombal** fronting the large park of **Eduardo VII**, beyond which sprawls modern Lisbon.

A view along Lisbon's Rua Augusta to the Triumphal Arch of the Praça do Commércio

The area within this canyon is all the average visitor to Lisbon needs to traverse—with the exception of **Belém**, the sight-filled suburb four miles west along the river.

Lisbon's delights are best savored on foot. The city's old yellow streetcars and buses imported from England, whose stops are marked by large signs with clearly posted routes, provide easy respites for the foot-weary. Even more convenient are Lisbon's taxis—the least-expensive in western Europe.

Meters in these black cars with green-blue roofs start at 130$00, and are unlikely to run beyond 600$00 (about $3.50) for local trips. A 10 percent tip is the norm. When their roof lights are lit, taxis can be hailed on streets, but are more readily found in stands beside hotels or tourist sights.

Buses charge by the number of zones traversed, starting at 140$00. Streetcars do likewise. *Módulos*, 10-trip tickets, cut both these costs in half and may be purchased at the Santa Justa elevator just south of Pr. Rossío. Even cheaper are 1350$00 special four-day unlimited-ride tourist passes, also available at the Santa Justa elevator.

Covering the sights of Lisbon requires a minimum of three days. The most expeditious way is by combining visits to sights in adjoining areas. Begin at the **Castelo de São Jorge**, at the top of its hill, meander down through the **Alfama**, and end with a tour of the **Cathedral** at the bottom. Or wander through **Pombal's Praça do Comércio** and explore the avenues leading to the **Praça Rossío**. From here, take an excursion up to the **Bairro Alto** and return along

Av. de Liberdade to finish at the **Parque Eduardo VII** and its botanical **Estufa Fria**.

A taxi or bus trip to the suburb of **Belém** yields the **Mosteiro dos Jerónimos**, the **Torre de Belém**, the **Museu de Marinha** and the **Museu Nacional dos Cochas**, all within walking distance of one another. Include the **Museu do Arte Popular** if interested. The **Museu Nacional de Arte Antiga**, located enroute to Belém, can readily be included in one long day. Because neither lies near other sights, both the **Museu Calouste Gulbenkian** and the church of **Madre de Dios**, with its wonderful azulejo tiles, require separate outings.

São Jorge Hill

Castelo de São Jorge ★★

> *Although it's best to taxi up to the castle, before walking down through the Alfama, bus #37 and trolleys #12 and #28 also stop nearby.*
> *Hours open: daily from 8 a.m. to sunset.*

It was on this hilltop that the Phoenicians first settled, though no one records who lived here before. Remains of a later Roman city are still being excavated, but the massive perimeter walls of the castle (and probably its 10 towers) were raised by Visigoths before 8th-century restoration and strengthening by the Moors. The remains of a 13th-century palace that stand inside the walls served as the principal palace of Portuguese kings for more than 300 years, not replaced until the 16th-century when Manuel I built a new one—later destroyed by the great earthquake of 1755—in the lower city. Afterwards the São Jorge palace became a prison, abandoned and fallen to ruin in the present century.

A haphazard garden reposes within the walls, populated by rare white peacocks, black-necked swans, ducks, ravens, chickens and the occasional flamingo. Walk the ramparts for the best orientation to the city. Southeast, spilling down the hill, is the aged Alfama quarter. To the east, in a valley, spreads the orderly avenues and plazas of Pombal's Baixa, with the Praça do Comércio beside the river. The Av. de Liberdade stretches straight as an arrow north to the large park of Eduardo VII. The Bairro Alto rises directly east of São Jorge hill. Even farther east, and south, the graceful bridge of the American-built Ponte 25 da Abril, whose 3323 feet of single span—the longest in Europe and second-longest in the world—curves gracefully cross the Tejo.

Four blocks east and downhill stands the former monastery of **S. Vicente de Fora**, interesting for the tomb of Catherine of Bragança, wife of Charles II of England. If it is a Tuesday or a Saturday and before 1 p.m., a trip to this church is worthwhile for the flea market that sets up in the street behind it, the **Feira da Ladra**. Most of the merchandise is junk by any standard, but there will be something to catch the fancy of those willing to search. *Free admission.*

Alfama ★

From São Jorge Castle walk to the church of Santa Cruz at the southeast corner of the grounds. Continue east behind its apse and follow R. de Santa Luzia going right downhill until it bends and narrows to stairs that enter the open plaza of Largo das

Portas do Sol. If coming from the lower town, taxi directly to Largo das Portas do Sol. Trolleys #28 and #12, as well as bus #37, also stop there. The route described below can be followed in reverse from the Cathedral, though it is uphill all the way.

The famed Alfama quarter—whose name probably derives from the Arabic word *al Hamman* (the baths)—presents a striking historical contradiction. Traditionally home to the city's upper crust, the rich residents fled at the onset of the great earthquake of 1755 to wait out the aftermath in the safety of their country estates. The poor people of Lisbon, on the other hand, had nowhere to go and many had lost their homes. They rushed to the abandoned Alfama and moved in, for this quarter had sustained less damage than any other because of the hill's granite base. When the rich returned, they chose not to live beside the poor, which is why the greatest concentration of old patrician houses survive in this poor section of Lisbon today.

The Alfama presents a slice of life from the 18th century. Buildings squeeze against one another, wash hangs from windows, braziers in doorways waft the scent of food, and children, animals and activity abound. Catch a glimpse of this earlier time in the mornings or late afternoons when the neighborhood is busiest. (But for safety's sake avoid the area after dark.) Before the cataclysm, most of Lisbon would have looked exactly this way (though somewhat cleaner).

The best introduction to the quarter is the Plaza of **Largo Das Portas do Sol**, named for a long-vanished gate, erected during Moorish rule, which was positioned to face the rising sun. On the right, at the southern end of the plaza, is the Museum of Decorative Arts.

Fundacão Ricardo do Espirito Santo Silva ★ ★

R. de São Tomé, 90, ☎ *(01) 886 2183.*
Hours open: Tues.–Sat. 10 a.m.–1 p.m. and 2:30–5 p.m.
This museum of decorative arts, housed in a 17th-century former palace of the Counts of Azurara, contains a remarkable collection of 17th- and 18th-century furniture and accessories displayed in rooms around a courtyard as they were used, rather than as in a museum. The furniture was donated by Sr. Ricardo do Espírito Santo, head of the bank of the same name and possibly the richest man in Portugal. The foundation supports a school in its annex where students study old crafts, such as wood inlaying. *Admission: 500$00, for 30 minute tours.*

Santa Luzia, opposite, has tiles inside depicting the palace that occupied the site of the Praça do Comércio before the earthquake.

Walk west from the museum (across the plaza) to descend the steps of Beco de Santa Helena on the right. Halfway down take the first left along Beco do Garces then left again to ascend R. do Picão, which enters **Largo do Salvador**. At number 22 is a rare remaining 16th-century mansion, formerly belonging to the Counts of Arcos. Its balcony is later Baroque. Return to the southern end of the largo to take the small **R. da Regueira**, which forks left of the R. do Picão on which we entered. It is a street of small shops and restaurants. At **Beco das Cruzes**, the first alley on the right, an 18th-century house rises with carved ravens supporting an overhanging second story. A few feet down Beco das Cruzes a quaint *azulejo* panel surmounts a door on the left, and beyond it an old arch crosses the street. Back on R. da Requeira again, a few steps sees it opens to a fountain on whose left are the steps of the **Beco do Carneiro**—so narrow that houses almost touch across the alley. There's a lovely view from the top.

Return to the fountain to follow **R. de San Miguel** (opposite Carneiro) where tiny antique shops line the way. **Beco da Cardosa**, the second left, is worth ascending for a short way to see 16th- to 18th-century houses branching off its blind alleys. Proceed a few steps along R. de San Miguel to the church of **San Miguel** which contains some fine Baroque woodwork. Largo de San Miguel (which fronts the church) is crossed by **R. de San Pedro**, the quarter's most animated street. Walk along it to the right into **Largo de San Rafael**, with its one remaining tower from the 14th-century city walls. West of the largo, R. de João da Praça leads in two blocks to the **Cathedral** of Lisbon.

Cathedral ★★

Largo da Sé. From the northern end of the Praça do Comércio go east two blocks to R. da Madalena, which runs north-south. Three blocks north at the church of Madalena, turn right on R. de Santo Antonio da Sé for three short blocks. (Another route is described in the Alfama section above.) Bus #37 and trolleys #28 and #11 stop at the Cathedral.

Hours open: daily 9 a.m.–noon and 2:30–6 p.m. Open Mon., Wed. and Fri. to 7:30 p.m.
After capturing Lisbon from the Moors in 1147, Afonso Henrique ordered a cathedral built for his English bishop. By the end of that century a Romanesque cathedral was completed, including defensive capabilities for a city that did not yet feel safe from attack. Over the centuries Gothic additions and, later, Baroque decorations were appended. But after the cathedral suffered great damage in the 1755 earthquake, it was reconstructed to its earlier style, producing the bare but imposing church on view today.

The facade is particularly harmonic, with massive crenulated towers and solid walls leaving only small Romanesque apertures for the rose window, bells and entry portals. It is all quite stately. Inside, a pure Romanesque barrel vault rests on plain pillars that lead to a simple lantern at the crossing. The aisles paralleling the nave, however, are surmounted by an elegant Gothic triforium. Yet somehow, the reconstruction removed the life from the cathedral, leaving it cold.

To the left, upon entering, a baptismal font dating from 1195 is said to have christened Saint Anthony of Padua. The church altar is 18th-century; behind it is a fine 14th-century Gothic ambulatory. The third chapel on the right (south) contains endearing 14th-century tombs of Lopo Fernandes Pacheco, a close friend of Afonso IV, and his wife, María Vilalobos. Just to the right is the entrance to a lovely, though damaged, 13th-century cloister. On the right in the south transept is the entrance to the sacristy, which serves as the treasury. It contains relics of Portugal's patron Saint Vincent in a lovely mother-of-pearl casket. *Admission: 100$00 to the museum and cloisters.*

Santo António da Sé, on the site of the birthplace of Saint Anthony of Padua, is west of the Cathedral facade.

Baixa

This is the "new" Lisbon, built in one intense decade by Pombal after the great earthquake leveled the old. Straight lines and ordered vistas reflect the rationalism of the 18th century—one of Pombal's rules was that buildings could include no overhangs or curves. The intent was to construct a commercial district anchored at either end by large plazas for public gatherings. Despite the office buildings and banks that have replaced most of the old shops, and the herd of cars that now fills the formerly dramatic expanse of the Praça do Comércio, the Baixa remains more or less as Pombal envisioned it.

Praça do Comércio   ★

The Baixa begins by the river at the Praça do Comércio. Most Lisboetas call it "Tereiro do Paço" (Terrace of the Palace), still memorializing the royal residence on this site before the earthquake. This huge square opening to the wide river lapping at its steps harkens to Venice. The plaza is closed on three sides by pink arcades housing government offices, including courts at its north end. Here, by waiting a while on weekdays, formally robed barristers and judges can be seen.

In the center of it all stands an equestrian **statue of José I**, king during Pombal's era. Machado de Castro cast this large work in the finest 18th-century style, reminiscent of statues of the French Sun King. As it happened, Dom José fell ill during the statue's creation so he did not sit for his portrait, which perhaps explains the ornate helmet and visor that all but obscures his face. A bronze medallion in the front depicts Pombal. When Pombal was removed from office in disgrace, the craftsman who made the medallion was ordered to destroy it. Unable to bring himself to melt his own work, he hid it instead, and later it was found and replaced.

The northeast corner of the plaza, beside the post office, was the spot where King Carlos I and his heir were gunned down in their carriage by assassins.

Rossío

A handsome **triumphal arch** in the northern arcade of the Praça do Comércio leads out to a series of parallel avenues, each built and named for a trade—*Sapateiros* (Cobblers), *Prata* (Silversmiths) *Aurea* (Goldsmiths). The center Rua Augusta is now a pedestrian mall. All the streets lead north over seven short blocks of stores and banks to the main square of the city known as the **Rossío**, although its official name is Praça Dom Pedro IV.

Yet the statue in the center of Pedro IV that lends the official name to the square is actually of Maximilian, the French emperor of Mexico. A ship transporting the statue to Mexico from France had sailed into Lisbon just as word arrived of Maximilian's death. The Portuguese were able to buy the now-useless statue for a pittance, and changed only a few details to adapt it for their own king.

To the left of the Teatro Nacional stands the main train station of Lisbon, the **Estação de Rossío**. Its 19th-century lobby mimics either the Manueline or the Moorish with such exuberance that it is difficult to tell which. North of the station is the **Pr. dos Restauradores**, whose central obelisk commemorates those who rose against the Spanish in the 17th century to regain independence for Portugal. In the northwest corner of the plaza stands the huge **Palácio Foz**, which now serves as the

Direcão-General do **Turismo** (☎ *346 33 14*), and provides maps along with answers to tourist questions—including where to find rooms when none seems available.

From the northern end of the plaza flows the grand avenue of Lisbon, **Av. da Liberdade**, straight (but uphill) for one mile to the large Eduardo VII park. This boulevard was laid out in the 19th century for promenades by the well-to-do. Originally it was walled and gated for their protection. The gates and walls are gone today but the promenade is composed of playful mosaics on the sidewalks, and presents vistas bordered by palms and water gardens. Because the hotels and office buildings that line it are of no great interest, a taxi is a good way to reach the park at its end.

The park, **Parque Eduardo VII**, is named for Queen Victoria's son who visited Lisbon several times to shore up the shaky monarchy of Carlos I who, despite these efforts, was assassinated. At the northwest (far) corner of the park visit the tropical lushness of indoor gardens.

Estufa Fria ★

Parque Eduardo VIII. ☎ *(01) 68 22 78.*
Hours open: daily 9 a.m.–6 p.m.; until 5 p.m. in winter; sometimes closed for lunch
Called the "Cold Greenhouse" because wooden shutters, instead of glass, maintain the temperature. Inside reside an acre of plants, ferns and flowers connected by paths, tiny bridges, fountains, ponds and streams. The Estufa Quente (Hothouse) nearby maintains desert flora, and well deserves its name in the summer. *Admission: 75$00.*

Going due west of the southern end of the park (left if your back is toward the river) along Av. Joaquim de Aguiar for four short uphill blocks then one long block along its continuation Av. Pacheco (about half a mile in all) brings one of Lisbon's most interesting examples of modern architecture. Designed by the Portuguese Tomás Taveira, **Amoreiras** is an imposing post-modern red and blue complex containing 10 theaters, 60 cafés and restaurants and almost 400 shops of all kinds. It remains open until 11 p.m. seven days a week to provide glimpses of what appeals to the Portuguese, some of which may appeal to you as well.

Barrio Alto

One block back toward the river from the Rossío, narrow R. de Santa Justa heads west to the Santa Justa Elevator that rises conveniently up the steep slope of the Bairro Alto. This wonderful cast-iron lift is an 1898 design of Gustave Eiffel, the man responsible for another famous monument in Paris. A one-way ride costs 140$00. Alternatively, the funicular (for the same fare) will take you up to fine city views from the terrace of São Pedro de Alcantara. The funicular entrance is just north of the Office of Tourism in the Pr. dos Restauradores. Either of these routes permits you to walk downhill through the barrio. If you prefer an uphill hike, walk west from R. da Conceição in the Baixa up C. de São Francisco and take a right (northward) turn at the top. After a deep breath, follow the directions above in reverse.

The curves of this steep slope defeated Pombal's efforts to construct his usual grid of orderly avenues in the quarter. Today the hill is a place for cafes and, especially on its southern slope, called the **Chiado**, the site of Lisbon's best stores. In 1988 terrible fires destroyed a score of shops including Lisbon's two largest department stores. The area has not completely recovered, although plenty of establishments remain.

Igreja do Carmo   ★ ★

Largo do Carmo, ☎ (01) 346 04 73. The Santa Justa elevator stops at this church. (If arriving by the funicular, visit Igreja São Roque first, then go south down R. Oliveira to the pleasant Largo do Carmo, which presents this church at its end.)

Hours open: Mon.–Sat. 10 a.m.–1 p.m. and 2–6 p.m. Closed Sunday and holidays.

Construction on a Carmelite church began at the end of the 14th century, although problems with its foundation delayed completion for years. It was finished in the finest Gothic style to become the second-largest church, after the Cathedral, in Lisbon. Then the great earthquake toppled its ceiling. For some reason the church was never rebuilt, so it serves today as dramatic evidence of that cataclysm. Past the entry comes a startling grassy sward and the church's skeletal walls, apse and arches. All is quiet inside, and moving. The former apse functions as a dull archaeological museum. *Admission: 300$00.*

South of the church R. Garret cuts across, lined with better shops. If tired or thirsty, try **A Brasileira** at No. 120, where the poet Fernando Pessoa hangs out as he always did, now as a seated bronze statue. Shops continue on surrounding streets down the slope of the Chiado. For the church of São Roche, go west through the square in front of Igreja do Carmo, then north along R. Oliveira to Largo Trindade Coelho faced by the classical facade of São Roque. (Or, from the funicular, follow São Pedro de Alcantara south from the terrace for one block.)

Igreja São Roque   ★ ★

Largo Trindade Coelho, ☎ (01) 346 03 61.

Hours open: daily 10 a.m. to 5 p.m. The museum is closed on Monday

An unremarkable 16th-century exterior encases an elegant Baroque interior that includes what may be the most sumptuous and costly chapel in the world.

The nave's flat wooden ceiling is a trompe l'oeil vault painted with scenes of the Apocalypse. Four ornate chapels line each side. Proceeding down the right side, note lovely *azulejos* and a fine painting in the third chapel. Continuing around, the chapel of São João Baptista is last on the left before the high altar, and unique in the world. In 1742 King João V commissioned a chapel of semiprecious stones to be built in Rome. Upon its completion, it was blessed by the Pope, dismantled, transported on three ships and reconstructed again in Lisbon in 1750. Lapis lazuli dominates, but there are elements of rare green porphyry, amethyst, jade and several sorts of marble. What appears to be a painting above the altar is also of stone, a finely detailed and polished mosaic, as are the others in the chapel. Note the chandeliers and their "chains."

After a look at the sacristy *azulejos*, located to the left of the São João Baptista chapel, exit the church for an inspection of its treasures in the **Museu de São Roque**, to the right of the church entrance. One bowl hefts at more than 30 pounds of gold, a miter is covered in Brazilian diamonds, and a pair of gilded silver candlesticks together approach one ton. *Admission: 150$00, free on Sunday.*

Following the west side of the church along R. de S. Pedro Alcantara brings the **Instituto do Vinho do Porto** in two short blocks at No. 45. In this comfortable old mansion more than 100 brands and vintages of wine are dispensed by the glass, at very fair prices starting at 150$00, although the good stuff will cost twice that price. If you like what you sipped, they will sell you a bottle. The old clublike atmosphere is from an age long past. Continuing along R. Alcantara as it bends left and changes the street name to **R. Dom Pedro V**, brings you to Lisbon's best antique shops crowded together for four blocks.

Belém

Belém is a 20-minute taxi ride for 8 km west of the center of Lisbon along the river. It is served by buses #12, #14, #27, #28, #29, #43 and #49, and trolleys #15, #16 and #17. Faster public transportation is the train that covers the distance in 10 minutes and departs every 15 minutes from the Cais do Sodré station, along the river due west of the Praça do Comércio.

Belém, Portuguese for Bethlehem, was Lisbon's original port from which maritime explorers sailed into the unknown and returned with the fruits of their discoveries to enrich Lisbon beyond the dreams of most countries. Some of this bounty stayed in Belém. Manuel I constructed the first complete Manueline structure, the **Mosteiro dos Jerónimos**, in thanks for Vasco da Gama's opening of the spice trade, financed by a five percent tax on the sale of all spice goods. Manuel also built a fortress in the river to protect the shipping—the **Torre de Belém**. Within three blocks of these aged sights are the **Museu de Marinha** (Maritime Museum) and the **Museu Nacional dos Cochas** (Coach Museum), each described below.

Flat, filled with parks and marinas, Belém is a treat to wander through (if you ignore the highway and train tracks). Buses #27 and #43 from the Pr. Pombal stop at the Mosteiro dos Jerónimos.

Note: All Belém museums close on Monday.

Torre de Belém   ★★

Av. da India, ☎ *(01) 301 68 92.*

Hours open: Mon.–Sat. 10 a.m.–6:30 p.m. (in winter until 5 p.m.) Open Sun. 10 a.m. to 2 p.m. Closed Mon. and holidays. In the river off the riverine Av. Marginal at Av. Torre de Belém.

Belém Tower is a virtual icon of Lisbon. When it was constructed in 1521, the tower stood farther out in the river, which lapped against the Mosteiro dos Jerómmos in those times, but centuries of silting has brought the banks out to meet the tower. It was planned both for a river lookout and as an armed fortress to defend Portuguese shipping, paired with São Sebastião fortress across the river. In truth it looks more cute than robust, but elegant at the same time, with its lovely porch, delicate third-story terraced windows and precious Moorish-influenced details. The inside is plainer and more Gothic in feeling, with stone spiral staircases and bare walls. Its lower recesses served as a very damp prison in the 19th century. *Admission: 400$00 (250$00 in winter), Sunday free.*

Mosteiro dos Jerónimos   ★★★★

Pr. do Império, ☎ *(01) 362 00 34. From the Museu Popular head north across the open park of the Pr. Império, which the monastery borders.*

Hours open: Tues.–Sat. 10 a.m.–6:30 p.m. (in winter until 5 p.m.) Open Sun. 10 a.m. to 2 p.m. Closed Mon. and holidays.

Henry the Navigator had built a small monastery on this site in the 15th century, and Vasco da Gama passed a night in prayer nearby before setting out to "discover" India. When he returned, his king, Manuel I, ordered Henry's simple structure replaced by a richly endowed monastery for his own patron saint Jerónimos in thanks for the bounty flowing over the new trade route. The original plans were drawn by the French architect Diogo Boytac, a brilliant innovator, who was taken from a commission at Setúbal for the job.

Seventeen years later, after the basic lines were complete, Boytac was succeeded by João de Castilho, who brought along the Fleming João de Ruão, and the French sculptor, Nicolas Chanterene, to whom most of the decoration is due. Work was complete by 1572, in the rapid time of less than 75 years. Centuries later, a long extension was added west of the entrance in a style appropriate to, but without the fine taste of, the rest. By great fortune, the earthquake of 1755 caused only slight damage to the complex, so this masterpiece remains in essentially its original state. Thanks to renovations in 1994, it glistens today.

The white limestone monastery consists of a compound whose southern side, facing the Pr. Império, is the south wall of the church of Saint Mary, while the three walls of the grand cloister extending north complete the sides of a square. On the southern side, facing the park, an elegant porch to the right of the entrance inserts intricacy into an otherwise monolithic facade. João de Castilho carved this busy canopy containing statues of the four Sybils, four prophets and four church fathers, including Saint Jerónimos, all surrounding the Virgin and child. Above the Virgin are two scenes from Saint Jeronimo's life. Below, on the central pillar, is a fine carving of Prince Henry the Navigator holding a large sword while pointing to the coat-of-arms of his native Porto.

The soaring church interior is vast, with aisles rising as high as the nave. Exquisite fan vaulting rises on paired columns whose diameters decrease for perspective as they proceed to the front of the church. Left, after the first chapel, is the tomb of Vasco de Gama borne on the back of six lions. There would be no grand church if it were not for his pioneering voyage. The tomb opposite honors Camões, Portugal's great poet, though his body actually lies in an unmarked pauper's grave. The star vaulting at the transept crossing is sublime.

The end of the church consists of a royal pantheon that tells the sad story of ascendancy and riches, followed by the loss of it all, a fitting morality tale for a church.

Manuel I, the Fortunate, to whom this monastery is due, reposes in what would normally be the apse. His son and successor, João III, lies right. (Evidently one animal from India made a strong impression on the sculptor—all the tombs are borne on the backs of elephants.) Both kings lie beside their Spanish queens, both named

María, whose marriages would bequeath Portugal to Spain after Manuel's family ran out of descendants.

In the transept to the right lie the remains of Manuel's grandsons, allegedly including those of King Sebastião. Sebastião's early death precluded children, giving the crown to his aged uncle, Cardinal Henri. In the left transept are tombs of three of Manuel's children, including the cardinal-king, Dom Henri, whose death after a six-month reign ended the dynasty.

Exit through the west entrance to enter the cloisters through the gift shop. The cloisters enclose a large space in a two-story arcade of wide arches punctuated by spires. The vaulting is fine and the sculpture incredibly rich. It is all so twisting and intricate that the carved stone almost moves. The galaxy of animals, vegetables and twisting ropes carved on columns and walls earn this monastery its fame and created the Manueline style. Close inspection reveals some fantastic creatures indeed.

The second story is elegant, if less exuberant. A doorway leads to the upper choir of the church, with 16th-century stalls handsomely carved from brazilwood. *Admission to the cloisters: 400$00 (250$00 in winter).*

Museu da Marinha ★★

Pr. Império, ☎ (01) 362 00 34. Entrance is at the west end of the Heronymite Monastery.
Hours open: Tues.–Sun. 10 a.m.–5 p.m. Closed Mon. and holidays.
This museum consists mainly of ship models, fascinating to those willing to study them, plus an occasional splendid barge of state. Three anchors from Columbus' Niña stand by the entrance. Inside are models of ships from the era of the great Portuguese discoveries. Most are naos, a heavier form of the caravels that Columbus chose as well for his voyage to the New World, a Portuguese invention adopted from the Moors. Without the innovation of their free lateen rigging that allowed sailing closer to the wind than stationary square sails had, Africa could not have been rounded. Some of the uniforms on display are splendid in a Gilbert-and-Sullivan way. *Admission: 300$00; free on Wed.*

Museu Nacional dos Coches ★★★

Pr. Afonso de Albguquerque, ☎ (01) 363 80 22. R. de Belém parallels the south face of the Heronymite Monastery and leads eastward in two blocks to the museum.
Hours open: Tues.–Sun. 10 a.m.–1 p.m. and 2:30–5:30 p.m., until 6:15 in summer. Closed Mon. and holidays.
Housed in the expanse of the former indoor royal riding school on the grounds of the Palace of Belém (now the home of the president of Portugal) is this museum filled with nothing but amazing coaches.

True gilded fantasies are parked in long rows. It should be remembered that their function was to impress, and anyone would admit that the least of them would turn heads if it rolled past today. Favorites are the coach of José I, the king at the time of the great earthquake, the huge carriages of João V, a 17th-century French litter, and the miniature coach of Carlos I, used when he was a child, which adds pathos to the thought of his later assassination. Amid all the gilt below, don't fail to look up at the lovely ceiling frescoes. *Admission: 400$00; free on Sun.*

Other Sights

Museu Nacional de Arte Antiga   ★ ★ ★ ★

R. das Janelas Verdes, ☎ *(01) 397 60 01. The museum is located along the river by the Jardim 9 de Abril at 95 R. das Janelas Verdes in the district of Lapa, which is halfway between Belém and the Praça do Comércio. A walk along the river from the Praça do Comércio would cover less than a mile and a half, although a taxi is certainly quicker. Trolley #19 and buses #27, #40, #49, #54 and #60 pass by.*

Hours open: Tues.–Sun. 10 a.m.–1 p.m. and 2:30–5 p.m. Closed Mon. and holidays.

This certainly is the finest museum extant of Portuguese painting, and includes much more. It is housed half in the 17th-century palace of the Count of Alvor, where Pombal lived for a while, and half in a modern addition whose west end provides the entrance.

The inside has just been remodeled, so exhibits may have been moved. Get a floor-plan at the desk, and please forgive us if our directions are a little off.

Inside and downstairs is the chapel of Santo Alberto, preserved from a former convent on this site. Its wooden sculpture is admirable, as are its *azulejos*. Rooms follow displaying Portuguese furniture, tapestries and carpets. Before entering the old building, opposite the entrance, ascend to the mezzanine to view a fine collection of porcelain, both from, and inspired by, the Far East. Two early 17th-century screens from Japan show the arrival of the Portuguese, the first people of European physiognomy that the insular Japanese had seen. The name for these screens comes from the Japanese word for "southern barbarian," and oversized noses show what most impressed the Japanese about these foreigners. Also on the mezzanine are collections of gold pieces and polychrome sculpture.

The second floor is devoted to Portuguese painting, including the one acknowledged masterpiece of the nation. It is a polyptych of six wood panels painted in the middle of the 15th century for the Lisbon church of Saint Vincent, since destroyed. The artist is Nuno Gonçalves, and this is his only attributable work. The painting portrays both famous Portuguese and segments of lower society, all listening to Saint Vincent, who is depicted in the center of both middle panels. All the faces are so vibrant that one wonders where this artist could have gained a skill that ranks with the European geniuses of the period.

The great Flemish painter Jan van Eyck's early 15th-century visit to Portugal influenced a century of Portuguese artists. Most notable among his artistic descendents is the 16th-century painter Frei Carlos, whose *Annunciation* bears comparison with the master. In a different vein are the charming Portuguese primitives, especially an anonymous 15th-century *Ecce Homo* with a shrouded upper visage, and *a Vision of Hell* in which hell is a kitchen presided over by an Indian Satan. Seek out the canvases by Josefa de Óbidos for a rare but talented female eye.

Farther on are rooms dedicated to the 19th-century Domingos de Sequeira, a sort of Portuguese Goya—he, like Goya, lived in exile and produced wondrous drawings and etchings, in addition to oils. His paintings appeared in Paris exhibitions where he bested Delacroix and Gérricault, among others. Outstanding are his portraits, especially those of the Viscount of Santarém and his family, the young Count of Farrobo, and the artist's own children.

Past the bookstore on the ground floor of the new building, the old building begins with a superb collection of silver tableware, mainly French, from the firm of Germain. French furniture follows. Across a landing is the entrance to the museum's European masterpieces. The stars are a Dürer painting of *Saint Jerome*, which once hung in the Heronymite Monastery, and an astonishing Bosch of *The Temptations of Saint Anthony*. Saint Anthony is painted four times throughout the picture, never once looking at all the sinners demonstrating sins of excess. There is also a lovely *Virgin and Child with Saints* by Holbein the Elder, an interesting Bruegel depiction of beggars, and a fine self-portrait by Andrea del Sarto. Of the Spanish paintings, the best is Ribera's *Martyrdom of Saint Bartholomew*, although there is also a Velázquez portrait of *Maria of Austria* and a Zurbarán canvas of the *Twelve Apostles*. Admission: 250$00; free Sun. morning.

Museu Calouste Gulbenkian ★★★★

Av. de Berna, 45, ☎ (01) 795 02 36. The museum is located in Lisbon's north, about a half-mile past the end of the Parque Eduardo VII. Av. de Alcantara, which is renamed Av. António Augusto Aguiar, follows the east edge of the park and leads to the Pr. da Espanha. Turn right to the Parque de Palhava and the museum. Trolleys #24 and #27, and buses #16, #26, #31 and #56 all stop nearby.
Hours open: Tues.–Sun. 10 a.m.–5 p.m. Open 2–7:30 p.m. on Wed. and Sat. in summer. Closed Mon. and holidays.

Before World War I the Armenian Calouste Gulbenkian negotiated an agreement to broker all the oil Iran sold to the West for a five percent commission. This made him one of the richest private citizens in the world. During World War II, however, Britain made him unwelcome for his refusal to sever ties with the Iranian embassy in Vichy France. When Portugal welcomed him on the rebound, he became a citizen and established a billion-dollar foundation, the largest in Europe, to aid the Portuguese arts. Upon his death in 1955, he donated his private art collection to the country.

In breadth and quality his collection was the finest remaining in private hands. Gulbenkian was a passionate collector, desiring only the best; his tastes were wide and his pockets incredibly deep. His great coup was in purchasing several works, including two Rembrandts, from the Hermitage during the late 1920s when Russia needed hard currency. Gulbenkian's bequest included funds to erect the museum, completed in 1969, designed expressly to display each part of the collection to best advantage.

What makes this collection special is that it is at once modest in size and astonishingly high in quality. Gulbenkian was not a collector who strove to complete a series, but a lover of art who purchased individual works because they captivated him. Consequently, it is a museum of stars, rather than the sort providing examples of the breadth of art genres.

Of the earliest art the Egyptian collection takes first place. The first example is an elegantly proportioned Old Kingdom alabaster chalice. A fine bronze funerary statue, a lovely wooden one of the Lady Henut-tawy, and a simple death-mask in gold follow. The Assyrian low relief is monumental. Those with an interest will find the Greek coins superb.

A highlight of the museum is its collection of Middle Eastern carpets, Korans, ceramics and clothes. There are also refined, delicate Far Eastern porcelains and an elegant silk hanging. The European art collection begins with several jewel-like medieval ivories and illustrated medieval manuscripts, including a fine *Book of Hours*, but moves quickly to paintings. Outstanding early works are Van der Weyden's *Saint Catherine*, Dirk Bouts' *Annunciation*, and a haunting *Portrait of a Young Girl* by Domenico Ghirlandaio. After a fine Hals, a Van Dyke portrait, and a Ruysdael landscape, are the two fine Rembrandt's—*Alexander* (sometimes called *Pallas Athene*), and the disturbing face of the *Portrait of an Old Man*. Eighteenth- and 19th-century French paintings and sculpture are choice, including a Fragonard, the De La Tour pastel of *Duval de l'Epinoy*, a nice Houdin sculpture of Diana, and several Corots. French furniture ranges from elegant to ornate. An impressive display of costly silver tableware leads to rooms of English painting and later French canvases, including seldom-seen canvases by Manet, Fantin-Latour (see his perfect "Still Life" with a knife overhanging a table) and Dégas, among others. Another favorite is a haunting Renoir of the recumbent "Madame Claude Monet." The exhibit ends with an overwhelming exhibit of Lalique art, nouveau jewelry and glass. *Admission: 200$00; free Sun.*

Adjoining the museum is the **Gulbenkian Museum of Modern Art**, with the same opening hours. Inside canvases fight each other rather schizophrenically. Some come out of the revolutionary realism favored by the former dictator Salazar, others adamantly refuse to follow this official line to cover all the genre of the modern era from cubism through abstraction, to neo-realism and surrealism. All in all, the collection is rather fun.

Igreja da Madre de Deus, and Museu Nacional do Azulejo   ★ ★ ★

R. Madre de Deus, 4, ☎ (01) 795 02 36. Located one block inland from the river, about 4 km west of the Praça do Comércio, at R. Madre de Deus, 4. Trolleys #3, #16, #24, #27, and buses #13, #18 and #42 stop there.
Hours open: Tues.–Sat. 10 a.m.–5 p.m. Open Sun. 10 a.m.–2 p.m. Closed Mon. and holidays. Admission: 200$00; free on Sun.

This monastery was founded at the beginning of the 16th-century by Donha Leonor, the widow of King João II. Here *azulejo* tiles can be seen *in situ* inside an exquisitely decorated little church, and their development is explained by displays in the museum housed in its cloisters.

Although the church (to the right of the entrance) was substantially rebuilt after the great earthquake, much of the earlier art survived inside, along with the outside Manueline west entrance. Twisted columns lining the portal support an arch in which fishnets and pelicans entwine. The fishnet was Leonor's symbol, the pelican was her husband's. Inside all seems stunningly rich. Lower walls are lined with 18th-century Dutch *azulejos*, deeper blue than the Portuguese examples. The walls above are crowded with paintings of Saint Francis, on the right, and Saint Clare, on the left. Overhead, the barrel-coffered ceiling also contains paintings, this time primitives of the life of the Virgin. The altar is gilded Baroque and holds a fine pulpit.

Steps lead down to the surviving part of the original church whose walls are lined with 16th-century *azulejos* from Seville. The main Renaissance cloister extends off this chancel, and beyond it is a lovely Manueline cloister. The *azulejo* museum can be entered from the main cloister, but first climb to the upper gallery for more of the church. Here the chapel of Saint Anthony is tiled with 18th-century *azulejos* depicting the saint's life, above which are more early primitive paintings. Next comes the *coro alto*, the nun's choir, all in gilt with still more paintings. Finally, the sacristy is lined with Portuguese *azulejos* from the 18th century and still more 16th century primitives.

For more wonderful azulejos, visit the following sight.

Quinta do Marquêses de Fronteira   ★ ★

Largo de Domingo de Benfica, 1, ☎ *(01) 778 20 23. In Parque Florestal, 3 miles north-*
west of the Baixa, a half mile southwest of the Zoo. Buses #15, #16, #41, #46, #54 and
#63 stop at the zoo, but a taxi is best.
Hours open: Mon.–Sat. 10:45 a.m.–5 p.m. Sat. only by guided tour.
This is the private residence of a most noble Portuguese family and has been so since the 17th century. Since it is still lived in, only six of the palace rooms are open to visitors, but they are not your normal rooms. A visit is worthwhile, both to see how the very old rich live and for the peaceful formal gardens.

Inside the palace, the Battle Room is covered in charming azulejos depicting the engagements of the War of Restoration, in which the Portuguese regained their freedom from Spain. The dining room is decorated with prized Delf azulejos in inky blues, among the first imported into the country. The terrace, covered in fantastic azulejos depicting the various arts, overlooks the lovely gardens. At its end is a chapel, older than the palace, decorated with mosaics made of broken Ming china. Be warned that some of the modern art displayed in the old kitchen is rather risque.
Admission: 300$00 to gardens; 700$00 to the palace; 500$00 for guided tour (in Portuguese).

Shopping

The best and largest concentration of **antique** stores congregate along R. Dom Pedro V and its continuation, R. da Escola Politécnica, in the Bairro Alto (see direction under "Sights"). Some of the material is religious, but there are also antique ceramics and furniture. Prices are not low. An outstanding selection of antique *azulejos* is offered by **Solar**, at #70, along with other old things.

A fascinating store for browsing is the **Centro Antiquaro do Alecrim** for drawings from old books, many handcolored. It is located at *R. do Alecrim, 48-50* (near Sant'Anna, described below). What could be more typical of Portugal than a souvenir of **cork**? **Casa das Corticas**, at *R. Escola Politecnica #4*, the continuation of R. Dom Pedro V, sells nothing else and has invented surprising, if not always serious, uses for the material.

For **ceramics** and **azulejos**, besides the fine antique ones at Solar mentioned above, see **Sant'Anna** occupying *#95-7 on R. do Alecrim*, the southern continuation of R. de San Pedro de Alcantara that leads from R. Dom Pedro V to R. Garrett. In addition to a large selection of **tiles**, the store also carries its own line of **ceramic pieces**—boxes, planters, candelabra, etc. Its only true competitor is **Fabrica Ceramica Viuva Lamego**, a fair distance away at *#25 Largo do Intendente* (by the Intendente metro stop in the north of the city). Designs here are more colorful, but less sophisticated than at Sant'Anna.

For fine bone **china**, there are several outlets of the well-known **Vista Alegre** factory. The best is at *Largo do Chiado, 18*, one block north of R. Garrett. In addition to prices that are about 20 percent less than those in the United States for the china, exquisite French Baccarat **crystal** is also sold at a great discount. Unfortunately, the outlets do not ship. For the well-known Portuguese crystal, Atlantis, the place to go is **Cristalissimo** at *R. Castilho, 149*, in the Meridien hotel.

The finest **embroidery** is sold in Lisbon, brought from the islands of Madeira and the Azores which remain bastions of the craft. However, cheaper copies from China make the Portuguese versions seem less of a buy. The best-known shop is **Madeira House** at *R. Augusta 131-5* in the Baixa. The selection is large, but not quite up to the quality carried at **Madeira Superbia** on *Av. Duque Loulé, 75-A* (the street that leads east from Pr. Pombal in front of the Parque Eduardo VII). The highest quality of all is carried by the prestigious **Principe Real** at *12-14 R. da Escola Politécnica* (the continuation of R. Dom Pedro V) in the Barrio Alta.

Needlepoint carpets from the village of Arraiolos are famous enough to lend their name to the style. Several stores in Lisbon sell arraiolos, but one is superior in selection, quality and honesty. People do almost as well from **Casa Quintão** on *R. Ivens, 30-4 (off R. Garrett in the Chiado)* as in the village where the rugs are made. If $2000 sounds like a lot for an eight-by-10-foot carpet, price comparable ones in the United States.

For **handcrafts** of great variety at inexpensive prices from all the regions of Portugal go to **Filartesanato**, which is toward Belém on the waterfront west of the Tejos bridge, *Ponte 25 de Abril*, in the Feira Internacional de Lisboa.

For an interesting shopping experience visit Lisbon's giant **shopping mall**, **Amoreiras** (*at Av. Duarte Pachecho, 1 km due west of the Pr. Pombal;* free buses from the Pr. Pombal; open until 11 p.m.). Captivatingly post-modern outside, it is a more pedestrian mall within that contains almost 250 stores, a supermarket, 10 movie theaters and a chapel. There is everything from Vista Alegra, to Marks and Spenser, shoe shops, hair dressers and 50 restaurants. A visit will give a sense of Portuguese tastes.

Then there is the famed Lisbon **flea market**, the *Feira da Ladra* (Thieves' Market). It is held Tuesdays, until 1 p.m., and Saturdays, from early morning until sunset. All the stalls are open-air and fill the Campo de Santa Clara, three blocks east of São Jorge Castle. Trolley #28 and bus #12 stop there. As with any such market, 99 percent of the goods are uninteresting, but there remains that one percent and the hope of a treasure. Diligence can uncover interesting craftswork. Bargaining is expected.

Directory

Airport

Portela airport (☎ *(01) 80 20 60* for flight information) is 8 km northeast of the center of the city and handles both international and domestic flights. By taxi (about 2000$00) the trip should take half an hour in traffic. Aero-bus expresses depart every 20 minutes or so, and make stops along Av. de Liberdade for under $3. Most airlines have offices in Pr. Marquês de Pombal, including TAP at #3-A, ☎ *(01) 57 50 20.*

Buses

The main depot is **Rodoviária Nacional** at *Av. Casal Ribeiro, 18* (☎ *(01) 534 54 39*) near the Pr. Duque de Saldanha (an eight-block walk from the Pr. Pombal along Pereira de Melo). Three buses go daily to Faro in the Algarve, two *expressos* travel to Porto, and 14 leave for Coimbra.

Changing Money

Banks are found primarily in two areas—in the Baixa, *just north of the Pr. Comércio and in the Pr. Restauradores*. They are open only on weekdays, close for lunch from 11:45 until 1, then close for good at 3 (service after 2:45 is chancy). Banco Pinto & Sotto Mayor in the Pr. dos Restauradores stays open until 7:30 p.m. A small *Cambio* with rates as good as a bank's at *R. do Ouro, 283*, just south of the Rossío opens on Saturday from 10 a.m.–5 p.m.

City Tours

The following firms offer half-day tours for about 4,500$00, usually departing at 9:30 a.m. and 2:30 p.m. **Citirams** (☎ *(01) 352 25 94*) located at Av. Praia da Vitória, 12, **Marcus & Harting** (☎ *(01) 346 92 71*) at Rossío, 45-50 is another, **Portugal Tours** (☎ *(01) 352 29 02*) at R. Estefania, 122-4 still another, as well as **RN Greyline Tours** (☎ *(01) 57 75 23*) on *Av. Fontes Pereira de Melo at 14*. Most such tours depart from the Pr. Pombal.

Trains

Four train stations serve Lisbon. International trains and trains from the north use **Santa Apolónia** station (☎ *(01) 888 41 42*; information: ☎ *(01) 87 60 25*). The station is a 15-minute walk along the river east of **Praça do Comércio**. Eight *Rapidos* leave daily for the three-and-a-half hour trip to Porto, two fewer on Sunday.

They also stop at Coimbra in two hours. Rossío station handles passengers from Sintra and Estremadura, the near north. It is located west of **Pr. Rossío** *(☎ (01) 8346 50 22)* at the beginning of the Pr. Restauradores. Electric trains to the near beaches Estoril and Cascais leave from **Cais do Sodré** *(☎ (01) 347 01 81)* by the river just west of the Praça do Comércio. The cost is less than $1. Trains for the Algarve and south leave from **Sul e Sueste in Barreiro** *(☎ (01) 207 30 28)* on the south bank of the river. Tickets include the price of a ferry that crosses the river at the Praça do Comércio.

Excursions

Lisbon serves as a hub for some special excursions. The longest is to **Batalha** ★★★★, 120 km north. Batalha monastery is the premier Gothic and Manueline structure in the country, outshining even Lisbon's Mosteiro dos Jerónimos. With a two-hour train ride each way the visit will consume a day, but by car other sights—such as the monastery of **Alcobaça** ★★★— could be combined in one excursion. By train lovely **Óbidos** ★★, a walled medieval town, requires a change at Caçem and a trip of almost three hours each way. At less than 100 km away, travel time by car should be an hour and a half. The huge Baroque palace complex at **Mafra** ★★ is a half-day excursion including a train ride of an hour and a half each way. By car it can be combined with Portugal's version of Versailles at **Queluz** ★★, otherwise a separate train trip. The haunting beauty of **Sintra** ★★★ was immortalized by Byron and can be reached by frequent trains in 45 minutes. For beaches, there are elegant ones at **Cascais** ★ and **Estoril** ★, near to each other as well as to Lisbon, half an hour away. Long, uncrowded beaches surround **Setúbal** ★, 55 miles south of Lisbon, a 45-minute train ride with frequent service. All the foregoing sights are described under their own headings in this chapter, except Mafra which is treated as an excursion from Queluz, and Alcobaça which is an excursion from Batalha.

By car, for **Cascais** and **Estoril,** follow the river west along Av. 24 de Julho which has been renamed Av. Marginal, before turning into scenic N-6 for 25 k, to Estoril, another 2 km for Cascais. The beautiful beach of **Do Guincho** is 12 km further west along N-247-7. For **Sintra** follow the same route into Estoril where a sign directs a right turn for N6-8 to Sintra in 23 km. For **Mafra** go east at Pr. Pombal on Periera de Melo, which reaches the circle of Pr. Saldanha in three blocks. Take Av. da República north as it becomes Campo Grande with a planted center strip. After the race course on the right, follow signs right to A-8 and Torres Vedras. Stay on A-8 for 32 km to exit for Malveira and another 11 km west on N-117. For **Queluz** turn left at the Pr. Pombal along R. José António de Aguiar which becomes A-5, the expressway to Estoril. Take the first exit for N-117 to Sintra; which becomes N-249 and brings Queluz in about 7 km.

For **northern points** take the autoestrada A-1 by going east at Pr. Pombal on Periera de Melo, which reaches the circle of Pr. Saldanha in three blocks. Take Av. da República north as it becomes Campo Grande with a planted center strip. After the race course on the right, turn left on Mel. Craveiro Lopez, which bends around the airport and funnels into the autoestrada A-1 to the north. For **Óbidos** exit at Aveiras de Cima in 37 km. Take N-366 northwest toward Caldas da Rainha, 41 km away, turning south at its outskirts on N-8 for the final 7 km. For **Alcobaça** follow the directions for Óbidos to Caldas da Rainha, but continue through Caldas to take N-8 north for 26 km. For **Tomar** exit A-1 at exit 7 in 80 km to go west on N-243 to Entroncamento, then north on N-110 for 19 km to Tomar. For **Batalha** take exit 9 for Fátima and Batalha. Go east on pretty N-356 for a final 22 km.

For destinations **south** and **east** of Lisbon cross on the Ponte 25 Abril by following the river west along Av. 24 de Julho to signs for the bridge at Av. de Ceuta, then north for two blocks to the circle of Largo de Alcantara, turning west to reach the ramp. Autoestrada A-2 reaches **Setúbal** in 48 km. From there, N-10 east for 35 km to Cruzamento de Pegoães joins N-4 to **Évora** in another 67 k. For the **Algarve** take N-10 from Setúbal for 21 km to Marateca to join N-5 south for 31 km to Alcácer do Sal, where the designation becomes N-120. Bear right in 18 km to continue on N-120 along the coast to the western Algarve in about 180 k. A faster route to the central Algarve is to continue on to Grandola, instead of bearing right on N-120, to take N-259 southeast, turning south on N-262 in about 20 km toward Azinheira dos Barros, and stay on the road as it becomes N-264 for a leg of 204 k.

POUSADA DE DONHA MARIA I

Largo do Palácio, Queluz, 2745
☎ *(01) 435 61 58, FAX (01) 435 61 89*
$140 per double; 24 rooms: 22 doubles, 2 suites

★ ★ ★ ★

This "little" pink and white confection is located across the plaza from the pink and white confection that is the Royal Palace of Queluz. Some of the staff lived here when the palace was in operation. Opened in 1995, it is all glistening inside. This happens to be one we saw under construction, so it is a shock for us to see what looks like a period building created from hardly any surviving remains. Yet it looks and acts the part of an ancient edifice, with comfortable, high-ceiling guest rooms. Ask for one facing the palace across the plaza.

Dining

In this case you have to cross the street to eat. The right wing of the palace is the former kitchen of the palace, now made over into the dining room. It is pleasant rather than grand—after all it was the kitchen—although some pains are taken to make it so. There is a huge, freestanding fireplace, high-beamed ceiling, original azulejos and a marble table groaning with food, but the decor is polished copper and the seats ladder-back chairs. You are here for the experience, more than for the cuisine, which tries to be special by claiming ancient recipes although they taste much like dishes available elsewhere. Leak or shellfish soup are subtle starts for a meal, but smoked swordfish is better. All is festive and fun, not everyone can say they dined at a palace, and the vanilla soufflé is divine. It is expensive, however—figure on about $40 per person, à la carte.

Directions

Only 12 km north of **Lisbon**, directions for Queluz are included in the "Excursion" section of Lisbon. **Sintra** is 15 km west along N-249.

By **train**, take the frequent Sintra line from Lisbon.

Pousadas Nearby

Palmela: 52 km	Setúbal: 58 km
Óbidos: 89 km	Batalha: 142 km

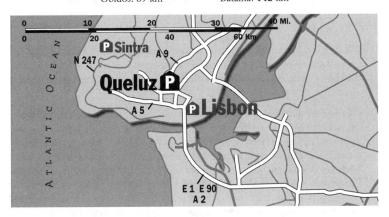

Sights

By a tradition going back to the mid-17th century, the second son of Portugal's king was given the use of a hunting lodge at Queluz. In 1747 the second son was Dom Pedro, who extensively rebuilt the lodge to transform it into a royal summer residence. At this first stage the edifice was too small for a proper palace, about one-third the present size. Then Pedro married his niece, Maria Francisca, who had been betrothed to France's Louis XV. She greatly admired Versailles where she had lived for a while. The new building had to become more grand and more French for her.

Starting over in 1758 under the direction of a French architect, Jean-Baptiste Robillion, the palace seen today was constructed as a sort of Portuguese Versailles, complete with formal gardens in the French manner. It required demolition of five earlier rooms to make a suitable throne room. And the outside was painted salmon. Here then is a palace built for a queen. For, by a tortuous course Maria eventually came to the throne, and this palace was her favorite residence. When she went insane in her later years, it became her place of confinement.

Although surrounded by a modern town today, the palace interior and gardens spreading behind transport the visitor into a more delicate Baroque age.

Palácio Real de Queluz   ★ ★ ★

Hours open: Wed.–Mon. 10 a.m.–1 p.m. and 2–5 p.m. Closed Tues.

Formerly fronted by a grand courtyard, the exterior is reached today by something resembling a parking lot. The low, undramatic outside fails to impress, although there is that unexpected color. The inside is another matter, as is the rear facade facing the garden.

While there is plenty of gilding and mirrors inside, a clear feel of French design, the overall sense is of a delicacy that does not come from the north. It would be a heresy to claim that the effect is more successful than the famous and grand French palaces of the era, so we say no more.

The stunning Ambassadors' Hall is roofed with a fine painting of a concert in pale pastels. Although the room's function in later years was to receive diplomats, hence the name, it was designed originally for musical entertainments, as it looks. Lovely *azulejos* of orange trees line the corridor outside. A very French Queen's boudoir prefaces the columned bedroom of the later regent, Donha Carlota (a veritable dwarf at four feet five inches) painted with scenes from *Don Quixote*. The breakfast room, next, is charming. After a mirrored dining room with a fine Arraiolos carpet, come three rooms for princesses, elegant dressing rooms, then an imposing music room with almost-perfect acoustics.

Glass and crystal in profusion characterize the throne room, probably the most Versaille-like part of the palace. Still, this one is special because of a softening lent by green-blue touches. The chapel contains paintings by Queen Maria and her sisters. Its intense colors make it the least engaging of the rooms, although such a strong statement is understandable given its purpose.

Outside, the palace rear presents a very French look, impressive in its formality. The pavilion on the left (if facing the palace) is original in its pillared design. The formal gardens are serene. *Admission: 400$00 for guided tour of the palace, 200$00 in winter; 50$00 for the gardens.*

Excursions

How about another palace, one sumptuous and rich, instead of Queluz' delicacy? Mafra Palace-Monastery is 29 km north on N-117, which becomes N-9.

Here is Portugal's most magnificent Baroque confection. Like Batalha, it was a king's offering in return for a favor from God, even if the favor this time was more personal than military. It was commissioned by João V in thanks—after three heirless years of marriage—for the birth of his daughter. Construction began in 1717 on this palace-church-monastery complex covering 10 acres. Eighteen years and two German architects later the monastery was completed—built, it is said, of Brazilian gold and diamonds.

The king wanted to overwhelm, and drained a rich treasury to do so, plunging Portugal into economic decline. Fifty thousand workers were employed at the height of the construction, not finished for 18 years. There are more than 800 rooms in the complex, brightened by 4500 windows. The length of the plain dark facade exceeds 200 yards. In the center is the classic pediment and high belltowers of the basilica, from either side of which the wings of the palace stretch to terminate in bulbous domed extensions. Most of the stone inside is marble, what is not is painted faux-stone. The left (south) wing housed the Queen and her staff, the right was for the King, and night visits entailed an appreciable, rather tiring, walk.

Mosteiro de Mafra   ★★

Entrance to the complex is through the Queen's door, the third left from the basilica
Hours open: Wed.-Mon. 10 a.m.–noon and 2–5 p.m. Closed Tues.

The **basilica** is elegant in proportion and consists of a fine barrel-vaulted ceiling on fluted columns, culminating in a large rose-and-white cupola. All the decoration is rich marbles. In particular the ornate sacristy is virtually a museum of the stone's variety.

The **palace** may be visited only by a guided tour. When inspecting the ornate furniture keep in mind that when João VI fled to Brazil in 1807 to avoid capture by the French, he took the best furnishings from this palace with him. What we see today is his rejects or mid-19th-century replacements. So little of the furniture is special, though some is interesting. The wood beds of the monks are almost elegant in their simplicity; some of the medical devices in the infirmary are funny or chilling, depending on your mood.

In the palace, note the game boards, one similar to a pinball machine. Special rooms include a trophy room in which everything is made of antlers or skins (a bit of pathos, when one remembers that the room was decorated for Carlos I who was killed by an assassin in the Pr. da Comércio in 1908); the mirrored queen's dressing room; the audience chamber with a trompe l'oeil ceiling; and an ornate throne room. Note the faux-stone walls throughout. Most dramatic is the 200 yard view down the main corridor, from one end to the other, that separated the king's from the queen's bedroom.

One room in all the complex is truly unforgettable. The gilded, marbled library, almost 100 yards long, is truly a cathedral for books. It can only be called awesome. *Admission: 400$00, for guided tours of the palace (200$00 in winter).*

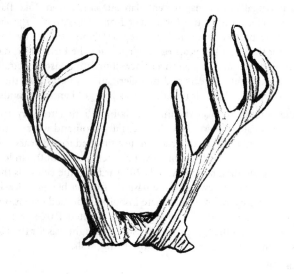

POUSADA DE PALMELA

Castelo de Palmela, Palmela, 2950
☎ *(01) 235 12 26, FAX (01) 233 04 40*
$150 per double; 28 rooms: 27 doubles, 1 suite

★ ★ ★ ★

This is a special hotel whose grounds merit half a day's sightseeing. It is situated in the confines of Palmela castle, a fortress that dates from even before Afonso Henrique, Portugal's first king, in the 12th century. West of the castle stands a 15th-century monastery in which the pousada is lodged, with a modern extension adjoining. A former mosque, made over into a church, in turn destroyed in the 1755 earthquake, stands in ruins in front of the castle. Around the whole are crude perimeter walls built by the Moors, surrounded by a complex 17th-century outer wall. The pousada is an example of good restoration, preserving the feel of the Renaissance monastery while providing every modern comfort. The former cloisters, now walled in with glass for all-weather comfort make as serene a spot for a drink as anyone could wish. Rest well knowing that you are staying where Mitterand of France slept along with the Queen of Denmark (not on the same night). On the other hand, the bedrooms, lodged in monks' cells, are spartan, although their marvelous views are anything but.

Dining

The restaurant is large and cold in feeling, the former refectory for the monks. This is soon atoned for by exceptional, award-winning pousada food. Consider *Arroz de Frutas do Mar na Cataplana* (rice and shellfish cooked in a sort of double wok that steams the dish), *Vitela Assada com Alecrim* (wood roasted veal with rosemary), *Sapateira Recheada* (stuffed crab), *Coelho Guisado com Feijão* (rabbit stew with red beans) and *Linguado com Cerveja Preta* (sole cooked in ale). Soups are fabulous, and range over a version of gazpacho, cream of vegetable and a rich fish soup. A lovely dessert is pears stewed in muscatel *(Peras Cozidas em Vinho Moscatel)*. The local wine is a very drinkable Pedras Negras red. Set-course meals are available for about $22.

Directions

From **Lisbon** cross on the Ponte 25 Abril by following the river west along Av. 24 de Julho to signs for the bridge at Av. de Ceuta, then north for two blocks to the circle of Largo de Alcantara, turning west to reach the ramp. Autoestrada A-2 reaches Setúbal in 40 km. From **Évora** take N-114, which joins A-6 to reach the Palmela exit in 87 km, then 4 km more to the city. High above the city, the pousada cannot be missed.

Pousadas Nearby

Setubal: 8 km	Queluz: 50 km	Évora: 100 km
Torrão: 100 km	Santiago do Caçem: 114 km	

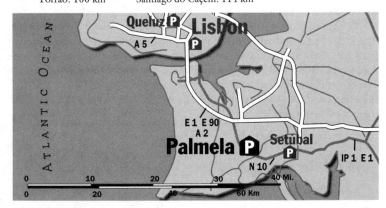

Sights

History was made in this castle. In 1484 a plot against the king was foiled; the ringleader, the Bishop of Évora, was arrested and imprisoned in the Palmela Castle. He died a few days later, probably poisoned. Today the most interesting building is the 15th century church of the monastery, in simple, inspiring Romanesque style. The view from the top of the tower keep is awesome, reaching Lisbon on a clear day, while, at the foot of the castle walls stands the 18th century church of St. Peter's whose interior is dramatically covered with azulejos depicting the saint's life.

Excursions

Most convenient is a trip to Setubal, 8 km away. See the description under its heading below, and also a description of beaches at Serra da Arrábia and at Tróia under its "Excursions."

POUSADA DE SÃO FILIPE

Castilo de São Filipe, s/n, Setúbal, 2900
☎ *(065) 52 38 44, FAX (065) 53 25 38*
$150 per double; 14 rooms: 13 doubles, 1 suite

★ ★ ★ ★

The Spanish built this fortress at the end of the 16th century to defend the kingdom of Portugal, which they had appropriated, and to cow the citizens in the city below with mighty guns. They chose a spot with the wonderful view that visitors to the pousada now enjoy. Guests stay in the former guards' quarters in bedrooms that are charmingly rustic, and getting to them requires wandering the fortress corridors, which is no chore at all. This is not the most beautiful, elegant or well-designed pousada, but all is forgiven for the view from its terrace. Reservations are usually necessary. Don't neglect the little chapel passed along the climb. Its interior is covered with fine azulejos.

Dining

The dining room is on the second floor for views. Setúbal is the oyster center of the country; look for them in season. The fish soup is special, but an interesting pumpkin cream soup makes for a choice. Stick to seafood, such as delicate bass *(robalinho)* or red mullet *(salmonete)*, rather than roasts. An orange tort *(torta de laranja)* is redolent of the fruit. A set-course meal is available for under $25 and includes local wine. The area is proud of its Muscatels, which are quite sweet, but Periquitas are available as well.

Directions

The pousada on high is visible as soon as Setúbal is reached. It is west of the center, above the port, along R. de São Filipe, well marked by pousada signs from the main Av. Luiza Todi. Parking is outside the wall, necessitating a steep climb with luggage.

Pousadas Nearby

Palmela: 8 km	Torrão: 100 km	Santiago: 103 km
Óbidos: 148 km	Batalha: 205 km	

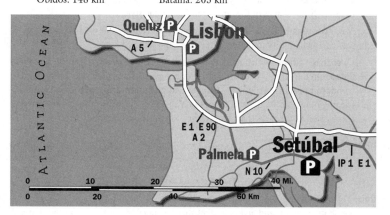

Sights

The industrial center and port of Setúbal makes it the third-largest city in Portugal. Although the city is not particularly attractive, neither is it as ugly as its economic functions might suggest. What makes it worth a stop is the intriguing small church of Jesus, the first Manueline building, and the fine beaches in its environs.

From **Lisbon**, **south** and **east**, Setúbal is entered along Estrada da Graça, which feeds into its continuation Av. Luisa Todi, with a planted center strip. In a few blocks the large park of Das Escolas appears on the right. Here parking is available.

From the parking lot head east for one long block along Av. Luisa Todi to turn left on Av. 22 de Dezembro, which reaches the church of Jesus in about the same distance. From the bus station on Av. 5 de Outubro or the train station just east, head west along Av. 22 de Dezembro for about four blocks.

Igreja de Jesus   ★★

Pr. Miguel Bombarda
Hours open: Tuesday–Sunday 9 a.m.–noon and 2–5 p.m. Closed Monday and holidays.
This hall-church was begun in the last decade of the 15th century by Boytac, the architect who originated the Manueline architectural style. He finished the church, but not the adjoining convent, because his master called him for the grander commission of the Hieronymite monastery in Belém. Given the shock of the interior even today, one can imagine how inventive the device of twisted columns would have seemed at the time. True, the columns are merely two pillars twisted into one mass, but they appear to grow down from the ceiling rather than support it from the ground, as columns had always done before. The effect is arresting, and led to the twisting, living shapes of the developed Manueline style.

A wainscotting of lovely *azulejos* from the 17th century follows both walls, and a particularly harmonious design of tiles lines the altar.

Outside is a cloister with a monastery surrounding it, now serving as the **Museu da Cidad**. On the ground floor are some nice *azulejos*. The upper floors are devoted to wonderful primitive paintings attributed to an anonymous "Master of Setúbal." Clearly influenced by the stiff figures of Van Eyke, the artist managed to convey a compassion in the faces that is his (or her) own. *Admission: free.*

Excursions

Tróia

The 8 km strip of sand and pine trees that separates the river Sado from the ocean is a highly developed beach resort, including an 18-hole Robert Trent Jones golf course. Despite the development of this peninsula, unspoiled beach remains on the ocean side and south.

A car ferry leaves the commercial port of Setúbal (the Doca Comércio) every half-hour in season (every hour out-of-season) for a 20-minute trip.

Serra da Arrábida

The Arrábida mountain range lines the 40 km southern coast of the Setúbal peninsula, forming high limestone cliffs over the ocean, broken here and there by sandy coves. The scenery is dramatic.
Follow Av. Luisa Todi west to N-379-1. After about 20 km signs for **Portinho do Arrábida** point to a steep and narrow 1 km descent. For safety it is best to leave one's car at the top, though the walk back is tiring. The bay forms a perfect curve of fine white sand embracing clear waters. Unfortunately, there are no hotels, although some private houses accept guests.

POUSADA DO CASTELO

Paço Real, Óbidos, 2510
☎ *(062) 95 91 05, FAX (062) 95 91 48*
$150, double; 9 rooms: 6 doubles, 3 suites

★ ★ ★

Yes, Óbidos is charming; and yes, this is the most heavily booked pousada in the county, but its popularity stems unaccountably from touting by guide books and tourist brochures. Success has undone whatever chance Castelo had of being a fine hotel. After all, why should the management care, when its rooms fill no matter what? The hotel is dingy, with narrow stone corridors lined by doors painted shed-brown. Rooms are small, cold in feeling, and not particularly comfortable. Best are the suites with exposed castle walls, but at exorbitant prices. All of this is criminal, for the building truly is a medieval castle and could be at least comfortable. It includes a splendid baronial hall, suits of armor dotting the way, and windows deeply set in thick fortress walls, all materials for a special hotel. This is the one failure of the pousada system. Still, it is an opportunity to live in a castle for a while, but only if you book months ahead.

Alternative Accommodations

Estalgem do Convento

R. Dom João de Ornelas (just outside the town walls), ☎ *(062) 95 92 17, FAX (062) 95 91 59, Telex 44906. 31 rooms.*

A better choice is the Estalgem do Convento, installed in a modest former convent. Appropriately whitewashed with dark wood details, this hotel is appealing, and sparkles with cleanliness. At the same time it is too pristine and sterile to feel quite comfortable, but at $70 a night who can complain? Large antique furniture lines the corridors and inhabits some of the rooms, and the bedrooms are well-designed. Good food is served in the patio restaurant for a moderate price.

Albergaria Rainha Santa Isabel

Rua Direita, ☎ *(062) 95 93 23, FAX (062) 95 91 15, Telex 14069. 20 rooms.*

The Albergaria Rainha Santa Isabel installed in one of the old houses in the heart of the village provides a sense of the aged village atmosphere. Bedrooms are cozily furnished and there is an elevator to the upper floor. A room costs $70.

Dining

Expensive meals are served in the dining room, also baronial with its beamed ceiling, but even the meals are not the best value. However, if one is staying elsewhere, a lunch or dinner here does provide a leisurely look at the inside of a veritable castle. Of the soups, leak, caldo verde or fish soup are better than the shellfish version. Entrées generally are bland, so the best choice is a delicate spotted bass with butter sauce *(lombos de cheme com molho)* or lamb *(borrego)*. A three-course set meal is available for about $25, plus drinks.

Alternative Dining

Alcaide   ★

R. Direita, Óbidos, ☎ *(062) 95 92 20. Closed Monday and November.*

The dining room is festooned with ivy and the tables dressed with checkered cloths. Outside, a balcony overlooks an orchard. The owner is from the Azores so menu choices include unusual dishes. Everything is tasty, and prices hover around $20.

Credit Cards: A, D, M, V.

Directions

From **Lisbon** take A-8 north for 79 km, which changes to N-8. From **Coimbra** and north, go south on A-1 to exit 9 at Leiria in 52 km. At Leiria pick up N-1 south for 16 km to Cruz da Légua, where N-8 goes to Caldas da Rainha in 46 km, and Óbidos in 8 km more.

Pousadas Nearby

Batalha: 53 km	Queluz: 85 km
Castelo de Bode: 120 km	Condeixa: 122 km

LISBON AND SURROUNDINGS

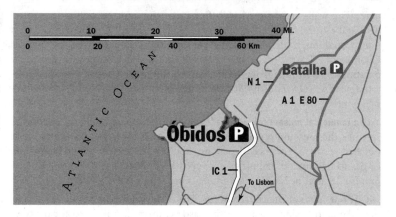

Sights

Óbidos is so quaint it hardly seems real. This tiny walled town surrounding a proper castle has changed hardly at all since the Middle Ages. Originally a sea bay lapping the town hill necessitated a fortress to guard against seaborne attack. When the Moors seized the fortress, they surrounded the small village grown beside the bastion with perimeter walls. After Christians reconquered Óbidos in 1148, they fitted the fortress out as a castle and several times restored the village walls—the last time being in the 16th century. By then the bay beside the town had entirely silted up, leaving the fortifications without purpose, and reducing the importance of the village. This preserved it from change. In 1228 King Dinis paused at Óbidos on his way elsewhere. His wife so admired its charm that he gave it to her as a present. By tradition Óbidos remained a fief of the reigning Queen of Portugal until 1833.

The village is so small that it takes only an hour to savor, but the narrow precipitous streets should not be attempted by car. Park beside the main gate, the Porta da Vila, and tour the curving streets on foot.

Azulejos mark a shrine just inside the Porta da Vila. The main street of the village is the quaint R. Direita that rises straight up to the castle. It goes past little whitewashed houses, roofed in orange tiles, with flowers on windowsills and beside doorways, to lead into the main square of the village around a pillory and fountain.

The tree-shaded **Church of Santa Maria** ★, in the square to the right, dates to the late 17th century, although its Romanesque portal shows earlier antecedents. In 1444, 10-year-old Dom Afonso V married his 8-year-old cousin here. The walls are covered with floral *azulejos*, and the ceiling is painted with arabesques, fanciful Brazilian natives and cherubs. On the left wall is an unexpected finely detailed Renaissance tomb, claimed to be by Nicolas Chanterene. To the right of the main altar are captivating 17th-century paintings by a woman from Seville, named Josefa de Óbidos, who was cloistered nearby. *(Open daily 9:30 a.m. to 12:30 p.m. and 2:30–7 p.m.; in winter to 5 p.m.)*

The **municipal museum** ★ is also located in the square, behind the church. In truth the museum is not very interesting except for one wonderful room devoted to the paintings of Josefa de Óbidos. There is an admirable quality of passion about the paintings conveyed by diffused light. *(Open Tuesday-Sunday 10 a.m. to 12:30 p.m. and 2–5 p.m.; admission: 100$00.)*

R. Direita ends at the church of São Tiago, old but redone in the 18th century. An arch beside it leads to the castle courtyard, now used for parking. To the left, steep stairs ascend the crenulated **ramparts** for a walk with nice views of the countryside. A fortunate hole in the walls looks out on one of the charming windmills of the area.

The **castle** ★ is suitably imposing. Square towers anchor its corners, the right-hand one being the main, castle keep, while round towers incongruously line the rear. In the 16th century the castle was outfitted as a palace when a Manueline door and front windows were added. Today it serves as one of Portugal's most popular pousadas. Anyone can walk inside for a look.

Excursions

Batalha, Alcobaça and Fátima are close. The latter two are discussed in the Batalha section.

POUSADA DO MESTRE AFONSO
DOMINGUES

Batalha, 2440
☎ *(044) 962 60, FAX (044) 962 47*
$100 per double; 21 rooms: 19 doubles, 2 suites

★ ★ ★

The best news about this pousada is its location. The great monastery of Batalha is fronted by a large paved square; this hotel sits at one side. However, it looks like an ordinary inn and so it was until the pousada people took it over. Stay only for convenience to the sights (it's about 20 km equidistant from Alcobaça and Fátima), for this is a bare-bones hotel of no aesthetic appeal. Guest rooms are cramped, the lobby is tiny and always crowded, as is the restaurant. Noise from the highway is a problem. Try for a room overlooking the monastery so you at least have something to look at.

Dining

There is little to say about the appearance of the dining room, for it is merely a functional place to eat. Always crowded because tourists throng to eat at this restaurant so close to their sight-seeing, service is rushed and frequently inattentive. All told, the food is merely passable. Specialties include shrimp in cream sauce *(gambas com natas)*, flambéd steak with mushrooms *(bife Mestre Afonso)* and seafood stew with fish, bread and eggs flavored by coriander *(açorda de marisco)*. All are à la carte. Set two- and three-course meals include blander choices except for a tasty roast pork loin with olives *(lombo de porco com azeitonas)*. The wine list is extensive. The set course meals include local wine for about $20.

Directions

There are two routes from **Lisbon**. Fastest is the autoestrada A-1 north for 99 km to exit 6, then N-1 south past Leiria to Batalha in 20 km more. Slower, but including a visit to **Alcobaça** and **Óbidos**, is A-8 north for 95 km where it becomes N-1 at Caldas da Rainha, then 46 km more. From **Coimbra** take N-1 south for 81 k. Or enter the auto-estrada, A-1, 10 km south of Coimbra to exit 9 at Leiria in 52 km, then turn south from Leiria on N-1 for 11 km. From **Tomar** take N-113 west to Leiria in 45k, then N-1 south for 11k.

Pousadas Nearby

Óbidos: 53 km	Condeixa: 60 km	Castelo de Bode: 92 km
Queluz: 153 km	Palmela: 176 km	Setubal: 190 km

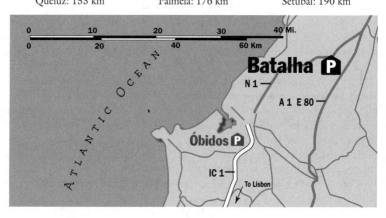

Sights

The town is aptly named by the Portuguese word for battle, for its founding was due to a fight that changed the course of history. A mighty army from Castile had invaded to contest the claims of King João I—who had usurped the Portuguese throne one year previously. On Aug. 14, 1385, the Castilian army lined the plain of Aljubarrota, 12 km south of Batalha, swelled by a large body of Portuguese nobles supporting the prior royal house. In addition, the Spanish brandished 16 of the new weapons of the day—cannons. Twenty-year-old João I, with no artillery and backed by a much smaller complement of knights—although aided by citizen-soldiers and 500 Englishmen—faced this host almost twice his numbers. He vowed that if success came his way he would endow a monastery, for it seemed that only a miracle could save him. João won a resounding victory, and construction of a monastery began three years later in this valley near the site.

The first stage of construction comprised the church, founder's chapel, royal cloister and chapterhouse, finished by 1436. The first architect, Afonso Domingues, was Portuguese, but the second, Houguet, was a Norman who lent the feeling of the English Gothic, reminiscent—in those areas where perpendiculars are emphasized by pillars and spires—of Westminster Cathedral.

King João's son Dom Duarte finished the founder's chapel and added an octagonal chapel behind the apse, although it was never completed. In turn, his successor appended a second cloister named—after himself—the Afonso V Cloister. Manuel I decorated various parts in the exuberant style named for him, before turning his attention to his own Hieronymite monastery outside Lisbon. His successor, João III, added dormitories and a third cloister (subsequently destroyed), before stopping work for good in 1550 to concentrate on his own building at Tomar. By that time, however, a century and a half of building by the mightiest monarchs of Portugal had created a monastery of surpassing majesty, one today designated by UNESCO as part of humanity's world heritage.

Mostairo de Santa Maria da Vitoria ★★★★★

Hours open: daily 9 a.m.–6 p.m., (until 5 p.m. in winter).

Setting off the square monastery is a sweeping plaza containing a modern mounted statue of Nuno Álvarez Pereira, the general at the battle of Aljubarrota. The exterior limestone of the monastery, weathered to a warm ochre, culminates in a flamboyant facade of scores of small spires, but no tower or belfry. To the right is the dome of the founder's chapel; cloister walls spread left. A lovely flamboyant window surmounts the richly carved main portal filled with copies of the original statues, except for those at the top. Buttresses and lacy balustrades run in all directions providing no focus for the eye, a characteristic of this structure built by various sovereigns with different ideas.

The church interior startles with plainness, after the exuberance outside. That same simplicity allows the grand sweep of the vaulting to soar. Dappled colors from the stained glass (modern, except for Manueline glass at the chancel end, and above in the choir) swathe the floor, and great piers seem to anchor the ceiling from possible flight. Pass reverently by the tomb of Mateus Fernandes by the main entrance door, the architect who embellished the Capelas Imperfeitas.

To the immediate right, through a splendid doorway, is the moving **Capela do Fundador** (Founders Chapel), a square room lit by an octagonal lantern. Under delicate stone canopies beneath the lantern lies the joint tomb of the founder, João I, and his wife, Philippa of Lancaster. The king wears the insignia of the Order of the Garter, founded by Philippa's grandfather, Edward III of England. As a moving touch, he holds his wife's hand.

The rear wall contains the tombs of the exceptional sons of these parents. The one on the left holds the few remains of Dom Fernando, who had been left a hostage after an abortive attack on Tangier failed. Humiliation and imprisonment led to his death, probably of dysentery. When his body was hung from the walls of Fez, his heart was removed by compatriots, embalmed and interred here. The third tomb from the left, bearing a Gothic canopy, is that of Dom Henrique, duke of Viseu, known as Prince Henry the Navigator. His features here look quite different from those painted by Nuno Gonçalves in his masterpiece of *Saint Vincent* in Lisbon.

The artistic highlight of the monastery is the **Claustro Real** (Royal Cloister), entered through the north wall of the church by the transept. Erected by Afonso Domingues, the first architect of Batalha, in pure, elegant Gothic style. Manuel I found it cold in feeling. He ordered his architect Mateus Fernandes to add Manueline embellishments to the columns and insert tracery to half-fill the arches. Manuel had a good eye—the combination is superb, though reconstructed today.

The **chapterhouse** is entered from the east side of the cloister. The boldness of its 60-foot expanse of unsupported vaulting amazed contemporaries. According to one story, the architect employed convicts to build it, since the dangers of its unproven construction were too great to risk the lives of honest men. Another story says the architect had to sleep beneath the vaulting for one night to convince doubters of its safety. Safe it is, for it survived the convulsions of Lisbon's 1755 earthquake. Today the room contains Portugal's Tomb of the Unknown Soldier (from WWI, for Portugal remained neutral in WWII), perpetually guarded. The east window is lovely 16th-century glass.

From the northwest corner of the Royal Cloister the adjacent **cloister of Dom Afonso V** may be entered. This slightly smaller cloister makes a nice contrast to its larger neighbor, for it is pure Gothic, and most elegant. Exit from its southeast corner to the outside, then round the chapterhouse to enter the **Capelas Imperfeitas**.

The chapels are entered through one of the great doorways in Portugal. Manuel's architect Mateus Fernandes covered every inch of this soaring Gothic portal with decoration.

"Inside" (a strange term for a roofless room), Dom Duarte's simple original design is apparent—an octagonal rotunda radiating seven chapels. He died before it was complete. Under Manuel I, Mateus Fernandes planned an octagonal roof supported by pillars, but was taken off the job before its completion, leaving stumps of the pillars, profusely carved, and a structure still unroofed. In 1533, in reaction to his father's exuberant decoration, Manuel's son added a sober balcony, but nothing more. And so it remains, somehow more moving in its incompleteness than the finished rooms. Although intended as a pantheon for the kings who succeeded João I, the chapel contains only the tomb (mutilated by the French) of one son, and of Dom Duarte and his wife, Leonor of Aragón, opposite the entrance, along with those of a noble and an infante (prince). *Admission: 400$00 to the abbey (250$00 in winter).*

Directory

Buses

The stop *(☎ (044) 965 05)* is behind the monastery in Largo da Misericórdia, an easy walk. Inquire at the Café Frazão for information. Frequent service is available to Alcobaça and to Nazaré, with a change in Alcobaça. There are four buses daily to Fátima and six express runs to Lisbon.

Excursions

Fátima and **Alcobaça** ★ ★ ★ each lie about 20 km away. For Fátima take N-356 east for 20 km; for Alcobaça take N-1 south for 6 km to branch southwest along N-8 for 12 km.

Fátima

Fátima and Santiago de Compostella in Spain constitute the great pilgrimage sites of the peninsula, with Fátima receiving greater numbers. It must count as one of the world's great ironies that this, holiest site in the Iberian peninsula, is named for Fatima, the daughter of the founder of Islam.

Fátima became holy when, on May 13, 1917, the sky suddenly brightened, causing three young children to look up to see the Virgin Mary standing in an oak tree. Their report was met with disbelief by most, but the children staunchly claimed that Mary promised to return on the same day of each ensuing month, pledging a miracle for her sixth and last appearance. Increasingly large crowds gathered on each succeeding 13th to hear Mary call for peace, a particularly appropriate message for World War I times. On Oct. 13, the sixth month, 70,000 people collected in a driving rainstorm. At noon the sun came out, spun in orbit and plummeted toward the earth. Then everything returned to normal, with no evidence of the rain.

The **Basilica of Fátima** stands at the end of an immense esplanade. This neoclassical church can hold 300,000 inside, but only those who are suitably attired—no shorts, no bare arms, no slacks on women—are permitted entrance. Inside, two of the three children who first saw the vision are buried. The **Capelinha das Apariçoães** on the esplanade is a modern structure surrounding the site of the visitation—alas, the oak tree is no more. The **Museu-Vivo Apariçoães**, which provides a sound-and-light show of the miraculous events, stands on the park grounds. Near the park, on R. Jacinto Marto, is the **Museu de Cera de Fátima**, a wax museum that attempts—sometimes in eerie ways—to make the events real.

Note: The 12th and 13th of each month are pilgrimage times. The town fills to overflowing on those dates in May, and almost so every October.

Alcobaça

The reason for the existence of the town and for the tourists is the Abbey of Santa Maria, containing the finest church in Portugal.The monastery is ancient, founded by the first king of Portugal, Afonso Henriques, to repay a vow to God for helping him capture the city of Santarém from the Moors. Work began in 1178 and finished in the first quarter of the 13th century for a cloistered order of Cistercians sent from France by Saint Bernard himself. Thus, the style of the buildings is the earliest, most monumental, and simplest Gothic, making this the finest surviving Cistercian structure anywhere.

Inside reposes a relic of one of Portugal's great romances. At the beginning of the 14th century, Dom Pedro, heir to the Portuguese throne, was betrothed to a Castilian princess. A lady-in-waiting named Inês de Castro travelled with Pedro's bride to Portugal, and the young groom fell instantly in love—not with his wife-to-be, but with the noblewoman accompanying her. Aware of his son's infatuation, Pedro's father banished Inês from the kingdom. When Dom Pedro's wife died five years later, Pedro brought Inês back to live with him, fathering two children. The king was enraged at this flouting of royal command and at the fact that the children's mother was Spanish. The King sent, or at least allowed, assassins to kill Inês.

As soon as the throne came to Pedro he viciously murdered two of the assassins, then disinterred Inês' remains, dressed her in regal robes, and ordered the nobles of the realm to kiss her skeletal hand as the reigning queen of Portugal. Then he buried her in high state in the Monastery of Santa Maria at Alcobaça and constructed his own tomb opposite, so his feet would face hers and his first sight on resurrection would be of his beloved.

Mostairo de Santa Maria

Hours open: daily 9 a.m.–7 p.m. (until 5 p.m. in winter).

The church facade was greatly changed by Baroque additions in the 17th and 18th centuries, but the central portal is original, if not its statues. The limestone outside has just been cleaned to glisten whitely, and show clearly how dismal the facade is. To the left extends a wall hiding ranks of cells that once housed 100 monks.

The interior of the church was altered over the centuries, but desecration by the French during the 19th-century Peninsular War led to removing later additions to reveal the pure, awesome Cistercian original—one of Portugal's most moving sights.

An unusually narrow nave accentuates the football field of length that makes this the largest church in the country. Columns are close-set and massive. Engaged pillars along the aisles are curiously truncated 10 feet above the floor to gain space for choirstalls, since removed, now providing a lovely perspective. Lighted only by the rose window of the nave and two others in the transepts, and barren of surface decoration or even side chapels, the effect is a purity that seems more modern than its venerable age.

To the left of the entrance is the Sala dos Reis containing statues—of no great artistic merit—depicting the kings of Portugal, in addition to *azulejos* portraying Afonso's victory at Santarém and the history of the monastery.

In the south transept (left) lies the 14th-century tomb of Inês de Castro resting on crouching figures, including, it is reputed, that of one of her assassins. Opposite, in the north transept, is the man who loved her, Dom Pedro. As Pedro commanded, they lie feet to feet, although with a fair distance between. Both effigies are carved of soft limestone in a florid Gothic style, but both were damaged by the French, as is apparent in the plaster reconstruction of Inês' nose. She does look beautiful, nonetheless, protected by six gentle angels surrounding her. A frieze at the top of the sarcophagus interweaves the coat of arms of Portugal with that of the de Castro family. Tomb sides depict scenes from the life of Christ. Carved on the end of the tomb's head is a crucifixion scene. Appropriately, the finest carving faces Pedro: a most realistic scene of the Last Judgement at her feet.

The effigy of Pedro looks severe, lending credence to his nickname "the Cruel." The sides of his tomb present scenes from the life of Saint Bartholomew, his patron saint, while the head-end shows Pedro's last moments. The carving at the foot is an exceptional composition of the wheel of fortune, whose details repay study. They depict events from the lives of this pair including Inês' murder. On both tombs is written *Até ão fim do mundo*—"until the end of the world."

A chapel off the south transept contains the tombs of Afonso II and III, from the 13th century, along with a strange—and mutilated—terra-cotta group surrounding St. Bernard, carved by a monk in the 17th century. Behind the high altar a charming Manueline door seems to grow vegetation as it leads to a sacristy with reliquaries emptied of their contents by some pillager or other. A door in the north aisle leads to a lovely 14th-century cloister of silence, whose upper story was added two centuries later. Arches between twisted columns are capped by roses looking out to orange trees. Here and there lie some of the statues that once graced the Cathedral portals.

The chapterhouse, entered from the north side of the cloister, is a room of round-arch doorways, windows, and graceful vaulting, although lined by distracting terra-cotta statues produced by monks in the 18th century. Stairs lead to a cavernous Gothic dormitory. From the west side of the cloister the monastery kitchen may be entered. A stream running through it was intended for washing dishes rather than, as some say, to provide the monks with fish. The colossal fireplace and chimney were tiled in the 18th century. Look up for a six story sight of the sky. Next to the kitchen is the solemn space of the refectory whose stairs, built into the end wall, lead to a fine lector's pulpit.

Where to Eat

As if heaven-sent, a hearty restaurant waits right beside the monastery.

Trindade   ★

Pr. Dom Afonso Henriques, 2, *(044) 423 97.*
This is not one of those restaurants near a monument that lives for tourists, but a venerable local bistro that thrives because it serves tasty, hearty food. The specialty is *açorda marisco*, a stew of shellfish and bread that is done very well here. There is also an inexpensive tourist menu. Credit Cards: V.

Moorish Castle above the forests of Sintra

SINTRA
★ ★ ★

Accommodations

We sympathize with anyone who does not want to leave Sintra after a day. Mountain nights are wonderful, the Moors' castle is lighted, and there are a number of exceptional accommodations in the area.

Palácio de Seteais

Rua Barbose do Bocage, 8 (1.5 km outside Sintra on N-375 which is reached by going west from the palace on R. Pedroso), Sintra, 2710. 29 rooms, plus 1 suite.

The Palácio de Seteais is the most tasteful, elegantly grand hotel in Portugal. "Seven sighs," which is what its name means, is what you will exhale on seeing it. It is a French chateaux more lovely than any we have had the good fortune to stay at in that country. Built in the 18th century by a Dutch businessman, it was taken over by the fifth Marquis of Marialva, the Royal Chamberlain, before transformation into a hotel. Now it is run by the Tivoli Hotel Corporation in Lisbon. An appropriately long driveway leads to the palace atop a bluff overlooking miles. Most rooms face palatial formal gardens, with views to the sea on clear days. The decor is pastel, working with the warm glow of ancient floors. Delicate frescoes cover ceilings and walls; fine antiques grace the rooms. Everything is perfect, including the bedrooms fitted with antiques or replicas. Three special bedrooms (which is almost a redundancy in this case) incorporate hand-painted murals. There is a pool and two tennis courts. For what it offers, prices are reasonable at just over $225 for a double, only $50 more for a suite, and you can knock off $100 in the winter. Other than at that time, reservations will be needed. If you cannot spend the night, go for an elegantly beautiful $40 lunch or dinner, or even for cocktails just to see the place, and you'll wish you could stay.

Quinta da Capela

Estrada da Monserrate, Sintra (about 2 km farther along the road past the Palácio de Seteais above, past Monserrate, then look carefully for a marked turn), Sintra, 2710, ☎ (01) 929 01 70, FAX (01) 929 34 25. 5 rooms, plus 3 suites.

Next best is the Quinta da Capela. From the outside this 18th-century building looks more like a farm than a villa, but inside it is sedate, yet cozy. Two outlying cottages contain two rather ordinary bedrooms and kitchenettes. The bedrooms in the main house are more elegant by far. There is a tiny ancient chapel in the garden, a pool and lovely views, and the young manager-caretaker is as likable as can be. The most expensive double apartment just passes $150. Breakfast is served and all the rooms either contain or have access to a kitchen. The quinta is closed out of season, and must be reserved far in advance in season.

Quinta de São Thiago

Estrada de Monserrate, Sintra (about 1 km farther along the road past the Palácio de Seteais above, then a marked turn along a treacherously steep and bumpy road, Sintra, 2710, ☎ (01) 923 29 23. 14 rooms.

Close behind is the Quinta de São Thiago, a lovely 16th-century villa owned by a British and Portuguese couple who extend themselves for their guests. Much of the furniture is antique and there is the feel of staying in a fine house rather than at a hotel. A swimming pool and a tennis court are provided, but not air conditioning. Reservations should be made far in advance. Rooms cost $125.

Caesar park Penha Longa

On the road to Lagoa Azul-Malveira, N-9, 7 km south of Sintra, Sintra, 2710, ☎ (01) 924 90 11; FAX (01) 924 90 07. 158 rooms.

For a different sort of stay, there is the Caesar park Penha Longa, with golf course in a natural reserve with 15th century buildings on the grounds. It's a modern hotel complex with some lovely touches.

Dining

For ambiance to spare and the best food in the area, reserve at the Monserrat restaurant of the **Palácio de Seteais Hotel**. Good food in pleasant surroundings is served at Galeria Real.

Solar de São Pedro ★

Pr. D. Fernando, 11-12 (just off the main street in São Pedro, where it makes a sharp bend left), São Pedro, 2710, *(01) 923 18 60, FAX 9(01) 24 06 78. Closed Wed.*
Locals consider this the best food in town. The cuisine is Portuguese but with French touches, served in a dim vault nicely decorated by azulejos. Meals run about $30. Credit Cards: A, D, M, V.

Restaurant Monserrat ★★★

In the Palácio de Seteais hotel, Av. Bocage, 8 (1.5 km outside Sintra on N-375, which is reached by going west from the palace on R. Pedroso), Seteais, 2710, *(01) 923 32 00.*
A lovelier dinner area would be hard to imagine, including fantastic views over the countryside. The food is elevated to match its surroundings, and four-course set meals can be had for about $40. OK, maybe the romance of the setting affected our taste buds, but it probably will do the same to yours. Eating here is an experience not to be missed. Credit Cards: A, D, M, V.

Galeria Real ★

R. Tude de Sousa (on the main street in São Pedro), São Pedro, 2710, *(01) 923 16 61. Closed Monday evening.*
This is a pretty, second-floor restaurant located in a warren of antique shops. The ceiling is hand-painted beams, the floors tiled, and flowers decorate each table. Codfish soufflé is the delicious specialty. Otherwise the menu is not adventurous. $25 should cover a meal. Credit Cards: A, D, M, V.

Restaurante Tulhas ★

R. Gil Vicente, 4 (behind the Office of Tourism), Sintra, 2710, no phone. Closed December.
Housed in attractively converted grain silos, the food tastes and looks like more than the $20 it costs. Veal in madeira sauce is a specialty.

Alcobaça ★

R. da Padarias, 7 (the street runs uphill from the tourist office, just west of the Palácio Real), Sintra, 2710, *(01) 923 16 51. Closed Wednesday and December.*
This is an eminently local place that serves standard Portuguese dishes at very fair prices. If the cooking wasn't good, it wouldn't be so crowded. Credit Cards: none.

Directions

Sintra is located 28 km northwest of **Lisbon**; directions are included in the "Excursion" section of Lisbon. From **Mafra** take N-9 south for 31 km.

Pousadas Nearby

Queluz: 16 km   Óbidos: 120 km   Batalha: 150 km

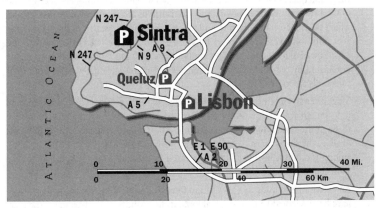

Sights

The magical mountains surrounding Sintra are lush with eucalyptus and camellias, gardenias and bougainvillea in season. Byron lauded this "glorious Eden" in *Childe Harolde* and wrote his mother that it is "perhaps the most delightful (village) in Europe." There is a Black Forest quality about the mountains, which appropriately shelter a castle worthy of King Ludwig of Bavaria. In the most dramatic setting imaginable, Sintra offers a palace, a fantasy castle and a ruined fortress of the Moors. While tourists arrive by the bus-full, they are quickly absorbed into the vastness of surrounding nature. A day would cover the sights comfortably.

Actually three Sintras wrap around the mountain. The Vila Velha clusters near the Palácio Real of Portugal's kings. To the north is the new town, called Estefania, with the bus and train station along the way, and to the south is the formerly separate town of São Pedro, which hosts a famous crafts market.

From **Lisbon** N-249 becomes the winding Estrada de Chão de Meninos, then Av. D. F. de Almeida, to end at Largo de Albuquerque. Turn left here along R. Dr. Alfredo Costa, which bends right to change its name to Av. Volta do Duche, leading into the parking of the Pr. de República beside the Palácio Real. From **Mafra** Av. Henrique Salgado leads into the Largo de Albuquerque, from which point the Lisbon directions can be followed.

Palácio Real   ★★★★

Pr. da República, ☎ *(01) 923 00 85.*
Hours open: daily 10 a.m.–1 p.m. and 2–5 p.m.

Kings and queens favored the mountain air of Sintra for their summers since the end of the 14th century. Even before, the Moors had built a summer palace on the spot, which Dom João I tore down to build the central, and oldest part of the present palace. Additions were made over the years—including the left 16th-century wing added by Manuel I—producing a jumble of styles. It is a Gothic-Mudejar complex dominated by two clumsy conical chimneys, though individual windows and their surrounds are lovely.

Magnificent rooms inside are lined with some of the finest *azulejos* in the world and hold remarkable antique furniture. Past the **kitchen**, with its gigantic fireplaces, through the **Guest Room**, with some interesting furniture, comes, in the **Sala dos Arabes**, the first example of these *azulejos*—blue, green and white Mudejar tiles, among the oldest in the country, imported from Spain in the first decade of the 16th century.

An exterior patio leads to the exquisite **Chapel**. Its adorable frescoed walls of doves have been restored to their original look, its fine Mudejar inlaid ceiling is the marvelous original, and its patterned tiles form a carpet. After the Chinese room with an ivory pagoda donated by the Emperor of China in 1809, comes the **Sala de Afonso VI**, whose 15th-century *azulejo* floor is said to have been worn away by that king's pacing during nine years of imprisonment. A lovely muslim hanging brightens the room. Along the next corridor hangs a 16th-century Brussels tapestry of the Portuguese royal coat of arms, with an unusual oriental carpet below it. Then comes the wonder of the **Sala dos Brasoães** (Coats of Arms Room).

This space was designed for views and light, which makes the 18th-century azulejo hunting-scenes lining the walls gleam with remarkable effect. But the purpose of the room is to display its incredible artesonado dome of the coats of arms of Portugal's first families. At the top is that of the Portuguese royal house, gilded and repainted to reflect the next dynasty; the arms of King Manuel's children surrounding his, then 80 more are arranged by their importance at court. Under the dome lies quite a carpet.

Farther along comes the **Sala das Sireias** with a lovely ceiling of mermaids playing instruments, above fine azulejos from Seville. Next is the 15th-century **Sala de Pegas** (Room of the Magpies), named for the birds on the ceiling hold a rose and the legend *Por bem* ("for the good"). Tradition had João I ordering the multiple images after being caught by his wife presenting a rose to a lady of the court and uttering "It's all for the best," a story that hardly makes sense. More likely, the magpies represent the king, and the rose represents his queen, who was indeed from the House of Lancaster.

Across the central patio the **Sala dos Cisnes** can be admired. This imposing audience hall is named for the swans embellishing a magnificent ceiling painted in the 17th century; the woodwork is also masterly. *Admission: 400$00 for guided tour; 200$00 in winter.*

There are various options for the 3-km, almost-vertical climb to the Castelo dos Mouros and the Palácio da Pena atop the highest peaks in the Sintra mountains. The most pleasant journey is to walk, encouraged by the thought that the return is downhill. It will take an hour to the Castle of the Moors, plus another to the Pena Palace, depending on your pace. A map is available from the tourist office. Alternatively, a taxi will cost about 3000$00 for the round trip to either, including an hour's wait, or 4500$00 to both. In summer buses travel daily at 10:45 a.m., 3 p.m. and 4 p.m. for 150$00. A half- day bus tour throws in Cabo de Roca, the westernmost point of Europe, for 4500$00; check at the Office of Tourism for times. For romantics there are horse-drawn carriages that will cost about 6000$00.

By car head west (uphill) from the palace, past the post office on R. Pedroso. At the Estalagem dos Cavaleiros, now boarded up, where Byron stayed, turn left and then turn sharply left at the next opportunity only to take an immediate right. The road twists and winds back on itself until reaching a parking place. From here a 10-minute walk remains up to the Moors' Castle. For the Palace of Pena continue to a "T," then turn right as a sign directs.

Castelo dos Mouros ★

Estrada da Pena
Hours open: Tues.–Sun. 8 a.m.–sunset. Closed Mon.
Although called a castle, this was actually a fortress, built in the eighth or early ninth century, then captured by Christians in the 12th. It has fallen into romantic ruins, although the perimeter wall still stands with corner towers. Some restoration was attempted in the 19th century, but given up. On a clear day there are heavenly views from atop a tower inside the walls. Also on the grounds is a Romanesque chapel dating to the 12th-century Reconquest. *Admission: free.*

Palácio Nacional da Pena ★★★

Estrada da Pena, ☎ *(01) 923 02 27.*
Hours open: Tues.–Sun. 10 a.m.–1 p.m. and 2–4:45 p.m. Closed Mon.
Queen Maria II came to the throne in 1836 and married Friedrich of Saxe Coburg-Gotha, an old titled German family of three cousins, each of whom married a queen. Cousin Leopold became King of the Belgians, cousin Albert became the consort of Queen Victoria in England while Fernando II, as the Portuguese know him, became the King of Portugal. A tinge of homesickness led him to import a German architect to build a palace at Sintra. Ferdinand had pretensions to art and worked closely on the design. What resulted was the beginning of the Victorian style, although we call it by the name of his cousin-in-law.

Outside the castle is part Moorish, part Gothic, part Baroque, tinged with Manueline—a confection of crenulations, minarets, turrets and drawbridges—a castle for the child in us all. The interior is another matter, consisting of patterns and colors jumbled on each other to create that dark, cozy, romantic cluttered look we call "Victorian."

Over the drawbridge and through a tunnel, then up a "Manueline" double stair, are remains from a Manueline monastery cloister with fine *azulejos* and a lovely alabaster altar. Then the pantry and dining room of the palace are entered to provide a foretaste of what lies in store. One special feature of this building is that the rooms actually looked lived in. Note the lace, the feathers and ornately carved furniture. This and the rooms that follow remain almost exactly as they were in 1910 when the royal family fled to exile. Their taste, however we evaluate it, is therefore evident to all.

The apartments of King Carlos include his workroom with unfinished canvases of nymphs and fauns. The bathrooms are a delight. After the chapel come bedrooms for the women, including the marvelous painted stucco of the Queen's Room, feeling Moorish. Then comes the Sewing Room, all oriental in style, and then the Private Living Room of a style unique to Fernando.

And so it goes, each chamber unique, each betraying the same "overdone" look that somehow works. Note the Arabian Room frescoed with trompe l'oeil mosque scenes, and the India Room, named for its furniture, with a playful Bavarian chandelier forerunner of the art nouveau. The multifarious ballroom furniture is a treat. *Admission: 400$00; 200$00 in winter.*

Directory

Trains and Buses

The train station is on Av. Dr. Miguel Bombarda (☎ *(01) 923 26 05)*, halfway between the Vila Velha and the new town of Estefania. Trains serve Lisbon every 15 minutes, stopping at Queluz. Trains connect with Óbidos, but connections elsewhere are difficult.

The bus station is across the street from the train station and is best for surrounding towns.

Excursions

Sintra is readily combined with **Mafra**, 22 km north along N-9 or with **Queluz**, 16 km east along N-249. Descriptions are contained in this chapter under the Quesluz heading. A pleasant excursion for those interested in wine is to the remarkable vineyards of **Colares**, 6 km west of Sintra. What makes its wines special is that vine roots are buried deep in sand which protected them from the phylloxera blight that struck Europe in 1865. All other vines in Europe succumbed and later had to be grafted to American roots that were immune to the blight.

SOUTHERN PORTUGAL

The beach at Praia da Rocha has become as commercial as Miami Beach.

Southern Portugal covers the vast plains of the region called the Alentejo, the breadbasket of the country. Here rolling hills are crowned by groves of olive and cork trees while the land between grows wheat and feeds sheep. Renaissance Évora reposes here, along with the grand castle-pousada at Estremoz, and the grand baroque castle at Vila Viçosa. This is also the route to Portugal's great beaches of the Algarve, although only two pousadas are situated there. Summer temperatures are hot, but there are more pousadas for cooling off in this area than anywhere else in the country.

The major sight of the Alentenjo is lovely **Évora**, with a Manueline convent, grand azulejos in a tiny chapel and a Roman temple. **Elvas** offers much to see as well, from substantial fortifications, to lovely squares, to a castle and pretty church. But, for churches, the one to see is the Templar church at **Tomar**, a wondrous Manueline confection with an often pictured window built around a mysterious templar church. Nearby are he fairy-tale ruins of castle **Amouril**. There are shopping opportunities for world renowned embroidered carpets at **Arraiolos** and for antiques at **Borba**. **Algarve** beaches are the finest in Europe, well worth a sit in the sun.

The following towns and pousadas are covered in this chapter.

Town	Pousada Name	Rating	Page
Alvitó	Castilo de Alvitó	★★★★	*page 544*
Arraiolos	da Assuncão	★★★★	*page 592*
Beja	São Francisco	★★★★	*page 561*
Castelo de Bode	São Pedro	★★★	*page 565*
Elvas	Santa Luzia	★★★	*page 554*
Estremoz	Rainha Santa Isabel	★★★★	*page 548*
Évora	dos Lóios	★★★★	*page 578*
Flor da Rosa	Flor da Rosa	★★★★	*page 546*
Sagres	do Infante	★★★★	*page 570*
São Bras	São Bras	★★★	*page 557*
Sta. Clara-a-Velha	Santa Clara	★★★	*page 552*
Santiago do Cacem	Quinta da Ortiga	★★★	*page 586*
Santiago do Cacem	São Tiago	★★★	*page 590*
Serpa	São Gens	★★★	*page 588*
Sousel	São Miguel	★★★	*page 563*
Torrão	do Gaio	★★★	*page 595*
Vila Viçosa	Dom João IV	★★★★	*page 575*

To savor the region, stay three or four nights in the upper Alentejo. A surplus of great pousadas in this area make for difficult choices. Try two nights at any two of the following: Estremoz, Vila Viçosa, Évora, or Flor de Rosa. Stay at least two nights in the Algarve, either at Sagres, near beach, or at São Bras, away from the beach for quiet and exploring. A rest on the way south from the upper Alentejo can be made at Santa Clara or, if driving straight from Lisbon, at one of the two pousadas in Santiago do Cacém.

Southern Portugal

P	PARADOR	PRIMARY ROAD
(castle)	CASTLE	SECONDARY ROAD
		SCENIC ROAD

0   10   20   30   40 Mi.

0   20   40   60 km

Leiria
Batalha
Obidos
Sao Pedro
Abrantes
Marvão
Monsanto
Flor da Rosa
Lisbon
Sousel
Estremoz
Elvas
Setúbal
Evora
Feri
Portel
Alvito
Moura
Santiago
Beja
Serpa
Aroche
Almonaster la Real
Ala
Alcoutim
Ayamonte
Castro Marim
Sagres
S. Bras de Alportel

ATLANTIC OCEAN

PORTUGAL

SPAIN

GULF OF CÁDIZ

N

©FWI

POUSADA CASTELO DE ALVITÓ

Largo do Castelo, Alvitó, 7920
☎ *(084) 483 43, FAX (084) 483 83*
$125, double; 20 rooms: 20 doubles

★ ★ ★ ★

SOUTHERN PORTUGAL

This special parador languishes off the beaten track, located in the wrong place. Too far north to serve as a reasonable stop on the way to the Algarve, and too close to the more elegant Estremoz pousada to win over that competition, Alvitó is meant for those who want to be where the crowd hasn't been. On its own it stands up to the best of the pousada system. Imagine a perfect 15th century fortress, complete with crenulated walls anchored by corner towers, yet a fortress owned by a government bureaucrat, not a king, it is so stylish and small. Finally, locate that fortress in a quiet village in the upper Alentejo for a taste of the rolling plains and special food of this region, and near a large artificial lake for swimming and boating. The capper is that this fortress was just remodeled as a pousada in 1993, making crisp rooms surrounding an interior courtyard on two floors. Their size and decor are inviting. Outside is a garden with palms and cypresses enclosing a graceful pool. The management aims to please those who make the effort to visit, as does a staff still learning the ropes.

Dining

A lovely dining room is still covered by original Gothic vaulting. The special soup of the region is a garlic soup with floating egg and bread, called *açord à alentenjana*, but there is a savory potato soup *(de batata)* as well. For a change the codfish is enjoyable, this time stewed with aromatic herbs *(com Ervas Aromáticas)*, or in the form of codfish cakes *(Pataniscas)*. Meats include a pork with coriander *(Porco com Coentros)*, fricassee of chicken *(Frango de Fricassé)* and roast lamb with spinach *(Borrego Assado à Alentejana)*. Here you can try a nice red Redondo with your meal or a Borba, which is also the house wine. A set-course meal is available for about $20, and includes house wine.

Directions

From **Lisbon** take A-2 south toward Setúbal then east to the exit for Montemor-o-Novo in 97 km. South of town pick up N-2 south for 60 km to N-257 east, just before Odivelas, which reaches Alvitó in 18 km. From **Faro**, in the Algarve, take N-2 north for 167 km to N-257 east just past Odivelas, for a final leg of 18 km. From **Évora** take N-18 south for 55 km to Vidigueira, then N-258 west for 15 km.

Pousadas Nearby

Torrão: 26 km	Évora: 41 km	Beja: 45 km
Serpa: 74 km	Estremoz: 87 km	Santiago: 114 km

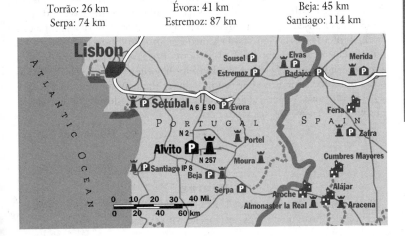

POUSADA DA FLOR DA ROSA

Flor da Rosa, 7430
☎ *(045) 99 72 10, FAX (045) 99 72 12*
$125 per double; 24 rooms: 24 doubles
★ ★ ★ ★

The present town is so small as to be overwhelmed by the massive fortified monastery in its midst, surrounded by a crenulated wall. Its buildings resemble small forts, for the Knights of Malta constructed the monastery in the
middle of the 14th century. On the right stands an elegantly simple church
with a most impressive nave. Its small cloister is lovely with flowers. This is a
favorite spot for those who take the small trouble to come here, and since
1995 it has housed a pousada inside to bring the enjoyment of a night alone
(well, with a few other guests) in a medieval monastery declared a national
monument. Less pleasant are the bedrooms, boxes with spare furnishings in
a modern addition. The gems are seven in the original buildings. But this is
not a hotel for sitting in your room. Wander the halls and lounges oozing
style and history. When the architecture pales, try the lovely garden for refreshing the senses. Or, there is a pool.

Dining

The restaurant provides nice views over the countryside. There is quite a
selection of Portuguese soups—gazpacho with sausage (*gazpacho á alenteja-*

na), delicate tomato, egg, bread and coriander *(açorda)* and cabbage *(caldo verde)*. A delicate fresh-water fish is lightly grilled *(assada de peixes)*, or there is lamb stew *(ensopado de borrego)* or jugged chicken *(frango na púcara)*, in addition to the usual cod dishes. A set-course meal is available for about $20.

Directions

From **Lisbon** take the autoestrada A-1 north for 81 km to exit 7 at Entroncamento, then IP-6 east for 48 km to join N-116 east for 59 km, the last bit on N-246, to Alpalhão. Take N-245 south for 12 km. From **Estremoz** take N-245 north for 63 km. From **Évora** take N-18 northeast for 46 km to Estremoz, then follow the directions above. From **Coimbra** take the autoestrada A-1 south for 92 km to exit 7 at Entrocamento, then follow the Lisbon directions from there.

Pousadas Nearby

Marvão: 43 km	Sousel: 45 km	Estremoz: 63 km
Elvas: 92 km	Évora: 110 km	

Excursions

Quaint **Marvão** ★★ is 2 km south on N-245 to Crato and 21 km on N-119 east to **Portalegre**, where N-359 reaches the village in 20 km. Both are described in the Northern Portugal chapter. **Estremoz** ★★ lies 63 km south along N-245, with directions to nearby **Évora** ★★★ and **Elvas** ★. All these are described in this chapter.

POUSADA DA RAINHA SANTA ISABEL

Largo Don Dinis, Estremoz, 7100
☎ *(068) 33 20 75, FAX (068) 33 20 79*
$150 per double; 33 rooms: 30 doubles, 3 suite

★ ★ ★ ★

Save up for this one and reserve months in advance. It's your chance to walk where kings walked and slept, if not in the same room, at least in the same building where they dreamed. A saint also spent time here, and the king granted Vasco da Gama an audience but did not invite him to stay the night. This is the most elegant of all the pousadas, and, befitting the flagship, service is exceptional too. Everything is monumental, from marble entry stairs, to a lofty reception area, to lounges scaled for coronations. Antiques abound amid velvets and marble; and the corridors are stately. Most rooms include canopied beds and the views that royalty came to enjoy. For all this the cost counts as a great bargain and the experience and unobtrusive pampering make a stay memorable.

Alternative Accommodations

Hotel Convento de São Paulo

Aldeia da Serra, Redondo 7170, ☎ *(068) 99 9 1 00, FAX (068) 99 91 04. 16 rooms.*
Believe it or not, there is an equally special hotel 15 km south on the road to Redondo, (go south on N-381 looking for signs in 15 km). The Hotel Convento de São Paulo is an ancient monastery fitted with modern conveniences. When your car arrives at an iron gate, it is electronically opened to let you drive a private road to a veritable edifice from the 14th century, although what survives is mainly from the 16th. No money has been spared to restore its former glory yet provide all the luxury anyone could wish for. There are tennis courts and a pool, vast gardens and

about five square miles of private forest for walks. The hotel interior is enchanting, and includes a lovely cloister in the center. But it is the 50,000 azulejos covering its corridors that astonish; no one who visits will ever forget them. The dining room is the cavernous original in which the monks ate, still covered with frescoes that are damaged but serene. All this will cost over $150, but you will talk about it for years. Here, too, we have had some of our best meals in Portugal, served by the most attentive staff. We drool every time we think of the tomato soup.

Dining

Fittingly, the restaurant dwells in a huge pillared hall covered by sweeping arches. Candelabra and tapestries continue the regal tone, complemented by high-backed chairs, good china and crystal. The cooking is considered the best of the pousada system. Soups include a gazpacho with mingled sausage *(gazpacho à alentejana)*, but other starters include a delicate smoked sword-fish *(espadarte fumado)* and a terrine of turbot with some caviar *(terrine de cherne com caviar)*. Game is a specialty, when available. Generally on the menu is a delicate white fish in coriander flavored wine sauce *(ensopado de cação)* or lamb in white sauce *(ensopado de borrego)*. Of course there is a perfectly done roast lamb or pig. The wine list is ample, providing special wine for your meal. A reserva from Borba or Redondo will match the meal, or, more special, a rare Frangoneiro. A set-course meal is available for about $25.

Alternative Dining

Águias d'Ouro ★★

Rossio, 27, ☎(068) 221 96.

Past a rather dingy bar comes style and service upstairs that are far more elegant than the prices. You will see unfamiliar dishes on the menu because the cooking is more adventurous than at most establishments, and good. If pheasant casserole is available, go for it. But there is an *ementa turistica* for about 2000$00 for those on a budget or who cotton to its selections. Credit Cards: A, D, V.

Directions

From **Lisbon** take A-2 south toward Setúbal then east past the exit for Montemor-o-Novo in 97 km where N-4 is picked up for a final 63 km. From **Évora** take N-18 northeast for 46 km. From **Marvão** take N-359 to Portalegre in 21 km, then N-18 south for 59 km. From the **Algarve** take N-264 north from Albufeira for 70 km to Ourique, outside of which N-123 heads east, then feeds into N-391 going north toward Beja just before Castro Verde. Circle Beja in 60 km to take N-18 north for 78 km to Évora. From there continue on N-18 north for 46 km. From **Guarda** take N-18 south past Castelo Branco, Portalegre and Estremoz for 289 km.

Pousadas Nearby

Vila Viçosa: i7 km	Sousel: 18 km	Elvas: 39 km
Arraiolos: 43 km	Évora: 46 km	Flor da Rosa: 63 km

Sights

Through the town walls the sandy expanse of the main square, Pr. Rossio, is reached for parking. Here a large regional fair, mostly for food, is held every Saturday, though some stalls remain through the week. It is known for cheeses. The south side of the square consists of the **town hall**, formerly a convent from the end of the 17th century, with a grand stair and fine azulejos. On the east, at #62b, stands a small regional **museum** displaying Alentejo scenes in miniatures carved by senior citizens, along with curiosities *(open Tues. through Sun. from 10 a.m. until 1 p.m. and from 3 p.m. until 5 p.m. for tours; admission: 100$00)*.

Head past the **pillory** at the north end of the Rossio to follow the alley on the right uphill. The old town is entered through 17th-century fortifications. Keep heading up to the castle past pretty whitewashed houses that are Manueline or older.

All that remains of the original castle is its rectangular **keep** bristling with battlements at the top. Three kings worked on it, finished by King Dinis in 1258. An octagonal room on the third floor is lined with fine windows, and the platform on the tower roof provides extensive views. (If closed ask at the pousada.) King Dinis later constructed a **palace** beside the keep for his lovely wife, Isabel of Spain, who became a saint. She died in what is today called the audience chamber. But an explosion at the end of the 17th century wrecked most of the palace, leading to restoration in the next century, and finally transformation into a luxurious pousada. Plain on the outside, it is grand within. Anyone can wander through and should, for a treat.

The castle square contains the attractive 16th-century church of **Sant Maria** (seldom open) with some nice paintings. Beside it is the former **Audience Hall** of the original palace, now a chapel, where Queen (Saint) Isabel died, with fine azulejos illustrating events from her life. Ask at the pousada desk for the key. *(open Tues. through Sun. 9 a.m. until noon and from 2 p.m. until 6 p.m. for tours; apply at the Municipal Museum on the south side of the square).*

Although the town's eccentric water jars are curiosities, more charming examples of ceramic work in the form of naive little figures and animals are also produced here and are sold around town.

Excursions

Arraiolos for carpets, **Redondo** for ceramics and **Borba** for antiques are nearby. **Évora** ★ ★ ★ is 30 miles distant with **Évoramonte** ★ passed on the way. Tiny **Vila Viçosa** ★, just 17 km east, with something for everyone is described under its own heading below. Borba is described under the Arraiolos entry and Évoramonte is discussed as an excursion from Évora. Read on for Redondo.

Redondo

*From **Évora** go east on N-254 for 34 km. From **Estremoz** go south on the scenic N-381 for 27 km.*

While the 16th-century church of Nossa Senhora da Anunciação in a pretty square is worth a look, this typical *alentejo* town is more often visited for its crafts. Conveniently located within less than 20 miles of both Évora and Estremoz, Redondo produces painted wood furniture and some good artisan ceramics. Small stores spread around the town selling these wares. A folk festival springs up on the first weekend in August.

POUSADA DE SANTA CLARA

Barragem de Santa Clara, Santa Clara-a-Velha, 7665
☎ *(083) 982 50, FAX (083) 984 02*
$100 per double; 19 rooms: 18 doubles, 1 suite

★ ★ ★

Waste not, want not. The Portuguese save the buildings that house the engineers of construction projects and turn them into pousadas. Here is one on a huge artificial lake where there is little to do except walk, swim and fish. If you want isolation and fine views of a lake surrounded by eucalyptus forest, this is your place. If so, sit on the long terrace, perhaps with a glass in hand, and drink in the panorama. The accommodations are comfortable, but nothing grand. They serve the purpose.

Dining

Meals include a stew *(caldeirad de achigã)* of the only fish the lake seems to provide, a rather bony creature. Simply done fried trout is also available, from fish caught elsewhere. Lamb stew *(borrego)* and braised kid *(cabrito)* are savory. Try the rice pudding for dessert. A set-course meal is available for about $20 and includes local wine.

Directions

From **Lisbon** take A-2 south toward Setúbal then east to join N-5 south in 54 km. Although it changes its designation inexplicably to N-120, it reaches the outskirts of Grândola in 44 km. Stay on N-120 as it passes Sines and goes south to Odemira in 106 km. Take N-123 east for 19km to Milharadas, then N-266 south to Santa Clara-a-Velha in 13 km of rough driving. Just past the town the first road going left reaches the pousada in 4 km. From **Faro**, in the Algarve, take the autoestrada for 33 km west to join N-125 west to **Portimão** in 28 km. Take N-124 north for 5 km to Porto de Lagos, then N-266 north for scenic, slow mountain driving to the first right before the village of Santa Clara-a-Velha in 49 km. The pousada is 4 km away.

Pousadas Nearby

Santiago: 87 km	Sagres: 103 km	São Brás: 125 km
Beja: 140 km	Serpa: 169 km	

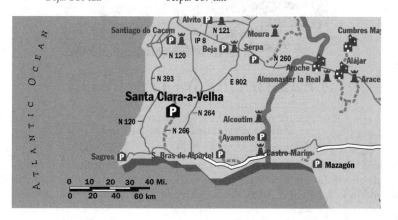

Pousada de Santa Luzia

Avenida de Badajoz (N-4), Elvas, 7350
☎ *(068) 62 21 94, FAX (068) 62 21 27*
$100 per double; 25 rooms: 24 doubles, 1 suite

★ ★ ★

This white-tiled, villa-like hotel from the 1940s recently became a pousada after failing as a private enterprise. The first floor is all spacious public rooms looking out on a fountained courtyard. Upstairs and annex bedrooms have recently been decorated colorfully and pleasingly. Not the most elegant pousada, it instead offers informality, making this a comfortable stopping place for those on their way to or from Spain. There is a pool and tennis court. However, a grand pousada beckons in Estremoz, just 39 km away.

Dining

It's too bad the dining room is not more attractive, but this is a busy restaurant, nonetheless, for it is a cut above the pousada average. Products of the sea are much in evidence. There is cod scrambled with egg and onions *(dourado)*, a kind of shellfish paella *(arroz de mariscos)*, monkfish stew *(cataplana de tamboril)* and sole stuffed with shrimp *(linguado recheado com gambas)*. Meats include a roast duck served over rice *(arroz de pato à pousada)* and pork with clams *(porco à alentejana)*. *Ensopado de borrego*, garlicky mutton, green pepper and bread stew, is special. Deserts are worth a try here. There is a prune cake *(sericaia com ameixas de Elvas)*, and ice cream with chocolate sauce *(gelado com chocolate)*. Some of Portugal's best wines are available, from nice Borbas reservas to superior Redondos. A set-course meal is available for about $20, including house wine.

Directions

From **Lisbon** take A-2 south toward Setúbal then east past the exit for Montemor-o-Novo in 100 km. Pick up N-4 east for 102 km. From **Évora** take N-18 northeast for 42 km to just before Estremoz, where N-4 goes east the rest of the 28 km. From **Badajoz** in Spain take N-4 west for 17 km. Spain's **Mérida** lies just 66 km farther east along N-V.

By **train** Elvas is just over five hours from Lisbon. Connections can be made from Marvão, but the trip takes more than three hours. There is an express **bus** from Lisbon that beats the train. A bus from Évora takes under two hours.

Pousadas Nearby

Vila Viçosa: 28 km	Estremoz: 33 km	Marvão: 67 km
Évora: 79 km	Flor da Rosa: 80 km	Arraiolos: 101 km

Sights

Standing by the Spanish border, Elvas' traditional business has been to defend Portugal against invasion. Its fortifications are not, as so often seen in Portugal, quaint relics of romantic struggles against Moors, but serious 17th-century ramparts that found good use during a siege as recently as the 19th century. Given the continual threat of attack, naturally the town of Elvas huddled within its fortified walls, which meant that houses had to be small and streets narrow to jumble in quaint ways.

Because Elvas was regained from the Moors a century later than Lisbon, Moorish relics are more in evidence. The occasional gateway or tower whose elegance catches the eye is surely a Moorish structure.

There are views of Elvas' imposing **aqueduct** ★ to the west as the town is approached. It took almost a century to build. Not completed until the early 17th century, the aqueduct runs for five miles, 100 feet high in places, forming an elegant, if somewhat chunky, line of arches and tiers that still carry water to the city.

The old town is entered through a gate in the south rampart wall a few blocks uphill after passing the pousada. Inside, Rua de Olivença leads up to the main square, the **Praça da República**, paved in geometric shapes. The former **town hall**, from the 16th century, stands on the near side housing the **tourist office**, and the squat **Cathedral** (or such was its employ until the bishop left in 1882) stands opposite (north). The Cathedral exterior looks like a castle, the interior is an impressive space with azulejos lining the walls.

A small street beside the right side of the Cathedral leads behind it into the pretty **Largo Santa Clara** surrounded by attractive houses. In the center of the triangular-shaped square a **pillory** dangling iron hooks stands as a reminder of times when punishment was public.

On the near (south) side of the square rises the octagonal-shaped church of **Nossa Senhora da Consolação** ★★. It was built in the 16th century during the Manueline era to duplicate the shape of an earlier Templar church that stood on the same site or nearby. Inside, it is a glory of colored *azulejos*, which line the walls and even the cupola supported by gilded marble columns.

At the north end of the square a **Moorish gate** beneath a logia is flanked by twin towers. Passing through this gate, ascend to the Largo da Alcaçova, then bear left, then right at the "T" to walk the lovely little Rua das Beatas to the **castle**.

Castle   ★

Hours open: Fri.-Wed. 9:30 a.m.–12:30 and 2:30–7 p.m.; closes at 5:30 p.m. in winter. Closed Thurs.

Original construction was Moorish, but the castle was reworked from the 14th through the 16th centuries. A walk along the top of the ramparts provides fine views of the countryside. The old governor's residence displays a reconstructed kitchen and bedroom.

For a different route back to the Olivença gate, follow the walls left from the castle.

A drive around the fortifications shows them to their best effect, including another fortress just southeast. This **Forte de Santa Luzia** is star-shaped to force attackers into cross-fire between the rays.

SOUTHERN PORTUGAL

Excursions

Vila Viçosa ★ is well worth the trip of 28 km west on N-4 to Borba then 6 km south on N-255. It is described under its own entry below.

The Alhambra's garden patio is set amid graceful arcades.

Most of the architectural legacy of the Moors is in Andalusia.

Jaén's castle parador has a medieval atmosphere.

Ronda conforms to a Moorish layout of winding streets and alleys.

POUSADA DE SÃO BRÁS

Estrada N-2, São Brás, 8150
☎ *(089) 84 23 05, FAX (089) 84 17 26*
$100 per double; 33 rooms: 32 doubles, 1 suite
★ ★ ★

The Algarve contains only two pousadas, this and one at Sagres described above. But São Brás is not what would be expected of a hotel in an area known for beach resorts. It is located in splendid isolation behind the sea in the hills. What it offers is peace and tranquillity, rather than international homogenization, a taste of the Algarve of the Portuguese less than an hour from fine beaches. The architecture is pure Algarve, gleaming white walls trimmed in yellow below an orange tile roof. A pool in back and a tennis court encourage exercise. There is little to note about the interior which is just a hotel, but views from upper floor guest rooms range over mountains and sea.

Alternative Accommodations

Similar isolation in more luxurious accommodations wait 10 km away in Santa Bárbara de Nexe.

La Réserve   ★ ★ ★ ★

Estrada de Esteval, Santa Bárbara de Nexe (Take N-125 northwest past the airport for 8 km to a right turn toward Loulé. In one mile comes Esteval, where a right turn toward Santa Barbara de Nexe brings the hotel in 2 km.), ☎ (089) 904 74; FAX (089) 904 02. 20 apartments.

La Réserve is a member of the Relais et Chateaux association, a group of elegant, luxury estates. In all of Portugal there is only one other. This hotel is uncharacteristically modern, rather than the historic properties usually affiliated with the group,

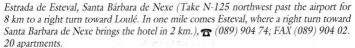

but it is luxurious anyway. Apartments have a distant sea view; the extensive gardens are lovely. Two swimming pools and a tennis court complete the complex. At $200, prices are high, but the comfort and elegance provided are higher for there are no more-relaxing accommodations in the Algarve. Conveniently alongside stands one of the finest restaurants (described below) in Portugal. Note, credit cards are not accepted and the hotel is closed from the second week of November through the first week in December.

The nearest beach town is Faro, capital of the Algarve. Two hotels stand out in this resort.

Eva   ★★★

Av. da República, Faro (occupying the north end of the harbor), ☎ *(089) 80 33 54, FAX (089) 80 23 04, Telex 56524. 150 rooms.*

Eva is an eight-story modern hotel that overlooks the yacht harbor and beyond. Bedrooms are pleasant (renovated in 1997) the management efficient, and there is a rooftop pool. The hotel is also a bargain because prices for rooms with a sea view run about $150. There is also a courtesy bus to the beach.

Casa de Lumena   ★★★

Pr. Alexendre Herculano, 27, Faro (two blocks east of the harbor), ☎ *(089) 80 19 90, FAX (089) 80 40 19.12 rooms.*

At $50 for a double room the Casa de Lumena is a less expensive but more interesting choice. The hotel was the home of Portugal's sardine king over a century ago who was the richest man in town. It sits on a lovely quiet square. Although by no means grand, it is tastefully restored and dotted with fine furniture. Each bedroom is different but all are appealing, and the most expensive remain well within the moderate-price category. The establishment is run by an English couple who keep it spotless. All told, the hotel is a pleasure to stay.

Dining

For some reason the dining room is circular which ruins any chance at intimacy. The food, however, is a cut above the pousada average. Start with cream of shellfish soup *(creme de mariscos)*. Follow with shrimp kabob *(espetada de gambas)*, calamari in butter sauce *(coquinhos com molho manteiga)*, veal with mushrooms *(vitela com cogumelos)* or fried fish with shrimp sauce *(filetes de peixe com molho de camarão)*. Orange cake *(tartade laranja)* finishes the meal. Beware of the local red wine, a raw Lagoa. A set-course meal is available for about $25.

Alternative Dining

La Réserve   ★★★★

Estrada do Esteval (see the hotel of the same name above), ☎ *(089) 902 34, FAX (089) 904 02.*

Closed Tuesday, and from the second week of November through the first week in December.

This restaurant ranks with the finest in the country, both for the quality of its French-inspired dishes and the elegance of their presentation. Salmon marinated in mustard and duck Vendome is memorable, as is the smoked swordfish. Furthermore, two can dine and be pampered for $80, the cost of one at a fine Lisbon restaurant. Reservations are required. Credit Cards: none.

Cidade Velha ★★

Rua Domingos Guieiro, 19 (beside the city hall and cathedral, through the old city walls 1 block east of the port), ☎ *(089) 271 45.*
Closed for Saturday lunch, and Sunday.

This is the leading restaurant in Faro proper. It is a romantic place installed in a former bishop's mansion, decorated with pink tablecloths and fresh flowers under soft lighting. The food is inventive, very good indeed and should cost no more than $35. All that prevents us from recommending it more strongly is the fact that while we dine here we think about La Réserve above. Credit Cards: M, V.

Directions

North for 2 km past São Brás on N-2. Look for parador sign indicating a right turn.

Pousadas Nearby

Sagres: 109 km	Beja: 125 km	Sta. Clara: 124 km
Serpa: 154 km	Santiago: 161 km	

SOUTHERN PORTUGAL

Excursions

Faro is located 18 km south on N-2. Tiny **Almansil** contains an appropriately tiny church, stunningly covered in azulejos. **Loulé** is a crafts town. Almansil is 9 km south on to the autoestrada, 7 km west, then 3 km south on N-125. For Loulé follow the same route, but go north on N-125 for 6 km.

Faro

Because Faro is the capital of the Algarve and serves as the airport for the area, it crowds with tourists. What it offers is a beach near a true city. Its harbor area is attractive, and an interesting old town is reached through ancient city walls, yet a shantytown rings its outskirts.

Although more attractive towns exist elsewhere in the Algarve, accommodations in Faro are generally scarce because many of those who land here venture no farther. As a result, its island beach, although attractive, is covered with sunbathers. Bus #16 serves this beach from the Office of Tourism in the harbor. The better shops congregate on the pedestrian Rua Santo António that goes west from the harbor.

Airport

Faro Airport (*(089) 81 82 81)* is 10 km west of the city and serves Europe. A bus connects with Faro for 100$00; a taxi should cost no more than 1000$00, a little more with the night surcharge. Settle on a price before getting in. TAP is located on *R. D. Francisco Gomes, 8* at the beginning of the harbor garden (*(089) 221 41).*

Shopping

Crafts, ceramics and other things line the pedestrian R. de Santo António, which leaves the harbor at the garden.

Almansil   ★

So small is the church of São Lourenço that the inside startles. It glistens and dances in azulejos covering every inch, including an amazing ceiling.

Loulé

Loulé is a center for baskets, mats and hats of palm and esparto, as well as for copperware, fine wrought iron, some pottery and beautiful colored harnesses (although the latter are hard to find these days).It is no chore to search through the shops that huddle under the ancient fortress in the center of the town. While there, notice the lacy chimneys that seem almost artworks, certainly with that order of individuality. Saturday is the bustling festive market day, but individual craftspeople in the town sell every day but Sunday.

POUSADA DE SÃO FRANCISCO

Largo Don Nuno Alvares Pereira, Beja, 7800
☎ *(084) 32 84 41, FAX (084) 32 91 43*
$125 per double; 34 rooms: 33 doubles, 1 suite

★ ★ ★ ★

From far across the endless wheat plains of the Alentejo Beja shines, all white, shimmering in the heat. This is the hottest part of a warm country, so the parador nestles within cool convent walls. Parts date to the 13th century, such as the lovely Chapel of the Tombs, but the mass is 18th century baroque that still retains the original shape of a quadrangle enclosing a cloister and garden. Guests are lodged in the former monks' cells, much altered to provide a comfort and spaciousness the monks only dreamed about. All has been renovated to a sparkle. There is a tennis court, and a pool to cool away the Alentejo heat.

Dining

The restaurant is set in a hall of dignified columns. Alas, the food is not exalted. Catfish with pepper or gratiné of cod with cream sauce are the fish options. Meats are stewed, as in veal fricassee, lamb in olive oil or chicken. However, there is a roast pork loin or roast lamb. A set-course meal is available for about $20, including beverage.

SOUTHERN PORTUGAL

Alternative Dining

Os Infantes   ★

Rua dos Infantes, 14, ☎ *(084) 227 89.*
Although not the most elegant place in town, the Infantes serves the most tasty
Alentejo food, and at very low prices. A full dinner can be consumed for as little as
$15. It will be good. Credit Cards: A, M, V.

Directions

From **Lisbon** take A-2 south for 106 km to join N-259 east for 52 km.
From **Évora** take N-18 south for 78 km. From **Faro**, in the Algarve, take N-2
north 99 km to Castro Verde, where N-391 goes the rest of the way in 46
km.

Pousadas Nearby

Serpa: 29 km	Alvitó: 37 km	Torrão: 61 km
Évora: 78 km	Santiago: 78 km	Arraiolos: 100 km

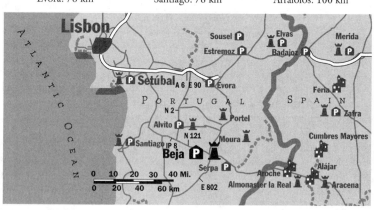

Sights

The **Regional Museum** is worth a visit for the building as well as the art. It
was a convent built in the 15th century, as the Gothic balustrade shows. Inside it is all baroque, gilded and carved. In particular, the chapterhouse is resplendent with azulejos.

The town **castle** from the 13th century is worth seeing to appreciate that
not all old royal structures are lovely.

Pousada de São Miguel

Sousel, 7470
☎ *(061) 55 11 60, FAX (061) 55 11 55*
$90 per double; 32 rooms: 28 doubles, 4 suites

★ ★ ★

This rambling new pousada (1993) on a hilltop overlooking rolling plains is crisply modern. Its reason for being is to cater to the sportsperson. Hunting and fishing are the thing. If that is of interest or the quiet of the countryside appeals, it would be a fine choice. The guest rooms are very comfortable, furnished with calming dark wood. Otherwise try the elegance of the pousada at Estremoz, 18 km away, or the antique charm of the Hotel Convento de São Paulo in Aldeia da Serra, 17 km further along.

Dining

Of course game is the specialty, covering rabbit *(lebre)*, duck *(pato)* and partridge *(perdiz)*. They do a nice roast lamb with rosemary as well. Set-course meals are available from $20.

Directions

Look for a sign for N-372 going west, the Cano-Caso Branca road. Take the first left and aim for the white pousada on its hill.

Pousadas Nearby

Estremoz: 18 km	Vila Viçosa: 35 km	Flor da Rosa: 45 km
Elvas: 57 km	Arraiolos: 61 km	Évora: 64 km

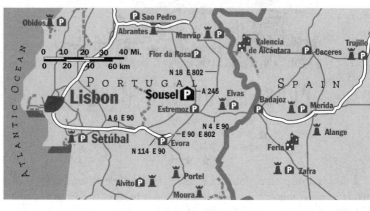

Excursions

Nearby **Estremoz** ★★ and **Évora** ★★★ are well worth the trip.

POUSADA DE SÃO PEDRO

Largo do Castelo, Castelo de Bode, 2300
☎ *(049) 38 11 59, FAX (049) 38 11 76*
$100 per double; 25 rooms: 24 doubles, 1 suite

The reason for a stay is to see two sights—the splendid Templar church at Tomar and the magical castle at Amouril. As to the pousada, the building was erected in the 1950s to house engineers constructing the Castelo de Bode dam. Today it is a hotel that offers quiet and the best view of the dam. Although why someone would want to contemplate a dam when the lake above is so lovely, is hard to fathom. The structure is not particularly imposing and high tension lines rather spoil what scenery there is. On the other hand, the hotel was remodeled after a terrible fire in 1991 to very comfortable standards and is a pleasant place to spend a night. Even better is the annex, a largish house 100 feet from the pousada. It is tastefully decorated, prices are 20 percent less than in the main hotel and the views take in the attractive pousada rather than the unattractive dam.

Alternative Accommodations

Dos Templários

Largo Candido dos Reis, 1 (beside the public garden), ☎ *(049) 32 17 30, FAX (049) 32 21 91. 171 rooms, plus 5 suites.*

If you want to stay in Tomar rather than drive into the countryside, there is the Dos Templários, whose best feature is the views it provides of the convent on its hill and ample grounds for strolling. Otherwise, it offers the services expected of a first-class hotel and ordinary bedrooms, but, considering its prices of under $100, there is no reason to complain.

Dining

The cooking is simple but few complain about a very fresh trout cooked with almonds. Otherwise the menu is unimaginative and consists of bland choices. A set-course meal is available for about $20, including local wine.

Alternative Dining

Chez Nous   ★

> *In Tomar, on Rua Dr. Joaquim Jacinto, 31 (between the two river bridges),* ☎ *(049) 31 47 43. Closed Tuesdays.*
>
> Unlike the other restaurants in town that strive for blandness, the French taste of the owner irrepressibly infuses his food. There are interesting beef dishes, and cod combinations even the Portuguese never thought of.

Directions

From **Lisbon** take the autoestrada A-1 north for 101 km to exit 7, then IP-6 for 18 km to Torras Novas. From there 10 km on N-110 north past Santa Clara brings a sign that directs to 6 km on N-358 to Castelo de Bode. From **Coimbra** and **north** take the autoestrada A-1 south to exit 7, then follow the preceding directions.

Pousadas Nearby

Batalha: 76 km   Condeixa: 82 km
Óbidos: 108 km   Marvão: 115 km

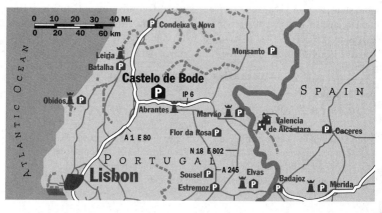

SOUTHERN PORTUGAL

Excursions

Fátima of the miracles lies on the way to **Batalha** ★★★★ and its incredible monastery, a trip of 50 km. Both are described in the Central Portugal chapter under "Batalha." The charming fortified hilltop town of **Marvão** ★★★, described under its own heading in this chapter, is 130 km east on IP-6, then joining N-118 around Abrantes. **Coimbra** ★★★ is 115 km northwest by taking N-113 for 45 km to Leiria, then N-1 north for 70 km. Both are described in the Northern Portugal chapter, Coimbra under the heading for Condeixa.

Nearer to hand, for **Tomar** ★★★ with its lovely convent-church, take N-358 west for 6 km back to N-110 for a 7 km jaunt north. For **Amouril's** ★ fairy-tale castle, take N-358-2 south for 10 km, under the overpass for the highway, then take the first right along the river toward Tancos, looking for the castle in the river in 4 km. When spotted, take the first left toward the river.

Tomar   ★★★

Tomar, a quaint town of cobblestone streets, straddles the river Nabão. Its quaintness, however, is not what draws tourists. In woods above the town a church consecrated to secret rites was embellished over the centuries by some of the greatest architecture in Portugal. And, nearby, on an island in the center of the Tagus river, reposes the 12th-century castle of Almourol rising above its wooded slope, the most romantic castle in Portugal.

When Jerusalem was captured in 1119 during the Second Crusade, a group of French knights created the Order of Knights Templar for the purposes of defending the Holy Sepulcher to the death, and of protecting pilgrims in Palestine. Despite such vows, Jerusalem was soon lost, but the order continued, now as a military arm of the Catholic Church. Within a century 20,000 members could be counted. They manned 9000 castles throughout Europe, and most European banking lay tight in the Church's fist. Kings begged contributions from the order for their wars and tread carefully in its presence lest they antagonize such immense power. The order answered to no authority below the pope. Individual members, subject only to the master of the order, strode the streets of Europe in white tunics blazoned with a red Maltese cross, afraid of no one up to and including the rank of king. Their rites were shrouded in deep mystery, known to no outsider.

In 1128 the Knights Templar were given land to erect a castle in Portugal by Donha Teresa, the mother of the first king of Portugal. Their contribution to her son Alfonso's military success against the Moors was substantial. In 1147 the order traded their original land for acreage at Tomar and there built a castle on a hill, completed in 1160. A church followed two years later; then all was surrounded by fortress walls. By the 14th century, however, the power of the order had become too threatening to those in high places. Phillip V of France arrested the Master of the Knights Templar in 1307 and executed him. Pope Clement V decreed the disbanding of the order five years later.

But a sympathetic King Dinis resurrected the order in Portugal in 1320 by creating a similar organization with a new name—the Order of Christ. Later, Prince Henry the Navigator, as a third royal son, was given charge of this order in lieu of a throne. Its Maltese cross glowed fiery red on the sails Henry sent searching for undiscovered worlds. Prince Henry added to the Templar church at Tomar; Manuel I supplied a nave done in the Manueline style—including the most ornate, most photographed window in the country; and João III changed the order into a monastic brotherhood to which he contributed cells for the monks and a solemn neoclassical cloister. Additions were made over the course of five centuries, but none disturbed the lines of the 12th-century octagonal Templar church. This church and its later embellishments are what bring the visitors to Tomar.

The Convent of Christ reposes atop a wooded park on the west bank of the Nabão. Rua Serpa Pinto crosses the Ponte Velha and leads to the main square, Pr. da República. Here the 15th-century church of **São João Baptista ★** has an imposing later Manueline tower and a most elegant door. Inside hang lovely paintings (poorly lit) by one of Portugal's best artists, Gregório Lopes.

Parallel to R. Pinto, and three blocks south (left), Av. Dr. Candido Madureira climbs to the Sete Montes park, after passing the Office of Tourism. The road through the forest zigzags up to the 12th-century walls of the precinct to pass through a gate beside which stands the keep of the original castle. To the right are ruins of the palace built by Prince Henry. Parking is available.

Convento de Cristo   ★ ★ ★

Hours open: daily 9:30 a.m.–12:30 p.m. and 2–6 p.m. (closes at 5 p.m. in winter).

The complete monastery is a confusion of buildings, because it is formed of additions that spanned five centuries. All the additions were constrained by the desire to be close to, but not impinge on, the original Templar church. This goal is illustrated by the strange angle of the cloister walls protruding to the right of the entrance stairs, and in the constricted entrance to the church. The present entrance was added in the 16th century, designed by a Spaniard in his splendid Plateresque style. It is worth a moment's study of the exuberant, yet mannered Plateresque to compare it later with the riotous Manueline style of Portugal. A plaque marks the original entrance.

The present entrance leads into the nave with the original octagonal Templar church, known as the *Charola*, to the right. Although many authorities claim the Charola was modeled on the Holy Sepulcher in Jerusalem, its polygonal shape and cupola match the Islamic Dome of the Rock more than any Christian prototype. Eight painted piers support a two-story octagon with an altar in the center. Coats of arms may be discerned painted on the cupola above. Except for a few paintings, some choir stalls and a number of 16th-century polychrome statues of saints leaning against the piers, little decoration survived the damage wrought by the occupying French in the 19th century. Enough remains to give some sense of the original look, but not of its intended functions.

Some say the knights attended services on horseback, while others claim that this was a place for vigils by novices. There are stories telling how the orientation of the building and details of its design provide secret messages about the location of buried treasures. But for most people the pleasure of seeing an unusual architectural design from the hoary early Middle Ages suffices without rationales.

The nave was added on early in the 16th century to form a more typical church, although its construction required breaking through the west wall of the Charola. Exuberant Manueline decoration makes the hall airy, in contrast with the more intimate charola. A doorway to the north leads to the Cloistro do Cemitario, named for two 16th-century tombs laying within—one being that of Baltasar de Faria, the first Inquisitor-General of Portugal. The cloister was built by Prince Henry the Navigator and later covered with *azulejos.*

A portal from the south side of the nave lets out to the splendid two-story *Cloistro Principal,* added by João III in the middle of the 16th century. Its Renaissance neoclassicism derives, as its unadorned sweeping arch and columns suggest, from the Italian Palladio. At each corner a grand spiral stair leads up to the terrace of the adjoining Santa Barbara cloister for a view of the window that epitomizes the extreme of Manueline ornateness.

This **window** ★ is actually the central window at the end of the church nave viewed from outside. Although the identity of the artist is unknown, it was carved in 1510. At the bottom a bust of a sea captain sprouts roots of a cork tree that rises through seaweed, coral and pieces of chain up masts framing the window sides. Above are symbols of Manuel I—a shield and a cross between two spheres. "Cables" run from the window to two turrets, one wrapped in chain (left), the other by a buckle. If the latter is seen as a garter, then the turrets might represent the orders of the Golden Fleece and of the Garter, respectively. Many pieces have been broken and lost, which only make one wonder how it would look if complete.

The remainder of the convent is used as a hospital by the military and is presently off limits to tourists. *Admission: 300$00; 200$00 in winter.*

Castelo Almourol   ★

The tiny island in the wide, quiet Tagus is improbably densely wooded, so its castle rises above the trees. It is an archtypical medieval fortress, straight from all our imaginations—10 golden-hued stone towers that anchor walls surrounding a massive square keep. Because the island is a hill, castle parts stand at different elevations to lend the false perspective of a larger structure. Early in the morning, when mist envelopes the river, the castle floats in a dream.

A Roman fortress first crowned the site before the Knights Templar—as part of a strategy of recapturing land from the Moors and then raising defensive castles to retain it—built the present castle in 1171. In little more than a century the Moors had been driven so far south that this castle lost its defensive purpose and was abandoned. Abandoned it remains, although an appropriately weathered boatman is pleased to motor visitors either out to the castle or just around it for a nominal fee.

POUSADA DO INFANTE

Sagres, 8650
☎ *(082) 642 22, FAX (082) 642 25*
$110 per double; 39 rooms: 38 doubles, 1 suite

★ ★ ★ ★

This is the only pousada in the Algarve near the beach. It is a new structure styled as a monastery gleaming white atop a small promontory outside of town. It is quite imposing. The location is prime—beach lies below, while a pool and terrace above present the ocean stretching infinitely. Bedrooms are comfortable, with the same glorious views, although antiseptic in feeling. A tennis court and riding stables adjoin. As far as comfort goes, there are no complaints and the view is as good as a view gets, still, there is a coldness about the place. More warmth is to be found in some of the moderate choices below.

Alternative Accommodations

Residêncial Dom Henrique   ★ ★ ★

Sítio da Mareta (in a cul de sac off the Pr. República, on the cliff above Mareta beach),
☎ *(082) 641 33. 28 rooms.*

The Residêncial Dom Henrique puts the ocean in your back yard, for this is the closest hotel to Mareta beach. Views rival those of the pousada at half of its price. This hotel is the proverbial "charmer," including a funky bar in the garden, an aviary next door for soothing bird peeps, and outside a large, quaint house with guest rooms to rent. Every one is comfortable and the more expensive provide ocean and beach views. Demand one. The management is very accommodating.

Fortaleza do Beliche   ★★★

Estrada da Cabo São Vicente, in Belixe, Sagres 8650 (to the right along the road to Cape St. Vincent, about 5 km northwest of Sagres), ☎ *(082) 641 24.4 rooms.*

We hesitate to mention the Fortaleza do Beliche because only four rooms are available, but these are the most unusual accommodations in Sagres, if not the whole Algarve. The rooms are remodeled parts of a fort from the 17th century composed of thick rock walls, yet it was a little fort, so it oddly juxtaposes cuteness with stolidity. Nothing else is around the place, high on a bluff above the sea. Here you get true isolation and spectacular views, as well as a little beach down steep stairs that should be yours alone. Plus, the restaurant is the best in the area. The whole tiny operation is run by Enatur, the parador company.

Motel Os Gambozinos   ★★

At the Praia do Martinhal, 3.5 km northeast, off N-125 at the sign for "Martinhal", ☎ *(082) 643 18.17 rooms.*

More ordinary is the Motel Os Gambozinos. If a secluded hotel above a cozy deserted beach appeals, here it is. The hotel is shaped as a long bungalow, and run by a Dutch couple with the cleanliness one would expect of such proprietors. Rooms are simple and white, but charmingly decorated with little frescoes. Good taste is evident. A walk through the garden leads down to the beach, so that you feel in the country while staying at the seashore. Note, at these low prices air conditioning is not supplied. The restaurant below the hotel is good enough for a visit even if staying elsewhere.

Aparthotel Navigator   ★★

R. Infante D. Henrique, Sagres (next to the pousada), ☎ *(082) 643 54, FAX (082) 643 60, Telex 5717956 rooms.*

Another choice is the Aparthotel Navigator, a new tall, white structure grand from the outside, but more modest within. All its rooms are apartments with sitting rooms and include cooking facilities, which is a fine idea for a resort. While the decor is rather drab, the price is remarkably low for what it buys. Rooms numbered from 11 through 17 on each floor own the best views.

Dining

Fresh fish is the thing. Start with a tasty fish soup *(sopa do mar)*. Then choose between fried fish with mayonnaise *(peixe dourados com maionese)*, bream with butter sauce *(parguinho grelhado com molho manteiga)*, sole in the same sauce *(linguado)* or baked swordfish *(espardarte no forno)*. Unusual for pousadas, a nice grilled liver *(fígado de vitela)* can be had, or the usual meats. A set-course meal is available for about $20, which includes rather raw local wine.

SOUTHERN PORTUGAL

Alternative Dining

Sagres village is full of inexpensive and moderately priced restaurants. For food that is a cut above, one has to travel 5 km to Cabo São Vicente.

Moderate ($15–$30)

Fortaleza do Beliche   ★

5 km along the road to Cabo Vicente (at the traffic circle in Sagres, take the road to Beliche), ☎ *(082) 641 34.*

This establishment is run by the Enatur pousada system and offers four rooms for sleeping, discussed above, but primarily serves as a restaurant. It is installed in a tiny fort, hence the name, that can only be described as cute. The decoration used to be a rather phoney Henry the Navigator theme, but the restaurant was being renovated when we last stopped. After renovation, food and the view should continue to be good, and cost about $25, but we will check. Credit Cards: A, D, M, V.

A Tasca

In the little Sagres port, ☎ *(082) 641 77.*

This is the most popular restaurant in town, but not with us. It is a barn of a building decorated with wine bottles imbedded in patterns in cement walls. Tables are heavy wood. The large terrace outside, overlooking the port, is more pleasant. All indications make this seem a place where the fish would be fresh and the cooking authentic. However, while the fish is fresh enough, it is treated with no great care, a lack of seriousness that extends to wait-people too rushed to care either. If meals had cost half what they do, we would have felt twice as charitable.

Directions

From **Lisbon** autoestrada A-2 reaches **Setúbal** in 50 km. From there N-10 east for 21 km reaches Marateca to join N-5 south for 31 km to Alcáçer do Sal where it changes its designation to N-120. For the more scenic route, bear right in 18 km to continue on N-120 along the coast to the western Algarve in about 180 km. A faster route is to continue to Grândola and take N-259 southeast, turning south onto N-262 in about 20 km toward Azinheira dos Barros. Stay on the road as it becomes N-264 for a leg of 204 km. The trip of 272 km takes less than five hours except in busy summer, and ends near Albufeira, roughly the center of the Algarve. The recommended route, however, is to Évora to see some of Portugal's finest sights, and spend the night there, or at the elegant Estremoz pousada, before traveling on. Directions to Évora are included in the "Excursion" section of "Lisbon"; the leg from Évora to the Algarve is described below.

From **north of Lisbon**, skirt Lisbon by turning east onto N-10 just before Vila Franca de Xira (a crafts center for brass, rugs, and objects made of horn), 35 km before the capital. In 49 km N-10 reaches Cruzamento de Pegões, where attention is required in order to remain on N-10 for a southern swing of 14 km to Marateca, from which the Lisbon directions apply. From **Évora** N-18 heads southeast toward Beja, 78 km away. Continue south along N-122 which changes its designation two times—to N391, then to N-123—in the 60 km to Ourique. A final leg on N-264 ends near Albufeira after 79 km.

From **Spain** the shortest drive is from Ayamonte, which is a direct 159 km from Seville. A bridge now crosses the Guadiana River to Vila Real de Santo Antonio at the eastern extreme of the Algarve. From north of Andalusia follow directions to Évora, then the directions above.

Sagres is the westernmost town in the Algarve, reached by going west on the autoestrada to its end, then west on N-125. West of **Lagos** N-125 deteriorates, as fewer tourists and towns result in less upkeep. In 23 km from Lagos, Vila do Bispo is reached; N-125 ends and N-268 is picked up turning south for a final 10 km to Sagres.

Daily **flights** of 40 minutes connect Lisbon with Faro. The regular **train** from Lisbon to Faro takes about seven hours, with the regular **bus** taking as long and being only slightly cheaper. Special *"Alta Qualidade"* buses streak to Albufeira in 4.5 hours. Express buses take five hours, and cost more than the express train that does the same trip in four hours.

Pousadas Nearby

Sta. Clara: 103 km	São Bras: 120 km	Santiago: 141 km
Beja: 190 km	Serpa: 219 km	

Sights

Sagres is the only true town on the Sagres Peninsula, a land—as the sparse vegetation indicates—of almost constant wind. Here Prince Henry the Navigator resided, and his energies and finances fueled the Portuguese exploration of the world. Living at the southwesternmost tip of Europe, Prince Henry came as close to participating in those discoveries as his political duties allowed.

The present village of Sagres on the sheltered east side of a small promontory is newer, consisting of but three streets paralleling the water. It is popular with fishermen, backpackers and nature lovers. The village is spreading and dusty, rather like a frontier town, but the three peninsulas—one east, one south and Capo to the west—are lovely. Scenic coves around the town provide beach shelter from the wind.

Prince Henry lived about 5 km west of the village on the naked extremity of **Cabo São Vicente**. Today as then, the cape is desolate, and awesome for it.

Sir Francis Drake destroyed Henry's monastery in a raid just before the time of the Spanish Armada and burned his great maritime library. Today, nothing but the land is as Henry knew it. A 16th-century fortress has been partly reconstructed, and inside stands a 14th-century sailors' chapel. A compass marked on the grounds dates from after Henry's time. Close to the cliff edge a lighthouse presents awesome views of waves whipped into froth by wind and rocks.

While the town beaches are serviceable, there is a quieter one in **Praia do Martinhal** reached by leaving town on N-268 toward Vila do Bispo. Turn right at a sign in 2 km. A truly spectacular beach lies beyond Vila do Bispo, by continuing on N-268. In the little town a sign to the "praia" directs a left turn that becomes a bumpy road circling steep hills for 3 km on the way to a string of three scenic beaches. The first beach, called **Castelejo**, starts from a precipitous headland at its south end and stretches to craggy offshore rocks on the north. The sand is long and fine. There, **Restaurant Castelejo** serves mouthwateringly fresh fish. The road continues to a second and third beach, neither so large or lovely as the first, but useful if crowds push you on. Since these beaches line the western Atlantic, they tend to receive breezes even when other Algarve beaches swelter airlessly.

If these beaches are not isolated enough, try **Praia da Bordeira** with a Big Sur magnificence. Long rolling waves crash against sand dunes, and there is nothing around. In fact the beach is so deep it looks like the desert. It is reached over a bumpy dirt road after a turn from N-268 at "Carrapateira", 13 km north of Vila do Bispo. There is a decent restaurant just before Citio da Rio.

Shopping

Hippercerâmica Paraíso in Raposeira, which is 3 km east of Vila do Bispo on N-125, is a barn of a place on the highway that sells the cheapest **pottery** in the country. While some pieces can be ghastly, prices are amazing for attractive plain planters and serving dishes.

For reasonably priced hand-woven **sweaters**, go to the fort on Capo São Vicente, where mobile stands generally display their wares.

Bikes and **mopeds** can be rented either at the GULP gas station on the circle entering town or at the kiosk called "do Papa" on the main street into town.

POUSADA DOM JOÃO IV

Praça do Paca, Vila Viçosa, 7160
Area Code: 068
$125 per double; 33 rooms: 30 doubles, 3 suites

★ ★ ★ ★

This is one special pousada and brand new in 1997. The town was the seat of the last ruling family of Portugal who bestowed a castle, convents and churches, all around one huge square, to immortalize itself. The present pousada is housed in the Convent of the Chagas, which was also the mausoleum of the family Duchesses. They reside in a church with exquisite azulejoed walls. The pousada is elegant, decorated with baroque details and rampant marble. Guest rooms are more ordinary, but whiling away time amid such splendor is a special treat. Try for a room overlooking the square.

Dining

The restaurant was not finished at our last visit. All we can say is that set-course meals will begin at about $20.

SOUTHERN PORTUGAL

Directions

From **Lisbon** take A-2 south toward Setúbal then east to pass the exit for Montemor-o-Novo in 103 km and join N-4 going east. In 63 km comes Estremoz, 11 km later, at Borba, turn southeast on N-255 for 6 km. From **Badajoz**, in Spain, cross the border and take N-4 west for 45 km to Borba, then turn southeast on N-255 for 6 km.

Pousadas Nearby

Estremoz: 17 km	Elvas: 34 km	Sousel: 35 km
Arraiolos: 60 km	Évora: 63 km	Flor da Rosa: 81 km

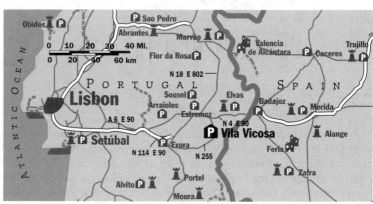

Sights

It seems incongruous that this little town of orchards, flowers and white-washed houses should contain a huge palace, plus a splendid convent and a fortress. The explanation is that it was the seat of the Duke of Bragança, the most powerful family in Portugal during the years of Spanish occupation. Here the duke and his family lived in the highest style. Then the duke became king in 1640 and left Vila Viçosa for the capital, which ended the festivities for this little town.

Entering from Borba you pass the huge square called the Terreiro do Paço (Terrace of the Palace), fronting the long, multi-windowed facade of the Ducal Palace.

Paço Ducal   ★

Terreiro do Paço, entrance in the center.
Hours open: Tues.–Sat. 9:30 a.m.–1 p.m. and 2–6 p.m. Closes an hour earlier in winter.
Understand that when the eighth duke left for Lisbon to be crowned king, he took
most of the good stuff with him. The palace is still owned by the Bragança family,
who have restocked it as best they could, but they aren't kings anymore, so the
highlights of the palace are the rooms rather than what furnishes them.

The palace was built from the 16th through the 17th centuries in an Italian Renaissance style. It includes a main, public wing whose walls are covered with azulejos
and whose ceilings are delicately frescoed, and another wing for the family that contains more intimate articles, including paintings done by the penultimate King Carlos, who was assassinated in Lisbon. *Admission: 600$00 for a guided tour. The
museums of coaches and of armor costs 100$00 more.*

The **Convento das Chagas**, which houses the bodies of the Bragança Duchesses
amid fine azulejos, occupies the south side of the square and is now a pousada.
Opposite the palace is the **Mosteiro dos Agostinhos**, full of white marble tombs for
all the dukes, set off by rococo gilt. Back a little way along the Borba road stands the
whimsical **gate** to the former royal forest. This often-pictured Manueline depiction
of stone knots is one of the last surviving parts of a wall that hemmed deer inside the
hunting area.

Continuing past the Paço, the Av. Duque de Bragança climbs to the old town and
its **castle**. This is a stout citadel raised in the 13th century and strengthened in the
17th. Inside is a collection of picturesque houses and churches.

Excursions

Estremoz ★★ is 17 km away and **Évora** ★★★ is 63 km away by N-18
after Estremoz. Each is described under its own heading in this chapter.
Borba for antiques is only 6 km away and described in the section on Arraiolos.

POUSADA DOS LÓIOS

Largo Conde de Vila Flor, Évora, 7000
☎ *(066) 240 51, FAX (066) 272 51*
$150 per double; 30 rooms: 28 doubles, 2 suites

★ ★ ★ ★

Installed in a late 15th-century convent, the elegance of its surroundings makes this a special pousada. As a result it is heavily booked. Rooms envelope a lovely two-story cloister, used for dining in the summer. One of the great doorways in the world, a Gothic-Moorish fantasy, leads to the former chapterhouse. There is even a pool in back. However, all the beauty of this pousada is exhausted in its public rooms—the bedrooms are another matter. They are small, with doorways only a child could walk through upright, and furnished forgettably. Still, to say that the location is convenient to the sights is an understatement. It is one. Would that the management cared more.

Alternative Accommodations

The pousada at Estremoz is better and, at 46 km, close enough for a day-trip to Évora. Also see the wonderful **Hotel Convento de São Paulo** described in the Estremoz entry, which is even closer.

Estalagem Monte das Flores

Monte das Flores (at the traffic circle beside the walls that presents N-114 toward Lisbon, instead take N-380 toward Alcáçovas for 4 km to a sign directing a turn along a private road), ☎ *(066) 254 90, FAX (066) 275 64.17 rooms.*

A less expensive option three miles from Évora is the Estalagem Monte das Flores which provides an opportunity to sample the style of a rich Alentejana farm. It's comfortable and horsey, bright and relaxed. Each bedroom is cheerily decorated and comfortable rather than deluxe. Sports are available from tennis to horseback-riding to swimming.

Dining

As with the rest of the hotel, the dining room combines the exceptional with the banal. It is located in the original cloisters whose arches are glassed to provide comfort and a spectacular view of the courtyard. The tables and chairs are more pedestrian, as is, unfortunately, the food. You best hope is game, if in season. Otherwise there is the usual gazpacho with sausage (*gazpacho à alentejana*), which is not bad, and a host of bland roasts and fish. The wine list features good local Borbas, Redondos and Reguengos. A set-course meal is available for about $20.

Alternative Dining

Fialho   ★ ★

Travessa das Mascarenhas, 14 (north of the Pr. do Giraldo for about 5 blocks to the Pr. J. A. de Aguiar, from which this little lane goes north), ☎ *(066) 230 79.*
Closed Monday, the first three weeks of September, and from the last week of December until after New Year's.
The restaurant is perhaps the best in the entire Alentejo. It is an old tavern with crockery hanging from the walls, made special by blue and white tiles all around. The food is traditional Portuguese, absolutely authentic and covers dishes you will not find elsewhere. Try the *Sopa de Panela*, full of sausage, chicken and fresh mint. We prefer the lamb or the game to the pork. A meal will cost $30 or more, and reservations are recommended. Credit Cards: A, D, M, V.

Cozinha de Santo Humberto   ★

Rua da Moeda, 39 (this street leaves the west side of Pr. do Giraldo), ☎ *(066) 242 51.*
Closed Thursday, and November.
This is where the locals come for a good homey meal, since Fialho's prices are a little steep for every day. Since they live here, they know best. The building dates from several centuries ago, and anything old the owner could find is hung on the walls. Flowered tables and comfortable seating are pluses, for local dishes well prepared. Fixed-course menus cut the bill at Fialho above in half. Credit Cards: A, D, M, V.

Directions

From **Lisbon** take A-2 south toward Setúbal then east past the exit for Montemor-o-Novo in 97 km. Join N-114 east for 30 km. From the **Algarve** take N-264 north from Albufeira for 70 km to Ourique, outside of which N-123

SOUTHERN PORTUGAL

heads east, then feeds into N-391 going north toward Beja just before Castro Verde. Circle Beja in 60 km. to take N-18 north for the final 78 km. From **Guarda** take N-18 south past Castelo Branco, Portalegre and Estremoz for 289 km. From **north of Lisbon** follow directions to Lisbon but exit A-1 at villa Franca, 35 km north of Lisbon, for N-10 going to Cruzamento de Pegões in 49 km. There N-4 goes east to Montamor-o-Novo in 37 km, from which N-114 reaches Évora in 30 km more.

Direct **trains** from Lisbon depart four times daily and take about three hours. Trains from Faro, in the Algarve, consume just under six hours (costing less than 1000$00). All told the **bus** is better, with expresses from Lisbon taking only 2.5 hours. From Elvas there are two daily departures and the trip takes under two hours.

Pousadas Nearby

Arraiolos: 22 km	Alvitó: 41 km	Estremoz: 46 km
Torrão: 46 km	Sousel: 64 km	Flor da Rosa: 94 km

Sights

Évora is a special town. It is a kind of Portuguese Florence—with bright houses topped by red-orange roofs—as well as a Portuguese Seville—gloriously flowered. UNESCO declared the town a world treasure.

Évora thrived during Roman times and was designated a *municipium*, giving it the right to coin money. Later, the Moors conquered it and held on for 450 years. It was liberated in 1166 by an outlaw knight named Geraldo Sem-Pavor (Gerald, the Fearless), whose reputation in Portugal is similar to El Cid's in Spain. To storm the town he impaled lances in the walls for his troops to climb like stairs. Once in Portuguese hands, the royalty found Évora more congenial than Lisbon, and spent as much time in residence as their duties permitted. During this period—from the 14th through the 16th centuries—Évora flourished as Portugal's Athens, a city filled with palaces, churches and art. But when the Avís dynasty died out in 1579 and the Spanish took over Portugal, Évora became a forgotten city consigned to preserving relics from its time of glory.

All the sights lie within the walls of the old city, and most are concentrated at the very center. They comprise monuments marking every era of greatness—from a Roman temple to 16th-century mansions. At least a day is required to savor them properly.

Anyone arriving during the last week in June will find Évora at its most festive. This is the fair of São João, which includes folk dancing, and stalls selling food or local crafts.

Parking is generally possible in the Pr. do Giraldo. If full, there are spaces in two blocks along Rua Nova, which runs east from the northern end of the plaza.

Arrivals from **Lisbon** reach the city walls, but are prevented by one-way streets from proceeding farther east. Turn left along the Estrada da Circunvalacão for a quarter of a mile to turn right through the next entrance into the walls. Inside, the street first is called Rua Candido dos Reis, then Rua João de Deus, before it enters the Pr. do Giraldo for parking. From the **Algarve and south** turn left onto Rua A. J. D. Almeida at a large intersection one block before reaching the city walls. It leads to a traffic circle in two blocks; take the left-hand road, Estrada do Circunvalacão past gardens to turn right through the walls along Rua da República, which arrives in five blocks at the Pr. do Giraldo for parking. From **Guarda**, **Estremoz** and **northern** areas turn right at the city walls along Estrada da Circunvalacão, through the aqueduct and then left at the next entrance through the walls. Inside the walls the street is first called Rua Candido dos Reis, then Rua João de Deus, before entering the Pr. do Giraldo for parking.

If no parking is found here, turn left at the end of the plaza for four short blocks then right along R. de Santa Clara. After three tiny blocks turn right again and take the next left (R. de São Domingos) to parking around the Pr. Joaquim António de Aguilar.

Start at the **Pr. do Giraldo**, the elongated main square almost exactly in the center of the walled town. A fine 16th-century fountain plays in the center. Interesting houses and arcades surround the square, now lined with cafés but formerly the site for immolating victims of the Inquisition. On the east side, a low arcade covers the sidewalk. About half way along, *Rua 5 de Outubro* leads uphill past attractive crafts shops to open wide in the Largo Marquês de Marialva. Adjoining the cathedral on its left side is the **Museu de Évora**. Further left one cannot help but notice a Roman temple.

Cathedral   ★★★

> Hours open: Tues.–Sun. 9 a.m.–noon and 2–5 p.m. Closed Mon. and holidays.
> The cathedral was begun late in the 12th century and finished by the middle of the 13th in the earliest Gothic style. With a few exceptions, it retains its original design. The monolithic facade flanked by square towers presents a fortress face, broken by the deeply recessed porch of the entrance. Each side of the entrance is lined by a 14th-century series of the Apostles, most of whom seem to have the same face, but the animals are delightful.
>
> The interior is disconcerting because its stone blocks are picked out with bright mortar, producing a checkerboard effect that fights with the solidity that should be

conveyed. Still, the lantern above the transept crossing is elegant, and the fine rose windows lighting the transepts are originals. Not so the retable. The old one is now displayed in the Museu de Évora; what presently overlooks the altar is an 18th-century work in marble, quite out of keeping with the style of the cathedral. At the end of the north transept a carved portal with a marble head is attributed to Chanterene.

After buying tickets near the main entrance, a fine Gothic cloister may be entered from the south transept. The heaviness of the cloister reflects an early Gothic aesthetic, although lightened by circles of Moorish open tracery. Statues of evangelists stand in each corner. At the southeast corner a chapel contains the moving sepulcher of the founding bishop of the cathedral, his head held gently by angels. All the carving in this chapel merits appreciation.

The glory of the treasury, housed in the tower beside the west entrance, is a 13th-century French ivory statue of the Virgin that opens to show events from her life (an odd wooden replacement-head sits on her shoulders). In addition to the usual sacerdotal vestments and ecclesiastical plate there is an impressive cross in gilded, enameled silver studded with more than 1000 precious and semi-precious stones. *Admission: 250$00 for cloisters and museum.*

Museu de Évora   ★ ★

Largo do Conde de Vila Flor.
Hours open: Tues.–Sun. 10 a.m.–12:30 p.m. and 2–5 p.m. Closed Sun. and holidays.
The museum is housed in the grand former bishop's palace from the 17th century. Sculpture is displayed chronologically on the ground floor. A fragment of Roman bas-relief of a vestal virgin's lower half is notable for the subtle depiction of her diaphanous dress. There are some fine medieval tombs and outstanding Renaissance carvings by Nicolau Chanterene, especially the effigy of Bishop Afonso. Displayed on the second floor is a good collection of Portuguese primitive painting. The main attraction is in room two—a colorful 13-picture series of the life of the Virgin from the late 15th century, the original retable of the cathedral. It is Flemish work, by the look, although Italian buildings serve as backgrounds. *Admission: 200$00.*

Proceeding northward past the museum, enter another large plaza, the Largo Conde de villa-Flor. In its center, framed by the open plaza, is a **Roman Temple**. A part of the 16th-century building at the northwest corner of the largo belonged to Vasco da Gama before his appointment as Viceroy of India. Later the building housed the first Office of the Inquisition in Portugal. To the west is the **Convento dos Lóios** beside the **Igreja de São João Evangelista**, and beyond it, north, is the **Palace of the Dukes of Cardaval** beside a garden affording views of the countryside over remains of the Roman town walls.

Templo de Diana   ★

Largo do Conde de Vila Flor.
This lovely second-century temple in the ornate Corinthian style, is called Diana's temple, although there is really no evidence that shows who was worshipped in it. Its base remains, along with 14 of the original 18 granite columns sandwiched by marble capitals and bases.

It owes its fine state of preservation to continued use through the centuries, so its stones were not carted away for building material. During one period, it served as a stronghold; during another, as the municipal slaughterhouse.

Paço dos Duques de Cadaval   ★

Largo do Conde de Vila Flor.
Hours open: Tues.–Sun. 10 a.m.–noon and 2–6 p.m. Closed Mon.
The palace was built in the 14th century by João I, founder of the House of Avís, and incorporated a turret from the medieval city walls as its northern tower. Later, he presented it to the ancestors of the Cardavals whose descendants substantially remodeled the facade in the 17th century. Two kings—João III and João V—lived inside, but the palace today is still owned by the Cadaval family, who also own the Church of Saint John the Evangelist adjoining. A museum displays a gallery of the dukes, along with two fine Flemish bronze plaques. *Admission: 200$00, for a ticket good for São João Evangelista as well.*

Igreja de São João Evangelista   ★★★

Largo do Conde de Vila Flor.
Hours open: Same hours and charge as the Paço dos Duques de Cadaval above.
This tiny church contains some of the finest **azulejos** in Portugal. After the 1755 earthquake, it was extensively remodeled, although the flamboyant Gothic entry remains from the original church, 200 years old by the time of the quake. Inside, the nave is lined with chapels forming a pantheon of the Melo family. But it is the amazing *azulejos* that captivate. They are by the greatest artist in the medium, Antonio Oliveira Bernardes, at the height of his powers in 1711. Note the *trompe l'oeil azulejo* window! The sacristy holds some unexceptional paintings, but also one of a pope, whose eyes not only follow the viewer, but whose feet seem to as well.

The convent of São João now is a most elegant pousada whose former chapterhouse door ranks with the great portals in Portugal. Next to the cloisters of São João stands a large library from 1805 connected by an arch to the bishop's palace. Pass under the arch and turn left to face a **Manueline mansion** with a mashrabiya balcony (for looking out without being seen). Continue past a tower next to the **Paláco do Condes de Bastos**, originally a Moorish palace, although the facade is 15th century. Parts of first-century Roman town walls are visible.

Returning to the rear of the cathedral and passing around the apse, continue south along the charming Rua do Cenáculo. In one block take the right arm of the "T," Rua da Freina de Baixo, which leads in a short block to the **mansion of Garcia de Resende** on the left side. The Manueline decoration of the second-floor windows is worth a look. Turn right to pass between two towers of the Medieval town wall into the picturesque **Largo das Portas de Moura**. An elegantly simple Renaissance fountain plays in the center of the square and a number of fine houses border it. Especially grand is the 16th-century **Corovil mansion** at the southern end, with twin arcades and horseshoe arches.

Return toward the two towers, turning left just before reaching them to travel two blocks along Rua Misericórdia, past the rococo **Igreja da Misericordia**, into the small Largo de Alvaro Velho. At its southwest end, steps lead down the picturesquely arched **Travessa da Caraça** to enter the Largo de Graca with a **Renaissance church** of the same name. Its facade is done in Italian classical style, topped by four rising atlantes. Leaving the largo by its west end opposite the church, turn left for a few feet along Rua da República to take the first right into the Pr. 28 de Maio, dominated by **Igreja de São Francisco**.

Igreja de São Francisco   ★ ★

Pr. 1 de Maio.
Hours open: Mon.–Sat. 9 a.m.–1 p.m. and 2:30–6 p.m. Open Sun. 10 a.m.–11:30 a.m. and 2:30–6 p.m.
The grandiose entry portico is formed of rounded, pointed and horseshoe arches, which about covers the genre. Inside, the aisleless nave is dizzyingly high. As is the case with the Cathedral, stones are picked out by white mortar, the peculiarity of this town. Except for the altar—with two galleries to either side—the church is relatively free of decoration which lets the architecture speak well.

But what everyone remembers about this church is not elegant architecture but its gruesome chapterhouse, entered from the left of the altar. Here the bones of perhaps 5000 dead have been collected as a reminder of what awaits us all. The sign at the entrance translates: "We bones who are here await your bones." *Admission: 50$00.*

Opposite the church is the misleadingly named **Museu de Artesonato**, for it is actually a store. At the lower end of the square a public garden is bordered on the south by part of the imposing 17th-century town walls. A bandstand in the park presents summer concerts beside ruins of one royal palace and a copy of part of another. The Pr. do Giraldo, from which we began, is two blocks.

Trains and Buses

The train station (☎ *(066) 221 25)* is located half a mile to the southeast of town along a continuation of Rua da República. Good connections are available from or to just about anywhere.

The bus station (☎ *(066) 221 21)* is near the church of São Francisco on Rua da República. Again, service is excellent to the rest of the country.

Excursions

Marvão ★ ★, pretty as a medieval postcard, lies northeast along N-18 for 105 km to Portalegre, then 16 km farther north on N-359. **Elvas** ★ ★, only 89 km northeast, is similar in its medieval-Moorish character to Évora. The medieval town of **Estremoz** ★ ★ offers a lovely castle made into one of the most elegant pousadas in the country, pleasant houses and local pottery. Attractions even nearer at hand include the embroidered carpet-making village of **Arraiolos**, and the antique shops of **Borba**. All, except Borba, are described under their own headings in this chapter, with direction to Évora that can be followed in reverse. Borba is described under the Arraiolos heading.

Also near are the fortified town and Gothic castle of **Évoramonte** ★, and the similar, but more evocative fortified village of **Monsaraz** ★ ★.

Note also, that this area has the highest concentrations of mystic Celtic dolmans—tombs built of massive boulders—and menhirs—circular places of worship formed by rock rings—in the country. They may be seen in their splendid isolation in the countryside. The Tourist Office provides a map of their locations.

Évoramonte   ★

Follow **Évora's** *Estrada de Circunvalacāo northward to turn left on N-18, toward Estremoz. Évoramonte lies north about 33 km along N-18. Signs for "Castelo d'Evoramonte" in the modern village point to a steep road up to the castle.*

Tiny Évoramonte's moment in history came in 1834 when King Pedro IV and his younger, more absolutist, brother Miguel duked it out for the Portuguese crown a few miles away. After winning, Pedro signed a treaty with his brother in a house in Évoramonte that still commemorates the event with a plaque.

The village castle and massive walls were built long before, in the 14th century, on Moorish and Roman foundations. As with many such castles, renovation occurred in the 16th century, but, unlike most, the renovation did not significantly change the style from the massive Gothic original. What is startling about this castle, however, is the vanilla color of a preservative covering its walls. Otherwise, it is a fine castle with four cylindrical towers that offer breathtaking views. Note the Manueline carved rope that "ties" the parts of the castle together, knotted at the entrance.

Monsaraz   ★ ★

Follow the Estrada de Circunvalacāo southward around Évora to turn right on N-18 going south toward Beha. In about 15 km N-256 bears east for 35 km, where a sign just before the Guadiana river directs a 4 km turn left to Monsaraz.

About two kilometers after turning onto the road to Monsaraz, look left to see a prehistoric megalith away from the road about 12 feet high surrounded by smaller stones. It conveys a tinge of the feel of Stonehenge. Who raised it is a subject of controversy, but, whoever it was did a lot of other building in this area.

Beginning in the 13th century, almost all towns near the Spanish border were fortified for defense. Monsaraz was no different. But when fortification ceased to be important, Monsaraz had nothing else to offer, so it has stayed the way it always was—today for our enjoyment. The village consists of just four cobblestone streets, lined with houses that are small and individual as only very old houses of the same general style can be. Many bear arms of the owners and most retain their outside stair—a style dating from the 16th–17th centuries.

Its ruined castle was rebuilt in the 13th century and given an outer massive perimeter wall in the 17th. Later, a small bullring with benches was added inside. Few places in the world so preserve the atmosphere of a Renaissance village; the experience is unique.

SOUTHERN PORTUGAL

POUSADA QUINTA DA ORTIGA

Apartado 67, Santiago do Cacem, 7540
☎ *(069) 228 71, FAX (069) 220 73*
$90 per double; 14 rooms: 14 doubles

★ ★ ★

Why does undistinguished Santiago do Cacém own two pousadas? The city is nicely located to serve as a stopover to break the long drive from Lisbon to the Algarve, but the original pousada proved too small, so the pousada people took over this sylvan quinta (country house) in 1991 to provide quiet rest for those pushing south. The estate consists of ten acres of grass and woods. Two buildings that feel like houses serve as the hotel. Guest rooms are boxes that are homily decorated. Across the lawn waits an attractive pool. There are stables for those who ride.

Dining

The cozy dining room features window alcoves and a restfully dark atmosphere. The food is authentic and the staff helpful. Here might be the place to try omnipresent cod, such as with cream sauce *(com natas)*, with smoked ham *(com presunto)*, as codfish cakes *(pataniscas)* or as a soufflé with herbs *(caldeira com ervas)*. Otherwise, they do a nice lamb, either roasted leg *(perma de borrego)* or with spinach *(borrego á alentejana)*. A set-course meal is available for about $20, which includes local wine.

Directions

Take N-261-3 toward Sines for 5 km, looking sharply for a parador sign to turn right. At the "T" turn left and look for the drive on your right in 100 yards.

Pousadas Nearby

Beja: 78 km	Torrão: 79 km	Alvitó: 86 km
Santa Clara: 88 km	Serpa: 107 km	Setúbal: 109 km

POUSADA SÃO GENS

Estrada N-260, Serpa, 7830
☎ *(084) 537 24, FAX (084) 533 37*
$100 per double; 18 rooms: 16 doubles, 2 suites

★ ★ ★

T his is an unusual pousada. On a hill surrounded by infinite plains sits a modern structure overlooking the land and its pool. Such modernity is attractively out of place, though it serves well as a stopover on the long drive from Spain to Portugal. There is a nice second floor terrace for lovely views while sipping an aperitif. Guest rooms are ample and all have balconies and French doors for the same glorious panorama.

Dining

The restaurant sits high above the plains with huge windows. The usual Portuguese soups are done well, including a not often featured cream of chicken that is less successful. Try the trout with fresh mint *(truta com hortelã)* for a treat or lamb, either stewed *(ensopado)* or roasted *(assada)*. The local goat cheese (Serpa) is as creamy as can be. A set-course meal is available for about $20 and includes a glass of wine.

Directions

From **Lisbon** take A-2 south toward Setúbal then east to link up with N-5 south in 54 km. N-5 south inexplicably becomes N-120 before reaching Grândola in 49 km. Take N-259 east which becomes N-260 after Beja and reaches Serpa in 96 km. From **Faro**, in the Algarve, take N-2 north for 79 km to Castro Verde, just past which N-391 north leads to Beja in 46 km and N-260 reaches Serpa in 29 km. From **Évora** take N-18 south for 78 km to Beja and N-260 east for 29 km to Serpa. From **Seville** in Spain take N-630 north for 35 km to join N-433 northwest for a scenic drive to the border in 144 km. N-260 west in Portugal reaches Serpa in 37 km.

Pousadas Nearby

Beja: 29 km	Alvító: 74 km	Torrão: 80 km
Santiago: 107 km	Évora: 111 km	

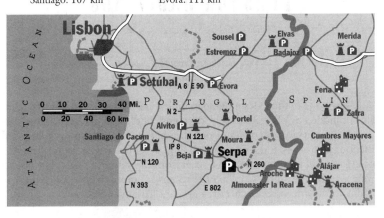

SOUTHERN PORTUGAL

POUSADA SÃO TIAGO

Estrada de Lisboa, Santiago do Cacem, 7540
☎ *(069) 224 59, FAX (069) 224 59*
$90 per double; 8 rooms: 8 doubles

★ ★ ★

This is one of the oldest pousadas, built in 1947, but just renovated. It is almost hidden by old trees to provide a sense of the country while in the city and screen out city sounds. The pousada is heavily booked, but try for one of the four bedrooms in the original building rather than those in the plain annex. Inside all is cool in feeling, a relief from the summer's heat, but not as welcome during winter's chill. Guest rooms are more than adequate in size and colorfully decorated. There is a pleasant garden and a pool.

Dining

Service and food earn high marks at this pousada. The kitchen, intelligently, does not try to offer great variety at any given meal, opting to change the menu often instead. This means that you cannot be sure what will be offered, but the sole *(linguado)* and soups are reliable choices. A fine choice of wines is provided, including Colares, Portugal's finest. A set-course meal is available for about $20 including local wine.

Directions

Take N-261-3 toward Sines for 5 km, looking sharply for a parador sign to turn right. At the "T" turn left and look for the drive on your right in 100 yards.

Pousadas Nearby

Beja: 78 km	Torrão: 79 km	Alvitó: 86 km
Santa Clara: 88 km	Serpa: 107 km	Setúbal: 109 km

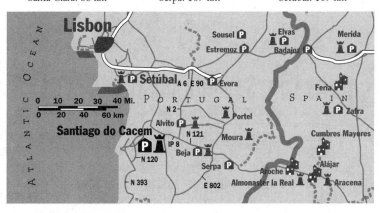

POUSADA SENHORA DA ASSUNÇÃO

Arraiolos, 7350
Area Code: 068
$125, double; 32 rooms: 30 doubles, 2 suites

★ ★ ★ ★

Brand new in 1997, this parador is located in a village world-renowned for its needlepoint carpets. A pretty 16th century convent on the outskirts of town with Manueline details and Mudejar windows now accepts 20th century guests. On the premises stands quite a church—faced with azulejos and capped by a remarkable tromp-l'oeil interior. The first floor of the pousada consists of the public rooms surrounding the former convent cloister, windowed to allow comfort in all seasons. Guest rooms range around the second floor, are comfortable and tasteful, but could be larger. Only the two suites, furnished with antiques, are in any way special. Tennis courts, swimming pool and horses are available. We will have to wait to see how professional is the service. The only problem is that this pousada sits in an area crowded with others, including the more elegant ones at Estremoz and Évora close by.

Dining

The restaurant is utterly lovely, surrounding an interior patio. Meals were not yet being served when we visited, so we await reports on the cooking.

SOUTHERN PORTUGAL

Directions

From **Lisbon** take A-6 south then east for 99 km to just past Montemor-o-Novo where N-4 goes the final 20 km. From **Évora** take N-370 north for 22 km.

Pousadas Nearby

Évora: 22 km	Alvitó: 63 km	Estremoz:63 km
Elvas: 91 km	Portalegre: 102 km	Flor da Rosa: 127 km

Sights

For more than two centuries this village has been in the carpet business. Portuguese exploration of the east brought an awareness of Indian and Persian carpets, which soon became the rage in upper-class households. By the middle of the 17th-century homegrown copies were being produced in the area around Arraiolos. In time, fashions changed to favor more formal Aubusson styles from France, and Arraiolos kept pace.

Today the carpets are still produced by the same techniques used two centuries ago. Rather than tied, as are oriental carpets, women in Arraiolos embroider with wool in gros point on a linen canvas. Styles and colors cover a wide range; in fact, almost any design or color scheme can be custom-made. Being entirely created by hand, these carpets are not cheap—costs run about $120 per square yard. What they are is future heirlooms since they easily stand up to a century of wear, retain their colors (being naturally died wool), and do not burn.

Rua Dr. Manuel Pinto, the main street of Arraiolos, consists of little more than shops selling *tapetes*. A cooperative at the corner of the main square carries a large selection where prices should be less, although they generally turn out to be about the same as those charged by the retail shops. Other than at this cooperative, some gentle bargaining may pay off in savings.

If you tire of shopping, Arraiolos provides a lovely 14th-century **castle** for exploring perched on the highest ground. Also, just south of the town hall in the main square, stands **Misericórdia** with elegant azulejos inside.

Excursions

The many glories of **Évora** are 22 km south on N-370 and described below under its own heading. Close at hand, too, are **Borba** for antiques (east on N-4, past Estremoz, for 54 km) and **Monsaraz** for a medieval castle and village (back to Évora on N-370 for 22 km, then east on N-18 for about 15 km to join N-256 east for 34 km to a turn north as directed, just before crossing the Guadiana River). Both are described below.

Borba

Borba is famed in Portugal for fine marble quarried from nearby mountains. You will seldom see so much calcite in such a small town. But for us, Borba stands for antiques. This quaint little town devotes three running blocks of its main street to store after store—we once counted 20. Note, these are not the high-priced fancy shops that the word antique may bring to mind, but those dusty, second-hand places where costs range from a few dollars to a few thousand, and the fun is in the exploring.

If you need some excuse to come for browsing, the main square, Pr. do Cinco de Outubro, is bordered by an 18th-century **town hall** and the pleasant 16th-century church of **São Bartolmeu** known for its azulejos. In the town center, at the junction of the road to Vila Viçosa, stands a little park with a fine marble (what else?) fountain in the center.

Monsaraz   ★

About two kilometers after turning onto the road to Monsaraz, look left to see a prehistoric megalith away from the road about 12 feet high surrounded by smaller stones. It conveys a tinge of the feel of Stonehenge. Who raised it is a subject of controversy, but, whoever it was did a lot of other building in this area.

Beginning in the 13th century, almost all towns near the Spanish border were fortified for defense. Monsaraz was no different. But when fortification ceased to be important, Monsaraz had nothing else to offer, so it has stayed the way it always was—today for our enjoyment. The village consists of just four cobblestone streets, lined with houses that are small and individual as only very old houses of the same general style can be. Many bear arms of the owners and most retain their outside stair—a style dating from the 16th-17th centuries.

Its ruined **castle** was rebuilt in the 13th century and given an outer massive perimeter wall in the 17th. Later, a small bullring with benches was added inside. Few places in the world so preserve the atmosphere of a Renaissance village; the experience is unique.

POUSADA VALE DO GAIO

Torrão, 7595
☎ *(065) 66 96 10, FAX (065) 66 96 10*
$90 per double; 13 rooms: 13 doubles

★ ★ ★

Again the Portuguese have turned the house of the head engineer on a damming project into a pousada, this time a rustic dwelling nestled in woods on the edge of a lake. Views of the lake are fine, and the location is close enough to N-2, a major highway to the Algarve, to provide a sensible rest-stop on the trip south. There is a cozy veranda and abundant quiet. Note, this is not luxury; it is sylvan rustic.

Dining

The staff is most willing, but the kitchen is not gourmet. So stick to local dishes, which means pork or game. However, the cream of watercress soup is subtle. Set-course meals start at about $20.

SOUTHERN PORTUGAL

Directions

From **Lisbon** take A-2 south toward Setúbal then east to the exit for Montemor-o-Novo in 97 km. Exit onto N-114 south for 3 km until it joins N-2 south for 44 km to just short of Torrão, where N-5 toward Alcácer goes west. Look in about 5 km for a semi-paved road to the left with a "Pousada" sign. From **Faro**, in the Algarve, take N-2 north for 181 km to N-5 east just past Torrão, for a final leg of 5 km and a left turn at the "Pousada" sign.

Pousadas Nearby

Alvitó: 34 km	Beja: 59 km	Santiago: 67 km
Évora: 76 km	Setúbal: 80 km	Serpa: 88 km

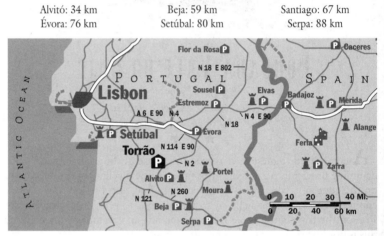

SOUTHERN PORTUGAL

NORTHERN PORTUGAL

The stairs to Bom Jesus near Braga are extraordinary.

At 150 miles long by 100 miles wide, northern Portugal comprises about half of the country. Mountains mark its eastern half to divide Portugal from Spain, still harboring medieval forts that once defended against its avaricious neighbor. Mountains continue across the northernmost part, forming Portugal's most scenic national park, Peneda Gerés. Sealed in the northeast corner, isolated Bragança survives from another time. Lovely beaches line the west coast at Aveiro and at Viana do Castelo.

The major metropolis of the north is Porto, with a clutch of attractive sights. Nearby is Guimarães, the birthplace of the country. Almost exactly in the center of the country is the other main metropolis, Coimbra, which hosts an ancient university. Extensive Roman ruins lie to its south, and, further south, stands Tomar with an intriguing church built by the Knights Templar. Northern Portugal can easily consume a packed week of sight-seeing.

Working up the country, the first sight is **Tomar**, with its mysterious Templar church later embellished by the great architects of Portugal. Nearby is the fairytale castle of **Amouril**. **Coimbra**, next, presents an ancient university partly housed in a royal palace and the premier museum of Portuguese sculpture. In splendid isolation on the eastern border stand a string of medieval fortresses anchored at **Almeida**. **Aveiro**, crisscrossed by canals owns miles of lovely beach, and is not far from elegant **Viseu** which boasts of churches and native art. **Porto** a number of fine churches and, of course, the bottlers of port wine. **Guimarães** retains some remains of the first castle in the country along with a magnificent restored medieval castle. Far north stands the scenic natural park of Penada **Gerés** and isolated **Bragança**, which retains a way of life from a century ago.

The following towns and pousadas are covered in this chapter.

Town	Pousada Name	Rating	Page
Albergaria-a-Velha	Santo António	★★★	*page 643*
Alijó	Barão de Forster	★★★	*page 659*
Almeida	Senhora das Neves	★★★★	*page 671*
Amarante	São Gonçalo	★★★	*page 667*
Aveiro	da Ria	★★★★	*page 608*
Bragança	São Bartolemeu	★★★	*page 645*
Caniçada	São Benito	★★★	*page 650*
Caramulo	São Jerónima	★★★	*page 653*
Condeixa-a-Nova	Santa Cristina	★★★★	*page 622*
Guimarães	Nossa Senhora da Oliveira	★★★★	*page 616*
Guimarães	Santa Marinha	★★★★★	*page 637*
Manteigas	São Lourenço	★★★	*page 657*
Marvão	Santa Maria	★★★	*page 633*
Miranda do Doura	Santa Catarina	★★★	*page 620*
Monsanto	Monsanto	★★★	*page 614*
Porto	None		*page 600*
Póvoa das Quartas	Santa Barbara	★★★★	*page 618*
Valença do Minho	São Teotónio	★★★	*page 669*
Viana do Castelo	Monte de Santa Luzia	★★★★	*page 662*
Vila Nova da Cerveira	Dom Denis	★★★★	*page 665*

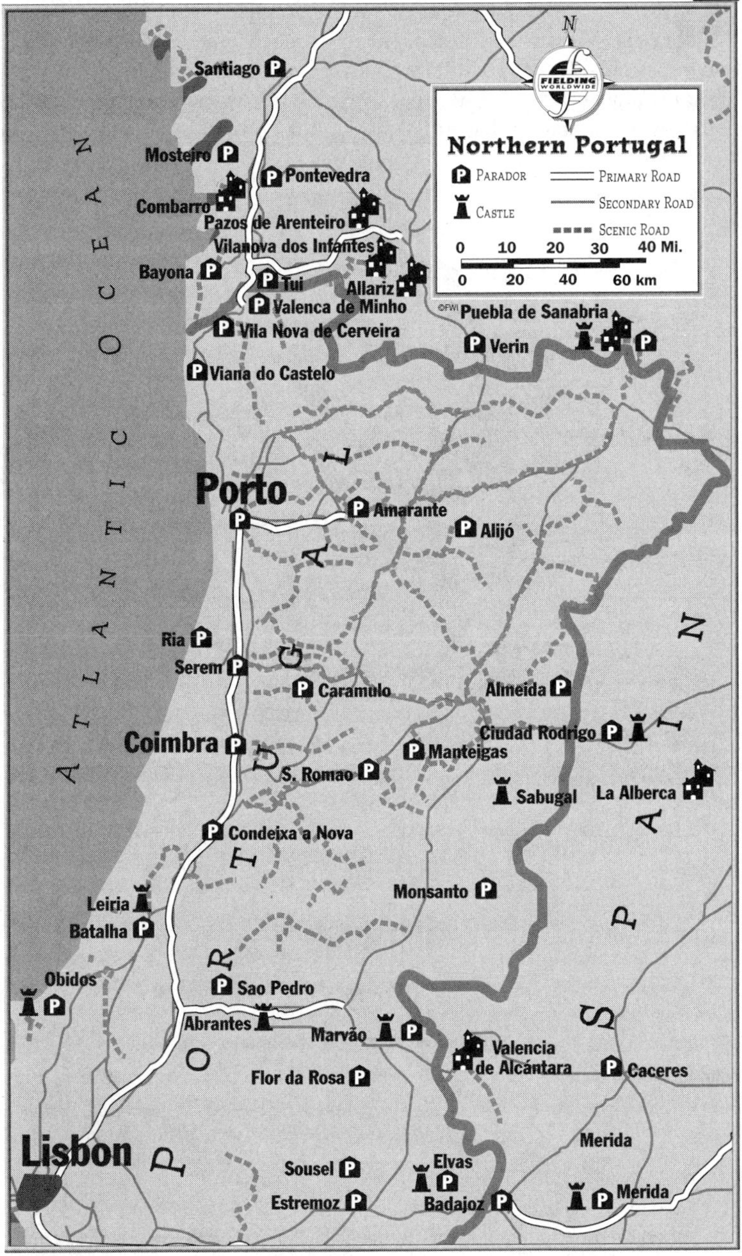

Northern Portugal

🅿 PARADOR	── PRIMARY ROAD	
♜ CASTLE	── SECONDARY ROAD	
	▬▬▬ SCENIC ROAD	

0   10   20   30   40 Mi.

0   20   40   60 km

Santiago 🅿

Mosteiro 🅿

Combarro 🅿 Pontevedra

Pazos de Arenteiro 🅿

Vilanova dos Infantes

Bayona 🅿   🅿 Tui   Allariz

🅿 Valenca de Minho

🅿 Vila Nova de Cerveira

🅿 Viana do Castelo

Puebla de Sanabria

🅿 Verin

Porto

🅿 Amarante

🅿 Alijó

Ria 🅿

Serem 🅿

🅿 Caramulo   Almeida 🅿

Coimbra 🅿   Ciudad Rodrigo 🅿 ♜

🅿 Manteigas   La Alberca

S. Romao 🅿   ♜ Sabugal

🅿 Condeixa a Nova

Monsanto 🅿

Leiria ♜

Batalha 🅿

Obidos

♜ 🅿   🅿 Sao Pedro

Abrantes ♜   Marvão ♜ 🅿

Flor da Rosa 🅿   Valencia de Alcántara   🅿 Caceres

Lisbon

Merida

Sousel 🅿   ♜ Elvas

Estremoz 🅿   Badajoz 🅿   ♜ 🅿 Merida

ATLANTIC OCEAN

PORTUGAL

SPAIN

To savor the region, stay two nights at the Condeixa pousada while visiting Coimbra and Tomar. For beach, spend as much time as you wish at the Aveiro pousada. If mountain forts appeal to you, spend a night at the Manteigas or Almeida pousadas. Porto is worth a night, even though there are no pousadas there. Stay at elegant Santa Marinha pousada in Guimarães if you want the hotel experience of a lifetime.

PORTO
★★

Accommodations

Hotel Infante de Sagres   ★★★★★

Pr. Dona Filipa de Lencastre, 62 (one block west of Av. do Almada, about halfway along), Porto 4000, *(02) 201 90 31, FAX (02) 31 49 37, Telex 26880. 68 rooms, plus 8 suites. There is a Sheraton and a Meridien, both modern high-rises that provide expected services at about $175 per double.*

The Hotel Infante de Sagres is one of the great hotels of Europe and, unquestionably, the most luxurious in Porto. Although built in the 1950s with a perfectly ordi-

nary exterior, no cost was spared inside to make it as grand and lovely as could be.
It is richly Victorian in style, replete with elegant paneling, crystal chandeliers, velvet
wallpaper and wrought ironwork. We would nominate its Dona Filipa restaurant as
the most elegant in the country, and for once the lighting is subdued. Bedrooms are
truly spacious, with marble bathrooms, although their vaguely *directoire* decor is
not up to the exalted standards of the public spaces. But what is truly outstanding is
the service, for there are as many people providing assistance as spending the night.
The guest list of this hotel includes the royal, great and famous. Anywhere else in
Europe a hotel of this caliber would cost three times its $150 per double price.

Albergaria Miradouro ★★

*Rua da Alegria, 598 (3 blocks east and 2 north of the Trinidade train station, which is just
north of the Trinidade church at the top of the Rua do Almada), Porto 4000,* *(02) 57
07 17, FAX (02) 57 02 06. 30 rooms.*

Much less expensive at under $75 and somewhat charming, is the Albergaria Mira-
douro, a 13-story modern building in a quiet neighborhood that offers dramatic
views of the city and the river traffic. The decor is tasteful and the walk to sights is
downhill. Its Portucale restaurant is one of the best in the city.

Albergaria São João ★★

*Rua do Bonjardim, 120 (although one-way in the wrong direction, Rua de Fernandes
goes east from the Trinidade church to reach the hotel in 4 blocks), Porto 4000,* *(02)
208 02 61, FAX (02) 32 04 46. 14 rooms.*

Similar in price is the Albergaria São João which occupies the top floor of a modern
building, yet is cozy with antiques and a fireplace. The bedrooms are large and intelligently laid out so that each includes a sitting area. The location is most convenient.

Rex ★★★

*Pr. da República, 117 (this major plaza is 1 block west of the Trinidade train station),
Porto 4000,* *(02) 200 45 48, FAX (02) 38 38 82. 21 rooms.*

For $50 the Rex is remarkable. It is a converted townhouse overlooking a gardened,
serene square. The house is a neoclassic charmer with marble staircase, paneled
wood and intricate stucco ceilings. Really, it is inexpensive, despite its more luxurious look. The bedrooms are lovely, with painted stucco ceilings, and larger than
alternatives at this low price.

Dining

Portucale ★★★

*Rua da Alegria, 598 (in the same building as the Albergaria Miradouro, 3 blocks east and
2 north of the Trinidade train station, which is just north of the Trinidade church at the
top of the Rua do Almada), Porto 4000,* *(02) 57 07 17, FAX 5(02) 7 02 06.*

The dramatic view alone would make this place special, but it also serves the best
food in the city. The dining room is pleasantly decorated with modern hangings,
and the tables are attractively dressed with good linens, silver, china and flowers.
Despite the stunning views, an intimate feeling is maintained. Both *tipas á moda do*

Porto (in casserole with white beans, bacon, chicken and sausage) and *cabrito a serrana* (kid stewed in red wine) are superb. Dinner, however, approaches $50. Reservations are required, as is a coat and tie. Credit Cards: A, D, M, V.

Mesa Antiga ★★

Rua de Santo Ildefonso, 208 (Leave the southeast corner of Pr. da Liberdade at the southern end of Av. do Almada on Rua de do da Bandeira. In one block, round the church to enter Rua de Santo Ildefonso for one block), Porto 4000, *(02) 200 64 32. Closed Saturday and the first two weeks of October.*

Old wood and blue-and-white *azulejos* create the proper cozy atmosphere for food that is prepared with care. This is a family-run place, where the main work is done in an improbably small kitchen. Try the tripe, or sole in delectable green sauce, or any daily special. Reservations are advised and the meal should cost half that at the Portucale. Credit Cards: M, V.

Chez Lapin ★★

Cais da Ribeira, 42, Porto 4000, *(02) 264 18.*

Let us get the bad part out of the way first. This restaurant is so tiny as to be claustrophobic, the decor is happenstance, and the noise level is extreme. However, the reason for the noise is that it is always full, for the food is indeed good. The claustrophobia soon disappears in the convivial atmosphere. Fish are the thing here, fresh and grilled perfectly. An equally minuscule upstairs is a bit quieter.

Aquário Marisqueiro ★

Rua Rodrigues Sampaio, 179 (a step or two east of the Pr. do General H. Delgado, which fronts the city hall), Porto 4000, *(02) 200 22 31. Closed Sunday and holidays.*

This is fish heaven. Clams are good, as is shellfish *açorda* (a bread thickened stew) and sole done any which way. Prices are about the same as at the Mesa Antígua. Reservations are required. Credit Cards: M, V.

Directions

From **Lisbon** take A1 north for 299 km. From **Tui,** in Spain, after crossing the border take N-13 south for 113 km. From **Coimbra** a drive north on N-1 of 9 km allows a connection to the autoestrada A-1 for the final 131 k. From **Évora** take N-114 northwest to Montemor-o-Novo in 30 km, where N-4 goes west to Cruzamento de Pegões in 37 km. There N-10 goes northwest to Vila Franca de Xiro, where the autoestrada A-1 is picked up for a speedy 314 km.

Train service is frequent from most parts of the country, although most disembark in the Campanha station, which is a distance from the center of the city. Change there for a five-minute ride to the Estacão São Bento in the heart of town. A Lisbon express train takes about three hours, twice the time from Coimbra. **Buses** almost double those times, although they are as convenient as trains from nearer departures, such as Braga and Viseu. At 4.5 hours, the bus beats the train handily from Guarda.

Of course, a **plane** is fastest. Pedras Rubras airport is 14 km south of the city. A taxi from the airport costs less than 3000$00. Alternatively, the #56 bus takes about 45 minutes to reach Pr. de Lisbôa, one block west of Av. dos Aliados, and costs less than $1.

Pousadas Nearby

Aveiro: 48 km	Guimarães: 55 km	Sérem: 61 km
Amarante: 74 km	Caniçada: 90 km	Caramulo: 100 km

Sights

The present city of Porto (known to the British as Oporto, confusing the Portuguese *O Porto* "the port") occupies the site of the Roman town of Portus, sprawling down the long, steep north bank of the Douro, 6 km from the sea. With almost a million people in the extended agglomeration, it is easily the second-largest city in Portugal and the one most single-mindedly devoted to commerce.

Portugal in general, but Porto in particular, also has a long history of close ties with England. In the 17th century, France closed its borders to imports of English clothing, and in response Charles II forbade the importation of French wines, leaving English thirsts unslaked. The English began sending their cloth to Portugal, trading for wine from Porto. This arrangement was formalized in the Methuen Treaty of 1703, which stipulated that the two countries would remain perpetual friends. Soon Englishmen came to Porto, bought up inland vineyards along the Douro, and formed shipping companies for the wine that floated down the river to Porto. Whether to prevent spoilage or to satisfy the English palate for sweet drink, a method was developed for adding grape brandy to the wine to stop its fermentation while half of the grape sugar still remained. It produced a sweet, fortified wine of as much as 30 percent alcohol that is called after its place of embarkation, *port*. To earn the name, wine originally had to age in Villa Nova de Gaia, across the river from Porto. Famous port houses, such as Sandeman, still maintain "lodges" (warehouses) there today, although aging now is permitted anywhere along the Douro littoral.

Porto today presents the face of a 19th-century commercial port—full of granite-trimmed buildings, few more than three stories high. The heart of the city is the wide, grass-lined, Av. dos Aliados, which runs five blocks inland from, and perpendicular to, the river.

All of the sights lie south of this landmark. The **Cathedral ★★**, with a fine altar, stands two blocks directly south; the church of **San Francisco ★★**, the non-plus-ultra of the Baroque, southeast a block from the river beside the **Palácio da Bolsa ★**, containing one impressive hall in the style of the Moors. Lining the river in front of San Francisco is the **Cais (quay) de Ribeira**, the oldest and most picturesque quarter. Across the river in **Villa Nova de Gaia** stretches a row of **port lodges ★** for free tours and tastings.

Cathedral   ★

> *Terreiro da Sé.*
> *Hours open: daily 9 a.m.–12:30 p.m. and 2–5:30 p.m.*
> Of the 12th-century Romanesque fortress church in which João I married Philippa of Lancaster in 1387, little can be seen, since so many decorative additions now cover it over. The central window of the facade is lovely Romanesque, but the church entrance is Baroque. Baroque is the dominant decorative theme of the interior, covering a simpler Romanesque space.
>
> A treasure graces the Chapel of the Holy Sacrament in the north (left) transept. Its retable and altar front of chased silver from the 17th century is a marvel of mannered figures that seem to move in the dim light. A door at the end of the south transept (right side) leads to a solemn 14th-century cloister whose upper tier was wrapped in charming *azulejos* in the 17th century. *Admission: 100$00 to the cloisters.*
>
> Toward the river in the Cathedral plaza is a fine 18th-century **Bishop's Palace**, now an office building. A lane behind the apse of the Cathedral leads to R. Dom Hugo and the 18th century building at number 32 that serves as the **Museu Guerra Junqueiro** for interesting decorative arts (open Tues. through Sat. from 10 a.m. until 12:30 and from 2 p.m. until 5; on Sun. from 2 p.m. until 5:30; admission 100$00).
>
> A lane leading left just before that museum leads downhill to cross the access road to the Ponte de Dom Luis I for the church of **Santa Clara**, covered inside in 18th-century carved gilt. The ceiling is elegant. Remains of the old **city walls** stand behind the church.

If the above sights do not appeal, descend the western flank of the Cathedral hill through the quaint and dirty Old Town to emerge into sunlight again at Av. Mousinho de Soveira. It goes south for about one block to the Pr. Infante Dom Henrique, at the rear of the church of **São Francisco**. Adjacent to the north side of the church is the **Palácio da Bolsa**.

Igreja São Francisco ⭐⭐

R. do Infante Dom Henrique, ☎ *(02) 200 64 93 (Museum across the plaza at Rua da Bolsa, 44).*
Hours open: Mon.–Sat. from 10 a.m.–1 p.m. and from 2–5 p.m. (in winter closed from 12:30–2 p.m., but open until 7 p.m.) Closed Sun.
Be prepared for a shock, for behind its Gothic exterior lies an interior decorated from the 17th through the 18th centuries with the most dazzling and fantastic of all the Baroque confections in Portugal. Gilt is everywhere in dizzying profusion. When your eyes begin to smart, it's time to leave.

The tour of the nearby museum starts in eerie catacombs, whose gloom is the perfect contrast to the gilt next door. You walk on what seem to be doors that house the last remains of a reputed 30,000 mortals. Afterwards, there is a museum of mixed oddities, then the rich Sala de Sessões presided over by a painted bishop, who seems to be eyeing your warm body avidly. *Admission: 350$00.*

Palácio da Bolsa ⭐

R. Ferreira Borges, ☎ *(02) 200 44 97.*
Hours open: Mon.–Fri. 9 a.m.–6 p.m. Open Sat. and Sun. 10 a.m.–noon and 2–5 p.m. (in winter open Mon.–Fri., closes noon to 2, open until 5:30 p.m.).
This is the Stock Exchange, built in 1834 on the ruins of the convent of neighboring São Francisco. What makes a visit worthwhile is a hall, called the Salon de Arabe, a huge oval room that took 18 years just to decorate in a style loosely derived from Spain's Alhambra. The ornateness is luxuriant, and the inlaid parquet, besides being fine work, still exudes a pleasant smell. *Admission: 400$00, for guided tour.*

Past the west end of the Bolsa a right then an immediate left brings the Largo São João Novo, named after the church there. Opposite the church is the **Museu de Etnografia i Historia**. Exhibits are a mishmash of 19th-century and early 20th-century curiosities and folk pieces that are generally interesting. (Open Tues.–Sat. 10 a.m. to noon and 2-5 p.m. Closed Sun., Mon., and holidays. Admission: free.)

Returning to the Pr. Infante Dom Henrique at the rear of the church of São Francisco, descend Rua da Alfandega that leaves its southeast corner. On the right the house where Henry the Navigator was purportedly born, now hosts art exhibits. Farther downhill and right at Rua da Reboleira is the **Center of Traditional Arts and Crafts**, for a look or a purchase. Down to the river and upstream (east) is the area called **Ribeira**, a lively district full of restaurants.

Vila Nova de Gaia ⭐

This is the name for the area across the river where port wine is warehoused in what the trade calls "lodges." They line the bank opposite the center of Porto, all clearly marked by neon company signs. One can walk or taxi—taxis are entitled to a surcharge for crossing the river—across the lower level of the Ponte de Dom Luis I.

(Buses #57 and #91 also make the trip.) Do not fail to notice the lovely **Maria Pia railway bridge** upstream (east), designed by Gustave Eiffel of the Paris tower fame, and the newer **Arrabida road bridge** downstream, crossing in a single span measuring 1000 feet.

All the lodges offer free guided tours and samples. All are open on weekdays from either 9 or 10 a.m. to noon and from 2–5 p.m. A few, such as Sandeman, Calém and Real Vinicola, are open on Saturday as well in the summer. Note that three such tours bring most people to the edge of intoxication. A few of the better ones are:

Sandeman
Largo Miguel Bombarda, 2. ☎ *(02) 30 40 81.*

Real Vinicola
Rua Azevedo Magalhães, 314. ☎ *(02) 30 54 62.*

Ferreira
Av. Diogo Leite, 70. ☎ *(02) 30 08 66.*

Calém
Av. Diogo Leite, 2. ☎ *(02) 39 40 41.*

Directory

Airport
Pedras Rubras international airport is 16 km north of the city (☎ *(02) 948 21 41).* A taxi will cost under 2.000$00. Buses #44 and #56 connect with the central Pr. do Lisbõa for 150$00. The main TAP office is at *Pr. Mouzinho de Albuquerque, 105* in the Boavista rotunda (☎ *(02) 69 98 41),* which is a mile east of the Pr. da República at the top of the R. do Almada.

Information
Located at Rua Clube dos Fenianos, 25 (☎ *(02) 31 27 40)* on the west side of the city hall. Lots of information is available about port tastings, boat trips up the Douro and vineyard tours.

Shopping
Shopping is fun in Porto because one sees unusual products and the good shops are concentrated. Better stores accumulate on the streets leading off **Pr. da Liberdade**, at the south end of Av. dos Aliados. Especially good are **R. dos Clérigos**, going west of the square, **R. da Sa Bandeira**, going northeast, and the parallel **R. de Sta Catarina**. The latter two host numerous shoe shops. For all-in-one shopping there is a large mall called **Centro Comércial de Brasileiraon Av. da Boavisto** parallel to the river, northwest of the center.

Of course port wine is on sale all over town, but more fun to buy after touring the lodge itself, see above.

A small flea market can be found almost every day in front of the Cathedral square.

Excursions

The most peaceful Porto excursion is a **cruise** up the Douro river—and the most ideal cruise is to Pinhão with an overnight in Regua. Including all meals for two days and sleeping accommodations, the trip costs about 20,000$00 per person. This and shorter trips are conducted by **Endouro Turismo** at *R. da Reboleira, 49 (☎ (02) 208 41 61)*. Or, for those with less money or time, there are cruises of the river bridges offered by **Cruzeiro das Quatro Pontes**. Boats depart on the hour from a dock in Villa Nova de Gaia, behind the Ferreira port lodge. Service runs from May through Oct.; between 10 a.m. and 6 p.m., except Sun.

Porto is 50 km from the fine beach and canals of **Aveiro ★**, and 65 more from elegant **Viseu ★★** with its museum. Aveiro is described under its own section above, Viseu in the Amarante section above. **Guimarães ★★**, Portugal's birthplace, is 24 km southwest of it, described under its own heading above.

One special excursion of about 60 miles from Porto is to visit the lovely manor house of Mateus, so familiar from the wine bottles of that name. Incidentally, the Solar (as it is called) has no connection with the winemakers who simply pay for the right to include its picture on their bottles. See the Aljitó section above for a description.

From downtown Porto the simplest route to Mateus is to take R. do Dr. Magalhães Lemos going east from a block north of the Pr. da Liberdade. It soon changes its name to R. do Passos Manuel, before entering a square at which one should continue in the same direction, now on R. de Mornado Mateus. Turn left at the next square to take the first right onto Av. de Ferão de Magalhães going north. The avenue feeds into the main Estrada da Circunvalação around Porto. Go left (west) to the first exit onto A-3 toward Braga. But take the first exit onto A-4 toward Amarante and Vila Real. In 62 km at Amarante, join N-15 to Vila Real in 36 km. Go 1 km on N-15 past Vila Real toward Sabrosa to a sign for a right turn to Mateus.

POUSADA DA RIA

Estrada N-327, Aveiro, 3870
☎ *(034) 483 32, FAX (034) 483 33*
$110 per double; 19 rooms: 18 doubles, 1 suite

★ ★ ★ ★

Water on three sides adds drama to this modern building, whose plentiful windows make the most of a setting on a tranquil lagoon. An inside-outside papyrus and goldfish pool adds a nice touch to the airy interior, while views of seaweed-harvesting boats plying the lagoon provide restful days in rooms that are comfortable but of no great style. Tennis is available too, at this heavily booked pousada. There is a pool, but it is a walk to seaside beach that spreads for miles.

Alternative Accommodations

The pousada offers the best accommodations near the beach, but there are two better hotels if that requirement is loosened.

Palácio de Águeda   ★ ★ ★ ★

Quinta da Borralha, Águeda (Scenic N-230 heads east from Aveiro before angling southerly along the Vouga river to Águeda in 22 km. Take N1 south for 2 km to Quinta da Borralha), ☎ *(034) 60 19 77, FAX (034) 60 19 76. 42 rooms, plus 6 suites.*

The first is one of the great hotels of the country, located in Águeda, 24 km south of Aveiro along N-1. Lying behind a wall and gate that suggests a ranch in the countryside, the Palácio de Águeda is situated in a boring industrial city, and not in the best part of town. But behind the gate, glistening white with delicate yellow trim, stands a veritable palace, a former manor house of the Counts of Borralha. Substantially renovated by a Frenchman with perfect taste and deep pockets, the Águeda is as lovely as any hotel in the country. Interior colors are oranges and browns, and Islamic motifs characterize many of the public rooms, for the owner spends part of his year in Morocco. Formal gardens stretch behind. Bedrooms are large and elegant, and their bathrooms are grand. All facilities are available, and the setting is restful behind its wall. Live like a noble for a night, at a price that barely crests the expensive. The only thing that prevents us from going all out for this hotel is the management, which, although willing and agreeable (you will be enchanted by the young women in their "school-girl" uniforms at the desk), is not up to truly first-class service. In most cases, however, this should not distract from a pleasant night in a truly memorable hotel.

Paloma Blanca ★★★★

Rua Luís Gomes de Carvalho, 23, Aveiro (near the east end of Av. Dr. Lourenço Peix-inho, close to the train station), ☎ (034) 38 19 92, FAX (034) 38 18 44. 49 rooms.
In Aveiro stands the Paloma Blanca, an almost perfect little hotel. The house is a former Moorish-style mansion surrounding a tropical garden, which most rooms overlook. The interior is replete with rich deco paneling in the reception and bar. Tasteful antiques, including old machines, fill the nooks and crannies. Bedrooms are large, comfortable, include semi-antiques and are decorated with exceptional style. This may be the cleanest hotel in the country, and adds the extra bonus of free underground parking. Don't tell the owner $70 is too low for such good taste.

Dining

A rather sedate, large room looks over the colorful seaweed collecting boats plying the lagoon. Here reasonably good food is served. A delicate consomme laced with port *(caldo rico com Porto)* or a cream of vegetable soup *(creme de legumes)* can start the meal. Here is the place to try eels at their best, if you have the stomach for it. A stew-pot of the critters *(caldei-rada de enguias)* is featured by the chef. Of course there are other options. Roast pork with prunes *(lombo de porco assado com ameixas)*, codfish with cream sauce *(bacalhau espiritual)*, hake with a port and mayonnaise sauce *(pescada assada à São Jacinto)*, or braised suckling pig with pepper sauce *(le-itão à Bairrada)* are all well put together. Local wines from Bairrada are ex-cellent values. Set-course meals begin at $20.

Alternative Dining

Centenario ★★

Largo do Mercado, 9, Aveiro (opposite the covered market, a third of the way along Av. Dr. Lourenço Peixinho, then a right down Pereira da Silva and down the steps right again), ☎ (034) 227 98. Closed Tuesday, and the first two weeks of May.
Although its prices hover at $20 for a meal, this restaurant, with its modern paneled dining room, looks like more. A must to begin is *Sopa do Mar*. Fish and meat are equally good, so order any of the specials with confidence. Credit Cards: M, V.

O Mercantel ★

R. António dos Santos Le, 16, Aveiro (near the Rossio), ☎ (034) 280 57. Closed Mon.

¢

Here is a restaurant run by a man who started out selling the fish. When he turned his hand to cooking, it turned out that he was very good, as various prizes have proved. Nothing fancy in his restaurant, just good food served at lower prices even than Centenario. Credit Cards: A, D, M, V.

Directions

From **Lisbon** take the autoestrada A-1 north for 264 km to the exit for North Aveiro. After going west for 3 km toward the city, join N-109 north for 23 km to Ovar, then go south for 15 km on N-327, past Torreira, to see the pousada on the left. From **Porto** take the autoestrada A-1 south for 28 km to the exit for Sta. Maria da Feira but go west toward Maceda and join N-109 going south for 7 km where it branches onto N-327 south for 18 km past Torreira to see the pousada on the left. From **Coimbra** take the autoestrada A-1 north for 50 km to the North Aveiro exit and follow the Lisbon directions from there.

Pousadas Nearby

Sérem: 45 km	Caramulo: 95 km	Condeixa: 106 km
Guimarães: 132 km	Póvoa das Quartas: 155 km	Manteigas: 175 km

Sights

Aveiro stands beside a huge lagoon extending north for 45 km and west for 10 km beside the ocean. It is an unusual city with the flavor of a Dutch burgh, situated near good beaches. Its canals are plied by high-bow, flat-bottomed, punted boats, not dissimilar to gondolas—except for brightly paint-ed bow emblems and the fact that they serve not as water-taxis, but as seaweed collectors.

Parking should be available along the Canal Central and its extension, the Canal do Cojo, in the city center.

Aveiro has had its ups and downs. Until the end of the 16th century it thrived as a port for cod fishing. In the 17th century, however, a storm shut Aveiro's lagoon from the sea so it quickly silted up, leading to two centuries of economic depression for the city. Because of the loss of its port and the malarial marshes that formed after the silting, Aveiro's population declined by two-thirds. Then, in 1808, the sandbar was breached by engineers, mak-ing Aveiro a port again. Today the city lives off fish, plentiful salt from the huge lagoon for the salted cod of Portugal, and seaweed for fertilizer.

Aveiro's main interest for tourists will be her beaches, but it is an attractive town as well with pleasant sights. Imposing mansions line the **Canal Central**; the **Convent of Jesus** ★ contains a pretty church and museum of worthwhile paintings; and a boat tour of the **ria** ★★ (lagoon) is a pleasant outing with local color to see. The **Vista Alegre** china factory hums 7 km south near Ilha-vo on N-109. Although the secrets of the manufacturing process are guard-ed, there is a museum showing the development of this ware from clumsy beginnings, and, of course, a shop selling the finished product.

The last half of August is a special time to visit Aveiro. This is the time of the Festa da Ria consisting of boat races, folk-dancing and a contest for the best-decorated seaweed-collecting punts. Accommodations, however, are scarce at that time.

The sights of Aveiro are central and compact. All roads converge on the main square of town, the Pr. Humberto Delgado, which is actually a wide bridge over the Canal Central. West of this bridge the canal is lined with ec-centric buildings. Here too is the **tourist office**, which provides information about boat trips through the lagoon. Branching off, farther east, runs the wide shaded main avenue of town, Dr. Lourenço Paixinho, lined with stores. The city **train station**, festooned with charming azulejos, waits eight pleasant blocks along this avenue. On the way, look for the headquarters of the local Communist Party on the south side of Av. Paixinho, set back from the street, with azulejos of St. Anthony.

The 16th-century church of **Misericordia** flanks the east side of Pr. Repúbli-ca, a short block south of Delgado. With a nice doorway and *azulejos* facade, it faces an elegant 17th-century **Town Hall** opposite. Two blocks west runs a large, pleasant municipal park with an eccentric building overlooking a wood bridge over the pond. By following Rua da Grande Guerra south past the church front, the second left leads to the **Convent of Jesus**, housing a surprisingly good regional museum that stands opposite the Cathedral, separated by a fine Gothic cruizeiro (pillory).

Convento de Jesús and Museu de Aveiro   ★★

R. Santa Joana Princesa.
Hours open: Tues.–Sun. 10 a.m.–12:30 p.m. and 2–5 p.m. Closed Mon.

The convent and its church were built in the 15th century but decorated in the early 18th. The church interior contains some of the finest Baroque gilded work in Portugal, finding its apex in the vaulted front chancel.

At the end of the 15th century the city received Donha Joana, the young sister of King João II. She was a celebrated beauty who had captivated Louis XI of France and almost married Richard III of England, but had decided to give up this world to enter a convent in Aveiro. She devoted the last 18 years of her life to sewing hair shirts and was beatified for it. Scenes from the life of Saint Joana line the church walls. The choir contains the memorable tomb of this saint, one that required 12 years to manufacture as the intricacy of the polychrome marble mosaic demonstrates. Despite its complexity, it manages to be moving.

Installed in the cloisters and former convent, in rooms of great interest for their azulejos and painted ceilings, is a museum containing a mixed lot of sculpture, polychromed wood, crucifixes, furniture and Vista Alegre porcelain. Best are the primitive paintings, including a 15th-century portrait of Saint Joana which some attribute to the great Nuno Gonçalves. The survey of Baroque gilt is stunning. *Admission: 350$00.*

The closest beach is **Praia de Barra**, on the sandbank 13 km due west. Proximity to Aveiro makes it crowded, however, while other beaches remain secluded. Twenty-six km farther south along N-109 and then a 5 km run west on N-334 brings **Praia de Mira**, a most attractive beach livened by stilted houses. Here fishing boats are still hauled by teams of oxen. Northern beaches require circling the lagoon on N-109 to Estareja in 20 km, then turning west on N-109-5 to bridge over to **Torreira**, which is an attractive, upscale little resort bordering a fine beach. In fact one beach or another runs 13 km south beside pine forests to **São Jacinto** beach, opposite Aveiro. São Jacinto beach stretches long and flat, like our New Jersey shore, although the town is rather rundown. It can only be reached by road through this circle through Torreira, or by an Aveiro ferry.

Shopping

The Vista Alegre factory, museum and store are planted in the company town of Vista Alegre a mile south of the town of Ilhavo, which is 7 km south of Aveiro by N-109. The factory does not allow tours without special arrangements, but a quaint little museum depicting the development of this ware is open Tuesday through Friday from 9 a.m. until noon and from 2 p.m. until 4:30. The adjoining store, open weekdays from 9 a.m. until 6 p.m., offers a fine selection that includes pieces not seen elsewhere. It charges about the same prices as other outlets in Portugal, although about 20 percent less than in the United States *(Lugar da Vista Alegre, 3830 Ilhavo; ☎ 034 32 23 65.)*

Excursions

Coimbra ★★ with a fine museum, churches and university stands 50 odd km south off the autoestrada. **Porto ★★** waits 53 km north at the end of that same highway.

POUSADA DE MONSANTO

Rua da Capela, 1, Monsanto, 6085
☎ *(077) 344 71, FAX (077) 344 81*
$85 per double; 10 rooms: 10 doubles

★ ★ ★

Salazar awarded this village the prize as the most charming city in Portugal. In this case the dictator's taste is not too far wrong. Mammoth boulders perch precariously on the steep side of the hill to which Monsanto clings. Granite houses tumble down the hill, seeming almost to be boulders too. The tiny parador is located in the center of the village, reached by a series of narrow turns. It is a simple structure made of granite blocks that blends well with the old townhouses. Decoration is supplied by colorful embroidered wall hangings from Castelo Branco and Portalegre. Guest rooms are plain but adequate.

Dining

The intimate dining room is on the second floor with a wall of windows to take in the town and countryside. Both the pork soup *(sopa da matança)* and bean soup with coriander *(sopa de favas com coentros)* are hearty. Veal stew *(vitela estufada com ervas)* and a stew of veal, sausage and rice *(panela no forno)* can be recommended. Try the different cheesecake *(tigelada de requeijão)* for dessert. Set-course meals begin at $20.

Directions

From **Lisbon** take the autoestrada A-1 north for 81 km to exit 7, then IP-6
east for 48 km to Abrantes where N-118 is entered. Go east on N-118 for 44
km to join IP-2 north to **Castelo Branco** in 65 km. Take N-233 north for 25
km to São Miguel de Acha, then N-239 east for 20 km and look for a sign to
turn right. From **Évora** take N-18 north for 46 km to **Estremoz**, then continue for 163 km to Castelo Branco and follow the directions above.

Pousadas Nearby

Alameida: 119 km	Manteigas: 130 km
Marvão: 160 km	Castelo de Bode: 190 km

Sights

There is little to do but amble to the castle for a destination. It was built in
the 12th century, but a munitions explosion in the 19th century blew its top.
Today it is a romantic ruin of granite walls and stairs, covered in lichen, but
strewn with flowers in spring. The view extends for miles.

Excursions

The string of medieval border **fortresses** described in the Almeida section
are anchored by Monsanto in the south. Reverse the directions to visit them
from here.

Pousada de
Nossa Senhora da Oliveira

Rua Santa Maria, Guimarães, 4800
☎ *(053) 51 41 57, FAX (053) 51 42 04*
$100 per double; 16 rooms: 10 doubles, 6 suites
★ ★ ★ ★

If two pousadas served the same town one would hope for a difference in what each offered. This one is for city mice. It is constructed from a block of 16th-century townhouses, now joined by interior corridors, so it has the feel of an old village inn. Best of all, it is located at the corner of a very pretty square, right in the heart of town. Were it not for the "other" pousada in the neighborhood, this one would get high marks for its charm and historic flavor. But it has no chance against the grandeur of its sister the Santa Marinha.

Dining

Dim yet busily festive, this is a popular place to eat although the food is nothing special. Cabbage soup *(caldo verde)* is decent, as is the grilled trout *(truta grelhada)* and braised duck *(pato no forno)*, if not overdone. Save room for a creme caramel *(leite creme queimado)*, although we could do without the pine nuts. Go for a Vinho verde, if a white wine is in order, or a Dão otherwise. Set-course meals start at about $20.

Directions

From **Lisbon** take the autoestrada A-1 north for 297 km to Porto. From **Porto** take A-3 north for 34 km to join A-7 west for 21 km.

Pousadas Nearby

Amarante: 50 km	Caniçada: 58 km	Viana do Castilo: 71 km
Valença: 93 km	Vila Nova: 96 km	Alijó: 110 km

POUSADA DE SANTA BÁRBARA

Estrada N-17, Póvoa das Quartas, 3400
☎ *(038) 596 52, FAX (038) 596 45*
$100 per double; 16 rooms: 16 doubles

★ ★ ★ ★

This is an attractive, well-managed hotel, nestled amid the pines. The question is why anyone would stay here. True, it presents a lovely view of the mountains of the Estrela range, but the pousada at Manteigas, only 25 miles away, sits atop the same mountains you would look at, with even more spectacular views. Nor is this hotel sited for a convenient rest-stop on the way to somewhere else or near especially appealing sights. In any case, it provides views and quiet, a pool and tennis court. The modern design almost works; guest rooms are ample with terraces for the mountain views.

Dining

A dining room attractively set looks out on the same lovely mountains. The food is about average for pousadas. If you have stayed at a few, you will notice few surprises on the menu. There is a nice liver done with an onion marinade *(imperador de cebolada)*, eggs are added to the tomato soup and veal is covered with a cream sauce *(bifinhos de vitela com natas)*. Set-course meals cost about $20.

Directions

From **Lisbon** take the autoestrada A-1 north for 158 km to exit 11 for **Coimbra**. Circle the southern half of the city to pick up N-17, first going south then east for 85 km. From **Porto** take the autoestrada A-1 south for 103 km to the north Coimbra exit. Join IP-3 going east 39 km to pick up IC-7 for 12 km just to reach N-17 going east. Stay on N-17 for 58 km.

Pousadas Nearby

Manteigas: 56 km	Caramulo: 69 km	Condeixa: 94 km
Sérem: 117 km	Almeida: 133 km	Aveiro: 174 km

Excursions

The museums of **Viseu** ★★, discussed in the Caramulo entry, are 11 km north along N-17, then 40 km north along N-231. The many delights of **Coimbra** ★★, discussed under the Condeixa heading, are 84 km southwest along N-17.

POUSADA DE SANTA CATARINA

Estrada de Barragem, Miranda do Douro, 5210
☎ *(073) 410 05, FAX (073) 410 65*
$85 per double; 12 rooms: 11 doubles, 1 suite

★ ★ ★

This is another of those former houses by a dam built for engineers and later turned into a pousada. This time it was a joint Portuguese-Spanish project so the house is larger and fancier. The question is why would anyone travel the distance to come here? True, there is a nice view of the dam and lake from the lofty perch of the pousada, but the surrounding terrain is poor scrub and there are no sights nearby. There is little to do but sit on one of several verandas and stare at the water until it is time to move on.

Dining

Pity the chef who has few mouths to feed and no near source of supplies. He does what he can. Melon with prosciutto *(melão com presunto)* or cabbage soup *(caldas verde)* are acceptable starters. After that, codfish with olives *(bacalhau à Monteteso)* of braised kid *(cabrito assado)* are your best options. Set-course meal start at $20.

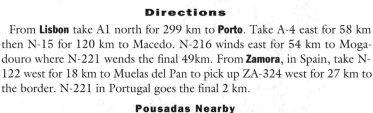

Directions

From **Lisbon** take A1 north for 299 km to **Porto**. Take A-4 east for 58 km then N-15 for 120 km to Macedo. N-216 winds east for 54 km to Mogadouro where N-221 wends the final 49km. From **Zamora**, in Spain, take N-122 west for 18 km to Muelas del Pan to pick up ZA-324 west for 27 km to the border. N-221 in Portugal goes the final 2 km.

Pousadas Nearby

Bragança: 82 km   Alijó: 135 km   Almeida: 157 km

Excursions

Bragança, described under its own heading, is 62 km north on N-218 then 20 km west in IP-4.

POUSADA DE SANTA CRISTINA

Condeixa-a-Nova, 3150
(039) 94 40 25, FAX (039) 94 30 97
$100 per double; 45 rooms: 45 doubles

★ ★ ★ ★

This pousada is lovely and a hub for a multitude of things to see and do. It also serves as a comfortable rest-stop on the way from Lisbon to the north. Altogether, it offers a great deal. The Santa Cristina is new, erected on the substantial plot of a former mansion, and decorated with molding and furniture saved both from the original mansion and from a house of the same owner in Lisbon that burned. Remodeling produced a lovely light-and-airy effect saved from any coldness by the older touches. This is among the most pleasant and comfortable of the pousadas, and graced by a young, attentive and enthusiastic management. There is even a pool and a tennis court in a pleasant rear garden.

Alternative Accommodations

Palace Hotel of Buçaco   ★ ★

Foresta do Buçaco, ☎ *(031) 93 01 01, FAX 93 05 09). 62 rooms.*
One of Portugal's most famous hotels resides in the nearby forest of Buçaco, the Palace Hotel of Buçaco. It is not our favorite by a long shot, although forest elves seems to have affected other travel writers who are unanimous in their praise. Viewed more soberly, the hotel is eerie, with overtones of *The Shining*. Of course its effect depends very much on the person, but one thing we feel confident about is that no one would consider the food very good or the service gracious. The bedrooms are a mixed lot that vary enormously in size. Some are impressive, but most would be at home in an institution, and an old one at that. With all our complaints

it must be acknowledged that this is an unusual hotel, for former royal residences do not accept most of us as guests. Some of the decoration is remarkable, and the setting is quiet and sylvan. It is very expensive at the 30,000$00 level, but with fixed-price meals that are more moderate in cost. We can only hope that the new management may correct some of the problems.

Nearby Coimbra, a largish city, should have some nice accommodations. Unfortunately, there is only one wonderful hotel, that costs about $125, and two more ordinary recommendations, both in the $75 range.

Quinta das Lágrimas ★★★

Santa Clara, Coimbra (☎ 44 16 15, FAX 44 16 95). 35 rooms.
The Quinta das Lágrimas used to be one of Coimbra's tourist sights, now it has just opened as the one grand hotel in town. It is an 18th century palace on substantial lovely grounds and is deluxe through and through. Located in Santa Clara, across the river from the main city, just off N-110-2.

Astória ★★

Av. Emidio Navarro, 21, Coimbra (on the avenue that parallels the river, just north of the bridge), (☎ 220 55, FAX 220 57, Telex 42859).64 rooms.
The Astória is a 1920s hotel with the froufrou of the era to lend individuality and interest is in fine repair and holds comfortable bedrooms. It exhibits the most character of any Coimbra hotel.

Dom Luís ★★

Quinta da Verzea, Coimbra (on N-1 to Lisbon, 2.5 km south of town),
Otherwise, there is the Dom Luís, Coimbra's newest hotel and most stylish. It's about a mile outside the city, but offers views and quiet.

Dining

The kitchen stands up to the high standards of the hotel. Cream of tomato soup *(creme de tomate)*, cream of spinach *(creme de espinafres)* or a hearty bean soup *(sopa de feijõ)* nicely whet the appetite. Then there is a choice to be made between kid en croute *(cabrito assado com migas de grelos)*, fresh salmon with capers *(truta salmonada com alcaperras)*, roast hen with pepper sauce *(gilinha assada com molho do leitão)* or grilled codfish with olive oil *(tibornada de bacalhau)*. The local Bairrada wines are exceptionally pleasant. Set-course meals begin at about $20.

Alternative Dining

Ramalhão ★★★★

R. Tenente Valadim, 24, in Montemor-o-velho (Montemor is 29 km west of Coimbra, just off N-111, the road to Figueira da Foz), *68 94 35. Closed Sunday night, Monday and October.*

Here is one of the great restaurant finds in Portugal, and it is appropriately difficult to locate. Take a right off the Montemor main square. About a hundred yards along this road, with the backs of houses on the right side, look very closely for a tiny, dimly-lit sign on one rear fence. (There is a more visible entrance on Tenete Valadim, but it is difficult to drive up this street or park when you arrive). Inside, the restaurant is as cozy as can be and always full, because those in the know return again and again. They realize that this place serves the most elevated of truly authentic Portuguese cooking. The food is by no means fancy, sauces are seldom employed, but the combinations are those the Portuguese developed over the ages. Many will find the dishes somewhat dry and too lightly seasoned, but everyone will discover new tastes. From some seats you can look past the bar into the improbably small kitchen to spot the two venerable women who produce the meals. They instill absolute confidence. Dishes change daily, so it makes little sense to go with any special dish in mind. Put yourselves in Sr. Ramalhão's hands and relax, for he is a most enchanting owner. A meal can cost up to $50, but is worth it. Reserve to prevent disappointment. Credit Cards: M, V.

Zé Manuel   ★★

Beco do Forno, 12 (a little street behind the Hotel Astória). ☎ *237 90.*

Don't be put off by the unassuming entrance, or even by the less-assuming inside with walls plastered in notes and papers, plain wood furniture set around, and an open kitchen in view. The customers come for the food, not the decor, and the upstairs is a bit nicer. The *sopa da pedra* is hearty and the *açorda de mariscos* as good as it gets, but almost any dish will please, especially at prices that should not top $15.

Pedro dos Leitões   ★★

On N-1 in the village of Mealhada, 21 km north of Coimbra. ☎ *220 62.*

This little village is the roast suckling pig center for the country. Restaurants line the road, all announcing *leitao assado*. This particular large establishment is generally mobbed for lunch. It roasts the little critters over glowing coals, pricing the pig by weight, so you can satisfy either a large or small appetite for a pittance. Credit Cards: V.

Directions

After the turn off of N-1 or A-1, keep left at the main square in Condeixa, for about 1 km.

Pousadas Nearby

Batalha: 63 km	Castelo de Bode: 82 km	Sérem: 86 km
Póvoa das Quartas: 89 km	Óbidos: 116 km	Marvão: 194 km

Sights

Near Condeixa stands Portugal's best preserved Roman city, Conímbriga.

Conímbriga ★ ★

Hours open: daily 10 a.m.–1 p.m. and 2–8 p.m.; until 6 p.m. in winter. The museum opens at 10 a.m. and closes at 6 p.m.; closed Mon. in winter.

A sign in the Condeixa town square, one block after the turn off N-1, directs to a 2 km run on N-347 at which point a sign on the right points to the ruins.

Originally, Conímbriga lay on the main road between the two large Roman centers of Braccaria (modern Braga) and Olissipo (now Lisbon), and prospered from passing traders and the good farmland surrounding it. The city was founded in the first century, or a little before, but artifacts dug from the site show that Celts preceded the Romans by as much as 900 years. The city's heyday came in the third century A.D. when huge villas were constructed, the largest so far unearthed from the Roman world. By the end of that century, fear of barbarians caused a defensive wall to be built around the town that consumed parts of these splendid villas for building material. By the fifth century the town had fallen to the Swabians and was gradually abandoned thereafter. This exodus accounts for the preservation of the remains, for there has been no construction on the site since. Excavation began almost 100 years ago, although so far only about one-third of the site has been dug and the most important city monuments have just recently been made available to the public.

Start in the museum, whose maps, maquettes and artifacts provide some orientation and a sense of what will be seen. The entrance to the ruins passes the **House of the Fountains ★** on the right, named for the unusually large pond in the center with provisions for water jets. Fine mosaics cover the floors, including hunting scenes and a chariot drawn by four horses. Through the city gates and to the right is the **House of Cantaber**, one of the largest homes known from the Roman world. There are several pools and, at the rear, private baths, a great luxury in this era of public bathing. The path continues to the city forum, donated by the emperor Flavian. Other remains are difficult to decipher, but lovely mosaics reward the intrepid explorer. *Admission: 300$00 (200$00 in winter).*

Excursions

Coimbra, Portugal's third-largest city, tumbles down a steep riverbank by the gently flowing Mondego river. The city is situated midway between Lisbon and Porto, making it a convenient stop along the way. To encourage visits, the city offers a fine museum, and a regal university quarter, plus mansions, monasteries and churches, including the most imposing Romanesque church in the country. Portugal's most extensive Roman remains stand nearby at **Conímbriga** (see above), while the enchanted forest of **Buçaco** and a vast beach at **Figueira da Foz** both lie less than an hour distant.

Coimbra ★ ★ ★

Although Coimbra has been occupied since Roman times, in its earliest days it was an insignificant appendage of nearby Conímbriga, the administrative seat of a Roman province. But when repeated sackings—first by barbarian Swabians, then by Moors—caused Conímbriga to be abandoned in the ninth century, many of its remaining citizens fled to Coimbra, making it a kind of descendant of the abandoned Roman town. Even Coimbra's name is probably a corruption of "Conímbriga."

When he assumed his crown in 1139, Afonso I, Portugal's first king, chose Coimbra—then the largest city in Christian hands—as his capital. It remained the seat of the government for two centuries, breeding the first six kings after Afonso, until the court moved permanently to Lisbon in 1255. Portugal's original university was established in Coimbra in 1308. Later it, too, moved to Lisbon, but complaints about boisterous students sent it back to Coimbra again, where it remains to dominate the town both literally, high on the hill, and figuratively, as the major institution in the city.

The city divides into three parts. Above the east bank stands the university quarter—the Velha Alta, site of the medieval city; at its feet lies the Baixa, or lower town; and, lastly, on the west bank of the river sprawls the newer town, which retains some old monasteries and churches that originally stood outside the medieval city. We divide our discussion of the sights into those on the Velha Alta hill, which include most of what is noteworthy, and those located elsewhere. We suggest starting with the university, as walking downhill is always easier.

Parking is a problem in Coimbra. Two options exist. From **Lisbon** Coimbra is entered on the east bank of the river. The road runs to the Ponte Santa Clara, which crosses to the west bank. Turn left along Av. Emidio Navarro, with a divided center on which parking may be possible. If full, continue to the plaza in front of the train station, where the avenue ends. Turn right there through the Largo das Ameias, then take the first left along

Av. Fernão de Magalhães. Parking is often available in two blocks in a large square on the right. From **Porto**, by continuing straight, one travels along Av. Fernão de Magalhães. After passing through the large plaza of Largo do Arnado, bear right to continue on Av. Magalhães, and parking should be available in the large park on the left in three blocks. If full, continue along Av. Magalhães for two more blocks where it ends at the Largo das Ameias. Turn right, then take the next left along Av. Emidio Navarro, where parking often is available in the center divider.

Climb or taxi up the Velha Alta hill, then walk down. Begin at the Porta Ferrea of the Velha Universidade (Old University). Ask the taxi to stop in the Pr. Dom Dinis, then turn west between two colleges.

Velha Universidade ★ ★ ★

Hours open: times of buildings are different and change with the university year, and some require small admission charges, but the hours from 10 a.m. to noon and 2-5 p.m. will generally find everything open.

During its first two centuries of existence, the university passed between Coimbra and Lisbon, but settled here for good in 1537 under orders from King João III. Before that time, only degrees for priests were conferred and the caliber of the education was mediocre by any standard. Dom João, determined to raise the quality, first donated his Coimbra palace to house the university magnificently, then hired Andre de Resende from the University of Paris to whip the faculty into shape. In his inaugural address the new rector accused the faculty of gross ignorance and sloth. Continuing his quest for excellence, the king offered impressive stipends to attract scholars of international repute, including Erasmus. Although that renowned scholar declined, other fine academicians accepted, lifting the caliber of instruction. A school of liberal arts was established, expanding the student population beyond prospective clergy, and soon after a college of law was inaugurated, followed by a college of pharmacy.

By the end of the 16th century, about 1500 students, mostly non-cleric, were in residence and the reputation of the university ranked with the very best in Europe. Although the institution was to suffer ups and downs over the following centuries— at times even selling degrees for a fee—today, with an enrollment of almost 15,000 students, it stands again as the premier Portuguese institute of higher learning. Famous residents have included Luis Vas de Camões, Portugal's greatest poet; Saint Anthony of Padua; and Dr. António Salazar, who served as a professor of economics before taking on the job of Portugal's dictator. Today some students still wear the traditional uniform of black capes with ribbons on the sleeve to indicate their college. Light blue indicates science; darker blue, liberal arts; violet, pharmacy; yellow, medicine; and red, law. Students in their final year sport wider ribbons than underclassmen.

This is the only university in the world lodged in a king's palace, the part entered through the 17th century **Porta Ferrea** (Iron Gate). Here the grey **Patio das Escolas** presents the most interesting buildings of the university, which today mainly house the law school. In the center stands a **statue of João III**, who donated all this. Naturally, his palace was much altered for educational purposes.

NORTHERN PORTUGAL

To the left is São Pedro College, a 16th-century addition, in which the royal family once stayed when visiting the university and where college rectors live today. To the right, facing the open end of the "patio," an imposing gallery, the **Via Latina**, is appended to the front of the original palace. Called the "Latin Way" because only Latin could be spoken here in earlier times, stairs ascend to the gallery, inside of which, a door to the left marked "reitoria" leads into the **Sala dos Capelos**. Before remodeling this was the throne room of the palace. Portraits of kings of the first two dynasties look down on the university ceremonies that take place here today. Overhead hovers a most remarkable painted ceiling. To the left of this hall is the sumptuous **Sala do Exame Privado,** featuring portraits of former rectors below a brilliant ceiling. It is hard to imagine focusing on an exam in such a room.

Returning to the courtyard and continuing counterclockwise leads to the clumsy clock tower in the corner. It summoned students to their classes and earned one frequently rung bell the name "The Goat." Continuing, a part of the former palace is passed, at whose approximate center is a fine Manueline portal leading into a corridor on whose left is the **University Chapel**. Tickets for admission (250$00) to the chapel and library (farther along) are available in the bookstore down this corridor.

The chapel ceiling is painted, *azulejos* line its walls, but its most impressive feature is an 18th-century organ, a fantasy of gilded wood. Over all, the chapel is a complex of bright pattern on pattern.

Outside, and farther along, waits the Baroque entrance to the **library**. (If the door is closed, ring the bell.) It was a gift from King João V in 1724. You can guess whose coat-of-arms is blazoned over the door. There is no library in the world that can compare with its always ornate, sometimes elegant, finely crafted Baroque decoration that covers every surface. It simply must be seen. At the library's end glowers a portrait of its royal donor encased in the most ornate frame imaginable. All three rooms are awesome, making one wonder how readers surrounded by such visual stimulation could concentrate.

Proceed back through the Porta Ferrea, through its plaza, then left (north) along Rua de Miranda, which passes between several colleges of the university to open up into the large Largo da Feira, down a flight of stairs. Nestled between university buildings on the north side of the square is the **Se Nova** (New Cathedral). To the left of the square is the former **bishop's palace** and the church of **São João de Almedina**, both built in the 12th century, although the bishop's palace was modified in the 16th. Today the palace houses the excellent **Museu Machado de Castro**. Note the **Moorish tower** by the entrance.

Museu Machado de Castro   ★ ★

Largo Dr. José Rodrigues, ☎ *237 27.*
Hours open: Tues.–Sun. 10 a.m.–12:30 p.m. and 2–5 p.m. Closed Mon. Admission: 500$00.

This museum displays the best collection of native sculpture in the country, and some fine painting and objets d'art in a building that add its own interest.

The collection begins to the right side of the entry courtyard with early sculpture. A Visigoth angel hovers charmingly. Resting his mace on his shoulder, a mounted knight in limestone is outstanding both as a composition and as a rare secular work from the Gothic era. Besides, it's adorable. More 15th-century work follows, of which an assemblage of three knights in mail at the Sepulcher, and a pregnant Virgin by Master Pero stand out.

In the 16th century Coimbra became the artistic center of Portugal by enticing Nicolas Chanterene, Jean de Rouen (Ruão) and Philippe Houdart (Hodart) from France. Here they were joined by the Portuguese Castilho brothers—João and Diogo. Their sophisticated work betrays a strong Italian influence, and is of the highest quality. Among other things, what attracted them to Coimbra was easily worked fine white limestone from nearby Ança. They initiated Renaissance sculpture in Portugal and are responsible for most of the fine Manueline carving throughout the country. The museum displays an admirable assemblage of their work. See Chanterene's *Virgin Reading*, Rouen's *Entombment* and Houdart's *Paschal Feast*. By the 17th century, wood replaced stone as the medium of choice and, with a few exceptions, the quality of sculpture declined.

The ceilings on the second floor deserve as much attention as the exhibits. A representative display of Coimbra pottery shows its development from the 17th century on. The best paintings are in two rooms devoted to Renaissance religious works by Portuguese and Flemish artists. Quentin Matsys is always interesting, and, on the Portuguese side, there are compelling works by the Master of Sardobal (or his school), the Master of Santa Clara and three sensitive paintings by Josefa de Óbidos.

The basement is formed of the remains of an eerie Roman cryptoporticus, a two-story platform (the lower story of which is closed) that once elevated a Roman forum that stood on this site. Today Roman and Visigothic artifacts are displayed in the nooks and crannies of this creepy structure.

Walk around the river end of the museum along Rua de Borges Carneiro, which winds in a block to the Old Cathedral.

Se Velha ★★

Largo da Sé Velha, ☎ *252 73.*
Hours open: daily 9:30 a.m.–12:30 p.m. and 2–7 p.m.
This church was erected when Coimbra first became the capital of Portugal in the 12th century. That the town did not yet feel safe from the Moors is evidenced by the fortress facade of the church, complete with merlons on top. Overall it's the most imposing Romanesque church in the country. The main facade (west) is pure Romanesque; the later, now crumbling, north portal is one of the first constructed in a Renaissance style, and the apse includes a rare and lovely Romanesque gallery.

The interior is awesome. Here the second and third kings of Portugal were anointed. The fine Gothic retable of the Assumption of the Virgin rising above the four Evangelists was carved by two Flemings. Its surrounding foliage contains charming figures, including a pig playing the bagpipe. The chapel in the south transept (to the right) holds a semicircular retable by a member of the Coimbra school, and the chapel of São Pedro to the left, lined by nice *azulejos*, presents a crumbling retable of the life of Saint Peter by Jean de Rouen.

Cloisters lie through the first door in the south aisle, and up. These are very early, 13th-century Gothic, although the bays are filled with tracery as would become the style two centuries later. In the first chapel on the left stands a fine font carved by Jean de Rouen. The chapterhouse holds the tomb of Dom Sisnando, the first Christian governor of Coimbra after its reconquest. There are indications that he was of Moorish blood. *Admission: 150$00 to the cloister.*

Descend the stairs of Escades de Quebra-Costas opposite the Cathedral front, and take an immediate right along the narrow Rua de Sobre-Ripas to reach two mansions standing across from each other. On the left side of the lane is the 16th-century **Casa Sub-Ripas**, privately owned, with a Manueline doorway; on the right side is the **Casa do Arco**. In a few steps farther, the lane passes beneath an arch to reach the **Torre do Anto**, remaining from the old city walls. Today it houses the Coimbra Regional Handcraft Center, an extensive display of local crafts. As it is an artists' cooperative, the pieces are for sale as well as for looking. Return to the beginning of the lane again to head down across the little square for a right turn through the **Almedina gate**, surmounted by a tower. This gate is 12th century, part of the medieval city walls, and still bearing the Moorish name of "The City." After angling left, a cross street is reached. Turn right onto the main shopping street of Coimbra, Rua Visconde da Luz, to reach the open Pr. 8 de Maio in a few blocks and the **Mosteiro de Santa Cruz**, in a building half of which now is occupied by the town hall. This is the lower town (Baixa). Behind the Mosteiro, east, is a fine open Pr. do Comércio surrounded by townhouses and shops. São Tiago from the 12th century, in the northwest corner, has a nice timber ceiling.

Mosteiro de Santa Cruz ★★

Pr. 8 de Maio, ☎ 229 41.
Hours open: daily from 9 a.m.–noon and from 2 p.m.–6:30 p.m.

The original monastery, built in 1131 before Portugal had a king, preceded even the Old Cathedral. Portugal's first two monarchs—Dom Afonso I and his son Dom Sancho I—were buried here. However, the church needed major renovations by the beginning of the 16th century, and the result of that rebuilding is what one sees today. As the burial place for the first kings, this church held a special place in royal hearts, so, although small, it is richly endowed with art. It was in this church that King Pedro forced the courtiers of Portugal to kiss the skeletal hand of his deceased love Inês.

The present church facade was designed by Diogo de Castilho and decorated with statuary by Jean de Rouen and Nicholas Chanterene. These three were the shining lights of a special assembly of artists who gathered in Coimbra early in the 16th century and were responsible for much that is wonderful in Manueline art. Sadly, the stone has weathered badly, and what remains is spoiled by an 18th-century doorway, so it is difficult to appreciate what should have been a seminal piece of architecture.

Fortunately, there is no problem with deterioration inside. A Manueline ceiling covers a nave lined with *azulejos*. The octagonal pulpit is an extraordinary piece of carving, probably by Nicholas Chanterene. On either side of the altar lie the tombs of Kings Afonso I, the first King of Portugal, and his son, Sancho I, left and right, respectively. Originally, they had been buried in the courtyard in front of the church, but were disinterred and installed in these tombs early in the 16th century. It is thought that Diogo de Castilho designed the anachronistic Gothic tombs and that Chanterene did the carving.

Left of the altar is the entrance to the sacristy. Some of the paintings are worth attention, but the period furniture is more interesting. The cloister is unusually simple Manueline, with bas relief for the most part instead of the usual high relief. Stairs lead up to the *coro alto*, which contains choir stalls carved and gilded along the top. The work is superior. *Admission: 150$00 to the sacristy and cloister.*

Buçaco ★★

From **Lisbon** take A-1 north for two exits past Coimbra to Mealhada in 199 km. Head east for Luso on N-234 for 7 km. Signs direct to the forest entrance. From **Porto** take the A-1 south for 84 km to the Mealhada exit and follow the directions above. From **Coimbra** follow the river road, Av. Emidio Navarro, to take a right through the plaza, Largo das Ameias, in front of the train station. Turn left at its end onto Av. Fernão de Magalhães, which connects with N-1 going north to Porto. At Mealhada, the suckling pig capital, in 21 km turn east onto N-234 which reaches Luso in 7 km.

Five **buses** daily stop at Buçaco on their way to Viseu. The last bus from Buçaco leaves at 6:45 p.m.

Buçaco Forest ★★

Follow signs to the forest entrance.

Buçaco National Forest crowns a peak of the Serra do Buçaco. Something is enchanted about its lovely waterways interspersed with palms, its ancient trees and vales of ferns. Monks thought so, and chose the forest for their solitary contemplations as early as the sixth century. Popes thought so, and from far away Italy forbade women to enter the forest, while decreeing excommunication to anyone damaging a tree. Kings thought so, and supported royal hunting lodges on its grounds for centuries, before erecting a final royal retreat in 1910. There is nothing to do except walk—cars aren't allowed—and little to observe except nature, which, if the season is right, will overpower with mimosas, camellias, magnolias, hydrangeas and lilies-of-the-valley.

True, there is the odd little chapel to come upon unexpectedly, and also, smack in the center, a gingerbread confection of a former royal palace, designed by an Italian who had worked on theater sets. It seems the king wanted a Manueline building three centuries after the style had become passe, so he was given a stage set. This fantasy of Renaissance times is a truly strange place to wander through and spend a day in, which one can. It now serves as a hotel for 60 guests who reserve months in advance.

The tourable forest, landscaped to suggest nature, extends only about half a mile by a quarter of a mile wide, although there are some steep hills. Several walking trails are laid out, the best entered off the far side of the Palácio Hotel past a small 17th century monastery where a sign points to the "Fonta Fria." This "fountain," more a series of pools and cascades, leads down to a lake, then through a fern valley. All is still, dark and ferny as the trail leads past almost 700 different species of tree. Here and there are remains of stone hermit huts, just large enough to lie in.

Figueira da Foz ★

Follow Coimbra's river road, Av. Emidio Navarro, to take a right through the plaza in front of the train station, Largo das Ameias. Turn left at its end onto Av. Fernão de Magalhães, which connects with N-1 going north to Porto. In just a kilometer or two look for the turn onto N-111 west, which reaches Figueira in 45 km. About half way, the romantic ruins of the **castle of Montemor-o-Velho** are passed.

Figueira da Foz is one of the most popular resorts in Portugal, but mainly with the Portuguese and Spanish, rather than we non-Iberians who have yet to make its discovery. Its appeal is a huge two-mile-long beach of impressive depth. There is little to do but walk, swim and bask, although the village is prosperous and attractive. A **casino** housed in a former palace opens in the afternoon. At the northern end of the beach, two miles away, reposes the almost unspoiled fishing village of **Buarcos ★**.

Shopping

Condeixa is the outlet for all the charming blue-and-white and polychrome ceramics seen throughout Portugal that copy 17th- and 18th-century pieces. Most factories are located in the Zona Industrial, which is the first left after the Condeixa main square. Another factory is located immediately left after the turn from N-1 at the light for Condeixa. These factories are not set up to sell to retail customers, but they will anyway and wrap and ship. The issue is what you will find for sale, for most of what is on hand is ear-marked for orders. Alternatively, take N-347, the road to Conímbriga, as a sign in the square directs. After about 1 km there will be a sign for two Artessanados, one on the left, another on the right. Both display a good selection, much of which they have painted themselves. At these shops and at the factories the lack of a common language should present no difficulty.

POUSADA DE SANTA MARIA

Marvão, 7330
☎ *(045) 932 01, FAX (045) 934 40*
$100 per double; 29 rooms: 28 doubles, 1 suite

★ ★ ★

Portugal has a surplus of fairy tale hilltop villages surrounded by medieval walls commanded by ancient castles. Excursions from Almeida in this chapter cover ten such sites, and an equal number more could have been added. However, everyone agrees that Marvão is the most charming of the lot—the one to see, if seeing just one. Best of all, it contains a pousada smack in the center of the tiny village. Three old townhouses were joined to create this hotel. Its comfortable decor and spectacular views make it one of the nicer places to stay in Portugal. There is no attempt at elegance or grandeur, just cozy relaxation, including wood fires when there's a chill in the air.

Alternative Accommodations

Estalagem Dom Dénis

Rua Dr. Matos Magalhães, ☎ *932 36. 7 rooms.*
The Estalagem Dom Dénis is a quiet, inviting place, with comfortably solid furnishings. A cheerful reception sets just the right tone and a stay costs only $50.

Dining

The restaurant is set on the roof inside a wall of glass for views so lovely that the food may be forgotten. Start with a most unusual soup of goat and giblets *(sarapatel de cabrito)* or a truly tasty tomato soup *(sopa de tomate).* Clams with coriander sauce *(ameljoas com molho de coentros)* make a nice appetizer. Then you should be ready for roast lamb *(borrego assado)* or kid stew *(cabrito guisado)*. Local wines from Portalegre are fine values. Set-course meal begins at about $20.

Directions

From **Lisbon** go north along the autoestrada for 112 km to exit 7 for Entroncamento. Follow signs for Entroncamento and N-3 east. Continue on N-3 east for 40 km to little Rossio, where N-118 is picked up. In 59 km Alpalhão is reached. Take N-246 east to Castelo de Vide in 14 km. There N-246-1 goes southeast to Portagem in 9 km for a turn north on N-359 for 4 km. From **Évora** take N-18 north, through **Estremoz**, for 105 km to Portalegre. Outside that city N-359 twists through mountains to Portagem in 17 km. Marvão is 4 km farther north on N-359. From **Coimbra** get to exit 7 for Entroncamento on the autoestrada A-1, 112 km south of Coimbra. From there the Lisbon directions apply.

Pousadas Nearby

Portalegre: 17 km	Flora de Rosa: 40 km	Estremoz: 76 km
Sousel: 80 km	Elvas: 115 km	Évora: 122 km

Sights

Marvão exudes a calming atmosphere and shows prettiness at every hand, but there is not much else to see in the tiny village butted against the eastern border with Spain. Sufficient variety in nearby excursions, however, justifies a stay overnight.

Since we are more accustomed to villages nestling in valleys, the initial sight of Marvão is surprising—perched atop a steep hill with houses seeming to strain to reach even higher. The reason, of course, was for defense. The village castle was raised at the close of the 13th century and surrounded by curtain walls. A second wall was added to envelop the whole in the 17th century.

From the access road—that circles all arrivals around the peak—the village seems utterly impregnable. And so it has proven to be. Dazzlingly white-washed houses, sporting orange tile roofs, cling to the walls. Hardly any are newer than the 17th century, so a walk through the cobbled street to the castle is hardly different today than it would have been three centuries ago, save for the odd TV aerial and telephone wire.

Rua do Espirito Sant leads to the castle, past handsome wrought-iron balconies. Four successive fortified gates must be passed to reach the fortress, which essentially consists of one massive keep. On a clear day the view from the walls is as fine as any in the country—looking east one sees Spain, a mere five miles away. Next to the castle stands a white chapel that serves both the **Office of Tourism** and the **Museu Municipal**, whose most interesting exhibits are mannequins in local costumes. *(Open daily 9 a.m. to 12:30 p.m. and 2-5:30 p.m. Admission: 200$00.)* The Office of Tourism maintains a list of inexpensive bed-and-breakfast rooms or even small houses rented by the locals.

After walking the town, consider a drive north, following signs for Santo António das Areias for several dozen prehistoric dolmens peacefully reposing in a sylvan chestnut grove.

Excursions

Past **Portalegre**, famed for tapestry, is the intriguing Knights' Templar monastery of **Flor de Rosa ★**, an outing of 36 km each way. Both are described under their own headings in this chapter.

Portalegre

Take N-359 southwest for 21 km. The road leads into Largo A. J. Lourinho. The tapestry workshop is one short block south and another east.

Flor da Rosa ★

After 2 km from Portalegre on N-18 toward Alpalhão, take N-119 west for 34 km to Crato. There take N-245 north for 3 km.

Castelo de Vide ★

From Marvão regain the highway N-246, south of the village. Go west for 11 km.

Standing even higher than Marvão, Castelo de Vide presents a similar picture of white-washed houses. The main square, **Praça Dom Pedro V**, is ringed with 17th-century buildings and an 18th-century mansion. Beside the church of Santa Maria in the square, a sign shows the way up to the castle. To the right is the **Judiaria**, the ancient Jewish quarter.

The Judiaria is a jumble of small houses, many with two entrances, one for business, the other for family. Houses are small and crowded together because an ordinance decreed that Jews had to live separately from Christians and be locked inside their quarters each night.

Uncharacteristically, the **castle** lies inside its own walls outside of the village. Its keep suffered damage from an explosion, but the 12th-century tower that leads to it is of interest. A 17th-century **church** on the site contains nice *azulejos*. Downhill from the Judiaria is a picturesque square, the **Fonte da Vila**, whose fountain waters are reputed to have curative value and certainly taste sweet.

Castelo Branco ★

From Marvão continue past Castelo da Vide on N-246 for 25 km to Alpalhão. There N-118 continues in the same direction for 15 km to join IP-6 going north for 65 km.

Head straight through the city along Av. 1 de Maio, which feeds into Rua de Se. Rua de Se bends left, then changes its name to Campo da Patria, as it climbs to the gardens of the former Bishop's palace.

The **gardens** of the former Episcopal Palace are a formal fantasy of clipped ornamental hedges, pools and unexpected statues, showing that those Bishops knew how to live. *(Open daily from 9 a.m. until 6 p.m.; admission: 150$00.)* To the left is the Episcopal Palace itself, with the **Museu Tavares Provença** installed inside *(Mon-Sat. from 10 a.m. until 12:30 and from 2 p.m. until 5:30; admission: 150$00)*. Its most interesting exhibits are a series of *colchas*, embroidered bedspreads, for which this town has been famous since the 16th century. They are linen, embroidered with brightly colored figures in large-stitched silk thread. Originally, young women made them for their trousseaux. At the workshop, adjacent to the museum, pieces may be bought or commissioned.

POUSADA DE SANTA MARINHA

Estrada da Penha, Guimarães, 4800
☎ *(053) 51 44 53, FAX (053) 51 44 59*
$125 per double; 51 rooms: 49 doubles, 2 suites

★ ★ ★ ★ ★

Do not judge this one by its whitewashed exterior suggesting a huge factory. Actually, it is a former convent, founded in the 12th century but completely restored in the 18th. Inside it is palatial, but even more impressive is its elegant taste. In fact it would be difficult to decide whether this or Rainha Santa Isabel in Estremoz is the most elegant of all the pousadas, but no question that this is the most imposing. The fortunate will stay at both. Hallways are high and wide enough to ride horses through, as happened in olden days, and tiled with luscious azulejos. You will never suspect that a terrible fire in 1951 destroyed much of the grand corridor, so skillfully has it been reconstructed. Bedrooms are formed from the original monks' cells, which you would not suspect either, for they are grand today. Some include canopied beds, far from a monk's original equipment. As this is the flagship of the entire pousada chain, the service is always on its efficient toes. Even the meals in a magnificent hall (hard to envision as the originally monastery's kitchen) are a treat. The only true surprise comes with the bill—the price of a room barely crosses the expensive line.

Dining

Huge, arched and pillared, the dining room is grand as it can be. The food cannot attain such elevation, but is a cut above that served at most pousadas. Scrambled eggs with sausage *(ovos mexidos com chouriço)*, prosciutto with figs *(presunto com figos)* or asparagus tart *(tarte de espargos)* make elegant appetizers. Roast veal with mushrooms *(vitela assada à vimaranense)*, trout meunière *(truta à Moleira)* or salmon with garlic *(salmão estufado com alho)* complete a nice meal. A delicate rice pudding, or your choice from the dessert cart, will top off the diner well. The wine list is extensive; your waiter will recommend a special bottle. Set-course meals begin at a reasonable $20.

Directions

In Guimarães, take N-101 east, the road to Penha, for 2 km where the pousada can be seen to the left.

Pousadas Nearby

Amarante: 50 km	Caniçada: 58 km	Viana do Castilo: 71 km
Valença: 93 km	Vila Nova: 96 km	Alijó: 110 km

Sights

Guimarães is Portugal's birthplace. Henri, second son of the Duke of Burgundy, came to Spain to help Alfonso VI battle the Moors and received the king's illegitimate daughter as his reward. When Henri and Teresa married in 1095 they were given the County of Portucale, as northern Portugal was then known, for a wedding present. At the time Guimarães was not even a village—only the site of a monastery—but the newlyweds took one of the monastery towers, fit it out as a noble's residence, and settled in. In that tower of Mumadona Monastery, their son Afonso was born in about 1110. After his father's death, he declared his territory independent from Spain and assumed the title of King of Portugal.

Today Guimarães thrives on weaving, cutlery manufacturing and tanning. Handwork still is practiced in the form of ox yokes, embroidery and linen damask. Industrial Guimarães surrounds the older sights, leaving the center attractive with squares, gardens and monuments. Parking is where one finds it, but should be available at the Paço dos Duques on the green hillside below the castle. Note that, in addition to the sights, a sufficient reason for visiting Guimarães is to spend the night in the magnificent *Pousada de Santa Marinha*, the flagship of the pousada chain.

From **Braga** Rua de São Gonçalo funnels into Rua de Gil Vicente, which bends left after passing the post office and receives the name Av. Henrique Delgado. Either the first or second right thereafter leads to the castle.

Castelo ★

Hours open: daily 10 a.m.–12:30 p.m. and 2-5 p.m.

First built in the 10th century, this castle is not only the oldest but among the most imposing in the country as well. Old walls of indeterminate great age surround a castle consisting of a massive keep amid seven towers of various heights. Each is topped by triangular merlons that make the whole look fierce. Originally there was but one tower, remodeled in the 11th century to serve as a palace in which Afonso I, the first king of Portugal, was born. Additions over the centuries greatly expanded that original; then the whole became a prison early in the 19th century. Soon after, the complex was abandoned and used as a quarry for public buildings throughout Guimarães. Prime Minister Salazar decided that this was one of the most historic buildings in the nation and, in 1940—recapturing as many of its stones as could be found—set about restoring it.

With so much alteration, it is no longer clear which tower was the original—the one in which the first king was born—or even if that tower still exists. Regardless, the monolithic complex is suitably awesome for a national monument, and its walls provide fine views. *Admission: free.*

Just outside the castle walls is the Romanesque chapel of **São Miguel** from the 12th century. Peering inside, a font can be seen from an earlier church that is said to be the one used to christen Afonso. The floor consists of early tombs of those who fought the Moors.

Below the grassy hill is the grey, fortresslike Palace of the Dukes of Bragança.

Paço dos Duques de Bragança ★★★

Hours open: daily 10 a.m.–5:30 p.m.

In about 1420 Don Afonso, an illegitimate son of the first king of the Avís line, constructed this huge manor house for himself and his wife. Later he would be named the first duke of the Bragança dynasty that grew powerful enough to rule Portugal in later times. The duke wanted a new palace because the castle on the hill was not modern enough for his needs, nor certainly for his bride-to-be Beatriz. For her he joined four buildings, each with a corner tower, to form a cloister in the center. The style is that of the late Gothic in Burgundy, since the duke, a diplomat who had traveled to northern Europe, employed a French architect. The large number of brick chimneys (39) was unusual and remains a striking feature, showing how important comfort was for owners. However, since some of the chimneys never functioned, ostentation must have figured prominently in the design.

The palace was abandoned in the 17th century and suffered horribly until Prime Minister Salazar ordered its repair in 1940, at the same time that the castle was receiving similar treatment. In the case of the palace, because Salazar intended to live in it, renovation—rather than restoration—was performed. The present structure, therefore, provides an interesting study of the difference between fixing the old without depriving it of its look of age, and making the old perfect again. Today the building functions as a museum displaying the noble lifestyle of some indeterminate century, for there are pieces inside from the 14th through the 19th centuries, in a building without the nicks and wear of its age.

Despite complaints about its renovation, the palace provides a good idea of what a late medieval palace would have been like. Still, it is the furnishings that are of primary interest—from Aubusson and Gobelins tapestries, to antique Persian carpets, Chinese porcelain, and 17th-century Portuguese furniture. In addition, the ceilings in the dining hall and banquet hall are restored wonders, and the second floor chapel is splendid. Three still lifes by Josepha de Óbidos repay seeking out. *Admission: 300$00 for a guided tour, 200$00 in winter.*

Proceed downhill by taking the first left, **Rua Santa Maria**, which passes the front of the Convent do Carmo. Many houses lining the way are from the 14th and 15th century. A square is soon passed with the former **convento de Santa Clara**, now the town hall. Continuing, the Largo de São Tiago is reached, at the end of which stands the 16th-century **Paços do Concelho**, a former town hall. Past it the Largo de Oliveira ★ opens up, impressively medieval, at its east side, next to the pousada, is the church and convent of **Our Lady of the Olive Tree**.

Nossa Senhora da Oliveira ★

Largo da Oliveira, *(053) 412 65.*
Hours open (museum): Tues.–Sun. 10 a.m.–12:30 p.m. and 2–5 p.m. Closed Mon.
This convent is the descendant of the original 10th-century monastery that Henri of Burgundy and his wife found occupied this site when they first arrived. As its name indicates, the founding had something to do with an olive tree. Legend has it that in the seventh century Visigothic nobles approached the shepherd Wamba in his fields to beg him to be their king. By way of refusal, he thrust his staff into the

ground and vowed that he would not accept unless his olive staff flowered. It did and he did. In the 10th century a monastery commemorating the miracle was constructed on this spot.

An unusual 14th-century Gothic canopy covering a cross prefaces the church, to commemorate a 14th-century victory over the Moors. The church facade is of the same era, although its tower is 16th-century Manueline. The church interior is older, 12th century, but redecorated in this century and of little interest. What is interesting are the Romanesque cloisters whose second floor serves as a fine museum. Called the Museu Alberto Sampaio, it can be entered just south of the church.

An astonishing collection of rich ecclesiastical plates are displayed. Also on view is a tunic that João I, the first king of the House of Avís, wore in the battle of Aljubarrota where he defeated Portuguese nobles and their Spanish allies to secure his throne. The most amazing work on display, however, is a 14th-century gilt triptych altarpiece donated by João after that battle. One story claims that he captured it from the Spanish, another contends that he commissioned it afterwards. Whatever its origins, it is a masterpiece displaying the Nativity in the center panel, the Annunciation and presentation at the temple on the left panel, and the adoration of the Magi and shepherds on the right. Elsewhere, chalices, monstrances and elegant crosses all fight for attention. *Admission: 200$00; free on Sun.*

A grand vista at the end of the square leads down (southeast) to the church of **Santos Passos**, majestic from a distance, although of little interest inside. Walk toward it to take the second right along the Alameda da Liberdade gardens for one block to the church of São Francisco to the left.

São Francisco ★
Largo de São Francisco.
Hours open: Tues.–Sun. 10 a.m.–12:30 p.m. and 2–5 p.m. Closed Mon.
Of the original 15th-century church only the main portal and apse remain, the rest being 17th century. One cannot fail to notice the tile-covered mansion next door that seems positioned to announce that the reason for entering the church is for sublime blue-and-white Delft *azulejos* lining the chancel walls. *Admission: free.*

For those interested in archaeology a walk to the **Martin Sarmento Museum** is in order. Continue to the west end of the Alameda gardens, where the **Office of Tourism** is found. Turn right to walk through the plaza, continuing north along Rua Paio Galvão, which passes more garden to reach the Gothic **São Domingos** in one block on the left, with the museum installed in its cloisters.

Museu Martins Sarmento
R. de Paio Galvão, ☎ (053) 41 9 69.
Hours open: Tuesday-Sunday 10 a.m.–noon and 2–5 p.m. Closed Mon.
Named for the archaeologist who excavated Citânia de Briteiros (see the Braga entry under "Excursions"), this museum displays the smaller objects found there and elsewhere in the area. Included are two headless statues of Celtiberian warriors holding round shields, and—most dramatic of all—the Colossus of Pedralva, all 10

feet of him. Some of the smaller bronze pieces are surprising, such as dolphins and a hermaphrodite figure. *Admission: 300$00.*

Excursions

A pleasant two-stop outing is possible for those interested in lace and a stroll through a pretty town. Take Rua Donha Constanca de Noranha, the road that follows the southern edge of the castle park, which leads to N-101 toward Amarante. In 7.5 km comes **Trofa** where, on a nice day, all the women will be tatting on their doorsteps. Feel free to inspect their wares. A command of Portuguese is unnecessary; the will to communicate finds a way.

In 25k more, the town of **Amarante ★** is entered. It lies pretty-as-a-picture in the mountains along the clear Tamega River. The newer houses are 18th century. Wooden balconies overhang the river which is spanned by a fine massive bridge from 1790. There is a 16th-century convent and church; if some sight-seeing objective is necessary, just across the bridge. The most pleasant course is to walk and stop frequently to look around.

POUSADA DE SANTO ANTÓNIO

Estrada N-1, Albergaria-a-Velha, 3750
☎ *(034) 52 32 30, FAX (034) 52 31 90*
$80 per double; 13 rooms: 12 doubles, 1 suite

★ ★ ★

This winning hotel was built in 1942 (although recently remodeled) with some sweep and style. On a knoll for views and extensive, well tended grounds, there is much to be said in favor of these accommodations. The problem is a location that only serves for a rest on the drive to Porto and north, for there is not much to see in the area. The pousada at Aveiro, just 52 km away, would serve the same stopover purpose and allow a day at the beach, instead of just a swim in the pool. Be that as it may, the guest rooms here are ample, if a bit old fashioned, but comfortable nonetheless.

Dining

Dark wood beams and wainscotting lend a pleasantly old-fashioned tone to the dining room. It is a room served by a chef with taste. Cream of vegetable soup *(creme do vouga)* is flavorful as is the cream of asparagus *(creme de espargos)*. For once there is a delicious cod dish, with peppers, ham and mushrooms *(bacalhau com cogumentos a Santo António)*. There is an excellent sucking pig with pepper sauces *(leitão à bairrada)* as well. Save room for a

confection of whipped cream and egg *(natas do Céu)*. Local wines can be quite good, especially a Garrafeira. Set-course meals begin at $20.

Directions

From **Lisbon** take the autoestrada A-1 north 244 km to the exit for Albergaria-a-Velha. In 5 km east on IP-5 join N-1 south for just over 3 km, a little past the town of Sérem. From **Coimbra** take the autoestrada A-1 north for 50 km to the exit for Albergaria-a-Velha, and follow the directions above. From **Porto** take the autoestrada A-1 south for 53 km to the exit for Albergaria-a-Velha, and follow the directions above. From **Viseu** take IP-5 for 52 km east to join N-1 south for about 3 km, a little past the town of Sérem.

Pousadas Nearby

Aveiro: 21 km	Caramulo: 53 km	Porto: 62 km
Condeixa: 64 km	Póvoa das Quartas: 112 km	Manteigas: 136 km

Excursions

Aveiro ★, described above, is a fast 21 km west. **Viseu ★ ★** for fine art, described under the Caramulo section, is 4 km north on N-1 then 62 km east on IP-5.

POUSADA DE SÃO BARTOLOMEU

Estrada de Turismo, Bragança, 5300
☎ *(073) 33 14 93, FAX (073) 234 53*
$90 per double; 16 rooms: 15 doubles, 1 suite

★ ★ ★

Although this pousada was built in the late 1950s and retains the feel of that era, a recent renovation changed it for the better. Its best feature remains a spectacular view of the citadel. Craft pieces from the region are used for decoration; the bedrooms are wood with cork ceilings for soundproofing. It remains a peaceful place with balconies for meditative views, despite a lack of style.

Alternative Accommodations

Bragança ★

Av. Dr. Francisco de Sá Carneiro, ☎ *(073) 33 15 79. 42 rooms.*

The Bragança is a modern hotel that primarily serves businesspeople, but its location is central and the bedrooms are comfortable, with some providing views of the citadel. Altogether, it's a reasonable choice at under $100, if the pousada is full.

Residential São Roque ★

Rua da Estacada, 26-7 7th-8th floors, ☎ *(073) 38 14 81, FAX (073) 269 37. 36 rooms.*

For about $50 the Residential São Roque offers guest rooms that look out to the citadel and are decorated pleasantly.

Dining

Dining on the terrace is a warm weather treat. Something must atone for the bland food of this region. The best starter is a nice watercress soup *(sopa de agriões)*. Otherwise, stick to the simplest things, such as grilled veal or roast pork. One exception is a tasty veal stewed in red wine *(vitela no Tacho)*. Set-course meals start at about $20.

Alternative Dining

Solar Bragançano ★★

Praça da Sé, 34 (smack in the cathedral square), ☎ *(073) 238 75.*
This is both Bragança's most attractive restaurant and the one with the best food and value for your dining dollar. Housed in a fine 18th century building, there are tables outside in warm weather to watch the passing scene. The bill should be less than $30. Credit Cards: D, M, V.

Lá em Casa

Rua Marqués de Pombal. ☎ *(073) 221 11. Closed Monday.*
Rustic bare stone walls and crockery decoration lend a homey feel. The cooking is more adventurous than at the competition, yet you would have to gorge to earn a bill of more than $20. Credit Cards: A, D, M, V.

Directions

From Lisbon take the autoestrada A-1 north to Porto for 297 km. From **Porto** the autoestrada A-4 speeds east to Amarante, where a slow-going N-15 twists directly to Bragança in 250 km. From **Viseu** N-2 goes north to Villa Real in 108 km, then the scenic but twisty N-15 going east reaches Bragança in 160 km more. From **Guarda** take N-16 north to Celorico da Beira in 22 km, then N-102 north to Macedo de Cavaleiros in 172 km. North of that town N-15 goes northwest to Bragança in a final 41 km. From Spanish **Zamora** (which is 62 km north of **Salamanca**) N-122 goes west to the border where it changes its designation to N-218 for a trip of 114 km.

By **train** from Porto the trip takes eight hours, for the train does not average as much as 20 m.p.h., but the views are awesome and the carriages are turn-of-the-century wooden ones (with primitive rest rooms) to enchant railway buffs. **Buses** are faster by a factor of two.

Pousadas Nearby

| Miranda do Douro: 84 km | Alijó: 118 km | Amarante: 137 km |
| Caniçada: 200 km | Guimarães: 231 km | |

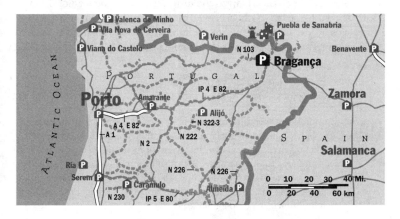

Sights

Bragança is tucked into the northeast corner of Portugal, a good 200 km from any area of interest to tourists. It lies in the heart of the province called Trás-os-montes, "behind the mountains" and indeed it is behind in many senses. The area is poor—because rolling hills keep farms small and unprofitable—and isolated politically and socially from the rest of Portugal by its mountain barrier. The inhabitants live in a different time from ours, and the reason for visiting is to view this older way of life. Farmhouses throughout the countryside are hand-built of stone, with slate, tile or thatched roofs, and nestle into bucolic hillsides covered in grass and scrub. Slate or granite cribs hold wheat away from rodents, but with crosses on their ends to suggest cemetery vaults. Wood-wheeled carts—pulled by lyre-horned oxen and driven by bearded men—will often be seen.

The town of Bragança is known for the imposing walls of its citadel, its ancient **keep ★**, its early medieval **town hall ★** and its importance for Portuguese history. In the 17th century when the Spanish controlled Portugal, the duke of Bragança was the foremost citizen in the country. He led the opposition against this foreign domination, and, after defeating the Spanish, became King João II, fathering the last dynasty in Portugal and enduring until the revolution of 1910.

Bragança stands at an elevation of half a mile, but is still overlooked by an amphitheater of hills. All roads converge on the Cathedral square, with parking below the romantic citadel high upon its hill. (Parking is also available beside the citadel entrance.) Given the insistent draw of the medieval citadel above, the 16th-century Cathedral need detain no one apart from a glance at its azulejos inside. Head up toward the ramparts along Rua do Conselheiro Abilio Beca to reach the **Museu do Abade de Baçal**.

Museu do Abade de Baçal   ★

R. do Consilheiro Abíla Beca, 27, ☎ *(073) 232 42*

Hours open: Tuesday–Sunday 10 a.m. to 12:30 p.m. and 2–5 p.m. Closed Monday and holidays.

This mansion is a former 16th-century bishop's palace, remodeled two centuries later. Two bishop's litters are displayed on the ground floor among archaeological pieces, including, in the garden, two crudely carved rocks called *berrões*. Generally just over a yard long, and usually depicting either boars or bulls, several hundred of these carvings have been discovered in the countryside of Trás-os-montes province. Their function—and the culture and dates of the carvers—is unknown. Certainly they are pre-Christian, in purpose if not date.

Several second-floor ceilings of the palace are notable, including one carved with fruit. Rooms display ecclesiastical paraphernalia—some elegant, some curious—as well as paintings—some nice work by Abel Salazar, from this century—and ethnographic pieces—including a scold's bridle with a tongue depressor to silence the offender. *Admission: 200$00.*

Continuing up toward the citadel, the first church passed on the right is **São Vicente** ★, in which Pedro the Cruel claimed to have married his mistress Inês de Castro. The present 17th-century facade covers a much older structure. Inside is a fantastic three-dimensional Christ from the 19th century flying across the ceiling. (**Note**: *churches in Bragança are not easy to get into. Luck will find them open, otherwise all that can be done is to ask anyone who passes.*)

Just before the citadel, to the left, is **São Bento** ★ with a nice Renaissance portal. The nave is a wooden barrel-vault covered in Renaissance trompe l'oeil, while the chancel is sheltered by a fine Mudejar ceiling.

The crenulated walls around the citadel are of indeterminate age, but appear to be 15th-century renovations of earlier fortifications. If so, they are in remarkable repair. The **castle** ★★ consists mainly of a tall square keep with turrets and towers surrounding. It was built by Dom Sancho I in 1187 and reinforced in the 15th century. There is a drawbridge, a dungeon and tiny doorways leading to unexpected rooms and corridors. The so-called Torre de Princesa actually held a queen captive—Donha Leonor, the wife of Dom Jaime—who was suspected of infidelity. The keep now serves as a military museum. Beside it stands a pillory on a boar-shaped *berrõe.*

To the left of the castle is **Santa Maria** with another painted nave ceiling. Beside it is a unique pentagonal structure, the **Domus Municipalis** ★. It is the oldest surviving town hall in Portugal, if not in the world, dating to the 12th century. The orange tile roof is incongruously bright, and the building has often been restored but it retains its original plan of a single large chamber. Clearly its function was not to house officials, but to serve as a meeting hall for general discussion of municipal affairs. Below the hall is a large cistern for supplying water to the citadel during times of siege.

POUSADA DE SÃO BENITO

Estrada N-304, Caniçada, 4850
☎ *(053) 64 71 90, FAX (053) 64 78 67*
$110 per double; 29 rooms: 29 doubles

★ ★ ★

Located in Portugal's largest natural park, this pousada is appropriately rustic like its mountain setting. It provides simple comforts with a view that is anything but. Unfortunately the sublime view is only presented from the lounge, for the bedrooms come with small shuttered windows to keep out the cold. In addition, the rooms are minuscule with low ceilings. A small terrace helps, but such matters are attended to by the lounge with high massive rafters and picture window (unfortunately tinted against the sun). There is a pool and a tennis court.

Dining

The kitchen does well enough. Either the leek *(alhos porros)* or cream of spinach soup *(espinafres)* start the meal well. Trout meunière *(truta à bela moleira)* can be fresh and delicate, a sort of duck risotto or paella *(arroz de pato à moda de Braga)* is tasty, or try the garlicky fried pork chop *(costeleta de porco com legumes salteados)*. When game is available, it is always fresh. The wine list contains a number of fine *vinho verdes*, fresh, slightly petillant whites. Ignore the reds in favor of an Aliança or, a more expensive Frei João. Set-course meals are available starting at about $20.

Directions

From **Porto** take A-3 north for 57 km to **Braga**, then N-103 east for 28 km to Cerdeirinhas, just past which N-304 reaches the pousada in 6 km. **Amarante** take N-101 north for 56 km to Braga, then follow the directions above.

Pousadas Nearby

Guimarães: 41 km	Vila Nova: 94 km	Amarante: 98 km
Valença: 107 km	Aljitó: 167 km	Bragança: 198 km

Sights

Massive Peneda Gerês Park covers 175,000 acres in a horseshoe that comprises in each arm the respective mountain ranges of Peneda and Gerês. Highest peaks attain about 5000 feet and spill precipitously down to rushing valley streams.

Since the landscape is elevated and carved from granite, it is covered in pines, ancient oaks, firs, ferns and heather, although wildflowers burst forth in the spring. The vegetation is as dense as the poor soil permits because of the highest rainfall in the country. Fauna include stags, golden eagles, wild horses, boar and goats. Several lakes have been formed by modern dams, but more common are racing streams, because the water rides over impenetrable granite.

NORTHERN PORTUGAL

Cars may be driven through the park. Of course there are abundant opportunities for walks, but the first official trail is still under construction. Your feet will instead follow the paths worn down by humans and their animals for centuries.

Peneda-Gerês Park   ★★

The best tour begins along N-304 at the Saúde entrance, just north of Cerdeirinhas. It winds downhill, passing the Pousada São Benito high on its hill to the left in about 2 km. The first bridge over the Cávado passes a village submerged by the rising waters of the nearby dam. Then comes an intersection at which N-308-1 to the right for Gerês should be taken.

A second bridge is crossed that leads into the park proper. The road follows the lake and then a rushing stream to the pleasant spa of Caldas do Gerês in a narrow scenic valley. Here a base can be made for further explorations and a map for drives and walks secured from the office of tourism.

From Gerês there is the choice of continuing on through the nature preserve and past a section of Roman road, or of taking a more spectacular, although rough road, west. For the latter, backtrack for 1 km from Caldas do Gerês to take a forest track on the right toward Lamas. After 3 km comes the Fragra Negra Fountain, where a hike up the stairs is rewarded by a glorious view. The track runs on through forest and rocky outcrops, before descending, soon after a crossroad, to São João do Campo, then on to the Vilarinho das Furas Dam.

POUSADA DE SÃO JERÓNIMO

Estrada N-230, Caramulo, 3475
☎ *(032) 86 12 91, FAX (032) 86 16 40*
$90 per double; 12 rooms: 12 doubles
★ ★ ★

Portugal boasts of three pousadas sited in beautiful mountains. This is one of them. Located near the decaying health spa of Careulo and not far from lovely Viseu, there is more to do here than at Caniçada, although its mountains and scenery are more beautiful than at Manteigas. The pousada is modern and so tiny it is more house than hotel. Indeed, except for adjoining bathrooms, the guest rooms also are more like those of a house than a hotel. There is a kidney-shaped pool in the garden out back.

Dining

Unfortunately the restaurant specializes in bland turkey with vegetables, codfish with eggs and beef with cream, give you the theme. The best choice would be leek soup *(sopa de alho Francés)* to start and grilled trout *(trutas grelhadas)*. Have a Dão with the meal. Set-course meal begin at about $20.

Directions

From **Lisbon** take the autoestrada A-1 north for 194 km pass **Coimbra** and join IP-3 northeast toward Viseu. In 64 km turn west onto N-230 toward, then past Campo de Beisteros for a total of 10 km. From **Porto** take the autoestrada A-1 south for 103 km until just before Coimbra to join IP-3 and follow the directions above. From **Guarda** take IP-5 for 61 km to exit for Viseu. Ring the city to join IP-3 going south for 23 km to exit onto N-230 going west for 10 km.

Pousadas Nearby

Sérem: 60 km	Póvoa das Quartas: 78 km	Manteigas: 101 km
Aveiro: 117 km	Guimarães: 175 km	

Excursions

Decaying **Caramulo** hopes to attract visitors with a vintage car museum. A more interesting outing would be to lovely **Viseu** ★★ for fine art. It lies 7 km west to take IP-3 north for 23 km.

Viseu is a peaceful, attractive city that serves as the capital of the Dão wine region. In many ways it is a typical Portuguese town, but the typical features seem more enchanting in Viseu. There are the usual stands of 16th-century houses, a large cathedral and cathedral square. But the 16th-century houses, untypically, are arranged on wide streets to show them to fine effect; the Cathedral is grand; and its square is surrounded by especially imposing buildings. While every town in Portugal seems to display a pretty whitewashed baroque church with details picked out by contrasting stone, Viseu's Miseracordia church has the loveliest face of them all.

Unique to Viseu were the two Renaissance artists who lived and worked here, combining forces to decorate the Cathedral. Today their production is enshrined in a fine museum. Gaspar Vaz joined Vasco Fernandes in the early part of the 16th century, to decorate the Viseu Cathedral altar. Led by these masters, a school of painting known as the Viseu School produced the finest Portuguese paintings of the era. In particular, the later works of Vasco Fernandes excel in sensitive portraiture and vibrant color. To the Portuguese he is known simply as "O Grão Vasco," the Grand Vasco.

From **Lisbon**, **north** and **west** N-2 becomes Av. Emidio Navarro as the Pavia river is crossed. Turn right just after the first plaza along Av. Cap. Silva Pereira, which reaches the major intersection of Largo de Santa Cristina in three blocks. A left turn would lead to parking in two blocks, but parking is often available in the more interesting main plaza, Pr. da República (a.k.a. Pr. Rossio) by taking a soft right on R. Formosa for two blocks. From **Guarda** N-16 becomes Rua 5 de Outubro in the town and goes straight to the major intersection of Largo de Santa Cristina. Here a sharp left would lead to parking in two blocks, but parking is often available in the more interesting main plaza, Pr. da República (a.k.a. Pr. Rossio), by continuing straight for two blocks.

The splendid Cathedral square, Largo da Sé, stands on the highest part of the town, tying together, as if the bow of ribbons, the convoluted streets of the old town that rise to meet it.

Two blocks below, the tree-lined, small park of the **Pr. da República** incorporates the very Baroque **São Francisco** with fine azulejos inside. Here resides a bronze statue of **Prince Henry the Navigator**, for he was the very first Duke of Viseu. Enter the stately **Town Hall** along the long side of the square to admire nice azulejos, fine woodwork and the courtyard. From the northwest corner of this plaza, R. Nunes de Carvalho climbs to meet the Cathedral, passing through a remaining gate in the original town wall just before disgorging in the Cathedral square.

This square is an open plateau overlooking the town. On its east side stands the grey Cathedral; beside it, on the north, is the former Bishop's palace, now the **Grão Vasco Museum**; and on the west is the lovely **Miseracordia church**. Once this was the loveliest square in the country, anchored at both ends by picturesque churches of different eras and styles. Now it is a parking lot. Look above the cars or blot them out with your hand to see what the plaza could have been.

Cathedral ★★

Largo da Sé.
Hours open: daily 9 a.m.–noon and 2–7 p.m. The treasury closes at 5 p.m.
Little that is visible remains from the 12th-century original, remodeled, as was the case with so many churches in Europe, in the 16th and 17th centuries and then redecorated in the 18th. Twin towers outside are legacies from that original church, but topped by 18th-century crowns. The 17th-century facade seems an afterthought, as bored-looking Evangelists march around the portal. Yet, a surprisingly elegant space waits inside.

Although the aisles were removed in the 16th century, original massive, early Gothic columns remain, and overhead, the ceiling has been redone with graceful ribs in the form of ropes knotted at intervals. Keystones present the coats of arms, respectively, of the first bishop, Alfonso V, and of King João II. The barrel ceiling above the altar was painted in the 17th century, and a century later the original altar retable by Vasco and others was removed to the Grão Vasco museum in favor of the present Baroque confection.

Azulejos line the north transept (left) leading to a sacristy, roofed by charmingly painted wood, then to stairs up to the high choir. The stalls are lovingly carved into fanciful animals. From here the upper level of a fine Renaissance cloister may be entered.

Before descending to the ground floor, a visit to the chapterhouse and the Cathedral treasury is worthwhile. Among miscellany, the treasury contains two lovely

13th-century Limoge coffers and a 12th-century Bible. The experience will be heightened if the guide is the sacristan, who delights in performing sleight of hand. The ground floor of the cloisters blends neoclassical arches on Ionic columns with 18th-century *azulejos* on the walls. The chapel of Our Lady of Mercy contains a fine retable in low relief of the Descent from the Cross. Note the elegant Gothic doorway that leads back to the Cathedral. *Admission: 100$00, to the treasury.*

Museu Grão Vasco ★★

Largo da Sé, ☎ (032) 262 49.
Hours open: Tuesday-Sunday 9:30 a.m.–12:30 p.m. and 2–5 p.m. Closed Mon.
In this former bishop's palace fine carvings are displayed on the ground floor along with a collection of Virgins of lesser interest, ceramics, Arraiolos carpets, and a small group of interesting early paintings. The second floor is devoted to furniture and ecclesiastic plates, with a few nice watercolors by the 19th-century painter Alberto de Sousa. But it is the third floor for which the museum is proudly named. Here are the paintings of Vasco Fernandes, the Grand Vasco, who spent his last 30 years in Viseu creating his finest works.

In room one hangs part of the former retable of the Cathedral. The work is by several hands as the lower figures reveal. *Saint Peter* on his throne and the *Martyrdom of Saint Sebastian*, with a background reminiscent of Holland, show a fine aptitude for the painter's art, although whether these were painted by Vasco Fernandes or by Gaspar Vaz remains in dispute. Room two is entirely devoted to the Grand Vasco, and the *Crucifixion* in luminous reds and yellows is memorable. Room three contains two masterworks by Gaspar Vaz: a triptych of the Last Supper and *Christ in the House of Martha*. Room four presents a fine series of 14 panels from the Cathedral retable depicting the life of Christ. Note Balthasar in the *Adoration of the Magi* panel depicted as an Indian from newly discovered Brazil. *Admission: 300$00, free on Sunday.*

Igreja de Misericordia ★

Largo da Sé.
Although the interior is of slight interest, the exterior, completed in 1775, presents—silhouetted against the open sky—the Portuguese Baroque church par excellence. Elegant stone window-surrounds echo the curves of the central roofcomb. The towers are stately and the balcony above the door is a fine touch. This example makes it evident that an earlier gap between ecclesiastic and secular architecture has narrowed. For without its small cross and towers, this facade could as easily preface a grand mansion.

Stairs at the rear of the Cathedral, by the south end of the apse, lead down to **Rua Direita**, a pedestrian walk lined with fine 18th-century houses. In two short blocks the street intersects with another. Turn back left along **Rua dos Andrades** to traverse three short blocks of 16th-century houses, some corbelled, interspersed with crafts shops. Rua Direita continues right from this meeting and soon arrives at Rua Formosa, a right turn on which leads back to the Pr. da República.

Pousada de São Lourenço

Estrada de Gouveia, Manteigas, 6260
☎ *(075) 98 24 50, FAX (075) 98 24 53*
$85, double; 22 rooms: 22 doubles
★ ★ ★

Perched at an elevation almost a mile high, this pousada is appropriately rustic, has a cozy fire when it's cold and provides views for 50 miles. Its outside is all mountain stone, the inside warm woods. Bedrooms are functional enough, and the management is so gracious that a warm sense of community grows among the guests and staff. Mountain walks are spectacular, but tiring because of the elevation.

Dining

A cozy dining room is just the place for trout caught in the fresh waters of the Zezare River. Since it can be overwhelmed by the onion marinade the pousada features, have it simply grilled. For a more hearty entrée after a brisk mountain walk, order pork ribs with sausage and mashed potatoes *(batata de caçoila com enchidos)*, smoked sausage with turnip greens *(grelos à pastor com enchidos da região)*, roast pork loin with herbs *(lombo de porco assado com carqueija)*, roast mountain kid *(cabrito assado à serrana)* or chicken stew *(frango estufado com legumes)*. Local Serra cheese can be sublime. Set-course meals start at less than $20.

Directions

From **Lisbon** take the autoestrada A-1 north for 81 km to exit 7, then IP-6 east for 50 km to Abrantes to join N-118. Go 44 km east to join IP-2 north, which changes to N-18 before reaching Covilhã in 117 km. Take winding N-339 west for the final 13 km. From **Évora** take N-18 north through **Estremoz** for 261 km to Covilhã, then N-339 west for 13 km. From **Viseu** take IP-5 east for 68 km to **Guarda**, then N-18 south for 43 km to Covilhã. Finally, N-339 winds the last 13 km. Guarda is a straight drive from Spanish **Salamanca** along N-620 which changes its designation at the Portuguese border to N-16. The distance is 157 km. Then follow the directions above from Guarda.

Note: Having once driven from the other direction, from N-17 through Gouveia, we would never do it again.

Pousadas Nearby

Póvoa das Quartas: 47 km	Monsanto: 95 km	Carmulo: 104 km
Almeida: 114 km	Condeixa: 147 km	Sérem: 150 km

Excursions

See the excursions from Almeida for the wonderful string of ancient fortresses in the area.

POUSADA DO BARRÃO DE FORRESTER

Alijó, 5070
☎ *(059) 95 92 15, FAX (059) 95 93 04*
$85 per double; 20 rooms: 20 doubles

★ ★ ★

This pousada, along with the one at Amarante, is for touring the vine-yards for port wine. Indeed, it honors an early innovator in port production, a Scott named James Forrester who was dubbed a baron *(barão)* by the Portuguese king, then managed to drown in the Douro. The building is a classic Portuguese country villa, white with details picked out by granite, and comfortable rather than grand. Its guest rooms look over rolling acres of vines. They are ample in size, though a little too "coordinated" for our taste. There is a pool in the rear and a terrace. However, the pousada at nearby Amarante is more sylvan, equally close to the sights of the area and more convenient to most destinations.

Dining

The dining room is cozy with a beamed ceiling and tile floor. Vines are painted on the wall to remind you where you are. Of course start with a port for an aperitif, either red or white. The bar carries over twenty, including some rare (and costly) vintages. Two unusual soups head the menu—cream of onion *(cebola)* and cream of spinach *(espinafres)*, although the marinated sardines *(sardinhas de escabeche)* are hard to pass up. The most savory main course is a local trout stuffed with ham *(trutas com presunto)*, but rabbit stew *(coelho a caçador)*, braised liver *(iscas de fígado)* and grilled veal *(vitela grelhado)* are also good. Finish with fresh pears soaked in sweet muscatel *(peras em vinho moscatel)*. The local Alijó wines are quite good. Set-course meals start at about $20.

Directions

From **Lisbon** take the Autoestrada A-1 north for 300 km through **Porto** to join A-4 going east. In 58 km, after Amarante, it changes designation to N-15, then to IP-4 and reaches N-122 in 65 km. The pousada stands beside the post office in Alijó.

Pousadas Nearby

Amarante: 70 km	Bragança: 101 km	Guimarães: 120 km
Almeida: 153 km	Caniçada: 160 km	Manteigas: 175 km

Excursions

Peso da Régua administers the port traffic. It is 40 km west along scenic N-322-3 toward Pinhão, then across the Douro to follow N-222. Along the way you will pass the quintas (like French wine chateaux) of famous port bottlers, such as Sandeman, Fonseca, and Croft. Arrangements can be made to visit the warehouses in Régua, either from the pousada or at the Instituto do Vinho do Porto in Régua. Some visits include lectures; most include samples.

The other nice outing is to the lovely **Palacio de Mateus ★**, the one pictured on the Mateus wine bottle. Take N-122 north for 23 km to join IP-4 going west toward Vila Real. In 18 km look for a sight to Mouços and Mateus going left for 4 km.

Solar de Mateus   ★

Hours open: 9 a.m.–7p.m., in winter open 9:30 a.m.–1 p.m. and 2 p.m. until 5 p.m.

This stands as the most elegant of all the Baroque manor houses in Portugal, perhaps because it was designed by an Italian. Suitably prefaced by a grand lawn lined by cedars, the house facade seems magical. A grand double staircase under a family escutcheon forms the center, whose deep recess emphasizes the sweep of wings on either side. Although somewhat busy, this design of whitewash facade with details picked out in granite epitomizes the Portuguese national style.

The house still is inhabited by the family who owns it, although not in summer, of course, which is beach time. As a result only certain parts are included on the tour. Left of the front is a fine Baroque chapel. Inside the main building is a grand hall with an extraordinary carved wood ceiling, almost matched by another in the main salon. Some of the furniture is attractive, and there is a small museum with pieces we wouldn't mind owning at all. After the tour, wander through one of the most beautiful gardens in the country. *Admission: 750$00 for a guided tour; 550$00 for the gardens only.*

POUSADA DO MONTE DE SANTA LUZIA

Monte de Santa Luzia, Viana do Castelo, 4900
☎ *(058) 82 88 89, FAX (058) 82 88 92*
$110 per double; 53 rooms: 50 doubles, 3 suites

★ ★ ★ ★

T he site could hardly be more splendid. Surrounded by green, high on a bluff overlooking Viana and the sea, stands this *modernista* white building. It was constructed as a grand mansion a century ago, then added to and remodeled in the 1930s. Done in art deco inside, with furniture designed for the building and plenty of crystal chandeliers. Guest rooms are spacious. This is a special hotel, first-class all the way. Of course there is a pool and tennis courts.

Alternative Accommodations

Viana Sol ★

Largo Vasco da Gama (near the river, three blocks southwest of the Pr. da República), ☎ *82 89 95, FAX 82 89 97, Telex 32790. 65 rooms.*
If the pousada is full, the Viana Sol is a possibility. The hotel's asset is that it provides a full range of facilities for under $75 per double. Bedrooms are spare but pleasant.

Dining

Attractive meals are served amid gleaming crystal and crisp linens. It all looks a bit better than it tastes. The cabbage soup *(caldo verde)* is dependably good, however, as is roast lamb *(borrego assado)* and roast pork loin with paprika sauce *(lombo de porco assado à Vianense)*. For wine, remember that this is the area where delicate vinho verdes are made. Set-course meals begin at $20.

Alternative Dining

Os 3 Potes   ★★

Beco dos Fornos, 7 (just off the east side of the Pr. da República). ☎ *82 99 28. Closed Monday.*

Installed in the 16th-century public bakery, the remodeled restaurant retains a rustic feel, lightened by delicate touches. The food is surprisingly good at about the same cost as the pousada's meals, and simple *caldo verde* is delicious. On summer weekends folk dancing can be a trifle touristy, although it's for the Portuguese, rather than for foreigners. Credit Cards: M, V.

Directions

On Monte Santa Luzia, 6 km north of town. Estrada Santa Luzia leaves the main Av. 25 de Abril at the hospital.

Pousadas Nearby

Vila Nova: 40 km	Valença: 51 km	Guimarães: 66 km
Caniçada: 82 km	Amarante: 136 km	Aveiro: 112 km

Sights

This elegant resort town is situated on the north bank of the River Lima estuary at the foot of green hills. Viana owes its appearance to the fact that it achieved prosperity exactly at the height of King Manuel's reign, so affluent citizens built their mansions in the Manueline style. Then prosperity drained away, so the 16th-century mansions were never replaced by more up-to-date styles.

The central **Praça da República**, with surrounding mansions and center fountain, is one of the loveliest squares in Portugal. Three blocks west, along Rua Manuel Espregueira, stands a fine 18th-century palace, which, since it's now the **Municipal Museum**, may be toured. *(Open Tues.–Sun. 9:30 a.m. to noon and 2–5 p.m.; closed Mon.; admission: 120$00.).* Just below the summit on which the pousada sits (see below) are remains of a first-century Celtiberian Citânia, or village.

As to swimming, the beach along the river is gravelly, but a ferry from the port goes to an island offshore every half-hour, and the attractive **Praia do Cabedelo**. In addition, there are pristine beaches a short car-ride north.

Excursions

Porto ★ ★ lies 62 km south along N-13. **Guimarães** ★ ★ is close as well. Take N-103 for 54 km to Braga then N-101 for 22 km.

POUSADA DOM DINIS

Praça da Liberdade, Vila Nova da Cerveira, 4920
☎ *(051) 79 56 01, FAX (051) 79 56 04*
$100 per double; 29 rooms: 26 doubles, 3 suites

★ ★ ★ ★

Respect for what was old governed the remodeling of this 15th century fortress complex. Rather than add new buildings or cut up old ones, various original structures of the garrison were simply adapted to hotel uses. Thus, this hotel counts as a small village. Three buildings constitute the guest accommodations, another serves as the restaurant, another as the bar and lounge, still another as the reception area. That means you walk outside to dine or commune with other guests. Unless it's cold or rainy, the effect is that of actually being a member of a garrison from 300 years ago. Guest rooms are unusually large, furnished with lovely beds and include a terrace. This is a quiet, atmospheric hotel.

Dining

The restaurant building owns the best view over the Minho River, which lends a nice atmosphere. What you want is local fish from the river, and different choices are available at each meal. If not fish, try the pork chunks with sausage *(rojões à Minhota)*, a local specialty. Refreshing white vinho verdes are available—splurge on an Alvainhos. Set-course meals begin at $20.

Directions

From **Lisbon** take the autoestrada A-1 north for 299 km to Porto. Take A-3 for 57 km to **Braga** then N201 for 57 km to N-303 for the final 18 km. From **Tui**, in Spain, after crossing the border take N-13 south for 15 km.

Pousadas Nearby

Valença: 15 km   Viana do Castelo: 36 km   Guimarães: 93 km
Caniçada: 107 km   Amarante: 143 km

Sights

Once this was the New Town, as its name says, but that was in the early 13th century. It began as a planned fortress town to defend against Spanish invasion. Two hundred years later this, no longer new, town was substantially remodeled to about what you see today. Unusually, the plan was oval in shape. Much of the solid stone walls remain that resisted French and Spanish attacks as late as the early 19th century. Around the fort a little town has grown. Pretty **Igreja Matriz** stands near the pousada.

POUSADA SÃO GONÇALO

Estrada N-15, Amarante, 4600
☎ *(55) 46 11 23, FAX (55) 46 13 53*
$85 per double; 15 rooms: 15 doubles
★ ★ ★

Like the pousada in Alijó nearby, this hotel is situated for a visit to the vineyards for port wines. São Gonçalo, however, is located high in lovely mountains for fine walks and views. Dating to 1942, it is one of the first of the pousada chain and monolithicly simple in construction out of local mountain stone. Inside all is spacious including the guest rooms. The whole has recently been renovated to a sparkle.

Dining

With windows over the mountains, the dining room presents views more pleasant than its meals. Cabbage and boiled potatoes set the tone of stews, from kid and lamb to rabbit. For amusement try the tornedo Rossini which stacks ham and an egg atop the steak and toast. A couple of glasses of good port will help, as will the local Vila Real wines. Set-course meals begin at about $20.

Directions

From **Lisbon** take the Autoestrada A-1 north for 300 km through **Porto** to join A-4 going east. In 58 km, after Amarante, it changes designation to N-15 for a final 16 km.

Pousadas Nearby

Guimarães: 53 km	Alijó: 69 km	Caniçada: 108 km
Bragança: 123 km	Almeida: 150 km	

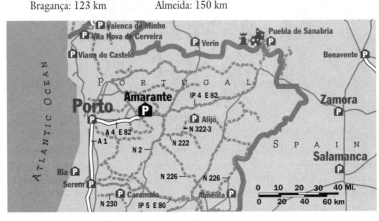

Excursions

Peso da Régua administers the port traffic. It is 16 km east on N-15 to join N-2 south for 19 km. Arrangements can be made to visit the warehouses in Régua, either from the pousada or at the Instituto do Vinho do Porto in Régua. Some visits include lectures; most include samples.

The other nice outing is to the lovely **Palacio de Mateus ★**, the one pictured on the Mateus wine bottle. Take N-15 for 22 km to Vila Real, then 3 km south to Mateus. See the description under the pousada at Alijó above. **Amarante★** is perhaps the prettiest town in the country flowing along the clear Tamega River. It lies 16 km west along N-15. The newer houses are 18th century. Wooden balconies overhang the river which is spanned by a fine massive bridge from 1799. There is a 16th century convent and church; if some sight-seeing objective is necessary, just across the bridge. The most pleasant course is to walk and stop frequently to look around.

POUSADA SÃO TEOTÓNIO

Valença do Minho, 4930
☎ *(051) 82 42 42, FAX (051) 82 43 97*
$95 per double; 16 rooms: 16 doubles

★ ★ ★

There is good and bad news about this pousada. The good news is that it commands a sweeping view over the wide Minho River across a turn-of-the-century iron bridge by Gustav Eiffel to the bluffs on the Spanish side. And, for fun, the hotel sits inside substantial 18th century fortifications on a grassy swathe. The bad news is that Valença is a touristy little town, stuffed with Spanish visitors on any holiday. The village is crisscrossed by narrow cobbled streets leading to quaint plazas bordered by attractive houses, all, unfortunately, interspersed with tourist shops. As to the pousada, it is low slung modern, with guest rooms that range from dowdy to plain. Five of the rooms overlook the river (1, 4, 5, 6 and 11); ask for one. As for us, we would travel on 12 km farther to Vila Nova or 51 km to Viana do Castelo for more interesting accommodations and surroundings.

Dining

Pleasant food is served overlooking the river. The *caldo verde* (cabbage soup) is good, as is the spinach soup *(sopa de espinafres)*. The best entrées are either a stew of kid in red wine *(caldeirada de cabrito à Serra de Arga)* or

pork chunks with sausage *(rojões de porco à Menhota)*. If you have never tasted truly fresh salmon ask whether any from the river Minho is on the menu. You can't do better in a white wine than a local vinha verde; Monção is a pleasant red. Set-course meals begin at $20.

Directions

From **Tui**, in Spain, drive across the Minho and into Valença's fortress walls. From **Porto** take A-3 north for 57 km to Braga then N-201 north for 71 km, the final 6 km on highway. From **Guimarães** take N-101 north for 22 km to **Braga** then N-201 north for 71 km.

Pousadas Nearby

Vila Nova: 14 km	Viana do Castelo: 51 km	Guimarães: 93 km
Caniçada: 102 km	Amarante: 143 km	Alijó: 211 km

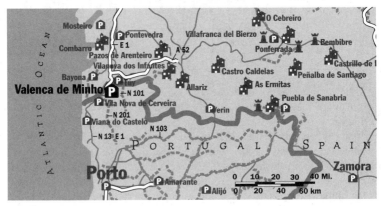

Sights

Not one but two 18th century forts constitute the town, joined by a bridge over a deep ditch. It is fun to wander the forts and inspect old cannons.

POUSADA SENHORA DAS NEVES

Almeida, 6350
☎ *(071) 483 43, FAX (071) 483 83*
$100 per double; 21 rooms: 21 doubles
★ ★ ★ ★

The reason for the trip is to visit a remarkable string of ancient forts guarding the border with Spain. Most are medieval, but that in Almeida is serious 18th century. Although within the fortress walls, the pousada is just a motel-like box. It offers a comfortable place to rest but no architectural or historical interest. The care, in this case, was spent on the bedrooms which are pleasantly light. As a nice touch, four-poster beds are covered with pretty white matelassé spreads.

Dining

As long as the chef remains, this pousada will serve some of the best food in the chain. Starters range from a subtle fresh cream of mushroom soup *(avelundado de coqumelos)*, to chicken liver pate *(terrina de aves)*, to salmon mousse *(mousse de Salmão)*, to mussels soaked in vinagrette on kebabs *(espetadinha de mexilhão a pescador)* to asparagus and shrimp tart *(tartelete de espargos com camarão)*. Lamb braised in wine *(carneiro à moda de Algodres)*, or tenderloin of pork flambéed in orange vermouth *(lombo de porco em vermute com laranja)* or lamb braised in red wine *(fornos de Algodres)* make unusual and well designed main courses. Local wines from Pinhel are good values, al-

though the wine list includes a number of French bottlings as well. Set-course meals start at about $20.

Directions

From **Lisbon** take the autoestrada A-1 north for 180 km to the **Coimbra** exit. From there the fastest, but less scenic route, is to go north on N-1 from Coimbra for 7 km to pick up IP-3 to Viseu in 87 km. From **Viseu** take IP-5 east for 93 km past **Guarda** to a turn north for 9 km on N-324, then 9 km north on N-340.More scenic, if you have the time, is to take a 5 km jag from the A-1 into Coimbra. Follow the river along Av. F. de Magalhães, then Av. E. Navarro to signs for N-17 and Guarda. N-117 heads southeast for a bit before turning northeast. The scenery is lovely, but the road is slow going for 138 km to Celorico da Beira. On the outskirts of that town, IP-5 east completes the final 22 km to Guarda. Continue on IP-5 for 23 km more to a turn north for 9 km on N-324, then 9 km north on N-340 to Almeida. From **Porto** take either the autoestrada or N-1 south to Albergens-a-Velha in 46 km. There take IP-5 east to Guarda in a further 133 km and follow the directions above. From **Évora** N-18 leads northeast to Estemoz in 46 km and continues through Portalegre and Castelo Branco to reach Guarda in a total of 289 km. Follow the directions above. From **Tomar** go south on N-110 to the outskirts of Entroncamento to pick up N-118 going east. In 76 km it reaches Alpalhão where N-18 leads to Guarda in 160 km more. From there follow the directions above. Almeida is an easy drive from Spanish **Salamanca** along N-620 which changes its designation at the Portuguese border to IP-5 for a further 15 km to a turn north on N-324 of 9 km and continue on N-340 for 9 km more. The distance is 147 km.

Pousadas Nearby

Manteigas: 86 km	Póvoa das Quartas: 110 km	Monsanto: 119 km
Carmulo: 132 km	Miranda do Douro: 165 km	Amarante: 180 km

Sights

This peaceful village displays formidable 18th-century **fortifications** in the form of a six-pointed star. This style is named Vauban, after its originator, who is said to have personally worked on Almeida. Monolithic in design, the walls force attackers to concentrate where they become easy targets for fire from two sides. Almeida's fortifications are double: should one wall be breached, another could still be defended. In spite of the cleverness of the construction, the fort was stormed—once by the Spanish and later by the French. Attractive mansions dot the town within the fortifications.

Excursions

Both **Évora ★★★★**, described in the Southern Portugal chapter, and **Porto ★★**, described in this, can be reached in a half-day. But the reason for the trip to Almeida is the score of fortresses in the countryside around it. Note that there is no requirement that all 20 must be seen. A sameness grows about them because all repose in tiny towns perched on hilltops, and all date from the same medieval era. Nonetheless, some have features that distinguish them, so the whole group would constitute an instructive two-day excursion. A car is the only practical way to reach every one. Here is a selective sampling. North of Almeida in 20 km along N-332 lies Castelo Rodrigo.

Castelo Rodrigo

Do not be misled by the quiet and intimacy of this little village within fortified walls—its early citizens had passion. In the 16th century, when the lord of their castle helped Felipe II of Spain acquire the Portuguese crown, the populace set fire to his castle. So today it is a ruin, with a bit of romance about it.

Take N-222 north through Figueira to pass Almendra for 21 km and joint N-222 for 4 km more to Castelo Melhor.

Castelo Melhor

The little village clings to the side of a rocky peak below a fine medieval wall steadied by strong round towers. Alas, the castle inside is gone, replaced by grass.

Continue on N-222 as it descends and bends to meet the highway N-102. Take the highway south (left) for about 21 km to the village of Marialva, about 1 km to the right.

Marialva ★

The old walls above the modern village gird the ghost town of an earlier village. The castle and walls date to the beginning of the 13th century, and the old village seems to have been abandoned for at least two centuries. A time warp is contained within the walls. There are remains of the castle keep, a tower wall, a church with a Manueline doorway, a 15th-century pillory and various aged houses, all empty.

Continue south along N-102 for 22 km to turn right on N-226 for Tancoso in 4 km.

Trancoso ★

In the 13th century King Dinis strengthened the original ninth-century Moorish walls and built a castle inside. Here he married his 12-year-old bride, Isabel of Castile, who later became a saint. As a wedding present Dom Dinis gave the village to his bride. Although it still retains some 16th-century houses, the walls at the northern end with their castle and squat keep are more interesting. (If it's closed, apply at the town hall.) Through the town old houses will be spied with two doors—one for trade, the other for family and friends. These are remainders of a formerly substantial Jewish community. South of Almeida on N-340 for 9 km, then south on N-324 for 41 km brings Sabugal.

Sabugal ★

This time the castle is a bit later—14th century. It is also quite complete since it has been restored. The five sides of the keep are unusual, and the ensemble of fortifications forms a pretty picture. (If it's closed, apply at the town hall.)

West in 10 km comes Sortelha.

Sortelha ★

All in granite and surrounded by boulders of the same material, the town huddles inside 13th-century fortified walls. Most of the houses inside the walls are empty, as is the imposing castle, artfully fitted into the living stone. The scene is memorable. Try to get the keys for **Igreja Matriz** from the house next door, for its lovely Moorish ceiling is delectable.

West for 7 km to Carvalhal then a jag north of 8 km brings Belmonte.

Belmonte ★★

The pretty Belmonte square is full of attractively restored mansions, but the monolithic granite **fortress** above exerts its pull. King Dinis erected it in the 13th century and it looks so right that it seems a movie set. (Open daily 9 a.m. to noon and 1-5 p.m.; admission 100$00.) Here Pedro Alvares Cabral, the discoverer of Brazil, was born. The coat-of-arms of the Cabral family is blazoned on the gate—two goats for *cabra*, which means goat. The church of **São Tiago** stands beside the keep. Its simple interior (with faint frescos) contains the Cabrals' tombs.

Two km north of Belmonte along N-18, a dirt road to the right toward Comeal da Torre shortly brings **Torre Centum Cellas**, a curious Roman tower. The three-story square structure is constructed of granite without mortar and dates at least to Roman times. Its function is debated, but its abundant windows argue against a fortress or watchtower.

HOTEL INDEX

RESTAURANT INDEX

INDEX

A

F

Fielding's Spain

"Worth reading even if you never go to Spain."
—Arizona Republic

In an easy-to-pack size, this in-depth guide captures the rich heritage, allure and flavor of Spain like no other guidebook on the market. Written by Hoyt Hobbs and Joy Adzigian, a renowned husband-and-wife travel-writing team, it offers the reader the perfect balance of education and entertainment.

With 1325 listings, hotel and restaurant comparison charts, a glossary, b/w photos and detailed maps. 672 pages, 5" x 7-1/4".

Available Now
$18.95
CAN $23.95
ISBN 1-56952-127-1

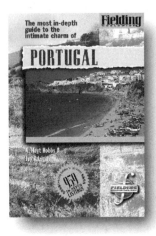

Fielding's Portugal

"Our best sources of information were fellow tour-goers and Fielding's Spain and Portugal."
—The New York Times

Discover the history, romance and intimacy of Portugal, Western Europe's best-kept travel secret. This land of passion and beauty will stir your soul. Visit enchanting castles, charming villages, spectacular beaches and dine on local cuisine.

More than 950 in-depth listings of accommodations, restaurants and attractions, b/w photos, detailed maps, comparison charts, 5" x 7-1/4".

Available Now
$16.95
CAN 20.95
ISBN 1-56952-102-6

Order Your Guide to Travel and Adventure

Title	Price	Title	Price
Fielding's Alaska Cruises and the Inside Passage	$18.95	Fielding's Indiana Jones Adventure and Survival Guide™	$15.95
Fielding's America West	$19.95	Fielding's Italy	$18.95
Fielding's Asia's Top Dive Sites	$19.95	Fielding's Kenya	$19.95
Fielding's Australia	$18.95	Fielding's Las Vegas Agenda	$16.95
Fielding's Bahamas	$16.95	Fielding's London Agenda	$14.95
Fielding's Baja California	$18.95	Fielding's Los Angeles	$16.95
Fielding's Bermuda	$16.95	Fielding's Mexico	$18.95
Fielding's Best and Worst	$19.95	Fielding's New Orleans Agenda	$16.95
Fielding's Birding Indonesia	$19.95	Fielding's New York Agenda	$16.95
Fielding's Borneo	$18.95	Fielding's New Zealand	$17.95
Fielding's Budget Europe	$18.95	Fielding's Paradors, Pousadas and Charming Villages of Spain and Portugal	$18.95
Fielding's Caribbean	$19.95	Fielding's Paris Agenda	$14.95
Fielding's Caribbean Cruises	$18.95	Fielding's Portugal	$16.95
Fielding's Caribbean on a Budget	$18.95	Fielding's Rome Agenda	$16.95
Fielding's Diving Australia	$19.95	Fielding's San Diego Agenda	$14.95
Fielding's Diving Indonesia	$19.95	Fielding's Southeast Asia	$18.95
Fielding's Eastern Caribbean	$17.95	Fielding's Southern California Theme Parks	$18.95
Fielding's England including Ireland, Scotland and Wales	$18.95	Fielding's Southern Vietnam on Two Wheels	$15.95
Fielding's Europe	$19.95	Fielding's Spain	$18.95
Fielding's Europe 50th Anniversary	$24.95	Fielding's Surfing Australia	$19.95
Fielding's European Cruises	$18.95	Fielding's Surfing Indonesia	$19.95
Fielding's Far East	$18.95	Fielding's Sydney Agenda	$16.95
Fielding's France	$18.95	Fielding's Thailand, Cambodia, Laos and Myanmar	$18.95
Fielding's France: Loire Valley, Burgundy and the Best of French Culture	$16.95	Fielding's Travel Tool™	$15.95
Fielding's France: Normandy & Brittany	$16.95	Fielding's Vietnam including Cambodia and Laos	$19.95
Fielding's France: Provence and the Mediterranean	$16.95	Fielding's Walt Disney World and Orlando Area Theme Parks	$18.95
Fielding's Freewheelin' USA	$18.95	Fielding's Western Caribbean	$18.95
Fielding's Hawaii	$18.95	Fielding's The World's Most Dangerous Places™	$21.95
Fielding's Hot Spots: Travel in Harm's Way	$15.95	Fielding's Worldwide Cruises	$21.95

To place an order: call toll-free 1-800-FW-2-GUIDE
(VISA, MasterCard and American Express accepted)
or send your check or money order to:
Fielding Worldwide, Inc., 308 S. Catalina Avenue, Redondo Beach, CA 90277
http://www.fieldingtravel.com
Add $4.00 per book for shipping & handling (sorry, no COD's), allow 2–6 weeks for delivery

International Conversions

TEMPERATURE

To convert °F to °C, subtract 32 and divide by 1.8. To convert °C to °F, multiply by 1.8 and add 32.

Fahrenheit	Centigrade	
230°	110°	
220°		
210°	100°	Water Boils
200°		
190°	90°	
180°	80°	
170°		
160°	70°	
150°		
140°	60°	
130°		
120°	50°	
110°		
100°	40°	
90°	30°	
80°		
70°	20°	
60°		
50°	10°	
40°		
30°	0°	Water Freezes
20°	-10°	
10°		
0°	-20°	
-10°		
-20°	-30°	
-30°		
-40°	-40°	

WEIGHTS & MEASURES

LENGTH

1 km	=	0.62 miles
1 mile	=	1.609 km
1 meter	=	1.0936 yards
1 meter	=	3.28 feet
1 yard	=	0.9144 meters
1 yard	=	3 feet
1 foot	=	30.48 centimeters
1 centimeter	=	0.39 inch
1 inch	=	2.54 centimeters

AREA

1 square km	=	0.3861 square miles
1 square mile	=	2.590 square km
1 hectare	=	2.47 acres
1 acre	=	0.405 hectare

VOLUME

1 cubic meter	=	1.307 cubic yards
1 cubic yard	=	0.765 cubic meter
1 cubic yard	=	27 cubic feet
1 cubic foot	=	0.028 cubic meter
1 cubic centimeter	=	0.061 cubic inch
1 cubic inch	=	16.387 cubic centimeters

CAPACITY

1 gallon	=	3.785 liters
1 quart	=	0.94635 liters
1 liter	=	1.057 quarts
1 pint	=	473 milliliters
1 fluid ounce	=	29.573 milliliters

MASS and WEIGHT

1 metric ton	=	1.102 short tons
1 metric ton	=	1000 kilograms
1 short ton	=	.90718 metric ton
1 long ton	=	1.016 metric tons
1 long ton	=	2240 pounds
1 pound	=	0.4536 kilograms
1 kilogram	=	2.2046 pounds
1 ounce	=	28.35 grams
1 gram	=	0.035 ounce
1 milligram	=	0.015 grain